Francine Johnson

April 120

MW01196483

"Although I part ways with the authors on their account and critique of Catholicism and its beliefs, there is much in this book that is very helpful in introducing the Christian student to the variety of ways in which Evangelical Protestant apologists have contributed to the intellectual life of global Christianity."

—*Francis J. Beckwith*, professor of philosophy and church-state studies, Baylor University

"Drs. House and Jowers have done a wonderful job at providing, in a single volume, a full-orbed education in the defense of the faith. We haven't seen a book like this in a long time that delves into the definitions, the methodology, the history, the issues, and the practice of this crucial but neglected field of Christian apologetics. I would like to see a more robust Christian response to the intellectual challenges of our time, and this book provides a solid foundation for exactly that. It ought to be digested by every thoughtful believer."

—*Craig J. Hazen*, founder and director of the graduate program in Christian apologetics, Biola University, editor of the journal *Philosphia Christi*, and author of the novel, *Five Sacred Crossings*

"Wayne House and Dennis Jowers have given us an understandable, practical, and informative apologetic work that will surely be recognized for its balance, articulation, clarity, and theological and philosophical insights. I highly recommend this book to anyone needing a more thorough and comprehensive grasp of the Christian apologetic task."

—*Joseph Holden*, president and professor of theology and apologetics, Veritas Evangelical Seminary.

"Wayne House and Dennis Jowers have crafted a *tour de force* in Christian apologetics. This power-packed book covers all the basics, biblically and historically, and it does a whole lot more as well. It offers rich insights into some of the most critical issues confronting Christians today and lays out practical solutions grounded in solid biblical theology. You won't find a clearer presentation of apologetic essentials in print. Whether neophyte or expert, you will learn from this book!"

—*Chad Meister*, professor of philosophy and theology at Bethel College, and coeditor of the award-winning *God Is Great, God Is Good* and *The Cambridge Companion to Christian Philosophical Theology.*

"*Reasons for Our Hope* is a clear, thorough, and accessible introduction to a wide range of issues in apologetics. The book's real strength lies in its treatment of apologetic methodology and the biblical and historical basis of apologetics. It is a delight to see this book published, and I hope it gets into the hands of those who want to know the reasons for our hope."

—*J. P. Moreland*, distinguished professor of philosophy, Talbot School of Theology, and author of *The God Question*

REASONS FOR OUR HOPE

An Introduction to Christian Apologetics

H. WAYNE HOUSE
AND DENNIS W. JOWERS

ACADEMIC

NASHVILLE, TENNESSEE

Reasons for Our Hope
Copyright © 2011 by H. Wayne House & Dennis W. Jowers

All rights reserved.

ISBN: 978-0-8054-4481-0

Published by B&H Publishing Group
Nashville, Tennessee

Dewey Decimal Classification: 239
Subject Heading: APOLOGETICS\CHRISTIANITY—APOLOGETIC WORK\
DOCTRINAL THEOLOGY

Printed in the United States of America

1 2 3 4 5 6 7 8 9 10 11 12 • 17 16 15 14 13 12 11
SB

To
Leta
my wonderful wife of forty-four years
and to
Judy A. Jowers

TABLE OF CONTENTS

Part Three
Apologetic Problems

Part Four
How to Use Apologetics in Engaging the World

ACKNOWLEDGMENTS

The authors of this work would like to thank all who have contributed directly or indirectly to the volume's production. We owe a special debt of gratitude to the patient and consummately professional staff of B&H: especially, John Landers, the editor who initiated this project, B&H academic publisher James Baird, and B&H projects manager Dean Richardson. We are also deeply indebted to Robert Bowman and Roy Zuck, whose insightful suggestions have led to substantial improvements in the work.

Professor Michael J. Adams, president of Faith Evangelical Seminary, likewise deserves our thanks for supplying a work environment conducive to scholarship and adroitly managing the institution from which we derive our primary income. Our wives, to whom we have dedicated this volume, naturally, have assisted us in more ways than we can enumerate. We would be highly remiss, finally, if we did not acknowledge our debt to the God from, through, and to whom are all things (Rom 11:36). *Soli Deo gloria.*

We would also like to mention persons who have reviewed and provided research in the writing of the book, namely, Rob Bowman, Gordon Carle, Robert Drouhard, Joseph Holden, and Steve Rost.

FOREWORD

Never before has apologetics been needed more. The Judeo-Christian framework in which the gospel alone made sense has been destroyed by secularism, pantheism, and postmodernism. We are attempting to preach that the gospel is the absolute truth of God, that Christ is the Son of God, that His resurrection is a supernatural act of God to a generation that does not even believe in God, not the theistic God of Scripture who alone must be embraced for salvation. As Francis Schaeffer insisted, we must do preevangelism before we can do evangelism effectively. We need to stop apologizing for the gospel and start doing apologetics for the gospel.

The Barthian fideistic aversion to apologetics must be overcome. We need to obey the biblical mandate to give "a reason for the hope that is in you" (1 Pet 3:15), "to contend for the faith" (Jude 3), and to "know how you should answer each person" (Col 4:6). Of course, the Word of God, like a lion, does not need to be defended; it merely needs to be expounded. But that is not the question, which is: Is the Bible the Word of God? No Christian would accept the claim of a Muslim that "the Quran does not need to be defended; it merely needs to be expounded." And neither should we expect them or anyone else to accept without evidence our claim that the Bible is the Word of God.

We need to follow the example of the Master Apologist, our Lord and Savior, who gave witnesses, performed miracles, pointed to fulfilled prophecy, and reasoned with His opponents in favor of the truth He presented. If our Lord saw the need for apologetics throughout His ministry and did it in many different ways (see our book, *The Apologetics of Jesus*[1]), then how much more should we.

---

[1] Norman L. Geisler and Patrick Zukeran, *The Apologetics of Jesus: A Caring Approach to Dealing with Doubters* (Grand Rapids: Baker, 2009).

As C. S. Lewis noted a generation ago,

> A century ago our task was to edify those who had been brought up in the Faith; our present task is chiefly to convert and instruct infidels.[2]

Elsewhere he added,

> To be ignorant and simple now—not to be able to meet the enemies on their ground—would be to throw down our weapons, and to betray our uneducated brethren who have, under God, no defense but us against the intellectual attacks of the heathen. Good philosophy must exist, if for no other reason, because bad philosophy needs to be answered.[3]

Professors House and Jowers make a noble effort to fill this gap. Few contemporary books on the topic are more comprehensive, more systematic, better documented, or better illustrated than this one. Of course the reader, like the reviewer, will not agree with all their views. Nonetheless, everyone can learn from them how to be better able to defend the faith once for all delivered to the saints.

Norman L. Geisler, Ph.D.
Professor of Apologetics
Veritas Evangelical Seminary
(www.VeritasSeminary.com)

---

[2] C. S. Lewis, "Christian Apologetics," in *God in the Dock: Essays on Theology and Ethics,* ed. Walter Hooper (Grand Rapids: Eerdmans, 1970), 94.

[3] C. S. Lewis, *The Weight of Glory* (San Francisco: HarperCollins, 2001), 58.

PREFACE

Sensible persons instinctively recoil from making potentially disastrous decisions without considering reasons for and against the action they propose to take. They do not so much as cross the street, for example, without looking both ways to ensure that their path is clear. Yet well-meaning Christians every day call persons to renounce their present worldview and lifestyle and embrace Christianity instead without explaining why they should consider Christianity true. Unlike every worldview, every political campaign, even every sales drive that appeals to reasonable people, too much of today's evangelism mounts no argument for the truth or goodness of what it promotes. Is it any wonder that many regard the gospel as incredible or worse?

This is not to deny the efficacy or the necessity of that "demonstration of the Spirit and of power" to which Paul refers in 1 Cor 2:4 (ESV): the work of the Holy Spirit whereby He brings sinners to a suprarational, unmistakable knowledge of Christ. God's kindness in supernaturally authenticating the gospel message, however, does not absolve Christians of the responsibility to be "always . . . prepared to make a defense to anyone who asks you for a reason for the hope that is in you" (1 Pet 3:15 ESV) and earnestly to "contend for the faith that was once for all delivered to the saints" (Jude 3 ESV).

One can insist on the necessity of rationally defending the Christian faith, furthermore, without diluting Scripture's teaching on the impotence of fallen human reason to grasp the gospel's truth. As all biblical Christians admit, "The natural person does not accept the things of the Spirit of God, for they are folly to him, and he is not able to understand them because they are spiritually discerned" (1 Cor 2:14 ESV). This great truth entails that, apart from the operation of the Holy Spirit, preaching is powerless to regenerate sinners. That does not imply, however, that preaching is unimportant or unnecessary.

Likewise, the inability of arguments on Christianity's behalf to bring sinners to saving belief in Christ without the regenerating work of the Holy Spirit does not render such arguments superfluous. Otherwise, the prophets, Christ, and the apostles would not have employed such arguments extensively themselves, and Paul would not have commanded Christians to "know how you should answer each person" (Col 4:6), including, presumably, those who delight in ridiculing the Christian faith.

Numerous persons in today's industrialized West, moreover, refuse even to consider whether Christianity might be true because they firmly believe that one cannot be both a Christian and a person of intellectual integrity. Even if Scripture did not mandate rational argument on Christianity's behalf in passages like 1 Pet 3:15 and Col 4:6, therefore, missiological necessity alone would require contemporary Christians to learn how to defend their faith with reasons. The time is ripe, accordingly, for an up-to-date and comprehensive introduction to apologetics, the art and science of rationally defending the Christian faith.

Reasons for Our Hope: An Introduction to Christian Apologetics is precisely such a book. Divided into four parts, it discusses, first, introductory questions about apologetic methodology and the foundations of apologetics as an academic and practical discipline; second, the history of apologetics in Scripture itself and in the subsequent life of the church; third, specific problems addressed by contemporary apologists for the Christian faith; and, fourth, the practical application of the information and arguments set forth in the preceding three sections.

The first section, in particular, includes a description of the discipline of apologetics, consideration of objections to it, a summary of the reasons for its necessity, and a broad survey of approaches to defending the Christian faith. This section also encompasses a treatment of the concept of worldview and an outline of the principal worldviews that compete with Christianity for human beings' allegiance.

After a preliminary critique of these, this section goes on to explore the subdisciplines of apologetics and discuss various conceptions of the nature of truth, a foundational question for apologetics or any other science. It addresses, moreover, the nature of Christian faith, the relation of this faith to its rational grounds, and the problem of the seeming disproportion of the absolute commitment demanded by Christianity to the apparently incomplete evidence for its truthfulness. After considering the character and interrelations of natural and supernatural revelation and their implications for natural theology, then, the section concludes with a defense of the conceivability of human beings' knowing and speaking truthfully about God.

The second part of the book consists of a broad overview of the history of Christian apologetics, which extends from biblical times to the present. Beginning with the inspired apologetic arguments of the Old Testament prophets, this section explores the development and usage of apologetic arguments in the apostolic period, the patristic era, the Middle Ages, the Reformation era, the Enlightenment and post-Enlightenment periods, and the present. Besides historical detail, this part of the book offers choice specimens of apologetic arguments Christians have employed through the centuries. These include, for example, Irenaeus's arguments against the Gnostic idea of a secret apostolic tradition that contradicts the New Testament, John of Caesarea's explanation of why Christ can have two natures without being two persons, William Paley's "watchmaker argument" for God's existence, and Blaise Pascal's famous wager for theism.

The book's third section, then, confronts specific problems with which contemporary apologists must grapple. It discusses, for instance, how one can reconcile the existence of a good God with the presence of massive evil in the world and how one ought to respond to scientific claims that appear to contradict Scripture. This section addresses, moreover, the search for the historical Jesus, Scripture's credibility vis-à-vis other ancient historical writings, and the plausibility of miracle reports in a world that seems to operate by uniform laws of nature. The superiority of Christianity over other religions also receives attention in this section, as does the challenge postmodernist philosophies pose to any worldview that lays claim to being true.

The work's fourth and final main division, then, shows how one can apply the information learned in the preceding sections to the actual work of persuading unbelievers, with the Spirit's aid and by His power, to accept the truthfulness of Christianity. The chapters in this section explore strategies and specific arguments to employ when attempting to reason with adherents of new religious movements, secularists, postmodernists, Muslims, and practitioners of Eastern religions such as Hinduism and Buddhism.

Without attempting to minimize the necessity or the importance of the proclamation of the gospel and the converting work of the Holy Spirit, this volume defends the view that rational argument on Christianity's behalf has a vital role to play in the life of the contemporary church. For Scripture mandates the use of apologetic arguments to persuade unbelievers to embrace the true religion and supplies numerous precedents for the use of such arguments. The low esteem in which many hold Christianity's intellectual credentials, moreover, frequently renders it impossible even to gain a hearing for the gospel without some demonstration that Christianity deserves the attention of thinking people; and Christians who study and employ apologetic arguments usually find their own faith powerfully confirmed. The study of apologetics thus bolsters not only the credibility of the church's witness but also the depth of conviction with which believers themselves hold the truths of the Christian faith. These benefits, the authors of the present work believe, suffice abundantly to justify the study of their book's topic: Christian apologetics.

H. Wayne House and
Dennis Jowers

GENERAL ABBREVIATIONS

AD	*Anno Domini* (the year of the Lord)
b.	born
BC	Before Christ
c.	*circa* (about)
cp.	Compare
chap(s).	chapter(s)
d.	died
e.g.	*exempli gratia* (for example)
etc.	*et cetera* (and so forth)
ibid.	*ibidem* (in the same place)
idem	the same author as previously mentioned
i.e.	*id est* (that is)
n.	note
p(p).	page(s)
viz.	*videlicet* (namely)

BIBLE BOOK ABBREVIATIONS

Gen	Genesis	Nah	Nahum
Exod	Exodus	Hab	Habakkuk
Lev	Leviticus	Zeph	Zephaniah
Num	Numbers	Hag	Haggai
Deut	Deuteronomy	Zech	Zechariah
Josh	Joshua	Mal	Malachi
Judg	Judges	Matt	Matthew
Ruth	Ruth	Mark	Mark
1 Sam	1 Samuel	Luke	Luke
2 Sam	2 Samuel	John	John
1 Kgs	1 Kings	Acts	Acts
2 Kgs	2 Kings	Rom	Romans
1 Chr	1 Chronicles	1 Cor	1 Corinthians
2 Chr	2 Chronicles	2 Cor	2 Corinthians
Ezra	Ezra	Gal	Galatians
Neh	Nehemiah	Eph	Ephesians
Esth	Esther	Phil	Philippians
Job	Job	Col	Colossians
Ps(s)	Psalms	1 Thess	1 Thessalonians
Prov	Proverbs	2 Thess	2 Thessalonians
Eccl	Ecclesiastes	1 Tim	1 Timothy
Song	Song of Songs	2 Tim	2 Timothy
Isa	Isaiah	Titus	Titus
Jer	Jeremiah	Phlm	Philemon
Lam	Lamentations	Heb	Hebrews
Ezek	Ezekiel	Jas	James
Dan	Daniel	1 Pet	1 Peter
Hos	Hosea	2 Pet	2 Peter
Joel	Joel	1 John	1 John
Amos	Amos	2 John	2 John
Obad	Obadiah	3 John	3 John
Jonah	Jonah	Jude	Jude
Mic	Micah	Rev	Revelation

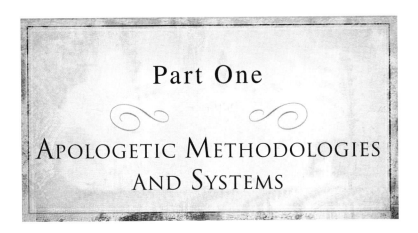

Part One

APOLOGETIC METHODOLOGIES AND SYSTEMS

This section examines the history and nature of apologetics. A brief historical sketch of the use of apologetics throughout church history is given first. This is followed by a survey of the more common forms of apologetics developed by Christians in response to those philosophical, scientific, and biblical challenges faced by the church.

Chapter 1

INTRODUCTION TO APOLOGETICS

I.   WHAT IS APOLOGETICS?

A.   Meaning of the Term *Apologetics*

THE ENGLISH WORD *APOLOGETICS* IS A transliteration, not a translation, of the Greek legal term *apologia*[1] (ἀπολογία), which was used to describe a rational defense of one's position in a court of law.[2] In the Greek world a similar word, "*dialegomenos,* 'to argue,' was used of Greek logicians and philosophers."[3] (The NASB renders this word "reasoning" in Acts 18:4,19; and 19:9.) In the Greek court system "*Apologia* originally referred to a defendant's reply to the speech of the prosecution, as in Plato's record of Socrates' *Apology.*"[4] Paul used the verb *apologeomai* (related to the noun *apologia*) this way in his defense before the Roman governors Felix and Festus and King Agrippa II (Acts 24:10; 25:8; 26:2,24).[5] Though the word is not used, a good example of the activity is found in Stephen's speech in Acts 7.

Apologetics, then, is a *defense (apologia)* of one's position or worldview as a means of establishing its validity and integrity. It is an attempt to establish the truth of the matter and to present *a convincing argument in support of it.* This is what the apostle Peter meant when he tells every Christian to "be ready to give a defense [*apologia*] to anyone who asks you for a reason for the hope that is in you" (1 Pet 3:15). The apologetic task, then, is an "activity of the Christian mind" which attempts to demonstrate the validity of the gospel message in what it proclaims as absolute truth. As Pinnock summarizes, "An apologist is one who is prepared to defend the message against criticism and distortion, and to give evidences of its credibility."[6]

---

[1] The Greek term is composed of two words, *apo* and *logia* (ἀπό and λογία), similar to *logos*, for "word" or "logic."

[2] C. H. Pinnock, "Apologetics," in *New Dictionary of Theology*, ed. D. F. Wright, S. B. Ferguson, and J. I. Packer (Downers Grove, IL: InterVarsity, 1988), 36.

[3] R. B. Mayers, *Balanced Apologetics: Using Evidences and Presuppositions in Defense of the Faith* (Grand Rapids: Kregel, 1984), 2.

[4] Ibid., 3.

[5] The term occurs as a verb or a noun 18 times in the New Testament.
As a verb: Luke 12:11; 21:14; Acts 19:33; 24:10; 25:8; 26:1,2,24; Rom 2:15; 2 Cor 12:19.
As a noun: Acts 22:1; 25:16; 1 Cor 9:3; 2 Cor 7:11; Phil 1:7,16; 2 Tim 4:16; 1 Pet 3:15.

[6] Pinnock, "Apologetics," 36.

Apologetics as a practice began in the early pages of the Old Testament (see chap. 9) and continued through the ministry of Jesus (see chap. 10) and the early church (see chap. 11). In the second century it became a separate branch of study with men such as Justin Martyr (c. AD 100–165) and Tertullian (c. AD 155–220) as they sought to defend the Christian faith from attacks by the Roman philosophical community and persecutors and to try to help Christianity gain currency as a legitimate religion.

The word *apologetics* carries a regrettable negative ring to many people today, even within the Christian community. This is due to several reasons, two of which are mentioned here (see pp. 16–20 for additional reasons). Some may wrongly believe that the discipline of apologetics relates to apologizing for our beliefs. Others may view apologetics as suspect because of an unfortunate experience with an aggressive individual who tried to persuade them to his particular belief. These improper perspectives belie the important place that the practice of apologetics has held within the advancement of the Christian faith. A robust defense of the Christian faith has been a prominent hallmark of the church from its very beginning, even to the practice of Jesus Himself, the apostles, and other Christians throughout the last two millennia.

Table 1.1 — What Is Apologetics?	
Definition	Defense of one's position or worldview to establish its validity and integrity
Aspects of Apologetics	• Destructive: seeks to "dismantle" arguments against Christianity • Creative: offers evidence to support the truthfulness of the Christian faith
Extrabiblical Use	• Plato used the term in *The Apology* in reference to a defense of Socrates. • Josephus used an apologetic for the Jewish people in *Against Apion*. • Justin Martyr defended Christianity to the Roman emperor Marcus Aurelius.
Biblical Use	• Elijah defended Yahweh against the priests of Ba'al (1 Kgs 18). • Peter said be able to give a defense (*apologia*) (1 Pet 3:15). • Jesus defended His claims before adversaries (Matt 22:34–45; John 5:31–46).

Adapted from H. W. House and J. Holden, *Charts of Apologetics and Christian Evidences* (Grand Rapids: Zondervan, 2007), 14, chart 1.

B. Applications of the Term Apologetics

In its current usage in evangelical Christianity *apologetics* may be defined as "the science and art of defending Christianity's basic truth-claims."[7] This is the sense that developed in the history of the church from its earliest days. Apologetics is not the same as theology, the systematic organization and presentation of the truths of Scriptures. Apologetics, however, may use theology, philosophy, and other disciplines to set forth reasons for the legitimacy of Christian truth and to show how alternative truth systems are contrary to Christianity.

Consequently, the practice of apologetics may be seen in at least three ways, the first two directed against those who challenge Christian truth and the third as evidence for the Christian in building up his faith. The first two purposes of apologetics are negative and defensive in approach, correcting incorrect and often malicious perspectives of Christian truth and also arguing against false claims of truth, while the third purpose has a positive intent, to build believers in the faith.

First, then, the truths of Christianity must be defended from attack by others. This sense is expressed by the apostle Peter when he wrote, "But honor the Messiah as Lord in your hearts. Always be ready to give a defense to anyone who asks you for a reason for the hope that is in you. However, do this with gentleness and respect" (1 Pet 3:15–16).

Second, the claims of others against the truths of Christianity must be shown to be false. This sense is spoken of by Paul when he wrote, "Since the weapons of our warfare are not worldy, but are powerful through God for the demolition of strongholds. We demolish arguments and every high-minded thing that is raised up against the knowledge of God, taking every thought captive to obey Christ" (2 Cor 10:4–5).

Table 1.2 Applications of Apologetics	
Defense	The truths of Christianity must be defended from attack (1 Pet 3:15).
Offense	The claims of others against Christianity must be shown false (2 Cor 10:4–5).
Support	Apologists should seek to strengthen the faith of other Christians by teaching them the logical and biblical basis of the Christian faith (2 Tim 2:24–26).

Third, the apologist has the task of strengthening the faith of other Christians by setting forth the truth claims of Christianity and support for them to other Christians as well as to non-Christians. This is a positive approach in giving logical arguments for Christianity and its various doctrines. As believers are taught the logical and biblical basis of our faith, they are strengthened intellectually and spiritually. This helps them

---

[7] G. R. Lewis, *Testing Christianity's Truth Claims: Approaches to Christian Apologetics* (Chicago: Moody, 1976), 21.

avoid becoming an easy prey for atheistic professors, cultists of various stripes, and philosophers of the popular culture. Christianity is a reasonable faith and as such may be articulated in careful and provable arguments.

Doctrines such as creation, the Trinity, the deity and humanity of Christ, and the resurrection of Jesus, among others, are often not addressed in the evangelical church, yet these are the teachings of the Bible regarding which the Christian is often challenged, undermining his or her faith. John Warwick Montgomery emphasizes the importance of including apologetics in the life of the church.

> Finally, the 21st century Apologist needs to take Apologetics far more seriously. He needs to incorporate Apologetics into every aspect of his or her ministry: every sermon, every class, every evangelistic activity. We have woefully neglected our responsibility to train our young people in the solid case for Christianity, and then we wonder why they depart from the faith under the influence of secular university instruction. We give our parishioners and our missionaries no foundation in the defense of the faith, and then wonder why our evangelistic efforts show so little fruit in a world where people have long moved beyond accepting something just because someone else believes it.[8]

Failure to take seriously the responsibility of training Christians properly in what God has given in Scripture leaves the church with little to offer the world regarding the truth of the gospel, and also an anemic view of God, Christ, and other areas of theology required for a vibrant Christian faith. Evangelicalism is at risk, as Daniel Wallace writes:

> Even with the proliferation of Bibles today, Christians are reading their Bibles less and less. I believe the evangelical church has only 50 years of life left . . . because of marginalization of the Word of God. We need another Reformation! The enemy of the gospel now is not religious hierarchy but moral anarchy, not tradition but entertainment. The enemy of the gospel is Protestantism run amock [sic]; it is an anti-intellectual, anti-knowledge, feel-good faith that has no content and no convictions. Part of the communal repentance that is needed is a repentance about the text. And even more importantly, there must be a repentance with regard to Christ our Lord. Just as the Bible has been marginalized, Jesus Christ has been "buddy-ized." His transcendence and majesty are only winked at, as we turn him into the genie in the bottle, beseeching God for more conveniences, more luxury, less hassle, and a life without worries or lack of comfort. He no longer wears the face that the apostles recognized. . . . The God we worship today no longer resembles the God of the Bible. Unless we return to him *through* a reading and digesting of the scriptures—through a *commitment* to the text, the evangelical church will become irrelevant, useless, dead.[9]

---

[8] J. W. Montgomery, "Defending the Hope That Is in Us: Apologetics for the 21st Century," lecture at the Hope for Europe conference of the Evangelical Alliance, Budapest, Hungary, April 27–May 1, 2002, http://www.jwm.christendom.co.uk/unpublished_essay.html (accessed June 1, 2010).

[9] D. B. Wallace, "The History of the English Bible, Part IV: Why So Many Versions?" (March 19–21, 2001), http://bible.org/seriespage/part-iv-why-so-many-versions (accessed June 1, 2010).

We can heartily agree and believe that the church must turn back to the conviction of the Lord's brother Jude, "to contend for the faith that was delivered to the saints once for all" (Jude 3). The task of apologetics requires not only a fervor of spirit but also an intellectual commitment to the revelation of God in Scripture.

II. WHY IS APOLOGETICS NEEDED?

A. There Is Opposition to Christian Truth

1. Scientific dogma

We live in a world in which scientific inquiry is considered equal to scientific truth. The public perception is that to speak of "science," which simply means knowledge, is to state fact. Such is not the case. There is a difference between scientific methodology and scientism, the latter referring to a philosophy or worldview and the former referring to a procedure of determining truth. The problem is that few, even within the community of scientists, are aware of the distinction between these two.

J. P. Moreland, for example, rightly points out that until the nineteenth century most scientists in Europe and the United States were creationists, daily performing scientific experiments and involved in many scientific disciplines, including biology, without any believing they were being unscientific. Interacting with the work of Neal Gillespie,[10] Moreland makes the important observation that the move from the creationist model to the Darwinian model was not primarily about scientific evidence but was a philosophical change regarding the meaning of "science."[11] Many scientists have moved from a theistic view of the world, in which scientific discoveries thrived, to a naturalistic view of science, in which only views that support philosophical naturalism are allowed.[12] If this is not true, then until about 1859, virtually no scientific work was being done by the overwhelmingly creationist scientists of Europe and America, and little until the emergence of Darwinism as the new prevailing scientific theory.

The scientific method (a) involves the procedure used by scientists in discovering truth about the material world, (b) is largely inductive in nature, and (c) can never be perfectly followed. The popular perception of the scientific method is that a scientist (a) poses a problem, (b) makes an educated guess (hypothesis), (c) tests the hypothesis through observation or experimentation, (d) states a theory (if the hypothesis checks

---

[10] N. Gillespie, *Charles Darwin and the Problem of Creation* (Chicago: University of Chicago Press, 1982).

[11] J. P. Moreland, "Intelligent Design and the Nature of Science," in *Intelligent Design 101*, ed. H. W. House (Grand Rapids: Kregel, 2008), 44.

[12] Thus the definition of science argued by the judge in a federal court in Arkansas specifically outlawed any theory of origins that was not naturalistic (see *McLean v. Arkansas Board of Education*, 529 F. Supp 1255). His five criteria for science (guided by natural law, explained by natural law, testable against the empirical world, tentative conclusions, and falsifiable) have been contested by several science philosophers as being overreaching, if not demonstrably false. See H. W. House, "Darwinism and the Law," in *Intelligent Design 101*, 197–200.

out), and (e) raises the theory to a fact if repeated testing corroborates the theory. The tentative nature of scientific "truth" is unacceptable to many within the scientific community who believe that their scientific investigations have no metaphysical elements or implications. In fact, however, philosophy enters into any scientific study and lies at the bottom of the scientific method itself. The truth about the scientific method, according to the late Austrian philosopher of science Sir Karl Popper (1902–94) in his monumental work, *The Logic of Scientific Discovery*,[13] is that scientists do not really do science according to what is called the scientific method, first proposed by Francis Bacon (1561–1626).[14] Popper says scientists could not work that way even if they wanted to. He argued that science can be done only by using a deductive method.[15] The idea that one starts with collecting observations and data indiscriminately and then fits them into theories simply does not follow. They must start first with some theory or concept[16] that guides them in the collection of data.

Similar to Popper are the instructive words of Albert Einstein in a conversation with atomic physicist Werner Heisenberg about quantum theory.

> "Possibly I did use this kind of reasoning," Einstein admitted, "but it is nonsense all the same. Perhaps I could put it more diplomatically by saying that it may be heuristically useful to keep in mind what one has actually observed. But on principle, it is quite wrong to try founding a theory on observable magnitudes alone. In reality the very opposite happens. It is the theory which decides what we can observe."[17]

Einstein's reasoning regarding quantum theory would seem to apply to any type of reasoning. A person cannot follow any area of human knowledge without first having a theory to lead the investigation. As Theodore Dalrymple argues, a person without prejudice or preconceived thoughts would need to be Cartesian, beginning anew in every intellectual quest, an unlikely and doomed enterprise.[18] No intellectual pursuit can begin or proceed without the investigator having in mind the parameters of his study and some idea of what he already believes to be the case regarding his inquiry. Without this theory, he or she would have limitless items to examine without any idea of what to include or exclude from the study.

---

[13] K. R. Popper, *The Logic of Scientific Discovery* (London and New York: Routledge, 1992, reprint).

[14] "Scientific method," http://www.physicalgeography.net/fundamentals/3a.html (accessed August 15, 2007).

[15] For further information on Popper and his view of inductive versus deductive reasoning, see S. Thornton, "Karl Popper," in *Stanford Encyclopedia of Philosophy*, ed. E. N. Zalta; http://plato.stanford.edu/entries/popper (accessed August 15, 2007).

[16] "Science, in Popper's view, starts with problems rather than with observations—it is, indeed, precisely in the context of grappling with a problem that the scientist makes observations in the first instance: his observations are selectively designed to test the extent to which a given theory functions as a satisfactory solution to a given problem" (ibid.).

[17] Albert Einstein, quoted in W. Heisenberg, *Physics and Beyond: Encounters and Conversations,* trans. A. J. Pomerans (New York: Harper and Row, 1971), 63.

[18] T. Dalrymple, *In Praise of Prejudice: The Necessity of Preconceived Ideas* (New York: Encounter, 2007), chaps. 1, 7, 9, 21.

Science, then, requires one or more assumptions before the so-called scientific method can be employed. As I (Wayne) have stated elsewhere:

> Science, for example, assumes the existence of an external world, which might be debated philosophically since this is understood through sense organs and it is not certain how accurate they are; it assumes that the external world is orderly; it assumes that the external world is knowable; it assumes the existence of truth; it assumes the laws of logic; it assumes the reliability of our cognitive and sensory faculties to serve as truth-gathers and as a source of justified beliefs in our intellectual environment; it assumes the adequacy of language to describe the world; it assumes the existence of values used in science (e.g., "test theories fairly and report test results honestly"); it assumes the uniformity of nature and induction; and it assumes the existence of numbers.[19]

Some who have absolute confidence in science have actually embraced "scientism" in addition to science, a view that elevates science above all other forms of knowledge. J. P. Moreland, in writing about Intelligent Design, reveals the bias of those who hold this "scientism."

> A few summers ago, *Time Magazine* published a cover story on how the universe will end. One of the article's premises was that for centuries humankind has tried to figure this out. Unfortunately, the only way people could approach this question was through religion and philosophy, which amounted to nothing but idle speculation. Now, said the article's writers, science has moved into this topic. For the first time in human history, we have actually gained knowledge and answers to our questions. The theory of knowledge presupposed in the article is this epistemology of scientism that is at the center of the debate.
>
> We aren't arguing just about what is true fact. The struggle is about who has a right to say what we can know. Postmodernists and naturalists do not believe there is knowledge outside the hard sciences, and this explains why evolution is embraced with a confidence that extends far beyond its justification. Methodological naturalism is responsible for the marginalization of religion in public discourse.[20]

"*Scientism* is the belief that the scientific method is the only method for discovering truth,"[21] a claim that is patently false. Such a view is accepted only in the masses

---

[19] H. W. House, "Darwinism and the Law: Can Non-Naturalistic Scientific Theories Survive Constitutional Law?" *Regent University Law Review* 13 (2000–2001): 432, drawing on the thoughts of J. P. Moreland, *The Creation Hypothesis* (Downers Grove, IL: InterVarsity, 1994), 17. See J. W. Klotz on the reliability of sense impressions and logic in scientific investigations (*Genes, Genesis, and Evolution*, rev. ed. [St. Louis: Concordia, 1970], 4–6).

[20] J. P. Moreland, "Intelligent Design and the Nature of Science," in *Intelligent Design 101*, 55.

[21] N. L. Geisler, "Scientism," in *Baker Encyclopedia of Christian Apologetics* (Grand Rapids: Baker, 1999), 702 (italics his).

because of the ambiguous use of terms in which science is broadly used for all forms of objective knowledge, as Moreland explains:

> Scientism is the view that science is the very paradigm of truth and rationality. If something does not square with currently well-established scientific beliefs, if it is not within the domain of entities appropriate for scientific investigation, or if it is not amenable to scientific methodology, then it is not true or rational. Everything outside of science is a matter of mere belief and subjective opinion, of which rational assessment is impossible. Science, exclusively and ideally, is our model of intellectual excellence.[22]

A host of other fields exist besides sciences that are concerned with physical and metaphysical reality. For example archaeology studies the physical remains of ancient civilizations and uses some scientific methods to ascertain a people group's history, cultures, customs, and the like, but it is not restricted to science. Archaeologists are required to use historical accounts, literature, inscriptions, pottery, and other artifacts to determine the truth about the civilizations studied, much of which does deal with science, which studies repeatable and physical phenomena. Moreover, even science is required to approach its study by the use of logic and mathematics, neither of which is science for both are nonphysical in nature.

2. *Contemporary humanism*

Contemporary humanism is a threat to Christian theism, and thus it must be confronted with truth. Man-centered religion has been with the human race from the fall in the garden of Eden. In its current manifestation, however, self-interest is not the only consideration of humanism, but it rejects the being of God altogether.

Several components identify secular humanism today, including its commitment to scientism, a philosophical stance, intolerance of Christianity, an emotional appeal, and a missionary zeal. Richard Dawkins, for example, criticizes creationists in these words: "It is absolutely safe to say that if you meet somebody who claims not to believe in evolution, that person is ignorant, stupid, or insane (or wicked, but I'd rather not consider that)."[23] For Sir Julian Huxley, evolution was an essential part of secular humanism. The acceptance of naturalistic evolution brought with it the view that nature operates by random forces; that no intelligence is needed to produce the world as we know it, with its denial of God and the embracing of the random and mindless forces of nature.[24] Additionally, Harold Urey, a Nobel laureate, has said, "[A]ll of us who study the origin of life find that the more we look into it, the more we feel that it is too complex to have evolved anywhere. . . . We all believe as an article of faith that

---

[22] Moreland, *The Creation Hypothesis*, 14.

[23] R. Dawkins, "Ignorance Is No Crime," *Free Inquiry Magazine* 21 (Summer 2001): n.p.

[24] See the discussion regarding the centrality of evolution to secular humanism in J. W. Whitehead and J. Conlan, "The Establishment of the Religion of Secular Humanism and Its First Amendment Implications," *Texas Tech Law Review* 10:1 (winter 1978): 47–54.

life evolved from dead matter on this planet. It is just that its complexity is so great, it is hard for us to imagine that it did."[25]

Humanism accepts only a one-story, nonmetaphysical universe. Humanists and evolutionists are naturalists and reject as reality anything that cannot be empirically verified.[26] Thus nonmatter is unreal, so that even humans consist of only physical properties; even mental processes are explainable in physical terms. Secular humanists hold such a view with blind faith.

A good example of this "leap in the dark" type of faith is illustrated in the words of Julian Huxley (1887–1975). He presents an interesting account of the mechanism of natural selection, much of which is held to be true by creationists and evolutionists.[27] There is little question that on a horizontal plane of evolution, often known as microevolution, organisms react and adapt to new circumstances. This has been observed in nature and in the laboratory. The "leap of faith" is to believe that because there are adjustments of living things to environment, this transfers—by extrapolation—to a vertical form of evolution, namely, macroevolution, in which organisms develop from lower forms to higher forms. This belief that certain genetic adaptations among certain organisms in response to environments can produce totally new organisms has not been observed. This extremely high improbability of occurrence did not keep Huxley from claiming an amazing ability of natural selection. In fact it emboldened his view that the paradox, as he says, is strength. Note his words about natural selection and what we have called vertical evolution:

> "That is all very well," you may say, "It seems to be true that natural selection can turn moths black in industrial areas,[28] can keep protective coloration up to the mark, can produce resistant strains of bacteria and insect pests. But what about really elaborate improvements? Can it transform a reptile's leg into a bird's wing, or turn a monkey into a man? How can a blind and automatic sifting process like selection, operating on a blind and undirected process like mutation, produce organs like the eye or the brain, with their almost incredible complexity and delicacy of adjustment? How

---

[25] H. C. Urey, quoted in R. C. Cowen (nature science editor of *Christian Science Monitor*), "Biological Origins: Theories Evolve," *Christian Science Monitor* (January 4, 1962): 4.

[26] See the definition of science fostered by Judge William R. Overton in the *McLean* opinion, the first element being naturalism: "1) It is guided by natural law; 2) It has to be explanatory by reference to natural law; 3) It is testable against the empirical world; 4) Its conclusions are tentative, i.e., are not necessarily the final word; and 5) It is falsifiable" (*McLean v. Arkansas Board of Education*, 529 F.Supp. 1267 [E.D. Ark. 1982]). Note the perspective of the National Association of Biology Teachers: "Explanations or ways of knowing that invoke metaphysical, non-naturalistic or supernatural mechanisms, whether called 'creation science,' 'scientific creationism,' 'intelligent design theory,' 'young earth theory,' or similar designations, are outside the scope of science and therefore are not part of a valid science curriculum" (National Association of Biology Teachers, "Statement on Teaching Evolution" [policy adopted by NABT Board on March 15, 1995, revised 1997, 2000, 2004, and 2008]); http://securewebcc.com/nabt/files/pdf/Evolution_Statement.pdf (accessed December 7, 2009).

[27] J. Huxley, *Evolution in Action* (New York: New American Library, 1953; reprint, New York: Mentor, 1957), 33–53.

[28] This example has been demonstrated to be a faulty study. See J. Wells, *Icons of Evolution: Science or Myth?* (Washington, DC: Regnery, 2000), 137–58.

can chance produce elaborate design? In a word, are you not asking us to believe too much?" The answer is no: all this is not too much to believe, once one has grasped the way the process operates.[29]

Huxley then continued by saying that "[n]atural selection is a mechanism for generating an exceedingly high degree of improbability," calling this a paradox whose improbability is only apparent.[30] In fact he postulates, "The clue to the paradox is time. The longer selection operates, the more improbable (in this sense) are its results."[31]

Is there no limit to this kind of "wishful thinking"? Given enough time, even though only one favorable mutation in a million[32] might prove beneficial, he believes that progress can be made (improvement, as he says) that will eventually produce a man from a lower primate. He discusses this idea using odds calculated by H. J. Muller regarding the likelihood of producing a horse from a lower organism (unnamed). By chance alone it would not occur, but chance and natural selection, he argues, could do such a feat. But the numbers he posits are staggering beyond all reasonable belief since chance is not a casual agent no matter how much time is put into an equation.

Given the faith that Huxley had in the power of natural selection to effect change, he believes that there is an unbelievably high improbability of creating a horse only through chance (by random mutations). After writing of the immensely vast number of favorable mutations required to produce a horse, he says:

> Of course, this could not really happen, but it is a useful way of visualizing the fantastic odds against getting a number of favourable mutations in one strain through pure chance alone. A thousand to the millionth power, when written out, becomes the figure 1 with three million noughts after it: and that would take three large volumes of about five hundred pages each, just to print! Actually this is a meaninglessly large figure, but it shows what a degree of improbability natural selection has to surmount, and can circumvent. One with three million noughts after it is the measure of the unlikeliness of a horse—the odds against it happening at all. No one would bet on anything so improbable happening; and it *has* happened. It has happened, thanks to the workings of natural selection and the properties of living substance which makes natural selection inevitable.[33]

Huxley has tremendous if not also incredulous faith in the power of natural selection, and he is willing to assume that the kinds of changes that occur within an organism of a particular species or genus may cause upward movement to produce higher forms of life, something just believed but never demonstrated.

Not all evolutionists would concur that natural selection has such power as Huxley believes. Steven Stanley has argued that the extremely slow operation of natural

---

[29] Huxley, *Evolution in Action*, 40.
[30] Ibid.
[31] Ibid., 41.
[32] Ibid., 42.
[33] Ibid., 41–42 (italics his).

selection cannot account for the major features of evolution (he opts instead for sudden and major changes),[34] and Murray Eden believes that given the high implausibility of randomness in creating new species, there is need to wait for the discovery of new natural laws to explain the process of evolution.[35]

Another aspect of secular humanism is its antagonism toward Christianity. The *Humanist Manifesto I* of 1933 stated that "the nature of the universe depicted by modern science makes unacceptable any supernatural or cosmic guarantees of human values."[36] To the surprise of some of his colleagues, Huxley declared in Chicago that he was an atheist: "In the evolutionary system of thought there is no longer need or room for the supernatural."[37] According to Huxley, "Darwinism removed the whole idea of God as the creator of organisms from the sphere of rational discussion."[38] Though Huxley's statement would make atheism the natural result of evolutionary thought, the true motivation of Darwinism, in our view, is to provide a substitute for God as Creator, so that there is no need for a god of any type. As Harvard zoologist Ernst Mayr stated:

> Thus, the Darwinian revolution was not merely the replacement of one scientific theory by another, as had been the scientific revolutions in the physical sciences, but rather the replacement of a world view, in which the supernatural was accepted as a normal and relevant explanatory principle, by a new world in which there was no room for supernatural forces.[39]

Another component of secular humanism is its emotional appeal. For example George Gaylord Simpson, when discussing the alternative evolutionary perspectives and their advocates, says that there was considerable confusion of theories that brought emotion that was blinding.

> The relatively few first-hand investigators of evolution who abandoned causalism did so, for the most part, because they despaired of finding an adequate naturalistic theory and could not endure the void of having no

---

[34] S. M. Stanley, "A Theory of Evolution above the Species Level," *Proceedings of the National Academy of Science* 72 (1975): 640–50.

[35] M. Eden, "Inadequacies of Neo-Darwinian Evolution as Scientific Theory," in P. S. Moorhead and M. M. Kaplan, *Mathematical Challenges to the Neo-Darwinian Theology of Evolution* (Philadelphia: Wistar Institute, 1967), 109. "Aside from the pre-Darwinian postulate that offspring resemble their parents, only one major tenet of neo-Darwinian evolution can be said to retain empirical content: namely, that offspring vary from parental types in a *random* way. It is our contention that if "random" is given a serious and crucial interpretation from a probabilistic point of view, the randomness postulate is highly implausible and that an adequate scientific theory of evolution must await the discovery and elucidation of new natural laws—physical, physic-chemical and biological. Until such time, neo-Darwinian evolution is a restatement in current terminology of Darwin's seminal insight that the origin of species can have a naturalistic explanation" (ibid). See the interaction of D. Gish with Stanley and M. Eden in "Crack in the Neo-Darwinian Jericho, Part II," http://www.icr.org/article/89 (accessed October 29, 2007).

[36] *Humanist Manifesto I*, http://www.americanhumanist.org/about/manifesto1.html (accessed October 29, 2007).

[37] J. Huxley, "The Evolutionary Vision," in *Issues in Evolution*, vol. 3 of *Evolution after Darwin*, ed. S. Tax and C. Callender (Chicago: University of Chicago Press, 1960), 252.

[38] J. Huxley, "'At Random': A Television Preview," in *Issues in Evolution*, 45.

[39] E. Mayr, "Evolution and God," *Nature* 240 (March 22, 1974): 285.

theory at all. Others, among them a number of professional and amateur philosophers, sounded a note of hope which was often quite plainly hope of drawing meaning from something not understood or, and this is particularly striking, hope of finding that science did, after all, confirm what were in reality their intuitive or inherited and popular prejudices. This tendency to confirm prejudice accounts for the great popularity that finalist theories have sometimes enjoyed among those incompetent to judge them adequately from either a scientific or a philosophical point of view.[40]

The religious tone of this attitude comes through in his quotation of the following comment by J. Arthur Thomson:

> To be content with the religious answer—always apt to become a soft pillow to the easy-going—is to abandon the scientific problem as insoluble, and there can be no greater impiety than that. It is surrendering our birthright—not for a mess of pottage, it is true, but for peace of mind. Therefore man is true to himself when he presses home the question: How has this marvellous system of Animate Nature come to be as it is?[41]

That scientists are not dispassionate observers and formulators of scientific truth becomes obvious the more one reads the promoters of macroevolutionary theory (versus microevolutionary fact). This blind emotional attraction to evolution causes them to argue for the fact of evolution and to deny an intelligent Creator, even when they can provide no satisfactory answer to causation. Simpson expresses this sentiment.

> This is not to say that the whole mystery has been plumbed to its core or even that it ever will be. The ultimate mystery is beyond the reach of scientific investigation, and probably of the human mind. There is neither need nor excuse for postulation of nonmaterial intervention in the origin of life, the rise of man, or any other part of the long history of the material cosmos. Yet the origin of that cosmos and the causal principles of its history remain unexplained and inaccessible to science. Here is hidden the First Cause sought by theology and philosophy. The First Cause is not known and I suspect that it never will be known to a living man. We may, if we are so inclined, worship it in our own ways, but we certainly do not comprehend it.[42]

Secular humanism is also characterized by missionary zeal in propagating its views. Simpson argued that evolution should be taught in every school,[43] but Huxley expressed this in a way that causes the appeals of a fundamentalist Christian to appear tame:

> Two or three states in your country still forbid the teaching of evolution, and throughout your educational system evolution meets a great deal of

---

[40] G. G. Simpson, *The Meaning of Evolution: A Study of the History of Life and of Its Significance for Man* (New Haven, CT: Yale University Press, 1949), 273.

[41] J. A. Thomson, *Concerning Evolution* (New Haven, CT: Yale University Press, 1925), 52.

[42] Simpson, *The Meaning of Evolution*, 279.

[43] G. G. Simpson, "One Hundred Years Without Darwin Are Enough," http://www.stephenjaygould.org/ctrl/simpson_evolution.html (accessed October 29, 2007).

tacit resistance, even when its teaching is perfectly legal. Muller, the Nobel Prize-winning geneticist, has written an admirable paper called "One Hundred Years without Darwin Are Enough," in which he points out how absurd it is still to shrink from teaching evolution—the most important scientific development since Newton and, some would say, the most important scientific advance ever made. Indeed, I would turn the argument the other way round and hold that it is essential for evolution to become the central core of any educational system, because it is evolution, in the broad sense, that links inorganic nature with life, and the stars with the earth, and matter with mind, and animals with man. Human history is a continuation of biological evolution in a different form.[44]

The victory of humanism over theism is not long-lived and has never been complete. The vast majority of people still believe in God, though not necessarily the God of Judeo-Christianity, but humanism has never been acceptable to the hearts and minds of most people. As Judge Robert Bork has written regarding the evidence for intelligent design:

Religion will no longer have to fight scientific atheism with unsupported faith. The presumption has shifted, and naturalistic atheism and secular humanism are on the defensive. Evidence of a designer is not, of course, evidence of the God of Christianity and Judaism. But the evidence, by undermining the scientific support for atheism, makes belief in that God much easier. And that belief is probably essential to a civilized future.[45]

3. *Contemporary liberal theology*

Apologists must not only concern themselves with those who are outside the Christian church but must contend for the faith against those inside the church who would pervert the purity and clarity of the gospel. The apostle Paul wrote of two men who had strayed from the truth, Hymenaeus and Philetus, who taught falsely that the resurrection of believers had already taken place and had harmed the faith of some believers (2 Tim 2:16–17). And Jude 3 encourages believers to contend earnestly for the faith, in the context of challenging false teaching in the church.

Often the teaching of Christian leaders in liberal denominations and heretical groups on the fringe of the Christian movement is more successful in leading Christians astray than pseudo-Christians cults, world religions, or movements like the Jesus Seminar. Churchmen and theologians have undermined the truthfulness of Scripture by embracing the rationalism of the Enlightenment or postmodernism.

Within the church are people who reject the authority of the Bible, viewing the Scriptures as a human attempt to understand God and to explain Jesus' ministry in

---

[44] J. Huxley (comments of Huxley et al.), "'At Random': A Television Preview," in *Issues in Evolution*, 42.

[45] R. H. Bork, *Slouching Towards Gomorrah: Modern Liberalism and American Decline* (New York: Regan, 1996), 295.

nonsupernatural terms. In the past pastors like Harry Emerson Fosdick (1878–1969) spoke against the substitutionary sacrificial death of Christ on the cross and focused instead on a selfless example of sacrifice that inspires Christians and others to act similarly.[46] In speaking against the Fundamentalist movement of his day, Fosdick represents the theological liberalism of his and our day:

> It is interesting to note where the Fundamentalists are driving in their stakes to mark out the deadline of doctrine around the church, across which no one is to pass except on terms of agreement. They insist that we must all believe in the historicity of certain special miracles, pre-eminently the virgin birth of our Lord; that we must believe in a special theory of inspiration—that the original documents of the Scripture, which of course we no longer possess, were inerrantly dictated to men a good deal as a man might dictate to a stenographer; that we must believe in a special theory of the Atonement—that the blood of our Lord, shed in a substitutionary death, placates an alienated Deity and makes possible welcome for the returning sinner; and that we must believe in the second coming of our Lord upon the clouds of heaven to set up a millennium here, as the only way in which God can bring history to a worthy denouement. Such are some of the stakes which are being driven to mark a deadline of doctrine around the church.[47]

Not only avowed liberals, like Fosdick, have challenged the inspiration and inerrancy of the Bible, but some in the broader stream of evangelicalism beginning in the 1960s, such as Dewey Beegle,[48] began to do so, necessitating the eventual formation of the Council on Biblical Inerrancy. Still others such as Clark Pinnock[49] and Greg

---

[46] H. E. Fosdick, *The Modern Use of the Bible* (New York: Macmillan, 1932), 231–32. His most complete explanation of the purpose of the death of Jesus on the cross, to our knowledge, is that given to a young man named Ted, clearly indicating that he rejected the view of God as a judge demanding satisfaction for man's sinful acts, in which Christ became man's substitution (H. E. Fosdick, *Dear Mr. Brown: Letters to a Person Perplexed About Religion* [New York: Harper & Row, 1961], 128–38). It is clear that he saw Christ's death as a voluntary act to rescue humans from their sin, and as an example for each of us to follow, but he repudiated the thought that God was offended by man's sin and that the holy God needed to punish sin, something that Christ satisfied by His death on the cross.

[47] H. E. Fosdick, "Shall the Fundamentalists Win?" *Christian Work* 102 (June 10, 1922): 717. Following these remarks Fosdick says that a true liberal believes that a person has a right to hold whatever opinion he wishes. His concern is whether "anybody has a right to deny the Christian name to those who differ with him on such points and to shut against them the doors of the Christian fellowship? The Fundamentalists say that this must be done" (ibid.). Though not directly responding to Fosdick, J. G. Machen expressed the sentiments of the Fundamentalists to such a charge as given by Fosdick: "We are not asserting at this point in our argument that the founders of the Christian movement had a right to legislate for all subsequent generations. That is a matter for further investigation. But what we are asserting now is that the founders of the Christian movement, whoever they were, did have an inalienable right to legislate for all those subsequent generations that should choose to bear the name 'Christian.' Conceivably we may change their program; but if we do change their program, let us use a new name. It is misleading to use the old name to designate a new thing" (J. G. Machen, *What Is Christianity? And Other Addresses* [Grand Rapids: Eerdmans, 1951], 19).

[48] D. M. Beegle, *The Inspiration of Scripture* (Philadelphia: Westminster, 1963).

[49] C. H. Pinnock et al., *The Openness of God: A Biblical Challenge to the Traditional Understanding of God* (Downers Grove: InterVarsity, 1994).

Boyd[50] have struck at the historic views of Christian orthodoxy, advocating erroneous views of God's nature by redefining the omniscience of God as well as other divine attributes,[51] so that a reformation of classical theism needs to emerge.

Former evangelicals and fundamentalists, such as Barr[52] and Ehrman,[53] have rejected Christianity and the Bible, often having a major impact on the nature of the debate about Christian truth. The ongoing assault against biblical truth and truthfulness will continue so long as scholars set human reason[54] against the biblical revelation given to mankind by God.

B. The Nature of Human Beings and the Gospel

Another reason apologetics should be practiced is that humans are able to interact with the truth of the Christian faith. This is so for at least three reasons. First, the natural bent of mankind to reject God (Rom 3:10–20) demands that we encourage people to embrace the truth of the gospel. Though the truth is clear, the sinful heart, mind, and will of individuals are rebellious against God. Apologetics serves to offer proof of God's truth, but it also places the hearer in a position of responsibility.

Second, apologetics speaks to truth that may be comprehended by the human being. It is rational. This is different from existential religious experience found in some liberal Christian thought and in eastern religions. The *imago Dei* ("image of God") is present in every human being. Regeneration may occur only through the Holy Spirit overcoming unbelief within each person, but it is possible for the sinful man or woman to understand logical arguments and persuasive evidence in which the capability to receive the gospel through the Spirit's work may be effected. If this were not true, there would be little reason for Jesus to rebuke His hearers for not embracing His teaching. Moreover, the preaching of Paul at Lystra, Athens, and elsewhere presupposed that his audience could understand and embrace the truth of what he said. Lastly, the apostle Peter specifically calls believers to give an answer to every man for the hope within us (1 Pet 3:15). Why should anyone give such an apologetic if the hearer is incapable of understanding it?

Third, the revelation of God is central in any Christian apologetic. A believer may try to convince someone of truth, and that person may understand to some degree what is said, but ultimately his or her acceptance of the message is based on the fact that God has revealed Himself to mankind and leads the hearer to receive it (John 6:37–39,64–65; 2 Thess 2:13–14).

---

[50] G. A. Boyd, *The God of the Possible: A Biblical Introduction to the Open View of God* (Grand Rapids: Baker, 2000).

[51] Though many evangelicals reject "open theism" and process theism, they nevertheless deny classical theism's acceptance of attributes such as simplicity, timelessness, omniscience, impassibility, etc. For a response to this new theism, see N. L. Geisler and H. W. House, *The Battle for God* (Grand Rapids: Kregel, 2001).

[52] J. Barr, *Fundamentalism* (Philadelphia: Westminster, 1978).

[53] B. D. Ehrman, *Lost Christianities: The Battle for Scripture and the Faiths We Never Knew* (New York: Oxford University Press, 2003); and idem, *Misquoting Jesus: The Story Behind Who Changed the Bible and Why* (New York: HarperOne, 2005).

[54] This is not to deny the need for human rationality and logic.

III. WHY DO SOME CHRISTIANS REJECT APOLOGETICS?

A. They Believe That the Bible Needs No Defense

Some people argue that since the Bible is the Word of God, and God needs no defense, then the Bible needs no defense. True, God is more than capable of defending Himself as the omnipotent Creator and Sustainer of the universe. Also the Bible is true in spite of attacks that have been made against it. However, many individuals are not aware that this is the case and may have been taught differently. One's defense is not so much of the Bible or of God; instead it is a matter of correcting incorrect thinking about them. Even Jesus in His debates with the Pharisees, Sadducees, and Herodians sought to correct wrong thinking about God and the Scriptures. Young people in universities hear little but negative views of the Bible and Christian truth and are generally ill prepared by their local churches to confront such claims. In the words of Gordon Lewis:

> The question has to do with the image of the Bible in the minds of young people who for twelve to sixteen years of public school education have heard the Bible's authority questioned and its teachings challenged. To defend is to act, speak, or write in favor of something. Shall these people hear nothing in favor of the Bible's truth? *As far as they are concerned* does the Bible need no defense?[55]

Failing to provide biblical argument for these young people and for older people as well means surrendering the truth of Christ to the foolishness of man. In the words of J. Gresham Machen, "Certainly a Christianity that avoids argument is not the Christianity of the New Testament."[56]

B. They Believe That Christianity Is a Matter of Faith, Not Reason

Some believe that Christians need not defend Christianity because its essence is faith, not proof. One might quote Heb 11:6, "Now without faith it is impossible to please God, for the one who draws near to Him must believe that He exists and rewards those who seek Him." The writer of Hebrews was not arguing here for blind faith. Some people believe that faith is merely believing something without any facts to substantiate it, but this is certainly not the faith spoken of in the Bible. When Paul spoke to the Greeks at the Areopagus, he adduced evidence from both nature and logic (Acts 17:22–31). Moreover, when he wrote about the resurrection of Jesus, he encouraged faith in Him based on eyewitness testimony and biblical prophecy (1 Cor 15:1–11). To believe something without any evidence or reason to accept it is no more than wishful thinking. Faith, though needing evidence, does not need absolute proof, merely adequate proof. As Lewis explains:

> We trust those who have given signs in word or deed of being trustworthy. So traditional analyses of faith have included in them the elements of

---

[55] Lewis, *Testing Christianity's Truth Claims*, 25 (italics his).
[56] J. G. Machen, *What Is Christianity? And Other Addresses* (Grand Rapids: Eerdmans, 1951), 127.

knowledge, assent, and commitment (*notitia, assensus,* and *fiducia*). The Sunday school boy was mistaken in defining faith as "believing what you know ain't true." Rather, as David Elton Trueblood has said, "Faith is not belief without proof, but trust without reservation."[57]

Christians cannot force someone to accept the gospel and cannot persuade someone of the truth of the Christian message without the work of the Holy Spirit. But the Spirit of God uses words, both those of Scripture and of believers, to open the hearts of men and women to accept Christ.

C. They Have Fear or Are Uncomfortable with Confrontation

Some Christians are uncomfortable with apologetics because they do not believe themselves capable of interacting on an intellectual level with unbelievers. Certainly some people are more timid than others and so will find the apologetic task more difficult than others. Nonetheless all Christians are called to tell others of their faith in Christ and to be faithful (2 Tim 2:11). When they do this, inevitably questions and objections will arise. Christians must be able to respond to them by doing more than inviting them to church to have the "professional" soul winner do the job.

Some Christians confuse arguments on issues with attacks against a person. Sometimes those involved in theological debate or apologetic persuasion may become overzealous, and this must be avoided. This is no excuse, however, for Christians to withdraw from the responsibility to defend the faith.

Answers must be given by speaking the truth in love (Eph 4:15). This indicates that there is "true truth," a phrase used by Francis Schaeffer. Unfortunately even the truth loses its force when not accompanied by love. As Peter wrote, one's answers should be given "with gentleness and respect" (1 Pet 3:16). Paul said, "Your speech should always be gracious, seasoned with salt, so that you may know how you should answer each person" (Col 4:6). Kelly Powers rightly says:

> Christians need to share with others in a way that brings glory to God. There are people who claim to be Christians who insult people and do not share the Word in love. Peter uses the word "reverence." This simply means to show respect as well as being a person who shows no partiality. It is important to have a gentle attitude and show respect towards those who do ask questions because in this attitude the Lord will be glorified.[58]

D. They Want to Accentuate the Positive and Downplay the Negative

The notion of always being positive is not just raised in regards to Christian apologetics; one hears the idea in popular culture as well. "Don't say no to your child; redirect his or her attention." "Don't be negative to someone because it might harm his self-esteem." However, a negative word may be just as beneficial as a positive one,

---

[57] Lewis, *Testing Christianity's Truth Claims*, 26–27 (italics his).
[58] K. Powers, "Apologetics: A Defense for the Faith (1 Pet 3:15)," http://www.afcministry.com/What_Is_Apologetics.htm (accessed August 18, 2007).

depending on the circumstances. God gave Moses many negatives in the Ten Commandments, and Jesus criticized bad theology and bad practice when He denounced the Pharisees, Sadducees, and Herodians.[59] Pointing out false ideas may be just as important as providing true ideas. This is repeatedly demonstrated in the prophets and apostles in the Bible as they interacted with unsaved and disobedient people.

Of course to point out error is not sufficient. One must also supply true ideas to take the place of bad ideas. Only when Christians know the Scriptures and are skilled in logical arguments can they be most beneficial to those who need the gospel.

E. They Believe It Is Either Ineffective in Evangelism or Hurts Evangelism

Some Christians believe that apologetics is ineffective in evangelism and may even hinder it. Lewis says, "Apologetic argument may not create belief, but it creates the atmosphere in which belief can come to life."[60] It creates a favorable environment in which belief may be nourished. The benefit of apologetics to evangelism may be illustrated by the conversion of the great church father Augustine.

> For example, many factors contributed to the conversion of Augustine. The corrective for his materialistic and skeptical notions was the philosophical reasoning of Plotinus. Augustine's confidence in astrology was removed by the argument of Nebridius. Erroneous impressions of biblical and Christian teachings were clarified by the expository preaching of Ambrose. And that pastor demonstrated Christian compassion for this troubled young man. With the evidences for the truth of Christianity which Ambrose added, Augustine's intellectual problems with the faith evaporated. But his moral struggle continued. Assistance came in the form of the counsel of older Christians and the testimonies of committed men of similar age and gifts. Still he said, "not yet." Finally his mother's prayers were answered as he read a verse of Scripture (Ro 13:13–14) and received Christ as his Lord.[61]

Another factor must be considered. Western culture is rapidly becoming biblically illiterate, so that quoting a text of Scripture is not immediately believed or even recognized. As Craig Hazen says:

> In years past it was not unusual that a believer could quote the Bible or "preach the Word" and have a good chance of engendering respect and perhaps deep reflection on the part of the unbeliever. This was possible because the Bible still carried significant cultural authority. An unbeliever would be likely to consider its words because there was a widespread recognition that the Bible was at the foundation of western civilization and brought wise counsel on many issues—even if the whole text was not considered true or without error by the skeptical recipient. Those days, however, are gone. There is a better than ever chance today that a person will actually consider

---

[59] To be critical does not mean merely to point out others' faults; it may also mean to attempt to see things more clearly in order to be as accurate as possible.

[60] Lewis, *Testing Christianity's Truth Claims*, 23.

[61] Ibid., 33–34.

you immoral for quoting the Bible because the Bible is often viewed, inappropriately of course, as misogynist, racist, violent, religiously exclusive and the basis for much of the conflict in our world.[62]

When Jesus spoke to a crowd of Jewish people, they shared belief in the Old Testament. When Peter spoke to the Jews on the Day of Pentecost, it was the same. When Paul spoke in the synagogues of the Jews, there was no debate on authority. However, when Paul came before pagans who had no knowledge of Scripture, he used another approach. He started from where they were and moved to the gospel (see chap. 3, "Approaches to Apologetics," and chap. 30, "Engaging the Muslim," for additional discussion of this).

Table 1.3 Excuses for Rejecting Apologetics	
Unnecessary	The Bible needs no defense because it is the Word of God.
A matter of faith	Christianity is a matter of faith, not reason. Therefore it needs no reasonable defense.
Timidity	Confronting others is uncomfortable, and some think they are not capable of arguing effectively.
Too negative	Apologetics is often negative, and negativity is not helpful.
Ineffective or detrimental	Apologetics may actually be detrimental to evangelism, because people will be put off by someone arguing with them.

IV. WHY SHOULD CHRISTIANS BE INVOLVED IN APOLOGETICS?

A. Preparing Non-Christians for the Gospel

1. Preevangelistic benefit of disarming pretense (Rom 1:18–32)

Paul described the state of mankind in Romans 1 as both ungodly and unrighteous, and for this reason God's wrath is manifested against humanity. *Ungodliness* describes mankind's irreverent attitude toward God, and *unrighteousness* is the sinful behavior that flows from the ungodly. These terms are descriptive of those who suppress the truth. Mankind is not a blank slate when it comes to both a knowledge of God and moral standards, but people willfully resist what they know to be true.

Romans 1:19–20 gives a good description of natural revelation, which means God's existence is made evident by what has been made, and particular truths (natural

---

[62] C. Hazen, "Defending the Defense of the Faith," in *To Everyone an Answer*, ed. F. J. Beckwith, W. L. Craig, and J. P. Moreland (Downers Grove, IL: InterVarsity, 2004), 44.

theology)[63] about His nature are derived from what has been made, namely, His eternal power and divine nature. Essentially there is an incipient form of the cosmological argument present in these verses, which means the unregenerate are capable of apprehending rational arguments for God's existence and nature. The problem, however, lies in mankind's fallen nature, which causes the lost to suppress these truths. While it is true that rational arguments for God's existence cannot bring the lost to a saving knowledge of Christ, such arguments do assist in showing them that positing the existence of God is not unreasonable. Furthermore the Holy Spirit can certainly use rational argumentation to convict the lost of their sinfulness.

2. *Persuading nonbelievers to turn from false religion to the true religion of Christianity (Acts 17:16–34)*

Paul's use of reason is clearly demonstrated in Acts 17 when he encountered both Stoic and Epicurean philosophers as well as Greek idolatry. In this setting he addressed those who were very religious, but they worshipped false gods. His apologetic method included references to Greek literature to support his understanding of the nature of God. This is not to say that he depended on Greek literature for such support, but wisely he used it to establish common ground with his audience and to persuade them to consider seriously his understanding of God. His argument paved the way for a powerful presentation of the gospel.

3. *Helping Christians to give a reasonable answer for the hope within them (1 Pet 3:15)*

Because God is a God of reason, and rational thought is an integral part of human life, faith, if truly from God, is by its very nature rational. Thus when a believer faces challenges to his faith, giving a strong defense of Christianity is certainly in keeping with its rational nature. The conversion of Augustine is a classic case in point. As a Manichean, Augustine struggled with particular aspects of Manichean teaching. When he sought answers to his questions, he was disappointed with the weak answers given to him by a particular Manichean teacher. He eventually approached the Christian preacher Ambrose, who answered Augustine's questions about Christianity and thereby influenced the brilliant searcher of truth to leave Manicheanism.

4. *Contending for the faith in light of false teaching in the world (Acts 19:8–10; Jude 3)*

With the publication of the novel *The Da Vinci Code* in 2003, a renewed debate ensued regarding the historical reliability of the Gospels, the origin of Christianity, Christ's deity, and the legitimacy of the canon of Scripture. More recently atheistic literature from Richard Dawkins, Daniel Dennett, and Sam Harris has made the

---

[63] "Natural theology refers to knowledge of God acquired through nature. Natural theology does not stand in contradiction to divine revelation nor does it exclude such revelation. In fact natural theology is dependent upon divine revelation for its content" (R. C. Sproul, J. Gerstner, and A. Lindsley, *Classical Apologetics* [Grand Rapids: Zondervan, 1984], 25).

best-seller lists, challenging the existence of God and the moral integrity of Christianity. While many bemoan the appearance of such material, these vigorous challenges to the Christian faith give Christians an opportunity to respond with superior arguments and thoroughgoing refutations of the criticisms. When critics of Christianity go public, they open the door of opportunity for capable Christians to show that such attacks are fraught with defective argumentation and devoid of the facts. Contending for the faith (Jude 3) can and often does become an evangelistic opportunity.

B. Maturing of Christians

Apologetics is a powerful tool for dealing with attacks against the Christian faith. However, the value of apologetics is not limited to responses to critics. From the standpoint of Eph 4:11–12, apologetics equips believers to be confident in and assured of their faith. Paul admonished Timothy to embrace and teach sound doctrine, one aspect of which is apologetics that establishes in believers a firm foundation of truth (2 Tim 4:2–5). Such a foundation helps eliminate doubts in the new convert, encourages saints in their trust in God, and gives believers a reason for their hope in Christ.

Anyone who has studied the Scriptures knows that it has many difficult passages. Apologetics that addresses Bible difficulties helps clarify many of those passages and reassures believers that the Scriptures are trustworthy and understandable.

C. Defending the Glory of God

In Romans 1 Paul described the state of mankind as that which dishonors God and seeks to establish man as the measure of all things. Apologist Francis Schaeffer devoted his entire life to showing that man left to himself truly becomes a fool. Schaeffer was a master at showing how the wisdom of man devoid of God is like the foolish builder who builds on sand. According to 2 Cor 10:5 believers are to destroy the foolish speculations and high-minded things that oppose God.

Table 1.4 Reasons for Apologetics	
Prepares for the gospel	Apologetics • Disarms non-Christian pretense. • Persuades non-Christians away from false religions. • Prepares Christians to answer the challenges of critics.
Maturity	Apologetics equips believers to be confident in and assured of their faith.
Defense	Apologetics shows the glory of God's wisdom as opposed to the foolishness of man's wisdom.

V. WHAT ARE SOME RESULTS FROM THE STUDY OF APOLOGETICS?

Apologetics does not simply impart truth and provide rational arguments for the historic Christian faith. It also enriches the spiritual and intellectual lives of every believer who seeks to understand the Scriptures. The study of apologetics contributes to the believer's spiritual formation by strengthening one's understanding of the things of God and assisting in the interpretation and application of propositional revelation.

This chapter has examined some of the more popular forms of apologetic categories employed today. The field is vast and challenging and deserves to be studied with vigor. The arguments of nineteenth-century philosophers who published tomes against the Christian faith were mere phantasms that did not rise to the level of sound argument. In the modern period Christian apologists like C. S. Lewis and Francis Schaeffer, to mention only two, raised the clarion, "The emperor has not clothes!" Numerous "naked" philosophies and ideologies are still parading about, begging for a hearing. The fields are ripe for many more apologists who have the courage for a good contest.

Chapter 2

WORLDVIEWS

I. WHAT IS A WORLDVIEW?

A WORLDVIEW IS A PARTICULAR PARADIGM or framework each person embraces, through which all reality is viewed and interpreted. A worldview is "the sum of a person's basic assumptions";[1] "a set of ideas, beliefs, convictions, or values that provides a framework or map to help you understand God, the world, and your relationship to God and the world";[2] a filter through which we process information;[3] and the way one views the whole world.[4]

James Sire offers one of the more detailed definitions of a worldview:

> A worldview is a commitment, a fundamental orientation of the heart, that can be expressed as a story or in a set of presuppositions (assumptions which may be true, partially true or entirely false) which we hold (consciously or subconsciously, consistently or inconsistently) about the basic constitution of reality, and that provides the foundation on which we live and move and have our being.[5]

Ronald Nash points out that a worldview must include at least five critical areas of belief: God, metaphysics, epistemology, ethics, and the nature of man.[6] Worldviews must first begin with the question of God. Does He exist or not? How this question is answered will have definite implications for questions related to existence, knowledge, ethical behavior, and humanity. Certainly the nonexistence of God automatically limits one's worldview perspective to an exclusively humanistic approach to existence, and

---

[1] K. D. Boa and R. M. Bowman Jr., *Faith Has Its Reasons: Integrative Approaches to Defending the Christian Faith*, 2nd ed. (Colorado Springs, CO: Paternoster, 2006), 91.

[2] D. A. Noebel, *Understanding the Times*, 2nd ed. (Manitou Springs, CO: Summit, 2006), 16.

[3] W. Corduan, *No Doubt About It: The Case for Christianity* (Nashville: B&H, 1997), 66.

[4] N. L. Geisler and W. D. Watkins, *Worlds Apart: A Handbook on World Views*, 2nd ed. (Grand Rapids: Baker, 1989; reprint, Eugene, OR: Wipf & Stock, 2003), 11.

[5] J. W. Sire, *The Universe Next Door: A Basic Worldview Catalog*, 5th ed. (Downers Grove, IL: InterVarsity, 2004), 20.

[6] R. H. Nash, *Life's Ultimate Questions: An Introduction to Philosophy* (Grand Rapids: Zondervan, 1999), 14.

man becomes the measure of all things. On the other hand if there is a God, how does a theistic perspective shape one's view of reality?

In the realm of metaphysics a worldview must be able to deal adequately with such questions as these: What is God's relationship to the universe? Did mankind get here by naturalistic forces or special creation? Is the universe a closed system? Does one's existence and the existence of the universe have any purpose?[7]

Everyday people make ethical decisions that impact their lives and the lives of others. A person's worldview wields a tremendous influence on his ethical decision-making. The twentieth century witnessed the implications of ethics driven by nontheistic worldviews. Nazi Germany, Stalinist Russia, and Maoist China exemplified the tragic consequences of ethics derived from worldviews wholly focused on humanism.

II. WORLDVIEW AND TRUTH

Though competing worldviews may agree in many areas, the areas of disagreement must be given serious consideration because they will identify matters of truth that have a critical bearing on life. E. F. Schumacher gives an interesting description of how he came to understand how his secular worldview eventually proved inadequate.

> All through school and university I had been given maps of life and knowledge on which there was hardly a trace of many of the things that I most cared about and that seemed to me to be of the greatest possible importance to the conduct of my life. I remembered that for many years my perplexity had been complete; and no interpreter had come along to help me. It remained complete until I ceased to suspect the sanity of my perceptions and began, instead, to suspect the soundness of the maps.
>
> The maps I was given advised me that virtually all my ancestors, until quite recently, had been rather pathetic illusionists who conducted their lives on the basis of irrational beliefs and absurd superstitions. . . . Their preoccupation with religion was just one of their many signs of underdevelopment, not surprising in people who have not yet come of age. . . . The maps of *real* knowledge, designed for *real* life, showed nothing except things which allegedly could be *proved* to exist. The first principle of the philosophical mapmakers seemed to be "If in doubt, leave it out," or put it into a museum. It occurred to me, however, that the question of *what constitutes proof* was a very subtle and difficult one.[8]

Here Schumacher is discussing the age-old problem of epistemological certitude. It is not enough to claim to know something. The point is, how does one know, and can a person know anything with reasonable certitude? Roderick Chisholm asks, "How do we decide, in any particular case, whether we have a genuine item of knowledge?"[9]

[7] Ibid., 15.

[8] E. F. Schumacher, *A Guide for the Perplexed* (New York: Harper and Row, 1977), 1–3 (italics his).

[9] R. Chisholm, *The Problem of the Criterion* (Milwaukee: Marquette University Press, 1973), 5.

Chisholm presents two sets of questions that are foundational in the pursuit of truth: "What do we know? What is the extent of our knowledge?" "How are we to decide whether we know? What are the criteria of knowledge?"[10]

Every worldview must address these questions, but by what criteria? According to Chisholm, there are three options: skepticism, methodism, particularism.[11]

Skepticism is ultimately self-defeating, for skepticism must by its very nature be skeptical of its own skepticism. Thus it renders itself inadequate as a viable epistemological option.

Methodism, which is empiricism, appeals to the senses as the starting point, and so the senses become the sole criteria of truth. Yet the problem here is, By what authority can empiricism be an adequate criterion of truth? As J. P. Moreland points out, "Methodism is not a good strategy because it leads to a vicious infinite regress."[12] Whatever an empiricist claims to know, he must provide criteria for justifying what he knows and then present criteria to justify his criteria.

The third option Chisholm presents is particularism, which is the view that people can know specific, clear items of knowledge, such as $2 + 2 = 4$. As Chisholm says, "I can know some things directly and simply without needing criteria for how I know them and without having to know how or even that I know them."[13]

A. The Nature of Truth

Jesus said He is "the way, the truth, and the life" (John 14:6). Pilate asked, "What is truth?" (John 18:38). And Paul said the church is "the pillar and foundation of the truth" (1 Tim 3:15). Two thousand years later postmodern culture is asking the same rhetorical question Pilate asked. Given the pluralistic drift so prevalent today, it is no surprise that the Son of the living God is viewed as one of many paths to truth and that the church is just one of many institutions that promote a truth.

At stake is whether objective truth exists. R. Scott Smith says, "Christians are increasingly accepting of ethical relativism, and in a climate that promotes pluralism, we are losing our understanding of Christian ethical and religious truths as being objectively true."[14] He defines objective truth as that which is "true for all people, whether or not anyone accepts them as true or talks about them as such."[15] For example simple mathematical equations such as $3 \times 5 = 15$ are objective, universal truths. Simply put, truth is what corresponds to reality, and this is known as the correspondence theory of truth.

Doug Groothuis identifies eight distinctives of biblical truth (see Table 2.1).[16]

---

[10] Ibid., 12.
[11] Ibid., 14–15.
[12] J. P. Moreland, *Love Your God with All Your Mind* (Colorado Springs, CO: NavPress, 1997), 139.
[13] Ibid., 140.
[14] R. S. Smith, *Truth and the New Kind of Christian* (Wheaton, IL: Crossway, 2005), 13.
[15] Ibid.
[16] These are the subheadings in D. Groothuis, *Truth Decay* (Downers Grove, IL: InterVarsity, 2000), 65–80.

Table 2.1 **Eight Distinctives of** **Biblical Truths**
• Truth is revealed by God.
• Truth exists and is knowable.
• Truth is absolute.
• Truth is universal.
• Truth is eternal and momentous.
• Truth is exclusive, specific, and antithetical.
• Truth is systematic and unified.
• Truth is an end, not the means to an end.

B. Major Tests for Truth

At face value, worldviews appear to be fluid, with persons changing their way of looking at the world at different periods of their lives and often based on different circumstances they have experienced. However, if there is such a thing as objective truth that is universal in scope and presented by a particular worldview, then that worldview by necessity is static. Worldviews in opposition to objective truth are relativistic and are ultimately inadequate. Furthermore to adopt a pluralistic approach to worldviews that limits truth to subjectivism conflicts with fundamental rules of logical thought, namely, the law of contradiction.

To escape the dilemma of a relativistic view of truth leading to pluralism, one must determine what the definitive tests for truth are. According to Ronald Nash, three tests for truth should be applied when evaluating a worldview: the tests of reason, experience, and practice.[17] The test of reason is the use of logic, specifically the law of noncontradiction. This is one of the three basic logs of logic, namely, the law of identity (A equals A), the law of the excluded middle (A or B), and the law of noncontradiction (A cannot be non-A). The law of noncontradiction affirms that two opposite things cannot both be true at the same time and in the same way (A cannot be non-A). For example a person cannot be in a classroom and not be in a classroom at the same time or in the same way. But of course a person could be in the same classroom at a different time or in a different way (present in body but not in mind).

The test of experience has to do with our experience of reality. Does the worldview hold to a correspondence theory of truth? Truth has been defined under a correspondence theory of truth as that which conforms to reality. If someone were to claim that the weather outside is beautiful with a warm sun and soft breeze, and yet when a

---

[17] R. H. Nash, *Worldviews in Conflict: Choosing Christianity in a World of Ideas* (Grand Rapids: Zondervan, 1992), 55.

person went outside, the weather was cold, and there was a terrible thunderstorm, this would be contrary to one's experience of reality.

The final test, that of practice, asks, How well does the worldview account for all of life? In other words, Is it comprehensive, or does it fall short? Can the worldview be lived out? This entails a universal perspective. It is not enough to say that a particular worldview can be lived out in a specific cultural context. One must ask, "Can the worldview in question be applied universally to all people regardless of cultural and geographical boundaries?"

Testing the truthfulness of a worldview provides a crucial safeguard against any worldview that would ultimately lead to despair. "Despair is one result of the failure to put the various parts of one's life together. Despair is essentially enthusiasm that has gone astray, that has lost its bearings; it is a zeal for things that either disappear when they are most wanted or fail to deliver all that they seem to promise."[18]

Table 2.2 Three Tests of a Worldview	
The test of reason	A worldview must pass the test of noncontradiction.
The test of experience	A worldview must correspond to the truth of experience in reality.
The test of universality	A worldview must be universally true, not just applicable to a particular culture.

III. THE FUNCTION OF WORLDVIEWS

By their very nature worldviews must be able to function logically (intellectual credibility) and be practical (livability). Worldviews speak to matters regarding ethics, metaphysics, the nature of man, and epistemology.

A. Statements of Faith

Worldviews are inherently religious. Even an atheist's assertion that there is no God is a religious statement. Even though he embraces a naturalistic, closed system regarding the universe, the assertion about God is a metaphysical statement about reality.

B. Ethical Guides

Metaphysically worldviews speak to issues about existence, in particular the quality of existence. Ethics deals with how people conduct themselves in relation to one another. Worldviews engage us in determining not only what constitutes ethical behavior but also by what authority right conduct is binding. Ethics not only involves con-

---

[18] Ibid., 49.

duct freely practiced but also conduct prohibited by a higher authority. All worldviews have an ethical component by which people make moral judgments.[19]

C. Linguistic Referees

Worldviews impact communication. When reading any literary work of any period of time or any culture, one may understand it properly only when he also comprehends the worldview espoused in that work.

Table 2.3 The Function of Worldviews	
Statement of faith	A worldview serves to explain.
Ethical guide	A worldview serves as a guide of one's ethical system.
"Linguistic referee"	A worldview serves to help people understand the ideas expressed by those who hold it.

IV. MAJOR WORLDVIEWS

A. Monotheism. The View That There Is Only One Divine Being[20]

1. Transcendent theism

The Creator, or Supreme Being, is wholly other, which is to say, He is totally distinct from what has been made. There are three categories of transcendent theists.

a. Trinitarian monotheism[21]

Historic, orthodox Christianity is unique among the monotheistic worldviews in teaching that God exists as one, yet within the Godhead there are three distinct persons: the Father, Son, and Holy Spirit, all three being coequal and coeternal. In this way Christianity's theological structure differs substantially from that of other world religions. A key distinction between non-Trinitarian and Trinitarian monotheisms is that Christianity is Christocentric, focusing on the incarnation, whereas all other monotheistic systems are only theocentric. Only in the incarnation of the eternal Son, as Jesus, has the revelation of the Trinitarian God been made evident. He has revealed

---

[19] R. H. Nash, *Faith and Reason: Searching for a Rational Faith* (Grand Rapids: Zondervan, 1988), 31.

[20] It is common to reserve monotheism for belief in a personal transcendent being, such as is found within Unitarianism and Trinitarianism, and thus exclude views such as pantheism, which, though believing in one God, rejects the personal nature of that God. But pantheism is included in this discussion following Geisler and Watkins, *Worlds Apart: A Handbook on World Views.*

[21] The Trinitarian nature of Christianity is demanded, and even developed, from the fact of the incarnation of God in Jesus the Messiah. Had Jesus not been recognized as God, there would have been no conundrum that required the early church to explain how the Father and Son, and eventually the Holy Spirit were a Trinitarian God.

the Father and has sent the Spirit. Carl Braaten carefully articulates the significance of this distinction.

> The whole gospel of the church rests on this christological tripod—these three interconnected legs of history, kerygma, and dogma, of Jesus of Nazareth as the risen Lord and as God's only begotten Son. When one of these legs is removed, broken, or shortened in the life, worship, and witness of the church, the door of hospitality opens to pagan spirituality and alien ideology.[22]
>
> Unlike Judaism, Islam, and Deism, the gospel is foundational to Christianity. Indispensable to the gospel is the fact that at the beginning of the Christian faith stands the figure of Jesus of Nazareth, his preaching of the kingdom of God, his intimate sense of being his Abba's Son, his way of accepting social outcasts, his table fellowship with sinners, and finally his obedient suffering and death on the cross. All that is concrete historical stuff, the granite foundation of the Christian faith.[23]

The Christological center of Christianity poses a significant problem for other worldviews. Jesus' proclamation that He is *the* way, *the* truth, and *the* life (John 14:6) solidifies the Christological bedrock on which Christianity is built. However, as Braaten points out, "One conspicuous trend is to debunk christocentric theology in favor of a theocentrism that places God at the center of the universe of faiths, relegating Christ to one among many ways of enlightenment, liberation, and salvation."[24] If theocentric pluralism is to succeed in equalizing all worldviews, it must diminish the influence of Christocentrism.

b. Non-Trinitarian monotheism

In contrast to the Christological focus of Trinitarian monotheism, some monotheists believe that God is only one person, that He does not exist in three persons. Jesus Christ was merely a great leader, and the Holy Spirit is nothing more than a force or power. Islam, Judaism, and Jehovah's Witnesses are examples of non-Trinitarian monotheism.[25] However, whereas Islam and Judaism reject the authority of the New Testament as God's revealed Word, Jehovah's Witnesses do believe the New Testament is God's propositional revelation to man.

c. Non-Trinitarian monotheism: Deism

Deism, which was an influential worldview in the eighteenth century, is making a comeback. Most recently the late atheist Antony Flew abandoned atheism and embraced a view of God that is more akin to Deism. Deism is "restricted to belief in

---

[22] C. Braaten, "The Gospel for a Neopagan Culture," in *Either/Or: The Gospel or Neopaganism,* ed. C. Braaten and R. Jenson (Grand Rapids: Eerdmans, 1995), 9.

[23] Ibid., 8–9.

[24] Ibid., 9.

[25] Modalists, who are non-Trinitarian monotheists, do acknowledge the deity of Christ.

a God, or First Cause, who created the world and instituted immutable and universal laws that preclude any alteration as well as divine immanence—in short, the concept of an 'absentee God.'"[26] Deists deny the occurrence of miracles, propositional revelation, and the efficacy of prayer.

As a worldview, Deism is essentially humanistic. Life is what people make of it, and there is no appeal to a Supreme Being for assistance. Since God has left people to their own devices, Deism by necessity defaults to an approach to existence that has much in common with atheism.

2.   *Nontranscendent monotheism*

Whereas transcendent monotheism understands God to be wholly distinct from and independent of what He has created, nontranscendent monotheism sees God as either one with the universe (pantheism) or bipolar (panentheism).

a.   *Pantheism*

"In pantheism God is all in all. God pervades all things, contains all things, subsumes (includes) all things, and is found within all things. . . . Pantheism views the world as God and God as the world."[27] This approach to reality is monism, which understands that "God and the universe are one thing, whereas Christianity is pluralistic in that it sees God as distinct from the universe."[28]

b.   *Panentheism*

Though it is easy to confuse panentheism with pantheism or to see them as similar, since they both share a nonclassic view of immanence, they are actually distinct worldviews. Unlike pantheism, panentheism is the view that "God and the world are ontologically distinct and God transcends the world, but the world is in God ontologically."[29] Since the panentheist acknowledges elements of God's transcendence and immanence, one would think it an expression of orthodoxy, but panentheism's *finite* nature of God's transcendence makes it a better candidate for nontranscendent monotheism.

Panentheism has also been identified as either bipolar or process theism. This worldview sees God and creation as mutually dependent on each other. The world exists and is part of God, and God cannot be God without creating something that enables Him to express His attributes.[30]

---

[26] E. C. Mossner, "Deism," in *The Encyclopedia of Philosophy*, ed. Paul Edwards (New York: Macmillan, 1967), 2:327.

[27] Geisler and Watkins, *Worlds Apart: A Handbook on World Views*, 75–76.

[28] N. L. Geisler, *Baker Encyclopedia of Apologetics* (Grand Rapids: Baker, 1999), 495.

[29] J. Cooper, *Panentheism: The Other God of the Philosophers* (Grand Rapids: Baker Academic, 2006), 27.

[30] Ibid., 29.

c. Finite godism

Various strains of finite godism exist, but the most popular is set forth by Rabbi Harold Kushner, who wrote the best-selling book *When Bad Things Happen to Good People.* Kushner believes God is limited in both power and perfection. He is limited by mankind in that He does not possess all power but leaves some for humans. The laws of nature, human nature, and moral freedom also limit what God is able to do.[31]

B. Atheism

Atheism, or naturalism as some prefer to call it, contends that God does not exist. All that exists came about as a result of evolution, or natural processes acting randomly over billions of years. What exists has no teleology, that is, no purpose; it merely exists for a brief period of time and then goes out of existence by death.

C. Polytheism

According to this worldview multiple gods exist who are finite and active in the world. They have varying degrees of power and influence and are either identified with nature or are beings with human qualities. Both the Old and New Testaments provide ample evidence for the existence of polytheism as far back as the garden of Eden. In Romans 1 Paul described naturalistic polytheism, which ascribes to various finite creatures the status of deity. This particular strain of polytheism is comparable to what Moses encountered in Egypt. When Paul visited Athens, he was deeply troubled by the rampant Greek polytheism (Acts 17), which is nothing more than amplified humanity.

Polytheism is not limited to ancient civilizations or primitive cultures. Modern polytheists include numerous religions such as some forms of Hinduism and African and Native American animism, as well as modern paganism.

A popular and growing polytheistic religion originating in North America is Mormonism. Though Mormons would deny it, the Mormon understanding of the Godhead is clearly polytheistic. Regarding the Godhead, LDS theologian Bruce McConkie states that the three personages of the Godhead, while they are "one God" in the sense of having all the same perfect attributes, "are three separate and distinct entities. Each occupies space and is and can be in but one place at one time, but each has power and influence that is everywhere present. The oneness of *the Gods* is the same unity that should exist among the saints."[32] In *The Pearl of Great Price*, one of the four books in what Mormons call the "Standard Works" and consider Scripture, Abraham 4 and 5 describes creation as a work of the "Gods": "And they went down at the beginning, and they, that is the Gods, organized and formed the heavens and the earth" (4:1).[33] Joseph Smith explicitly taught polytheism: "I will preach on the plurality of Gods. I have selected this text for that express purpose. I wish to declare I have always and

---

[31] Geisler and Watkins, *Worlds Apart: A Handbook on World Views,* 202–3.

[32] B. McConkie, *Mormon Doctrine* (Salt Lake City: Bookcraft, 1979), 319 (italics added).

[33] This account is clearly polytheistic. Furthermore it contradicts the monotheistic account of creation found in Moses 2 of *Pearl of Great Price.*

in all congregations when I have preached on the subject of the Deity, it has been the plurality of Gods. It has been preached by the Elders for fifteen years."[34]

D. Agnosticism

Though often confused with atheism, agnostics do not deny the existence of God. Instead they claim His existence either cannot be known or cannot be known with reasonable certainty.

V. IMPACT OF WORLDVIEWS ON MAJOR DISCIPLINES[35]

Worldviews can be divided into two major categories: the Christian worldview and non-Christian worldviews.[36] The significance of these two categories is made clear by what the worldviews affirm and deny.

A. The Christian Worldview

First, Christianity rests on an epistemological foundation that is distinct from all other worldviews. It affirms the existence of objective truth revealed by God in the form of propositional revelation found exclusively in the Old and New Testaments.

Second, Christianity affirms the Trinitarian nature of God, which Robert Reymond has summarized in three points: "(1) there is but one living and true God who is eternally and immutably indivisible . . . ; (2) the Father, the Son, and the Holy Spirit are each fully and equally God . . . ; (3) the Father, the Son, and the Holy Spirit are each distinct Persons."[37] Christ is not just a great prophet among many; He is the Son of God to whom "all authority has been given . . . in heaven and on earth" (Matt 28:18).

Third, affirmation of the centrality Jesus Christ as the way, the truth, and the life (John 14:6) is the heart and soul of Christianity. This is the gospel message, and the gospel is not theocentric, as stated earlier; it is Christocentric. The mission of Christianity is to go into all the world and proclaim the gospel, baptize converts, and teach them to observe everything Christ taught (Matt 28:19–20). Because mankind is hopelessly lost, dead in trespasses and sin, at enmity with God, and therefore in need of redemption in order to be in righteous fellowship with God, the missiological mandate is fundamentally Christological. The gospel, when it is proclaimed, challenges all other worldviews, and the gospel, when it is embraced, constitutes a paradigm shift from either a secular or non-Trinitarian worldview to Christianity. In contrast to

---

[34] J. F. Smith, ed., *Teachings of the Prophet Joseph Smith* (Salt Lake City: Deseret, 1976), 370.

[35] This section provides a brief overview of how worldviews impact the numerous areas of human inquiry. For a thorough, detailed treatment see D. Noebel, *Understanding the Times,* 2nd ed. (Manitou Springs, CO: Summit, 2006).

[36] When we say "Christian," we must give proper recognition to the dependence of Christianity upon the Hebrew Scriptures and the historic Jewish faith from which Christianity grew. They share much in common that is different from other worldviews, though the Trinitarian and Christological aspects of Christianity distinguish it from the Jewish faith.

[37] R. Reymond, *A New Systematic Theology of the Christian Faith*, 2nd ed. (Nashville: Thomas Nelson, 1998), 205–6.

Christianity, non-Christian worldviews consist of radically different views of reality and life. Atheism and agnosticism deny or doubt the existence of God, consider Jesus nothing more than a religious leader, reject propositional revelation, and scorn the gospel. Non-Trinitarian monotheistic and polytheistic worldviews do not fare much better. Though they acknowledge the existence of a divine being, the god they proclaim is not the God of the Old and New Testaments. Jesus Christ is nothing more than a great religious leader, propositional revelation is ascribed to numerous religious texts that are incompatible with the Judeo-Christian Scriptures, and the gospel is denied or trivialized.

One's worldview is not simply a way of interpreting all of life and reality in an intellectual vacuum, but a definitive philosophy of life that plays out in virtually every area of human endeavor. The various branches of human inquiry, such as philosophy, theology, sociology, history, biology, psychology, ethics, law, politics, and economics, are interpreted and applied in accord with one's worldview. This in turn radically affects all of society.

A Christian worldview is philosophically supernaturalist and Trinitarian with respect to the nature of God. It is not only embraced by faith but also is intellectually rational and justifiable. Regarding the existence of the universe and life, the Christian worldview teaches that all mankind, unlike the animal kingdom, is created in the image of God; and, unlike the animal kingdom, God has commanded mankind to take dominion over what has been made. Teleologically there is a definite purpose behind human existence. Since God is holy and just, people are ethically bound to moral absolutes derived from God's propositional revelation.

B. Non-Christian Worldviews

In contrast to the Christian worldview, all other worldviews, whether of a religious or secular nature, are inherently detrimental to mankind's spiritual and physical well-being. Though non-Trinitarian monotheistic worldviews such as Islam and Judaism have several things in common with Christianity (such as belief in moral absolutes, special creation, and supernaturalism), they do not see mankind as fallen and needing redemption. Without redemption people are hopelessly alienated from God and left to seek humanistic solutions to deep-seated moral problems that can be solved only by means of spiritual transformation in Christ.

An even worse cultural state of affairs is brought about by secular worldviews that totally deny the existence of God, and those worldviews that reduce God to finitude or a monistic understanding of reality. Essentially these worldviews approach life and reality from a humanistic perspective. Man is the product of naturalistic processes with no purpose for existing. Morality is reduced to what any given culture decides is right or wrong. Both divine and natural law are rejected, leaving only humanistic or oppressive theocratic (e.g., Islam) approaches that destabilize political security and negatively affect freedom, justice, and order.

A Christian worldview stabilizes, strengthens, and enhances mankind's existence in every possible way, whereas non-Christian worldviews ultimately lead to mankind's moral, spiritual, and physical decline.

VI. HOW DO YOU CHOOSE A WORLDVIEW?

Missiologist and philosopher Harold A. Netland writes, "Perhaps the most daunting task for the Christian apologist in the coming decades emerges from the fact of competing religious and secular worldviews and the accompanying problem of determining acceptable criteria for the assessment of alternative worldviews."[38] Given the fact that one may choose from numerous worldviews, the apologist faces a key question: "How do we determine which religious worldview is in fact true? On what basis do we accept the Christian worldview as in fact the true one?"[39]

Earlier this chapter discussed the nature of truth, the general epistemological problem of establishing an acceptable criterion for knowing truth, and the fact that truth can be known.[40] Since all the worldviews discussed claim to be knowledge, the issue to be addressed now is how to identify specific criteria by which one can evaluate all worldviews to determine which one can best justify its particular truth claims. To assess the epistemological integrity of a worldview adequately, the criteria must be universally self-evident and not bound by culture. Nash applies three tests to worldviews: reason, experience, and consistency in practice.[41] According to Geisler and Watkins, a worldview must be able to demonstrate consistency, comprehensiveness, livability, and be consistently affirmable.[42]

In the lists provided by Nash and by Geisler and Watkins, two criteria stand out that are universally self-evident: logic (in particular the law of noncontradiction) and ethics. The justification of applying logic universally is well stated by Netland:

> Although the term "logic" has many uses and meanings, strictly speaking it refers to the non-empirical and non-psychological domain consisting in certain principles, rules of inference, and relations that apply to propositions and arguments, and thus by extension, to thinking and reasoning. Logic in this sense is objective in that its reality is independent of the mental processes or psychological states of any human being. The basic principles of logic are normative: if reasoning and thinking are to be done correctly they must conform to these principles. Furthermore, their normativity is not dependent upon or restricted to particular linguistic or cultural contexts. They are translinguistic and transcultural. Basic logical principles and relations have extramental ontological reality; they are part of the "stuff" constituting

---

[38] H. A. Netland, "Apologetics, Worldviews, and the Problem of Neutral Criteria," in *The Gospel and Contemporary Perspectives: Viewpoints from Trinity Journal*, ed. D. J. Moo (Grand Rapids: Kregel, 1997), 140.

[39] Ibid., 140–41.

[40] See chap. 5, "How Do We Know the Truth?" for a detailed discussion of epistemology.

[41] Nash, *Worldviews in Conflict*, 55.

[42] Geisler and Watkins, *Worlds Apart: A Handbook on World Views,* 263–66.

reality. As such, they do provide some neutral criteria for the evaluation of competing worldviews or truth claims.[43]

Netland identifies three key principles of logic that are essential to meaningful, intelligible communication: the principles of *identity* (if a statement is true, then it is true), *noncontradiction* (no statement can be both true and false), and *excluded* middle (a statement is either true or false).[44]

Another criterion is moral virtue. Though all worldviews promote the same basic moral standards, not all worldviews can justify their respective moral positions. The atheist and Christian can both agree that the Holocaust was immoral. However, why it was immoral poses a problem for atheism because the atheist cannot appeal to a moral authority to justify his position. Furthermore atheism's evolutionary explanation for the origin and development of life undermines its ability to establish an objective morality, and so cultural relativism is the only logical recourse. But cultural relativism provides the justification needed by an individual, tyrant, despot, or the state to be morally self-determining.

On the other hand Christianity does have a moral authority, God, who has set forth specific moral principles that are universal. His moral principles have been revealed not only by means of propositional revelation but also in the conscience (Rom 2:14–16), so all people are aware of right and wrong.

Alister McGrath observes that "one of the most significant developments in the last decade or so has been the increasing realization that modern worldviews rest on distinctly vulnerable foundations."[45] In Rom 1:18–32, the apostle outlined the progressive deterioration of people who embrace ungodliness (irreverence toward God) and unrighteousness (moral decline) brought about by the suppression of truth (a biblical worldview). Christian apologetics is the bringing of the Christian worldview to bear on a world enslaved to foolishness masquerading as wisdom. McGrath is instructive when he says, "Christian apologetics centers on twin foci: on the one hand the truth and reliability of the Christian revelation, and on the other hand the need to relate it to, and demonstrate its transformative potential for, the human situation."[46]

---

[43] Netland, "Neutral Criteria," in *The Gospel and Contemporary Perspectives*, 151.

[44] H. A. Netland, *Dissonant Voices: Religious Pluralism and the Question of Truth* (Grand Rapids: Eerdmans, 1991), 183.

[45] A. McGrath, *Intellectuals Don't Need God and Other Modern Myths* (Grand Rapids: Zondervan, 1993), 144.

[46] Ibid., 211.

Chapter 3

APPROACHES TO APOLOGETICS[1]

DEFENSE OF THE CHRISTIAN FAITH IS central to the ongoing viability of Christianity in its struggle with false religions and ideologies and in assisting individuals to embrace the gospel of Christ. Those who share the good news of Jesus often encounter individuals who do not share the same view of the world, their need of salvation, the credibility and value of the Scriptures, or knowledge of Jesus as He is presented in the Bible.[2] The religions of the world make truth claims at considerable variance with what is set forth in Christianity,[3] including cults of Christianity.[4] Even in the West, where Christianity was once held to be the accepted religion, most people now have little knowledge of the biblical claims regarding Jesus Christ or of the need for salvation through Him.[5] Divisions of faith and fact and of the religious and the secular, and skepticism about the viability of objective truth claims, pervade the culture.

In view of this ignorance, rejection, or repudiation of Christian truth claims by potential converts, the evangelist must decide how to bridge this resistance to Christian truth. Does the Christian apologist and evangelist share with the potential convert any common ground that may serve as a basis for answering the unregenerate person's questions that are at variance with Christian claims? Or is the unregenerate "evangelee" totally incapable of understanding rational and evidentiary arguments

---

[1] This chapter in a different form appears in H. W. House, "A Biblical Argument for Balanced Apologetics," in *Reasons for Faith: Making a Case for the Christian Faith*, ed. N. L. Geisler and C. W. Miester (Wheaton, IL: Crossway, 2007). The present chapter is the basis for the *Reasons for Faith* chapter.

[2] See T. C. Muck for a discussion of how world religions and ideologies differ from Christian claims and Muck's suggestions on how to establish common ground with them ("Is There Common Ground Among Religions?" *Journal of the Evangelical Theological Society* 40 [1997]: 99–112). See also H. A. Netland, "Apologetics, Worldviews, and the Problems of Neutral Criteria," in *The Gospel and Contemporary Perspectives: Viewpoints from* Trinity Journal, ed. D. J. Moo (Grand Rapids: Kregel, 1997), 138–52.

[3] See H. W. House, *Charts of World Religions* (Grand Rapids: Zondervan, 2006).

[4] See H. W. House, *Charts of Cults, Sects, and Religious Movements* (Grand Rapids: Zondervan, 2000).

[5] Belief in God, Jesus, the Bible, and other Christian claims has continued to decline in the United States but are still much higher than in Europe. See the following polls on the World Wide Web: "Poll: Christian Beliefs," Blue Meme, http://bluememe.blogspot.com/2004/12/poll-christian-beliefs.html (accessed February 25, 2007); "Beliefs About Jesus' Resurrection Among Christian Laity & Clergy," http://www .religioustolerance.org/resurrec8.htm (accessed February 25, 2007); "Comparing U.S. Religious Beliefs with Other 'Christian' Countries," http://www.religioustolerance.org/rel_comp.htm (accessed February 25, 2007); "The Religious and Other Beliefs of Americans 2003," *The Harris Poll*, http://www. harrisinteractive.com/harris_poll/index.asp?PID=359 (accessed February 25, 2007).

without special revelation? How one answers these questions is determined by one's methodology, as well as by one's perspectives on God, creation, man, and sin.

Divine revelation includes two general areas: (a) general revelation found in creation and human conscience and (b) propositional revelation from God in the Bible. Apologists differ as to whether God intends to use the former, known as natural theology, to assist men and women in receiving salvation or whether Scripture alone is sufficient to lead an unregenerate person to salvation in Christ. The view that general revelation is a sufficient tool in evangelism is accepted in Roman Catholic theology (after Vatican II), and even by many Protestants (the heathens are not lost so long as they follow the general revelation that God gives). But those who believe special revelation is a necessary means to create faith in the unconverted (recognizing the preevangelistic value of general revelation) is largely within Reformed theology. The extent to which an unregenerate person is capable of responding in saving faith to either natural or special revelation is debated among theologians and apologists. Some believe that the Spirit of God may simply aid reason in helping a person accept evidence of God's existence and even truth regarding the redemptive work of Christ, whereas others believe that a synergism of human ability and divine assistance is inadequate. Only the efficacious and monergistic work of the Spirit of God can bring the unregenerate to salvation. In the midst of this debate is the matter of common ground. What may be a basis of discussion with a person still unconvinced of the truth of the gospel? Do believers and unbelievers share a common ground philosophically that provides a bridge over which believers may lead unbelievers to faith in Christ? What presuppositions of unregenerate persons hinder or help them come to the truth of the gospel?

I. METHODS OF APOLOGETICS

Based on their view of these issues addressed in the preceding paragraph, apologists may be grouped in one of four approaches to apologetics:[6] classical apologetics, evidential apologetics, presuppositional apologetics, and fideistic/experiential apologetics.[7]

---

[6] One may also include fideism, the view that Christian truths are beyond reason and should only be defended only by the Scripture. This view was held by S. Kierkegaard and K. Barth and to some extent by M. Luther. For discussion of the latter, see, H. W. House, "The Value of Reason in Luther's View of Apologetics," *Concordia Journal* 7 (1981): 40–53. For a brief overview of these four views, with their strengths and weakness discussed, see H. W. House and J. M. Holden, *Charts of Apologetics and Christian Evidences* (Grand Rapids: Zondervan, 2006).

[7] A recent book includes two other methods of apologetics to the three above: the Reformed Epistemology Method, and the Cumulative Case Method. Others could be included too. But the purpose here is not to discuss in detail all the various methodologies. For more information see S. B. Cowan, ed., *Five Views on Apologetics* (Grand Rapids: Zondervan, 2000), 15–20; K. D. Boa and R. M. Bowman Jr., *Faith Has Its Reasons: Integrative Approaches to Defending the Christian Faith*, 2nd ed. (Colorado Springs, CO: Paternoster, 2006).

A. Classical Apologetics

The first view is the "classical method."[8] It is generally practiced in two or three steps (i.e., philosophical, theistic, and evidential). First, the apologist approaches the person being addressed from first principles, such as the laws of logic or the fact of one's own existence. With this established, then the various theistic arguments for God's existence are given. The third step, building on the first two, is to demonstrate that certain empirical or historical evidences may be proved regarding matters such as the truthfulness of Scripture, miracles, or the resurrection of Christ. The classical apologist believes that the unconverted, though separated spiritually and ethically from the true God, nonetheless has a rational capacity to understand arguments and to draw truthful conclusions when false assumptions are set aside. The use of first principles and theistic proofs is often called "natural theology."[9]

Norman Geisler, a classical apologist, provides a helpful example of how this argument may be made:

The Steps. The overall argument in defense of the Christian faith can be stated in twelve propositions. They flow logically one from another:

1. Truth about reality is knowable.
2. Opposites cannot both be true.
3. The theistic God exists.
4. Miracles are possible.
5. Miracles performed in connection with a truth claim are acts of God to confirm the truth of God through a messenger of God.
6. The New Testament documents are reliable.
7. As witnessed in the New Testament, Jesus claimed to be God.
8. Jesus' claim to divinity was proven by an [*sic*] unique convergence of miracles.
9. Therefore, Jesus was God in human flesh.
10. Whatever Jesus (who is God) affirmed as true, is true.
11. Jesus affirmed that the Bible is the Word of God.
12. Therefore, it is true that the Bible is the Word of God and whatever is opposed to any biblical truth is false.[10]

Then Geisler concludes:

If a theistic God exists and miracles are possible and Jesus is the Son of God and the Bible is the Word of God, then it follows that orthodox Christianity is true. All other essential orthodox doctrines, such as the Trinity, Christ's atonement for sin, the physical resurrection, and Christ's second coming, are taught in the Bible. Since all these conditions are supported by good

---

[8] The term *classical* is used because this method was used by the first apologists of the second and third centuries of the Christian era.

[9] For further description see N. L. Geisler, "Classical Apologetics," in *Baker Encyclopedia of Christian Apologetics* (Grand Rapids: Baker, 1999), 154–56; for a critique of some classical apologists, see G. J. Zemek Jr., "Classical Apologetics: A Rational Defense," *Grace Theological Journal* 7 (1986): 111–23.

[10] Geisler, "Apologetics, Arguments of," in *Baker Encyclopedia of Christian Apologetics*, 36–37.

evidence, it follows that there is good evidence for concluding that orthodox Christianity is true.

And since mutually exclusive propositions cannot both be true, then all opposing world religions are false religions. That is, Buddhism, Hinduism, Islam, and other religions are false insofar as they oppose the teachings of Christianity. Therefore, only Christianity is the true religion.[11]

Some of the proponents of classical apologetics are Augustine, Thomas Aquinas, C. S. Lewis, William Lane Craig, Norman L. Geisler, and J. P. Moreland. Classical apologetics has been criticized for an overemphasis on the use of reason that appeals to make an infinite God subject to human logic and finite reason. Those who oppose classical apologetics because of these perceived errors believe it devalues Christianity and attempts to bring God down to the human level. They say God's ways are higher than man's, and people should not try to comprehend Him intellectually (Isa 55:8–9). Classical apologists respond that though God is certainly not subject to human logic or reason, viewpoints that are argued by persons regarding God need to be tested by rules of thought. Also, though God's ways are indeed *beyond* finite reason, they are not *contrary* to reason (Isa 1:18; 1 Tim 6:20).

B. Rational Evidential Apologetics

The second view is the evidential method of apologetics, named for its emphasis on evidences that serve as common ground for believers and unbelievers. This method shares with the classical method the belief that the unregenerate have the capacity to hear rational argument and to be convinced of certain truths, though there is the recognition in both views that sin distorts the way in which information is received. The evidentialists do not argue that truth claims made in Christianity may be demonstrated in an absolute way, but rather that they can be shown to be most likely true, that they are both *reasonable* and *highly probable*. Rather than using the two- or three-step deductive method of classical apologists, which seeks to prove God's existence *before* moving to the evidence, the evidentialist seeks to demonstrate God's existence, and other Christian claims inductively, and not in any particular order or rational relationship.[12] What is argued largely depends on what the concern or question of the potential convert might be, so that matters relating to biblical veracity, the existence of God, the possibility of miracles, historical and archaeological data, or even experiential issues may be discussed, and may overlap with classical apologetics at several points.

---

[11] Ibid., 37. References in the original quotation have cross-referencing to other articles in the *Encyclopedia*, which have been deleted from the quotation.

[12] G. R. Habermas, "Evidential Apologetics," in *Five Views on Apologetics*, 92. For further discussion of evidential apologetics, see Geisler, *Baker Encyclopedia of Christian Apologetics*, 42. For a spirited defense of evidential apologetics against the view that the proclamation of Scripture, apart from arguments regarding the truthfulness of Scripture, is adequate, see J. W. Montgomery, "The Holy Spirit and the Defense of the Faith," *Bibliotheca Sacra* 154 (1997): 387–95. For a presuppositional response to the value of evidences, see J. C. Whitcomb Jr., "Contemporary Apologetics and the Christian Faith, Part IV: The Limitations and Values of Christian Evidences," *Bibliotheca Sacra* 135 (1978): 25–33.

Some of the proponents of evidential apologetics are William Paley, John Warwick Montgomery, Joseph Butler, Bernard Ramm, and Josh McDowell. Critics of this method argue that empirical evidences are only *interpreted* through presuppositions and the framework of one's worldview. Thus they say these evidences should be properly joined with the philosophical assumptions of the evidence being discussed, and some critics say these assumptions should precede the evidentiary presentation. Evidentialists would respond that evidence is in fact not necessarily "self-evident" but instead provides a reason and high probability to conclude that the truths of Christianity are consistent with the facts. Also, philosophical considerations, it is argued, often involve empirical evidences, such as the cosmological and teleological arguments for the existence of God.

A Possible Solution to the Evidentialist-Presuppositionalist Difficulty

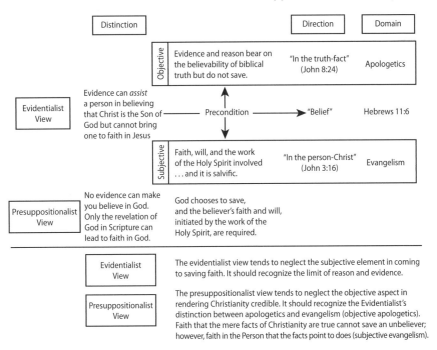

C. Presuppositional Apologetics

Advocates of the presuppositional method include Cornelius Van Til, Abraham Kuyper, and John Frame. They have a considerably different perspective on the possibility of common ground between the believer and unbeliever than the other two methods. This method assumes that people have certain presuppositions on which they base their beliefs. For example if people presuppose that God cannot exist, it is likely that no amount of contrary information or contrary argument will persuade them that He does. They will doubt the reliability of the information and explain away the arguments because for them the matter is already settled. The Christian presuppositionalist assumes the biblical revelation in all matters relating to conceptions of reality and logic. From a Christian perspective sin keeps the unregenerate sinner from sharing concepts of truth or morality with the regenerate who has been released from the bondage of sin and able to understand the wisdom of God. The Christian presuppositionalist's task is to demonstrate to the unregenerate person, who is using irrational methods and distorted truth, that only biblical presuppositions provide the necessary means to make sense of the world and life.[13] Thus the apologist must presuppose the special revelation of God in presenting a defense of Christian truth; all knowledge must be understood as presupposing the existence of the God of the Bible.

D. Fideistic/Experiential Apologetics

The fideistic or experiential method of apologetics is distinguished from the previous models of defending the Christian faith by its belief that apologetics should be accomplished by the experience of faith, not by fallen man's reason. That is, one's theological knowledge of God is discovered in the Scriptures and can be engaged and applied only by faith. No rational justification or proof is necessary as a defense. Fideism/experientialism often describes Christianity as beyond, above, or against reason. However, this is not to assert that Christianity is irrational but rather that some of its concepts and doctrines are inexpressible and unintelligible to the human mind. This is not to suggest that fideistic apologetists give no answer in defense of the faith; on the contrary they engage in both negative and positive aspects of apologetics. Negatively, fideism asserts that the use of rational argumentation is insufficient to reason for Christianity, and positively it argues for the sufficiency of the faith experience to discover and answer theological challenges. Some of the proponents of fideism are Martin Luther,[14] Søren Kierkegaard (who is credited with the idea of a "leap of faith" in regard to the Christian experience), and Karl Barth.

Opponents of fideism argue that the view is inconsistent, if not contradictory, on both biblical and philosophical grounds. This has been demonstrated, it is said, by the fact that God, in Scripture, encourages the use of reason regarding spiritual matters (Isa 1:18; 1 Pet 3:15). They also point out that it is not possible to believe in God without first believing that He exists (Heb 11:6). Moreover, a rational defense of fideism appears contradictory and self-refuting since reason is used to suggest that one should not use reason to defend Christianity. Fideists have responded that reason cannot be the basis for salvation or faith; God must be. Furthermore reasons are not adequate to enable a person to believe; instead God the Holy Spirit bears witness to the human mind and heart, a subjective act.

---

[13] For further discussion see Geisler, "Presuppositional Apologetics," in *Baker Encyclopedia of Christian Apologetics*, 607–8.

[14] However, see House, "The Value of Reason in Luther's View of Apologetics." Also, some argue that Luther was a precursor to fideist apologetics, not that he was an explicit fideist himself. See Boa and Bowman, *Faith Has Its Reasons*.

II.   EVALUATION OF APOLOGETIC APPROACHES

In reading apologists for these varying perspectives, one sometimes senses that they are like ships passing in the night. This is often a question of emphasis and definition of terms. Neither classical apologists nor evidential apologists, in general, believe that arguments for the existence of God or proof of biblical historicity will cause a person to embrace Christ;[15] they affirm that the reception of the gospel through the work of the Holy Spirit is necessary.[16] Also few presuppositionalists believe that the fallen person is incapable of acknowledging God's existence—in fact this is presupposed—or that certain facts of history or science, even miracles, are true. They only insist that none of this will cause the fallen person to embrace Christ—fallen man needs the gospel and the work of the Spirit of God. In reality apologists representing these different approaches reveal in their writings much that they hold in common: that there is the *sensus divinitatis* spoken of by Calvin in which humans have innate knowledge of God's existence; that there is objective truth to be known; that humans are fallen creatures; that unbelievers are incapable of embracing the truth of Christ apart from the divine work of the Holy Spirit; and that presenting rational arguments for God's existence, proof of the authenticity of the Scriptures, and evidence for the resurrection of Christ are never substitutes for the proclamation of the good news of Jesus' death, burial, and resurrection.

If, then, these competing methodologies have so much in common, when all the innuendos and misrepresentations are noted, may it be that they also have something to offer to apologists who desire to present the gospel of Christ to fallen humanity? We believe so.

Ronald Mayers points out that this division between classical/evidential apologetics and presuppositional apologetics is not something new. The ideas of these systems date back to the Greeks between Plato and Aristotle, and later between René Descartes

---

[15] Classical apologist W. L. Craig comments, "[W]hat about the role of the Holy Spirit in the life of an unbeliever? Since the Holy Spirit does not indwell him, does this mean he must rely upon arguments and evidence to convince him that Christianity is true? No, not at all. According to Scripture, God has a different ministry of the Holy Spirit especially geared to the needs of the unbeliever" (*Reasonable Faith: Christian Truth and Apologetics* [Wheaton, IL: Crossway, 2008], 46). "Warfield agreed with Calvin that proofs cannot bring people to Christ or even convince them of the divine authority of Scripture. Nonetheless, Warfield believed that the Holy Spirit exercises his convincing power through them" (Norman L. Geisler, "Warfield, B.B.," in *Baker Encyclopedia of Christian Apologetics*, 769). Bernard Ramm, an evidentialist, says, "[N]o well-grounded apologist will state that the philosophic demonstration of Christianity saves a man, but it is, to the contrary, quite evident that no man will give the necessary credence to the Word if he has certain mistaken notions and biased opinions about the facts and nature of the Christian religion" (B. Ramm, *Protestant Christian Evidences* [Chicago: Moody, 1953], 15).

[16] Montgomery says, "Ultimately a non-Christian must make a moral choice as to what he will do with the objectively sound case for Christianity. If he exercises his will to accept the Christ of the Scriptures, that act must be attributed to the Spirit alone as a pure gift of grace. But the monergistic event of conversion no more denigrates or renders superfluous the work of the apologist than it does the work of the preacher or evangelist who presented the saving message to the individual in the first place. The Holy Spirit does not create the gospel or the evidence for it; He applies what is preached and defended to produce salvation" ("The Holy Spirit and the Defense of the Faith," 392).

and John Locke.[17] The contrast is akin to the debate between deduction and induction, between the perspective of innate principles from which one must deductively construct his worldview and whether one must instead construct his view of reality inductively a little bit at a time.[18] Similarly presuppositionalists believe that we must presuppose God-first principles, such as rationality or truth, whereas evidentialists (and classical apologists, though they also accept deduction from first principles that both saved and unsaved share by virtue of the *imago Dei*) aver that a case should be built from the pieces of historical and scientific evidence that demonstrates the truthfulness of Christian truth claims.[19] After positing the ways in which these approaches to apologetics differ from their historical precursors, Mayers asks, "Must these two approaches to knowledge remain mutually exclusive, or nearly so, in Christian apologetics?"[20] He follows his question with a surprising, but encouraging, conclusion:

> It is the contention of a Both/And apologetic that both evidentialism and presuppositionalism are correct. God most definitely is the self-existent Creator, but He is also the One who not only makes our history possible, but has frequently joined us. As Creator, God is certainly the presupposition of everything. Presuppositionalism is correct: there is nothing if there is not God. Evidentialism is correct also, however, because this God has invaded our history and left a historical path that we can trace. The trail of evidence His invasions left behind include the archaeological remains that inductively support the truth of the Old Testament as well as the various evidences that establish the historical reliability of the Gospels and that point to Jesus as the incarnate God/Man and not simply a fine ethical teacher, as C. S. Lewis showed in his *Mere Christianity*.
>
> In one sense, presuppositionalism begins with God while evidentialism begins with man. They are both right! As Creator, God is primary and logically prior to all our thoughts. There is a difference, however, between logical priority and existential beginning. We are not God and thus must begin "where we are."[21]

Mayers is correct in his assessment. A common ground exists between nonpresuppositional (classical and evidential apologetics) and presuppositional apologetics, as stated earlier. John Calvin understood this. He began his monumental work, *Institutes of the Christian Religion*, with these words: "Our wisdom, in so far as it ought to be deemed true and solid wisdom, consists almost entirely of two parts: the knowledge of

---

[17] R. B. Mayers, "Both/And: A Biblical Alternative to the Presuppositional/Evidential Debate," in *Evangelical Apologetics*, ed. M. Bauman, D. W. Hall, and R. C. Newman (Camp Hill, PA: Christian, 1996), 35. See also R. B. Mayers, *Balanced Apologetics: Using Evidences and Presuppositions in Defense of the Faith* (Grand Rapids: Kregel, 1984).

[18] Mayers, "Both/And," 35.

[19] Ibid., 35.

[20] Ibid., 36.

[21] Ibid., 36–37.

God and the knowledge of ourselves. But as these are connected together by many ties, it is not easy to determine which of the two precedes, and gives birth to the other."[22]

Evangelical apologists agree that human depravity is total, and that sin has permeated the entirety of each human. This separates men and women from necessary association with God required for eternal life, and it also causes people to arrive at wrong presuppositions using faulty reasoning. Unregenerate persons deny the true God and live in ways contrary to Him. But this does not mean that the unregenerate cannot do anything on the human plain.[23] No one can deny that unregenerate people carry on life in ways similar to the regenerate. In the spiritual realm they can believe in a divine being and worship this being, though ignorantly. In the sphere of the intellect, the unregenerate can reason and research in the same manner as the regenerate, recognize at least some things that are true, and can even understand passages of Scripture. Moreover, they have effective actions no less than the saved, for they may excel in the arts and sciences. In the ethical and social realm, they can act with magnanimity toward family and friends, showing genuine love and concern, and even great sacrifice. These are all examples of what theologians have recognized since Calvin[24] as the common grace of God, though aspects of this doctrine may even be seen in Augustine.[25]

Dennis Johnson presents a good case for God's common grace for the unregenerate. They are able to use the *imago Dei* in such various positive pursuits as those stated in the previous paragraph, and to understand truth about the world and God.[26] Johnson's thinking was argued several hundred years earlier by Calvin, who said:

> Whenever we come upon these matters in secular writers, let that admirable light of truth shining in them teach us that the mind of man, though fallen and perverted from its wholeness, is nevertheless clothed and ornamented with God's excellent gifts. If we regard the Spirit of God as the sole fountain of truth, we shall neither reject the truth itself, nor despise it wherever it shall appear, unless we wish to dishonor the Spirit of God. . . . Shall we deny that the truth shone upon the ancient jurists who established civic order and discipline with such great equity? Shall we say that the philosophers were

---

[22] J. Calvin, *The Institutes of the Christian Religion*, trans. F. L. Battles, ed. John T. McNeill, Library of Christian Classics (Philadelphia: Westminster, 1960), 1.1.1.

[23] This appears to be acknowledged by C. Van Til, when he says, "The actual situation is therefore always a mixture of truth with error. Being 'without God in the world' the natural man yet knows God, and, in spite of himself, to some extent recognizes God. By virtue of their creation in God's image, by virtue of the ineradicable sense of deity within them and by virtue of God's restraining general grace, those who hate God, yet in a restricted sense know God, and do good" (*An Introduction to Systematic Theology* [Phillipsburg, NJ: P&R, 1979], 27).

[24] Summarizing Calvin's perspective, L. Berkhof says, "This is a grace which is communal, does not pardon nor purify human nature, and does not effect the salvation of sinners. It curbs the destructive power of sin, maintains in a measure the moral order of the universe, thus making an orderly life possible, distributes in varying degrees gifts and talents among men, promotes the development of science and art, and showers untold blessings upon the children of men" (*Systematic Theology*, rev. and enlarged ed. [Grand Rapids: Eerdmans, 1941], 434).

[25] Ibid., 433.

[26] D. E. Johnson, "Spiritual Antithesis: Common Grace, and Practical Theology," *Westminster Theological Journal* 64 (Spring 2002): 73–94.

blind in their fine observation and artful description of nature? Shall we say that those men were devoid of understanding who conceived the art of disputation and taught us to speak reasonably? Shall we say that they are insane who developed medicine, devoting their labor to our benefit? What shall we say of all the mathematical sciences? Shall we consider them the ravings of madmen? No, we cannot read the writings of the ancients on these subjects without great admiration. We marvel at them because we are compelled to recognize how preeminent they are.[27]

Johnson continues with important insight. He says that there is a great division within humanity between those born anew and those still dead in their sins, but common grace is a unifying element between these two extremes. Believers and unbelievers err in maintaining consistency when it comes to truth, though the unbeliever has a fundamental inclination to suppress the truth (Rom 1:18).[28] But common grace keeps the unbeliever from doing this at every instant. In contrast, the efficacious grace of God saves Christians and gives them a fundamental disposition to embrace God, though at times they fail in this commitment to God.

These two components—common grace and the innate properties of the *imago Dei*—may be put together. They enable an unregenerate person who has no spiritual life from God, and has total inability in himself, to appropriate the spiritual things of God. Neither common grace nor the *imago Dei* can save a person, but in concert they may help a person be sensitive to events, words, and gospel proclamation that the Holy Spirit may choose to use to bring him to Christ through the gospel (2 Thess 2:13–14).

A tremendous difference exists between stating a fact that is true and embracing that fact in some form of commitment. The unbeliever is capable of stating a fact. He or she may believe *that* something is true, but this is only half the battle with regard to becoming a person born from above. For example Jewish non-Christian Pinchas Lapide acknowledges that Jesus came back from the dead; he notes that this is the only reasonable explanation for the evidence. Yet even while acknowledging this, he does not consider Jesus the Messiah.[29] Others even in Jesus' day knew that Jesus died on the cross, or that He did marvelous miracles. However, the unregenerate may know as true the same things a regenerate person knows is true. But this is not enough. Though the man without the Spirit may know certain things about God (Rom 1:19–20), he is incapable of receiving or appropriating the things of God that relate to one's position before God and in God (1 Cor 2:14). There is a marked distinction between knowing truth and having the proper interpretation of the truth.[30] The latter is from the Holy Spirit, as the believer observes and meditates on the special revelation of God.

---

[27] Calvin, *Institutes of the Christian Religion*, 2.2.15, quoted in ibid., 75.

[28] Opinions differ on the meaning of "suppress" in Rom 1:18. See S. L. Johnson Jr., "Paul and the Knowledge of God," *Bibliotheca Sacra* 129 (January–March 1972): 67.

[29] P. Lapide, *The Resurrection of Jesus: A Jewish Perspective* (Philadelphia: Augsburg, 1983).

[30] On the importance of connecting facts to significance see A. E. McGrath, "Apologetics to the Jews," *Bibliotheca Sacra* 155 (April–June 1998): 136–38. McGrath says, "Christians need to do more than simply prove that Jesus died on a cross and rose again. They need to convey the significance of those facts for the fallen, lost world" (ibid., 137).

Mayers identifies three forms of knowledge: logical, empirical, and intuitive.[31] In Romans 1 Paul seems to assert these three forms. According to Paul God created a world that can be understood[32] and from which human beings, though fallen into sin, should be able to deduce the existence of God. Moreover, this knowledge of God is found within man. The problem in the passage, then, is not that man cannot know God and not that the way to this knowledge is inadequate. The problem is that humans suppress and distort knowledge of God, are without gratitude, and become futile and foolish. Nonetheless unsaved humans can come to know about God, the true God, without trusting this God. This is proved by the fact that Pharaoh and the Egyptians were able to know Yahweh in a nonsalvific way because of the proofs He gave to them of his existence, His power, and His identity (Exod 7:3–5; 10:1–2).[33]

So then, common grace is the common ground between the regenerate and unregenerate, but it does not substitute for the gospel. Regeneration does not come simply by knowing truths learned from creation, nature, conscience, or historical events and evidences.[34] The Holy Spirit may use events in one's life to bring comprehension of truth or God's common grace to place the unregenerate in the proper attitude or disposition to embrace the gospel (moving from believing *that* to believing *in*). On the other hand sin has a tremendous impact on both the regenerate and the unregenerate. Both are capable of believing truth and falsehood, of following an ethical or unethical course of conduct. God's special work of grace is what enables humans to rise above the impact of sin in their lives. This dynamic is seen in the apologetic ministry of the apostle Paul, his encounter with unregenerate Jews in Asia and Greece, and particularly unbelieving intellectuals in Athens.

III. CONCLUSION

Several approaches are available to apologists, from classical to evidential to presuppositional to fideist. Each has strengths and weaknesses, and each presents valid and useful apologetics. The Christian apologist, then, needs to understand each approach thoroughly and glean the best from each of them. Further, the apologist needs to be able to employ different approaches in different contexts. Every person will react and be reached differently, so there is no one approach that will work every time.

---

[31] Mayers, *Balanced Apologetics*, 36–57.

[32] "Something about human nature seems to prompt it to ask questions about the world. And something about the world seems to allow answers to be given to those questions" (A. E. McGrath, "Apologetics to the Greeks," *Bibliotheca Sacra* 155 [July–September 1998]: 263). The capacity for discovery in the universe is rare, yet this is available to humans on planet earth. For an excellent study of this truth, see G. Gonzales and J. W. Richards, *The Privileged Planet: How Our Place in the Cosmos Is Designed for Discovery* (Washington, DC: Regnery; Lanham, MD, 2004).

[33] See discussion by Mayers, *Balanced Apologetics*, 49–52.

[34] Though common grace may enable the fallen creature to exercise his innate abilities founded in the *imago Dei*, common grace cannot save, and apart from the regenerative work of the Holy Spirit a person will not receive the grace of God in salvation. As W. G. T. Shedd said, "Regeneration rests upon God's election and not upon man's preparative acts, upon special grace and not upon common grace" (*Dogmatic Theology*, 3rd ed., ed. A. W. Gomes [Phillipsburg, NJ: P&R, 2003], 781).

Defending the faith with an atheist will be vastly different from presenting the gospel to someone who already believes in some form of deity, for example. For this reason the approach taken by the apologist must match the person with whom he is defending the faith. This means the apologist needs to be able to discern where the person is spiritually, intellectually, and philosophically. Of course the apologist may discern this only by personal interaction.

Chapter 4

CATEGORIES OF APOLOGETICS

THOSE WHO ENGAGE IN THE STUDY of apologetics recognize basic types of apologetic activity. These six are: philosophical, theistic, religious, biblical, scientific, and cultural.

I. PHILOSOPHICAL APOLOGETICS[1]

Many would undoubtedly object to the use of philosophy for Christian apologetics based on Paul's warning against its use when he wrote, "Be careful that no one takes you captive through philosophy and empty deceit based on human tradition, based on the elemental forces of the world, and not based on Christ" (Col 2:8). Furthermore, it has been argued that the discipline of philosophy has pagan and secular roots in the early speculative systems of Thales, Heraclitus, Socrates, Plato, and Aristotle, and for that reason alone it should be avoided. In response to the first argument, Paul was most likely referring to a particular type of philosophical system, which later developed into Gnosticism. He may also have been referring to the kind of specious philosophical speculations he encountered in Athens in the systems of the Epicureans and the Stoics of his day. Also, one who rejects truth simply because of its origins is committing what is referred to as the "genetic fallacy." If this objection is true, then such benefits from modern medicine, science, technology, education, and logic must be avoided because of their pagan origins.

Since philosophical apologetics is a vast field of study, only a thumbnail sketch is presented here.[2] As formidable a tool as it is, philosophical reasoning does not in itself resolve all theological debate, for it is a supplemental feature of the disciplines of theology and apologetics. Its primary use is for clarification of certain principles of thought, such as the existence of God, the nature of truth, the nature of reality, and the like. One cannot offer an apologetic defense of the Christian faith without providing a cogent rationale for the acknowledgment of objective truth regarding the Bible, science, and other such fields of inquiry. The study of philosophy forces individuals to evaluate their own presuppositions, prejudices, and arguments carefully to see if they

---

[1] The following discussion is adapted from H. W. House and J. M. Holden, *Charts of Apologetics and Christian Evidences* (Grand Rapids: Zondervan, 2006), part 2, "Philosophical Apologetics."

[2] For an outline of all facets of philosophical apologetics, see ibid., charts 10–25.

conform to what is known about reality and to see if they are consistent with biblical truth. This will contribute to an understanding of the truth and a greater appreciation for the God Christians worship.

The various tools of philosophy assist in employing sound reasoning principles to form valid arguments. An argument is any group of statements or propositions in which one (the conclusion) is claimed to follow from the others. The two distinct types of arguments are referred to as inductive and deductive arguments. These require either good evidence to support the truthfulness of the premises, or the premises must be known universally to be true without need of evidential support. The inductive argument is also called the "reliable argument," and the deductive argument is also referred to as a "conclusive argument." The discipline of philosophy also seeks to identify various types of logical "fallacies," such as the *Quaternio Terminorum* (*Four Terms*) fallacy, the fallacy of the *Undistributed Middle* (the middle term is not placed in the correct order in the argument), the fallacy of the *Illicit* (*Undistributed*) *Major* (where the major term is in the conclusion but not in the major premise), the *Exclusive Premises* (two negative premises), and the *Existential* fallacy (two universal premises with a specific conclusion).[3] Knowledge of these philosophical "pitfalls" can assist the Christian apologist in recognizing specious arguments by recognizing their technical fallacies or "mistakes" in logical thinking. The idea is, of course, that if the logical progression of one's argument is in error, then the conclusion is at best unreliable or at worst, false.

This suggests that there are logical "laws," which is quite true. Four laws of logic are recognized universally: (1) The Law of Identity, wherein a statement or proposition is identical to itself (Exod 3:14), and is expressed formally as *A is A*. (2) The Law of the Excluded Middle, wherein every statement is either true or false, with no middle alternative (Matt 12:30), and is expressed formally as *A is either A or non-A*. (3) The Law of Noncontradiction, wherein no statement can be both true and false at the same time and in the same sense (1 Tim 6:20), and is expressed formally as *A is not non-A*. (4) The Law of Rational Inference, in which inferences or conclusions can be made by reasoning from a series of premises to a sound conclusion, and is expressed formally as *A is in B; B is in C; therefore A is in C*.

Some object to the validity of the laws of logic. Some argue, for example, that no laws of logic are absolutely certain. In response, however, the four laws stated above are self-evident and cannot be rationally denied. When one attempts to deny them, they must invariably rely on the very laws of logic they want to deny. For example if one said, "There are no laws of logic," then one has automatically assumed the very laws of logic, in that one must employ the laws of logic to make the distinction between the existence and nonexistence of laws of logic. Such a statement is "self-refuting." Another objection is that logic is simply man's reasoning and does not apply to God at all. This objection too is self-refuting since it uses "man's reasoning" and is a logical statement about God. The objection is either logical or it is not. If it is logical, then

---

[3] For a full discussion of these fallacies, see ibid., chart 13.

the objection defeats itself. If the objection is not logical, then it is illogical, and hence there is no reason for anyone to believe that the objection is true.

II.   THEISTIC APOLOGETICS[4]

Theistic apologetics historically deals with the classical arguments for the existence of God. The use of this apologetic category takes one into the realm of worldviews and their differences. The seven major worldviews are: atheism, polytheism, panentheism, finitism, pantheism, deism, and theism (see chap. 2, "Worldviews"). The adoption of any one of the seven worldviews will determine what one believes about the nature of God, the origin of the universe, God's relationship to that universe, the existence of miracles, truth, morality, life after death, and one's view of Jesus.

When one thinks of theistic apologetics, one usually associates this category with the classical arguments for the existence of God. The great proponent of those classical arguments was Thomas Aquinas. These have come down to us as the "five ways" of proving (yes, *proving*) the existence of God. Thomas Aquinas's arguments are the Argument from Motion, the Cosmological Argument, the Argument from Possibility and Necessity, the Argument from Perfection, and the Teleological Argument. These arguments (once Thomas Aquinas popularized them in the thirteenth century) proved to be a formidable phalanx of defense against the most incipient forms of atheism until Immanuel Kant (1724–1804) and the eighteenth-century philosophers mounted their concerted attack against them. Since then, many modern theologians have shied away from utilizing these classical arguments for the existence of God in their apologetic defense of Christianity.

Of the five arguments for the existence of God, the most formidable in the opinion of its opponents by far was the Teleological Argument, or the Argument from Design. The argument briefly goes something like this: There is an observable order or design in the world that cannot be attributed to the object itself (such as inanimate objects). This observable order argues for an intelligent being who established this order.

Another strong argument in support of God's existence is the Argument from Necessity. This argument postulates that all "things" that exist in the universe are finite beings and therefore as such cannot be the cause of their own existence. Every individual thing is a dependent thing, that is, dependent on some other thing for its existence. This is called "contingency." An infinite regression of finite, contingent things is impossible; therefore there must be a "necessary" Being that exists absolutely independently, that is, not dependent on anything else. This *necessary* Being is God.

The initial shock of the eighteenth-century Enlightenment onslaught has worn off over the years, and there has been a steady resurgence of interest in theistic apologetics as a means of arguing for the existence of God. However, this or any other apologetic tool is simply that—a tool. These tools are not intended to supplant the role of evangelism but to augment evangelism in whatever is appropriate for the occasion.

---

4 The following discussion is adapted from ibid., charts 26–33.

Not every situation will call for the Argument from Necessity or the Teleological argument. One must be sensitive to the leading of the Holy Spirit to know when such arguments as these are appropriate. With that in mind, it should also be emphasized that a thorough grasp of these ancient arguments is just as useful as preparatory means of evangelism today as they were centuries ago. Therefore after some reflection, it seems clear that the once-persuasive arguments of the eighteenth-century philosophers against the theistic proofs of God's existence were not as devastating as once believed and that the assumed demise of Christianity was greatly exaggerated.

III. RELIGIOUS APOLOGETICS[5]

This apologetic category deals with three theories on the origin of religion: the Subjective/Projection/Psychological Theory, the Evolutionary Theory, and the Original Monotheism Theory.

A. The Subjective/Projection/Psychological Theory

As stated earlier, after the Enlightenment attacks against the basis of the Christian faith, many Christians sought to make Christianity in particular and religion in general relevant to the prevailing "scientific" realities of the eighteenth and nineteenth centuries. One approach to the origin of religion was to treat it as a psychological phenomenon rather than the study of an objective Being within a historical context. Instead of being found within a verifiable historical context, religion resides within the realm of a person's emotions and feelings and is an extension of one's psychological desires. This theory explains religion in terms of symbols and behaviors rather than doctrinal propositions. Since religion begins at the level of the subconscious, the mental projection of God is not assumed as an object of faith at all but rather is viewed as only a subjective reality. Proponents of this theory were not unanimous in their psychological bases. Friedrich Schleiermacher, for example, began with the idea of absolute dependence, Ludwig Feuerbach proposed that man worships an idealized notion of the self, Sigmund Freud taught that religion is an idealized father image, Rudolph Otto asserted that religion is an encounter with the feeling of holiness, and Carl Jung defined religion in terms of primal images or archetypes that recur universally among humanity in dreams.

This theory obviously ignores the historical evidence in favor of religion. It also neglects the possibility that God placed the religious impulse within humans and therefore does not preclude the objective reality of religion. And why must one assume that "feelings" or "desires" are related to the way one understands God? One could simply assert that the subjectivist must have a psychological desire to distort the origin of religion.

---

5 The following discussion is adapted from ibid., charts 34–39.

B. The Evolutionary Theory

Although this theory has been expressed in various forms throughout the writings of some Greek philosophers, Charles Darwin first postulated the theory that religion evolves,[6] and later Herbert Spencer popularized the idea in the mid-nineteenth century. Spencer viewed religion as having progressed through various evolutionary stages of development, beginning with the most primitive expression, sometimes referred to as "manna" but more widely called spiritism or animism, which is the awareness of an invisible supernatural power or force in nature (which is often viewed as inhabiting animals, celestial bodies, and inanimate objects). Subsequent development found expression in ancestor worship, polytheism (belief in many gods), and in the pinnacle of religious development, monotheism (belief in one God). In this theory monotheism is believed to be the result of increased religious sophistication among developing peoples (such as the Jews). This theory rests on the presupposition that Darwin's theory of ascent, from simple to complex, over millions of years without the intervention of a creator, is true, as well as the assumption that monotheism is the most complex religious expression, whereas spiritism or "manna" is the simplest.[7]

The theory of the evolution of religion has been seriously challenged in the past 50 years or so. Although it has been credited with attempting a serious historical investigation into the origin and development of religious expressions, it has been demonstrated that the evolutionary theory has serious problems that have never been resolved. Several studies, such as Wilhelm Schmidt's *The Origin and Growth of Religion: Facts and Theories,* have proposed that earlier cultures believed in one ultimate god above all others, which directly challenges the religious evolutionary theory.[8]

C. The Original Monotheism Theory

This theory proposes that God is the primary source of religion. Wilhelm Schmidt has collected data from all over the world from each major continent and demonstrated an early belief in a sky God. Among the most ancient cultures of Africa and Australia, Schmidt found a strong worship of God without the practice of magic, the very opposite conclusion from that set forth in the evolutionary theory. The Abrahamic religions of Judaism and Christianity teach that at the beginning of creation there was only God. Man was created directly by God, who subsequently disobeyed Him and fell in spiritual, moral, and physical ruin. In the classical theism of Augustine, Anselm, and Aquinas, and of Judaism, this transcendent God is one, eternal, self-existing, merciful, and compassionate. In stark contrast to the evolutionary theory of religious progression, original monotheism proposes that instead of evolving to a belief in one God, there has been "devolution" on a massive scale from belief in the one God of creation.

---

[6] See C. Darwin, *Descent of Man and Selection in Relation to Sex* (New York: Appleton, 1871), 1:62–66.

[7] See W. Corduan for a presentation of the view that monotheism is the initial religion from which other forms devolved (*Neighboring Faiths: A Christian Introduction to World Religions* [Downers Grove, IL: InterVarsity, 1998], 24–35).

[8] For more on this topic, see ibid.

This departure follows a random pattern in the direction of henotheism, polytheism, and animism.

Proponents of original monotheism should be acknowledged for their investigation and appreciation of the historical and relational aspects of religion. In an age when the evolutionary theory has dominated all fields of human endeavor, their comprehensive treatment of the subject has provided ample information to supplement research in the field of religious studies and to challenge an established ideological hegemony. Some have accused proponents of original monotheism of bias in research even though it is a truism that all researchers have bias. The real questions are these: Which bias is true? Which theory best supports the data? Others have complained that original monotheism is contrary to the established theory of evolution and modern cultural anthropology. True, the view of original monotheism contradicts the conventional wisdom on the evolution of religion, but it should be pointed out that the real interloper on the historical scene is the evolutionary theory.

IV. BIBLICAL APOLOGETICS[9]

An easy way to understand biblical apologetics, among other things, is to think of the twin sciences of Old Testament and New Testament archaeology. The science of archaeology has provided an extensive confirmation of the historicity of the Old and the New Testaments, and particularly the latter. The evidence for its reliability is overwhelming.[10] Several things, however, should be kept in mind when reviewing archaeological evidence in relation to Christianity.

First, archaeological evidence does not stand on its own. It depends on various factors, such as the context of date, place, and materials at hand. The evidence is understood on the basis of the interpreter's presuppositions. This means that two individuals may look on the same evidence and come to different conclusions.

Second, archaeology is a specialized form of science that does not fit under the category of physics or chemistry. Archaeologists possess only the evidence left from the one time and place that civilization flourished. The discoveries cannot be repeated as in other sciences in a laboratory. At best, archaeology attempts to find plausible and probable explanations for the evidence that it brings to light. It cannot create laws as physics can. Therefore the best interpretation is the one that best explains the evidence at hand.

Third, archaeological evidence is fragmentary at best. Although archaeological artifacts and facts have been discovered, they comprise only a tiny fraction of all that occurred in that particular site or civilization. Hence the discovery of more data can alter the picture considerably. Many critical views of the Bible's historical veracity have been overturned by archaeological discoveries. For example, many held that the Bible

---

[9] The following discussion is adapted from House and Holden, *Charts of Apologetics and Christian Evidences,* charts 40–60.

[10] N. L. Geisler, "Archaeology, New Testament," in *Baker Encyclopedia of Christian Apologetics* (Grand Rapids: Baker, 1999), 46. The following discussion is based on this article.

was in error because it mentioned a people called the Hittites (Gen 23:10). However, the discovery in 1906 of the Hittite library in modern Turkey vindicated the biblical text.

A number of important archaeological discoveries have provided impressive evidence of the historical veracity of the Scriptures. Such evidence can lend considerable credibility to a presentation of the gospel in the right context. Following are just a few of the archaeological discoveries that shed light on Christianity and that can prove useful in biblical apologetics.

A. Archaeological Evidence Bearing on the Old Testament

1. Adam and Eve seal (c. 3500 BC)

This is a Sumerian seal found by E. A. Speiser which depicts a naked man and woman bowed in humiliation and being driven out, followed by a serpent (Gen 3:23).

2. Amarna tablets (c. 1400 BC)

In 1887 a peasant woman happened across a cache of ancient clay tablets with cuneiform inscriptions. Subsequent deciphering revealed the early conquests of Canaan by the Hebrews known by the name "Habiru." These tablets, along with other tablets discovered at Mari and Nuzi, confirm that the Habiru were well known in Mesopotamia by the early second millennium BC.

3. Black obelisk of Shalmaneser III (841 BC)

This obelisk was discovered in 1846 by A. H. Layard in the palace of Nimrud. It confirms the historical identity and military victories of the Assyrian king (and biblical figure) Shalmaneser III. Of great interest the obelisk portrays Israel's king, "Jehu, son of Omri," bowing in homage before Shalmaneser (2 Kings 9–10).

4. Ebla tablets (c. 2350 BC)

This amazing discovery by archaeologist Paolo Matthiae while excavating Tell Mardikh, south of Aleppo, Syria, yielded approximately 16,000 clay tablets that describe various cities such as Sodom, Zeboim, Hazor, Megiddo, Jerusalem, and Gaza, which were previously thought by critics to be mythological. In addition the tablets reveal names resembling such names as Nahor, Israel, Michael, Ishmael, and Eber used some 200 years later. Several deities named Dagon and Baal are also identified, and correlate with the biblical narrative.

5. Tell Dan inscription (ninth century BC)

In 1993 a stunning discovery was made by Tell Dan excavators in the area of northern Galilee near Mount Hermon. They unearthed a stone slab containing several lines of incomplete Aramaic inscriptions. Among the identifiable inscriptions were the first extrabiblical citations of King David, which read, "The House of David" and "The

King of Israel." Later discoveries also refer to Jehoram and Ahaziah, names mentioned in 2 Kings 8–9.[11]

B. Archaeological Evidence Bearing on the New Testament

1. James ossuary (AD 63—though still under debate)

This 20-inch-long limestone box is thought to have been the repository for the bones of James, brother of Jesus. The side panel of the box has an Aramaic script with the words, "James, son of Joseph, brother of Jesus." The authenticity of the ossuary is doubted by the Israeli Antiquities Authority (currently led by a political appointment rather than a scholar, who is antagonistic to the discovery) but is viewed by many scholars specializing in the field of palaeography, geology, and epigraphy as authentic.[12] If it is authentic, the ossuary would be the earliest extrabiblical evidence directly relating to James and Jesus.

2. Other Jewish ossuaries (AD 40–50)

Several other burial ossuaries near Jerusalem were found with the sign of the cross and various prayers directed to Jesus etched on them. They indicate an early belief in the significance of Jesus' death on the cross and the fact that He is God.

3. Pilate inscription (first century)

Antonio Frova discovered a stone slab at Caesarea Maritima with a Latin inscription that reads, "Tiberium Pontius Pilate Prefect of Judea." This is the only archaeological evidence found to date that gives Pilate's name and title.

4. Gallio inscription (first century)

In 1908 an inscription was found in northern Greece at the site of Delphi that identifies "Gallio" as "proconsul" being in office from AD 51 to 53, which corresponds to Luke's record in Acts 18:12–17.

5. Zeus and Hermes (first century)

In 1909 archaeologists unearthed several inscriptions and a temple near Lystra that identified Zeus and Hermes as the two most important gods of the city, since it was believed they visited the earth. These gods were expected to return in the future, which helps biblical scholars understand the strong reaction of the people when they thought that the expectation was realized in identifying Barnabas and Paul as Zeus and Hermes (Acts 14:8–12).

---

[11] Additional archaeological finds include the Babylonian Chronicles, the Balaam inscription, the Cylinder of Nabonidus, the Cyrus Cylinder, Hezekiah's Tunnel and the Siloam Inscription found in it, the King Hezekaih Seal, the Ketef Hinnom Silver Scrolls, and the Baruch Seal.

[12] For a general overview see C. A. Evans, *Jesus and the Ossuaries* (Waco, TX: Baylor University Press, 2003); and for a refutation of the view that this refers to Jesus Christ, see R. López, *The Jesus' Family Tomb Examined* (Springfield, MO: 21st Century, 2008).

The preceding is a mere sampling of the archaeological evidence available for examination. But biblical apologetics is not limited to archaeological evidence. Biblical apologetics also examines the writings of Jewish and pagan historians who confirm biblical history, such as Flavius Josephus, the Babylonian Talmud, Pliny the Younger, Tacitus, Mara bar Serapion, and Suetonius. Biblical apologetics also examines the references to Jesus in Paul's New Testament writings, the historical Christological heresies that plagued the early church, and the many messianic prophecies from the Old Testament fulfilled in Christ. A number of biblical apologists devote their time and energy to examining and critiquing the writings of the so-called Jesus Seminar. Still others study the writings of the church fathers on the nature of the resurrection body, for example, in relation to modern views.

6. *Meggido church (third and fourth centuries AD)*

Not all support for biblical teaching must be found in the period of the New Testament or immediately adjacent to the New Testament. Some have argued that the deity of Jesus was not established until Nicea in AD 325, but we know from archaeology, and not just the writings of the church fathers, that Jesus was viewed as divine much earlier. While excavating a new compound at the Meggido Prison in northern Israel, workers unearthed an ancient Christian church that dates to the third or fourth century. This is perhaps the oldest church found to date in Israel. In addition to the well-preserved mosaic floor with fish inlays, inscriptions were also found which read, "The God-loving Aketous has offered this table to the God Jesus Christ as a Memorial . . . Gaianus . . . Roman military officer . . . having sought honor, from his own money has made the mosaic." This archaeological find supports the view that Jesus Christ was considered God by his early followers, that Christianity was well established in Israel, and that Christianity appealed to various classes of people, all of which are either stated or alluded to in the New Testament.

V.   SCIENTIFIC APOLOGETICS

The eminent Christian philosopher J. P. Moreland has highlighted a glaring problem evident in the evangelical community today. Moreland writes:

> Undoubtedly the most important influence shaping the modern world is science. People who lived during the Civil War had more in common with Abraham than with us. From space travel and nuclear power, anesthesia and organ transplants, computers and brain bisections, to DNA research, optics, and lasers, ours is a world of modern science.
>
> If the church is to speak to the modern world and interact with it responsibly, it must interact with modern science. Christians cannot afford to promulgate a dichotomized stereotype of Christianity wherein a believer's

spiritual life is a private, individualized faith operating in some upper story (to borrow Francis Schaeffer's term) while his secular life is public and involves reason and argument.[13]

Simply stated, scientific apologetics is the use of scientific evidence and reasoning in support of the truth claims of Christianity and the entire biblical revelation regarding cosmology, history, geology, anthropology, and all other hard sciences. The world has seen countless scientific and technological achievements, and the world is permeated with a scientific methodological philosophy. The remarkable plethora of scientific accomplishments leads many to give "science" an almost divine status as an all-powerful panacea to solve any human problem and a host of challenges facing the human race.

In order to speak to our own age, it is essential to understand the fundamental scientific assumptions that most modern people today hold. Also the present age has been described as the most anti-intellectual period in all of church history. Pietism and fideism are rampant in the evangelical world. Christians ought not ignore the worldview of the present age and allow secularists and scoffers to set the agenda of the debate. Christians have been commanded to cast down every ideological stronghold that exalts itself over the knowledge of God: "We do not wage war in a fleshly way, since the weapons of our warfare are not fleshly, but are powerful through God for the demolition of strongholds. We demolish arguments and every high-minded thing that is raised up against the knowledge of God, taking every thought captive to the obedience of Christ" (2 Cor 10:3–5). Such strongholds as methodological naturalism[14] and naturalistic evolution must be challenged and refuted by *sound* scientific reasoning and biblical revelation in concert. One must not perform the two enterprises independently of each other, not in the present age of "science."[15]

Scientific apologetics, then, will examine views on the origin of life and of the universe. The naturalistic view, for example, holds that the universe was not created. It is either eternal, or if it did come into existence, it came from nothing.[16] Inherent processes within nature produced all that exists, including man. Atoms, time, motion, and chance have formed all that is in the universe. In refuting this view, young-earth creationists argue that God created the universe and all that is in it through direct action. This happened over a short period of time, according to the biblical text, in a single solar week. God did not use any indirect means or biological mechanism to bring His creation into being but employed direct action or contact. God created the universe initially out of nothing (Gen 1:1). From this universe He formed human be-

---

[13] J. P. Moreland, *Christianity and the Nature of Science: A Philosophical Investigation* (Grand Rapids: Baker, 1989), 11.

[14] Methodological naturalism is the idea that one can reason only along naturalistic lines and that no transcendent realities exist outside of time and space. For an excellent discussion of this idea that is epidemic in our society, see P. E. Johnson, *Reason in the Balance: The Case against NATURALISM in Science, Law & Education* (Downers Grove, IL: InterVarsity, 1995).

[15] This is because a mere critique of such ideologies as methodological naturalism, without an evangelical message, is not a true pattern of biblical evangelism as portrayed in the book of Acts.

[16] For an excellent critique of the fallacy of this reasoning, see R. C. Sproul, *Not a Chance: The Myth of Chance in Modern Science & Cosmology* (Grand Rapids: Baker, 1994).

ings and other parts of creation. Each species was created distinct from all others. God made man completely by a direct creative act and then created the woman from the man's own body. Between these two views of naturalism and young-earth creationism lie a number of intermediate views, such as deistic evolution, theistic evolution, and progressive creation.

The study of scientific theories of origins is important since it establishes the truth of one's cosmology (the view of the origin of the universe). Many theological inferences stem from one's cosmological orientation. If one is a creationist, then he is likely to hold to a high view of Scripture and its depiction of creation. If one is a Darwinian evolutionist, he will regard the universe as naturalistic and will view methodological naturalism as the only means of learning about the universe. Various fields of theology are directly affected by one's cosmology.

For example in the field of biblical studies if the Bible teaches creation *ex nihilo* by God but if a naturalistic evolutionary theory of the origin of the universe (such as the Big Bang theory) is accepted as true, then the Bible cannot be true as well (this would be a violation of the law of noncontradiction). If the Bible is not true in its entirety, then it cannot be the inerrant Word of God as Jesus Himself taught. If the Bible is not the Word of God, then it is not necessarily authoritative.

The doctrine of Christ is central to the Christian faith. If a denial of the doctrine of creation *ex nihilo* would destroy the doctrine of Christ, then that very denial would also destroy the Christian faith. Jesus believed and taught the doctrine of creation *ex nihilo* (Mark 13:19). Either creation is true or Jesus was wrong. If creation *ex nihilo* is not true, then the entire Christian edifice falls. Therefore Christianity demands creation *ex nihilo*.[17]

The arena of scientific apologetics is as vast as it is interesting. Modern evangelical writers, some of whom have already been cited, are accomplishing much fruitful work. It is a worthwhile endeavor for the scientifically inclined Christian apologist. It is a worthwhile endeavor for all Christians, whether one is heavily involved in science or not.

VI. CULTURAL APOLOGETICS

This category of apologetics interacts with the societal trends in matters of ethics, government, family, and religion. Christianity and Christian teaching have much to say in these matters.

In ethics Christianity's view of the sanctity of life stems from the theory of natural law, which is derived from the teachings of Christian philosophers. Since humans are created in the image of God, the Christian argues that innocent human life ought to be protected. Christian philosophers argue that God, not government, grants rights, such

---

[17] Admittedly such a dogmatic statement engenders controversy among evangelicals. However, it is impossible to refute the statement logically. For an excellent source for this kind of "creation *ex nihilo*" apologetics, see the website AnswersinGenesis.org.

as the right to life. This is why orthodox Christians oppose abortion and euthanasia. They believe that these acts violate a person's natural rights.

In matters of family, Christians support the biblical model of marriage, which consists of a husband and a wife. They reject the argument that the Bible does not speak on the family. Despite the militant (and largely emotional) arguments to the contrary, science is now beginning to catch up with Christian ethics in relation to what constitutes the most healthy arrangement of families. More and more evidence is mounting that there are definite societal benefits to traditional marriage, from healthy children to personal happiness, to the stability of the society itself.[18]

Though traditional religion's role in society is under pressure from groups like secular humanism (discussed in chap. 28, "Engaging the Secularist"), the case can be made that society benefits from a large number of its people adhering to the teachings of Christianity. Although individual believers do not always carry out the precepts of Christian teaching, nevertheless Christianity offers many benefits. It teaches care for others, stewardship of the planet's resources, opposition to greed, personal responsibility and a strong work ethic, and numerous other positive characteristics. Certainly these are all ideals that are healthy for society in general, not just for Christians.

VII. CONCLUSION

Each of six apologetics categories serves as a testament to the overwhelming amount of evidence in defense of Christianity. Christian theology is superior to philosophy, for it can prove the existence of God by using logic. It is also superior to the subjective/projective psychological and evolutionary explanations for the presence of religious belief in humans. The vast amount of knowledge obtained from archaeology continues to support the reliability of the biblical text. Christianity has answers to modern science and cultural issues. There is no excuse for Christians to remain uninformed about these matters. Moreover, it is imperative for Christian apologists to become well acquainted with these areas of apologetics.

---

[18] See L. J. Waite and M. Gallagher, *The Case for Marriage* (New York: Doubleday, 2000); G. T. Stanton and B. Maier, *Marriage on Trial: The Case Against Same-Sex Marriage and Parenting* (Downers Grove, IL: InterVarsity, 2004).

Chapter 5

How Do We Know the Truth?

I.   What Is Truth?

PILATE'S QUESTION TO JESUS' "WHAT IS truth?" (John 18:38) is as provocative and important a question today as it was in the first century. The question reflects humanity's innate desire to *know* what is true and to have right beliefs about ultimate reality, including God. Ronald Nash notes that "the major thinkers of the past believed one of life's crucial tasks was the discovery of truth about humans, the world in which they live, and the God whose existence makes everything else possible."[1] In theology, truth is an issue of primary significance, if not *the* issue. If theology is the reasoned attempt to understand and know God, ourselves, and the world truly, both conceptually and relationally/experientially, and if God *is* truth, then the question of truth for the theologian is a primary one.

Before the theologian asks whether what he has come to know or believe is or is not the truth (i.e., is one's theological and religious beliefs *justified* as being true belief—and thus *knowledge*), he or she must also ask what is meant by the concept of "truth," or "true." Is truth a *quality* of a thing? A designation of the relationship between knowledge of something and what is known? Is truth primarily the result of an activity, such as reason and rationality, or of experience and evidence? Is truth mainly a function of the exercise of a mind or minds? Or is truth (or things that are true) independent of mind and consciousness? Is truth mainly subjective and personal? Is truth relative to time, location, and the knower? How can one verify that his or her knowledge and beliefs are true? These questions are discussed in this chapter.

II.   The Nature of Truth

When one asks about the nature of truth, the question is not about what *is,* in fact, true—this is the task of metaphysics (in philosophy) and of theology proper. Rather, the question about the nature of truth relates to what theologians mean when they say they have arrived at a true belief about God or true knowledge of God. Is truth

---

[1] R. Nash, *Life's Ultimate Questions: An Introduction to Philosophy* (Grand Rapids: Zondervan, 1999), 228.

61

discovered or is it created? How is the quality "true" related to the activity of the mind? And how is it related to the formulation of theological propositions? What is the structure under which truth is apprehended? In relation to theology, "When asking about truth, we are specifically interested in finding what conditions a sentence, statement, belief, or proposition must satisfy to be true."[2] Three basic views of the nature and structure of truth have been posited.[3] They are as follows.

A. Foundationalism

This epistemological perspective holds that "some beliefs, basic or foundational beliefs, are justified apart from their relations to other beliefs, while all other beliefs derive their justification from that of foundational beliefs."[4] Knowledge and justification of one's beliefs and perceptions have a "two-tier structure."[5] The underlying structure is the "foundational" one, in which beliefs, perceptions, and knowledge do not need to be justified by their relation to some other, more basic belief. They are self-justified, or self-evident, or "properly basic" beliefs or items of knowledge.

In foundationalism first principles are self-evident and are the foundation of all knowledge.[6] These principles are logically related to each other and are seen sequentially in the following 12 principles: (1) existence (Being is), (2) identity (Being is Being), (3) noncontradiction (Being is not non-Being), (4) excluded middle (Either Being or non-Being), (5) causality (non-Being cannot cause Being), (6) contingency (a contingent Being cannot cause another contingent Being), (7) negative modality (a necessary Being cannot cause a necessary Being), (8) positive modality (only a necessary Being can cause a contingent Being), (9) existential causality (every contingent Being is caused by a necessary Being), (10) existential necessity (a necessary Being must exist), (11) existential contingency (a contingent Being exists), and (12) analogy (a necessary Being has similarity to the contingent Being it causes).[7]

The second tier of beliefs, knowledge, and perceptions are justified in relation to the foundational beliefs on which they depend. These beliefs and items of knowledge are not self-evidently true, nor are they properly basic. Instead they depend on the truth-value of more fundamental, *foundational* beliefs. Thus the foundationalist philosopher pays heed to causes and effects in relation to the knowledge he holds and the beliefs he deems true. A specific belief or item of knowledge that one holds might not be a properly basic or foundational one, which would mean that the justification for

---

[2] P. K. Moser, D. H. Mulder, and J. D. Trout, *The Theory of Knowledge: A Thematic Introduction* (New York: Oxford University Press, 1998), 60.

[3] "Truth," in *The Cambridge Dictionary of Philosophy*, ed. R. Audi, 2nd ed. (Cambridge, UK: Cambridge University Press, 1999), 931. Some authors also rightly include "relativism" as one theory of the nature of truth. Relativists hold that "truth" is always justified by and determined by individual persons, communities, and the local situation under which the knower works. For a helpful explanation of relativism see Moser, Mulder, and Trout, *The Theory of Knowledge,* 61–64.

[4] "Coherentism," in *The Cambridge Dictionary of Philosophy*, 154.

[5] "Foundationalism," in *The Cambridge Dictionary of Philosophy,* 321.

[6] N. L. Geisler, "First Principles," in *Baker Encyclopedia of Christian Apologetics* (Grand Rapids: Zondervan, 1999), 250.

[7] Adapted from ibid., 250. A detailed description of how each principle works is in ibid., 250–52.

believing it could be easily overturned if a more foundational belief shows the other belief to be false. One might, for example, be fully convinced that one has seen a ghost. However, that belief would be overturned when the perceiver discovers that he or she has actually seen a jokester wearing a white sheet or has discovered that he or she has in fact seen a ghost but in a dream. That the perceiver has seen a ghost is an inference based on a limited perception in a specific moment of time. That belief is in no way *foundational,* however, and should be held quite tentatively.

René Descartes is considered by many to be the father of classic, modern foundationalism. He sought to ground all his knowledge on a single, unassailable truth that needed no external verification by anything else. For Descartes that truth was *cogito ergo sum,* "I think therefore I am." As a thinking being, Descartes believed he must also be an existing being. All other knowledge and true beliefs (including his belief in the existence of God!) would be derived from that basis.

Classic foundationalism (there are two forms, ancient and modern)[8] holds that once the foundational belief is established, belief can be determined to be true (and thus knowledge) or false only in reference to and as a logical derivation of that true foundation. According to the classic perspective, foundational knowledge, once established, cannot be questioned because it is certain. The key question of course is whether the foundation has been correctly established. On this view then one must be sure that the foundational belief is indubitable and unassailable. For classic foundationalists, the only kinds of beliefs considered as potentially foundational are reason and experience—beliefs that can be publicly verified and held up unfailingly against scientific and rational scrutiny.[9]

B. Moderate Foundationalism

Moderate forms of foundationalism have also emerged, some in reaction to the stronger version of Descartes. These allow for foundational beliefs other than those of reason and experience, such as the belief that God is a "properly basic belief."[10] Moderate foundationalists also seek a more modest kind of justification of knowledge and belief. (These forms of foundationalism have been prefaced by adjectives such as "moderate," "soft," and "modest.") They recognize that for something to be deemed true, it must bear some public relation to an already established truth or recognized authority. Unlike classic foundationalists, however, moderate (or "weak") foundationalists hold that a foundational ("noninferential") belief can be justified as such simply by one's having *good reason* to believe it along with a corresponding lack of a negative reason to disbelieve it (what is called a "defeater"). Also "modest" foundationalism "implies that foundational beliefs need not possess or yield certainty, and need not deductively support justified nonfoundational beliefs."[11]

---

[8] Ancient classic foundationalism is represented by Aristotle and Aquinas, whereas modern classic foundationalism is represented by René Descartes. See J. P. Moreland and W. L. Craig, *Philosophical Foundations for a Christian Worldview* (Downers Grove, IL: InterVarsity, 2003), 113.

[9] Ibid., 112.

[10] See the work of Alvin Plantinga for his version of foundationalism known as "Reformed Epistemology."

[11] Moser, Mulder, and Trout, *The Theory of Knowledge,* 87–88.

Some theologians have suggested that the Bible is the foundation for all theological knowledge. For a proposition or belief related to or derived from the content of the Bible to be deemed true, one must show it to be true in relation to the already assumed truth of the Bible's veracity, trustworthiness, and so forth. Some other alleged fact then could not be considered true if it were not based on the foundation of Scripture's authority or inerrancy. Thus the truth of Scripture is logically prior to other truths, such as God's existence, His faithfulness, and so forth. Yet other theologians might make God's existence the foundation of all knowledge, so that one's doctrine of Scripture derives from and rests on the more certain knowledge of God's existence, faithfulness, and so forth.

C. Nonfoundationalism

Foundationalism, as a school of epistemology, has been described metaphorically as a building (often a pyramid) with first-order and second-order tiers of beliefs stacked one on top of the other. On the other hand nonfoundationalism (or coherentism) has often been depicted as a "web" of beliefs (or sometimes as a log raft), with no one particular belief holding a higher or more fundamental epistemological status than any other. (One could even hold simultaneously to any number of different belief systems or webs at a given time, assuming they are not fatally contradictory.) The beliefs that comprise one's particular web all hang together and are mutually dependent on one another for their veracity as true knowledge. Within a web, or matrix, or system of belief or knowledge, a causal relation exists between each item. That is, they are connected to one another, making up a paradigm, but it is difficult to explain the relationship in terms of specific causality. No indubitable, noninferential beliefs support the entire system. Rather, each supports the other with little attention to hierarchy.

Nonfoundationalism appeals less to those who desire a logically, rationally, or scientifically rigorous certainty for the justification of their beliefs and more to those who see belief and the structure of its justification to be more dynamic, organic, interconnected, and holistic. Nonfoundationalists also focus on the reality and importance of community in the process of forming beliefs and justifying knowledge. Similarly nonfoundationalism appeals to those who prefer the paradoxical, mystical, and less rational, scientific, and cognitive aspects of theology. Nonfoundationalists often focus on "faith" in the theological process as itself a way of knowing. Sometimes, though not always, coherentists are less concerned with whether specific beliefs can be shown to correspond with actual *facts* of the external or *real* world and more concerned with whether one is able to arrive at an internally satisfactory account of life, belief, meaning, truth, and knowledge. However, nonfoundationalists are not necessarily nonrealists when it comes to the question of the nature of truth. Nonfoundationalism addresses the *justification* of truth and knowledge, not the *nature* of truth and knowledge. Thus nonfoundationalists explore how entire systems, webs, or paradigms of knowledge can be justified as a whole.

Postmodern theology is often more concerned for coherence than it is for establishing knowledge on certain foundations. This is because postmodernism emphasizes the historical, cultural, and linguistic situatedness of knowledge. Humans are historical creatures, products of a time and a situation that are distinct from other times and situations. Thus the only way a person can hope to acquire justification is by appealing to criteria that are specific to his own situations, cultures, languages, experiences, and so forth. Thus truth can be verified only in relation to a given, local, individual situation.

In this postmodern context some theologians have proposed a "postfoundationalist" way of doing theology. These theologians have pointed out the demise of the stronger, more radical forms of Enlightenment foundationalism and have recognized many of the insights of postmodern thought (such as the linguistic, social, cultural, and historical embeddedness of thought, knowledge, and belief). They argue that rationality is not always a "responsible choice" of the knower. Rather, knowers have received a tradition, a language, a structure of rationality from which it is not always possible to escape. That is, people do not always begin the reasoning process from logical first principles from which they can then deduce second and third principles justified on unquestionable foundations. Rather, they often begin from *within* a web of belief, that is, a context.

In proposing a postfoundationalist theology J. Wentzel van Huyssteen distinguishes his approach from both foundationalism and nonfoundationalism (which he points out often degenerates into radical relativism). *Post*foundationalism, he says, recognizes contextuality, and yet he wishes to "point creatively beyond the confines of the local community, group, or culture towards a plausible form of interdisciplinary conversation."[12]

Postfoundationalism, van Huyssteeen states, is an alternative epistemological option that is concerned "to identify the shared resources of human rationality in different modes of reflection, and then to reach beyond the walls of our own epistemic communities in cross-contextual, cross-cultural, and cross-disciplinary conversation."[13]

Some coherentist views of justification are compatible with a realist view of truth. The realist view simply states that what one knows is true—there is a reality outside one's perceptions of it, even though these perceptions are limited. A coherentist view of justification can align with a realist view of truth because for some, coherence may be the only hope of epistemic verification, but *what* is actually being shown to be true is objectively and ontologically (and/or metaphysically) *real*.

III. HOW CAN TRUTH BE KNOWN?

A. Rationalism

This view is characteristically modern, deriving largely from the Enlightenment emphasis on reason and human rationality to acquire and apprehend truth. Human rationality has been a conscious source for theology throughout the centuries, from the patristic period through the medieval and Reformation periods. But it was given a subordinate role as the arbiter or instrument whereby revelation, whether general or

---

[12] J. W. van Huyssteen, *Essays in Postfoundationalist Theology* (Grand Rapids: Eerdmans, 1997), 4.
[13] Ibid.

special, was understood, interpreted, and appropriated. In the modern period reason began to take on a much more significant role, becoming in many cases a substitute for revelation or a determinant of what *could be* a divine revelation in the first place.

Descartes, who stated *cogito ergo sum* ("I think therefore I am"), is known as a founder of modern rationalism for his attempt to ground all his beliefs and understandings of God and reality in a deductive, rational process. His attempt was not for rationalism to usurp religion, but his philosophy has turned much of traditional theology upside down in later centuries.

Much of conservative evangelical theology in the modern period is known for its emphasis on the importance of maintaining rationally coherent, publicly defensible, and logically explicable theological methodologies.

B. Empiricism

Whereas rationalism appeals to universal rules of logic or the derivations of internal reasoning, empiricism finds the source of truth primarily in experience and observation, whether sense experience, scientific observations, or intuitions. Where rationalism relies on deductive reasoning and logic,[14] empiricism relies on inductive argumentation. The empiricist examines the available and relevant evidence and derives a conclusion from the "ground up," so to speak.

Empiricism was a reaction to the rising tide of Enlightenment rationalism, largely through the work of David Hume (1711–76), whose skepticism challenged the ideals of rationalism to prove by evidence what they could only exclaim by logical syllogism. The data of sensation must be the primary source of one's concepts for them to have meaning.[15]

Empiricism takes any number of forms in theology, though in most recent days as liberal theology's insistence on human experience of the divine as the ground and source of religious truth. The theology of Friedrich Schleiermacher (1768–1834), with its centering on the "feeling of absolute dependence" as the source and ground of ecclesial piety and communion, is probably the best example of this kind of empiricism in modern theology.

C. Correspondence

Truth can be defined as those statements, propositions, affirmations, and judgments that correctly correspond to its extramental referent in the real world. That is, truth-value is contained in indicative statements about reality regardless of what anyone else thinks or feels about the matter. Statements that accurately reflect the current state of affairs are true, and those propositions that do not accurately correspond to reality are false.

This perspective, though in a variety of forms, is a dominant understanding of the nature of truth throughout the course of theological history. Some trace it as far back as

---

[14] In rationalism truth is upheld by the structure of a proposition (e.g., "All bachelors are unmarried men. John is an unmarried man. Therefore, John is a bachelor.").

[15] Cf. Moser, Mulder, and Trout, *The Theory of Knowledge*, 106–7.

Aristotle, though Thomas Aquinas is thought to be the greatest advocate of the theory of correspondence.[16] "Truth is correspondence with the facts" or "truth is agreement with reality."[17] Something is said to be true if whatever is purported or asserted, by whichever medium of thought or communication (declarative statement, interrogative utterance, scientific conclusion, and so forth), adequately represents reality *as it actually is*. Thus a statement, a belief, a depiction, and so on, is true if it sufficiently and adequately represents the state of affairs to which it refers. One might say that a correspondence theory of truth places the search for knowledge (through theology, science, philosophy, etc.) and the importance of epistemology (the study or science of knowledge) in a subordinate relation to ontology (the study or science of existence) or to metaphysics (what lies beneath, beyond, or "under" the physical world). This is because the disciplines (or mediums) that attempt to acquire and/or apprehend knowledge are seeking after something that lies "out there," beyond the limitations of finite knowing and finite abilities to grasp truth completely and entirely.

Several objections have been raised against the correspondence theory.[18] The one discussed here is directed against that form of the theory envisioning correspondence as a "picturing relation." A sentence, proposition, or assertion corresponds to reality in that it pictures reality, what is the case. "Barack Obama is the president of the United States" is a statement that can be said to "picture" rightly the current state (in 2010) regarding America's governmental leadership. However, not all statements or assertions "picture" states of affairs. Statements in the subjunctive mood ("I would go to town if I had enough money") do not necessarily "picture" a single state of affairs in the actual world. Similarly "normative" statements that give a command or a directive to someone do not necessarily "picture" a state of affairs but may actually *bring about* a state of affairs in the actual world if they are obeyed. "Pass me the ketchup" does not picture a state of affairs; rather it creates the possibility of a new state of affairs in the world if the ketchup is passed to me.

Similarly work in the philosophy of language has focused attention on "performative utterances." These statements do in fact bring about a new state of affairs simply by virtue of the utterance being made by the proper authority in the appropriate situation. When a minister pronounces a man and woman "husband and wife," he or she does not "picture the world" by the statement; rather the performative utterance creates a new situation. In theology this distinction encourages the interpreter of Scripture, for example, to read the Bible not simply as a collection of propositions that "picture" a state of affairs but to be attentive to ways in which the biblical text may contain "performative utterances" that are "true" in that they bring about a new reality.

---

[16] M. David, "The Correspondence Theory of Truth" in *The Stanford Encyclopaedia of Philosophy*, http://plato.stanford.edu/entries/truth-correspondence (accessed September 20, 2008).

[17] "Correspondence Theory of Truth," in *Routledge Encyclopedia of Philosophy*, ed. E. Craig (New York: Routledge, 1998), 9:472.

[18] See Moser, Mulder, and Trout, *The Theory of Knowledge*, 66–67, to which this paragraph is indebted.

Nonetheless in theology a correspondence view of truth holds to the importance of representing God insofar as He has made Himself known and insofar as the possibility for knowing Him is available to the human mind. Theologians who hold to correspondence theories of truth utilize a variety of sources for acquiring knowledge; including revelation (special and divine), reason, experience, church authority, and so forth. Protestant (particularly evangelical) theologies typically focus on the priority of special revelation for acquiring knowledge that corresponds to ultimate reality. Some theologians are more optimistic than others regarding the nature of that knowledge *as it corresponds* to God's own knowledge. Some theologians say people can acquire only an indirect, analogical, or metaphorical knowledge of God. For others, God has so manifested Himself in His revelation that any true knowledge of Him (and of the world) will be fundamentally equal to the knowledge that He has of those things (though, of course, the *amount* of knowledge He possesses infinitely exceeds what man's knowledge could ever be).

Evangelical theologians have generally held to some form of the correspondence theory of truth. Those who empathize with the postmodern critiques of the modernist quest for indubitable certainty in knowledge have been more prone to reject—or at least modify—some aspects of the correspondence theory of truth in favor of coherence or pragmatist notions.

1. Criticism

Though the correspondence theory can be applied to some statements, it cannot be applied universally. For to say that the statement "God exists" is true only if it corresponds to a referent outside of God Himself would make the referent superior to God since He would be dependent on that outside referent for His existence. In addition, some statements that refer to singular events such as the beginning of first life have no verifiable referent and cannot be considered true as tested by the correspondence theory's own criteria.

2. Response

For verifiable objective truth to be possible, some kind of correspondence must exist between one's statements and the real world. The statement "Truth does not correspond to the way things actually are" purports to correspond to reality and therefore is self-defeating. God needs only to correspond to Himself perfectly as His ideas correspond to His being. In fact ultimately God is the "referent" to which all else must correspond. Finally, the verification of past events does not rule out the correspondence view of truth since there could be eyewitnesses to the event, or one could give the benefit of the doubt to those things and events that cannot be verified if other such related statements are found to be true. Besides, whether one can *verify* a statement has no bearing on the *truthfulness* of the statement since there are certain judgments most believe to be true apart from any verification. That is, if one could not positively *verify* a cause of first life does not mean that it is not true *ipso facto* that there was a cause of first life.

D. Coherence

Responding to foundationalism as a system of verification for meaning and justification for truth, W. V. O. Quine described the nature of truth (and belief) using the metaphor of a "web." Rather than a structural metaphor, such as a building or a pyramid, in which subordinate truths are entailed logically by more fundamental truths, Quine saw each belief as equally necessary and no more foundational than any other. So long as they exist in one's belief-structure, each part serves equally to validate the whole, and the whole serves to validate the parts.[19]

Pointing out the flaws in the correspondence theory of truth and specifically the foundational approach of Descartes, in which immediate ideas (perceptions) give rise to mediate ideas in an abstract sense, Harold Joachim emphasized the "concreteness" of the coherence notion of truth, "as a living and moving whole."[20] He defined the theory as "that systematic coherence which is the character of a significant whole. A 'significant whole' is an organized individual experience, self-fulfilling and self-fulfilled."[21] He pointed out that correspondence (between perceptions and ideas with reality) may be a symptom of the truth, but it does not serve to describe sufficiently the nature of truth.[22]

According to Joachin, truth is mind dependent because it is apprehended by finite knowers in a finite world. This is different from the correspondence view of truth, in which a person does not make or alter truth by his thinking. For Joachim, "Truth, if it is to be *for me*, must enter into my intellectual endeavour and emerge in my conscious thought as the result of a personal process, and as, in a sense, *my* personal possession. I must get to know it, and I must express it when known, and the expression is tinged with my personal individuality and is *my* judgement."[23] While truth may be in and of itself independent, "this independent truth lives and moves and has its being in the judgements of finite minds."[24]

Joachim's coherence view of truth was influenced by Georg W. F. Hegel (1770–1831) and thus was universal, single, and timeless, though apprehended differently throughout the world's historical development. Essentially, for Joachim, *all truth* coheres in a seemingly single, overarching system, though expressed and articulated differently by various individuals.

In the postmodern situation many view the coherence of truth as the best way to describe the nature and acquisition of truth. The postmodern view of coherence, however, differs from that expressed by Joachim. For many who are influenced by the philosophical and cultural notions of postmodernism, truth is not a universal, ultimate

---

[19] See J. E. Thiel, *Nonfoundationalism*, Guides to Theological Inquiry (Minneapolis: Fortress, 1991) for a helpful explanation of the influence of Quine's nonfoundational philosophy on contemporary theology.

[20] Ibid., 77.

[21] H. H. Joachim, *The Nature of Truth* (Oxford: Clarendon, 1906; reprint, New York: Greenwood, 1969), 76.

[22] Ibid., 19.

[23] Ibid., 21 (italics his).

[24] Ibid., 22.

phenomenon; rather it is a designation for a communally agreed-on standard of explaining the nature of reality, of God, or of how people ought to behave within a given community. That is, one could be said to believe something *truly* if what he believes represents and is validated by the local community of which one is a part. Beliefs and actions, then, *cohere* within the structure of language, culture, meaning, and reality that has been established in a particular community.

Stanley Grenz preferred a more holistic vision of theology's task than has been commonly represented by evangelicalism's doctrinal propositionalism. He sought to expand on the insights of George Lindbeck, whose "cultural-linguistic" view of religion likened religions to languages and religious doctrine to grammar. Grenz's intent was to "revise" evangelical theology in light of the current demands, and so he appropriated insights of postmodernity, while also attempting to remain faithful to the best of Christian tradition as its resources for theological authority.[25] He saw the task of theology as a second-order discipline, that of reflecting on the experiences of being the people of God. For Grenz, unlike the "propositionalist" theologians, theological doctrine is not an a priori, purely rational discipline that then leads to experience. Rather, the experience of the people of God in the local (and time-specific) Christian community of which they are a part, informed by the workings of the Holy Spirit in personal conversion and in the interaction with the community of faith, leads to doctrinal understandings. Theological truth is likened to a mosaic, with narratives, symbols, and images filling out the picture of what God is doing with and in His people. According to Grenz, theology must be seen as practical as well as propositional, as communal as well as individual, and the ultimate nature of and apprehension of truth is *holistic*.

> The contemporary situation demands that we as evangelicals not view theology merely as the restatement of a body of propositional truths, as important as doctrine is. Rather, theology is a practical discipline oriented toward the believing community. . . . Our participation in a faith community involves a basic commitment to a specific conceptual framework. Because faith is linked to a conceptual framework, our participation in a community of faith carries a claim to truth, even if that claim be merely implicit. By its very nature, the conceptual framework of a faith community claims to represent in some form the truth about the world and the divine reality its members have come to know and experience.
>
> To the extent that it embodies the conceptual framework of a faith community, therefore, theology necessarily engages in the quest for truth. It enters into conversation with other disciplines of human knowledge with the goal of setting forth a Christian worldview that coheres with what we know about human experience in the world.[26]

---

[25] S. Grenz, *Revisioning Evangelical Theology: A Fresh Agenda for the 21st Century* (Downers Grove, IL: InterVarsity, 1993).

[26] Ibid., 79.

Grenz was not saying that there is no truth "out there" apart from the communities' perceptions of it. Nor was he saying that theological propositions have no ontological import or that they do not describe ultimate reality. He was suggesting, rather, that there is no actual and existential perception of truth apart from what is mediated to persons through the experience of life in community, including the testimony of Scripture (as interpreted and taught by a community). For Grenz, the best way to understand truth (and thus the best way to understand the task and objectives of theology) is not as the correspondence between a proposition and the reality it represents but rather as a dynamic, holistic mosaic that incorporates all the elements of existence and reality in a single whole.

There is no one sole authority, such as Scripture or doctrinal tradition, to which one can refer in seeking truth. Rather, God has made Himself known in numerous ways in mankind's finite existence. For Grenz, Scripture testifies to the Word of God and thus mediates God's Word to its readers/hearers. By employing and appealing to every possible avenue in which the truth of God might be apprehended, people then "gain . . . identity as the people of God."[27]

1. Criticism

Coherence theory lacks any external referent by which to test the statements within a given system. One may construct any system, including a mythical one, that perfectly measures up to other statements within the system or one's personal experience, thereby making a mythical system true. But it is contradictory that a mythical system be considered true. Many liken the coherence theory to building a house without any foundation. Also, if two mutually exclusive systems such as Islam and Christianity are internally consistent, then both must be considered true systems. However, this is impossible because of their mutually exclusive nature. One would be left in agnosticism, which is self-defeating. Lack of internal consistency may reveal which system *cannot* possibly be true but cannot demonstrate which system *is* true.

2. Response

The law of noncontradiction shows that truth must cohere within a system for it to be considered true. Something cannot be true if it does not cohere with other statements in the system since it would then be considered contradictory. A real difference exists between a true system with pockets of error (i.e., Christianity) and a false system with pockets of truth (i.e., Islam). Therefore truth must necessarily cohere, and whatever does not cohere is necessarily false. Furthermore to assume there is extra-propositional "fact" to which one's statements must correspond is inadequate since one may not have direct access to these facts.

E. Existentialism

In existentialism truth is defined in terms of emotions, feelings, sincerity, or intentions. Statements and affirmations do not contain truth-value as in objectivism;

---

[27] Ibid., 136.

instead, truth is rooted in individuals' subjective characteristics. Atheistic existentialism, which developed from the works of intellectuals such as Friedrich Nietzsche, Edmund Husserl, Jean-Paul Sartre, and Albert Camus, embraces and promotes a thoroughgoing naturalistic worldview. However, as James Sire points out, existentialism departs from naturalism with respect to "human nature and our relationship to the cosmos. Indeed, existentialism's major interest is in our humanity and how we can be significant in an otherwise insignificant world."[28] Existentialism is closely connected with romanticism,[29] a movement that arose near the end of the eighteenth century and gained momentum within the literary community of the nineteenth century. Both movements were reactions to Enlightenment rationalism (modernity) and paved the way for twentieth-century postmodernism. One common thread that runs through romanticism, existentialism, and a related movement, phenomenology, is the nature and importance of human experience.[30] Ultimately existentialism, romanticism, and phenomenology are humanistic and see man as the measure of all things.

1. Criticism

A truth statement must correspond to its referent in the real world or else the statement possesses no more value than one's own opinion. If this is the case, there can be no objective truth; however, this conclusion must be false since to say, "There is no objective truth," is an objective truth-statement and is therefore self-defeating. Moreover, truth is found not in what one does not say but, rather, in what one does say. Feelings change from day to day; if truth is subjective, then truth changes as feelings change, leading ultimately to a breakdown of communication and moral behavior. Also if truth is subjective, no one could verify its validity since the basis for truth is located within the individual consciousness.

2. Response

Truth cannot be relegated to mere facts in the real world since many statements about things known universally to be true cannot be verified extramentally (e.g., by numbers and logic). Further, truth is often personal and cannot be divorced from the individual determining it. To do so would dismiss and subvert the vital element (subjectivism) and its relationship to truth.

F. Pragmatism

Pragmatism is the view that truth is a correlate of what works to bring about a desired result in the cognitive task—the task of seeking truth. William James, a well-known American pragmatist whose classic work *The Varieties of Religious Experience*

---

[28] J. W. Sire, *The Universe Next Door*, 4th ed. (Downers Grove, IL: InterVarsity, 2004), 114.

[29] M. Hunnex, *Chronological and Thematic Charts of Philosophies and Philosophers* (Grand Rapids: Zondervan, 1986), chart 24.

[30] An excellent study of the rise of romanticism in the nineteenth century and its current impact on American culture is R. Lundin, *From Nature to Experience: The American Search for Cultural Authority* (New York: Rowman and Littlefield, 2005).

in 1902 laid much of the groundwork for a psychological and individualistic study of religion, adhered to the "instrumentalist theory" of pragmatism. For James, "A proposition counts as true if and only if behaviour based on a belief in the proposition leads, in the long run and all things considered, to beneficial results for the believers."[31]

In places James seemed to agree with a measure of truth as correspondence. He states:

> Truth, as any dictionary will tell you, is a property of certain of our ideas. It means their "agreement," as falsity means their disagreement, with "reality." Pragmatists and intellectualists both accept this definition as a matter of course. They begin to quarrel only after the question is raised as to what may precisely be meant by the term "agreement," and what by the term "reality" when reality is taken as something for our ideas to agree with.[32]

James disagreed with the "intellectualists" or rationalists, who insisted, in his opinion, that truth is an "inert static relation." For these rationalists,

> When you've got your true idea of anything, there's an end of the matter. You're in possession; you *know*; you have fulfilled your thinking destiny. . . . Pragmatism, on the other hand, asks its usual question. "Grant an idea or belief to be true," it says, "what concrete difference will its being true make in any one's actual life? How will the truth be realized? What experiences will be different from those which would obtain if the belief were false? What, in short, is the truth's cash-value in experiential terms?"[33]

For James, truth is not a static or inert "property"; rather truth is something that "happens to an idea." Truth is verified through a process or event in which the cash value of an idea or belief is made clear to the one holding that idea.[34]

> Our account of truth is an account of truths in the plural, of processes of leading . . . and having only this quality in common, that they *pay*. . . . Truth for us is simply a collective name for verification-processes, just as health, wealth, strength, etc., are names for other processes connected with life, and also pursued because it pays to pursue them. Truth is *made*, just as health, wealth and strength are made, in the course of experience.[35]

More currently George Lindbeck has set the agenda for what is called "postliberal" theology. In his work *The Nature of Doctrine* Lindbeck seeks to articulate a vision for understanding religion and religious doctrine in a framework that would facilitate

---

[31] R. L. Kirkham, "Pragmatic Theory of Truth," in *Routledge Encyclopedia of Philosophy*, 478.
[32] W. James, *Pragmatism and Other Essays* (New York: Washington Square, 1963), 87–88.
[33] Ibid., 88 (italics his).
[34] Ibid., 89.
[35] Ibid., 96 (italics his).

ecumenical unity among Christian denominations while encouraging distinctive traditions to retain their unique—and thus seemingly opposed—doctrinal formulations.

Lindbeck identifies two prevailing models for understanding and conceptualizing religion—the cognitivist and the experiential-expressivist—and then presents a third, the cultural-linguistic, which he endorses as the best way (the most pragmatic!) to conceive of religion.

Cognitivist views of religion and doctrine prioritize propositional and scientific approaches to apprehending objective truth, and experiential-expressivist models of religion are grounded on the conviction that a universal experience (though experienced particularly in ecclesial community) of the transcendent and the divine (cf. Schleiermacher) gives rise to the expression of that experience through religious symbols, art, doctrines, ethics, and so forth.

In contrast the cultural-linguistic view suggests that the religious symbols and doctrines come before and give rise to the particular religious experience of those symbols. Thus religions provide a conceptual structure whereby an adherent to the particular religion *becomes* and *believes* what is prescribed within the linguistic (doctrinal) convictions of that particular faith community or tradition.

> Religion cannot be pictured in the cognitivist (and voluntarist) manner as primarily a matter of deliberately choosing to believe or follow explicitly known propositions or directives. Rather, to become religious—no less than to become culturally or linguistically competent—is to internalize a set of skills by practice and training. One learns how to feel, act, and think in conformity with a religious tradition that in its inner structure is far richer and more subtle than can be explicitly articulated. The primary knowledge is not *about* the religion, nor *that* the religion teaches such and such, but rather *how* to be religious in certain ways.[36]

Thus for Lindbeck truth is given in cultural-linguistic communities, and the religious doctrinal truths are teachings that exist for a pragmatic function: they are rules that provide ethical guidance, belief content, as well as structure for giving rise to religious experience and religious meaning in one's faith and existence.

Though Lindbeck is illustrative of a pragmatic understanding of truth, his view also has affinity with a view of truth as coherence, for its emphasis on the emergence and apprehension of truth as that which derives from a particular community of faith, belief, and practice. Indeed, the comparisons between Lindbeck and Grenz's revision of evangelical theology may be noted.

1. Criticism

If truth is defined by what works, it would be difficult to discover what is true since identical ideas, concepts, and propositions that contain truth-value yield differing conclusions for different people. Moreover, truth can "work" and bring intended

---

[36] G. Lindbeck, *The Nature of Doctrine: Religion and Theology in a Postliberal Age* (Philadelphia: Westminster, 1984), 35.

results, but occasionally *unintended* results are the end product, such as when parents feed, nurture, and love their children but unfortunately some of the children become tyrants. Moreover, someone may lie to gain some benefit or utility; however, it does not make their lie true since a true lie would be a contradiction. In addition, some suggest that function and utility are not in the same category as truth any more than a *functioning* car is a "true car."

2. Response

Without something practical or concrete by which to discover the truth-value of one's beliefs, he is left in subjectivism. Even the much-acclaimed scientific method seeks after general truth through results and experience. Moreover, it would seem to go against logic to reject as true the vital benefits that are accorded to an individual through belief in some things such as God that cannot be verified by empirical means.

IV. APPROACHES TO TRUE THEOLOGICAL KNOWLEDGE

Truth has commonly been held to have two facets: truth of being and truth of knowing. The former relates to how objects in the world correspond to "the exemplar or idea on which it depends."[37] The latter, truth of knowing, is the "knowing conformity of mind to being." It is the exercise of "judgment" regarding the perceived case of things.[38] Epistemology is the attempt to verify the judgments, the knowledge, that one has. This section compares various ways in which theologians have believed that people come to acquire truth. As introduced in chap. 3 ("Approaches to Apologetics"), different approaches to apologetics have different ways they approach theological knowledge. This section considers how rational evidentialism, revelational presuppositionalism, rational revelationism, and fideistic revelationalism explain epistemology.

A. Rational Evidentialism

Rational evidentialism is the view that truth is a characteristic of a claim, the merits of which are determined by whether evidence and/or experience can validate an assertion or hypothesis to be the case in a rational way. Much of early modern theology (Enlightenment) was driven by the desire for empirical verification, evidenced in the often-used designation of theology as "queen of the sciences." Evidential theologies generally focused more on the merits of natural theology than on that of revealed theology (at least for apologetic purposes) since the data of natural theology, it was assumed, can be more easily and more publicly verified. Not all evidentially minded theologians hold to the superiority of natural theology or natural things to revealed content (i.e., Scripture), but all would assert the importance of evidence and/or reason to supplement, support, clarify, and explain the data and meaning of revelation. After

---

[37] T. C. O'Brien, "Truth," in *Encyclopedic Dictionary of Religion,* ed. P. K. Meagher, T. C. O'Brien, and C. M. Aherne (Washington, DC: Corpus, 1979), 3577.
[38] Ibid.

all, God created everything (all matters of evidence); even the ability to reason can be seen as an "evidence" for God's existence.

However, the evidential turn of modernity also made its way into the data of revelation, giving rise to the predominance in some theological circles on the European continent, and later in England and America, of the historical criticism of the Bible. Miracles, since they cannot be historically verified, were deemed by some to be epistemically unjustified and therefore, if they were to be believed literally, could be believed on the strength of blind faith alone ("fideism").

In *The Openness of Being* E. L. Mascall writes a moderate defense of natural theology in which he upholds the importance of metaphysical reflection on the natural world (both empiricism and rationality) for Christian theology. He does not argue for the superiority of empiricism or rationalism in theology but for the significance of it in theology.

> Because I believe that God has created man as a rational animal and has endowed him with natural powers, of which reason itself is one of the most significant, I hold that in religious experience there is a common element which is highly important and which can be brought under rational examination. Furthermore, because I believe that all natural objects have the common characteristic of being created and sustained by God, I hold that rational investigation of them may disclose rational grounds for believing in his existence.[39]

In evangelical circles one also thinks of evidentialist apologetics,[40] which uses traditional arguments for God's existence (e.g., Aquinas's "five ways"), historical and archeological findings verifying the data of Scripture, scientific arguments for the reasonableness of a literal creationism, and so on, to provide unbelievers with reasons to believe in Christianity or at least to remove obstacles to believing.

Phillip Johnson has written extensively on the intersection of theology and science. He has argued for the evidential coherence and rationality for a Christian view of creation, contrary to the prevailing views of evolutionary science. He has drawn on traditional arguments for the existence of God (e.g., argument from design)[41] as well as on contemporary findings in science to make a case for the reasonableness of Christianity in the modern context.[42]

B. Revelational Presuppositionalism

Cornelius Van Til suggested that the knowledge of God and of the world (in the sense that *God* knows it) is essentially unavailable to unaided fallible humans. However, through special revelation, God has made truth known to humanity, which is

---

[39] E. L. Mascall, *The Openness of Being: Natural Theology Today* (Philadelphia: Westminster, 1971), 4.

[40] See J. McDowell, *Evidence That Demands a Verdict* for a popular example.

[41] See P. Johnson's chapter, "Is There a Blind Watchmaker?" in *Reason in the Balance: The Case Against Naturalism in Science, Law and Education* (Downers Grove, IL: InterVarsity, 1995).

[42] See also P. E. Johnson, *The Right Questions: Truth, Meaning and Public Debate* (Downers Grove, IL: InterVarsity, 2002).

ascertainable and knowable by Christians in analogy. Humanity's knowledge of God is thus a derivative knowledge and is thus not equal with God's knowledge, which is "self-contained" knowledge.[43] Van Til explained:

> By this is meant that God is the original and that man is the derivative. God has absolute self-contained system within himself. What comes to pass in history happens in accord with that system or plan by which he orders the universe. But man, as God's creature, cannot have a replica of that system of God. He cannot have a reproduction of that system. He must, to be sure, think God's thoughts after him; but this means that he must, in seeking to form his own system, constantly be subject to the authority of God's system *to the extent* that this is revealed to him.[44]

Van Til was concerned with what he views as a prevailing tendency in modern theology to see humanity "as the final reference point" and thus the final source of knowledge.[45] However, any epistemology that places humanity, rather than God, as its ultimate reference point cannot, Van Til posited, offer an optimistic account of the possibility of knowing anything at all. For Van Til, "The final reference point in predication is God as the self-sufficient One."[46] Thus the only true Christian epistemology is one that posits the existence of the triune God as well as the fact that this God has revealed Himself through the Scriptures.

This epistemology, which Van Til called the Reformed method of apologetics, "begins frankly 'from above.' It would 'presuppose' God."[47] The only way the data of the world, reason, and experience can be rightly interpreted is in light of the order (and "system") in which the God of the universe has placed it. "Reason and fact cannot be brought into fruitful union with one another except upon the presupposition of the existence of God and his control over the universe."[48]

How is God's "system" (including His presence and work in the world) and thus His truth to be learned and rightly understood? Only through the Scriptures. "Accordingly, the Bible must be identified in its entirety in all that it says on any subject as the Word of God. It is, again, only if history is considered to be what it is because of the ultimate controlling plan of God, that such a relationship between God's Word and all the facts of the universe can be obtained."[49]

Van Til's presuppositionalism is not a strict fideism, though at times it sounds like it. Rather, his was a view of truth that depended heavily on the regenerative power of the Holy Spirit and the convincing strength of the Word of God. As he wrote, "It is

---

[43] C. Van Til, *Christian Apologetics* (Phillipsburg, NJ: P&R, 1976), 9.

[44] C. Van Til, *A Christian Theory of Knowledge* (Phillipsburg, NJ: Presbyterian & Reformed, 1969), 16 (italics his).

[45] Ibid., 17.

[46] Ibid.

[47] Ibid., 18.

[48] Ibid.

[49] Ibid., 31.

through the heavenly content of the Word that God speaks of himself. Faith is not blind faith; it is faith in the truth, the system of truth displayed in the Scriptures."[50]

C. Rational and Propositional Revelationalism

For Carl F. H. Henry, "The God of biblical revelation is the God of reason, not Ultimate Irrationality; all he does is rational."[51] Henry does not assert, however, the supremacy of reason in coming to understand and know God. Rather, God can be truly known only through the revelation of Himself which He has provided in Scripture:

> Be they gods of secular philosophy or gods of the history of religion, the false gods can in principle be completely known for what they are simply through human inquiry and ingenuity. Given enough time and effort, any person can explore, expound and expose the nature of these "divinities." . . . But to speak of God and attribute specific characteristics to him apart from a basis in divine revelation is to play the gardener who, after spraying water into the sky from a hose, then welcomes the "rainfall" as "heaven-sent."[52]

For Henry, divine revelation takes the form of propositions. God communicates His nature, actions, and purposes through the meaningful, truthful (and inerrant) statements and stories of Scripture. That is, God communicates true *information* about Himself to the recipients of revelation. This communication, this information, is not itself salvific but is the precondition for salvation. It is necessary first to know *about* God before one can *know* God. By making this distinction, Henry set his view of biblical truth ("propositional revelationism") apart from the existential theologies that had become fashionable in various theological circles. They held that revelation was synonymous with redemption and that truth is *personal,* not *propositional.* It brings about a new reality, a new relation with God, rather than providing information about God.

Nevertheless, as James Emery White points out, Henry would deny being an adherent of a correspondence theory of truth because he did not wish to align himself with the evidential approach to apologetics. This does not mean, however, that Henry does not believe in ultimate truth to which one's apprehensions of it correspond. "While Henry would deny being an adherent of a correspondence theory of truth, his resistance to that label is epistemological, not ontological, in orientation. . . . What Henry ultimately offers is a modification of the correspondence theory of truth."[53]

White says that for Henry the knowledge of reality is not a correspondence in that knowledge is distinct from the reality it knows. Rather, Henry's correspondence theory is "an understanding of truth in terms of divine revelation, which gives us reality in

---

[50] Ibid., 33.

[51] C. F. H. Henry, *God, Revelation and Authority,* vol. 1 (Waco, TX: Word, 1979), 233.

[52] Ibid., 2:19.

[53] J. E. White, *What Is Truth? A Comparative Study of the Positions of Cornelius Van Til, Francis Schaeffer, Carl F. H. Henry, Donald Bloesch, Millard Erickson* (Eugene, OR: Wipf & Stock, 2006), 104.

true correspondence." The point is that whatever God reveals, one can know it just as God knows it.

Gordon Clark, another proponent of rational, revelational propositionalism (to whom Henry was dependent for his position), says that "knowledge . . . requires an existing object, and that object is truth—truth that always has and always will exist."[54] For Clark, "the object of knowledge is a proposition, a meaning, a significance; it is a thought. And this is necessary if communication is to be possible. . . . The truths or propositions that may be known are the thoughts of God, the eternal thought of God. And insofar as man knows anything, he is in contact with God's mind."[55]

D. Fideistic Revelationalism

Karl Barth insisted that there is no "point of contact" between humanity and the Word of God. God's revelation of Himself always comes to a humanity that cannot naturally receive and understand it. There is no "capability or property grounded in man" by or through which the experience of God's revelation (the Word of God in its three forms: Christ, preaching, Scripture) can take place.[56]

When theology expresses a real knowledge of God, it is because the Word of God has entered into the theologian's reality, making him or her into a "witness" of the truth of that reality. When one has truly heard the Word of God,

> there can be no question of any ability to hear or understand or know on his part, of any capability that he the creature, the sinner, the one who waits, has to bring to this Word, but that the possibility of knowledge corresponding to the real Word of God has come to him, that it represents an inconceivable *novum* compared to all his ability and capability, and that it is to be understood as a pure fact, in exactly the same way as the real Word of God itself.[57]

When one experiences the reality of the Word, one believes not on the basis of evidence, reason, or internal ability but because of the faith created by one's transformative encounter with revelation. Barth emphasized the freedom of God in revealing Himself through His Word to sinful, finite people:

> The fact of God's Word does not receive its dignity and validity in any respect or even to the slightest degree from a presupposition that we bring to it. Its truth for us, like its truth in itself, is grounded absolutely in itself. . . . Men can know the Word of God because and in so far as God wills that they know it, because and in so far as there is over against God's will only the impotence of disobedience.[58]

---

[54] G. Clark, *A Christian View of Men and Things* (Grand Rapids: Eerdmans, 1952), 318–19. See also G. Clark, *Language and Theology* (Jefferson, MD: Trinity, 1980).

[55] Clark, *Christian View of Men and Things*, 321.

[56] K. Barth, *Church Dogmatics*, ed. G. W. Bromiley and T. F. Torrance, 2nd ed. (Edinburgh: Clark, 1975), 193.

[57] Ibid., 194.

[58] Ibid., 196.

Donald Bloesch, in many ways a theological successor of Barth, states that in order to recover biblical, evangelical theology one must not adhere to presuppositionalism, foundationalism, evidentialism, or coherentism. Rather, he affirms "a *fideistic revelationalism,* in which the decision of faith is as important as the fact of revelation in giving us certainty of the truth of faith."[59]

Bloesch employs Barth's emphasis on the freedom of God to speak his Word to humanity, apart from human "a priori assumptions," "universal principles," or "transcendental ideals." Bloesch wishes to maintain a proper unity between the subjective and the objective elements of theology while keeping the sovereignty of God (and thus of His revelation) in its proper place over the insights of anthropology. For Bloesch, "In a theology of Word and Spirit we receive or hear the concrete speech of God, which makes an indelible impression on the human soul but can never be fully assimilated by the human mind. To know the full import of what is revealed, we must act in obedience to what we presently ascertain to be the will of God."[60]

For Bloesch, if theology has any "foundation," in the philosophical, epistemological sense of the word, it is God Himself, not sense impressions or "noninferential beliefs." However, theology is concerned with truth and with making and validating truth claims given in revelation but ascertained and understood in existence, faith, and obedience. Thus experience (and obedience) enables interpretation and understanding, and interpretation and understanding enables obedience.

V. CONCLUSION

There can be no doubt the human mind desires to know what is true. The question is, What is that truth? And more basically, Can a person even know truth? This chapter has discussed the fact that the truth is not only knowable but also that there is a certain path to knowing that truth. The strengths and weaknesses of both foundationalism and nonfoundationalism as a basis for knowledge have been discussed. Foundationalism is based in the rules of logic and argues that there are truths that form a foundation of understanding, whereas nonfoundationalism argues that truths are more of a web, interconnected, and not necessarily built on each other. The chapter then discussed different methods of how to find truth—rationalism, empiricism, correspondence, existentialism, and pragmatism—evaluating each for their strengths and weaknesses. Then four methods of finding theological knowledge were discussed: rational evidentialism, revelational presuppositionalism, rational propositional presuppositionalism, and fideistic revelationalism. The apologist should be well versed in these topics because they deal with the basic questions of philosophy. One must answer Pilate's question, "What is truth?" before one can answer the question of whether Christianity presents the truth.

---

[59] D. G. Bloesch, *A Theology of Word and Spirit: Authority and Method in Theology* (Downers Grove, IL: InterVarsity, 1992), 21.

[60] Ibid., 22.

Chapter 6

THE TENSION BETWEEN
FAITH AND REASON

SINCE GOD, WHO CANNOT LIE (TITUS 1:2), has revealed the doctrines of the Christian faith, these truths cannot conflict with right reason. Given the human penchant for misinterpreting these doctrines and for abusing the gift of reason, it is not surprising that the two frequently seem to be in tension. This chapter explores four models of how Christians ought to correlate their reason and their faith: fideism, Reformed epistemology, rational evidentialism, and rationalism. By a judicious application of the third model, one can do justice to the legitimate claims of both faith and reason while doing violence to neither.

I.   THE NATURE OF THE PROBLEM

A. Introduction

Before exploring the various models of how one should relate his faith to his reason, however, it is important to show what faith and reason are and why the relationship between the two might seem problematic. Reason, in the sense in which the term is employed in this chapter, is simply the faculty that governs or at least ought to govern human decisions about what is or is not true and what is or is not known. Just as one troubles one's conscience when he or she performs an act whose rectitude is suspect, so one "troubles" one's reason when he or she adopts a belief on the basis of insufficient evidence.

Since faith is complex, it is necessary to distinguish between the following four senses of the word.

1.   Faith, broadly speaking

In the widest sense of the term, faith is simply assent to a statement whose truthfulness one cannot directly verify but which one believes on the basis of credible testimony.

2. Saving faith

Saving faith, evangelical Protestants hold, consists of knowledge (*notitia*) of the articles of the Christian faith, assent (*assensus*) to those articles, and trust (*fiducia*) that God will act as He promises in those articles. Some people think that the assent of Christian faith conflicts with reason or at least strains the credulity of it.

3. Human and fallible faith

Faith, in the sense of assent, comes in at least two forms: divine and infallible faith, and human and fallible faith. Human and fallible faith consists in the kind of assent that a schoolchild gives to his teacher's statement, "There once was a man named George Washington." This faith is said to be human and fallible because the authority on which the assent is based is human and fallible.

4. Divine and infallible faith

The Christian's assent of faith accepts the teaching of Scripture as divine and infallible because the authority on whose account one believes is divine and infallible, namely, God, Scripture's primary author. Divine and infallible faith, in other words, consists of the Christian's assent to the teachings of Scripture not merely because he finds them plausible but because he trusts that the God who reveals them cannot lie (Titus 1:2). One believes propositions with divine and infallible faith because they are revealed by a divine and infallible God.

One might define the global assent of faith, which is essential to, though not sufficient for, becoming an authentic Christian as the act in which a human being accepts without reservation the truthfulness of all revealed propositions, not on account of their intrinsic probability but on account of the authority of the God who reveals.[1]

B. The Motive of Faith

The belief that God reveals the propositions of Scripture is known as the motive, or ground of faith. The motive of faith is the belief that a being who is divine and infallible reveals the propositions of Scripture. This belief may be called the motive of faith because it motivates one to repose divine and infallible faith in the teachings of Scripture. The motive of faith, then, is the rational basis of divine and infallible faith.

Once one has this motive, that is, once one has decided to assume that God, who can neither deceive nor be deceived, is the primary author of the propositions revealed in Scripture, the conclusion that these propositions are true follows inexorably from this assumption.

The motive of faith consists in the first two premises, considered collectively, of the syllogism below.

---

[1] For further discussion of divine and infallible faith and the motive of faith on which it is founded, see E. Stillingfleet, *Origines Sacræ, or a Rational Account of the Grounds of Natural and Revealed Religion* (Oxford: Oxford University Press, 1836), 1:277–92.

> What God affirms is true.
>
> God affirms the teachings of Scripture.
>
> Therefore the teachings Scripture are true.

As one can see, the conclusion follows from the premises with complete certainty. Divine and infallible faith follows from the motive of faith as surely as any belief can follow from any evidence. Seeming tension between faith and reason therefore does not arise because of any inadequacy in the motive of faith.

C. The Motives of Credibility

The tension arises, if it arises at all, rather, from the probable and incomplete character of the motives, or grounds, of credibility, namely, the evidence on the basis of which one determines that the Scriptures are the Word of God. An individual Christian's motives of credibility, for instance, might include archaeological evidence of Scripture's historical accuracy, the testimony of historians like Herodotus and Josephus to the occurrence of events mentioned in Scripture, instances of fulfilled prophecy, a sense of Scripture's majesty, and an acquaintance with Scripture's power to transform lives. All items of evidence that lead someone to believe that Scripture is God's Word make up his motives of credibility.

Weighty and numerous as these motives of credibility may be, they rarely if ever suffice to demonstrate that the Bible is God's Word in such a way as to eliminate all conceivable grounds for doubt. Few if any human beings, for example, possess sufficient knowledge to refute every objection to the inspiration of Scripture; and few if any could honestly claim expertise in more than a handful of the subjects relevant to the debate over Scripture's historical accuracy. Inevitably therefore the motives of credibility to which a given person has access will, at best, render probable grounds for his identifying Scripture as a revelation from God. The motives of credibility in and of themselves thus give rise only to a human and fallible faith. One needs this human and fallible faith nevertheless to obtain the motive of faith, from which divine and infallible faith springs. For when one first comes to accept that the Word of God is divinely revealed, he must do so either (a) with a human and fallible faith based on motives of credibility or (b) with a divine and infallible faith based on the motive of faith. One cannot come to believe, at least initially, that the Word of God is divinely revealed by a divine and infallible faith built on the motive of faith, however. For the motive of faith is itself that the Word of God is divinely revealed. One who wished to ground his initial acceptance of the motive of faith in the motive of faith would thus ensnare himself in a vicious circle.

Any additional revelation that taught that the Word of God is divinely revealed admittedly would enable one who knew of it to decide initially that the Word of God is divinely revealed with a divine and infallible faith. In order to accept that prior revelation with a divine and infallible faith and thus start the entire process of coming to belief with divine and infallible faith, however, such a person would require a third revelation to attest that the prior revelation is divinely revealed, and so on ad infinitum. "It is irrational," writes John Tillotson, "to expect that a man should have another divine revelation to assure him that this [the Word of God] is a divine revelation: for then, for the same reason, I must expect another Divine revelation to assure me of that, and so without end." The only alternative to moving from the motives of credibility, by an act of human and fallible faith, to the motive of faith is thus an impossible, infinite regress.[2]

The Christian apologist must conceive of the relation between faith and reason in such a way that the motives of credibility, which in themselves yield only human and fallible faith, nonetheless warrant acceptance of the motive of faith, which grounds the divine and infallible belief of authentic Christians.

II. FOUR MODELS OF THE RELATIONSHIP BETWEEN FAITH AND REASON

Any adequate concept of the relationship between faith and reason must satisfy at least three criteria. First, such a concept must honestly take into account the limitations of the motives of credibility. Second, it must in no way compromise the unconditional character of divine and infallible faith. Third, it must acknowledge the indispensability of motives of credibility to the eventual attainment of divine and infallible faith. The following four models of the faith-reason relationship are evaluated in accord with these criteria.

A. Fideism

Fideism is the view that faith consists in belief without evidence. In other words motives of credibility for embracing the Christian revelation as divine do not exist and would not be significant if they did. Most evangelical Christians have encountered this attitude in their interactions with other believers. Arguing from such texts as 1 Cor 1:17–2:16, fideists normally maintain that God communicates the knowledge of gospel truths to human beings exclusively through the foolishness of preaching and that to offer reasons for faith would be either irreverent or useless on three counts. First, fideists assert, a rational defense of Christianity would constitute preaching with the wisdom of words, which, according to Paul, makes the cross of Christ of no effect (1:17). Second, fideists charge that one who argues for the gospel causes the faith of his hearers to rest on the wisdom of men rather than the power of God (2:4–5). Third, fideists contend that those who attempt to demonstrate Christianity's truthfulness imply that rational argument, apart from the Holy Spirit, can secure belief in the gospel. According to Scripture, however, "the unbeliever does not welcome what comes from God's Spirit" (2:14).

Admittedly these arguments for fideism may appear persuasive when presented in isolation. "The first to state his case seems right until another comes and cross-examines him" (Prov 18:17). The third objection, however, presupposes a false di-

---

[2] J. Tillotson, sermon 220, "Of the Faith or Persuasion of a Divine Revelation," in *Works of Dr. John Tillotson*, 10 vols. (London: Richard Priestley, 1829), 9:212.

chotomy: either one must attempt to argue someone into the kingdom of heaven or one must forsake rational argumentation altogether. Nonfideist Christians typically opt for a third position. Yes, they acknowledge, "No one can say, 'Jesus is Lord,' except by the Holy Spirit" (1 Cor 12:3). The nonfideist believes, however, that the necessity of the Holy Spirit's work in regeneration no more dispenses a Christian from the duty to give a reason for his hope (1 Pet 3:15) than it dispenses him from the duty of evangelism. True, arguments will be fruitless without the regenerating work of the Holy Spirit, but so will the preaching of the gospel. If the insufficiency of human words for effecting salvation therefore does not absolve the Christian of the obligation to share the gospel, neither does it absolve him of the duty to "contend for the faith" (Jude 3).

As to the first and second objections, moreover, rational apologetics is not to be equated with the "persuasive words of wisdom" Paul denounced in 1 Cor 2:4. The same Holy Spirit who inspired Paul to write that verse also inspired Paul and other biblical heroes to employ rational arguments to persuade their hearers to turn from idolatry and worship the one true God (Deut 4:25–28; 1 Kgs 18:27; 2 Chr 25:15; Pss 115:4–8; 135:15–18; Isa 41:21–23,26; 44:7,19; 45:21; 46:10; 48:3–8; Hos 8.6, Acts 14:14–18; 17:22–31). Presumably the "persuasive words of wisdom" which Paul disapproved were the elaborate rhetorical devices employed by teachers of other religions to captivate gullible crowds. The Holy Spirit, in any event, does not contradict Himself and therefore did not condemn rational arguments for Christianity in 1 Corinthians 1 and 2. Fideism, although common, is thus difficult to defend.

B. Reformed Epistemology

Reformed epistemology is the view that a person may reasonably assent to the Christian faith if he considers the principal objections to Christianity available to him and finds these objections unpersuasive. Reformed epistemology, whose principal advocates are Alvin Plantinga and Nicholas Wolterstorff, differs from fideism in that it requires a person to take seriously (and to rebut) objections to the Christian faith. Yet it resembles fideism in that it allows for the possibility that an intellectually responsible person might accept Christianity without first demanding evidence for its truthfulness.

The truth or falsehood of Reformed epistemology, it seems, hinges on the plausibility of its concept of proper basicality, that is, what makes a statement worthy of belief even if one cannot prove it. Contemporary secular philosophy holds that three kinds of belief are properly basic: beliefs that are self-evident, beliefs that are derived from sense perception, and beliefs that are incorrigible (i.e., impossible not to believe).

Two factors, according to Reformed epistemologists, authorize one to receive the second kind (those derived from sense perception) as true. First, one possesses sense perception, a faculty whose purpose is to perceive physical objects in one's environment. Second, this faculty functions properly; one does not hallucinate, for example. Reformed epistemologists argue that it is at least conceivable that certain human beings might possess another faculty, the *sensus divinitatis*, or sense of divinity, whose purpose is to perceive the truthfulness of the Christian faith. If some human beings possess such a faculty and it functions properly in apprehending the truthfulness of the Christian faith, then humans can reasonably accept the Christian faith simply on account of these two factors, if no objections definitely falsify it.

Most human beings do not sense that anyone possesses a *sensus divinitatis*. Nevertheless, Reformed epistemologists argue, a person who believes that he experiences the operation of such a faculty within himself has no compelling reason to distrust his own experience. Until such a person encounters a compelling objection to the claim that he possesses a *sensus divinitatis*, it might seem that he should acknowledge that he does. One might object, however, that what a person believes to be an extraordinary faculty operating in new and surprising ways within himself could also be an ordinary faculty, the human intellect, malfunctioning badly. If someone for instance claimed that he possessed a faculty that enabled him to perceive that the Great Pumpkin appears annually at Halloween, few would take seriously the claim, notwithstanding their inability to disprove it.

Plantinga responds to this objection, which he himself first introduces into the literature,[3] by observing that Reformed epistemologists' ascription of proper basicality to Christian theism does not commit them to accepting *any* belief whatsoever as properly basic. While Plantinga's reply is correct, it hardly suffices to blunt the force of the objection. For as James F. Harris observes,[4] the objection does not sting because it implies that Reformed epistemologists might accept belief in the Great Pumpkin as properly basic. The criticism stings, rather, because it exposes Reformed epistemologists' inability to explain why Great Pumpkin believers, who believe that their *"sensus Pumpkini"* is properly functioning when it leads them to believe in the Great Pumpkin, are not entitled to regard their belief in the Great Pumpkin as properly basic.[5] One cannot reasonably claim therefore that some faculty justifies him in believing claims for which he can produce no evidence; and to this extent Reformed epistemology fails as an apologetic strategy. Its advocates nonetheless are to be congratulated for exposing what might be called the standard account of belief justification in twentieth-century philosophy as untenable. According to this standard account, one can justifiably believe a proposition true only because, and to the extent that, one can prove it on the basis of beliefs that are self-evident, derived from sense perception, or incorrigible. The problem with this dictum, naturally, is that it seems impossible to prove the dictum itself on the basis of the these three classes of beliefs. While Reformed epistemology

---

[3] A. Plantinga, "Reason and Belief in God," in *Faith and Rationality: Reason and Belief in God*, ed. A. Plantinga and N. Wolterstorff (Notre Dame, IN: University of Notre Dame Press, 1983), 16–93, 74–78.

[4] J. F. Harris, *Analytic Philosophy of Religion* (Dordrecht: Kluwer, 2002), 174. R. A. Christian develops essentially the same criticism in much greater detail ("Plantinga, Epistemic Permissiveness, and Metaphysical Pluralism," *Religious Studies* 28 [1992]: 553–73, esp. 567–72).

[5] Plantinga responds to this point, which he dubs the "Son of Great Pumpkin" objection, by noting that even if one accepted, as Plantinga himself does not, that Christian belief is warranted simply because it is properly basic, consistency would not oblige one to grant that belief in the Great Pumpkin might be warranted for the same reason (Plantinga, *Warranted Christian Belief* [New York: Oxford University Press, 2000], 346–49). This response, it seems, ignores the crux of the objection. Reformed epistemology's critics allege that, according to its principles, belief in the Great Pumpkin could be properly basic and thus minimally rational for Great Pumpkin believers. And this Plantinga not only fails to deny but explicitly grants (ibid., 346).

seems ultimately inadequate as a model of the relation between Christian faith and human reason, then it does contribute significantly to the overall enterprise of Christian apologetics.

C. Rational Evidentialism

Rational evidentialism is the belief that one can accept Christianity without being intellectually irresponsible if (a) one possesses sufficient motives of credibility to render it probable that one ought to believe it, and (b) one knows of no objections that outweigh or undermine those motives of credibility. This understanding of the relationship between faith and reason enjoys broad, though not unanimous, support from Christian theologians of all ages. It is, however, subject to a weighty objection.

Merely probable motives of credibility, one might charge, can never warrant the sort of absolute assent of faith that Christianity demands. This objection could be valid, however, only if imperfect evidence could warrant no absolute assent, or at least no absolute assent of great import; and this is manifestly false. For assent is neither more nor less than a particular kind of decision; and humans must constantly make absolute, irrevocable decisions on the basis of incomplete evidence simply in order to conduct their affairs.

One who ponders whether he should cross the street, for example, cannot know, in the strictest sense of the term, that he will survive the trip. Nevertheless he must decide absolutely. He can commit himself absolutely to crossing or to remaining where he is. Indecision, as long as it endures, constitutes an absolute decision to remain where he is. Whatever a person does in this situation, then, constitutes an absolute decision on the basis of imperfect evidence. Unless human beings are doomed to irrationality in this and all similar situations, it must be justifiable to assent (to decide what to believe) on the basis of defective evidence.

D. Rationalism

The final model for correlating faith and reason exists in two forms: crude and sophisticated.

1. *Crude rationalism*

Crude rationalism, encountered more often in conversation than in reading, claims that one can justifiably believe nothing except what one can verify through sense perception or reasoning. In this view the mere testimony of humans establishes nothing, and to believe something simply because one reads of it in a book is the height of absurdity. While this position has affinities with serious forms of philosophical skepticism, it appears for the most part on the lips of persons who wish vigorously to resist encouragements to religious faith and who have not reflected on their crude rationalism's implications. These implications include that one cannot know that the Revolutionary War took place; that Abraham Lincoln was once president of the United States; or even the date of one's birthday. For knowledge of these and countless other data, humans depend completely on human testimony.

2. Sophisticated rationalism

A more sophisticated version of rationalism consists in the claim that one can reasonably believe nothing that one cannot verify through sense perception, reasoning, or testimony either (a) to events analogous to one's own experience (the position of Ernst Troeltsch) or (b) by persons whose worldview is similar to one's own (the position of F. H. Bradley). Troeltsch's brand of this sophisticated rationalism seems manifestly less plausible than Bradley's. For even the most hardened secularists accept on the basis of testimony that nuclear bombs have exploded and that hypnotists have induced persons to do marvelous things, yet few persons have witnessed anything even vaguely resembling these phenomena.

Even Bradley's rationalism, moreover, is not above reproach. For, one might ask, how can one know that the worldview of some witnesses of atomic explosions corresponds even faintly to one's own? One could ask certain witnesses personally. Yet even if he did, believing their answers would constitute acceptance of testimony that is rather difficult to verify. In order to verify a witness's claims about his worldview, again one would have to rely on testimony including others' recollections of his conversation, his writings, and so forth. Even on Bradley's view, then, one cannot substantiate testimony without consulting yet more testimony. It seems therefore that if testimony is to possess any evidential value at all, as it does in the eyes of all rational people, then testimony must constitute a kind of warrant for belief in and of itself. This does not mean any and every form of human testimony merits credence; it does mean, however, that human testimony constitutes one of several factors that can contribute to the credibility of a statement. Neither Troeltsch's nor Bradley's form of rationalism therefore seems adequate as an account of the relationship between faith and reason.

E. Conclusion

Of the four models for correlating faith and reason studied in this section, rational evidentialism alone seems to satisfy the three criteria set forth in the introduction. The first two models, fideism and Reformed epistemology, run afoul of the second criterion, namely, that a plausible model must acknowledge the dominion of reason over all human decision-making. For, according to both of these models, one can justly embrace Christianity without any evidence for its truthfulness that is external to Christianity itself. It seems impossible, moreover, to reconcile any of the fourth model's three forms with orthodox Christianity without grotesquely exaggerating the force of Christianity's motives of credibility and thereby failing to meet the first criterion. Process of elimination thus indicates that rational evidentialism must be the most plausible among the models of the faith-reason relationship analyzed here, for it alone satisfies all three criteria.

III. CONCLUSION

Tension between faith and reason arises as a result of the disproportion between the motives of credibility, which provide merely probable evidence for the truthfulness of Christianity, and the absolute assent that every authentic Christian yields to the articles of the Christian faith. One can overcome this tension, as has been seen, by a twofold expedient. First, one must carefully distinguish between the motives of credibility, which establish only the probability that one ought to consider Scripture a divine revelation, and the motive of faith, which establishes without any doubt that the divinely revealed propositions of Scripture are true. Second, one must adopt and apply what has been described as the rational evidentialist position on the relationship between faith and reason.

Chapter 7

NATURAL THEOLOGY AND ITS CONTRIBUTION TO APOLOGETICS

NATURAL THEOLOGY CONSTITUTES AN INDISPENSABLE PREREQUISITE to the intelligent consideration of the historical evidence for Christianity. Therefore the present chapter explains the concept of natural revelation, defines natural theology itself, offers a thumbnail sketch of the history of natural theology, reviews common objections to the study of natural theology, and surveys a number of reasons for cultivating natural theology.

I. NATURAL REVELATION

Natural revelation, which constitutes the subject matter of natural theology, consists simply in God's revelation of Himself to human beings in nature. David wrote of natural revelation in Psalm 19:1–2: "The heavens declare the glory of God, and the sky proclaims the work of His hands. Day after day they pour out speech; night after night they communicate knowledge."

Also Job appealed to natural revelation when he exhorted his friends in Job 12:7–9: "But ask the animals, and they will instruct you; ask the birds of the sky, and they will tell you. Or speak to the earth, and it will instruct you; let the fish of the sea inform you. Which of all these does not know that the hand of the LORD has done this? The life of every living thing is in His hand, as well as the breath of all mankind."

Paul affirmed the reality of natural revelation when he wrote, "What can be known about God is evident among them, because God has shown it to them. For His invisible attributes, that is, His eternal power and divine nature, have been clearly seen since the creation of the world" (Rom 1:19–20).

These and other scriptural testimonies indicate that according to Scripture God reveals Himself to all human beings at all times through nature. Because this form of revelation requires no miraculous alteration of the course of nature, theologians refer to it as natural revelation. And, because this revelation pervades all of creation, theologians also refer to it as general revelation. The revelation of God's being and attributes through nature, then, constitutes natural, general revelation.

One ought carefully to distinguish this natural, general revelation from supernatural, special revelation, which consists in God's disclosure of Himself to particular human beings at particular times by means of a miraculous alteration of the course of nature. Besides occurring less frequently and impacting fewer people, this special, supernatural revelation differs radically from natural, general revelation in that it conveys information not only about God as Creator but also about God as Redeemer. It discloses not merely the God of the philosophers but the God of Abraham, Isaac, and Jacob. Scripture teaches that natural revelation suffices only to condemn those who know it and that belief of supernatural revelation constitutes, at least in adults, a prerequisite sine qua non of salvation.

II.   NATURAL THEOLOGY

Natural theology is the practice of inferring truths about God from the data of natural revelation. If constructing a sound natural theology were impossible (i.e., if one could learn no truths about God from the evidence of natural revelation), then natural revelation itself would seem superfluous. In this case it would not constitute an authentic revelation. Scripture's unequivocal witness to the reality of natural revelation therefore implies that one *can* construct a sound natural theology on its basis.

III.   HISTORICAL ROOTS OF NATURAL THEOLOGY

A.   Pre-Christian Natural Theology

Natural theology outside the biblical tradition first flowered in ancient Greece, the cradle of Western philosophy. Though numerous figures would merit treatment in a more extensive survey of natural theology before the Christian era, the following is limited to three: Anaxagoras, Plato, and Aristotle.

1.   *Anaxagoras (500/499–428/427 BC)*

To the pre-Socratic philosopher Anaxagoras of Klazomenae belongs the distinction of being the first Western philosopher on record to conceive of the cosmos as in some sense caused by one infinite, omniscient, and incorporeal being. Anaxagoras did not affirm the doctrine of creation *ex nihilo*, but neither did any other pagan thinker. The idea that all things originate from the creative power of God seems to have been so alien to conventional pagan views on these subjects that even the Christian apologist, Justin Martyr (c. 100–165), balked at affirming it.[1] The following fragment from his writings shows that Anaxagoras approximated Christian monotheism rather well for a person of his time and place.

> Mind is infinite and self-ruled. . . . It is the finest of all things and the purest, it has all knowledge about everything and the greatest power; and Mind controls all things, both the greater and the smaller, that have life. Mind controlled also the whole rotation, so that it began to rotate in the

---

[1] Justin, *First Apology,* chap. x, in *Ante-Nicene Fathers,* ed. A. Roberts and J. Donaldson (Peabody, MA: Hendrickson, 1994), 1:165.

beginning. . . . And the things that are mingled and separated and divided off, all are known by Mind. And all things that were to be—those that were and those that are now and those that shall be—Mind arranged them all.[2]

2. Plato (c. 427–347 BC)

The literary output of Plato is so vast and his thought so unsystematic that one cannot hope to offer in this format more than a few representative samples of Plato's reflections on natural theology. This section therefore presents one of Plato's arguments for the existence of God, an example of his manner of reasoning about the divine attributes, and a brief account of his concept of the material world's creation.

a. God's existence

Perhaps the clearest of Plato's arguments for the existence of a god or gods appears in the *Laws* 894e–895a (cf. *Phaedrus* 245c–245e), where he wrote, "When we have one thing making a change in a second, the second, in turn, in a third, and so on—will there ever, in such a series, be a first source of change? Why, how can what is set moving by something other than itself ever be the first of the causes of alteration? The thing is an impossibility."[3] Plato argued, in other words, that because an infinite regress of movers is inconceivable, any chain of moved movers must originate in something that exists independently of any other being's motion.

b. Divine attributes

Plato's brief yet enormously influential argument for divine immutability in his *Republic* 381b–c typifies his manner of discussing the divine attributes.

Socrates: [If God changes], does he change himself to the better and to something fairer, or for the worse and to something uglier than himself?"

Adimantus: It must necessarily be for the worse if he is changed. For we surely will not say that God is deficient in either beauty or excellence.

In other words Plato argued, through his usual mouthpiece Socrates, that God is perfect and that since He cannot change for the better, any change must necessarily be for the worse. Therefore he concluded that God will not change.

c. Creation

Before leaving Plato, it seems appropriate at least to introduce his discussion of creation in what was once his most celebrated dialogue, the *Timaeus*. Near the outset of his oration on the cosmos and its origin, Timaeus, the principal speaker in this

---

[2] Anaxagoras, fragment 12, §476, in *The Presocratic Philosophers: A Critical History with a Selection of Texts,* ed. and trans. G. S. Kirk, J. E. Raven, and M. Schofield (Cambridge, UK: Cambridge University Press, 1983), 363.

[3] All translations of Plato in this work are from *The Collected Dialogues of Plato: Including the Letters,* ed. E. Hamilton and H. Cairns; trans. L. Cooper et al. (Princeton, NJ: Princeton University Press, 1961).

dialogue, asks, "What is that which always is and has no becoming, and what is that which is always becoming and never is?"[4] Answering his own question, he continued,

> That which is apprehended by reason and intelligence is always in the same state, but that which is conceived by [mere] opinion with the help of sensation and without reason is always in a process of becoming and perishing and never really is. Now everything that becomes or is created must of necessity be created by some cause, for without a cause nothing can be created. The work of the creator, whenever he looks to the unchangeable and fashions the form and nature of his work after an unchangeable pattern, must necessarily be made fair and perfect, but when he looks to the created only and uses a created pattern, it is not fair or perfect.[5]

After pausing to confirm that this world is indeed created, Timaeus then posed a question of enormous import for the history of natural theology: "Which of the patterns had the artificer [creator] in view when he made it [i.e., the world]—the pattern of the unchangeable or the pattern of that which is created?"[6] He answered as follows:

> If the world be indeed fair and the artificer good, it is manifest that he must have looked to that which is eternal, but if what cannot be said without blasphemy is true, then to the created pattern. Everyone will see that he must have looked to the eternal, for the world is the fairest of creations and he is the best of causes. And having been created in this way, the world has been framed in the likeness of that which is apprehended by reason and mind and is unchangeable.[7]

Plato, then, had Timaeus conceive of the universe as consisting of three kinds of being: (a) a realm of Ideas, that is, unchanging, uncreated, ideal essences such as perfect goodness, perfect beauty, and perfect happiness; (b) a created, material world; and (c) a god, or demiurge, who creates the material world in the likeness of the Ideas.

Admittedly this concept of the universe might seem irrelevant to the Christian view of creation. Christianity acknowledges a creator and a material world, but Plato's uncreated ideas do not seem to fit in a universe with only one uncreated Being. However, Plato's Ideas live on in Christian natural theology, not as independent entities but as ideas or "reasons" in the divine intellect. Augustine, in fact, places a Christianized form of Plato's Ideas at the center of his theology of creation. Augustine asked:

> Who dares to say that God has composed all things irrationally? If that cannot rightly be said or believed, it remains that all things have been composed for a reason; neither is a man for the same reason as a horse—for it is absurd to suppose this. Single things, therefore, have been created for their own reasons. Where, however, ought one to judge that these reasons exist except in the very mind of the Creator? For he did not look at anything placed outside

---

4 Plato, *Timaeus* 27d.
5 Ibid., 27d–28b.
6 Ibid., 28c–29a.
7 Ibid., 29a.

himself so that he would establish what he established in accordance with it; for to think this is sacrilege. If these reasons for creating all things that were created are contained in the divine mind (in the divine mind there cannot be anything except that which is eternal and immutable), and Plato calls these principal reasons Ideas; not only are there Ideas, but they are true, because they are eternal and, in the same way, remain immutable.[8]

Thus Augustine reformed and ennobled Plato's creation account in the *Timaeus* in such a way that it contributes constructively to an authentically Christian theology of creation. Incidentally this achievement of Augustine constitutes proof that theology can profit from the critical appropriation of extrabiblical concepts without forfeiting its right to the name "Christian."

3. Aristotle (384–322 BC)

Aristotle's views are more systematic than those of Plato, Aristotle's teacher. This section discusses Aristotle's principal theistic argument, his general manner of discussing the divine attributes, and his position on the relationship of the world to God.

a. God's existence

Like Plato, Aristotle argued for the existence of God primarily from the impossibility of an infinite regress.

> Since everything that is in motion must be moved by something, let us take the case in which a thing is in locomotion and is moved by something that is itself in motion; and that again is moved by something else that is in motion; and that by something else, and so on continually. Then the series cannot go on to infinity, but there must be some first mover.[9]

From this extract it might appear that Aristotle scarcely improved on Plato's formulation of the argument from motion. One should note, however, that an extraordinarily complex argument for the impossibility of an infinite regress follows this passage immediately (an argument not discussed here).

b. Divine attributes

Aristotle's comments on the divine attributes are frequently short and sententious. In defense of the unmoved mover's immutability, for example, he writes simply; "The divine and most exalted suffers no change; for it would be a change into something worse."[10] In defense of divine unity he asserted, "The world refuses to be governed badly," and then he quoted the words of Odysseus from Homer's *Iliad*: "The rule of many is not good; one ruler let there be!"[11] Usually, however, Aristotle's discourses on

---

[8] Augustine, *On 83 Diverse Questions*, q. 46 (our translation).

[9] Aristotle, *Physics* 7.1.242a. All translations of Aristotle in the present volume are from *The Complete Works of Aristotle: The Revised Oxford Translation,* ed. J. Barnes, trans. J. L. Ackrill et al., 2 vols. (Princeton, NJ: Princeton University Press, 1984).

[10] Aristotle, *Metaphysics* 12.9.1074b, in *The Complete Works of Aristotle.*

[11] Ibid., 12.10.1076a; and *Iliad* 2.204.

the divine attributes are relatively lengthy and abstruse. The following excerpt from a much longer discussion of divine intelligence is representative.

> First, then, if "thought" is not the act of thinking but a potency, it would be reasonable to suppose that the continuity of its thinking is wearisome to it. Secondly, there would evidently be something else more precious than thought, viz. that which is thought of. For both thinking and the act of thought will belong even to one who thinks of the worst thing in the world, so that if this ought to be avoided (and it ought, for there are even some things which it is better not to see than to see), the act of thinking cannot be the best of things. Therefore it must be of itself that the divine thought thinks (since it is the most excellent of things), and its thinking is a thinking on thinking.[12]

It is, perhaps, worth recalling here Plutarch's account of Aristotle's response when his erstwhile pupil, Alexander the Great, upbraided him for publishing his "secret" doctrines. According to Plutarch, Aristotle said the works are published, and yet they are not published, for they are written in such a way as to be instructive only to those already acquainted with Aristotelian philosophy (*Alexander* 7).

Considerations of clarity aside, however, Aristotle did hit on an important truth when he concluded that God, in the strictest sense of the term, contemplates only Himself. If, as Scripture teaches, God is immutable and utterly independent of creation, He cannot acquire knowledge of creation by beholding creation's history as it occurs. For if He did behold creation in this manner, like a spectator at a sports event, then He would depend on something external to Himself for His knowledge and His mental states would change constantly along with the constant change of the scenes He beholds.

Instead God knows creation by beholding Himself and His eternal will, whereby He has eternally and unchangeably foreordained all things that come to pass. By contemplating Himself, God can know of all events simultaneously without depending on anything else for His supply of information or undergoing the slightest of changes. Aristotle did not err therefore by concluding that God thinks directly only about Himself. Aristotle erred, rather, by failing to recognize that God controls and foreordains every aspect of created history so that God can know this history simply by observing His own will. God thinks about things other than Himself by thinking about Himself.

c. The world and God

Aristotle denied that God could have created the universe at some particular moment. Instead he maintained that change (motion) must always have occurred and that changeable things, that is, things other than God, must always have existed. Among his arguments for the eternity of motion is the following:

---

[12] Aristotle, *Metaphysics* 12.9.1074b.

It is impossible that movement should either have come into being or cease to be (for it must always have existed), or that time should. For there could not be a before and an after if time did not exist. Movement also is continuous, then, in the sense in which time is; for time is either the same thing as movement or an attribute of movement.[13]

What Aristotle seems to mean by this is, the idea that motion began at some moment implies motion did not occur before that moment and that this consequence is absurd, because time itself constitutes a measure of motion. In other words, if there is no time, then where there is no motion, nothing strictly speaking is "before" motion's beginning. If the idea that motion began implies that something was "before" motion, then the proposal that motion began is ludicrous.

One can defeat this argument, naturally, simply by denying that the proposition, "Motion began at a certain point," implies the proposition, "Before that point, motion did not occur." This seems to be a plausible solution, and it occurred already to Augustine in the fourth century.[14] Nevertheless Aristotle's arguments for the eternity of the world proved a fertile source of heresies in the high Middle Ages. Along with Aristotle's objections to the immortality of individual souls and to creation ex nihilo, these arguments tempered considerably the benefits Christendom reaped from the rediscovery and Christianization of Aristotle's philosophy in this period.

B. Natural Theology in the Patristic Era

A number of distinguished Christian natural theologians appeared during the patristic era, which extends from the close of the first century of the Christian era until the death of Isidore of Seville (AD 636) in the West and the death of John of Damascus (AD 749) in the East. The following discussion is limited to the two greatest natural theologians of the period, Augustine in the West and Gregory of Nyssa in the East.

1. Augustine (AD 354–430)

The most notable of Augustine's contributions to natural theology that is not treated elsewhere in the present work is perhaps his argument for the existence of God from the nature of truth. This argument consists of these claims:

1. God is that than which there is no greater being.
2. If something exists that is greater than the human mind, either it or something greater than it is God.
3. Truth exists.
4. Truth is greater than the human mind.
5. Therefore truth, or something greater, is God.[15]

---

[13] Aristotle, *Metaphysics* 12.6.1071b.

[14] Augustine, *Confessions* 11.10.12–14.17, in *Nicene and Post-Nicene Fathers,* ed. P. Schaff and H. Wace (Peabody, MA: Hendrickson, 1994), 1:167–68.

[15] See Augustine, *On the Teacher* 7.14 and 15.39.

This argument fails indisputably. For if only a rock and a tree existed, a being "than which there is no greater being" would exist, namely, the tree. Of significance, nevertheless, is the fact that Augustine's argument initiated and to a certain extent inspired a long series of increasingly sophisticated ontological arguments for God's existence that played a prominent role in the natural theology of the next sixteen centuries. The argument's greatness, therefore, lies in its *Wirkungsgeschichte* (the history of its effects) rather than in any particular insight.

2. Gregory of Nyssa (c. 335–394)

The most distinguished natural theologian of the Christian East during the patristic era is Gregory of Nyssa. Representative of his achievements in this area is the following argument for the oneness of God. To one who believes that many gods exist, Gregory asserts, one ought to pose the question:

> "Does he think Deity is perfect or defective?" . . . If, as is likely, he bears testimony to the perfection in the Divine nature, then we will demand of him to grant a perfection throughout in everything that is observable in that divinity. . . . Whether as respects power, or . . . goodness, or wisdom and imperishability . . . in all he will agree that perfection is the idea to be entertained of the Divine nature. . . . If this, then, be granted us, it would not be difficult to bring round these scattered notions of a plurality of Gods to the acknowledgment of a unity of Deity. For if he admits that perfection is in every respect to be ascribed to the subject before us, though there is a plurality of these perfect things . . . he must be required by a logical necessity, either to point out the particularity in each of these things which present no distinctive variation . . . or, if . . . the mind can grasp nothing in them in the way of particular, to give up the idea of any distinction.[16]

Gregory reasoned this way:

1. If two beings differ in no respect whatsoever, they are in fact the same being.
2. Multiple, perfect beings, if they existed, would differ in no respect.
3. Therefore only one perfect being can exist.
4. Every deity is by definition perfect.
5. Therefore only one deity can exist.

One might object to this argument that the fourth premise seems gratuitous. However, since Gregory believes that a typical polytheist of his time would readily acknowledge its truthfulness and since Gregory sought by this argument not so much to demonstrate the veracity of monotheism as to persuade polytheists to embrace it, his employment of this unsubstantiated premise seems at least excusable.

---

[16] Gregory of Nyssa, *The Great Catechism*, in *Nicene and Post-Nicene Fathers*, 1:474.

C. Natural Theology in the Medieval Period

Natural theology reached its height in Christendom in the Middle Ages, a period that extends from the close of the patristic era until the Renaissance of the fifteenth century. Of the countless Christians who developed natural theology during this period, the most significant are Anselm, Thomas Aquinas, and John Duns Scotus. Inasmuch as Anselm and Aquinas receive considerable attention in chap. 12 ("Later Patristic and Medieval Apologetics"), the present section focuses on Duns Scotus.

1. The theistic argument of Duns Scotus (c. 1266–1308)

In various places in his vast corpus, Duns Scotus proposes an elaborate argument for the existence of God, which constitutes his most distinguished contribution to the discipline of natural theology. The argument, as it appears in Duns Scotus's *Ordinatio*, Distinction 2, Question 1, serves as a representative example of his natural theology as a whole.

2. The threefold primacy

Scotus's argument begins with a thoroughgoing case for the existence of a threefold primacy in the universe: a primacy of efficiency, finality, and eminence. He attempted to establish that at least one entity in nature, albeit not necessarily the same entity, holds first place among all beings in efficient causality, in final causality, and in eminence.

a. A being that is first in efficient causality

To demonstrate that some being constitutes an uncaused efficient cause and thus exemplifies the first element of his threefold primacy, Scotus marshals three arguments, two of which are noted here. First, he reasoned, the actual existence of effects proves the possibility of the existence of effects: the sort of things brought about by efficient causality. Since an infinite regress is inconceivable, Scotus maintains, any possible effect must originate in some efficient cause that is itself uncaused. If an effect is possible, Scotus concludes, a first, uncaused efficient cause must be possible as well.

In his third argument for the existence of at least one uncaused, efficient cause, Scotus asserted that the possibility of an uncaused efficient cause's existence means that such a cause actually exists. If an uncaused cause did not actually exist, Scotus reasons, then it could not possibly exist. For no other being could bring precisely this kind of cause into existence. Yet the first argument proves that it is possible for an uncaused efficient cause to exist; therefore Scotus concluded, an uncaused efficient cause must actually exist.

b. A being that is first in final causality

To demonstrate the existence of an uncaused final cause, Scotus proposed three similar arguments. First, the possibility that some entity might exist for the sake of some other entity implies the possibility of the existence of an entity that does not exist for the sake of anything else. Otherwise an infinite regress would ensue.

In other words Scotus reasoned that in the absence of an end that existed for the sake of no prior end, one could not have either an infinite or a finite chain of ends, each of which exists for the sake of the end that constitutes the prior link in the chain. In this case one would have no chain at all. For no end that depended on another end for its existence could initiate and support the entire chain's existence.

Second, Scotus argued that nothing could cause an end, which exists for the sake of no other end, to exist. For in the absence of such an end, no existing end could motivate an entity to cause it. Third, the possibility of such an end's existence implies that it actually exists. For if an uncausable end did not exist, its existence would be impossible; no other entity could cause the uncausable.

c. A being that is first in eminence

To demonstrate the existence of a being that excels all others in eminence or perfection, Scotus proposed three further arguments. First, if one allows for the possible existence of beings that are less perfect than others, then consistency demands that one also allow for the possible existence of a being that is the most perfect of all. Otherwise, Scotus argued, an infinite regress would ensue.

Second, the most perfect of all beings does not exist for the sake of an end, because the end for the sake of which something else exists is necessarily more perfect than that something else. Since then what exists for the sake of no end is uncausable, as Scotus has already argued, the most perfect being must be uncausable.

Third, the possibility of a most perfect being's existence thus implies that a most perfect being actually exists. For if an uncausable being did not exist, its existence would be impossible; and the most perfect being is uncausable. The existence of the most perfect being can be possible therefore only on the supposition that a most perfect being actually exists.

3. The identity of the first efficient cause with the first final cause and the most eminent being

By means of nine subordinate arguments Scotus established in the first stage of his broader case for God's existence that at least one being, although not necessarily the same being, is first among all beings in efficient causality, final causality, and eminence or perfection. In the second stage of his argument, Scotus attempted to prove that if an entity is the first efficient cause, it must also be the first end and the most eminent of all beings. To this end he proposes two arguments.

First, Scotus contended, the first efficient cause must itself constitute the being that exists for no end other than itself. For all agents act for some end. The first efficient cause, however, that brings every subordinate end into being cannot act for the sake of any other end than itself. For prior (logically speaking) to its causation of other things, no other end exists. The first efficient cause therefore must constitute the end, which has no other end than itself and for the sake of which all other ends exist.

Second, Scotus argued, the efficient cause of all other entities must also be identical with the most perfect being, because it constitutes the end for the sake of which all other entities exist and is therefore by definition more perfect than any of them. Scotus therefore concluded, that a being cannot be the first efficient cause without also being the most perfect being and the end for the sake of which everything other than itself exists.

4. The existence of at least one being who possesses the threefold primacy

In the third stage of his case for God's existence Scotus advanced two arguments to the effect that a being, which is the first efficient cause and therefore also the first end and the most eminent of beings, necessarily exists. In the first of these arguments, Scotus maintained that whatever enjoys the triple primacy must, on account of its status as first efficient cause, first end, and most excellent being, be self-existent (i.e., not dependent for its existence on any other cause).

In the second and more complex of the two arguments, Scotus reasoned as follows:

1. A being that exists can fail to exist only if something that is incompatible with it can exist, or some essential condition of its existence can be lacking.
2. No being's existence can be incompatible with the existence of an entity that is uncaused; since it is uncaused, moreover, such an entity requires for its existence nothing external to itself.
3. Therefore an entity that exists and that is uncaused cannot fail to exist.

Duns Scotus, correctly it seems, takes the first of these premises to be evident. On behalf of the second and crucial premise, he argued first that the absence of some condition cannot threaten the existence of an entity that exists of itself. Second, and more significantly, he asserted that if a being, whose existence might arguably prove incompatible with the existence of something that possesses the threefold primacy, existed, this being would exist either of itself or of another. Such a being, that is to say, would either be uncaused or be dependent on some cause other than itself for its existence.

If the being in question were uncaused, Scotus argued, it would itself constitute a being with the threefold primacy, and a being with the threefold primacy would, manifestly, exist. If the being in question were caused, however, it would be incapable of destroying the being with the threefold primacy; for no being that is caused by another can be more powerful than what caused it. Duns Scotus thus concluded that at least one entity, which possesses the threefold primacy, must exist.

5. Conclusion

In the fourth and fifth stages of his overall argument, Duns Scotus attempted to prove that only one being can possess the threefold primacy and that this being must be infinite. These stages of his argument are significantly more complex and are dependent on more controversial presuppositions than the first three. This argument is typical of medieval natural theology in its thoroughness and intricacy and yet distinctive insofar as it hinges on considerations of possibility and necessity: themes that Duns

Scotus developed more extensively than virtually any Christian thinker who preceded him.

D. Natural Theology in the Modern Period (1400–)

It is difficult to determine whether Christendom has progressed or declined during the modern period. On one hand through the Reformation God brought a renewed awareness to Western Europe of central gospel truths, and through the missionary movement of the nineteenth century, God increased the proportion of the world's population that professes to be Christian from one fourth to one third. On the other hand the forces unleashed by the Renaissance, the Enlightenment, and the French, Russian, and Chinese revolutions, among other events, made atheism, during a long stretch of the modern period, the official "religion" of one third of the globe. The same forces, moreover, have made atheism the de facto official religion of the intelligentsia worldwide, of Western Europe, and, to an extent many are unwilling to admit, of the United States.

The modern period witnessed a continuation of the medieval tradition of natural theology in the fifteenth and sixteenth centuries; a great flourishing of natural theology in response to the Enlightenment in the seventeenth, eighteenth, and nineteenth centuries; and then a virtually complete collapse of the enterprise of natural theology in the twentieth century. The present section surveys the accomplishments of the two most significant natural theologians of the modern period: Gottfried Wilhelm Leibniz and William Paley.

1. Gottfried Wilhelm Leibniz (1646–1716)

The masterwork of Gottfried Wilhelm Leibniz, philosopher, mathematician, theologian, scientist, historian, courtier, and diplomat extraordinaire, is almost certainly his *Theodicy*.[17] Because Leibniz affirmed in this work that the existing world is the best of all possible worlds,[18] it was scorned in Voltaire's novella *Candide*. However, this grotesquely implausible thesis played no essential role in Leibniz's argument. The work as a whole is a competent attempt to demonstrate the compatibility of evil's existence in the world with the existence of an omnipotent and morally spotless God.

a. God is not the creator of evil

To prove his point Leibniz appealed to four considerations. First, he argued, since evil is a privation, that is, a lack of necessary being rather than a being itself, God is certainly not the creator of evil.

b. God is not the origin of evil

Leibniz also contended that God as such is not even the origin of evil. Evil's origin, rather, lies "in the ideal nature of the creature, in so far as this nature is contained in the eternal verities which are in the understanding of God, independently of his

---

[17] G. W. Leibniz, *Theodicy: Essays on the Goodness of God, the Freedom of Man, and the Origin of Evil*, ed. A. Farrer, trans. E. M. Huggard (London: Routledge, 1951).
[18] Plato, incidentally, asserted the same (*Phaedo* 97c-d).

will."[19] By virtue of creatures' ideal natures, that is, the ideas of creaturely natures in God, he affirmed, "There is an *original imperfection in the creature* before sin, because the creature is limited in its essence; whence ensues that it cannot know all, and that it can deceive itself and commit other errors."[20] Leibniz argued in other words that because creatures are naturally imperfect and evil derives from this imperfection, the origin of evil must lie not in some imperfection in God but in imperfect creaturely natures. In Leibniz's view, the presence of such ideas in the divine mind does not compromise God's perfection, because finitude inevitably involves imperfection, and the creation of finite beings constitutes nevertheless an act of benevolence. Leibniz conceives of the divine ability to create the imperfect and potentially evil therefore as an aspect of God's perfection.

c. Evil is indispensable to the attainment of certain goods

Third, Leibniz considers the objection that a perfect God would not allow evil in His creation at all. It is not inconceivable, Leibniz responded, that a creation that contains some evil, but a great deal of good, might actually contain greater cumulative goodness than any possible universe from which evil is completely absent.

> Often an evil, brings forth a good whereto one would not have attained without that evil. Often indeed, two evils have made one great good. . . . Even so two liquids sometimes produce a solid, witness the spirit of wine and spirit of urine mixed by Van Helmont; or so do two cold and dark bodies produce a great fire, witness an acid solution and an aromatic oil combined by Herr Hoffmann. A general makes sometimes a fortunate mistake which brings about the winning of a great battle; and do they not sing on the eve of Easter, in the churches of the Roman rite:
>
> > O certainly necessary was the sin of Adam, that by the death of Christ has been destroyed!
> >
> > O happy fault, that merited so great a Redeemer![21]

Leibniz concluded that since one cannot reasonably exclude the possibility that a world with evil may contain more cumulative goodness than a world without evil, one cannot justly impugn God's goodness simply because He allows evil in the world.

d. God is not culpable for sinful human acts

In his fourth and final consideration Leibniz faced the objection that God does not merely permit human beings to perform sinful acts but actually causes them to sin. Surprisingly Leibniz accepts the fundamental accuracy of this charge. For he reasons, since (a) no creaturely event occurs without a cause, and (b) "effects follow their

---

[19] Leibniz, *Theodicy*, §1.20, p. 135.
[20] Ibid. (italics his).
[21] Ibid., §1.10, p. 129.

causes determinately,"[22] then (c) God, as the only uncaused cause, must constitute at least the ultimate cause of every creaturely act. He maintained, however, that this causation of sinful acts does not involve God in moral culpability. For God causes human acts only insofar as these acts exist and not insofar as they are evil and thus deprived of necessary elements of their being.

God's causality of sinful acts, Leibniz contended, resembles the causality exercised by a river current on vessels of differing mass; the relative slowness with which the bulkier vessels move derives solely from their own bulkiness and not from any defect in the current that moves them.

> The current is the cause of the boat's movement, but not of its retardation; God is the cause of perfection in the nature and the actions of the creature, but the limitation of the receptivity of the creature is the cause of the defects there are in its action. Thus . . . God is the cause of the material element of evil which lies in the positive, and not of the formal element, which lies in privation. Even so one may say that the current is the cause of the material element of the retardation, but not of the formal: that is, it is the cause of the boat's speed without being the cause of the limits to this speed. . . . God is no more the cause of sin than the river's current is the cause of the retardation of the boat.[23]

1. Why create morally imperfect beings? One may reply, naturally, that although this explanation absolves God of the charge of participating in sinful acts Himself, it does not absolve Him of responsibility for the existence of those morally imperfect creatures whose defects cause the divine action to terminate in human sin. Leibniz gave an answer to this objection, however, in his doctrine of the necessary imperfection of creatures.

> The imperfections . . . and the defects in operations [of creatures] spring from the original limitation that the creature could not but receive with the first beginning of its being, through the ideal reasons which restrict it. For God could not give the creature all without making of it a God; therefore there must needs be different degrees in the perfection of things, and limitations also of every kind.[24]

2. Are predetermined acts in any meaningful sense free? Again, however, one might reply that rational agents are responsible only for those acts that they freely perform and that if God predetermines all such actions, He cannot reasonably reward or punish human beings on those actions' account. Leibniz argued, however, that the freedom that moral responsibility presupposes cannot consist in the ability to do other than one actually does. For "the very nature of truth"[25] in his view renders future events determinate. Even if God did not know the future, the truth of propositions uttered

---

[22] Ibid., §3.360, p. 341.
[23] Ibid., §1.30, p. 141.
[24] Ibid., §1.31, pp. 141–42.
[25] Ibid., §1.37, p. 144.

today about events that will occur tomorrow would render the future determinate. After all, Leibniz explained, "It was true already a hundred years ago that we should write today as it will be true after a hundred years that I have written."[26] If it is true right now, by the same token, that Italy will defeat France in the World Cup competition in 2050, it is simply impossible that France will emerge the victor.

The idea of freedom as the ability to refrain from performing the acts one actually performs, Leibniz argued, is therefore incoherent. The true essence of freedom, Leibniz suggests, consists rather in "spontaneity and choice."[27] "When we act freely," he explained, "we are not being forced, as would happen if we were pushed on to a precipice and thrown from top to bottom; and we are not prevented from having the mind free when we deliberate, as would happen if we were given a draught to deprive us of discernment."[28] An act is free, in other words, so long as it is genuinely the agent's action and not something thrust on it by another and so long as the agent itself decides to perform the action or at least not to refrain from it. Since freedom in this sense of the word by no means excludes predetermination, Leibniz concluded one cannot reasonably assert that actions predetermined by God are therefore unfree. If predetermined acts are not unfree, then God does no one an injustice in punishing predetermined acts that transgress the moral law.

e. Summary

In his *Theodicy* Leibniz offered credible, albeit perhaps not compelling, arguments to the effect that divine predetermination of creaturely acts does not make God culpable. God may allow evil in order to achieve otherwise unattainable goods; and He is neither the creator nor the origin of evil. While Leibniz's view that the present world is the best of all possible worlds unquestionably mars the work, it by no means deprives his *Theodicy* of all usefulness.

2. William Paley (1743–1805)

The Anglican clergyman William Paley (1743–1805) wrote *A View of the Evidences of Christianity* and *Natural Theology*. At the outset of the latter work, arguably Paley's greatest, he introduced his famous "watchmaker argument."

> In crossing a heath, suppose I pitched my foot against a *stone*, and were asked how the stone came to be there: I might possibly answer, that for anything I knew to the contrary, it had lain there forever: nor would it perhaps be very easy to show the absurdity of this answer. But suppose I had found a *watch* upon the ground, and it should be inquired how the watch happened to be in that place; I should hardly think of the answer which I had before given, that for anything I knew the watch might have always been there. Yet why should not this answer suffice for the watch as well as for the stone? . . . For this reason, and for no other, viz. that when we come to inspect the

---

[26] Ibid., §1.36, p. 143.
[27] Ibid.
[28] Ibid.

watch, we perceive (what we could not discover in the stone) that its several parts are framed and put together for a purpose . . . ; that if the different parts had been differently shaped from what they are, of a different size from what they are, or placed after any other manner, or in any other order, than that in which they are placed, either no motion at all would have been carried on in the machine, or none which would have answered the use that is now served by it.[29]

From these data, Paley wrote, "the inference is inevitable, that the watch must have had a maker; that there must have existed . . . an artificer or artificers, who formed it for the purpose which we find it actually to answer."[30] In this passage Paley restated, albeit in an especially striking manner, a classic and even shopworn argument for God's existence: the teleological argument, or argument from design. He expressed himself so picturesquely, however, that his "watchmaker" analogy and his general approach to the subject have become synonymous with the teleological argument itself. Paley adeptly parried, moreover, a number of surprisingly contemporary-sounding objections, which are discussed in chap. 14 ("Enlightenment and Post-Enlightenment Apologetics").

E. Conclusion

A few of the other numerous distinguished natural theologians include (a) the panentheist, Neo-Platonist Plotinus (c. AD 205–270), who seems to have exerted a decisive influence on Augustine; (b) Bonaventure, who with Duns Scotus, advocated forms of the ontological argument; (c) Samuel Clarke (1675–1729), who argued for the necessary existence of a single, immutable cause of the universe in his *Demonstration of the Being and Attributes of God* (1704); (d) Thomas Chalmers (1780–1847), who, among his many other achievements, argued extensively for design in creation; and (e) the panentheist originator of process theology, Alfred North Whitehead (1861–1947).[31]

IV. OBJECTIONS TO NATURAL THEOLOGY

Natural theology's impressive pedigree notwithstanding, a number of twentieth–century theologians, including Karl Barth and Cornelius Van Til, maintain that one cannot construct a sound natural theology and ought not make the attempt. Among the reasons advanced by these theologians for their opposition to natural theology are the claims (a) that natural theology tends to usurp the prerogatives of revealed theology; (b) that natural theology implicitly minimizes the antithesis between believer and unbeliever; and (c) that natural theology lacks scriptural warrant.

---

[29] W. Paley, *Natural Theology,* in *The Works of William Paley,* new ed. (Philadelphia: Crissy & Markley, 1853), 387a–88a.

[30] Ibid., 388a.

[31] Some may include the pioneers of the Intelligent Design movement among the great advocates of natural theology. However, Intelligent Design advocates consistently deny that that theory is a form of natural theology.

A. Does It Marginalize Revealed Theology?

To the first claim, however, one can reasonably respond that theologians who treat the conclusions of natural theology as the sum and substance of Christian doctrine (e.g., John Cobb, Schubert Ogden, David Tracy, and Nels Ferré) typically deny the existence of special revelation (i.e., God's supernatural self-disclosure to particular persons at particular times, which forms the basis of revealed theology). This denial alone suffices to account for these theologians' departures from historic Christianity.

B. Does It Mitigate the Antithesis?

The second claim presupposes a highly disputable concept of the antithesis between believing and unbelieving human beings. The objection may have some merit, if the antithesis is primarily epistemic, that is, if believers accept Christianity and unbelievers reject it, primarily because God strengthens the believer's intellect and thus enables him to know data to which the unbeliever has no access. However, the objection seems groundless if the antithesis is primarily moral, that is, if believers accept Christianity, and unbelievers reject it primarily because the Holy Spirit empowers the believer's will to accept propositions that both he and the unbeliever know to be true.

Admittedly the believer-unbeliever antithesis has an intellectual as well as a moral component. The preponderance of scriptural evidence nevertheless indicates that unbelievers "by their unrighteousness suppress the truth" (Rom 1:18). They reject the truths of natural revelation not out of ignorance but from hostility to what they know to be true. If the antithesis, then, consists primarily in a moral gap between the regenerate and the unregenerate, a robust affirmation of natural theology actually aggravates the antithesis. For the guilt one incurs by rejecting a truth increases proportionally with one's certainty that it is, in fact, true. The more the unbeliever knows from and yet fails to heed natural revelation, the wider the moral gap or moral antithesis between believer and unbeliever grows.

C. Does It Lack Scriptural Warrant?

The third claim, namely, that natural theology lacks scriptural warrant, seems plausible only if one artificially distinguishes between natural theology and reasoning about God on the basis of natural revelation. In Rom 1:20 Paul wrote of God's "eternal power and divine nature . . . being understood through what He has made." Thus creation conveys knowledge about God to human beings. Of course creation does not convey this knowledge directly. For unlike Scripture it does not communicate in propositions, and simply by gazing at sticks and stones one cannot behold the divine nature, the vision of which God reserves for the "pure in heart" (Matt 5:8) in the next world (1 John 3:2).

Rather, creation conveys this knowledge indirectly, by supplying evidence from which ordinary humans can infer that the universe derives from an infinitely superior kind of being. This inference, at least in certain societies, is virtually effortless. When, however, human beings have grown so perverse that this inference does not come naturally to them, as in atheistic and polytheistic cultures, it seems advisable to elaborate this natural inference into logical arguments, in other words, to cultivate natural theology. This is precisely what Paul did in Athens:

> The God who made the world and everything in it—He is Lord of heaven and earth and does not live in shrines made by hands. Neither is He served by human hands, as though He needed anything, since He Himself gives everyone life and breath and all things. From one man He has made every nationality to live over the whole earth and has determined their appointed times and the boundaries of where they live. He did this so they might seek God, and perhaps they might reach out and find Him, though He is not far from each one of us. For in Him we live and move and exist, as even some of your own poets have said, 'For we are also His offspring.' Being God's offspring, then, we shouldn't think that the divine nature is like gold or silver or stone, an image fashioned by human art and imagination (Acts 17:24–29).

Here Paul presented two arguments. First, he reasoned, since God made all things, He must be infinitely greater than His creatures and therefore infinitely greater than "shrines made by hands" or "gold or silver or stone" (vv. 24,29). Second, Paul argued, God is not "an image fashioned by human art and imagination." That is God must be incapable of deriving benefits from human acts of devotion such as bringing sacrifices to "feed" the gods. For God could not bestow on creatures any good if He did not already possess it, and creatures could not offer any good thing to God if He had not already given it to them. A human cannot enrich God therefore by serving Him. He can offer God nothing that God does not already possess.

These two arguments of Paul, then, are nothing other than natural theology. Natural theology possesses clear scriptural precedent. Moreover, Scripture also affirms natural theology's two indispensable presuppositions: (a) that God has supplied sufficient data in natural revelation to warrant conclusions about His existence and nature and (b) that human beings are capable of inferring these conclusions from the available data. The fact that Scripture warrants the use of natural theology ought to be uncontroversial.

V.   REASONS TO CULTIVATE NATURAL THEOLOGY

A number of considerations indicate that natural theology is not merely unobjectionable and scripturally warranted but is also indispensable to the welfare of the church. These considerations include, first, that all revealed theology presupposes natural theology; second, that apologetics to nontheists requires natural theology; and third, that one cannot construct an integrated, Christian worldview without utilizing natural theology.

A.   Revealed Theology Presupposes Natural Theology

The fact that revealed theology presupposes natural theology appears from the role natural theology inevitably plays in persuading people to acknowledge the authority of

Scripture. One can hardly accept that Scripture constitutes God's Word before he accepts the fact that God exists, and one cannot reasonably grant that God exists simply because Scripture says He does. Instead, one must have recourse to natural revelation and infer from it that God exists. Only then, after one has established God's existence by means of natural theology, can a person reasonably consider whether Scripture constitutes God's Word.

The fact that Scripture is God's Word will not move someone to accept its entire truthfulness unless he knows from natural revelation that God is good and thus is honest. One cannot reasonably accept the fact that God is honest simply because Scripture says so. The testimony of Scripture to such matters can be rationally affirmed only if one considers Scripture the word of an honest God. Without the testimony of natural revelation to God's existence and honesty one cannot justly infer the truthfulness of God's Word from its divine inspiration.

One cannot reasonably grant the truthfulness of special revelation without learning from natural revelation, and one can learn from natural revelation only through some variety of natural theology. Thus revealed theology presupposes natural theology as a prerequisite. Since the church needs revealed theology, that is, reasoning on the basis of inspired Scripture, the church also needs natural theology.

B. Apologetics to Nontheists Requires Natural Theology

The church also needs natural theology in order to render God's message credible to atheists, pantheists, and polytheists. A robust, Christian faith presupposes beliefs about God's existence and character that one derives from natural revelation by a process of inference (i.e., by natural theology). If someone avowedly rejects theism, he could not embrace Christianity without accepting at least some form of natural theology. An effective apologetic to such an individual is inconceivable without at least an element of natural theology.

C. Natural Theology Is Integral to Any Full-Orbed, Christian Worldview

The church also needs natural theology because it constitutes an essential component of any thoroughgoing Christian worldview. With the aid of natural theology one can recognize indications of design in nature as well as principles of logic and ontology that reinforce the teaching of Scripture. Without natural theology, however, the Christian seems doomed to a bifurcated view of the world, in which the seemingly secular aspects of human experience seem irrelevant to special revelation. Natural theology therefore seems vitally necessary to the development of an integrated, Christian worldview.

VI. CONCLUSION

Natural theology infers truths about God from the data of natural revelation. Revealed theology excels natural theology in dignity in that the former plumbs truths of greater depth (e.g., the Trinity, the incarnation, the atonement) compared with the topics of natural theology (God's eternal existence and power). Nevertheless revealed theology also presupposes knowledge derived from natural theology, which one must possess in order to appreciate the value and authority of God's special revelation in Scripture. Although some have objected to the use of natural theology on the grounds that it tends to marginalize revealed theology, that it diminishes the antithesis between believer and unbeliever, and that it lacks scriptural warrant, these charges have been shown to be without merit. Instead, the church ought to encourage the cultivation of natural theology because it is basic to an integrated Christian worldview, it is useful for apologetics to nontheists, and it is indispensable as a step toward accepting special revelation.

Chapter 8

SPEAKING ABOUT GOD AND ULTIMATE REALITY

THIS CHAPTER SURVEYS AND REFUTES ARGUMENTS commonly advanced that all claims about God are necessarily either meaningless or unsubstantiated. Such arguments are especially pernicious in their influence because they induce those who accept their conclusions to refuse even to consider evidence for theism. Typically these arguments rest on three claims: (a) if God exists, He is utterly unknowable; (b) the limitations of human nature preclude the possibility that human beings might know Him; and (c) that statements about God violate certain standards of intelligibility.

I. IS GOD INTRINSICALLY UNKNOWABLE?

Arguments for God's intrinsic unknowability are usually as follows:

1. Knowledge presupposes a real distinction between its subject and its object.[1]
2. What is distinct from something else is finite.[2]
3. Thus human beings can know God only if He is finite.
4. God, however, is infinite.
5. Therefore human beings cannot know God.

This argument's fourth premise constitutes a tenet of orthodox, Christian theism. Its third premise and the conclusion (fifth point) follow from the premises that precede them. Any fault in the argument must therefore lie in its first two premises.

A. The Nature of the Distinction Between Knower and Known

The falsehood of the first premise becomes manifest when one grasps the difference between a real distinction and a merely rational distinction. A real distinction exists when two things are actually different. For example the Empire State Building and the Sears Tower are really distinct. By contrast two objects of thought are merely

---

[1] H. Mansel, for example, affirms this in *The Limits of Religious Thought* (Boston: Gould & Lincoln, 1860), 77–79.

[2] Ibid., 76.

rationally distinct when they constitute not objectively diverse entities but one and the same entity considered in different respects. John Doe as citizen, John Doe as human being, John Doe as father, and John Doe as son are rationally distinct but not really so. When a human being thinks of himself, the thinker and the object of thought are only rationally distinct, not really so.

The first premise—that "knowledge presupposes a real distinction between its subject and object"—thus crumbles when one differentiates real distinctions from rational distinctions. This constitutes an important result for the following reasons. First, God's infinity implies that He cannot consist in really distinct parts; for one cannot add to what is qualitatively infinite, and if God consisted in parts, one could conceivably always add another. Second, if God is absolutely "partless," or simple, then no real distinction can exist in His essence.[3] One cannot add to what is genuinely, qualitatively infinite.

These two considerations imply, third, that if knowledge actually presupposed a real distinction between subject and object, then God could not know Himself. In this case divine self-knowledge would require a real distinction within God's essence, precisely the kind of distinction that divine infinity renders inconceivable. Since God's self-awareness is worth defending, it is important that the above argument's first premise is false. Establishing this premise's falsehood, however, hardly suffices to counter the argument as a whole. For orthodox Christians, regardless of what they think of the first premise, universally grant that God is really distinct from human beings and that human beings nevertheless know something of God. To vindicate God's knowability, therefore, Christians must also refute the argument's second premise: "What is distinct from something else is finite."

B. The Infinite Verses the All-Encompassing

This dictum could be true only if by "infinite" one means something like "all-encompassing," and proponents of arguments like the one above employ the term "infinite" in precisely this sense. Christians, however, ascribe quite a different kind of infinity to God. God's infinity, according to classic Christian belief, consists in His being absolutely *in*-finite, that is, in no way infected with any trace of the finite.

This constitutes a more exalted concept of infinity than that presupposed by the above argument. One can admittedly conceive of material entities for whom the existence of anything other than them indicates some limitation in themselves. If a pit, for example, contains both granite and coal, this would imply among other things that the granite in the pit is quantitatively finite. Even if granite were infinite in extension and the universe consequently consisted in nothing but granite, the granite, however, would remain qualitatively finite. For it would admit of division into finite parts. A pantheistic god, who is infinite in the sense of "all-embracing," likewise would consist at least partially in the crudest of finite things, not excluding the filthy and the evil.

---

[3] Properly speaking, the three persons in the Trinity are identical with the divine essence and yet are distinct from one another. Although each is fully God, the distinctions between them are not, strictly speaking, "in" the divine essence.

Such a god would be inferior in the extreme to the qualitatively infinite God of the Bible, who is perfectly holy, pure, and so forth. Since the Christian God's infinity renders Him radically unlike any other entity, the Christian God need not compete with other entities for space like the pantheist's god, which either absorbs all entities or itself becomes in every respect finite. The infinity of the Christian God so exalts Him above the realm of the finite that finite beings not only constitute no threat to Him but are also the objects of His fatherly care. The Christian understanding of the infinite—a much truer and loftier understanding than that of the pantheist—therefore in no way means that finite creatures cannot exist alongside of, or rather beneath, the infinite God. Thus, the second premise of the above argument ("What is distinct from something else is finite") is false.

C. Conclusion

While the infinity that Christians ascribe to God does imply that He is incomprehensible to creatures, it does not render Him utterly unknowable. Since the key premises of the argument above, which is representative of philosophical arguments from the idea of deity to the impossibility of knowing God, are false, the charge that God's nature renders Him unknowable is unsubstantiated.

II.   DOES HUMAN NATURE PRECLUDE HUMAN KNOWLEDGE OF GOD?

The skeptic then cannot prove that God, if there is a God, is intrinsically unknowable. A skeptic who acknowledges this might argue that while angels or some other suprahuman beings might know God, human beings do not. Humans, the skeptic might argue, suffer from such severe limitations that they cannot hope to know Him. Arguments to this effect usually take one of two forms. First, many (including most notably David Hume, 1711–76) argues that humans derive all their knowledge from the senses, and that these do not supply adequate information to infer to God's existence. Second, some argue, following Immanuel Kant (1724–1804), that when one attempts to apply the categories of human understanding to realities that humans cannot observe, one inevitably becomes entangled in self-contradiction.

A.   The Origin of Human Knowledge in the Senses

According to many Christian philosophers as well as many atheist philosophers, humans derive all their knowledge through the medium of sense perception. In this way people gain knowledge of the principles of noncontradiction, causality, and sufficient reason, as well as an elementary and implicit knowledge of ontology (the nature of being).

According to most atheists of this persuasion, humans by contrast, acquire no knowledge of being as such and little in the way of first principles of reason. David Hume, in particular, believed that people cannot obtain through their senses any knowledge of a connection between causes and their effects. In Hume's view people merely observe a constant succession of certain events after others (e.g., a nail penetrating wood each time someone strikes it with a hammer). While this uniform experience may lead persons to believe that swings of the hammer cause the nail to sink into wood, Hume maintained, strictly speaking, they know only that the one event has followed the other every time they have experienced either event. Of the universal principle that every effect requires a cause, he asserts, human beings know nothing.[4]

Since, then, humans do not know that effects require causes, Hume reasoned, they do not know that the cosmos requires an uncaused cause, God. Hume believed that if human beings cannot know God as cause of the universe, they cannot know God at all. He thus denied that people can know anything of God.[5]

That Hume erred in denying that human beings know that all contingent things require a cause, however, appears from the following argument. People naturally know that the principle of contradiction (that X cannot be not-X at the same time in precisely the same way) is true. Hume and conventionally Christian philosophers grant that all human beings rightly believe in the principle of contradiction.

Every being, as presumably even Hume would grant, either does or does not suffice to account for its own existence. If a being suffices to account for its own existence, then necessarily it exists by itself; it depends on nothing else to initiate or sustain its being. If a being does not suffice to account for its own existence, however, it might not exist. If such a being were to exist, even for a moment, without any cause, this being would suffice to account for its own existence. In that case, however, a being that does not suffice to account for its own existence would suffice to account for its own existence: a patent contradiction. If then the principle of contradiction holds true, every being that does not suffice to account for its own existence requires a cause.

Regardless of Hume's objections humans can know that contingent beings, which might or might not exist, require a cause to explain their existence. Given this information, it seems evident that the existence of contingent beings presupposes the existence of some uncaused cause. For if a chain of uncaused causes either extended backward infinitely or moved in a circle, then either an infinite regress would ensue or causality would move in a circle (i.e., events in the present would cause events in the past, which in turn would cause the same events in the present). If one did not shrink from affirming either of these paradoxical theses, one would still face the problem of explaining how a chain, whether infinite or circular, which is composed entirely of beings that are not self-existent, can itself be self-existent. A fireplace composed entirely of bricks, after all, cannot be marble.

Human beings then, can know (a) that contingent beings exist; (b) that contingent beings require a cause, and (c) that the existence of contingent beings presupposes some necessary, uncaused being. Therefore Hume's reasoning seems inadequate to overthrow the conviction of theists that human beings can know, through the information supplied by natural revelation alone, that some uncaused cause exists.

---

[4] D. Hume in *Enquiry Concerning Human Understanding,* ed. L. A. Selby-Bigge, rev. P. H. Nidditch, 3rd ed. (1748; reprint, Oxford: Clarendon, 1975), sec. 7, part 2, 74–77.

[5] Ibid., sec. 11, 143–48; and sec. 12, part 3, 162–65.

B. Antinomies

Skeptics of human beings' ability to know of the existence of God, however, can also appeal to what Immanuel Kant characterizes as antinomies, or paradoxes, that arise when one attempts to understand things that one cannot sense. Human attempts to reason about things inaccessible to sense perception, Kant maintained, inevitably founder on the following four paradoxes.

1. The thesis, "The world has a beginning in time and is also limited in regard to space," seems evidently true. The truthfulness of its antithesis, "The world has no beginning, and no limits in space; it is infinite as regard to both time and space," however, seems no less evident.[6]
2. The thesis, "Every composite substance in the world is made up of simple parts; and nothing anywhere exists save the simple or what is composed of the simple," appears indisputably correct. Its antithesis, "No composite thing in the world is made up of simple parts, and there nowhere exists in the world anything simple," however, appears no less indisputably correct.[7]
3. The thesis, "Causality in accord with laws of nature is not the only causality from which the appearances of the world can one and all be derived. To explain these appearances it is necessary to assume there is also another causality, that of freedom," seems incontrovertible. Its antithesis, "There is no freedom; everything in the world takes place solely in accord with laws of nature," however, seems equally incontrovertible.[8]
4. The thesis, "There belongs to the world, either as its part or as its cause, a being that is absolutely necessary," appears incontestable. Its antithesis, "An absolutely necessary being nowhere exists in the world, nor does it exist outside the world as its cause," however, seems equally incontestable.[9]

When presented in this format, admittedly, Kant's arguments appear formidable. In order to prove that each of these four putative antinomies is false, one need merely show that Kant's arguments for one of each of the four opposed pairs of propositions are less than compelling. For Kant's point is that, if the categories of the human understanding applied to the suprasensory sphere, then human beings would be obliged to believe contradictions. To show that Kant's proof is invalid, one need merely show that his arguments for one out of each pair of propositions is not fully persuasive; and this seems relatively easy to accomplish.

On behalf of his first antithesis (that the universe had no beginning in time), Kant argued that if the universe had begun to exist at some moment of time, then an infinity of moments of time would have existed beforehand. Since nothing within this "empty time" would dictate that creation should start at this moment rather than that,

---

6 I. Kant, *Critique of Pure Reason* (1855; reprint, Aalen, Germany: Sirantia, 1982), B454–55, p. 396.
7 Ibid., B462–63, p. 402.
8 Ibid., B472–73, p. 409.
9 Ibid., B480–81, p. 415.

he reasoned, creation could not begin at all.[10] One can call this argument into question merely by observing that time could have begun simultaneously with creation. In this case the "empty time" in which, Kant believed, creation could not occur would never have existed.

Kant defended the second antithesis (that no simple substance exists) by arguing that human beings do not encounter simple substances in their experience and that, if they did, they could not know with certainty that these substances were actually simple.[11] This argument hardly proves, however, that no simple substance exists. It proves, rather, at most that a certain type of evidence for a simple substance's existence is unavailable to human beings, and absence of evidence is not evidence of absence.

On behalf of his third antithesis (that there is no freedom and that everything in the world takes place solely according to laws of nature), Kant argued that if a god could act freely, then it could act in such a way that its state before the action did not causally necessitate the act. Since a divine act not necessitated by the deity's prior state, in Kant's view, would violate the law of cause and effect, he concluded that it could not occur.[12] In reply to this argument, if God, as Christians believe, is timeless, then no amount of free, divine activity can generate a causal disconnect between prior and subsequent states of God's being.

In defense of the fourth and final antithesis (that a necessary being does not constitute the cause of the universe's existence), Kant proposed a trilemma: this being must consist in a component of the world, the world in its entirety, or some entity outside the world. In the first case, he maintained, the universe would have an uncaused beginning, which would violate the law of cause and effect. The second option, that the entire universe exists necessarily, is unthinkable, Kant argued, because what is composed exclusively of nonnecessary beings cannot itself constitute a necessary being. The third option, in which the necessary being transcends the world, is likewise unthinkable, he reasoned, because in order to initiate the chain of causes in which the universe consists, the being would have to act at some particular time; if he acts in time, however, he does not transcend the world.[13] Kant seemed not to consider the Christian view in which God's action in creating, governing, and consummating the world consists entirely in the one, eternal act of decreeing that all events occur in their appointed times.

Kant failed to substantiate at least one of each of his four pairs of opposing statements. His charge that human beings cannot reason about suprasensible beings without falling into self-contradiction, therefore, is false.

C. Conclusion

Neither Hume nor Kant, therefore, supplied good reason to believe that some limitation of human nature precludes the possibility that human beings might know of

---

[10] Ibid., B455, p. 397.
[11] Ibid., B465, pp. 403–4.
[12] Ibid., B473–744, p. 410.
[13] Ibid., B481–83, pp. 415–16.

God. The origin of human knowledge in sense perception, in contrast to Hume, does not prevent human beings from knowing of God because it does not prevent them from grasping the principle of causality. And this principle, as seen, dictates that contingent beings must originate in an uncaused cause. Kant's contention that the intellect encounters antinomies when it reasons about suprasensible matters, moreover, does not invalidate this conclusion. For as noted, his antinomies are not antinomies at all.

III.   ARE STATEMENTS ABOUT GOD UNINTELLIGBLE?

Neither the transcendence of God's nature nor the limitations of human nature, therefore, poses an insurmountable obstacle to human attempts to know God. A third potential objection to the possibility of knowing and speaking intelligibly about God, however, demands consideration. Verificationism (also known as logical positivism or logical empiricism) was a school of philosophy that flourished around 1930–50. In this view statements about matters of fact that are not empirically verifiable are meaningless.[14] Although this school of philosophers is now moribund, historical considerations render it important briefly to review and refute the verificationist objection to the possibility of meaningful knowledge about God.

A.   The Unverifiability of the Verifiability Criterion of Meaning

The most common criticism of verificationism has always been that its central claim is not empirically verifiable and is therefore by its own standard meaningless. This criticism is quite unfair. For the verificationists intended their criterion of meaning to apply only to statements of fact and regarded the verifiability principle as a definition or a logical rule. While verificationism labors under severe difficulties and enjoys no or almost no advocates among present-day philosophers, it is not patently self-refuting.

B.   The Problem of Universal and Near-Universal Claims

A more serious criticism of verificationism is that it appears to imply that all universal and many near-universal claims are meaningless. The statement, "No human being has ever contracted AIDS from contaminated drinking water," for example, seems meaningful and yet resists verification. Admittedly one can falsify the statement by producing a single case in which someone has contracted AIDS through drinking contaminated water. Also, one can confirm the statement by examining groups of AIDS patients and finding that none of them contracted the disease as a result of contaminated water supplies. One cannot, however, conclusively verify the claim in question for it seems that one could not conceivably eliminate all possibility that someone, somewhere had acquired the disease in this manner.

Certain verificationists, admittedly, modified the verifiability principle in such a way as to allow for the meaningfulness of statements like the one in question. Specifi-

---

14 See, e.g., A. J. Ayer, *Language, Truth, and Logic,* 2nd ed. (London: Gollancz, 1946), 5.

cally Rudolf Carnap and others proposed that claims that admit of no conceivable veri-fication might nonetheless be meaningful if they can be confirmed (i.e., if one can find data consistent with the claim that would tend to corroborate it).[15] By thus weakening the verifiability principle, however, these verificationists rendered it powerless to con-demn language about God. For one could plausibly identify numerous events (e.g., answers to prayer, religious experiences, or remarkable providences) as confirmations, although not verifications, of claims about God. Therefore strict verificationism dis-qualifies as meaningless such obviously meaningful statements as "No human being has ever contracted AIDS from drinking water." A form of verificationism sufficiently liberalized to allow for the meaningfulness of these statements also allows for mean-ingful language about God.

C. Fitch's Theorem

Another criticism of verificationism derives from Frederic B. Fitch's "Theorem 5": "If there is some true proposition which nobody knows (or has known or will know) to be true, then there is a true proposition which nobody can know to be true."[16] This theorem seems obviously true; for if someone is utterly ignorant of a proposition, he is also necessarily ignorant of his ignorance of this specific proposition. Fitch's Theorem 5, however, has a startling implication. All truths can be knowable only if all truths are actually known at least by someone at some time. From a Christian per-spective Fitch's theorem appears innocuous. For the existence of an omniscient God guarantees that all truths are both knowable and known regardless of the limitations of creatures.

The conventional verificationists' principles dictate, however, that (a) all authentic truths (i.e., all meaningful true statements) are verifiable and thus knowable; and yet (b) one cannot meaningfully affirm that God or any other suprahuman being exists. The verificationist thus finds himself in the unenviable position of having to maintain both that all truths are knowable and that many truths are unknown: a position Fitch's theorem shows to be untenable. Fitch's Theorem 5 therefore appears to constitute a definitive refutation of unreconstructed verificationism.

D. Eschatological Verification

John Hick has proposed that human beings can verify the accuracy of religious statements in the next life. Through such "eschatological verification," he reasons, religious claims might prove capable of satisfying the verifiability criterion of mean-ing.[17] Since one can regard "eschatological verification" as empirical only by an abuse of language, however, Hick's proposal has persuaded few that verificationism and a robust Christian faith are compatible.

---

[15] R. Carnap, "Truth and Confirmation," in *Readings in Philosophical Analysis,* ed. H. Feigl and W. Sellars (New York: Appleton-Century-Crofts, 1949), 119–27.

[16] The theorem appears in F. B. Fitch, "A Logical Analysis of Some Value Concepts," *Journal of Symbolic Logic* 28 (1963): 139.

[17] J. Hick, "Theology and Verification," *The Existence of God* (New York: Macmillan, 1964), 253–74.

E. Conclusion

As mentioned, verificationism has been an object of ridicule for decades among philosophers and enjoys no or almost no contemporary adherents. It has not fallen into obscurity because it refutes itself, for it does not. Rather, people distrust verificationism because it entails absurd consequences (e.g., that universal claims are meaningless and that all truths are knowable but not known).

IV. CONCLUSION

The claim that one can speak meaningfully and truthfully about God, a key presupposition of all theistic religions in all ages, thus emerges largely unscathed from the criticisms investigated here. Neither the putative unintelligibility of language about God nor the real incapacities of human beings nor even the more significant transcendence of the Almighty precludes the possibility of humans knowing God and expressing that knowledge in words.

Part Two

APOLOGETICS IN SCRIPTURE AND IN HISTORY

This section details the history of apologetics from the Old Testament all the way to contemporary apologetical methods. This section shows how biblical apologists, the church fathers, medieval theologians, the Reformers, Enlightenment apologists, and contemporary leaders have defended the faith. The discussion includes illustrations of how modern apologists can learn from and implement their methods.

Chapter 9

APOLOGETICS IN THE OLD TESTAMENT

CONTEMPORARY APOLOGISTS ARE NOT THE INVENTORS of apologetics. From the first chapter of the Bible the writers of Scripture presented truths of theism, including the nature of God, His view of history, and His work of redemption. The God of the Bible is inscrutable in His nature, but He has chosen to make Himself known through the universe that He has created and through His many acts in history. That God has designed the universe is evident through His handiwork observed in nature, often called general revelation; while He more clearly revealed Himself through the words of the prophets and apostles, discovered in their writings, the sacred Scriptures (called special revelation), and more fully in the coming of the living Word of God (the Logos), to teach, to heal, and to die for the sins of humanity.

The fact that God has so dynamically and clearly made Himself known is further evidence of His abiding love for His creatures, and His intent to save from among humanity those who place their trust in Him not only as Creator but also as Savior. This is unlike any religion in the world. Most religions are based on the philosophies of humans who allegedly had some special insight into the human condition and suggested various means to alleviate some of the difficulties of life. But none of these leaders could offer forgiveness of sins, peace with God, or hope of eternal life.[1]

This chapter focuses on the fact that Yahweh, the God of Israel, elected a people, revealed Himself to them, and then redeemed them for Himself as a special possession. To do this He was constantly involved in apologetic words and acts, either directly or through the authors of the biblical text or in the words and acts of the prophets whom He sent to Israel. The defining point, however, of God's acts on behalf of His people Israel was to deliver them from Egyptian bondage with His strong hand (Deut 4:34; 5:15; 7:8,19; 11:2; 26:8; Ps 89:10).

---

[1] See H. W. House, *Charts of World Religions* (Grand Rapids: Zondervan, 2006).

I. YAHWEH, THE REDEEMER AND CREATOR

A. The Being and Acts of God as the Foundation for Biblical Faith

1. The God who elects, reveals, and redeems

a. God's intent to elect a people for His name's sake

The Old Testament clearly demonstrates that the nation did not seek to serve God, but was instead elected by His sovereign grace.[2] In fact Yahweh indicated that His choosing of Israel was not founded in their greatness (Deut 9:1) or their righteousness (9:6). Instead His choice related to the promise He had made to the patriarchs (4:37; 7:8), revealing that He is a faithful God.[3] He had come to Abraham in Ur, calling him to go to a land unseen by him, a land and people through whom He would eventually bless the world (Gen 12:1–3; Gal 3:16). From the root Abraham grew a mighty tree that eventually enveloped the entire earth, branching through Isaac, Jacob, Israel, the prophets, and finally Christ. Thus the revelation of God occurred in history, in His historical acts of election and redemption; more than just Creator, He works within the creation.[4]

b. God desired to redeem a people to demonstrate His glory

God, however, not only wanted people to know who and what He is but also He came to save.[5] The defining moment in the history of Israel was the Exodus from Egypt. Matthew used the rabbinic interpretive method of *remez*[6] to describe the exodus

---

[2] B. Ramm, "Apologetics, Biblical," in *International Standard Bible Encyclopedia*, rev. and ed. G. W. Bromiley (Grand Rapids: Eerdmans, 2002): 1:189.

[3] "The Angel of the LORD went up from Gilgal to Bochim and said, 'I brought you out of Egypt and led you into the land I had promised to your fathers. I also said: I will never break My covenant with you'" (Judg 2:1).

[4] Though I do not fully subscribe to his statement, Ramm points out the importance of this dynamic relationship of Yahweh and His people Israel based on personal encounter rather than philosophical discernment. "(1) Israel did not first understand Yahweh as Creator and then as a consequence come to know Him as Elector, Revealer, and Redeemer; rather it was the other way around (cf. Vriezen, p. 187); (2) Israel's faith was not philosophically grounded in the sense of being a product of a rational interpretation of nature, religion, or experience" (Ramm, "Apologetics, Biblical," 1:189).

[5] A. J. Droge, "Apologetics, NT" in *Anchor Bible Dictionary*, ed. D. N. Freedman (New York: Doubleday, 1996): 302.

[6] Fructenbaum explains this interpretive method of literal fulfillment plus a type: "The second rabbinic category was *remez* which means 'hint' or 'clue' or 'suggestion.' Cooper dubbed this category as *literal plus typical* and the example is Matthew 2:15 which quotes Hosea 11:1. In the original context of the Hosea passage, it is not even a prophecy but refers to an historical event, that of the Exodus. The background to the Hosea passage is Exodus 4:22–23 which refers to Israel as the national son of God. Thus, according to Hosea, when God brought Israel out of Egypt, He divinely called His son out of Egypt. The *literal* meaning of the Hosea passage refers to the Exodus under Moses. There is nothing in the New Testament that can change or reinterpret the meaning of the Hosea passage nor does the New Testament deny that a literal exodus of Israel out of Egypt actually occurred. However, the Old Testament *literal* event becomes a *type* of a New Testament event. In the New Testament, an individual *Son of God*, the Messiah, is also divinely called out of Egypt. The passage is not quoted as a fulfillment of prophecy since it was not a prophecy to begin with, but quoted as a *type*. Matthew does not deny, change, or reinterpret the original

of God's Son, Jesus, from Egypt (Matt 2:15). When God appeared to Moses on Mount Horeb to reveal Himself, the focus of the text is His concern for the sufferings of His people Israel.[7] This gave rise to the revelation of His name, *Ehyeh*, "I am," and the response *Yahweh*, "He is."[8] He is the faithful God who had seen their sufferings and who was with His people. He had now come down to deliver them and bring them out:

> Then the LORD said, "I have observed the misery of My people in Egypt, and have heard them crying out because of their oppressors, and I know about their sufferings. I have come down to rescue them from the power of the Egyptians and to bring them from that land to a good and spacious land, a land flowing with milk and honey—the territory of the Canaanites, Hittites, Amorites, Perizzites, Hivites, and Jebusites." (Exod 3:7–8)

> Go and assemble the elders of Israel and say to them: Yahweh, the God of your fathers, the God of Abraham, Isaac, and Jacob, has appeared to me and said: I have paid close attention to you and to what has been done to you in Egypt. And I have promised you that I will bring you up from the misery of Egypt to the land of the Canaanites, Hittites, Amorites, Perizzites, Hivites, and Jebusites—a land flowing with milk and honey. (Exod 3:16–17)

This redemption of the people of Israel became the basis of the Passover and the equivalent to the cross in Old Testament theology, the event in which God saved His people.

> "Remember that you were a slave in the land of Egypt and the LORD your God redeemed you; this is why I am giving you this command today." (Deut 15:15)

> "Observe the month of Abib and celebrate the Passover to the LORD your God, because the LORD your God brought you out of Egypt by night in the month of Abib." (Deut 16:1)

> "Remember that you were a slave in Egypt, and the LORD your God redeemed you from there. Therefore I am commanding you to do this." (Deut 24:18)

> "Remember that you were a slave in the land of Egypt. Therefore I am commanding you to do this." (Deut 24:22)

---

meaning. He understands it literally, but the literal Old Testament event becomes a type of a New Testament event. In rabbinic parlance, it is a *remez* or a hint of another meaning in addition to the literal, in this case a *typology*." A. G. Fruchtenbaum, "Rabbinic Quotations of the Old Testament and How It Relates to Joel 2 and Acts 2" (italics his), http://www.pre-trib.org/articles/view/rabbinic-quotations-of-old-testament-and-how-it-relates-to-joel-2-acts (accessed December 8, 2009).

[7] "After a long time, the king of Egypt died. The Israelites groaned because of the difficult labor, and they cried out; and their cry for help ascended to God because of the difficult labor" (Exod 2:23).

[8] The Hebrew word *ehyeh* is a self-proclamation that God Himself made. The believer then responds in agreement that He is (*Yahweh*).

The end of all theology and human effort is to bring glory to God, and this in fact is the goal of all God's actions (Eph 1:6,12,14), including the deliverance of the Israelites from the hand of Pharaoh (Exod 9:16; Rom 9:17).

In contrast to all false gods of this world, ancient and modern, the God of the Bible desires to save and can truly deliver His people, both in struggles in this life and for all eternity.

2. The God of Israel is a living God in contrast with the gods of the nations

The Old Testament was written during a time when all the nations of the Mediterranean world had many gods. The purported deities were in the cycle of nature, and their worshippers sought to alter their lives by appealing to the various deities that were thought to have control over the rain, sky, life, and death. One sees the lifelessness and powerlessness of these gods in their inability to save or to reveal themselves to their followers. The true prophets of the God of Israel mocked these deities and rebuked their devotees. In the eighth century before Christ, the prophet Isaiah said, "All who make idols are nothing, and what they treasure does not profit. Their witnesses do not see or know anything, so they will be put to shame. Who makes a god or casts a metal image for no profit?" (Isa 44:9–10). Isaiah continued to mock the one who trusts in lifeless and powerless idols:

> It serves as fuel for man. He takes some of it and warms himself; also he kindles a fire and bakes bread; he even makes it into a god and worships it; he makes it an idol and bows down to it. He burns half of it in a fire, and he roasts meat on that half. He eats the roast and is satisfied. He warms himself and says, "Ah! I am warm, I see the blaze." He makes a god or his idol with the rest of it. He bows down to it and worships; he prays to it, "Save me, for you are my god." (44:15–17)

The God of Israel is unique, and incomparable.[9] In contrast to these deities, He is a living God. The phrase "the living God" is used 15 times in the Old Testament[10] and 13 times in the New Testament[11] and is an especially important one in contrast to the dead and breathless gods of the nations in the Mediterranean world and the ancient Near East. Ramm says that the Old Testament "speaks much more of the living God than of the true God. A living God does something; He possesses power; He is spirit; He can answer by fire (1 Kgs 18:24). The pagan gods are essentially lifeless, breathless,

---

[9] Yahweh asks for anyone to compare Him to another, emphasizing in the context that it cannot be done. "Who will you compare God with? What likeness will you compare Him to?" (Isa 40:18); "Who will you compare Me or make Me equal to?" (46:5). See C. J. Labuschagne, *The Incomparability of Yahweh in the Old Testament* (Leiden: Brill, 1966).

[10] Deut 5:26; Josh 3:10; 1 Sam 17:26 (2),36; 2 Kgs 19:4,16; Pss 42:2; 84:2; Isa 37:4,17; Jer 10:10; 23:36; Dan 6:20,26; Hos 1:10.

[11] Matt 16:16; 26:63; Acts 14:15; Rom 9:26; 2 Cor 3:3; 6:16; 1 Tim 3:15; 4:10; Heb 3:12; 9:14; 10:31; 12:22; Rev 7:2.

and powerless."[12] They can neither act on behalf of their people nor show themselves to be gods.

The fact that the gods of the nations were deities (Isa 41:24) existing only in the minds and physical representations of the people may be seen in the contest on Mount Carmel between Elijah and the prophets of Ba'al and Asherah (1 Kings 18). This is also seen in the foolishness of the people in Jeremiah's day who bowed down to blocks of wood. "They are both stupid and foolish, instructed by worthless idols made of wood!" (Jer 10:8). Later in the New Testament Paul denied that idols were true beings, when he wrote, "We know that 'an idol is nothing in the world,' and that 'there is no God but one'" (1 Cor 8:4).

The way the prophets presented Yahweh as alive over against the false deities of the nations may be seen in three ways. First, He is the Lord of history. Second, He communicates with His people to reveal Himself. Third, He reveals Himself not only as the Creator of Israel but also as the God of the universe.

a. The Lord of history

As the Lord of history, He is unsurprised by what occurs because He is in control of history (Dan 4:25). In Isa 41:1–10 Yahweh stated His majesty over the earth and over nations, calling Israel to trust in Him. He then challenged His hearers with the fact that idols cannot predict the future (vv. 22–23) and then He concluded about the idols, "Look, all of them are a delusion; their works are nonexistent; their images are wind and emptiness" (v. 29). As the Lord of history, He acts on behalf of His people and determines the destiny of men and nations.

b. The communicating God

Also false deities could not communicate with their worshippers. This lack of revelation is emphasized by Habakkuk: "What use is a carved idol after its craftsman carves it? It is only a cast image, a teacher of lies. For the one who crafts its shape trusts in it and makes idols that cannot speak" (Hab 2:18). In contrast, the God of Israel is one who clearly reveals Himself to His chosen people in both word and deed. This was most evident in His act of coming down and delivering His people, as discussed in Exodus 3. He gave Moses a sign of His intent through a miraculous rod and the instantaneous transformation of his hand to a leprous one and then back to normal. God continued that commitment in the mighty deeds that followed His challenge to Pharaoh. This revelation is seen in at least three forms, found in the Old and New Testaments, namely, miraculous events, divine speech, and incarnational revelations of God.

Yahweh made His existence known in miracles through His prophets. Some miracles were less spectacular or obvious, like the opening of Rachel's womb (Gen 30:22) or the budding of Aaron's rod (Num 17:1–9), whereas extensive evidence of His power are seen in the plagues against Egypt (Exodus 7–11), including the Passover (Exo-

---

[12] Ramm, "Apologetics, Biblical," 1:189.

dus 12), and the opening of the Red Sea for the Israelites to escape Pharaoh's army (14:22–30).

Divine speech includes audible statements of God to human beings. He spoke to Adam and Eve in the garden (Gen 2:16) to Samuel (1 Sam 3:4), and to a number of others like Cain, Noah, Abraham, and Moses. To others He spoke through dreams, such as Joseph and Daniel in the Old Testament, and to Joseph in the New Testament. Also He communicated to prophets and apostles through visions, such as Ezekiel, Zechariah, Paul, and John, the writer of Revelation. And He communicates today through the Scriptures, the written Word of God (2 Tim 3:16; 2 Pet 1:21).

God also revealed Himself in theophanies (Gen 16:7,13–14; 32:24–30). And the most complete revelation of God is that of Jesus the Christ, Son of God (John 1:14).

God's willingness to enter into intelligent and rational dialogue with His people may be seen in His word to the Israelites to reason with Him about their spiritual condition (Isa 1:18). Moreover, He revealed prophetic events as an apologetic for His unsurpassed greatness in contrast to the false deities of the nations around Israel (Isa 48:3–5).

c. The creating God

As Creator of the universe, God shows Himself to be the first apologist. He does not hide; He reveals Himself to the person who is willing to see.

The apostle Paul wrote in Rom 1:18–15 that God has revealed Himself through what He has created, and because of this all mankind is without excuse for rejecting Him.

The first verse of the Bible—"In the beginning God created the heavens and the earth" (Gen 1:1)—begins with a declaration of God's act as Creator rather than with an attempt to prove the existence of God. Yet this is a strong polemic against false religions and ideologies. The verse affirms God's existence (against atheism), that He is Creator of all that exists (against naturalistic evolutionism and dualism), that God is one (against polytheism), that God and the universe are distinguished (against pantheism or materialism), and that God is eternal (against finite godism).

II. THE PRACTICE OF APOLOGETICS THROUGH MEN OF GOD IN THE OLD TESTAMENT

A. The Polemical Nature of the Writings and Works of Moses

1. Polemic nature of the creation account (Gen 1:1–2:3)

What is often missed in a reading of the creation accounts in Genesis 1 and 2 is that they were not written to establish a theory of creation as such, though certainly deductions may be made regarding the nature of creation from the text. Instead, these chapters serve as a polemic against the pagan gods of Canaan, the land where the Israelites would soon enter. A grave danger was that the Israelites would embrace these pagan gods and abandon the true God who had delivered them from captivity in Egypt. The belief in monotheism in the ancient world was restricted to only one nation, Israel, and the pressure to conform to the surrounding nations, including the people of Canaan, would be strong.

The underlying creation myth of the ancient Near East was that the gods emerged from a precreation chaos that existed indefinitely in the past. This birth of the gods (called theogony) is in stark contrast to the God of Israel, who preexisted before the creation of the heavens and the earth. Also the material universe was not made from preexisting matter (creatio ex material) or out of the essence of God (creatio ex deo) but out of nothing (creatio ex nihilo). This totally foreign idea of creation could be found only in a faith community that was based on revelation from the God who was there when the universe began. This presentation by the eternal Yahweh (the I AM, Exod 3:14–15) is a direct challenge to the cosmology and theogony of the ancient world. As Otto Procksch states:

> This first word of the Bible expresses the basic relationship of God and universe that is present in creation. The term for creation (*bara'*) denies any relationship of God and cosmos through nature. God has not emerged from the cosmos as is suggested in the mythology of many peoples of the world, of which we need to think only of Egypt, Babylon, and Greece. Nor, as is suggested infrequently, has the world gushed forth from God through emanation, as Gnosticism maintains. Rather, God and cosmos are essentially distinct, underivable from one another, God is not the world and the world is not God; though certainly God does work in the world omnipotent, omnipresent, omniscient, available in it.[13]

Several of the terms used in Genesis 1 approximate those used in Canaanite religious literature but are distinguished from it. For example the word *tehom* ("formless") in Gen 1:2 is clearly an inanimate idea, not a powerful deity as in Canaanite thought. Moreover, the mythical sea creature of the Canaanite god Ba'al mythology, *tanninim* (1:21), as Gerhard Hasel notes,[14] is powerless inanimate creation in Yahweh's hands, in contrast to the struggle of the gods in Canaanite thought.[15]

---

[13] O. Procksch, *Theologie des Alten Testaments* (Gütersloh Bertelsmann, 1949), 454–58 (authors' translation).

[14] See G. Hasel, "The Polemic Nature of the Genesis Cosmology," *Evangelical Quarterly* (April–June 1974): 87. Hasel's article gives a number of instances in which the biblical account is poised against the mythological accounts of the ancient Near East.

[15] What enemy rises up against Baal,
What adversary against Him who mounteth the clouds?
Have I not slain Sea (yam), beloved of El?
Have I not annihilated River (Nahar), the great god?
Have I not muzzled the Dragon (Tannin), holding her in a muzzle?
I have slain the Crooked Serpent (Lotan-Leviathan),
The foul-fanged with Seven Heads.
(J. Gray, "Texts from Ras Shamra," in *Documents from Old Testament Times*, ed. D. W. Thomas [New York: Thomas Nelson, 1958], 129–30).

2. Miraculous rod confirms Moses and Aaron's credentials (Exod 4:3–4,30; 7:8–13)

Moses challenged the gods of Egypt when he threw down his rod at the feet of the Pharaoh (Exod 7:9–10). The magicians of Pharaoh were able to repeat this miracle,[16] but the rod from Moses and Aaron swallowed up their snakes, thereby demonstrating God's superiority over the Egyptian gods. This rod, symbolizing authority, was used in several signs against Egypt, which had enslaved God's people (7:15–20; 8:5–17; 9:23; 14:16).

3. God's acts against Egypt

Why did God choose to use Moses' rod to challenge Pharaoh (Exod 4:3–4,30; 7:8–13)? In Moses' first use it was directed against the snake, a favorite deity in Egypt. Each of the subsequent plagues against Egypt (7:17–12:30) was addressed to specific gods, demonstrating that these false gods were no match for the true God who made heaven and earth and controls the forces of nature, and even life itself.[17] The subsequent miracles, such as the pillar of fire and the dividing of the sea, revealed the power of God against all attempts of the supposed god Pharaoh to destroy God's people.[18]

Why suggest that these acts against Egypt are an apologetic by God? Pharaoh indicated in his first encounter with Moses that he was ignorant of Yahweh, the God of Israel (5:2). After the plagues he could make no such claim. Through these wonders the Egyptians would recognize Yahweh (7:5,17; 10:2). Moreover, He would bring honor and glory to Himself through this ordeal (14:18; Rom 9:17). Also this test between Yahweh and the gods of Egypt was an apologetic for the Israelites. Yahweh said He would deliver the people with a strong hand, so it was clear that it was He who had delivered them (Exod 6:1,6–7; 9:14; 14:31).

B. The Contest of Elijah with the Prophets of Ba'al and Asherah on Mount Carmel

Elijah gave evidence to Ahab and the prophets of Ba'al that Yahweh is the true God (1 Kgs 18:20–40). This is one of the most powerful passages in the Old Testament regarding God's revelation of Himself through apologetic means.

The occasion for the contest on Mount Carmel was the judgment of God on the northern kingdom of Israel for their abandonment of the covenant that God gave at Mount Sinai. In the giving of the covenant God promised to bless Israel if they were obedient but curses if they were unfaithful (Deut 11:13–17). Because Israel was

---

[16] For a suggestion on how this might have been done, see K. Butt, "Egyptian Magicians, Snakes, and Rods," Apologetics Press, http://www.apologeticspress.org/articles/698 (accessed November 5, 2007).

[17] See J. J. Davis, *Moses and the Gods of Egypt* (Grand Rapids: Baker, 1971), 79–152.

[18] B. Sparks set forth 61 Egyptian religious and literary texts that speak of various aspects of the account of the Exodus in the Bible (Sparks with D. N. Freedman in *Egyptian Exodus Parallels, Exodus and Conquest: A New Investigation*, Archaeological and Biblical Studies series, vol. 1 (San Diego: University of California at San Diego, 2007 [unpublished manuscript]).

following after other gods (1 Kgs 18:18), Yahweh had Elijah (meaning "My God Is Yahweh") declare a three and one-half year drought (1 Kgs 17:1; Jas 5:17–18).

The people of Israel had adopted the pagan god of Queen Jezebel, her name reflecting Ba'al even as Elijah's name reflected Yahweh (Eli-Yah or "My God Is Yahweh"). This god was thought to have many of the same characteristics Yahweh possesses. In Canaanite epic he is described as the rider of the clouds (cp. Yahweh in Pss 68:33; 104:3); he brings rain and harvest (cp. Yahweh in Deut 11:14; Ps 68:9; Jer 5:24); he could heal the sick and raise the dead (cp. Yahweh in 1 Kgs 17:17–24; Isa 26:19).

> Worship of Ba'al involved imitative magic, the performance of rituals, including sacred prostitution, which were understood to bring vitality to Ba'al in his struggle with Mot. It takes little imagination to see the connection between the human sexual act and rain watering the earth to produce fruit. It is interesting to note in passing that the biblical traditions use these same agrarian images of being fruitful or barren to describe vitality in human beings.[19]

Thus Ba'al was much like Yahweh in the minds of the people. But unlike Yahweh he required no moral standards as given by God in the Ten Commandments (Exod 20:1–16). Instead Ba'al appealed to the primal sexual desires of the people in worship, in that sexual rites were performed in the Canaanite temples to entice Ba'al to bring fertility to the land.

The people of Israel had not totally abandoned Yahweh for Ba'al; they simply blended the two together, similar to what they did at Sinai (Exod 32:8), and in the period of the judges (Judg 17:1–18:20). This is not dissimilar to the attitude present today in which one religion is viewed as the same as another or the notion that all religions lead to the same goal. "In God we trust," on the money of the United States does not specify in which God people are to trust. This attitude is not true of Elijah or Jezebel, for they had clear lines of demarcation.[20] This is evident in Jezebel by her support of the prophets of Ba'al while she relentlessly hunted and killed the prophets of Yahweh. Also Elijah revealed an absolutist view of religion in his challenge to the prophets of Ba'al in 1 Kgs 18:21–24.

Elijah then proceeded to set the claims and acts of Yahweh against the prophets of Ba'al and his consort Asherah. He came onto enemy territory to make his argument since Mount Carmel at that time was viewed as a mountain dedicated to the worship of Ba'al; he came as one person against more than 800 false prophets; he came in the face of the attempt of Jezebel to put him to death; he put himself at a tremendous disadvantage in the contest in which he depended on the faithfulness of God to honor His own

---

[19] D. Bratcher, "Ba'al Worship in the Old Testament," http://www.cresourcei.org/baal.html (accessed November 7, 2007).

[20] This thought stems from S. P. Lewis, in his sermon, "Let's Test Your Worldview for Consistency," Evergreen Presbyterian Church, Salem, Oregon, September 30, 2007.

word and Elijah's faithfulness (18:25–29). The one overarching goal to all this was to honor Yahweh and turn the people back to their covenant with God.

The purpose of the contest was to reveal to the people of God that the true God is Yahweh, not Ba'al, and that they should return to the covenant they made with Him at Sinai.

III. OTHER EXAMPLES OF THE PRACTICE OF APOLOGETICS IN THE OLD TESTAMENT

In other examples in the Old Testament, Yahweh revealed Himself more fully to His people and showed Himself to be the true God of the universe to those outside His covenant people. When the people of Israel approached the Jordan River to enter the promised land, He opened the river (Josh 3:14–17; 4:16–18). When Gideon sought advice as to his proper course of action, God gave double evidence of His message to this judge (Judg 6:36–40). The Philistines took the ark in battle, but God would not dwell among these pagan people in His ark. So He made the god Dagon fall repeatedly (1 Sam 5:1–4), and He brought plagues on the Philistines (5:9–12). He revealed His will by acting through nursing cows' acting against their instinct (6:7–14). He healed Hezekiah (Isa 38:21) and delivered Israel with a miraculous mighty hand (2 Kgs 19:29–37), and in Israel's captivity repeatedly He showed Himself to have no rival among foreign gods (Dan 3:23–27).

IV. CONCLUSION

In numerous places throughout the Old Testament, God was willing to prove His existence, power, and faithfulness to His covenant to those who were believers in Him and those who were not. The creation record reveals that He differed immensely from the gods of the nation to which the Israelites would settle. While in the desert He miraculously provided for the needs of the Israelites and in the land of Israel, and in their deportation He continued to show Himself the true God against all counterfeits. He accomplished this by direct acts and through His prophets.

Chapter 10

APOLOGETICS IN THE NEW TESTAMENT

I. INTRODUCTION

THE LITERATURE OF THE NEW TESTAMENT served several purposes. The Gospels were written, in part, to record the teaching of Jesus to His followers, and the Epistles were written to instruct and correct the doctrines and lives of the early Christians. However, these books also were

> written to promote and defend the Christian movement. As the early Christians attempted to appeal to the inhabitants of the Greco-Roman world at large, use was made of the strategies and methods of Hellenistic religious propaganda. The appropriation of such apologetic-propagandistic forms was essential if Christianity was to succeed in the face of competition from other religions.[1]

The apostolic writings defended the truths of Christ's preexistence, birth, incarnation, life, death, resurrection, and ascension. The earliest Christian preaching has apologetic elements (Acts 2:14–35; 22:1; 24:10; 25:8,16; 26:1,24; Phil 1:7,16; 2 Tim 4:16).

In the following centuries early Christian apologists sought to defend Christians and Christian truth from four groups: Judaism, paganism, the Roman Empire, and other competing forms of Christianity.[2]

A. The Vocabulary of Apologetics in the New Testament

The word *apologetics* does not actually occur in the New Testament,[3] but as discussed in chap. 1, the Greek word *apologia* refers to a defense of someone or something. According to Greek law an accusation (*kategoria*) was made against a person, to which he would respond with an answer or defense (*apologia*). If a person did not

---

[1] A. J. Droge, "Apologetics, New Testament," in *Anchor Bible Dictionary*, ed. D. N. Freedman (New York: Doubleday, 1992), 302–67.

[2] Ibid., 302.

[3] B. Ramm, "Apologetics, Biblical," in *International Standard Bible Encyclopedia*, rev. and ed. G. W. Bromiley (Grand Rapids: Eerdmans, 1979), 190.

have an answer, then he was said to be "without excuse" (*anapologetos*), a term Paul used in Rom 1:20 and 2:1.[4]

Bernard Ramm cites an example of this in the case of Socrates.[5] Socrates was accused (*kategoria*) of being an atheist in not accepting the gods of the city and a corrupter of the young men of Athens. Socrates made a famous defense (*apologia*), recorded by Plato in his *Apology*.[6]

Similar calls for "giving a defense" are in the writings of Peter and Paul, with the latter's speeches called "apologies" (Acts 22:1; 24:10; 25:8; 26:1,24). Paul desired to give a "defense" of the gospel (Phil 1:16), and Peter told believers always to be ready to give a defense (*apologia*) for the hope that is in them (1 Pet 3:15).[7]

B. The Classifications of Apologetics in the New Testament

1. *Apologetics is rational and evidential*

The people who heard Jesus were not asked to embrace Him apart from any proof about who He is. Luke, a protégé of Paul, indicated that his record of Jesus was not mere speculation or invented stories but was based on careful investigation. Luke described Jesus as showing Himself by many "convincing proofs."

> I wrote the first narrative, Theophilus, about all that Jesus began to do and teach until the day He was taken up, after He had given orders through the Holy Spirit to the apostles He had chosen. After He had suffered, He also presented Himself alive to them by many convincing proofs, appearing to them during 40 days and speaking about the kingdom of God. (Acts 1:1–3)

Similarly, John declared this about Jesus' miracles: "Jesus performed many other signs in the presence of His disciples that are not written in this book. But these are written so that you may believe Jesus is the Messiah, the Son of God, and by believing you may have life in His name" (John 20:30–31). On the day of Pentecost Peter said that the Lord confirmed his message. "Men of Israel, listen to these words: This Jesus the Nazarene was a man pointed out to you by God with miracles, wonders, and signs that God did among you through Him, just as you yourselves know" (Acts 2:22). As noted below, Jesus also gave a number of proofs for the truthfulness of His teachings and the nature of His person.

2. *Apologetics is revelational*

Though apologetics is concerned about rational evidence, it is also revelational in nature. Though one must use rational thought to understand revelation, one cannot come to knowledge of God apart from God's revealing Himself to humanity. Even though the gospel came first to the Jewish people, God's general revelation is for

---

4 Ibid.

5 Ibid.

6 *See* Plato, *The Apology of Socrates*, trans. D. F. Nevill (London, Robinson & Co., 1901).

7 Ramm, "Apologetics, Biblical," 1:189–92.

all peoples. He has revealed Himself in nature, demonstrating His divine nature and power (Rom 1:19–20), His goodness (Matt 5:45; Acts 14:17), and that He is near each person as he is groping for Him (Acts 17:27). However, many people have rejected this revelation (Rom 1:20–21), have walked in error (Acts 14:16), and therefore are without excuse (Rom 1:20; 2:1).

Since no one can receive adequate knowledge of God apart from God's making it known, understandably some people are suspicious of philosophy. Wise people, with all their wisdom, are still unable to come to a proper knowledge of God (1 Cor 1:20–22). Paul did not reject philosophy altogether, for he used philosophical method and arguments in his ministry. But he rejected philosophy that is contrary to Christ (Col 2:8).

3. Apologetics focuses on Christ and salvation

The two primary themes in the New Testament are Christology and soteriology. Though the Bible never seeks to prove the existence of God with philosophical proofs, at times it does present historical and theological proofs for Jesus. Bernard Ramm explains Jesus' apologetic method in these words:

> The apologetic method of Christ in these controversies was fivefold: (1) He appealed to the OT as being on His side rather than that of His opponents; (2) He argued from logic, e.g., when He demonstrated the logical absurdity in saying that He was in league with the devil in casting out demons (Mt. 12:22–25); (3) He argued from analogy in His parables and in various sayings; once, e.g., He argued that if it is right for a man to rescue a sheep on the sabbath, it ought to be more than right to heal a man on the sabbath (Mt. 12:9–12); (4) He appealed to the verifying function of signs (cf. Jn. 2:18–22; Lk. 7:18–23); (5) He placed great emphasis on the spiritual hearing of the Word of God as a self-authenticating experience (e.g., Jn. 5:24; 10:3; Mt. 11:15).[8]

II. THE APOLOGETICS OF JESUS

Jesus, as the Son of God, was the master of apologetics. He knew intuitively which methods would be most effective in proving His arguments and defending Himself. Several times after Jesus answered His opponents, they "marveled," unable to argue against Him (e.g., Matt 22:22 NKJV).

A. His Arguments against His opponents (Matt 22:15–46)

One of the best examples of Jesus' use of apologetic methods is in Matt 22:15–46. Here Jesus was engaged by several groups who opposed His teachings. He perfectly avoided being trapped by His opponents' arguments and proved that His teachings are correct.

---

[8] Ibid., 190.

1. Pharisees and Herodians

Jesus had been speaking in parables (21:28–44), and the Pharisees "perceived that He was speaking about them" (21:45 NKJV). They wanted to get rid of Him by putting Him to death, but they were afraid of the crowds (v. 46). So instead, "the Pharisees went and plotted how to trap Him by what He said" (22:15). Through the Herodians[9] they came up with something they thought would entrap Jesus. After trying to gain favor with Him by flattery (v. 16), they asked, "Is it lawful to pay taxes to Caesar or not?" (v. 17). They thought they had placed Him in a bind. If He said paying to Caesar was lawful, He would lose favor with the multitude, who resented Roman occupation with its heavy taxation and oppressive laws. If He answered in the negative, He would be branded as a rebel by the Roman authorities and most likely executed. So Jesus did not answer right away. Instead He asked for a coin used to pay the tax. When it was brought to Him, Jesus asked whose image and inscription were on the coin. They answered, "Caesar's." With this information Jesus then gave His answer: "Give back to Caesar the things that are Caesar's, and to God the things that are God's" (v. 21). Rather than engage His opponents in their game, Jesus effectively negated the entire question. This answer was so effective that it left the Pharisees and the Herodians speechless. They simply "went away" (v. 22).

2. Sadducees

That same day some Sadducees confronted Jesus. The Sadducees, liberals of their day, did not believe in the resurrection of the dead. They must have heard Jesus speaking about the resurrection because their question was designed to get Him to show that believing in the resurrection is foolish. They asked,

> Teacher, Moses said, if a man dies, having no children, his brother is to marry his wife and raise up offspring for his brother. Now there were seven brothers among us. The first got married and died. Having no offspring, he left his wife to his brother. The same happened to the second also, and the third, and so to all seven. Then last of all the woman died. In the resurrection, therefore, whose wife will she be of the seven? For they all had married her. (22:24–28)

This time Jesus pointed out the fallacy in their argument itself. He answered, "You are deceived, because you don't know the Scriptures or the power of God. For in the resurrection they neither marry nor are given in marriage but are like angels in heaven" (vv. 29–30). Jesus again negated the question, but He did so this time by pointing out their factual error. This might have been enough to end the argument, but Jesus had something else for the Sadducees. He added, "Now concerning the resurrection of the dead, haven't you read what was spoken to you by God: I am the God of Abraham and the God of Isaac and the God of Jacob? He is not the God of the dead, but of the

---

[9] The Herodians were the political party in support of King Herod. Since Herod was Rome's installed ruler, these men would have supported Rome's taxation policies. The Pharisees opposed this policy. Yet these enemies united in their opposition to Jesus.

living" (vv. 31–32). He showed why the Sadducees' question was wrong, but He also showed why the *basis* for their question (not believing in the resurrection) was wrong.

3. Lawyers

After the Pharisees and Sadducees both failed to trap Jesus, the Pharisees again went to Him. This time they used a lawyer[10] to test Him. The lawyers of Judaism had identified over 600 commandments in the Law. There had been centuries of debate over which were the really important ones, to be kept at all cost, and those that could be broken with little spiritual detriment. The lawyer asked Jesus, "Teacher, which command in the law is the greatest?" (v. 36). Jesus answered, "Love the Lord your God with all your heart, with all your soul, and with all your mind. This is the greatest and most important command. The second is like it: Love your neighbor as yourself. All the Law and the Prophets depend on these two commands" (vv. 37–40). In Mark's version of the account the lawyer agreed with Jesus, saying that to love God and one's neighbor is "more important than all the burnt offerings and sacrifices" (Mark 12:33). Jesus here showed the futility of arguing over the minor points of what commandments to keep and what to let slide. If one keeps these two commandments, he will show that he has a heart that is obedient to God.

4. Jesus questions His opponents

After the three previous encounters, Jesus took the argument to the Pharisees. They were gathered (perhaps trying to figure out what their next move would be), and Jesus asked, "What do you think about the Messiah? Whose Son is He?" (Matt 22:42). Of course these learned men knew the answer: the Son of David. Jesus then added, "How is it then that David, inspired by the Spirit, calls Him 'Lord': The Lord declared to my Lord, 'Sit at My right hand until I put Your enemies Your feet'? If David calls Him 'Lord,' how then can the Messiah be his Son?" (vv. 43–45). Verse 44 quotes Ps 110:1, which was widely held to be speaking about the Messiah. Not only were none of the Pharisees "able to answer Him at all, but also from that day no one dared question Him any more" (v. 46).

B. His Defense of Himself

Many times Jesus was attacked personally, especially after His enemies failed to discredit His teachings. Unable to discredit His words, they attempted to discredit His person.

1. His declaration of His deity

Despite the arguments of some scholars, Jesus claimed to be divine. In fact He not only claimed it; He also defended His claim against the ruling authorities from several standpoints.

---

[10] "Lawyer" here refers to one who was trained in the laws of Judaism, including the Pentateuch and nonbiblical Jewish law.

a. Jesus defended His identity as Lord (Matt 22:41–46)

As discussed earlier, Jesus silenced His critics by asking them a question they were either unable or unwilling to answer. This followed failed attempts to trap Him with trick questions. There is more to this argument, however, than His putting a stop to His enemies. He is also defending His deity here. Jesus had been called "the Son of David" many times during His ministry.[11] The people saw Jesus as the Son of David, and surely the Pharisees would have known this. They acknowledged that the Messiah would be the son of David.[12] Jesus then quoted Ps 110:1, where David called the Messiah his Lord. The language here is important. In Hebrew, David said, "Yahweh said to my Adonai." This refers to a conversation David heard between the Lord God and the one whom David called his "Lord." The context shows that David was clearly speaking about the Messiah. So David's Lord is the promised Messiah. But as Jesus asked, "If David then calls Him 'Lord,' how is He his Son?" (NKJV) Further the Messiah will sit at the right hand of God. When Jesus claimed this seat for Himself later,[13] the Jewish rulers used Jesus' words against Him to try to convict Him of blasphemy. How were the Pharisees to reconcile these two teachings? The only answer is that the Messiah would be divine and human, David's son and David's Lord. Not willing to admit this, the Pharisees could not answer, and they never attempted to question Him again.

b. Jesus defended His ability to forgive sins (Mark 2:10–11)

One of the most powerful evidences of Jesus' claim to deity is His forgiving of sins. God alone has this ability. When Jesus encountered a paralyzed man, He forgave his sins. The scribes watching Jesus rightly said, "Who can forgive sins but God alone?" (Mark 2:6). If Jesus can prove His ability to forgive sin, He proves He is divine. Jesus said to the scribes, "'Why are you thinking these things in your hearts? Which is easier: to say to the paralytic, "Your sins are forgiven," or to say, "Get up, pick up your mat, and walk"? But so you may know that the Son of Man has authority on earth to forgive sins,' He told the paralytic, 'I tell you: get up, pick up your stretcher, and go home'" (2:8–11). Immediately the once-crippled man got up and walked. It is easy to say, "Your sins are forgiven" (v. 5). But it is another matter entirely to enable a paralyzed man to walk. By performing this miracle, Jesus showed that He is divine.

c. Jesus defended His resurrection from the dead (Luke 24:39–40)

Sometimes Jesus even had to defend Himself from His own disciples. After His crucifixion and resurrection, Jesus appeared to His disciples. At first they were terrified and thought they were seeing a ghost. As proof that He was not a ghost Jesus "showed them His hands and feet." He told them that a ghost would not have bones and flesh as He did. Even this did not convince the disciples. So Jesus went a step further. He asked

---

[11] Examples include Matt 9:27; 15:22; 20:30; and 21:15.

[12] Many of the prophecies about the coming of the Messiah state that He would be in the kingly line as a descendant of David. Examples of these prophesies include Isa 3:5, 11:1; Jer 23:5; and Ezek 34:23.

[13] Matt 26:57–67; Luke 22:66–71.

135

for some food and He ate it (broiled fish). Apparently this was enough to convince them that He was in fact really resurrected in bodily form.

d. Jesus defended His equality (deity) with the Father (John 5:17–47)

John 5:17–39 gives an amazing look at how Jesus defended His equality with the Father and thereby His own deity. Jesus first claimed, "My Father is still working, and I am working also" (v. 17). The Jews immediately knew He was claiming deity; His claim to be equal to God meant He was claiming deity for Himself. Hearing this, the Jewish leaders wanted even more to kill Jesus. In His defense Jesus continued, "I assure you: The Son is not able to do anything on His own, but only what He sees the Father doing. For whatever the Father does, the Son also does these things in the same way" (v. 19). Jesus then claimed that the Father has given Him the authority to exercise judgment (v. 22) and to offer eternal life (vv. 24–26). Next He stated again that He can do nothing apart from God the Father and that He, the Son, does everything according to the will of the Father (v. 30). Knowing that they would question His testimony, He appealed to the testimony of John the Baptist, whom the people regarded as a prophet.[14] He said that "John was a burning and shining lamp" of testimony to Him, and that even the Jewish leaders "for a time . . . were willing to enjoy his light" (v. 35).

Yet Jesus said He had an even more powerful witness than John, namely, His works. There is no way Jesus could have performed His many miracles on His own. In fact the Pharisees, rather than trying to discredit the miracles, tried to discredit the source (Matt 12:24).[15] Jesus had healed the lame and the sick, and He would eventually even raise someone from the dead, Lazarus (John 11:1–44). The Jews could not argue against these facts. Jesus then said that the Father Himself testified about Him (John 5:31–32). This is seen at Jesus' baptism when God the Father said of Jesus, "This is My beloved Son. I take delight in Him!" (Matt 3:17). Jesus also stated that the Scriptures testify of Him (John 5:39), and even Moses testified about Him (v. 46), a reference to Moses' prophesy in Deut 18:18–19. "I will raise up for them a prophet like you from among their brothers. I will put My words in his mouth, and he will tell them everything I command him. I will hold accountable whoever does not listen to My words that he speaks in My name." Jesus said He came in His Father's name, and yet the Jewish leaders did not accept it (John 5:43).

In summary Jesus presented evidence from four sources: John the Baptist, Jesus' works, God the Father, and the Scriptures. Thus overwhelming evidence shows that He is in fact equal to the Father, as He said, and therefore He possesses full deity as God the Son.

---

[14] Matt 21:26; Mark 11:32.

[15] The Pharisees accused Jesus of casting out demons by the power of "Beelzebul, the ruler of the demons" (Matt 12:24). Jesus answered with the well-known phrase, "No city or house divided against itself will stand" (v. 25). Satan would not fight against himself (v. 26), so if Jesus was doing things harmful to Satan, He was not acting through the power of Satan.

2.   His declaration of His messiahship (John 11:25–27,41–45)

Jesus defended His mission as Messiah in a most extraordinary way. Lazarus, whom Jesus loved, fell sick and died. Jesus waited two days before journeying to Lazarus's hometown. He was greeted by Martha, Lazarus's sister, who was distressed that Jesus had not been there when Lazarus died, thinking Jesus might have healed him. However, Jesus had another plan. He told Martha, "I am the resurrection and the life. The one who believes in Me, even if he dies, will live. Everyone who lives and believes in Me will never die—ever. Do you believe this?" (John 11:25–26). She answered, "Yes, Lord . . . I believe You are the Messiah, the Son of God, who was to come into the world" (v. 27). After Lazarus had been dead for four days and others went to Lazarus's tomb, Jesus prayed, "Father, I thank You that You heard Me. I know that You always hear Me, but because of the crowd standing here I said this, so they may believe You sent Me" (vv. 41–42). Jesus then shouted, "Lazarus, come out!" (v. 43). Lazarus was immediately resurrected, and the people were amazed, and many believed (vv. 44–45). Jesus had proven He was sent by God by raising someone from the dead.

III.   THE APOLOGETICS OF GOD THE FATHER AND GOD THE HOLY SPIRIT

Since apologetics means providing convincing evidence, then the Father and the Holy Spirit may be understood as apologists. In creation God the Father reveals His existence and Being (Ps 19:1; Rom 1:19–20). Also God the Father and God the Holy Spirit gave evidence in Jesus' ministry that He is indeed the Messiah. This evidence occurred at Jesus' baptism (Matt 3:13–17), in His miracles, and by God raising Jesus from the dead (Acts 2:22,32).

A.   The Apologetics of God the Father

In two instances in the New Testament, the Father spoke audibly on behalf of Jesus. In these the Father gave His approval of Jesus and gave irrefutable evidence, namely, His baptism and transfiguration, that Jesus has the same authority as that of the Father.

1.   The baptism of Jesus

The first public approval from God the Father is given at Jesus' baptism: "This is My beloved Son. I take delight in Him!" (Matt 3:17). This declaration was important in the ministry of Jesus. John the Baptist had said that Jesus must "increase," but that he (John the Baptist) must "decrease" (John 3:30). John's baptism of Jesus introduced Jesus' public ministry. From then on, Jesus was the focus. The Father gave His approval to this transition. Many people had come to hear John and be baptized, and they heard this voice from heaven. Thus they knew that Jesus' authority was greater than that of John's, and that John's ministry was coming to a close. John had faithfully executed the mission God had given him, and now the Father's public declaration effectually endorsed Jesus, showing that Jesus has the Father's authority.

2. The transfiguration of Jesus

When Jesus took Peter, James, and John to a high mountain, probably Mount Hermon, Jesus' clothes appeared "white as the light" (Matt 17:2) The Father spoke again, saying, "This is My beloved Son. I take delight in Him. Listen to Him!" (v. 5). Again the Father gave His approval of Jesus, saying the same thing He had said at Jesus' baptism, but He added a command that they should listen to Jesus.

B. The Apologetics of God the Holy Spirit (John 16:7–11)

The Holy Spirit is also an apologist. He empowered Jesus to perform the Lord's evidential miracles (Matt 12:28; Luke 4:18). The Holy Spirit also convicts the world of sin, righteousness, and judgment (John 16:8). The apologetic activity of the Spirit in the church is also seen in Acts 15:28 and 1 Cor 14:24.

He convicts unbelievers "about sin, because they do not believe in Me; about righteousness, because I am going to the Father and you will no longer see Me; and about judgment, because the ruler of this world has been judged" (John 16:9). The convictions the Holy Spirit will bring are brought because of man's sin.

IV. THE APOLOGETICS OF THE APOSTLES

Besides Paul, other apostles used apologetics in defending both their actions and their teachings.

A. Peter

In Acts 2:6 Peter and other leaders were preaching in Jerusalem and "each one heard them speaking in his own language." Some were amazed at this (v. 12), while others began to mock them, accusing them of being drunk (v. 13). Peter defended their actions, saying, "Men of Judah and all you residents of Jerusalem, let me explain this to you and pay attention to my words. For these people are not drunk, as you suppose, since it's only nine in the morning" (vv. 14–15). Peter seems to be using a little humor to engage his critics. Since it was only nine in the morning, it was too early for the speakers to have gotten up and started drinking. After "warming up the crowd" as it were, Peter gave a serious defense of the group's actions from Scripture. He quoted the prophet Joel (2:28–30) to show that in the last days many signs will accompany the coming of the Messiah. In verses 25–28 Peter cited David's words promising life to those who believe (Ps 16:8–11). Finally Peter affirmed that Jesus, whom they crucified, was made "both Lord and Messiah!" (Acts 2:36), and that they needed to repent and believe (v. 38). This powerful sermon was a wonderful example of using Scripture to defend Christianity.

Later, in Peter's first letter he told all Christians to defend the faith (1 Pet 3:15–16).

B. Peter and John

When preaching in Jerusalem after Pentecost, Peter and John were confronted by the Sanhedrin, the Jewish ruling council. Peter and John had healed a man, crowds were coming in droves to hear them, and many were believing in Jesus. This disturbed the Sanhedrin, so they came up with a plan to silence John and Peter. They arrested them and brought them before the council, asking about the healing, "By what power or in what name have you done this?" (Acts 4:7). Peter and John saw a golden opportunity the council had unwittingly opened for them. They told the council they had healed the man "by the name of Jesus Christ the Nazarene—whom you crucified and whom God raised from the dead" (v. 10). Since the healed man was there in the crowd, the council could not argue against the apostles' point. So the Sanhedrin ordered the apostles to stop preaching about Jesus. Peter and John responded, "Whether it's right in the sight of God for us to listen to you rather than to God, you decide; for we are unable to stop speaking about what we have seen and heard" (vv. 19–20). The council knew these men had been with Jesus and that the crowd had seen them heal a man by Jesus' name, so the Jewish leaders were powerless to do anything about it. In the end they are forced to let Peter and John go.

C. Paul

Paul was a master at using the apologetic logic and Greek philosophy in confronting Gentiles, and in arguing from the Scriptures when addressing Jewish authorities.[16]

1. The Greeks (Acts 14:8–18; 17:16–34)

When Paul and Barnabas were in Lystra, a cripple "heard Paul speaking." Seeing that the man "had faith to be healed," Paul shouted to him, "Stand up right on your feet!" (Acts 14:5–10). The people of Lystra thought that the "gods" had come down to them and so they tried to offer sacrifices to Paul and Barnabas. But Paul and Barnabas "tore their robes . . . and rushed into the crowd, shouting: 'Men! Why are you doing these things? We are men also, with the same nature as you, and we are proclaiming good news to you, that you should turn from these worthless things to the living God, who made the heaven, the earth, the sea, and everything in them" (vv. 14–15).

The people had misunderstood the miracle, so Paul had to convince them by what power he had done the miracle. The Greeks believed in a myriad of gods, many of whom were said to control some aspect of nature. They also believed that at times these gods descended to earth to be among humans. Therefore Paul told them that the real God is over all things, and He was the power behind Paul and Barnabas's miracle. Moreover, he needed to dispel the notion that he and Barnabas were gods who had come into the world. Apparently they were successful in convincing some of the Lystrians of true faith because later Paul and Barnabas returned to Lystra, "strengthening the disciples by encouraging them to continue in the faith" (v. 22).

---

[16] For a discussion of Pauline apologetic methodology, see H. W. House, "A Biblical Argument for Balanced Apologetics: How the Apostle Paul Practiced Apologetics in the Acts," in *Reasons for Faith: Making a Case for the Christian Faith*, ed. N. L. Geisler and C. V. Meister (Wheaton, IL: Crossway, 2007), 53–75.

Another example is recorded in Acts 17:16–34. Paul was in Athens, the center of religious and political thought of the Greek world. Paul began by acknowledging their religious interests (v. 22). He observed that they even have an altar to "TO AN UNKNOWN GOD." This God, he said, is the Creator of the universe and everything in it. Therefore He does not live in temples or any other works built by human hands (vv. 23–25). Furthermore we are His offspring, and we have our very being in Him. Therefore, His nature cannot be found in gold, silver, or stone (vv. 28–29). God has appointed a day in which He will judge the whole world by one Man whom He has appointed. "He has provided proof of this to everyone by raising Him [Jesus Christ] from the dead" (v. 31). Apparently most of these Greek philosophers were willing to listen until Paul started talking about the resurrection. Some of them mocked Paul, some wanted to hear more, and a few believed and followed him. Paul used the philosophers' own logical arguments to prove the God of the Bible. Interestingly the philosophers did not argue against what Paul was arguing; they simply mocked him. They could not disprove what he said to them, so they attacked him personally.

2. To the Jews in the synagogues (13:13–41; 17:1–4)

Paul preached mainly in the synagogues as he traveled. In Antioch of Pisidia, as Paul proclaimed the gospel in the synagogue, he related the life of Jesus from John the Baptist's ministry through Jesus' crucifixion and resurrection. Then he told them that through this Jesus, who was resurrected, they may obtain forgiveness of sins by believing in Him (Acts 13:38–39). Many Jews followed Paul and Barnabas, and Paul was "persuading them to continue in the grace of God" (v. 43). The next Sabbath, "almost the whole town assembled to hear the message of the Lord" (v. 44). When the Jews saw this, they were envious, and "began to oppose" Paul and Barnabas. Despite this, many of the Gentiles believed because of Paul's testimony. "All who had been appointed to eternal life believed" (v. 48). Paul and Barnabas simply presented the facts about Jesus. When the Jews as a group began to oppose them, Paul and Barnabas declared that since the Jews rejected the message and judged themselves, "unworthy of eternal life" (v. 46), they turned to the Gentiles.

In another instance Paul used reason while he was teaching in the synagogue of Thessalonica. Paul taught there on three Sabbaths, where he "reasoned with them from the Scriptures, explaining and showing that the Messiah had to suffer and rise from the dead, and saying: 'This Jesus I am proclaiming to you is the Messiah'" (17:2–3). Some Jews were persuaded to believe, and many "God-fearing Greeks," among whom were some of the "leading women" of the city, also believed.

3. Before the Jewish leaders in Jerusalem (Acts 21:26–26:32)

After Paul traveled through Asia and Greece, he journeyed back to Jerusalem. His arrival at the temple stirred up the people there, especially some Jews from Asia who had heard of his activities in the region. They seized Paul and made false accusations of him, saying, "This is the man who teaches everyone everywhere against our people, our law, and this place. What's more, he also brought Greeks into the temple and has profaned this holy place" (21:28). These were lies, but the mob began to beat Paul until the Roman commander arrived with his troops. The commander could not ascertain what Paul had done because of the ruckus the mob was making, so he took him to the barracks. Arriving there, Paul convinced the commander to let him speak to the crowd. Paul silenced them by speaking in Hebrew, their native language. He gave his defense by beginning with his personal history. He reminded them that he was trained in Jerusalem by the famous Gamaliel. He said he was "zealous for God, just as all of you are today" (22:3). Paul admitted that he even persecuted the followers of Jesus, including even being sent to Damascus to ferret out the believers there (v. 5). He told his audience about his conversion on the way to that city, when Jesus appeared to him along the road (vv. 6–20). He told them that God sent him to the Gentiles (v. 21). At that point his defense was interrupted by the crowds who were yelling and throwing dust into the air (vv. 22–23). Paul shows that apologetics can include personal testimony. His conversion story is a powerful one because Jesus personally appeared to him. Many more remarkable conversions have occurred throughout the history of the church. While one's personal experience should never be used by itself, it can be a useful tool when used in conjunction with other apologetical methods.

The next day, after it was confirmed that Paul was a Roman citizen (vv. 25–29), the Roman commander wanted to know what Paul was accused of (v. 30). He gathered the chief priests and council together, and Paul again reminded them that he had lived "before God in all good conscience until this day" (23:1). The chief priest Ananias had Paul struck on the mouth, to which Paul said, "God is going to strike you, you whitewashed wall! You are sitting there judging me according to the law, and in violation of the law are you ordering me to be struck?"(v. 3). But as soon as Paul learned Ananias was the chief priest, he apologized, citing that the people should not speak evil of the rulers over them. Then Paul took a different approach. He saw that there were both Pharisees and Sadducees at the meeting, so he exclaimed, "Brothers, I am a Pharisee, a son of Pharisees! I am being judged because of the hope of the resurrection of the dead!" (v. 6). He knew this would cause division because the Sadducees did not believe in the resurrection. His comment had the desired effect. The assembly was sharply divided. By this he won the support of the Pharisees. The council was thrown into so much turmoil that the commander had to take Paul away from them (vv. 7–10). After learning of a plot on Paul's life, the commander sent him to Felix, the governor of the region (vv. 11–35). Here Paul gave another outstanding example of apologetical methods.

After the spokesman of the council tried to flatter the governor, he accused them of creating dissension "among all the Jews throughout the Roman world" (24:5), being a ringleader of a sect, and defiling the temple (v. 6). They said they would take care of the matter, but the commander, Lysias, intervened. Paul then gave his defense against these accusations. He stated what actually happened, and he argues that he had been worshipping in the temple 12 days when they attacked him. Moreover, he was purified according to Jewish custom and had no mob of his own while there. He accurately asserted that his accusers (the Asian Jews) were not present, so the accusations against him were hearsay. Felix, finding no guilt in Paul, but not wanting a riot, put off making a decision. He kept Paul under arrest for two years. At this time Felix was succeeded by Festus as governor (v. 27), and Paul's case was reopened. Once again the Jewish leaders "brought many serious charges that they were not able to prove" (25:7). Paul answered these complaints by citing the facts. He stated that he had done nothing "against the Jewish law, nor against the temple, nor against Caesar" (v. 8). Festus could find nothing wrong with Paul either, but he wanted to please the Jews.[17] So he asked if Paul would assent to going to Jerusalem to be judged (v. 9). Paul knew that would lead to his death so he appealed instead to Caesar.

Festus then summoned King Agrippa, a descendant of Herod, who was installed by the Romans as king of northern Israel. The Romans often consulted him in matters of religion, and he had authority to appoint the high priests.[18] Paul acknowledged that Agrippa was an expert in the law, and therefore he was happy to give his defense before him (26:1–3). Again, as he had done several times in the past, Paul gave his conversion story. Paul reminded Agrippa of who he was before his conversion (vv. 9–11), which all the chief priests knew. Then he reminded the king that it is nothing out of the ordinary to expect God to raise the dead. Paul told Agrippa that everything that had happened to Christ—His suffering, rising from the dead, and becoming a light to both Jews and Gentiles—had been prophesied (vv. 22–23). Agrippa tried accusing Paul of insanity, but Paul countered that he was speaking reasonably (vv. 24–25). "For the king knows about these matters. It is to him I am actually speaking boldly. For I'm not convinced that any of these things escapes his notice, since this thing was not done in a corner King Agrippa, do you believe the prophets? I know you believe" (vv. 26–27). Agrippa answered "Are you going to persuade me to become a Christian so easily?" (v. 28). Agrippa then told Festus that had Paul not appealed to Rome, he could have been released (v. 32).

Several things can be learned from Paul's example before the Jewish leaders. He showed that defending the faith should be done in a respectful manner. The Jews accused him of stirring up trouble, but Paul was careful not to do that. He was not distracted from the facts by their attacks. He continued to present the truth, arguing from Scripture and his own conversion experience that the gospel is true. Over and over, he reminded them that he used to think as they did, persecuting the followers of Jesus. He was no newcomer teaching some foreign religion from ignorance. He was trained in the law by a respected authority. He used the Law and the Prophets (of which these men were also experts) to show why Jesus of Nazareth is the predicted Messiah. The leaders were forced to overlook the facts in order to carry on with their accusations to such an extent that Festus (a Gentile) and Agrippa (a Jew) saw through their deception.

---

[17] The Roman authorities had a notoriously difficult time keeping the peace in the Jewish provinces. Many violent revolts had occurred in the past. The Roman governors and procurators found that appeasing the Jews, although by no means entirely successful, was less likely to cause revolt than harsh rule. So they would try occasionally to appease the Jewish leaders by doing them favors.

[18] H. W. Hoehner, "Herod, Herodian Family," in *Baker Encyclopedia of the Bible*, ed. W. A. Elwell and B. J. Beitzel (Grand Rapids: Baker, 1988), 972.

Many times Christians are accused of being ignorant of issues surrounding religion. So it is important for Christians to study and be knowledgeable so they can give logical, reasoned, and informed answers in defense of the gospel.

4. Paul's defense of his apostolic calling

To defend his calling to be an apostle, Paul wrote that "signs" (miracles) confirmed the authority of his apostleship. He wrote, "The signs of an apostle were performed with great endurance among you—not only signs but also wonders and miracles" (2 Cor 12:12).

In Phil 1:15–18 Paul gave a defense of the gospel's integrity, even in the face of impure intentions. He wrote,

> To be sure, some preach Christ out of envy and strife, but others out of a good will. These do so out of love, knowing that I am appointed for the defense of the gospel; the others proclaim Christ out of rivalry, not sincerely, seeking to cause me trouble in my imprisonment. What does it matter? Just that in every way, whether out of false motives or true, Christ is proclaimed.

Paul encouraged Timothy to "reject foolish and ignorant disputes" that lead to quarrels. However, he also told him he should gently and patiently correct those who oppose sound knowledge so that God may lead them to repentance, "to the knowledge of the truth. Then they may come to their senses *and* escape the Devil's trap" (2 Tim 2:23–26). Paul also encouraged Titus to "encourage with sound teaching and to refute" those whose teachings are contradictory to the gospel, because these teaching can "overthrow whole households" (Titus 1:9,11).

V. THE APOLOGETICS OF THE OTHER CHRISTIAN LEADERS

A. Stephen (Acts 6:8–7:60)

Stephen's defense just before he was martyred by stoning is one of the most powerful examples of courage and faith in the New Testament. He gave an impassioned defense against the charge of blasphemy brought against him in Jerusalem. Starting with Abraham, he told the story of the nation of Israel and how they rebelled, even though they were delivered by God from Egypt. Stephen said that they not only killed the prophets who told of the coming One but also killed that One Himself. He ended his speech when he saw a vision and he exclaimed, "Look! I see the heavens opened and the Son of Man standing at the right hand of God!" (7:56). The priests knew it was Jesus whom Stephen was claiming to see, and they had had enough. They dragged him out of the city and stoned him. As Stephen was being put to death, he cried out on behalf of those persecuting him, "Lord, do not charge them with this sin" (v. 60).

B. Apollos (Acts 18:24–28)

Apollos was an eloquent speaker and "powerful in the use of the Scriptures" (v. 24). Apollos "had been instructed in the way of the Lord" and "spoke and taught the things about Jesus accurately" (v. 25). Although he knew John the Baptist's teachings, he was further instructed by Aquila and Priscilla. Once Apollos knew the full gospel, he joined a group of believers in Achaia, where "he greatly helped those who had believed through grace. For he vigorously refuted the Jews in public, demonstrating through the Scriptures that Jesus is the Messiah" (vv. 27–28). Here again a New Testament apologist used the Scriptures in defending Christianity. Apollos taught accurately and knew the Scriptures, the points that are of utmost importance for Christians.

C. Jude

The apostle Jude exhorted believers to "contend for the faith" (v. 3). The reason, he said, was that "some men . . . have come in by stealth; they are ungodly, turning the grace of our God into promiscuity and denying Jesus Christ, our only Master and Lord" (v. 4). He then said, "These dreamers likewise defile their flesh, reject authority, and blaspheme glorious ones" (v. 8). Believers are to be on guard against these apostates, for they are in error and "have traveled in the way of Cain, have abandoned themselves to the error of Balaam for profit, and have perished in Korah's rebellion" (v. 11). Jude warned that these will creep into Christian gatherings (v. 12), though they are not believers themselves. Because of this, believers are not to stand by idly and allow them to flatter people "for their own advantage" (v. 16). Instead they should stand up to them and point out the errors in their teaching.

VI. CONCLUSION

The New Testament is full of instances of Christian apologetics. The apostles showed how different circumstances call for different methods, following both Jewish and Greek thinking in defending the faith. Of course Jesus, being divine, is the perfect example of how to defend the claims of Christianity and answer the challenges of skeptics. Christian apologists should know the Bible so they can "give a defense" of the gospel "with gentleness and respect" (1 Pet 3:15–16).

Chapter 11

Early Apologists of the Second and Third Centuries

APOLOGETICS, AT LEAST IN THE NARROWEST sense of the term, was of little concern to the earliest writers of the post-New Testament church. While apologetic themes can be discerned in the *Letter of Pseudo-Barnabas*, they are overshadowed in this and other Christian writings of the late first and early second centuries by the practical concerns of a movement struggling to establish itself in the face of bitter persecution.

By the time Aristides (d. c. AD 134) presented his *Apology*, perhaps the earliest uninspired work of Christian apologetics, to the Emperor Hadrian in c. AD 125, conditions had changed decisively. Persecution continued and even intensified during this period. In fact, a principal objective of second- and third-century Christian apologists seems to have been persuading pagans to cease this persecution. Yet the church by this time was reasonably well organized and widespread. Christian authors therefore turned their attention largely from ensuring the survival of the Christian movement to securing for Christianity at least limited acceptance in Roman society.

As Christianity began to flourish, moreover, Christian writers found themselves contending with Gnostic opponents bent on co-opting Christianity's appeal for the benefit of essentially pagan, anti-Christian ideologies. Theological innovators threatened to alter fundamentally the church's beliefs, and so Christian writers responded to these false teachers with an antiheretical apologetic. Also, Christian writers of the second and third centuries responded to unbelieving Judaism, the source of Christianity's earliest, best organized, and most embittered opposition.

This chapter discusses how Christian apologists sought to persuade pagans, Jews, and heretics to embrace orthodox Christianity or at least to cease persecuting it. The chapter shows how apologists in the second and third centuries tailored their arguments to their audience's outlook and how contingent, historical factors shaped the apologetics of this era.

I. APOLOGETICS TO PAGANS

Christian authors such as Aristides, Justin Martyr (c. 100–c. 165), Theophilus of Antioch (d. c. 183–85), Athenagoras of Athens (d. after 177), Tertullian (c. 160–c. 220),

Clement of Alexandria (d. before 215), and Origen (c. 185–c. 254) principally attempted to persuade their pagan readers to believe these tenets:

1. Christians are innocent of the crimes with which they are commonly charged.
2. Pagans who level such charges are ignorant of Christianity's true nature.
3. Pagan morals are corrupt.
4. Christian morals are pure.
5. Christian beliefs are endorsed by numerous pagan philosophers and poets.
6. Christianity is the oldest of all the world's religions.
7. Christianity is verified by the fulfillment of scriptural prophecies.

That the last claim should occupy a prominent place in apologetics to pagans might seem odd. For unlike Jews, pagans accept neither the Old or the New Testament as authoritative. One should note, however, that appeals to prophecy function differently in defenses of Christianity directed to pagans than they do in Christian works addressed to Jewish readers. In the latter one finds Christian authors demonstrating that Christ fulfilled Old Testament prophecies and that Jews who believed the Old Testament ought therefore to embrace Christianity. In the former, however, Christian authors show that Scripture accurately predicts events of which its human authors could not have known or even conjectured without supernatural assistance. This remarkable fact, it is argued, suffices to prove that the entire Bible is of divine origin. In other words, when addressing Jews, this era's apologists argue from the authority of Old Testament Scripture to the truthfulness of Christianity. When addressing pagans, however, they argue from the fulfillment of prophecies to the authority of Scripture as a whole, and acceptance of that is tantamount to acknowledging the truthfulness of Christianity.

A. The Innocence of Christians

The pagan masses in the second and third centuries, to a great extent at least, viewed Christians as atheists and libertines. Athenagoras, whose work illustrates how Christians attempted to clear their reputation, thus attempted in his *Embassy for the Christians* to prove that Christians are neither atheists, nor perpetrators of incest, nor cannibals.[1] As to the first charge, Athenagoras avers that it is absurd to charge with atheism those who worship

> one God, uncreated, eternal, invisible, impassible, incomprehensible, illimitable, who is apprehended by the understanding only and the reason, who is encompassed by light, and beauty, and spirit, and power ineffable, by whom the universe has been created through His Logos, and set in order, and is kept in being.[2]

---

[1] Athenagoras, *Embassy for the Christians* 3, in *Ante-Nicene Fathers*, ed. A. Roberts and J. Donaldson (Peabody, MA: Hendrickson, 1994), 2:130.

[2] Ibid., 10, in *Ante-Nicene Fathers*, 2:133.

If failing to acknowledge the official gods of the cities sufficed to qualify Christians as atheists, moreover, Athenagoras contended that the entire world, by this ludicrous standard, would be equally guilty of atheism.

> The very men who charge us with atheism for not admitting the same gods as they acknowledge, are not agreed among themselves concerning the gods. The Athenians have set up as gods Celeus and Metanira: the Lacedaemonians Menelaus; and they offer sacrifices and hold festivals to him, while the men of Ilium cannot endure the very sound of his name, and pay their adoration to Hector. . . .When, therefore, they differ among themselves concerning their gods, why do they bring the charge against us of not agreeing with them? Then look at the practices prevailing among the Egyptians: are they not perfectly ridiculous? . . . They look upon the brutes as gods, and shave themselves when they die, and bury them in temples, and make public lamentation. If, then, we are guilty of impiety because we do not practise a piety corresponding with theirs, then all cities and all nations are guilty of impiety, for they do not all acknowledge the same gods.[3]

As to the charge of incest, Athenagoras called attention to the saying of Christ, "Everyone who looks at a woman to lust for her has already committed adultery with her in his heart" (Matt 5:28). Athenagoras added that Christians have intercourse only with their wives "and that only for the purpose of having children. For as the husbandman throwing the seed into the ground awaits the harvest, not sowing more upon it, so to us the procreation of children is the measure of our indulgence in appetite."[4] He also noted that many Christians practice lifelong celibacy in order to obtain closer union with God; and no Christian marries a second time, even if his first spouse is dead. "For a second marriage," as Athenagoras understood it, "is only a specious adultery."[5]

A third charge commonly leveled against Christians was that they engaged in cannibalism, or "Thyestean feasts." In Athenagoras's view this too is unreasonable. For, he argued, cannibals are murderers; one must kill a human being before eating him. Yet Christians not only refrain from murdering adults; they also abhor abortions. "When we say that those women who use drugs to bring on abortion commit murder, and will have to give an account to God for the abortion," he asked, "on what principle should we commit murder?"[6] Christian avoidance of the gladiatorial games testifies similarly, in Athenagoras's view, to Christians' abhorrence of violence. "We, deeming that to see a man put to death is much the same as killing him," he writes, "have abjured such spectacles. How, then, when we do not even look on, lest we should contract guilt and pollution, can we put people to death?"[7]

In response to the charges of incest and cannibalism, Athenagoras reasoned from Christians' abstention from lesser vices such as licentiousness within marriage and

---

[3] Ibid., 14, in *Ante-Nicene Fathers*, 2:135.
[4] Ibid., 33, in *Ante-Nicene Fathers*, 2:146.
[5] Ibid.
[6] Ibid., 35, in *Ante-Nicene Fathers*, 2:147.
[7] Ibid.

abortion to the extreme unlikelihood of their engaging in the greater vices of cannibalism and incest. Athenagoras rebutted the charge of atheism by pointing to Christians' obvious reverence for the Christian God and by showing that pagans, no less than Christians, routinely reject the beliefs and practices of religions other than their own. The refusal of Christians to acknowledge the gods of the cities, he argued, is therefore no aberration from the natural order. This is the Christian application of a principle universally observed, namely, that one ought to embrace the beliefs and practices of one's own religion and reject the beliefs and practices of other religions.

B. Pagan Ignorance of Christianity

Tertullian, the fiery North African lawyer-turned-clergyman, insisted more than any other apologist of this period that pagans persecute Christians because they are ignorant of Christianity.

> The proof of their ignorance, at once condemning and excusing their injustice, is this, that those who once hated Christianity because they knew nothing about it no sooner come to know it than they all at once come to lay down their enmity. From being its haters they become its disciples. By simply getting acquainted with it, they begin now to hate what they had formerly been, and to profess what they had formerly hated; and their numbers are as great as are laid to our charge.[8]

Surely Tertullian employed some hyperbole here. Nevertheless he seems also to have stated the apologetically significant and still valid truth that skepticism toward Christianity is usually inversely proportional to knowledge of it.

C. The Corruption of Pagan Morals

All Christian apologists of this period condemned the morals of contemporary pagans as abysmal. Minucius Felix (early third century), for instance, noted that incest, although unheard of among Christians, is commonplace among pagans and is even celebrated by them. "Your records and your tragedies," he wrote, "which you both read and hear with pleasure, glory in incests: thus also you worship incestuous gods, who have intercourse with mothers, with daughters, with sisters. With reason, therefore, is incest frequently detected among you, and is continually permitted."[9] According to Minucius, moreover, murder and inhumanity permeate the religions of pagans. Since Saturn is said to have eaten his own children, Minucius wrote:

> With reason were infants sacrificed to him by parents in some parts of Africa, caresses and kisses repressing their crying, that a weeping victim might not be sacrificed. Moreover, among the Tauri of Pontus, and to the Egyptian Busiris, it was a sacred rite to immolate their guests, and for the Galli to slaughter to Mercury human, or rather inhuman, sacrifices. The Roman sacrificers buried a living Greek man and a Greek woman, a Gallic

---

[8] Tertullian, *Apology* 1, in *Ante-Nicene Fathers*, 3:17b.
[9] Minucius Felix, *Octavius* 31, in *Ante-Nicene Fathers*, 4:192b.

man and a Gallic woman; and to this day Jupiter Latiaris is worshipped by them with murder; and, what is worthy of the son of Saturn, he is gorged with the blood of an evil and criminal man.[10]

Added to these atrocities are the games at which pagans amused themselves by watching people being slain by the sword or eaten by wild beasts. "Who," asks Minucius, "does not shudder . . . at the teaching of murder in the gladiatorial games?"[11] Christian apologists of the second and third centuries portray the morals of pagan society as almost indescribably corrupt.

D. The Purity of Christian Morals

The apologists of this period demonstrated the moral bankruptcy of paganism in order to persuade their readers to adopt the starkly divergent, morally elevating religion of Christianity. In addition to indicting pagan culture for its decadence, the apologists of this era uniformly described Christian morality not only in theory but also in practice, as virtually spotless. Aristides for example claimed that Christians

> do not commit adultery nor fornication, nor bear false witness, nor embezzle what is held in pledge, nor covet what is not theirs. They honour father and mother, and show kindness to those near to them. . . . They do good to their enemies; and their women, O King, are pure as virgins, and their daughters are modest; and their men keep themselves from every unlawful union and from all uncleanness, in the hope of a recompense to come in the other world. . . . Falsehood is not found among them; and they love one another, and from widows they do not turn away their esteem; and they deliver the orphan from him who treats him harshly. And he, who has, gives to him who has not, without boasting. . . . And if there is among them any that is poor and needy, and if they have no spare food, they fast two or three days in order to supply to the needy their lack of food.[12]

Doubtless not all Christian congregations exemplified the ideals of holiness set forth here by Aristides. Nevertheless second- and third-century Christians evidently approximated this ideal to some degree; and Christian apologists were quick to seize on this fact as evidence of the truthfulness of Christianity.

E. Endorsement of Christian Beliefs by Pagan Philosophers and Poets

Neither did the apologists of this period neglect to exploit the countless testimonies of pagan philosophers and poets to Christian ideas such as monotheism, the futility of idol worship, God's providential care for the world, and the reality of future rewards and punishments. The most eager gatherer of such testimonies from this era is doubtless Clement of Alexandria, the extraordinarily learned head of the catechetical school (a quasi-seminary) in Alexandria, Egypt. For example, Clement

---

[10] Ibid., 30, in *Ante-Nicene Fathers*, 4:192a.
[11] Ibid., 37, in *Ante-Nicene Fathers*, 4:196b.
[12] Aristides, *Apology* 15, in *Ante-Nicene Fathers*, 10:283.

found intimations of monotheism in Antisthenes, Socrates, Plato, Cleanthes, and the Pythagoreans, among philosophers, and in Aratus, Hesiod, Euripides, Sophocles, and the legendary Orpheus, among the poets.[13] He accused such a diverse group of thinkers as Plato, Aristotle, Pythagoras, Heraclitus, Epicurus, Democritus, Empedocles, Antisthenes, Solon, Xenophon, Cleanthes, Parmenides, Metrodorus, Xenocrates, Homer, Euripides, Aeschylus, Pindar, Sophocles, Aratus, Hesiod, and Menander of plagiarizing doctrines from Moses and the biblical prophets.[14]

Clement suggested with only slight hesitation that Greek philosophy constitutes a sort of Old Testament for the Hellenic world, a schoolmaster to lead learned pagans to Christ. Philosophy, he wrote, is

> a kind of preparatory training to those who attain to faith through demonstration. "For thy foot," it is said, "will not stumble, if thou refer what is good, whether belonging to the Greeks or to us, to Providence" [cf. Pr 3:23]. For God is the cause of all good things; but of some primarily, as of the Old and the New Testament; and of others by consequence, as philosophy. Perchance, too, philosophy was given to the Greeks directly and primarily, till the Lord should call the Greeks. For this was a schoolmaster to bring "the Hellenic mind," as the law, the Hebrews, "to Christ" [cf. Gal 3:24]. Philosophy, therefore, was a preparation, paving the way for him who is perfected in Christ.[15]

Clement overreached, naturally, by comparing Greek philosophy with Old Testament Scripture. He did, however, present Christianity in an especially winsome way to a civilization that prized philosophy and high culture. He was almost the ideal teacher for the inquirer who was saturated with pagan learning and wished to embrace Christianity without renouncing his cultural heritage.

F. The Antiquity of Christianity

Within antique Roman culture popular opinion held that the most ancient writings are probably the most true. Most Christian apologists in this era therefore strive to demonstrate that the Hebrew Scriptures, and especially the Pentateuch, antedate the most ancient literature of Greece and other civilizations. One of the reasons Clement of Alexandria charged Greek authors with plagiarizing from Scripture was to bolster his case for the fact that much of the Bible was written before pagan writings were written. Homer and others could not have copied from Scripture, Clement reasoned, if Scripture had not existed before them.

The apologist of this period who lay the greatest stress on this argument from antiquity to truthfulness is probably Theophilus of Antioch, who devoted two substantial sections of his work, *To Autolycus*, to recounting ancient events recorded in Scripture and to constructing a scriptural chronology of world history. The concluding remarks

---

[13] Clement of Alexandria, *Exhortation to the Heathen*, in *Ante-Nicene Fathers*, ed. A. Roberts and J. Donaldson (Peabody, MA: Hendrickson, 1994), 191–93.

[14] Clement of Alexandria, *Stromata* 5.14, in *Ante-Nicene Fathers*, 2:465–75.

[15] Ibid., 1.5, in *Ante-Nicene Fathers*, 2:305b.

of Theophilus's chronological section indicate something of the importance he ascribed to this kind of argument: "These periods, then, and all the above-mentioned facts, being viewed collectively, one can see the antiquity of the prophetical writings and the divinity of our doctrine, that the doctrine is not recent, nor our tenets mythical and false, as some think; but very ancient and true."[16]

In these remarks Theophilus echoed the common conviction of Christians of his time that the Scriptures are the oldest documents available to human beings and that the Bible's teachings may therefore be regarded as true.

G. The Argument from Prophecy

Important as the argument from antiquity may have been to second- and third-century apologists, even more important was the argument from prophecy. Origen, for example, asserted that "the prophecies . . . are sufficient to produce faith in any one who reads them"[17] and that "the strongest evidence in confirmation of the claims of Jesus . . . [is] that His coming was predicted by the Jewish prophets."[18] Likewise Justin Martyr, after devoting approximately one third of his *First Apology* to a discussion of fulfilled prophecies, wrote, "Since, then, we prove that all things which have already happened had been predicted by the prophets before they came to pass, we must necessarily believe also that those things which are in like manner predicted, but are yet to come to pass, shall certainly happen."[19]

Naturally neither Justin nor Origen nor any of the other Christian apologists of this period expected pagans to accept Christianity on the basis of the authority of the Old Testament. Rather apologists of this era asserted that without the aid of inspiration no one can predict extraordinary occurrences accurately, in detail, and hundreds of years in advance. They demonstrated that the Hebrew prophets predicted in detail extraordinary occurrences in the career of Christ, and hundreds if not thousands of years in advance; and then they established that Jesus actually fulfilled those predictions. These considerations, as the apologists knew from personal experience, suffice with the aid of the Holy Spirit to persuade even pagans to embrace the Old Testament as Scripture and Jesus as the Messiah.

II. APOLOGETICS TO JEWS

Understandably the apologists of the second and third centuries largely failed to address the concerns of potential Jewish converts to Christianity. Given the intense hostility that had already developed between the two communities by this time, the apologists could scarcely have expected Jews to embrace the gospel in appreciable numbers. However, Justin Martyr in his lengthy *Dialogue with Trypho* and to a lesser extent Tertullian in his brief *Answer to the Jews* did grapple with Jewish objections

---

[16] Theophilus, *To Autolycus* 3.29, in *Ante-Nicene Fathers*, 2:120b.
[17] Origen, *Against Celsus* 1.2, in *Ante-Nicene Fathers*, 4:397b.
[18] Ibid., 1.49, in *Ante-Nicene Fathers*, 4:417b.
[19] Justin Martyr, *First Apology* 52, in *Ante-Nicene Fathers*, 1.180.

to Christianity. The following sections examine the efforts of Justin and Tertullian to vindicate the following three claims in a manner satisfactory to Jewish readers: (1) that Christians are justified in their nonobservance of the ritual prescriptions of the Mosaic law; (2) that Jesus is the Messiah predicted in the Old Testament; and (3) that the Old Testament does not contradict but rather confirms the Christian belief that Jesus is God.

A. Christian Nonobservance of the Mosaic law

Near the outset of Justin's largely fictitious dialogue with the Jew Trypho (whom some implausibly identified as the famous Rabbi Tarphon), Trypho expressed his amazement that Christians expect to receive divine favor from the God of the Old Testament although they neither circumcise their children nor observe the Jewish Sabbaths and feasts.[20] In response Justin observed that Jer 31:31 predicts God's institution of a new covenant with human beings, which differs from the covenant made with the Jews on Mount Sinai. "Law placed against law," Justin reasoned, "has abrogated that which is before it; and a covenant which comes after in like manner has put an end to the previous one."[21] The ceremonial law, Justin believed, was given exclusively to the Jews only because of the hardness of their hearts, and it has been completely annulled by Christ.

B. Jesus as the Old Testament Messiah

To demonstrate Jesus' identity as the Jewish Messiah, both Justin and Tertullian appealed to numerous Old Testament prophecies. Although Justin appealed to a greater number of prophecies, and thoroughly discussed Psalm 22,[22] the arguments of Tertullian, which were more cogent, are the focus of discussion here. Especially important to Tertullian among the prophecies he discussed are the predictions of the Messiah's coming and passion in Daniel 9 and the prediction of the Messiah's virginal conception in Isa 7:14. Regarding Daniel 9, Tertullian labored painstakingly to correlate the predictions of this chapter with secular chronology and thus to demonstrate that according to Daniel 9 the Messiah will come and die at precisely the time when Jesus came and died.[23]

Regarding Isa 7:14 Tertullian argued against those who maintain that the prophecy refers merely to conception and birth in a young woman. He said instead that the text's identification of the predicted conception and birth as a sign precludes this possibility.

> A sign from God unless it had consisted in some portentous novelty, would not have appeared a sign. . . . [If] you have the audacity to lie, as if the Scripture contained (the announcement) that not a "virgin," but a "young female," was to conceive and bring forth; you are refuted even by this fact,

[20] Justin Martyr, *Dialogue with Trypho* 10, in *Ante-Nicene Fathers*, 1.199.

[21] Ibid., 11, in *Ante-Nicene Fathers*, 1:200; cp. Tertullian, *Answer to the Jews* 3 in *Ante-Nicene Fathers*, 3:164–67.

[22] Justin Martyr, *Dialogue with Trypho* 98–106, in *Ante-Nicene Fathers*, 1:243–47.

[23] Tertullian, *Answer to the Jews* 8, in *Ante-Nicene Fathers*, 3:158–60.

that a daily occurrence—the pregnancy and parturition of a young female, namely—cannot possibly seem anything of a sign.[24]

While Tertullian failed to appreciate the linguistic questions underlying the dispute over the interpretation of Isa 7:14, he did propose an at least somewhat plausible argument for the Christian interpretation.

C. Jesus as God

Both Justin and Tertullian appeal to classic texts such as Psalm 110 in order to prove from the Old Testament that a Being exists who is God and yet is not identical with the Father. Likewise both Tertullian and Justin claimed that because the Father is invisible, the God whom Moses and the patriarchs are said to have seen must be, in Justin's words, "another God and Lord subject to the Maker of all things."[25] After the Council of Nicaea (AD 325), in which the church definitively determined that the Father and Son are of the same substance, such language would be unacceptable. For if the Father and the Son are of one substance, and the Father's substance is unalterably invisible, the Son's substance is no less unalterably invisible. Also, if the two are of the same substance, then the Son is equal to, rather than subject to, the Father. Before the debates of the fourth century about the relationship between Christ and the Father, however, talk of Christ as inferior to the Father in His divine nature was not at all uncommon.

III. ANTIHERETICAL APOLOGETICS

The foremost antiheretical apologist of the church's first three centuries was undoubtedly Irenaeus (c. 140–200), bishop of Lyons during the last quarter of the second century. He wrote two works of an apologetic character: *Against Heresies* and *Proof of the Apostolic Preaching*. In each of these works Irenaeus sought to refute the claims of the numerous and bewilderingly diverse sects of Gnosticism, a heretical distortion of Christianity whose adherents typically display the following five characteristics. They (1) distinguish sharply between a mere man Jesus and a heavenly, immaterial Christ; (2) believe in the emanation, in a descending, hierarchical order, of multiple divine beings from the supreme deity; (3) differentiate between the supreme deity and the creator of the cosmos; (4) conceive of salvation as a kind of restoration of lost unity with the supreme deity; and (5) consider themselves in possession of an esoteric tradition deriving from Christ and/or the apostles, whose contents diverge radically from conventional Christianity.

In these works Irenaeus offered an understanding of the rule of faith as a bulwark against heretics and presented a case against the existence of secret traditions deriving from Christ and the apostles, both of which bear on apologetic problems of today.

---

[24] Ibid., 9, in *Ante-Nicene Fathers*, 3:161b.
[25] Justin Martyr, *Dialogue with Trypho* 56, in *Ante-Nicene Fathers*, 1:223a.

Irenaeus's first contribution, his understanding of the rule of faith, consists in a theory of how one should adjudicate conflicting claims as to what constitutes the teaching of Jesus and the apostles. Quite simply, Irenaeus postulated the existence of an apostolic tradition independent of Scripture, that is, a rule of faith, to which one who doubts whether he has correctly interpreted Scripture may have recourse.

> Suppose there arises a dispute relative to some important question among us, should we not have recourse to the most ancient churches with which the Apostles held constant intercourse, and learn from them what is certain and clear in regard to the present question? For how should it be if the Apostles themselves had not left us writings? Would it not be necessary to follow the course of the tradition which they handed down to those to whom they did commit the churches?[26]

So reliable did Irenaeus consider this tradition that he seems to have regarded those without access to written revelation as more secure against the temptation to heresy than those who possess Scriptures they can misinterpret. Of those who, in the absence of written documents, have believed this faith, Irenaeus wrote:

> If anyone were to preach to these men the inventions of the heretics . . . they would at once stop their ears, and flee as far off as possible, not enduring even to listen to the blasphemous address. Thus, by means of that ancient tradition of the Apostles, they do not suffer their mind to conceive anything of the [doctrines suggested by the] portentous language of these teachers [i.e. Gnostics], among whom neither church nor doctrine has ever been established.[27]

Irenaeus, it seems, reposed a naïve confidence in the reliability of the church as a repository of apostolic tradition. None "of the rulers in the churches," he asserted,

> however highly gifted he may be in point of eloquence, teach doctrines different from these [i.e. the received orthodox faith] . . . ; nor, on the other hand, will he who is deficient in power of expression inflict injury on the tradition. For the faith being ever one and the same, neither does any one who is able at great length to discourse regarding it, make any addition to it, nor does one, who can say but little, diminish it.[28]

In Irenaeus's view, "Where the church is, there is the Spirit of God; and where the Spirit of God is, there is the church and every kind of grace; but the Spirit is truth."[29] Numerous persons throughout the history of the church have entertained similar concepts and accordingly have advised those who would shun the heresies of small sects like the Jehovah's Witnesses to use the tradition of the church as a key to interpreting Scripture.

---

[26] Irenaeus, *Against Heresies* 3.4.1, in *Ante-Nicene Fathers*, 1:417a.
[27] Ibid., 3.4.2, in *Ante-Nicene Fathers*, 1:417a.
[28] Ibid., 1.10.2, in *Ante-Nicene Fathers*, 1:331a.
[29] Ibid., 3.24.1, in *Ante-Nicene Fathers*, 1:458b.

Unquestionably, references to traditional interpretations can enrich one's understanding of Scripture and help preserve one from embracing errors already refuted in the history of the church. It is doubtful, however, whether one can identify any specific institution that has actually conformed to Irenaeus's ideal of the church as guardian of apostolic tradition over the centuries.

In his second, principal contribution to Christian apologetics, Irenaeus supplied two arguments to the effect that the apostles handed down no secret tradition that in any way contradicts or radically transcends their public teaching as recorded in Scripture. The Gnostics, whom Irenaeus opposed, claimed that Jesus and the apostles accommodated their public teaching to the tastes and capacities of their hearers and shared the full truth only in secret to a small circle of the enlightened. Irenaeus retorted, first, however, that the same reasoning that leads one to regard the public teaching as merely accommodated, if carried to its logical conclusion, would lead one to think that the traditions shared with the elite were also not the unvarnished truth but an accommodated representation thereof, suited to the tastes and capacities of elite hearers.

> If the Apostles used to speak to people in accordance with the opinions instilled in them of old, no one learned the truth from them, nor, at a much earlier date, from the Lord; for they say that he did himself speak after the same fashion. Wherefore neither do these men themselves know the truth; but since such was their opinion regarding God, they had just received doctrine as they were able to hear it. According to this manner of speaking, therefore, the rule of truth can be with nobody; but all learners will ascribe this practice to all [teachers], that just as every person thought, and so far as his capability extended, so was also the language addressed to them.[30]

No religion therefore that proclaims an esoteric doctrine that conflicts with its exoteric preaching can be credible. For if a person is willing to lie to the public in order to coax them nearer to the truth without unduly offending them, why should the same person not be willing to lie to his inner circle, insofar as their sensibilities and capacities might also be inadequate to receive the undistorted truth?

In his second argument Irenaeus observed that if Christ and His apostles had accommodated their teaching to the capabilities and preconceptions of their hearers, they would not have suffered martyrdom.

> Those . . . who delivered up their souls to death for Christ's gospel—how could they have spoken to men in accordance with old-established opinion? If this had been the course adopted by them, they should not have suffered; but inasmuch as they did preach things contrary to those persons who did not assent to the truth, for that reason they suffered. It is evident, therefore, that they did not relinquish the truth, but with all boldness preached [it] to the Jews and Greeks.[31]

---

[30] Ibid., 3.12.6, in *Ante-Nicene Fathers*, 1:432a.
[31] Ibid., 3.12.13, in *Ante-Nicene Fathers*, 1:435a–b.

The idea that Christ or the apostles taught some secret tradition and that this tradition, instead of Scripture, conveys the real meaning of Christianity, Irenaeus concluded, is therefore preposterous. "The doctrine of the Apostles," he wrote, "is open and steadfast, holding nothing in reserve; nor did they teach one set of doctrines in private and another in public."[32]

IV. CONCLUSION

In the face of persecution from without and heresy from within the apologists of the second and third centuries defended Christianity against the criticisms of pagans, Jews, and pseudo-Christian heretics. When addressing pagans, the apologists emphasized the falsehood of popular accusations against Christians, the ignorance of Christianity's opponents about its authentic nature, the corruption of pagan morals, the purity of the lives of Christians, the witness that pagan poets and philosophers supply to the superiority of Christianity, the superior antiquity of the Christian religion, and the fulfillment of the prophecies in Christianity's holy book.

When addressing Jewish audiences, however, the Christian apologists of this period broached a different set of topics. They explained, for example, how Christians reconcile their allegiance to the God of the Old Testament with their abandonment of the ceremonial law; how Christians can worship Christ without committing idolatry; how Christians can deem Christ divine without compromising monotheism; and how the prophecies and types of the Old Testament can predict the coming of a Savior radically different from that expected by conventional Jews. Again, when addressing teachers of error within the church, the apologists of this period turned to discussing a radically distinct complex of issues, including what constitutes the authentic "rule of faith," the continuing authority of the churches the apostles founded, and the inconsistency of heretical teachings both with themselves and with orthodox Christianity. The apologists of the second and third centuries displayed a remarkable capacity to adjust their arguments for Christianity to the needs and dispositions of different audiences. Like Paul, they became "all things to all people, so that . . . by every possible means [they might] save some" (1 Cor 9:22).

---

[32] Ibid., 3.15.1, in *Ante-Nicene Fathers*, 1:439b.

Chapter 12

LATER PATRISTIC AND MEDIEVAL APOLOGETICS (APOLOGETICS IN THE MIDDLE AGES)

THIS CHAPTER CONCERNS CHRISTIAN APOLOGETICS IN the period spanning from the fourth through the fifteenth centuries. The amount of time covered by this chapter limits the degree of detail with which the work of individual apologists in this period can be examined. This is regrettable, for during the period between the conversion of Constantine and the Reformation Christian thinkers cultivated the study of natural theology and reflected on the many puzzling and obscure aspects of the Christian faith.

Nevertheless, this chapter discusses the principal audiences for Christian apologists during this period and the main problems Christians addressed in order to persuade persons in these audiences to embrace the Christian faith. The principal audiences for Christian apologists of this period were heretics, that is, persons who, while professing to be Christians, believed doctrines inconsistent with the most basic truths of the Christian faith; and Muslims, who enjoyed extraordinary political power and a literary culture that rivaled that of the Christian West during this period.

Julian the Apostate sought to "repaganize" the Roman Empire and so Christian intellectuals fiercely resisted this movement. This struggle extended well into the Middle Ages and yet never proved completely successful.[1]

I. HERETICS

While countless heretics emerged during the troubled period covered by this chapter, those who posed the gravest and most direct threats to Christian orthodoxy were these: (a) the Arians, who flourished especially in the fourth century and denied that Christ is of the same substance (that is, that He is the same God) as the Father; (b) the Nestorians, who taught that the eternal Logos and the man Jesus were two, distinct persons; (c) the non-Chalcedonians (frequently regarded as Eutychians), who taught

---

[1] This chapter does not discuss pagans as one of the audiences of Christian apologetics in this period because of space limitations. The discussion of Christian antipagan polemics in the previous chapter must suffice.

that after the incarnation Christ possessed only one, divine-human nature; and (d) the Manicheans who taught cosmic dualism, the belief that equally primordial creators, one good and one evil, are responsible for the existence of the present universe.

This list does not begin to exhaust the range of heresies that plagued the period covered by this chapter. Nevertheless the four listed do constitute the most virulent heresies of this period.

A. The Arians

The Arians took their name from Arius (c. 280–336), an Alexandrian priest who became known for his denial that Jesus Christ is God. While the Arians marshaled a host of arguments against the orthodox belief in Jesus' deity, two difficulties in particular seem to have motivated their opposition to the orthodox doctrine. First, they considered affirmations of Jesus' full deity inconsistent with scriptural texts that portray Christ as subordinate to the Father; and second, they failed to perceive any difference between a Father and a Son who possess the same substance.

1. How can Jesus be equal to God the Father and subordinate to Him at the same time?

Orthodox defenders of Christ's deity address the first concern by calling attention to the distinction between Christ's divine nature and His human nature. One can reconcile scriptural texts that characterize Jesus as equal to the Father with scriptural texts that portray Him as subordinate, if one distinguishes between the natures to which the two classes of texts refer. Passages that portray Jesus as equal to the Father, the orthodox maintain, apply only to His divine nature; and texts that portray Jesus as subordinate to the Father apply to His human nature alone. "What is lofty," Gregory of Nazianzus (329–390) explained, "you are to apply to the Godhead, and to that nature in him which is superior to sufferings and incorporeal. But all that is lowly you are to apply to the . . . flesh."[2]

The following remarks by Augustine (354–430) supply an example of how one can apply this rule to the exegesis of scriptural texts.

> According to the form [i.e. the nature] of God all things were made through him [i.e. Christ; John 1:3]. According to the form [i.e. the nature] of a servant, he was made of a woman, made under the law [Gal 4:4]. According to the form of God, he and the Father are one [John 10:30]; according to the form of a servant, he came not to do his own will, but the will of him who sent him [John 6:38]. According to the form of God, as the Father has life in himself, so has he also given to the Son to have life in himself [John 5:26]; according to the form of a servant, his soul is sorrowful unto death, and: "Father," he says, "if it is possible, let this cup pass" [Matt 26:38–9]. According to the form of God, he is the true God and life eternal [1 John 5:20];

---

[2] Gregory of Nazianzus, *The Second Theological Oration* 29.17, in *Nicene and Post-Nicene Fathers*, 2nd series, ed. P. Sheff and H. Wace (Peabody, MA: Hendrickson, 1994), 2.7:307b–8a.

according to the form of a servant, he became obedient unto death, even the death of the cross [Phil 2:8].[3]

By invoking a simple distinction between Christ's human and divine natures Christian apologists of the fourth century established that one can reconcile statements that portray Jesus as God with statements that portray Him as subordinate to the Father without, like Arius, diluting Scripture's testimony to Christ's full deity. Thus these apologists removed one of the key stumbling blocks that prevented Arius and his followers from acknowledging that Christ is God.

2. *How can two distinct persons be identical to the same substance?*

The apologists of the fourth century prove less successful in answering the Arians' second quandary, namely, how can the Father and the Son be truly different if they are one and the same God, the same divine substance? The church father who came closest to resolving this dilemma satisfactorily in the patristic era was Augustine. He concluded that the Father and the Son differ not in their substance but in their relations to each other. "Although to be the Father and to be the Son are two different things," he wrote, "still there is no difference in their substance, because the names, Father and Son, do not refer to the substance but to the relation."[4]

Augustine reasoned, in other words, that since Scripture proclaims that there is only one God and that Jesus is God, the names "Father" and "Son" must not be intended to indicate that the Father and Son are distinct substances. Augustine observed, however, that the names "father" and "son," when used of human beings, designate not only two distinct substances but also two distinct relations: fatherhood and sonship. Since these names, when used of God, cannot indicate that the Father and Son are different substances, he concluded, they must signify that the two divine persons differ in their relations to each other. In other words the Father and the Son are precisely the same substance and yet really distinct from each other on account of their distinct relations.

How Augustine and his later disciples, especially Thomas Aquinas, substantiated and developed this concept of the intra-Trinitarian distinctions is beyond the scope of the present chapter. But Augustine's understanding of distinction through relation shows how one can adhere to a rigorous monotheism, admitting no distinction whatsoever between the one substance of the divine persons and yet meaningfully assert that the divine persons differ eternally and ontologically.

B. The Nestorians

The Nestorians take their name from Nestorius (381–c. 415), the one-time patriarch of Constantinople who scandalized the church by his assertion that the eternal Logos was one person and that the Man Jesus was another. Nestorius, unlike Arius,

---

[3] Augustine, *On the Trinity* 1.11.22, in *Nicene and Post-Nicene Fathers*, 1st series, ed. P. Schaff (Peabody, MA: Hendrickson, 1994), 1.3.30.

[4] Ibid., 5.5.6., in *Nicene and Post-Nicene Fathers*, 1.3.89.

understood that God is a Trinity, that is, three divine persons, each of whom is identical to the one divine nature. He is capable therefore of conceiving of three persons in one nature. Nestorius was incapable, however, of conceiving of one person, Jesus Christ, having two natures.

Nestorius failed to apply the nature-person distinction, which is essential to the doctrine of the Trinity, to his Christology and to understanding the being and activity of Christ. Nestorius failed to distinguish between the claim that Jesus has two natures, which is true, and the claim that Jesus is two persons, which is radically false. To accept Nestorius's claim that Jesus consisted of two persons—the divine person, the Logos, and the human person, Jesus—is dangerous. One need merely consider its implications for the doctrine of the atonement.

Protestant Christians rightly claim that even the slightest sin is infinitely wicked and merits infinite punishment because it offends God, who is infinitely benevolent and infinitely worthy of praise. "Whoever keeps the entire law, yet fails in one point, is guilty of breaking it all" (Jas 2:10). Since even a perfect human being is of only finite worth, the sacrifice of one who is merely a perfect human being could not pay the debt incurred by a single sin.

To obtain forgiveness from a righteous God, whose perfect justice allows no sin to go unpunished, human beings need a divine sacrifice; for God alone is of infinite worth. God's nature, however, is incapable of suffering. So if humans are to have any hope for salvation, a divine person must unite to Himself a human nature so that in that human nature the divine person can suffer and thereby offer a sacrifice to God on their behalf, a sacrifice that derives infinite value from the infinite value of the divine person who suffered.

If Nestorius were correct—that is, if the divine Logos is one person and Jesus who died is another—then no such infinitely valuable sacrifice has occurred. God has not purchased the church with His own blood (cf. Acts 20:28), and human beings have no hope for forgiveness of their sins. By claiming that Jesus exists as two persons instead of one person in two natures, Nestorius thus implicitly denied the possibility of salvation.

A thoroughly satisfactory response to Nestorius's error requires a clear distinction between nature and person in Christology. Regrettably Nestorius's foremost opponent, Cyril of Alexandria (385–444), did not elaborate such a distinction as clearly as one might like. He did, however, secure the condemnation of Nestorius's heresy by the Council of Ephesus in 431.

C. The Non-Chalcedonians

Non-Chalcedonians, as the name suggests, reject the ruling of the Council of Chalcedon that Christ is one person in two natures. This council, which convened in 451, endorsed this formula in the process of condemning Eutychianism, a heresy that takes its name from Eutyches (d. after 454), a monk of Constantinople who disgraced himself by stating that Christ possessed not two natures united in one person but only one nature. The fathers of the Council of Chalcedon regarded Eutyches's statement as

160

abhorrent because they understood it to mean that Christ possesses a mongrel of the divine and human natures and is therefore neither fully human nor genuinely divine.

The fact that the accepted formula, "one person in two natures," became immediately controversial was not because of widespread sympathy at the time for the position promoted by Eutyches. Virtually all educated persons who claimed to be Christians at the time of the Council of Chalcedon recognized that the divine nature is simple, immutable, impassible, atemporal, aspatial, and utterly incapable of being affected by the world.

1. Incompatible with Cyril's early Christology?

The expression "one person in two natures" became controversial for two reasons. First, it seemed incompatible with the early Christology of Cyril of Alexandria (c. 376–444). Although the Council of Ephesus did not declare that the God-Man had only one nature, Cyril himself, the Council's most influential theologian and virtually its living embodiment, spoke of "the one incarnate nature of the Word."[5]

Cyril did not intend by this phrase, however, to deny a real distinction between Christ's manhood and His deity. Cyril distinguished between the two much as one distinguishes between a human body and soul: entities that, though distinct from each other, together make up one human nature. Just as a body and a soul constitute one human nature, Cyril reasoned, so Christ's deity and humanity constitute His one nature. Numerous persons find the formula "one person in two natures" objectionable not because they are Eutychians, but because they employ the theological vocabulary and conceptual framework of the early Cyril, which conflicts with those of Chalcedon.[6]

2. Crypto-Nestorian?

Many skeptics of the "one person in two natures" formula consider it crypto-Nestorian. In the philosophical vocabulary of the time, the word "person" meant the hypostasis of a rational nature; and "hypostasis" means what enables any nature, rational or otherwise, to exist as a complete entity over against other things. Every distinct nature therefore possesses a hypostasis. The Council of Chalcedon's claim that Christ has two, distinct natures thus appears to many people tantamount to an assertion that Christ consists of two hypostases, or persons. If every distinct, existing nature has a hypostasis, skeptics of Chalcedon reason, one cannot say that Christ has two natures without implying that he has two hypostases.[7]

This objection is the central problem faced by orthodox defenders of the formula "one person in two natures": how can Christ have two natures without also having two hypostases or persons? The answer to this objection emerges principally in the works

---

[5] Cyril of Alexandria, *Epistle 46.3* ("Second Letter to Succensus," in *Cyril of Alexandria: Select Letters*, ed. and trans. L. R. Wickham [Oxford: Clarendon, 1903], 87).

[6] Cyril did acknowledge in 433 is his *Epistle* 39 the orthodoxy of the Formula of Reunion, which refers to Christ as one person with two natures.

[7] Severus of Antioch, for example, states this objection (*Ad Nephalium* 2:50, in *Severi Antiocheni orations ad Nephalium, ciusdem ac Sergii Grammatic epistulas matual*, ed. J, Lebon, Corpus Scriptorum Christianorum Orientalium 119, Scriptores Syri 64 [Louvain: Secrétariat du Corpus SCO, 1949]).

of John of Caesarea (early sixth century), who distinguished between the true dictum that no nature can exist distinctly without a hypostasis and the false claim that no nature exists distinctly without a hypostasis that is exclusively its own.[8]

John asserted that although Christ's human nature requires a hypostasis to exist as distinct, it does not require a merely human hypostasis that would constitute a second person in Him. Rather, John proposed, both of Christ's natures can subsist as distinct by virtue of Christ's one divine hypostasis. Even though there can be no distinctly existing nature without a hypostasis, John concluded, it is conceivable that Christ could possess two distinct natures supported by one hypostasis, the person of the eternal Logos. One can assert that Christ possesses two natures, therefore, without implicitly endorsing Nestorianism.

3. The significance of John's conclusion

This conclusion is significant for two reasons. First, it establishes the orthodoxy of the "one person in two natures" formula, which, unlike Cyril's "one nature" language, does not lend itself to a Eutychian interpretation. Second, the "one nature" formula of Cyril appears unacceptable in that it portrays Christ's divine nature as a part of a larger whole, which a simple and infinitely great nature cannot be.

D. The Manichaeans

The Manicheans, at least in the narrowest sense of the term, take their name from their third-century founder, Mani. In the present context the term "Manichaean" designates not only Manichaeans in the strict sense of the term but also Paulicians, Bogomils, Cathars, and Albigensians. These were disparate sects united by their belief in the existence of two gods, one good and one evil, who are responsible for the good and the evil, respectively, in the world.

The appeal of this view seems obvious; just as the presence of good in the world presupposes the existence of a good creator, the Manichaeans reason, so also does the presence of evil in the world presuppose the existence of an evil creator. Augustine, however, argued persuasively that this conclusion of the Manichaeans sprang from a misunderstanding of the nature of evil. The Manichaeans themselves, Augustine asserted, would concede that evil is what is contrary to nature.

> The establishment of this doctrine [as to the nature of evil] is the overthrow of your heresy. For evil is no nature if it is contrary to nature. Now, according to you, evil is a certain nature and substance. Moreover, whatever is contrary to nature must oppose nature and seek its destruction. For nature means nothing else than that which anything is conceived of as being in its own kind. . . . Here, then, . . . we see that evil is that which falls away from essence [= nature] and tends to non-existence.[9]

---

[8] See the brief but comprehensive statement of the position of John of Caesarea in his *Capitula XVII contra Monophysitas*, in *Johannis Caesariensis grammatic et presbyteri opera qual supersunt*, ed. R. Marcellus, Corpus Christianorum, Series Graeca 1 (Turnhout, Belgium: Brepols, 1977).

[9] Augustine, *On the Morals of the Manichaeans* 2.2, in *Nicene and Post-Nicene Fathers*, 2.4.69b–70a.

Augustine argued, in other words, that evil is not a nature, but a defect that in some way impairs a nature; and that any nature, to the extent that it is free from defect, is good. When one removes evil from a nature, what remains is good. When one removes the nature from evil, however, what remains is a mere lack of goodness, an absence of being or sheer nothingness.[10] Nothingness, naturally, requires no creator. Augustine concluded, accordingly that one can account for the existence of evil without denying that the good God created all things good; and that Manichaeism is therefore unwarranted.

E. Conclusion

In summary four principal heresies plagued the patristic church: Arianism, Nestorianism, non-Chalcedonianism, and Manichaeism. To these heresies, orthodox apologists responded: Gregory of Nazianzus and Augustine responded to Arianism; Cyril of Alexandria to Nestorianism; Leontius of Jerusalem to non-Chalcedonianism; and Augustine to Manichaeism. With the exception of Cyril of Alexandria, these apologists drew distinctions that allowed them to affirm elements of truth in their opponents' convictions while at the same time showing that these truths do not imply heretical conclusions.

II. Muslims

The period covered by the present chapter coincides roughly with the first 900 years of Islam, a religion whose military conquests made it impossible for Christian apologists to ignore. Muslims object to Christianity principally on two grounds. First, Christianity affirms the doctrine of the Trinity, which Muslims consider tritheistic. Second, Christianity rejects the prophethood of Muhammad, whom Muslims consider the greatest of all prophets, the "Seal of the Prophets." This section briefly considers Christian responses to both of these objections.

A. The Trinity

Theodore Abū Qurrah (c. 755–c. 830) presents in his *On the Trinity* a conventional Eastern Christian response to Muslim concerns about the compatibility of Christian Trinitarianism with faith in one and only one God. The failure of Muslims and Jews to recognize the monotheistic character of Christian Trinitarian faith, Theodore asserted, springs from a logically prior failure to grasp the distinction between "nature" and "person."

> I want those who deny Christian doctrine to know that some names refer to persons and others to natures. . . . The Father, Son, and Holy Spirit are three persons with one nature. . . . If you count them, you must not predicate

---

[10] Augustine, *Against the Epistle of Manichaeus* 33.36, in *Nicene and Post-Nicene Fathers,* 2.4.146a.

number of the name "God," which is the name of their nature. . . . Rather
you must count three persons and one God.[11]

When Christians confess that the Father, Son, and Holy Spirit are God, Theodore continued, they do not mean to set Father, Son, and Holy Spirit over against one another as
if they were independently existing entities. "The Father, Son, and Holy Spirit are not
like three men, divided in terms of place or differing in form, will, or state. . . . [Rather]
there is no difference among them at all, no difference that has an effect on the hypostasis of one of them—other than that each is different from the other."[12] One can safely
say that Theodore offered in this treatise an impeccably orthodox confession of faith
in the mystery of the Trinity. He recognized that one must distinguish between person
and nature in order to think correctly of the Trinity, and he asserted that the Trinitarian
persons consist in one, undivided essence, being distinguished not by their essential
qualities but by some other factor.

By failing to identify this other factor, however, Theodore considerably weakened
the apologetic force of his confession. Admittedly, he disabused Muslim readers of the
fantasy, propagated by the Qur'an (Sura 5:116), that Christians worship a Trinity of
God, Jesus, and Mary. Yet he failed even provisionally to answer the question of how the
Father, Son, and Holy Spirit can each be identical to the same essence while remaining
really and eternally distinct. He offered instead a few quaint analogies that, while possibly helpful to believers, answer no substantive objections to the doctrine of the Trinity.

Perhaps Theodore could have countered Muslim objections more persuasively if
he had been able to access the works of Augustine and Boethius (c. 480–c. 524) on
the Trinity, which were completed long before his birth and yet were largely unknown
to Eastern Christians before the early modern period. In the actual course of events,
however, neither Theodore nor his fellow Arab Christian apologists were able to fend
off serious criticism of the doctrine of the Trinity. As a result their attempts to defend
the doctrine were ineffectual.

B. Muhammad as a Prophet

John of Damascus (c. 676–749), one of the earliest Christian authors to write
against Islam, criticized the claim of Muhammad to prophethood on two grounds.
First, he noted that Muhammad, unlike Jesus or Moses, supplied no evidence for the
divine inspiration of his message; he neither performed miracles nor fulfilled prophecies. Yet the Qur'an itself stipulates that marriages and business transactions require
witnesses to validate them. If claims about such relatively unimportant matters require verification, John asked, how much more ought Muslims to demand verification from one who alleges to deliver revelations from God? "How is it," John asked
Muslims, "that when he [Muhammad] enjoined . . . in this book of yours [the Qur'an]
not to do anything or receive anything without witnesses, you did not ask him: 'First,

---

[11] Theodore Abū Qurrah, "On the Trinity," in *Theodore Abū Qurrah*, trans. J. C. Lamoreaux, ed.
D. Taylor, Library of the Christian East (Provo, UT: Brigham Young University Press, 2005), 175–93.
[12] Ibid., 184–85.

show us by witnesses that you are a prophet and that you have come from God, and show us what Scriptures there are that testify about you?'"[13] Since Muhammad failed to warrant his claim to prophethood, John concluded, acceptance of this claim is mere trifling with religion; it is irresponsible acquiescence to teachings that are potentially blasphemous.

Second, John asserted that Muhammad falsified his claim to prophethood by endorsing and practicing sexual immorality. John wrote that in the Qur'an Muhammad:

> plainly makes legal provision for taking four wives and, if it be possible, a thousand concubines—as many as one can maintain, besides the four wives. He also made it legal to put away whichever wife one might wish, and, should one so wish, to take another in the same way. Muhammad had a friend named Zeid. This man had a beautiful wife with whom Muhammad fell in love. Once, when they were sitting together, Muhammad said . . . "God has given me the command that you put away your wife." And he put her away. Then several days later: "Now," he said, "God has commanded me to take her."[14]

Muhammad also legislated, John noted, that a brother may marry his own brother's wife if and when his brother puts her away. The testimony of conscience against such practices, John argued, ought to disabuse Muslims of their misguided faith in Muhammad.

C. Conclusion

In opposition to Islam, then, late patristic/early medieval apologists such as Theodore Abū Qurrah and John of Damascus attempted first to vindicate the doctrine of the Trinity and Christian views about Jesus in general from Muslim reproach and second to challenge the Islamic world's culpably credulous confidence in the prophecies and person of Muhammad. It is difficult to assess the impact of Christian anti-Islamic apologetics in this period. However, then as now, attacking Muhammad proved easier than defending Christian doctrine and rendering it intelligible.

III. CONCLUSION

During the late patristic and medieval periods, Christian apologists sought principally to quell the upsurges of heresy that imperiled the church in these times. Controversies with Arians, Nestorians, and especially non-Chalcedonians merited the attention Christian thinkers of this era bestowed on them and probably considerably more. Nevertheless it is distressing to compare the quality and quantity of orthodox literature devoted to the Christological controversies with the few and relatively feeble efforts of Christian authors to respond to the challenge of Islam. Hopefully, Christian apologists will respond more vigorously to anti-Christian religions and ideologies that emerge in the future.

---

[13] John of Damascus, *Writings*, trans. F. H. Chase Jr. (New York: Fathers of the Church, 1958), 100 (Fathers of the Church 37:156).

[14] Ibid., 160–61.

Chapter 13

APOLOGETICS OF THE REFORMERS

THIS CHAPTER SURVEYS THE REFORMERS' CONTRIBUTIONS to Christian apologetics and especially the contributions of the two principal Reformers, Martin Luther and John Calvin. This chapter differs from the other chapters on the history of apologetics in this volume in that it focuses exclusively on arguments against the errors of late medieval Roman Catholicism. These are the kind of arguments that many would regard as interconfessional polemics rather than apologetics in the traditional sense of the term. The Reformers (and evangelical Protestant Christians who follow them) considered the errors they combated sufficiently grave to warrant visible separation of Christians from the Roman Catholic Church. Since evangelicals think of apologetics as addressing theological controversies of grave import, it seems appropriate to discuss the work of the Reformers in the present volume.

I. ISSUES TO BE CONSIDERED

A. Justification

The principal disagreements discussed in this chapter relate to the nature of justification, the relationship between the authority of Scripture and that of tradition, and the significance of the institutional church for salvation and the Christian life. On the first issue, broadly speaking, Catholics believe that the justification of which Paul wrote consists in an infusion of righteousness that encompasses regeneration, adoption, and sanctification, an infusion that removes all sin from the justified person and makes him so good that he merits eternal life in heaven. Luther and Calvin, by contrast, held that by "justification" Paul meant God's imputation or crediting of Christ's righteousness to sinners so that, notwithstanding the sinners' abiding corruption, God treats them as if they are as righteous as Christ.

Luther and Calvin do not deny that a divine infusion of righteousness occurs in every justified person. Thus the justified person lives a holy life. However, Luther and Calvin also insisted that this infusion of righteousness constitutes sanctification, not the justification on account of which God treats Christians as if they were righteous. Confusing justification and sanctification, Protestants argue, obliterates the distinction between Christians' right to be treated as righteous in God's sight, a right purchased for them by Christ's blood, and the Christians' own spiritual condition.

B. Scripture and Tradition

On the second issue, the relative authority of Scripture and tradition, Catholics of the Reformation period believed in the main that Christians possess two equally authoritative sources of revelation: Scripture and oral tradition. The latter consists, in the Reformation-era Catholic view, in a body of revealed information that the apostles communicated orally to their disciples and did not record in writing. In the classic Catholic view, God preserved this information in the belief of the faithful in churches whose bishops stand in apostolic succession. In this succession bishops received supernatural powers through the laying on of hands of the apostles, and these bishops passed these powers to other bishops by laying their hands on them and ordaining them. The rightful head of these bishops, the first among equals, Catholics maintain, is the bishop of Rome (the pope), who received the keys that Christ bestowed on Peter.

Sixteenth-century Catholics held that one can gain certain knowledge of truths revealed in tradition, even if they are absent from Scripture. If a belief is held by all the faithful, who are in communion with bishops in apostolic succession, and are in communion with the bishop of Rome, then that belief is true and divinely revealed. If some doctrine cannot be deduced from Scripture, this belief must reflect some tradition passed down orally from the apostles. Likewise, if an ecumenical council (a meeting of bishops from different parts of the world), solemnly sanctions a belief and the pope approves it; or if all the bishops in their ordinary capacity as teachers affirm some belief and the pope approves it; or if the pope alone solemnly affirms that a belief is divinely revealed, then Roman Catholics consider this belief to be divinely revealed. From the perspective of sixteenth-century Catholicism, if the belief in question is neither contained in nor deducible from Scripture, it must derive from apostolic, oral tradition.

If a particular interpretation of Scripture meets any of the four conditions mentioned in the preceding paragraph, then it is considered true and authoritative. If someone argued that Christians ought not believe some tenet because Scripture obviously says nothing about it, Reformation-era Catholics responded that the belief might derive from apostolic oral tradition. If someone charged that a Catholic belief contradicted the teaching of Scripture, that charge could not be accepted if the belief met any one of the four conditions previously outlined. For in this case the authority of the pope, of an ecumenical council, of the entirety of the bishops, or of the faithful as a whole would possess the authority to declare the dissenter's interpretation of Scripture incorrect.

The Reformers, by contrast, believed that the Bible alone constitutes the post-apostolic church's infallible source of knowledge. They believed that the Catholic view of Scripture and tradition was a warrant for imposing merely human teachings on Christians even when those teachings are unwarranted by Scripture or patently opposed to it. Since the Bible unmistakably condemns many of the teachings propagated by the pope and bishops, the Reformers held, the claim that those who affirm these teachings cannot err when they solemnly and unanimously affirm them, is manifestly false. The Reformers also rejected the theory of apostolic succession. They claimed that one who separates from those who claim to stand in this succession need not thereby deprive himself of any spiritual benefit.

C. The Significance of the Church

According to the Catholic position bishops who stand in apostolic succession and the priests whom they ordain possess the supernatural power to forgive sins a person commits after baptism. Second, Catholics of this period held that a person cannot obtain forgiveness for "mortal" sins committed after baptism without confessing those sins to a priest and receiving the priest's forgiveness (the sacrament of penance), or at least desiring the requisite confession and absolution. The Reformers, by contrast, considered faith in Christ the sole condition of forgiveness of sins. They rejected the notion that penance constitutes a sacrament. In the Catholic view the Christian receives forgiveness of mortal sins committed after baptism through the sacrament of penance administered by a priest. The Protestant view, by contrast, is that a person receives forgiveness for all his sins when he believes the divine promise of forgiveness for believers in Christ.

II. THE ARGUMENTS

One cannot reasonably regard the disagreements between Protestants and Catholics that necessitated the Reformation as mere misunderstandings or disputes about matters without practical significance. The two parties' views diverge much too radically for both sides to coexist in a single institution. The following section seeks first to explain in greater detail precisely what Reformation-era Roman Catholics believed about justification, the relation between Scripture and tradition, and the significance of the institutional church for salvation; and second to outline the principal arguments that Martin Luther and John Calvin employed against the Catholic position on these subjects.

A. Justification: The Roman Catholic Position

Protestants object to three aspects of the Catholic doctrine of justification, in particular the Catholic definition of justification, the ascription of merit to the justified person, and the denial that justification always entails remission of punishment for sins.

1. Definition

First, as already noted, Catholics define justification as an infusion of righteousness into the justified person's soul. The Council of Trent, convened by Pope Paul III in 1545 to define the Catholic position on disputed questions over against the Protestants, described justification as "not the remission of sins alone, but also the sanctification and renovation of the interior man through the voluntary reception of grace and of gifts, through which, from being an unjust man, he becomes a just man."[1] As a result of justification, the Council proclaimed, "We are renewed in the spirit of our mind,

---

[1] H. J. D. Denzinger and P. Hünermann, *Enchiridion symbolorum: definitionum et declarationum de rebus fidei et morum*, bilingual version of the 37th ed. (Barcelona, Spain: Herder, 1976), 1528.

and not only are we regarded, but we are truly called and are just, receiving justice within us."[2] This clearly is an antithesis to the Protestant understanding of justification as God's gratuitously regarding Christians as if they had lived as righteously as Christ.

2. Merit

Catholics believe that justification makes a human being so good that he merits eternal life, as a matter of justice and not merely of grace. "It must be believed," the Council of Trent taught, "that to the justified themselves, nothing further is lacking from being reckoned indeed, by these works that are performed in God, fully to have satisfied the divine law for this state of life and truly to have merited eternal life."[3] Again the Council declared:

> If anyone shall have said that the good works of the justified man are the gifts of God in such a way that they are not also the good merits of the justified man himself or that the one justified by these good works . . . does not truly merit increase of grace, life eternal, and his own attainment of life eternal (if, however, he shall have departed in grace) and also increase of glory: may he be anathema.[4]

Catholics believe, then, that one is justified not by grace instead of works but by both grace and works, a position the Reformers found not only unacceptable but positively abhorrent.

3. Satisfaction

Catholics hold that when God, through the mediation of a priest in the sacrament of penance, forgives postbaptismal sins, he thereby removes the guilt of those sins, but not the sinner's liability to punishment. The sinner himself, Catholics believe, either in this world or in purgatory, must bear the punishment he deserves for the sin in question. By his own suffering the sinner must satisfy or make satisfaction to divine justice. In the words of the Council of Trent, "If anyone shall have said that the entire punishment is always remitted by God at the same time as the guilt, and that the satisfaction of penitents is nothing other than the faith by which they apprehend Christ to have satisfied for them: may he be anathema."[5] Again, the Council stated,

> If anyone says that for sins, as to temporal punishment, little satisfaction is made to God through the merits of Christ by the punishments inflicted by him and patiently tolerated or imposed by the priest, but not voluntarily undertaken, as by fasts, prayers, almsgivings, or also by other works of piety, and that the best penance, therefore, is only a new life: may he be anathema.[6]

---

[2] Ibid., 1529.
[3] Ibid., 1546.
[4] Ibid., 1582.
[5] Ibid., 1712.
[6] Ibid., 1713.

The Reformers, by contrast, believed that only Christ can make adequate satisfaction for even the slightest sin and that the Catholic position on this question robs Christ of the glory due Him who has made a full atonement.

B. Justification: The Protestant Response

Luther and Calvin developed arguments to prove that the Catholic understanding of justification is false and that their Protestant alternative is true.

1. The Definition

a. Luther

Against the view that justification renders a human being so intrinsically righteous that he deserves salvation, Luther argued from Scripture that even justified persons continually commit mortal sins, that is, sins that are worthy of damnation, without thereby ceasing to be justified.

> This is clear from the Lord's Prayer, "Forgive us our trespasses" (Matt 6:12). This is a prayer of the saints. . . . But that these [trespasses] are mortal sins is clear from the following verse, "If you do not forgive men their trespasses, neither will your father forgive your trespasses" [Matt 6:15]. Note that these trespasses are such that, if unforgiven, they would condemn them, unless they pray this prayer sincerely and forgive others.[7]

Sins that suffice to condemn a human being are mortal. If saints must pray the Lord's Prayer throughout their lives, saints must be required to ask for forgiveness for mortal sins until death. Luther said this would be absurd if they did not continually commit such sins even after they received forgiveness in their initial justification.

Luther observed that according to Rev 21:7 nothing unclean shall enter the kingdom of heaven. If something debars one from heaven, it constitutes mortal sin. Yet even the slightest sin renders one unclean. Therefore even slight sins which, as Catholics and Protestants agree, all human beings constantly and inevitably commit, are mortal; and even justified persons commit multitudes of mortal sins. One can warrant this conclusion, Luther observed, more directly by numerous scriptural verses. Among those he cited are the following.

> "Do not bring Your servant into judgment, for no one alive is righteous in Your sight." (Ps 143:2)

> "Who can say, 'I have kept my heart pure; I am cleansed from my sin'?" (Prov 20:9)

> "Though a righteous man falls seven times, he will get up." (Prov 24:16)

> "There is certainly no righteous man on the earth who does good and never sins." (Eccl 7:20)

---

[7] Martin Luther, *Luther's Works*, ed. J. Pelikan and H. T. Lehmann, vol. 31 (St. Louis: Concordia, 1957), 46.

"I do not do the good that I want to do, but I practice the evil I do not want to do." (Rom 7:19)

"In my inner self I joyfully agree with God's law. But I see a different law in the parts of my body, waging war against the law of my mind and taking me prisoner to the law of sin in the parts of my body." (Rom 7:22–23)

"The flesh desires what is against the Spirit, and the Spirit desires what is against the flesh; these are opposed to each other, so that you don't do what you want." (Gal 5:17)

"If we say, 'We have no sin,' we are deceiving ourselves, and the truth is not in us." (1 John 1:8)

Luther recognized that Catholics do not believe that God seriously requires from human beings the perfect love demanded in, say, Deut 6:5: "Love the Lord your God with all your heart, with all your soul, and with all your strength." Luther replied to Catholics, "Of whom does he then demand it? Of stone and wood? Or of cattle? This is an error, for it is stated in Rom 3[:19], 'Now we know that whatever the law says, it speaks to those who are under the law.' Therefore it is a command for us and is demanded of us."[8] If God did not demand such perfect love of Christians, Luther charged, Christ would be guilty of falsehood when He stated that "until heaven and earth pass away, not the smallest letter or one stroke of a letter will pass from the law until all things are accomplished" (Matt 5:18). Luther concluded that the justified, who, as even Catholics agree, rarely if ever perform acts of perfect love, continually commit mortal sins.

Of course Luther did not insist on the sinfulness of the justified person in order to lower the standard of Christian living. He reacted, rather, to the Catholic teaching that concupiscence, that is, unlawful desire, does not constitute a sin. In the words of the Council of Trent:

> That concupiscence or kindling [of the fire of sin] remains in the baptized, this holy synod confesses and perceives; which, although it is left for struggle [*ad agonem*], does not suffice to injure those who do not consent to it and who manfully fight back through the grace of Jesus Christ. He who strives lawfully, therefore, shall indeed be crowned. This concupiscence, although the Apostle sometimes calls it sin,[9] the holy synod declares the Catholic Church never to have understood to be called sin, because it is truly and properly sin in the regenerate, but because it is from sin and inclines to sin. If anyone, however, thinks the contrary: may he be anathema.[10]

In spite of seemingly unmistakable biblical testimony to the contrary,[11] the Catholic Church teaches that concupiscence does not constitute sin in order to render its view

---

[8] Ibid., 31:62.

[9] Denzinger and Hünermann list Rom 6:12–15 and 7:7,14–20 as examples.

[10] Ibid., 1515.

[11] In Rom 7:7 Paul stated that he learned what sin is from the tenth commandment, which forbids unlawful desire (concupiscence).

of justification credible. For according to the Catholic doctrine of justification, the baptized person, so long as he retains the grace of justification conferred in baptism, commits no sin in the proper sense of the term. Again in the Council's words,

> If anyone denies that through the grace of our Lord Jesus Christ, which is conferred in baptism, that the guilt of original sin is remitted or, likewise, asserts that all that, which has the true and proper nature of sin, is not removed, but says that it is only scratched out or not imputed: may he be anathema. For in the regenerate, God hates nothing.[12]

The reality of concupiscence sharply contradicts this roseate portrayal of the most saintly Christian's nature in this life. Martin Luther insisted on the sinfulness of concupiscence and of all thoughts, words, and deeds that do not measure up to the standard of Deut 6:5 in order to show human beings guilty who imagine themselves free of mortal sin. Thus he sought, first, to induce persons to seek salvation through Christ rather than the "filthy rags" (Isa 64:6 KJV) of their own righteousness; second, to raise the standard of Christian morality; and, third, to show that whatever justification is it is not an infusion of righteousness that renders human beings worthy of eternal life in heaven.

b. Calvin

Since in Calvin's words, "He is said to be justified in God's sight who is both reckoned righteous in God's judgment and has been accepted on account of his righteousness," Calvin held that justification in the Pauline sense of the term "consists in the remission of sins and the imputation of Christ's righteousness."[13]

In defense of this definition of justification, Calvin offered at least two arguments. First, he contended, the word *justify* in Scripture means not to make righteous but to declare righteous. When Luke, for example, wrote that the people justified God (Luke 7:29), he did not mean that the people made God righteous. Instead he meant that they acknowledged God's righteousness and thereby praised Him. And when Christ rebuked the Pharisees for justifying themselves (Luke 16:15), He did not condemn them for acquiring righteousness; He condemned them, rather, for laying claim to a righteousness they did not possess.[14]

Second, Calvin argued that Paul employed the term *justify* in the sense of "to acquit the guilt of him who was accused."[15] In Romans 4, for example, after speaking of Abraham's justification, Paul illustrated the concept with these words: "Likewise, David also speaks of the blessing of the man God credits righteousness to apart from works. 'How joyful are those whose lawless acts are forgiven and whose sins are covered! How joyful is the man the Lord will never charge with sin!'" (Rom 4:6–7). The concept Paul illustrates in this passage is not an infusion of righteousness but an

---

[12] Denzinger and Hünermann, *Enchiridion symbolorum,* 1515.

[13] J. Calvin, *Institutes of the Christian Religion,* trans. F. L. Battles; ed. J. T. McNeill (Philadelphia: Westminster, 1960), §3.11.2, pp. 726–27.

[14] Ibid., §3.11.3, p. 727.

[15] Ibid., §3.11.3, p. 728.

acquittal, a verdict of "not guilty" pronounced on a person, notwithstanding his sins.[16] Calvin concluded that "justification" in the sense in which Paul employs the term signifies God's reckoning a person righteous and accepting him on that account.

2. Merit

a. Luther

In response to the Catholic claim that the justified person merits heaven, Luther argued that the Scripture passages that promise heaven to the saints as a reward for their good deeds need not imply that human beings can merit heaven. For, he observes, "reward is either a matter of worthiness or of consequence."[17] That is, the reward of an action may be a recompense for merit, but it also may be a mere consequence that follows some action. Scripture verses about heavenly rewards therefore do not by themselves resolve the question of whether human beings can merit heaven.

More important in this regard, in Luther's view at least, are two considerations. First, justified persons sin even in every relatively virtuous act inasmuch as they do not satisfy the divine standard of perfection. Although God Himself performs the good works of Christians in them, Luther contended, they are nonetheless sinful. "If someone cuts with a rusty and rough hatchet," he writes, "even though the worker is a good craftsman, the hatchet leaves bad, jagged, and ugly gashes. So it is when God works through us."[18] Therefore since all human works are sinful, no human being can merit heaven.

Second, the idea that human beings should seek to merit salvation by their own works, rather than by relying on the blood Christ shed on the cross, detracts, in Luther's view, from the honor of Christ. Those who argue that human beings merit their own salvation, Luther maintains:

> wish to make us more perfect than our Savior, because they attribute that which is the greatest to works and that which is least to Christ and faith. Even if Christ merits forgiveness of sins for us, we must still save ourselves. . . . These absurdities bring darkness into the minds of men. For they assume that Christ must not be the Savior, that he made us safe from original sin, and that we must later become perfect by ourselves.[19]

By these statements Luther did not intend to discourage good works or lower the standard of Christian morality. Rather, he insisted that the person who does not perform good works is a counterfeit Christian, whose faith is insincere. "Works are necessary to salvation," he writes, "but they do not cause salvation, because faith alone gives life. On account of the hypocrites we must say that good works are necessary to salvation. It is necessary to work."[20] Luther argued against the view that Christians merit

---

[16] Cf. Calvin, *Institutes of the Christian Religion*, §3.11.4, p. 729.
[17] Luther, *Luther's Works*, 33 (1971): 152.
[18] Ibid., 31 (1957): 45.
[19] Ibid., 34 (1960): 163–64.
[20] Ibid., 165.

salvation by their works. But this was not to discourage such works but to vindicate the honor of Christ.

b. Calvin

Like Luther, Calvin maintained that sin adheres even to the good works of justified persons and that God accepts them as sacrifices only because Christians offer them through the mediator, Jesus Christ.

> Because the godly, encompassed with mortal flesh, are still sinners, and their good works are as yet incomplete and redolent of the vices of the flesh, he can be propitious neither to the former [the persons] nor to the latter [the works] unless he embrace them in Christ rather than in themselves. In this sense we are to understand those passages which attest that God is kind and merciful to the keepers of righteousness.[21]

Calvin affirmed, therefore, that the good works of Christians are pleasing in God's sight without implying in the slightest that they merit eternal life; for it is Christ and not Christians who render their works acceptable to the Father.

3. Satisfaction

a. Luther

Against the Roman Catholic teaching that Christians can receive remission from the guilt of postbaptismal sins through the sacrament of penance, but that Christians themselves must suffer punishment for these sins nonetheless, Luther advanced two arguments. First this doctrine, he said, has given rise to grave abuses.

> This matter of *satisfactio*, "satisfaction," is the source and origin, the door and entrance to all the abominations of the papacy. . . . Had the notion of satisfaction not arisen, then indulgences, pilgrimages, brotherhoods, masses, purgatory, monasteries, convents, and most abominations would not have been invented, and the papacy would not have grown so rich and fat.[22]

Second Luther contended, the notion that sinners themselves must satisfy for their postbaptismal sins is patently inconsistent with Rom 11:6: "If [it, i.e., salvation is] by grace, then it is not by works."[23] The Catholic doctrine, he wrote, "is nothing but self-righteousness, a holiness based on works" of the sort that Scripture unequivocally condemns.[24]

b. Calvin

Against the doctrine that God remits the guilt but not the punishment of postbaptismal sins, Calvin argued that Scripture equates remission of guilt with remission of punishment. Jeremiah 31:31,34 affirms that God promised to remember the Christian's

---

[21] Calvin, *Institutes of the Christian Religion*, 3.17.5, p. 807.
[22] Luther, *Luther's Works*, 41 (1966): 199.
[23] Ibid., 138.
[24] Ibid., 199.

sins no more, and Ezek 18:24 states, "When a righteous person turns from his righteousness . . . [n]one of the righteous acts he did will be remembered."

> The statement that he will not remember their righteous acts means virtually this: he will not keep an account of them to reward them. The statement that he will not remember their sins [in Jer 31], therefore, means that he will not demand the penalty for them. The same thing is said elsewhere. "Cast . . . behind my back" [Isa 38:17]; "swept away like a cloud" [Isa 44:22]; "cast . . . into the depths of the sea" [Micah 7:19]. . . . Surely if God punishes sins, he charges them to our account; if he takes vengeance, he remembers them; . . . if he weighs them, he has not cast them behind his back; if he scrutinizes them, he has not blotted them out like a cloud; if he airs them, he has not cast them into the depths of the sea.[25]

By the same token, Calvin argued, if God does not remember the Christian's sins, He does not exact vengeance for them. If He has cast those sins behind His back, He does not weigh them. If He has blotted out the Christian's sins like a cloud, He does not scrutinize them. If He has cast them into the depths of the sea, He does not air them. In Scripture therefore a statement that God remits the guilt of sin also includes the fact that He remits the punishment.

God afflicts Christians in this life, Calvin reasoned, not to punish them for their sins but to discipline and purify them (Heb 12:5–11). One ought to distinguish, therefore, between "the judgment of vengeance" that God exacts from His enemies and the "judgment of chastisement" He lovingly inflicts on His children.[26]

> The one is the act of a judge, the other, of a father. For when a judge punishes an evildoer, he weighs his transgression and applies the penalty to the crime itself. But when a father quite severely corrects his son, he does not do this to take vengeance on him or to maltreat him, but rather to teach him and to render him more cautious.[27]

The truth that Christians suffer painful consequences for their sins in this life, Calvin argued, need not imply that the God who remits Christians' guilt does not also remit their punishment. When one considers the reality of God's fatherly judgment of chastisement, Christ's suffering of His people's punishment on the cross,[28] and the sinfulness of Christians' best works in this life,[29] one cannot reasonably conclude that Christians do or even can make satisfaction for postbaptismal transgressions.

C. Scripture and Tradition: The Roman Catholic Position

The Roman Catholic view on Scripture and tradition has been discussed earlier. This section includes two statements from the Council of Trent that document the

---

[25] Calvin, *Institutes of the Christian Religion*, §3.4.29, p. 656.
[26] Ibid., §3.4.31, p. 659.
[27] Ibid.
[28] Ibid., §3.4.30, p. 657.
[29] Ibid., §3.4.28, p. 655.

Catholic position. The first is an endorsement of a two-source theory of revelation, which ascribes equal authority to Scripture and unwritten apostolic traditions.

> The sacred, ecumenical, and general Tridentine synod . . . seeing that this truth and instruction [i.e., the truth and instruction of the gospel; the Christian revelation] are contained in the written books and in the unwritten traditions, which having been received by the Apostles from the mouth of Christ himself, or from the Apostles themselves, the Holy Spirit dictating, have come down even to us, transmitted, as it were, from hand to hand, following the examples of the orthodox Fathers, receives and venerates with an equal affection of piety and reverence all of the books, as much of the Old as of the New Testament, since one God is the author of each, and the traditions themselves, pertaining to faith as well as to morals, as either from Christ's own mouth or dictated by the Holy Spirit, and conserved by a continuous succession in the Catholic Church.[30]

The second, briefer conciliar pronouncement concerns the Catholic Church's rules for the interpretation of Scripture. "The synod decrees that no one . . . shall dare to interpret sacred Scripture contrary to that sense, which holy mother Church, whose it is to judge of the true sense and interpretation of the holy Scriptures, has held and does hold, or contrary to the unanimous consensus of the Fathers."[31]

D. Scripture and Tradition: The Protestant Response

The convictions enunciated in these two pronouncements of the Council of Trent run counter to one of the Reformers' most fundamental principles, namely, that Scripture alone possesses indisputable authority in the church. The following paragraphs survey a portion of Luther's and Calvin's responses to the Catholic position on this subject.

1. Luther

Against the Catholic concept of an authoritative interpretation of Scripture by the church, Luther argued, first, that the church fathers and councils contradicted each other on a massive scale.

> It is obvious that the councils are not only unequal, but also contradictory. The same is true of the fathers. If we should try to bring them into accord with one another, far greater discord and disputes would ensue than at present, and we would never get out of it. . . . All our labor and trouble would be futile, and the evil would only be aggravated.[32]

In Luther's view the "unanimous consensus of the Fathers," to which the Council of Trent appealed, simply does not exist. Councils and fathers thus offer no clear guidance as to the interpretation of Scripture or the governance of the church.

---

[30] Denzinger and Hünermann, *Enchiridion*, 783.
[31] Ibid., 785–86.
[32] Luther, *Luther's Works*, 41 (1966): 20–21.

Second, Luther reasoned that one ought to interpret Scripture by Scripture, regarding it alone as absolutely authoritative because this is precisely the procedure adopted by the fathers.

> One must know, that Scripture without any glosses is the sun and the whole light from which all teachers receive their light, and not vice versa. This can be seen from the following: when the fathers teach something, they do not trust to their own teaching. They are afraid it is too obscure and too uncertain; they run to Scripture and take a clear passage from it to illumine their own point. . . . In the same way, when they interpret a passage in Scripture, they do not do so with their own sense or words. . . . Instead, they add another passage which is clearer and thus illumine and interpret Scripture with Scripture.[33]

Protestants who acknowledge the church fathers as authoritative sources neither of oral tradition nor of scriptural interpretation follow the fathers more faithfully than the Catholics, in Luther's view, because they emulate the fathers' submission to the authority of Scripture.

Third, against the two-source theory of revelation espoused by mainstream, sixteenth-century Roman Catholicism, Luther argued that an authoritative oral tradition, especially when coupled with a living authority competent to identify, promulgate, and interpret it, would render Scripture superfluous. "If the Christian faith depended on men or were based on the words of men, what need would there be then for Holy Scripture? Or why should God have given it? Let us shove it under the bench."[34]

If God gave the church an authoritative tradition and an authoritative interpreter of this tradition, Scripture would be useless and even harmful. For unlike the tradition Scripture would be publicly available and thus subject to false interpretation, a platform, as it were, from which heretics could challenge the tradition and its infallible interpretation.

Both sides in this debate agreed that Scripture is unquestionably revealed and authoritative. If this is the case, however, then it seems a priori improbable that God would have supplemented this revelation with an amorphous but equally authoritative tradition, which could give rise to at least apparent conflicts between a written and an oral source of revelation. Naturally only historical evidence could determine definitively which, if either, of the two putative sources of revelation is actually revealed. Nevertheless, since God is not the author of confusion (1 Cor 14:33), He would reveal either one or the other as having divine authority. So if both parties of the debate agree that God revealed Scripture, considerations of antecedent probability heavily favor the Protestant view that Scripture constitutes the church's only source of special revelation.

---

[33] Ibid., vol. 39 (1970): 164.
[34] Ibid., 41 (1966): 49.

2. Calvin

The Catholics claim that God preserves the Catholic Church from error and that one ought therefore to trust her authorities' dicta about tradition and the interpretation of Scripture unconditionally. However, Calvin observed that according to scriptural prophecy the rulers and teachers of the church may lead her astray.

> Peter's words are clear: "As there were," he says, "false prophets among the ancient folk, so also among you there will be false teachers, secretly bringing in destructive heresies" [2 Pet 2:1 p.]. Do you see how he predicts that danger threatens, not from the common people, but from those who boast the title of teachers and pastors? Moreover, how often did Christ and his apostles foretell that pastors would pose the greatest dangers to the church [Matt 24:11,24; Acts 20:29–30; 1 Tim 4:1; 2 Tim 3:1 ff.; 4:3]? Indeed, Paul plainly shows that Antichrist will sit in no other place than the temple of God [2 Thess 2:4]. By this he means that the terrible calamity of which he there speaks will come from no other source than from those who will sit as pastors in the church.[35]

Calvin maintained therefore that Christians ought to be vigilant and protest when the church departs from the teaching of God's Word. The statement, "The church says so," Calvin insists, does not constitute a compelling theological argument. Of the numerous theologians of his time who affirmed the opposite, he observed:

> These utterly stupid men . . . [do not] realize that they are singing the same song that those once sang who were fighting against God's Word. For thus did Jeremiah's enemies array themselves against the truth: "Come, and we shall make plots against Jeremiah, for the law shall not perish from the priest, nor counsel from the wise, nor the word from the prophet" [Jer 18:18].[36]

According to Calvin, Scripture's warnings of massive apostasy led by authorities in the church ought to disabuse Christians of the illusion that their leaders always merit trust. In matters of theology and scriptural interpretation Calvin concluded that Christians ought by no means to place unreserved confidence in the teaching authority of the Catholic Church.

E. The Significance of the Institutional Church for Salvation: The Roman Catholic Position

A third principal disagreement concerns what Catholics regard as the sacrament of penance. In this rite one confesses at least his mortal sins to a priest and receives, according to Catholic belief, absolution through the priest's exercise of his power to forgive sins. Orthodox Catholics believe that every Catholic priest receives this power in ordination by virtue of the apostles' bestowal of it, along with the ability to communicate it, to bishops and their successors in ordination.

---

[35] Calvin, *Institutes of the Christian Religion*, §4.9.4, pp. 1168–69.
[36] Ibid., §4.9.5, p. 1169.

Sixteenth-century Catholics considered absolution through the sacrament of penance (or at least the desire for such absolution) indispensable to the salvation of persons who commit "mortal" sins after baptism. As the Council of Trent explains:

> For those who after baptism fall into sin, Christ Jesus instituted the sacrament of penance, when he said "Receive the Holy Spirit: whose sins you shall have remitted, they are remitted; whose you retain, they are retained" [John 20:22b–23]. Hence it must be taught that the penance of a Christian man after a fall is much different from his baptismal penance, and that it contains not merely cessation from sins and detestation of them . . . but also the sacramental confession of the same, at least in desire and to be made in its season, and sacerdotal absolution.[37]

F. The Significance of the Institutional Church for Salvation: The Protestant Response

This understanding of the Christian's repentance and restoration to grace was abhorrent to Luther and Calvin, each of whom denied that to achieve salvation one must have the aid of (or a desire for the aid of) one ordained by a bishop in apostolic succession. The doctrine appeared doubly repulsive to Calvin inasmuch as he considered it inconceivable that a believer could fall from saving grace. Calvin and Luther offered compelling arguments against the idea that absolution by a Catholic priest is necessary for salvation.

A priest possesses the power to forgive sins in the sacrament of penance, according to Catholicism, only if the Catholic account of the distribution of powers by the apostles to what Catholics consider their successors is correct. In this account the apostles ordained three orders of ministry: bishops (who correspond to the biblical *episkopoi*), priests (who correspond to biblical presbyters), and deacons. Bishops, the Catholic Church teaches, are the successors of the apostles, each of whom is to rule as a monarch in his own territory or diocese.

To the bishops, according to this theory, the apostles conveyed certain quasi-magical powers such as forgiving sins and bringing about (by the utterance of a few words) the transubstantiation of the Eucharistic elements. The apostles also bestowed on the bishops the right to rule over priests in their jurisdiction. Furthermore the apostles bestowed on bishops the power to ordain other bishops, priests, and deacons, and to pass on all of their quasi-magical powers to other bishops and (all except that of ordination) to priests. Thus the bishops were to perpetuate the existence of an institution whose bishops and priests possess the power, among other things, to forgive sins.

Luther and Calvin recognized, however, that the New Testament identifies the offices of presbyter and bishop, and it thus falsifies the Catholic position on the priesthood. The key scriptural verses in this regard are Acts 20:17,28; Phil 1:1; and Titus 1:5–7. Calvin explains:

---

[37] Denzinger and Hünermann, *Enchiridion*, 1542–43.

In indiscriminately calling those who rule the church "bishops," "presbyters," "pastors,' and "ministers," I did so according to Scriptural usage, which interchanges these terms. For to all who carry out the ministry of the Word, it accords the title of "bishops." So in Paul, when he has bidden Titus to appoint presbyters for each town [Titus 1:5], there follows immediately "for a bishop must be blameless" [Titus 1:7], etc. Elsewhere he greets a number of bishops in one church. And in The Acts it is related that he convened the Ephesian presbyters [Acts 20:17], whom he calls "bishops" in his speech [Acts 20:28].[38]

Since the narrative that legitimates the sacrament of penance is false, participation in this pseudo-sacrament is unwarranted. The Reformers, as already seen, had ample grounds for opposing the rite in addition to their historical objections. Sacramental penance gives honor to the priest, which in the Reformers' view God has reserved for Himself alone, and it fosters reliance on works and ritual for salvation. In these respects the rite is not only unwarranted, but from the Reformers' perspective it is positively sacrilegious.

III. CONCLUSION

In each of the three principal disputes of the Reformation—justification, the relative authority of Scripture and tradition, and the significance of the institutional church for salvation—the Reformers presented weighty, compelling arguments for their position. The issues discussed in this chapter hardly exhaust the range of subjects about which the Reformers disagreed with the Catholic Church. These other areas of disagreement included the propriety of invoking saints and angels; the existence or nonexistence of limbo; the status of marriage, extreme unction, and confirmation, which Catholics consider sacraments; the advisability of clerical celibacy and monastic vows; the relative authority of laity and clergy in the church; and the relationship of the church to secular governments.

---

[38] Calvin, *Institutes of the Christian Religion*, §4.3.8, p. 1060. See Luther's similar comments in *Luther's Works*, 39 (1970): 155.

Chapter 14

ENLIGHTENMENT AND POST-ENLIGHTENMENT APOLOGETICS

THE APOLOGISTS OF THE SEVENTEENTH, EIGHTEENTH, and nineteenth centuries struggled to counteract the baneful influence of this period's numerous critics of the Christian faith, including Herbert of Cherbury (1583–1648), John Toland (1670–1722), Thomas Hobbes (1588–1679), François-Marie Arouet (also known as Voltaire; 1694–1778), G. E. Lessing (1729–81), David Hume (1711–76), and Ludwig Feuerbach (1804–72). These men and others like them are largely responsible for the abandonment of orthodox Christianity by most of the European intelligentsia during this period. This chapter chronicles the efforts of Christian apologists to respond to the concerns of three groups of skeptics of Christianity in this era: deists, atheists, and those firmly committed to neither deism nor atheism but who question the rationality of religious belief.

I. APOLOGETICS TO DEISTS

Deism, which flourished in the seventeenth and eighteenth centuries, is the belief that one God exists, usually a God who rewards virtue and punishes vice, coupled with a denial that any of the revealed religions (Christianity, Judaism, and Islam), is literally true. Some well-known deists include Ethan Allen (1738–89), Thomas Paine (1737–1809), Benjamin Franklin (1706–90), and Thomas Jefferson (1743–1826). Deists, especially in the period covered by the present chapter, oppose Christianity and other revealed religions primarily on two grounds. First, they believe that a just God would not communicate a historical revelation to a relatively small number of persons and then require all of humanity to embrace it as a condition for salvation. Second, they believe a just God would make the authenticity of any revelation He might propose unmistakable so that no one could plead the excuse of ignorance. The following pages survey the responses to these difficulties proposed by Joseph Butler (1692–1752) in his *Analogy of Religion*, a work almost universally acknowledged to be the most incisive critique of deism ever composed.

A. The Scandal of Particularity

The first is Butler's response to the objection that a just God would not make belief in a historical religion, such as Christianity or Islam, a prerequisite of salvation. Historical religions, an objector may correctly observe, do not confine themselves to teaching only what everyone, everywhere, at every time may verify by inspecting natural revelation. Such religions claim, rather, to possess a *special* revelation, delivered to particular persons at particular times, a revelation that is accessible to some persons and yet at least potentially unknown to many others. If any historical religion is true, an objector could declare, God does not give every human being an equal opportunity to attain salvation; and this, in the view of many, would be an egregious injustice on the part of God.

In his response to this objection, Butler acknowledges that the Christian God, if He exists, distributes religious privileges unequally. Butler observed, however, that whatever God creates and oversees the natural order bestows favors with the same or perhaps even greater partiality.

> The Author of nature . . . appears to bestow all His gifts with the most promiscuous variety among creatures of the same species: health and strength, capacities of prudence and of knowledge, means of improvement, riches, and all external advantages. And as there are not any two men found, of exactly like shape and features: so it is probable that there are not any two, of an exactly like constitution, temper, and situation with regard to the goods and evils of life.[1]

Indeed, Butler asserted, profound inequalities in religious privileges would remain even if God supplied the same information about Himself to everyone.

> Were revelation universal yet from men's different capacities of understanding, from the different lengths of their lives, their different educations, and other external circumstances, and from their difference of temper and bodily constitution; their religious situations would be widely different, and the disadvantage of some in comparison with others, perhaps, altogether as much as at present.[2]

One might reply to all this that Butler has simply shown that the God of nature is as arbitrary and tyrannical as the God of Christianity, and thus he may have eased the unbeliever's transition from deism to atheism. There is much truth in this accusation. However, Butler addressed his argument to deists, who at least professed to acknowledge the existence of the God of nature and who rejected atheism. From the perspective of Butler's audience, then, his argument appears persuasive.

B. Obscurity of the Evidence for the Truthfulness of Christianity

If God actually required human beings to embrace Christianity as a condition of their salvation, an unbeliever might argue, God would have made the truthfulness

---

[1] J. Butler, *Analogy of Religion* (1736; reprint, London: SPCK, 1902), 224.
[2] Ibid., 229.

of Christianity unmistakably clear to human beings. In the present order of things, however, numerous persons lack demonstrative evidence of the truthfulness of Christianity. Therefore deists and many contemporary persons conclude that God does not require human beings to profess the Christian religion.

Butler observed in reply that the author of nature, if He exists, requires human beings constantly to make decisions of the utmost importance on the basis of imperfect evidence.

> Persons who speak of the evidence of religion as doubtful, and of this supposed doubtfulness as a positive argument against it, should be put upon considering, what that evidence indeed is, which they act upon with regard to their temporal interests. For, it is not only extremely difficult, but, in many cases, absolutely impossible, to balance pleasure and pain, satisfaction and uneasiness, so as to be able to say, on which side the overplus is. There are the like difficulties and impossibilities in making the due allowances for a change of temper and tastes, for satiety, disgusts, ill-health: any one of which render men incapable of enjoying, after they have obtained, what they most eagerly desired. . . . Hence arises that great uncertainty and doubtfulness of proof, wherein our temporal interest really consists; what are the most probable means of attaining it; and whether those means will eventually be successful.[3]

Human beings, in other words, simply cannot know whether their decisions about whom to marry, where to live, what career to pursue, what job to take, what school to attend, and so forth, will result in triumph or tragedy. Yet it would be insane not to make such decisions. For indecision itself constitutes a decision of sorts; if one refuses to decide which job to take, one decides, in effect, to be unemployed. The potential advantages to be gained by making certain decisions and the potential disadvantages that result from indecision, moreover, render it imperative that human beings make certain decisions under conditions of great uncertainty. One must, for example, choose some school to attend, for a diploma from any school is better than no diploma at all.

The potential advantages to be reaped by assent to Christianity, along with the potential penalties to be incurred by refusing such assent, thus seem to warrant acceptance of Christianity even under conditions of substantial uncertainty. If the Christian God and the God of nature are the same, and if the God of nature requires human beings to make decisions on the basis of incomplete evidence in secular matters, it seems only natural that the Christian God would require decisions under uncertainty in religious affairs as well.

Butler also observed that just as the God of nature and the Christian God allow human beings to be subject to moral temptations in order to test and improve their characters so the God of Christianity may subject human beings to intellectual trials for similar ends. "The very same account," he wrote, "is to be given why the evidence of religion should be left in such a manner as to require, in some, an attentive, solicitous,

---

[3] Ibid., 223–24.

perhaps painful exercise of their understanding about it; as why others should be placed in such circumstances as that the practice of common duties . . . should require attention, solicitude, and pains."[4]

That God would refuse to human beings the absolutely unambiguous evidence for the truthfulness of Christianity, which they may desire, does not therefore merely accord with God's analogous behavior in the moral sphere. This conduct also possesses an easily understandable rationale, namely, that God allows the evidence for Christianity to remain obscure in order to call forth in believers "a more careful and attentive exercise of the virtuous principle, in fairly yielding themselves up to the proper influence of any real evidence, though doubtful."[5] For, as Butler observed, diligent and conscientious consideration of the evidence of Christianity before one's conviction of its truth "is as really an exercise of a morally right temper . . . as is religious practice after."[6]

In any event, Butler maintained, even slight evidence that Christianity might possibly be true suffices to render a person who is aware of it morally obliged to determine to the best of his ability whether Christianity is actually true. Butler illustrated this point with the following analogy.

> Suppose a man to be really in doubt, whether . . . a person had not done him the greatest favour; or, whether his whole temporal interest did not depend upon that person. . . . In truth, it is as just to say, that certainty and doubt are the same; as to say, the situations now mentioned would leave a man as entirely at liberty in point of gratitude or prudence, as he would be, were he certain he had received no favour from such person, or that he [in] no way depended on him.[7]

Given the importance of Christianity and the consequences of embracing or rejecting it, if it is in fact true, one who so much as suspects that it might be true is therefore bound by duty and self-interest diligently to inquire into the evidence for it.

C. Conclusion

In his *Analogy of Religion* Butler seems to have undermined the deists' two most common rationales for rejecting Christianity: first, that a God of justice would not reveal a historical religion, and second, that a loving, competent God would make the truthfulness of any religion He revealed unmistakably evident. The prevalence of atheism in today's culture naturally limits the usefulness of a designedly antideistic apologetic like that of Butler. It does not, however, entirely eliminate it.

Two arguments in Butler's response to the second objection possess enduring relevance. The first is Butler's argument for the irrationality of applying standards of evidence in religious questions that radically diverge from those one applies in other areas of life. Just as one can be justified in taking intellectual risks in, say, forecasting one's

---

[4] Ibid., 236.
[5] Ibid., 235.
[6] Ibid.
[7] Ibid., 230–31.

performance in a job, so one, Butler argued, can reasonably act on less than perfect evidence when faced with the prospects of infinite gain or loss in questions of religion.

The second is Butler's argument that the nature of Christianity's claims renders even a slight amount of evidence in its favor sufficient to warrant a diligent inquiry into its overall plausibility. If Christianity is true, the guilt and penalty incurred by unbelievers has not fundamentally changed over the past two and a half centuries. If such considerations warranted earnest study of the evidence for Christianity in the mid-eighteenth century, presumably they warrant it no less today. The passage of time therefore has certainly decreased the relevance of Butler's apologetic; by no means, however, has Butler's *Analogy* become utterly useless.

II. APOLOGETICS TO ATHEISTS

Atheism, while relatively uncommon at the beginning of the period surveyed in this chapter, came to constitute the dominant view of religious questions within the European intelligentsia by the mid to late nineteenth century. A number of distinguished apologists for Christianity attempted, and did not completely fail, to stem the tide of unbelief. What little intellectual respectability Christianity retains, it owes largely to these individuals.

The principal intellectual difficulties that alienated Europeans (and to a great extent intellectual elites from around the world) during this period were two. First, it seemed and continues to seem to many that the idea of God is explanatorily idle; that it explains no significant set of phenomena that one cannot otherwise account for so that one can dispense with it without suffering a loss of understanding. Second, many persons then as now found the existence of a benevolent God irreconcilable with the prevalence of evil in the world. Since chap. 6 has already discussed this period's most successful attempt at reconciling the existence of God with the reality of evil (Leibniz's *Theodicy*), explicit treatment of this subject is not included here. However the chapter discusses the response of William Paley (1743–1805) to those who regard the concept of God as inessential to a right apprehension of the universe.

A. The Explanatory Idleness of Theism?

This period's most effective exponent of the view that human beings do require the God-hypothesis to account for a great deal of indisputable data was the Anglican clergyman William Paley. As mentioned in chap. 7, Paley introduced his famous "watchmaker argument" at the outset of his masterpiece, *Natural Theology*, as follows:

> In crossing a heath, suppose I pitched my foot against a *stone*, and were asked how the stone came to be there: I might possibly answer, that for anything I knew to the contrary, it had lain there forever: nor would it perhaps be very easy to show the absurdity of this answer. But suppose I had found a *watch* upon the ground, and it should be inquired how the watch happened to be in that place; I should hardly think of the answer which I had before given, that for anything I knew the watch might have always been there. Yet

why should not this answer suffice for the watch as well as for the stone? . . . For this reason, and for no other, viz. that when we come to inspect the watch, we perceive (what we could not discover in the stone) that its several parts are framed and put together for a purpose . . . ; that if the different parts had been differently shaped from what they are, of a different size from what they are, or placed after any other manner, or in any other order, than that in which they are placed, either no motion at all would have been carried on in the machine, or none which would have answered the use that is now served by it.[8]

From these considerations, Paley wrote, "the inference is inevitable, that the watch must have had a maker; that there must have existed . . . an artificer or artificers, who formed it for the purpose which we find it actually to answer."[9] Here Paley merely restated, though in an especially striking manner, a classic and even shopworn argument for God's existence: the teleological argument, or argument from design. The greatness of Paley's *Natural Theology* lies not in its argument as such but in its defense of the argument against eight surprisingly contemporary-sounding objections.

1. A God of the gaps?

Philosophical naturalists of Paley's time and today objected that any God who intelligently designs His creation is a mere "God of the gaps": a superfluous, supernatural explanation for particular phenomena that will in time be explained naturalistically. Paley, however, precluded the possibility that God could thus be explained away by investing creation with a certain degree of autonomy. Suppose, Paley asked, one found a watch that was constructed in such a way that it made other watches that reproduced themselves. This discovery would greatly increase the evidence that such a machine could originate only in the mind of an exceedingly wise designer.[10]

This discovery would remove the impression, moreover, that the designer is a being who periodically intervenes to fill gaps in natural processes. When one infers the existence of this kind of designer, therefore, one does not forestall scientific speculation about any individual phenomenon. One infers, rather, a truth about the universe and its origin, a truth about reality as a whole. Paley modified the argument from design in such a way that it led to a suprascientific, metaphysical conclusion, which can neither impede nor influence the conduct of natural science.

2. The unobservability of divine design

Opponents of the argument from design object that Paley can point only to the results of the design he postulated; the design itself is unobserved and unobservable so that one cannot verify by scientific means the existence of a designer. Paley's response is twofold. First, natural scientists themselves must constantly transgress the canon that limits the range of their inquiry to the observable in order plausibly to account

---

[8] W. Paley, *Natural Theology* (London: Richard Griffin, n.d.), 387a–88a (italics his).
[9] Ibid., 388a.
[10] Ibid., 389a–90b.

for the most mundane occurrences. Gravity, for example, influences even the simplest events in the physical universe, yet to human beings gravitational force is imperceptible. "Is it then to be wondered at," Paley remarked, "that it should, in some measure, be the same with the Divine nature?"[11]

Paley observed, moreover, that inferences from complexity to design need not depend on prior observation of the designing process.

> Nor would it . . . weaken the conclusion [Paley wrote of his watchmaker argument] that we had never seen a watch made; that we had never known an artist capable of making one; that we were altogether incapable of executing such a piece of workmanship ourselves, or of understanding in what manner it was performed; all this being no more than what is true of some exquisite remains of ancient art, of some lost arts, and, to the generality of mankind, of the more curious productions of modern manufacture. Does one man in a million know how oval frames are turned? Ignorance of this kind exalts our opinion of the unseen and unknown artist's skill if he be unseen and unknown, but raises no doubt in our minds about the existence and agency of such an artist.[12]

3. Flawed design?

To the objection that apparently designed organisms are nevertheless imperfect Paley replied that purposeful, complex organization in a being, which does not exist of itself, demands some explanation; and the observation that the same organism contains imperfections in no way obviates that demand, which apparently can be satisfied only by appeal to intelligent design.[13]

4. Vestigial organs?

A fourth objection was that certain parts of animals (e.g., putatively vestigial organs) are at least apparently unnecessary to the animal's function. Paley responded: "Superfluous parts, even if we were completely assured that they were such, would not vacate the reasoning which we had instituted concerning other parts."[14] Parts of the animal that exhibited the telltale marks of design would demand an explanation in terms of design regardless of the character of the animal's other parts.

5. Self-organizing properties of nature?

Skeptics of design arguments, however, frequently attempt to account for apparent purposefulness in an organism of nature by appealing to self-organizing properties of nature. Such tendencies, in the terminology of the eighteenth century, would be categorized as "laws of nature" or "principles of order." To this suggestion, however, Paley retorts:

---

[11] Ibid., 462b.
[12] Ibid., 388a.
[13] Ibid., 388b.
[14] Ibid.

It is a perversion of language to assign any law, as the efficient, operative cause of any thing. A law presupposes an agent; for it is only the mode, according to which an agent proceeds: it implies a power; for it is the order, according to which that power acts. Without this agent, without this power, which are both distinct from itself, the law does nothing; is nothing.[15]

If one wishes to conceive of a "principle of order" as something more substantial than a mere tendency, then one arrives almost inevitably at the idea of a designing intelligence. For unintelligent beings can hardly structure other beings in such a way that they fulfill their intentions; unintelligent beings have no intentions. "Order itself," Paley wrote, "is only the adaptation of means to an end; a principle [in the sense of a source] of order therefore can only signify the mind and intention which so adapts them."[16]

6. The insignificance of mere improbability

The philosophical naturalist, however, could reply that mere chance suffices to account for all the apparent design in the universe. "One atheistic way of replying to our observations upon the works of nature," Paley said, "and to the proofs of Deity which we think that we perceive in them, is to tell us, that all which we see must necessarily have had some form, and that it might as well be its present form as any other."[17] The legitimate insight that motivates this objection, it seems, is that so many different modes of organization for particular species and for the universe are conceivable that any particular mode, when ranged against the entirety of possibilities, will necessarily appear wildly improbable. Thus, improbability of organization alone does not suffice to prove design. As Paley explained, however, it is not improbability of arrangement alone that proves, say, a hummingbird to have been designed but improbability coupled with a precise adaptation of a complex system of parts to useful ends.[18]

7. Faulty examples

Paley answered by way of anticipation the objection that because one or more of his examples of design seems inapt, therefore the idea of design in nature is implausible.

> If we had never in our lives seen any but one single kind of hydraulic machine, yet, if of that one kind, we understood the mechanism and use, we should be as perfectly assured that it proceeded from the hand, and thought, and skill, of a workman, as if we visited a museum of the arts, and saw collected there twenty different kinds of machines for drawing water, or a thousand different kinds for other purposes. Of this point, each machine is a proof, independently of all the rest. So it is with the evidences of a Divine agency. The proof is not a conclusion which lies at the end of a chain of

---

[15] Ibid., 388b–89b.
[16] Ibid., 400b.
[17] Ibid., 398b.
[18] Ibid., 398b–99a.

reasoning, of which chain each instance of contrivance is only a link, and of which if one link fail, the whole falls; but it is an argument separately supplied by every separate example. An error in stating an example [therefore] affects only that example.[19]

Paley reasoned, in other words, that even a single instance of manifest design in nature suffices to prove that a suprahuman author of this design exists.

8.   *Human ignorance*

Paley also responded to the objection that human knowledge of nature is too limited to warrant acceptance of the argument from design. Paley's answer, in short, was that human beings are indeed ignorant of much of nature but that this does not imply that they know nothing at all. "True fortitude of understanding," he explained, "consists in not suffering what we know, to be disturbed by what we do not know. If we perceive a useful end, and means adapted to that end, we perceive enough for our conclusion. If these things be clear, [it is] no matter what is obscure. The argument is finished."[20]

9.   *Conclusion*

In the period under consideration Christian apologists replied cogently and forcefully to the atheist charges that (a) the God hypothesis can be explained as "idle," and that (b) the existence of evil discredits Christian belief in a single, morally perfect, and omnipotent Creator. The devastating Lisbon earthquake of 1755 and Voltaire's mockery in his novella *Candide* of Gottfried W. Leibniz's thesis that "this is the best of all possible worlds" eventually discredited Leibniz's *Theodicy*, which actually constituted the period's most powerful treatment of the subject from a Christian standpoint. Also the triumph of Darwinism in late nineteenth-century biology brought Paley's *Natural Theology* into disrepute. Although the Christian apologists of this period strove mightily to combat atheism founded on the supposed explanatory idleness of theism and on the problem of evil, these issues remain key factors in twenty-first-century rationales for atheism.

III.   Apologetics to Undogmatic Skeptics

The third audience of Christian apologists in the Enlightenment and post-Enlightenment periods consists in what one might describe as undogmatic skeptics, that is, persons who regard with suspicion all claims to certain knowledge, including those made by atheists and deists. Such persons, also numerous today, tend to consider their beliefs mere hypotheses, which they accept only provisionally and conditionally and which admit of no irrefragable proof, and which they must be prepared to revise. Repulsed by the tendency of Christians to demand unconditional acceptance of claims

---

[19] Ibid., 401b.
[20] Ibid., 401a.

for which they provide, at most, slight and ambiguous evidence, these persons refuse assent to Christianity and stand aloof from it.

To persuade such a person to embrace Christianity one must convince him that doubt is not always and in all contexts an intellectual virtue, that it is sometimes foolish or impossible to remain cognitively uncommitted. The Christian apologists who most successfully carried out this task in the Enlightenment and post-Enlightenment period were Blaise Pascal (1623–62) and John Henry Newman (1801–90).

A. Blaise Pascal

Posterity remembers the short-lived polymath Blaise Pascal as a distinguished scientist, mathematician, theological polemicist, and apologist for the Christian faith. His most distinguished contribution to Christian apologetics is his famous wager, which he set forth in his *Pensées*.

> "Either God is or he is not." But to which view shall we be inclined? Reason cannot decide this question. Infinite chaos separates us. At the far end of this infinite distance a coin is being spun which will come down heads or tails. How will you wager? . . . Let us weigh up the gain and loss involved in calling heads that God exists. Let us assess the two cases: if you win you win everything, if you lose you lose nothing. Do not hesitate then; wager that he does exist.[21]

The wager Pascal proposed seems especially relevant to the dilemma of the undogmatic skeptic because it supplies him with a pragmatic rationale for embracing theism in spite of his generalized skepticism. Regardless of whether one can know, in the strictest sense of the term, that God exists, Pascal argued, compelling reasons dictate that one ought to believe this nonetheless.

One who reads the paragraph just quoted in isolation or hears an account of "Pascal's Wager" secondhand, however, is likely to form a radically false concept of the nature of Pascal's apologetics. For this passage, especially if one includes elements not included in the quotation, seems to reflect an almost total lack of confidence in reason's ability to discern the truth about God. Read in isolation, moreover, this selection makes Pascal appear oblivious to the difficulties posed by the diversity of theistic religions for his wager. Since the passage fails to address whether one ought to believe in the God of Christianity, the god of Islam, the God of Judaism, the god of Sikhism, or the god of the Baha'i, reading the quotation out of the context could easily lead one to believe that Pascal ignored this vital question.

However, Pascal fully recognized that one must demonstrate Christianity's superiority to other theistic religions in order to induce a rational inquirer to embrace it. Thus his *Pensées* abound with passages in which Pascal attempted to prove non-Christian religions implausible. "Any man," he wrote, "can do what Mahomet did.

---

[21] B. Pascal, *Pensées*, trans. A. J. Krailsheimer (1669; reprint, Harmondsworth, UK: Penguin, 1966), §418, pp. 150–51.

For he performed no miracles and was not foretold."[22] Against paganism, he asserted, "heathen religion has no foundations today. It is said that it once had them in oracles that spoke. But what are the books that assert this? Are they so reliable by virtue of their authors? Have they been so carefully preserved that we can be certain that they are not corrupt?"[23] Speaking more broadly, Pascal wrote:

> I see . . . makers of religions in several parts of the world and throughout the ages, but their morality fails to satisfy me and their proofs fail to give me pause. Thus I should have refused alike the Moslem religion, that of China, of the Romans, and of the Egyptians solely because, none of them bearing the stamp of truth more than another, nor anything which forces me to choose it, reason cannot incline towards one rather than another.[24]

This passage, in particular, shows Pascal's sensitivity to the dilemma of the skeptic who is sympathetic to religion in general and yet so baffled by the diversity of religions as to be reluctant to profess any religion at all. Pascal not only criticized non-Christian religions but also employed a multitude of traditional, apologetic arguments for the truthfulness of Christianity.

For instance he tirelessly cataloged fulfilled prophecies[25] in order to prove Christianity's veracity. "The most weighty proofs of Jesus," he affirmed, "are the prophecies."[26] Pascal also pointed up the evidence supplied by miracles and proposed arguments from Christianity's unique suitability to the needs of human beings. In fact he seemed to embrace the entire panoply of traditional apologetic arguments in his list of proofs for Christianity.

> PROOFS—1. The Christian religion, by the fact of being established, by establishing itself so firmly and so gently, though so contrary to nature—2. The holiness, sublimity, and humility of a Christian soul—3. The miracles of Holy Scripture—4. Jesus Christ in particular—5. The apostles in particular—6. Moses and the prophets in particular—7. The Jewish people—8. Prophecies—9. Perpetuity: no [other] religion enjoys perpetuity—10. Doctrine, accounting for everything—11. The holiness of this law—12. By the order of the world.[27]

Although Pascal did consider the heart an organ of religious knowledge distinct from reason, he by no means discounted reason as a legitimate and necessary factor in religious decision-making. "If we submit everything to reason," he argued, "our religion will be left with nothing mysterious or supernatural. If [however] we offend the principles of reason our religion will be absurd and ridiculous."[28] Pascal fully recognized the significance of rational argument in the process of conversion to the Christian faith.

---

22 Ibid., §321, p. 127.
23 Ibid., §243, p. 103.
24 Ibid., §454, p. 176.
25 See esp. ibid., §323–48, pp. 127–32; and §483–98, pp. 183–203.
26 Ibid., §335, p. 130.
27 Ibid., §482, p. 181.
28 Ibid., §173, p. 83.

"The way of God, who disposes all things with gentleness," he asserted, "is to instill religion into our minds with reasoned arguments and into our hearts with grace."[29] While Pascal offered a pragmatic rationale for embracing the Christian faith in his wager, he recognized that such arguments cannot warrant Christian belief without the aid of other considerations. So he buttressed his practical case with the kind of evidential arguments that characterize conventional Christian apologetics.

B. John Henry Newman

John Henry Newman is better known for his role in the revival of Anglo-Catholicism in the Church of England and his later advocacy of Roman Catholicism than for any contributions to Christian apologetics. Newman, however, did produce one great work on apologetics, *An Essay in Aid of a Grammar of Assent*.[30] This book is highly relevant to the concerns of undogmatic skeptics in his time and the present. Newman primarily addressed the question of how the arguments for the Christian faith—which can at best show the truthfulness of Christianity to be quite probable—can justify the absolute assent to Christianity involved in living, wholehearted Christian faith. He wrote,

> How it is that a conditional acceptance of a proposition,—such as is an act of inference—is able to lead as it does, to an unconditional acceptance of it,—such as is assent; how it is that a proposition which is not, and cannot be demonstrated, which at the highest can only be proved to be truth-like [i.e. probable], not true, . . . nevertheless claims and receives our unqualified adhesion.[31]

1. Does partial evidence warrant only partial assent?

To accomplish this task Newman sought to refute the dictum of the English philosopher John Locke (1632–1704) that one ought to proportion one's assent to the power of the arguments for that to which one assents. According to Locke, in other words, one ought to give absolute, wholehearted assent only to what is demonstrable; and yield only, say, 75 percent assent to that which is only 75 percent likely to be true.[32] In opposition to this suggestion, Newman argued that everyone, including Locke, yields absolute assent to countless propositions that do not admit of absolutely certain, quasi-mathematical proof.

> We are sure beyond all hazard of a mistake that our own self is not the only being existing; that there is an external world; and that the future is affected by the past. . . . We laugh to scorn the idea that we had no parents though we have no memory of our birth; that we shall never depart this life, though

---

[29] Ibid., §172.

[30] J. H. Newman, *An Essay in Aid of a Grammar of Assent* (1870; reprint, Notre Dame, IN.: University of Notre Dame Press, 1979).

[31] Ibid., 135.

[32] Cf. J. Locke, *Essay concerning Human Understanding* (1689; reprint, ed. P. Nidditch; Oxford: Oxford University Press, 1975) §4.19.1, pp. 697–98.

we can have no experience of the future; that we are able to live without food, though we have never tried; that a world of men did not live before our time; or that that world has had no history; that there has been no rise and fall of states, no great men, no wars, no revolutions, no art, no science, no literature, no religion.[33]

Newman thus affirmed that it is impossible and absurd not to assent unconditionally to many propositions that admit of no absolutely indubitable proof. Yet one might reply to Newman that even if one must admit exceptions to Locke's rule, it seems reasonable to apply his rule when thinking about speculative propositions, whose truth is questionable at best.

Responding to this counterobjection, Newman argued that Locke's rule is incoherent because it confuses assent with an aspect of inference. Statements of the proposition "If x, then y," are conditional, and therefore they have various degrees of probability. If then the act of assent consists in the mental equivalent of just such a conditional statement, this act can admit of various degrees and one can easily adjust the degree of one's assent so that it corresponds with a proposition's degree of probability. However, if the act of assent consists in the mental equivalent of a simple assertion, "x is y," it is unconditional, and as such it admits of no degrees. In this case one either assents absolutely, or one does not assent at all; and the idea of adjusting the degree of one's assent to a proposition is absurd. Newman naturally advocated the second of these alternative positions.

According to the paradigm Newman and his opponents share, assent constitutes an act that presupposes and follows on inference. A human being first weighs the evidence for a proposition and finds it conclusive or lacking. Only then after this process does the person assent to or withhold assent from the proposition. If assent is conditional, however, Newman argued, assent is nothing but the final step in inference, and if in accord with the shared paradigm, assent followed inference, assent would merely repeat an aspect of an already completed process. An act of assent in addition to inference would be superfluous.

Presumably the process of human reasoning does not include utterly superfluous steps. So Newman concluded that if assent is conditional, there is no such thing as a distinct act of assent.

> If assent is a sort of reproduction and double of an act of inference, if when inference determines that a proposition is somewhat, or not a little, or a good deal, or very like truth, assent as its natural and normal counterpart says that it is somewhat, or not a little, or a good deal, or very like truth, then I do not see what we mean by saying, or why we say at all, that there is any such act. It is simply superfluous, in a psychological point, and a curiosity for subtle minds, and the sooner it is got out of the way, the better.[34]

---

[33] Newman, *An Essay in Aid of a Grammar of Assent*, 149.
[34] Ibid., 140.

Newman argued, however, that human experience reveals a number of situations in which assent can be present and inference absent, and vice versa. He noted, for example, that persons frequently adopt a belief on the strength of some argument and then retain the belief long after they have forgotten the supporting argument; in other words persons often infer the truth of a proposition, assent to it, and then continue to assent to it in the absence of the inference. Also it is not unheard of for persons to assent to some proposition on the basis of an inference, retain the memory of the inference perpetually thereafter, and yet gradually withdraw their assent with no more warrant than a vague suspicion that one's argument might be incorrect or reflect a distaste for the truth to which one formerly assented. In such persons the inference remains while the assent has long departed. Again, persons sometimes possess an irrefragable argument for some truth and yet never assent to it at all out of animosity for the truth itself or persons who are identified with it. Such persons have the inference but never possess the corresponding assent. Also untold numbers of persons assent to propositions with no rational basis at all and maintain their assent doggedly until they die. Such persons definitely possess assent and yet usually do not even pretend to possess an underlying inference. Newman concluded then that inference and assent must constitute distinct acts.[35]

If this is the case, Newman reasoned, assent must always, by its nature, be unconditional, that is, absolute. For if assent were conditional, it would constitute a mere aspect of inference; and this it certainly is not, as the possibilities of inferring a truth without assenting to it and vice versa prove. One cannot therefore withhold full assent to that which he really assents; rather one either assents with his whole heart or does not assent at all. Newman concluded that Locke's contention that one ought to yield only qualified assent to propositions whose truthfulness one cannot demonstrate is not only false but also incoherent.

2. Certitude and the illative sense

Having refuted Locke, Newman then proceeded to address the question of how a person can achieve certitude of truths that cannot be established demonstratively, truths such as the historicity of Christ's resurrection. On the nature of the problem he addressed, Newman is his own best expositor.

> Certitude is a mental state. Those propositions I call certain, which are such that I am certain of them. Certitude is . . . an active recognition of propositions, such as it is the duty of each individual himself to exercise at the bidding of reason, and, when reason forbids, to withhold. And reason never bids us be certain except on an absolute proof; and such a proof can never be furnished to us by the logic of words, for as certitude is of the mind, so is the act of inference which leads to it. Every one who reasons, is his own centre; and no expedient for obtaining a common measure of minds can reverse this truth;—but then the question follows, is there any criterion of the

---

[35] Ibid., 141–44.

accuracy of an inference, such as may be our warrant that certitude is rightly elicited in favour of the proposition inferred, since our warrant cannot, as I have said, be scientific.[36]

Newman's warrant for discerning which concrete inferences, that is, inferences about subjects that do not admit of precise demonstration, are sound and which are not is what he calls the illative sense. This is a kind of quasi-intuitive mental faculty by which one bridges the gap between probability and certainty in deciding questions of concrete fact. Through this illative sense, Newman asserted, one can reach a conclusion:

> not by any possible verbal enumeration of all the considerations, minute but abundant, delicate but effective, which unite to bring him to it [the conclusion]; but by a mental comprehension of the whole case, and a discernment of its upshot, sometimes after much deliberation, but, it may be, by a clear and rapid act of the mind, always, however, by an unwritten summing-up, something like the summation of terms, plus and minus of an algebraical series.[37]

This power of "supra-logical judgment,"[38] Newman insisted, does not supplant but rather supplements, logic in the ordinary sense of the term. He affirmed, nevertheless that the illative sense constitutes the source of the first principles by which logic is governed,[39] and that the illative sense "is a rule to itself . . . [which] appeals to no judgment beyond its own."[40] Disappointingly, however, Newman gave no persuasive account of why one should regard the illative sense as reliable, and to this extent he failed to explain how one can justifiably arrive at unconditional assent to propositions about concrete affairs.

3. Summary

In his *Grammar of Assent*, Newman addressed two concerns of undogmatic skeptics, in particular. First, he demonstrated that one not only ought not but cannot proportion one's assent to a proposition in such a way that it accords with the degree of probability with which one infers it to be true. Rather, Newman argued, one either assents absolutely or does not assent at all. Second, Newman postulated the existence of a faculty for concrete judgment, which he termed the "illative sense," to explain precisely what warrants concrete inferences, that is, inferences about matters of fact whose soundness one cannot verify by logic in the conventional sense of the term. Newman's hypothesis that the illative sense meaningfully reinforces the credibility of concrete inferences is, as we have seen, questionable.

---

[36] Ibid., 271.
[37] Ibid., 232.
[38] Ibid., 251.
[39] Ibid., 240.
[40] Ibid., 283.

C. Conclusion

In the period under consideration, the most distinguished Christian apologists who addressed the concerns of what may be called "undogmatic skeptics" were Blaise Pascal and John Henry Newman. Pascal has received acclaim for his wager, an argument peculiarly suited to the undogmatic skeptic, because it entirely bypasses the delicate questions of warrant and evidence. As noted, however, the concept of the wager by no means exhausted Pascal's contribution to Christian apologetics. He explored numerous other arguments in favor of Christianity, many of which compensated for the commonly acknowledged weaknesses of the wager, when considered in isolation.

John Henry Newman addressed the concerns of undogmatic skeptics even more directly and intensively than Pascal. Newman is best known for his hypothesis that an "illative sense" suffices to justify human certitude in matters that do not lend themselves to precise calculation. His proof of the distinctness of inference and assent, in which he affirms that assent is always unconditional, seems to constitute a greater accomplishment. Why? Because it disproves the assumption that a rational person cannot yield absolute assent to claims grounded in merely probable evidence.

IV. CONCLUSION

Christian apologists in the Enlightenment and post-Enlightenment periods sought to address three audiences opposed or at least resistant to historic Christianity: deists, atheists, and undogmatic skeptics. Deists object to Christianity on the grounds that only an unjust God could make salvation contingent on acknowledgment of a historical revelation and that if God demanded belief in such a revelation, He would make its veracity easy to recognize. In response to these objections, Joseph Butler observed that the God of nature, whom deists profess to worship, unquestionably favors some human beings over others to an extraordinary degree and that He demands obedience to the moral law and yet does not render such obedience easy.

Atheists, the second primary audience for Christian apologetics in this period, deny the existence of God because in their view one can explain the workings of the universe without Him and because if a good God existed, He would not tolerate the kind of evil that afflicts the world. To the first objection, namely, that the God hypothesis is explanatorily "idle," William Paley responded by defending the traditional, teleological argument against criticisms made by atheists of that time and today. To the second objection Leibniz, whose treatment of the problem of evil was discussed in chap. 6, defended the possibility that a good God might create, sustain, and even govern precisely such a world as the present one. Leibniz accomplished this in a way that neither presupposed nor implied his absurd thesis that the world as human beings know it is the best of all possible worlds.

Undogmatic skeptics, persons who abstain from firm conviction in all areas as a matter of principle, were the third audience of Christian apologetics in the Enlightenment period. As seen, Blaise Pascal and John Henry Newman responded to their audiences' distinctive concerns: Pascal, by constructing his famous wager, which bypasses the undogmatic skeptics' suspicion of Christianity's credibility by justifying Christian faith on nonepistemic grounds; and Newman, by deconstructing the claim that only absolute certainty can warrant absolute assent. Virtually all the apologetic arguments surveyed in this chapter possess at least limited relevance for Christian apologetics in the twenty-first century.

In addition to the apologists discussed in this chapter, several others are also relevant to present-day apologetics. These include Samuel Clarke (1675–1729), who vindicated theism against the philosophical criticisms of Benedict Spinoza (1632–77) and Thomas Hobbes (1588–1679) in his *Demonstration of the Being and Attributes of God*; Nathaniel Lardner (1684–1768), whose *Credibility of the Gospel History* constitutes a massive apologetic for the historical accuracy of the New Testament; François René de Chateaubriand (1768–1848), who attempted in his work, *The Genius of Christianity*, to manifest Christianity's beauty and its contributions to civilization; and Friedrich August Tholuck (1799–1877), who attempted to manifest the self-validating character of Christian experience in his highly emotional and partially autobiographical dialogue, *Guido and Julius; or, Sin and the Propitiator Exhibited in the True Consecration of the Skeptic*.

Chapter 15

CONTEMPORARY APOLOGETICS

INGRAINED SECULARIST PREJUDICE, REINFORCED SIGNIFICANTLY BY evangelical contempt for higher learning, renders the average intellectual of today singularly unreceptive to arguments on behalf of the Christian faith. Not surprisingly then Christian apologists of the twentieth and twenty-first centuries have failed to reverse the tide of secularism that has swept the West since the late seventeenth century. Yet this period does not lack distinguished apologists.

Audiences addressed by Christian apologists in this period include (a) persons who are tempted to waver in their Christian faith, (b) persons who are disenchanted with at least nominal Christianity, (c) persons of romantic and literary sensibilities, and (d) what one might call reasonable skeptics. This chapter discusses issues of importance to each of these audiences and explains how at least one twentieth-century apologist addresses these concerns.

I.   PERSONS TEMPTED TO WAVER IN THEIR FAITH

A. Introduction

Christians who struggle with doubts and require reassurance of the credibility of the gospel have existed in all ages. The almost complete collapse of the presumptive, at least nominal, Christianity that once characterized virtually all of Europe and North America, however, has increased the number of such persons to unprecedented proportions. The crisis of confidence in Christianity that has beset all strata of Western, industrialized societies over the past century has given rise to a school of apologetics known as "Reformed epistemology" (discussed in chap. 6), whose arguments seem to be primarily tailored to doubting Christians.

According to this school of thought, one cannot prove Christianity true by objective, rational means, but one can rationally treat it as "properly basic," that is, as a belief, like the reliability of one's sense perception or memory, for which no proof is needed. The present section discusses arguments characteristic of this school, which can prove useful in apologetics to both nominal Christians and non-Christians.

This section summarizes the responses of Alvin Plantinga, the most distinguished exponent of Reformed epistemology, to five of what he calls *de jure* objections to Christian belief. By *de jure* objections he means:

arguments or claims to the effect that Christian belief, whether or not true, is at any rate unjustifiable, or rationally unjustified, or irrational, or not intellectually respectable, or contrary to sound morality, or without sufficient evidence, or in some other way rationally unacceptable, not up to snuff from an intellectual point of view.[1]

These arguments are especially convenient for skeptics of Christianity and therefore especially pernicious from a Christian perspective because they purport to supply reasons why one should not even bother considering the question of whether Christianity is true. De facto objections to Christianity—arguments that Christianity is not merely unwarranted but is demonstrably false—at least place this issue squarely on the table.

B.   Is Meaningful Discourse About God Impossible?

First among the *de jure* objections scrutinized by Plantinga is the claim that human beings could not meaningfully refer to God even if God actually existed. Since God, if He exists, is infinitely unlike all other beings, the objector reasons, it is futile to attempt to know or speak of Him. His sheer greatness outstrips the capacity of human language to refer to Him. Plantinga commences his critique of this objection by asking whether it is coherent.

> Initially, the answer seems to be no; one who makes the claim [that one cannot meaningfully refer to God] seems to set up a certain subject for predication—God—and then declare that our concepts do not apply to this being. But if this is so, then, presumably, at least one of our concepts—*being such that our concepts don't apply to it—does* apply to this being. Either those who attempt to make this claim succeed in making an assertion or not. If they don't succeed, we have nothing to consider; if they do, however, they appear to be predicating a property of a being they have referred to, in which case at least some of our concepts do apply to it, contrary to the claim they make. So if they succeed in making a claim, they make a *false* claim.[2]

Even if one disregards its self-refuting character, moreover, the warrants for this thesis are most implausible. Plantinga observes, for instance, that the achievements of contemporary science refute the claim that one cannot meaningfully refer to what one has not or cannot experience.[3] The much-vaunted Kantian antinomies (pairs of equally sound arguments for contradictory conclusions) are, according to Plantinga at least, not antinomies at all.[4] Kant claimed that attempts to apply human concepts to extra-phenomenal things in themselves lead inevitably to self-contradiction. But Plantinga states that this is simply false. Plantinga concludes that the objection to Christian belief from the alleged inability of human beings to speak of God is so lacking in coherence and warrant that it does not constitute an authentic objection.

---

[1] A. Plantinga, *Warranted Christian Belief* (Oxford: Oxford University Press, 2000), ix.

[2] Ibid., 6 (italics his).

[3] Ibid., 34.

[4] Ibid., 21–27. We argue for the same conclusion in this work's chap. 7.

C. Classical Foundationalism

Plantinga then examines the *de jure* objection to Christian belief from the putative impossibility of warranting it in a way that satisfies the standards of classical foundationalism. Plantinga defines classical foundationalism as the assumption that

> a belief is acceptable for a person if (and only if) it is either properly basic (i.e., self-evident, incorrigible [one cannot help believing it], or evident to the senses for that person), or believed on the evidential basis of propositions that are acceptable and that support it deductively, inductively, or abductively [in the manner that factual evidence supports its most plausible explanation].[5]

This assumption is highly problematic, in Plantinga's view, first, because "it appears to be self-referentially incoherent: it lays down a standard for justified belief that it doesn't itself meet."[6] It seems difficult, initially at least, to defend classical foundationalism, as Plantinga defines it, against this criticism. Second Plantinga sets forth a plausible account of how one could reasonably assent to Christianity without satisfying the requirements of classical foundationalism. After posing the question of how a Christian could justifiably believe in God without evidence acceptable to the classical foundationalist, he writes:

> The answer seems to be pretty easy. She [the Christian] reads Nietzsche, but remains unmoved by his complaint that Christianity fosters a weak, whining, whimpering, and generally disgusting kind of person: most of the Christians she knows or knows of—Mother Theresa, for instance—don't fit that mold. She finds Freud's contemptuous attitude toward Christianity and theistic belief backed by little more than implausible fantasies. . . . She thinks as carefully as she can about these objections and others, but finds them wholly uncompelling. On the other side . . . , she has a rich inner spiritual life . . . ; it seems to her that she is sometimes made aware, catches a glimpse, of something of the overwhelming beauty and loveliness of the Lord: she is often aware, as it strongly seems to her, of the work of the Holy Spirit in her heart, comforting, encouraging, teaching, leading her to accept "the great things of the gospel.". . . After long, hard, conscientious reflection, this all seems to her enormously more convincing than the complaints of the critics.[7]

As Plantinga admits, a person could accept objectively false religious beliefs on such grounds as these. Yet, as he observes, such a person would not behave irresponsibly or unreasonably in embracing those beliefs. He concludes that the allegation that Christianity cannot satisfy classical foundationalism's standards of proof, even if it is true, need not constitute a debilitating objection to Christian belief.

---

[5] Ibid., 84–85.

[6] Ibid., 93; cf. 94–99.

[7] Ibid., 100–101.

D. The Historically Conditioned Character of Human Knowledge

Plantinga then addresses the *de jure* objection to Christian belief from the histori- cally conditioned character of human knowledge. This is the objection that one who believes in Christianity believes in it by virtue of certain factors in his environment and would not believe it if he lived in a radically different environment. The point of the objection is that one cannot liberate oneself sufficiently from one's cultural back- ground to differentiate, at least in matters religious and philosophical, between what is objectively true and what merely seems to be true because of social and cultural condi- tions prevailing in particular places at particular times. One cannot reasonably believe in Christianity, the objector reasons, because one cannot distinguish it from commonly accepted but objectively unwarranted assumptions held in one's cultural milieu.

One could respond to this objection by examining the evidence for Christianity and showing that unlike mere prejudices it does not wither under intense scrutiny. Plantinga, however, opts for a distinct and more devastating mode of refutation. The thesis that one cannot justifiably believe here and now what one would not have be- lieved elsewhere at some other time is self-refuting.

> Suppose I accept [this thesis], which is a religious or philosophical belief. Isn't it clear that there are times and places such that if I had been born there and then, I would not have accepted it. If I had been born in nineteenth- century New Guinea, or medieval France, or seventeenth-century Japan, I would (very likely) not have accepted [it] . . . ; so according to [this thesis, it] . . . is not warranted for me; and once I see that it isn't warranted, I have a defeater for it; so I shouldn't believe it.[8]

The thesis in question then crumbles under its own weight. Even if one regards this ar- gument as mere dialectical gamesmanship, Plantinga continues, common sense should suffice to establish its falsehood. "Had Einstein been born in the eighteenth century," he writes, "he would not have believed special relativity; nothing follows about spe- cial relativity."[9] Moreover, Plantinga observes, many contemporary persons believe that invidious discrimination against persons on the basis of their race is intrinsically unjust. Had these persons been raised in ancient Sparta or Nazi Germany, they might well have thought differently. If the thesis in question were true, this would imply that one should not consider invidious racial discrimination unjust, a conclusion that is false and absurd. In Plantinga's view therefore the objection to Christianity from the historically conditioned character of human knowledge has little to recommend it.

E. The Arrogance of Christian Faith?

Fourth, Plantinga responds to another *de jure* objection to Christian belief. This charge is that Christianity is culpably egotistical; it is arrogant to think that one's own religious beliefs are correct even though they contradict the considered judgments of countless intelligent and sincere persons. "These charges of arrogance," Plantinga

---

[8] Ibid., 428.
[9] Ibid.

writes, "are a philosophical tar baby: get close enough to use them against the Christian believer, and you are likely to find them stuck fast to yourself."[10] For, Plantinga explains, the critic who urges this objection seems to behave just as arrogantly as does the Christian.

> If *contradicting* others is arrogant and egotistical, so is *dissenting*. For suppose you believe some proposition that I don't believe: perhaps you believe that it is wrong to discriminate against people simply on the grounds of race, while I, recognizing that there are many people who disagree with you, do not believe the proposition. . . . I think the right thing to do is to abstain from belief. Then am I not implicitly condemning your attitude, your believing the proposition, as somehow improper—naïve, perhaps, or unjustified, or unfounded, or in some other way less than optimal. . . . Am I not guilty of intellectual arrogance? Of a sort of egoism, thinking I know better than you, arrogating to myself a superior status with respect to you?[11]

As Plantinga observes, while the Christian lays claim to knowledge others do not possess, the critic who objects to this pretension lays claim to a virtue others do not possess. If then it is arrogant to claim that one is more knowledgeable than others, Plantinga asks, is it not at least as arrogant to claim that one is more virtuous? One who believes that it is arrogant to contradict others' beliefs, therefore, by this very belief falls into arrogance; for this belief contradicts the beliefs of numerous others. Plantinga reasons therefore that if the thesis in question is true, "Nobody can believe without being arrogant. . . . [This thesis] is either true or false; if the first, I fall into arrogance if I believe it; if the second, I fall into falsehood if I believe it; so I shouldn't believe it."[12]

F. The Freud/Marx Objection

Fifth, Plantinga considers the *de jure* objection to Christianity that Christian faith is irrational because it is the product of either: (a) wishful thinking (Freud) or (b) a corrupt social order (Marx). One who proposes such an objection, Plantinga observes, seems to presuppose that the only evidence theism or Christianity possesses is that persons actually believe in it. The objector regards an alternative account (even if implausible and unwarranted) of the origins of Christianity and theism sufficient to debunk them. By supplying a nonreligious account of the origins of religious belief the objector seeks to prove that no data whatsoever demand a religious explanation. Religious belief is required to explain nothing, in the objector's view; it is "explanatorily idle."[13]

Plantinga discredits the objector's contention by pointing to realities besides Christian theistic belief that Christian theism explains.

---

[10] Ibid., 444.
[11] Ibid., 445 (italics his).
[12] Ibid., 446.
[13] Ibid., 369.

> Even if the existence of theistic belief can be "explained" . . . without pos-
> tulating the existence of God, it might still be that theism itself explains lots
> of *other* things. Theistic belief is only *one* of the things that theism can be
> invoked to explain. Theism has also been used to explain the fine-tuning of
> the universe; the existence of propositions, properties, and other abstract
> entities; the origin of life; the nature and existence of morality; the reliabil-
> ity of our epistemic faculties; and much else besides. Hence the fact that it
> is explanatorily idle with respect to *theistic belief* doesn't by itself show that
> it is explanatorily idle *tout court*.[14]

One might wish to add to this that, even with respect to theistic belief, theism is not
explanatorily idle if it supplies a more probable explanation for such belief than alternative theories. Plantinga also notes that little evidence seems to confirm nontheistic
accounts of theistic belief such as those of Freud or Marx. These accounts derive their
credibility, rather, from the presupposition that theism is false, in which case something like what they propose must be true.

In this case, however, the Freud-Marx objection, the only one of the five *de jure*
criticisms considered that Plantinga does not find self-refuting, can have warrant only
if one can establish, on the basis of some *de facto* objection, that Christianity is false.

G. Conclusion

If the five categories of *de jure* objections that Plantinga addresses are sufficiently
broad to encompass all *prima facie* reasonable arguments to the effect that Christianity lacks warrant regardless of its *de facto* truth or falsehood, it follows that no *de jure*
objection by itself suffices to prove Christian belief irrational. Four of the five varieties
of such objections are self-refuting, and the fifth is credible only if it is backed by a
substantial *de facto* criticism.

The importance of this finding can hardly be overestimated.

> What it shows is that a successful atheological objection will have to be to
> the truth of theism, not to its rationality, justification, intellectual respect-
> ability [etc.]. . . . Atheologians who wish to attack theistic belief will have to
> restrict themselves to objections like the argument from evil, the claim that
> theism is incoherent, or the idea that in some other way there is strong evi-
> dence against theistic belief. . . . This fact by itself invalidates an enormous
> amount of recent and contemporary atheology; for much of that atheology
> is devoted to *de jure* complaints that are allegedly independent of the *de
> facto* question. If my argument . . . is right . . . , there aren't any sensible
> complaints of that sort.[15]

Although Reformed epistemology disappoints anyone seeking arguments that one
ought to embrace Christianity because concrete evidence proves it true, even an evidential apologist can find much of use in the work of Reformed epistemology's most

---

[14] Ibid., 370 (italics his).
[15] Ibid., 191.

distinguished advocate. The flaws of his exclusively defensive apologetic notwith-standing, Plantinga does supply arguments with the potential to open skeptical minds to the possibility of warranted Christian belief.

II.   PERSONS DISENCHANTED WITH CHRISTIANITY

The second primary audience for Christian apologetics in the twentieth and twenty-first centuries consists in individuals who in their childhood were nominal Christians and have come to regard Christianity as illusory and passé. Such persons tend to be receptive to Christian apologetics insofar as they do not regard Christianity as alien and bizarre. To persuade these people to embrace the gospel, however, one must convince them that a reasonable person of today can believe it.

The Christian apologist who excels at this task more than any other is C. S. (Clive Staples) Lewis. In his book *Mere Christianity* he addresses the problem of those to whom Christianity appears illusory. He does this by articulating an argument from moral awareness to the existence of God, and by implicitly posing the famous "tri-lemma" about Christ, that He is a liar, a lunatic, or the Lord.[16]

A.   An Argument from Moral Awareness to the Existence of God

One can conveniently divide Lewis's theistic argument from moral awareness into seven segments. The first two are arguments for the reality of the moral law from the phenomenon of quarreling and from the tendency of those who deny its existence implicitly to appeal to it. In the next four segments Lewis argues that one cannot rea-sonably reduce the objective standards of the moral law to a matter of instinct, conven-tion, convenience, or utility. Rather, one must accept it for what it is: a law that defies attempts to explain it away or replace it with some less imposing reality. In the seventh step of his argument for God's existence, Lewis argues that human awareness of the moral law presupposes the existence of an intelligent, morally upright being, which is responsible for informing human beings of the moral law's contents. The following summarizes Lewis's reasoning in brief compass.

---

[16] Josh McDowell admittedly first enunciates the trilemma in the memorable words, "liar, lunatic, or Lord" (*More Than a Carpenter* [Wheaton, IL: Tyndale, 1980], 25–34). He clearly drew inspiration from the following words of Lewis (in *Mere Christianity* [London: Macmillan, 1952], 40–41), which he quotes in *More Than a Carpenter*, 25–26:

> I am trying here to prevent anyone saying the really foolish thing that people often say about Him: "I'm ready to accept Jesus as a great moral teacher, but I don't accept his claim to be God." That is the one thing we must not say. A man who was merely a man and said the sort of things Jesus said would not be a great moral teacher. He would either be a lunatic—on a level with the man who says he is a poached egg—or else he would be the Devil of Hell. You must make your choice. Either this man was, and is, the Son of God: or else a madman or something worse. You can shut Him up for a fool, you can spit at Him and kill Him as a demon; or you can fall at His feet and call Him Lord and God. But let us not come with any patronising nonsense about his being a great human teacher. He has not left that open to us. He did not intend to.

1. Simple quarrelling

In his first argument for the reality of the moral law, Lewis appeals to the ubiquitous, all too familiar phenomenon of quarreling. When one person criticizes another for, say, cutting in line in front of him or breaking a promise to him, Lewis observes, the person criticized rarely replies, "There is no right or wrong; therefore I am above criticism." Rather in almost every case, the human being criticized, or at least one who lacks the humility to admit that he was wrong, argues that, given the circumstances of the case, he committed no offense. When abstract questions of morality enter into the discussion, each party insists that he is right and the other is wrong.

> It looks, in fact, very much, as if both parties had in mind some kind of Law or Rule of fair play or decent behavior or whatever you like to call it, about which they really agreed. And they have. If they had not, they might, of course, fight like animals, but they could not *quarrel* in the human sense of the word. Quarreling means trying to show that the other man is in the wrong. And there would be no sense in trying to do that unless you and he had some sort of agreement as to what Right and Wrong are; just as there would be no sense in saying that a footballer had committed a foul unless there was some agreement about the rules of football.[17]

In the petty quarreling in which human beings constantly engage, Lewis asserts, all human beings implicitly affirm the existence of a moral law.

2. The testimony of those who deny the objectivity of morality

Lewis recognizes that many persons, especially when it is convenient for them, assert that right and wrong are purely subjective. Yet, he notes, the same persons instantly, albeit only implicitly, contradict themselves when someone offends them. "Whenever you find a man who says he does not believe in a real Right and Wrong," Lewis notes, "you will find the same man going back on this a moment later. He may break his promise to you, but if you try breaking one to him he will be complaining 'It's not fair' before you can say Jack Robinson."[18] Even those who profess to deny the existence of an objective moral code, Lewis concludes accordingly, constantly bear witness to its existence.

3. Mere instinct?

Someone may object, Lewis realizes, that the universal testimony of human beings to the objectivity of the moral law need not indicate that human beings are aware of a moral law. It might imply merely that human beings possess a moral instinct. To this objection, Lewis responds, first, that knowledge of the moral law cannot consist in a mere instinct because human beings call on this knowledge to regulate other instincts. "This thing that judges between two instincts," Lewis asserts, "that decides which should be encouraged, cannot itself be either of them. You might as well say that

---

[17] Lewis, *Mere Christianity*, 3–4 (italics his).
[18] Ibid., 5.

the sheet of music which tells you, at a given moment, to play one note on the piano and not another, is itself one of the notes on the keyboard."[19]

Again, Lewis observes, second, that one's conscience, that is, one's awareness of the moral law, frequently favors a weaker instinct over a stronger one. "You probably *want* to be safe," writes Lewis, "much more than you want to help the man who is drowning: but the Moral Law tells you to help him all the same."[20] Conscience in fact frequently stirs one to stimulate an instinct "so as to get up enough steam for doing the right thing."[21] Hence he reasons, conscience cannot itself constitute an instinct. "The thing that tells you which note on the piano to play louder," he writes, "cannot itself be that note."[22]

Third, Lewis remarks, "If the Moral Law was one of our instincts, we ought to be able to point to some one impulse in us which was always . . . in agreement with the rules of right behavior. But you cannot."[23] As Lewis explains, if conscience is a mere instinct instead of an awareness of some reality, then human beings would possess an instinct that always urges them to do good. Since human beings possess no such instinct, one cannot reasonably relegate conscience to the moral and intellectual status of an instinct.

4. Social convention?

Others may object, Lewis realizes, that the moral law is not an objective reality but a mere convention, instilled in persons by their culture and upbringing. This objection, in Lewis's view, rests on a misunderstanding. People who mistake the moral law for a social convention

> are usually taking it for granted that if we learn a thing from parents and teachers, then that thing must be merely a human invention. But, of course, that is not so. We all learned the multiplication table at school. . . . But surely it does not follow that the multiplication table is simply a human convention.[24]

Also items of knowledge that one learns from authority need not be mere conventions. That parents teach morals to their children, he asserts, does not settle the question of whether the moral law is a product of human imagination. What does settle this question, Lewis maintains, is the reality of moral progress and its opposite. "Progress," Lewis observes, "means not just changing, but changing for the better. If no set of moral ideas were truer or better than any other, there would be no sense in preferring civilised morality to savage morality, or Christian morality to Nazi morality."[25]

---

[19] Ibid., 8.
[20] Ibid., 9 (italics his).
[21] Ibid.
[22] Ibid.
[23] Ibid.
[24] Ibid., 10.
[25] Ibid., 11.

Few if any persons naturally would seriously deny that some systems of morality are objectively better, truer at least in some sense of the term, than others. If, however, "your moral ideas can be truer, and those of the Nazis less true," Lewis asserts, "there must be something—some Real Morality—for them to be true about. The reason why your idea of New York can be truer or less true than mine is that New York is a real place, existing quite apart from what either of us thinks."[26] The morals of Aleksandr Solzhenitsyn can be truer than those of Joseph Stalin only if, and precisely because, they conform to a real moral law that is independent of human thought.

5. *A matter of convenience?*

Others may object that even if morality is not a mere instinct or convention, it nevertheless does not constitute a law that governs or ought to govern human conduct; it could consist simply in the convenience of the individual. To this objection Lewis replies that it is absurd.

> We might try to make out that when you say a man ought not to act as he does, you only mean . . . that what he does happens to be inconvenient to you. But that is simply untrue. A man occupying the corner seat in the train because he got there first, and a man who slipped into it while my back was turned and removed my bag, are both equally inconvenient. But I blame the second man and do not blame the first. I am not angry—except perhaps for a moment before I come to my senses—with a man who trips me up by accident; I am angry with a man who tries to trip me up even if he does not succeed. Yet the first has hurt me and the second has not.[27]

Since morality frequently approves what is inconvenient for a person and blames another person for what is convenient and perhaps even highly advantageous, Lewis concludes, morality surely does not consist in what is convenient for an individual.

6. *The greatest good for the greatest number?*

The notion that morality consists in convenience for an individual, one might object, is frivolous and unworthy of refutation. Yet a more egalitarian version of the same idea commands the allegiance of an entire school of philosophers, the utilitarians. These defend some form of the principle that one ought to do what is good or right, because it yields the greatest benefit to the greatest number of persons. Lewis's response to this proposal is instructive. He deems it not false but tautological. Saying that a person ought to do good because it conduces to the welfare of all humanity, Lewis asserts, is like saying that one ought to play football because only thereby can one score goals. "For trying to score goals," Lewis explains, "is the game itself, not the reason for the game, and you would really only be saying that football was football—which is true, but not worth saying."[28]

---

[26] Ibid., 12.
[27] Ibid., 14–15.
[28] Ibid., 15–16.

Also, Lewis reasons, it is not absurd to identify moral behavior with behavior that conduces to the greatest good of the greatest number, but it is absurd for one who thinks this to proceed to say that one ought to be moral because it conduces to the greatest good of the greatest number. This in Lewis's view is like saying one should not steal because one should not steal. When asked the question of why one should seek the greatest good for the greatest number, Lewis responds that one cannot reasonably answer, "Because it is the greatest good for the greatest number." Rather, one must appeal to a law, which is universally known, binding on all, and just without exception, and which human beings intuitively know is sufficient of itself to justify and even mandate action in accord with it. One must reach a transcendent "This is right" and "This is wrong," Lewis believes, in order to answer the question of why humans ought to be moral. Any answer short of this will be either tautological, like "The greatest good of the greatest number," or false, like "It will get me great rewards in heaven."

7. The moral law as a clue to the nature of the universe

Having established that an objective, binding moral law exists and that it is at least dimly known by all human beings, Lewis ponders the implications of human awareness of this law. In order for every human being without exception to know of this self-validating and supremely authoritative law, Lewis reasons, something must exist that controls at least much of the universe—something that is (a) sufficiently intelligent to know this law, (b) sufficiently upright to desire to inculcate it in others, and (c) sufficiently powerful to render all humans aware of it. There must be, in Lewis's words:

> Something which is directing the universe, and which appears in [or manifests itself to] me as a law urging me to do right and making me feel responsible and uncomfortable when I do wrong. I think we have to assume it is more like a mind than it is like anything else we know—because after all the only other thing we know is matter and you can hardly imagine a bit of matter giving instructions.[29]

Given the entire sweep of biblical teaching about God, these conclusions may seem meager. They appear sufficient, however, to undergird the central argument of Lewis's book, namely, that Jesus is either a madman, a fraud, or God incarnate, and that, since He is neither a madman, nor a fraud, He must be God incarnate, which is equivalent to saying that Christianity is true.

B. The Trilemma: Liar, Lunatic, or Lord

Jesus, Lewis asserts, claimed to be God in the fullest sense of the term. The monotheism that He shared with His Jewish listeners renders ludicrous any other interpretation of such sayings as "The Father and I are one" (John 10:30) or "Before Abraham was, I am" (8:58). If one disputes the authenticity of such sayings, Lewis observes, one still ought to confess that Jesus claimed to be God because such a claim is implicit in His authority to forgive sins. Referring to this claim, Lewis writes:

---

[29] Ibid., 20.

Unless the speaker is God, this is really so preposterous as to be comic. We can all understand how a man forgives offences against himself. You tread on my toe and I forgive you, you steal my money and I forgive you. But what should we make of a man, himself unrobbed and untrodden on, who announced that he forgave you for treading on other men's toes and stealing other men's money. . . . This is what Jesus did. He told people that their sins were forgiven and never waited to consult all the other people whom their sins had undoubtedly injured. He unhesitatingly behaved as if He was the party chiefly concerned, the party chiefly offended in all offenses.[30]

Someone could rationally behave in this way, asserts Lewis, only if he were "the God whose laws are broken and whose love is wounded in every sin."[31] A person might assert that a lunatic could claim as much as Jesus did, yet His words were not the words of a madman (John 10:21). Alternatively one might assert that Christ's claim to deity, implicit in His claim to forgive sins, betrays a satanic ambition to be like God (Gen 3:5) and be worshipped as such. Yet Christ's deeds were hardly satanic. Lewis concludes that one can reasonably account for Christ's constant, albeit frequently implicit, assertions of His deity only by accepting that these assertions are in fact true. Christ is evidently not a liar or a lunatic; therefore He must be Lord (1 Cor 12:3).

C. Conclusion

In summary C. S. Lewis in his *Mere Christianity* attempts to manifest the truthfulness of Christianity in general to persons who have had some contact with nominal Christianity but have become disenchanted with Christianity. His argument proceeds in two stages. First, after arguing extensively for the reality and objectivity of the moral law, he argues that human awareness of this law presupposes the existence of a morally upright, intelligent, and powerful suprahuman being: something that at least resembles what Christians mean by the word *God*.

Second, he demonstrates that Jesus spoke in ways that no wise but merely human teacher would. Rather, Jesus claimed directly and indirectly that He is God. Thus He must either be an incredibly audacious liar, a raving lunatic, or God. Since Christ's words and deeds show Him to have been neither a fraud nor a madman, an intellectually responsible human being must conclude that Christ is God.

III. Persons of Literary and Romantic Sensibilities

The third primary audience of Christian apologetics in the twentieth century consists in persons of literary and romantic sensibilities. These are people who combine intelligence with a pronounced tendency to think with the right hemisphere of their brains and who are moved more by ten lines of poetry than a thousand pages of dry, scholastic argumentation. The most distinguished Christian apologist to address this

---

[30] Ibid., 40.
[31] Ibid.

audience primarily during the twentieth century is G. K. (Gilbert Keith) Chesterton (1874–1936), a person who fits the romantic mold in an eminent degree and therefore speaks with special power to persons of kindred temperaments.

A. A Specimen of Chesterton's Apologetics

Chesterton's central argument in his book *Orthodoxy*, probably his greatest work of Christian apologetics, is that Christianity must be true because it captures the unsuspected truths, the paradoxical necessities, the irrational rationalities of life.

> Actual insight or inspiration is best tested, by whether it guesses . . . hidden malformations and surprises. If our mathematician from the moon saw the two arms and two ears [of a human being], he might deduce the two shoulder-blades and the two halves of the brain. But if he guessed that the man's heart was in the right place [an unexpected exception to the rule of bilateral symmetry], then I should call him something more than a mathematician. . . . This is exactly the claim which I have since come to propound for Christianity.[32]

As an example of Christianity's insights into the surprising and paradoxical, Chesterton notes that in order to change the world for the better, one must love it and hate it at the same time. One must "hate it enough to change it, and yet love it enough to think it worth changing."[33] Unlike merely "rational" moralities, ancient and modern, Chesterton asserts, this is exactly what Christianity urges one to do. Christianity, moreover, encourages both childbearing and virginity, ferocity in war and abject submission, extravagance in ceremony and brutal self-denial, limitless mercy and inhuman severity.

> The Church not only kept seemingly inconsistent things side by side [love and hate, sorrow and joy, restraint and abandon, etc.]. . . . What was more, it allowed them to break out in a sort of artistic violence otherwise possible only to anarchists. . . . Historic Christianity rose into a high and strange *coup de théatre* of morality—things that are to virtue what the crimes of Nero are to vice. The spirits of indignation and of charity took terrible and attractive forms, ranging from that monkish fierceness that scourged like a dog the first and greatest of the Plantagenets to the sublime pity of St. Catherine, who, in the official shambles, kissed the bloody head of the criminal.[34]

It is precisely this tendency not to dilute seemingly inconsistent virtues into a bland mixture but to inflame them both to a fever pitch that, according to Chesterton, proves Christianity true.

> Those insult Christianity, who say that it discovered mercy; anyone might discover mercy. In fact everyone did. But to discover a plan for being merciful and also severe—that was to anticipate a strange need of human

---

[32] G. K. Chesterton, *Orthodoxy*, in *Collected Works of G. K. Chesterton*, ed. D. Dooley (1908; reprint, San Francisco: Ignatius, 1986), 286.

[33] Ibid., 275.

[34] Ibid., 301.

nature. . . . Anyone might say that we should be neither quite miserable nor quite happy. But to find out how far one may be quite miserable without making it impossible to be quite happy—that was a discovery in psychology. Anyone might say, "Neither swagger nor grovel." . . . But to say, "Here you can swagger and there you can grovel"—that was an emancipation.[35]

Christianity's ability to combine seemingly incompatible truths and virtues in such a way as to meet the needs of human nature and to do so in ways otherwise not thought of by human beings is, in Chesterton's view, an unmistakable mark of its divine origin. Only supernatural agency, he asserted, can account for this "huge and ragged and romantic rock, which, though it sways on its pedestal at a touch, yet, because its exaggerated excrescences exactly balance each other, is enthroned there for a thousand years."[36]

B. Conclusion

Few intelligent readers can fail to be delighted by prose as scintillating as Chesterton's. Yet many could read Chesterton's *Orthodoxy* without being moved in the slightest to embrace the faith he extols in its pages. For regardless of how powerfully Chesterton's reasoning (if one can call it reasoning) appeals to sculptors, playwrights, and trombone virtuosos, it seems hardly suited to the tastes and intellects of, say, certified public accountants. For persons of certain temperaments, Chesterton's *Orthodoxy* constitutes the ideal apologetic, but only for persons of certain temperaments.

IV. REASONABLE SKEPTICS

The fourth audience of Christian apologetics in the twentieth and twenty-first centuries consists in what may be called "reasonable skeptics," that is, persons who are intent on believing what the evidence available to them indicates and willing at least in principle to do so even when its implications prove distasteful or inconvenient. The Christian apologist who most effectively addresses the concerns of these persons is Richard Swinburne (b. 1934), presently Emeritus Nolloth Professor of the Philosophy of the Christian Religion at Oxford University.

Swinburne's masterpiece, *The Existence of God*, constitutes an elaborate attempt to establish on the basis of scientific models of inference that the creative activity of the Christian God constitutes the most plausible explanation for the existence of the present universe. A comprehensive account of Swinburne's lengthy and complex argument is naturally out of the question in a work of this sort. A summary of Swinburne's refutations of seven common objections to theistic arguments, however, should suffice to convey a sense of the genius and power of Swinburne's reasoning.

---

[35] Ibid., 303.
[36] Ibid.

A. Are Unobservable Causes Inadmissible?

Swinburne replies, first, to the dictum, supposedly established by David Hume and Immanuel Kant in the eighteenth century that one cannot reasonably infer the existence of an unobservable cause from observable effects. If this were the case, Swinburne observes, one could not reasonably acknowledge the reality of protons, neutrons, neutrinos, quarks, and countless other entities contemporary scientists consider real, notwithstanding their unobservability. "Both Hume and Kant," writes Swinburne, "wrote when science had not had the success it has had today in discovering the unobservable causes of observable events."[37] This partially explains their willingness to embrace the principle that one cannot reasonably argue from the existence of perceptible beings to that of an imperceptible being. "It is sufficient," however, Swinburne observes, "to reflect on the evident success of chemistry and physics, in providing good grounds for believing in the existence of atoms, electrons, photons, etc., to realize that that principle is quite mistaken."[38]

B. Can One Explain Away a Fine-Tuned Universe?

Second, Swinburne points out the absurdity of the contention, frequently heard in discussions of theistic arguments, that since one could not exist unless the universe were ordered, and even fine-tuned, in the way in which it is, one should not be surprised at the order displayed by the universe or think that it demands some special explanation. In response to this claim Swinburne notes (a) that the earth possesses more order than is required for human existence; and (b) that human existence requires the existence of order only on the earth so that, even if the objector were correct, order in the extraterrestrial domain would demand explanation.[39] He states, however, that these responses do not strike at the most basic flaw in the objector's reasoning—a flaw he seeks to manifest by way of the following analogy.

> Suppose that a madman kidnaps a victim and shuts him in a room with a card-shuffling machine. The machine shuffles ten packs of cards simultaneously and then draws a card from each pack and exhibits simultaneously the ten cards. The kidnapper tells the victim that he will shortly set the machine to work and it will exhibit its first draw, but that, unless the draw consists of an ace of hearts from each pack, the machine will simultaneously set off an explosion that will kill the victim. . . . The machine is then set to work, and to the amazement and relief of the victim the machine exhibits an ace of hearts drawn from each pack. The victim thinks that this extraordinary fact needs an explanation in terms of the machine having been rigged in some way. But the kidnapper, who now reappears, casts doubt on this suggestion. "You ought not to be surprised," he says, "that the machine draws only aces

---

[37] R. Swinburne, *The Existence of God*, 2nd ed. (Oxford: Clarendon, 2004), 58, n. 4.
[38] Ibid., 58.
[39] Ibid., 156.

of hearts. For you would not be here to see anything at all, if any other cards had been drawn."[40]

The kidnapper, Swinburne observes, obviously misunderstands the issues at stake. For the victim does not assert that his mere perception of a mere precondition of his existence demands explanation. There is nothing remarkable about a person's perceiving realities (say, his mother and father) without which he could not exist. What is remarkable and what does demand explanation, rather, is the existence of a wildly improbable and yet obviously advantageous precondition. The fine-tuning of the universe, according to Swinburne, is no less improbable and no less advantageous than the machine's drawing only aces of hearts; it seems therefore that this fine-tuning demands explanation no less than the machine's peculiar draw of cards.

C. Does Explaining the Parts Suffice to Explain the Whole?

Swinburne responds, third, to Hume's claim that one need merely identify a cause for each member of a series of states (say, the series of states of affairs that constitutes the history of the universe) in order to explain the existence of the entire series. This claim arises, naturally, in arguments over whether one must posit a single cause for the existence of the entire universe. When the theist asserts that such a cause must exist, the atheist may respond by raising the possibility of an infinite series of causes extending backward in time. In this event the theist typically responds with words such as these: "If such an infinite series existed, each particular entity could, indeed, be correlated with a non-divine cause; the existence of the series as a whole could be accounted for, however, only by positing a cause that transcends the series."

Hume's principle becomes relevant in arguments of this nature. To this kind of reasoning Hume responds that correlating each member of a series with a particular cause of that member suffices to explain the existence of the series as a whole. Hume's principle, Swinburne acknowledges, proves correct in certain circumstances.

> This principle clearly holds, for any finite set of effects, where none of the causes of any member of the collection of effects is itself a member of the collection of effects. . . . If a full cause of one lamp's lighting up is its being connected to a battery, and a full cause of a second lamp's lighting up is its being connected to a different battery, then a full cause of the two lamps' lighting up is the connection of the two to batteries.[41]

In other words a series of entities can be accounted for by correlating a particular cause with each member of the series if no member of the series causes the existence of another member. This is the grain of truth in Hume's principle that renders it attractive to intelligent persons. In the case typically envisioned in arguments about the existence of God, however, each member of the series of states of affairs in the universe is not correlated with a particular cause outside of the series; the atheist usually denies that

---

[40] Ibid., 156–57.
[41] Ibid., 141.

anything outside of the series exists. Rather, the atheist claims that each member of the series is caused by the one preceding it in a chain that extends backward eternally.

In this case, Swinburne asserts, Hume's principle becomes untenable. For here one cannot reasonably invoke the collection of causes as an explanation of the series; the collection of causes is identical with the series. Unless the existence of the series is to remain completely unexplained, one must appeal to some cause that does not belong to the series itself. To be consistent, therefore, the atheist must regard the existence of the universe as an inexplicable, brute fact; he cannot reasonably consider the existence of the universe self-explanatory.[42]

D. Can One Reasonably Speculate About the Origins of Something Unique?

Fourth, Swinburne criticizes Hume's oft-repeated claim that one cannot reasonably speculate about the origin and development of the universe because there is only one universe. Hume reasons that one can know that a given human being was born of a human mother, for example, only because one knows that the human species is such that its members are born of mothers. As a general rule, that is, one can reasonably infer the origin of an entity only from one's more direct knowledge of the origins of other entities of its kind. The universe, however, in a certain sense at least, belongs to no kind. It is utterly unique. So Hume concludes that one cannot plausibly reason from the universe's existence in a certain state at a certain time to the manner or source of its origination because one has not and cannot observe the origination of any other universe.

Swinburne finds Hume's claim unpersuasive for two reasons. First, he notes:

> This objection has the surprising and, to most of these writers [i.e. those who echo Hume's contention] unwelcome, consequence, that physical cosmology could not reach justified conclusions about such matters as the size, age, rate of expansion, and density of the universe as a whole (because it is the only one of which we have knowledge); and also that physical anthropology could not reach conclusions about the origin and development of the human race (because, as far as our knowledge goes, it is the only one of its kind).[43]

Critics of theistic arguments who fervently believe in Big Bang cosmology and neo-Darwinist accounts of human origins would find these consequences unpalatable. This ad hominem argument, however, only hints at the root error in Hume's case, namely, the initially plausible thesis that uniqueness radically differentiates the universe from the objects within it. In his second and decisive counterargument, therefore, Swinburne asserts:

> Uniqueness is relative to description. Every physical object is unique under some description, if you allow descriptions that locate an object by its spatial position. . . . Thus my desk is the one and only desk in such and such

---

42 Ibid., 141–43.
43 Ibid., 134.

an apartment; and that apartment is the penultimate one on the left in a certain row. And, even if you allow only descriptions in qualitative terms—for example, the one and only existing desk of such-and-such a shape, such-and-such a weight, with such-and-such carvings on its legs, and scratches on its top situated in an apartment that is the penultimate one in a row of apartments—it is still plausible to suppose that most physical objects have a unique description. . . . The universe [therefore] is no more "unique" than the objects it contains.[44]

Swinburne argues, in other words, that Hume's objection defeats itself by implying that the origins and development of most if not all physical objects in the universe are insusceptible of rational investigation. Hume's objection proves too much. Swinburne explains, moreover, that the universe does possess properties in common with entities within it. "It is, for example, like objects within it such as the solar system, a system of material bodies distributed in empty space. It is a physical object and, like other physical objects, has density and mass."[45] Hume's assertion that one can rationally investigate the origins only of those entities that possess properties in common with others therefore does not imply that human beings cannot reach justified conclusions about the origins of the universe.

E. What Is the Force of Cumulative, Probabilistic Arguments?

Swinburne responds next to the objection that no combination of arguments, each of which when considered in isolation does not render God's existence probable, can render God's existence probable when considered as a whole. While the assertion that ten bad arguments are no better than one bad argument may seem plausible, he explains, human beings constantly and justifiably reach conclusions on the basis of accumulations of pieces of evidence, no one of which suffices to establish the conclusion implied by the whole. To illustrate his point, Swinburne proposes the following example:

That Smith has blood on his hands hardly makes it probable that Smith murdered Mrs Jones, nor (by itself) does the fact that Smith stood to gain from Mrs Jones' death, nor (by itself) does the fact that Smith was near the scene of the murder at the time of its being committed, but all these phenomena together (perhaps with other phenomena as well) may indeed make the conclusion probable.[46]

Common experience testifies therefore that multiple arguments, none of which renders a conclusion probable on its own, may render the same conclusion probable when considered together.

---

[44] Ibid., 134–45.
[45] Ibid., 135.
[46] Ibid., 12.

F. Can Different Theistic Arguments Support the Same Conclusion?

Swinburne replies, sixth, to the objection that one cannot combine particular theistic arguments into a plausible, cumulative argument for the existence of God, because particular theistic arguments imply different conclusions. Arguments from the necessity of a first cause, for example, imply by themselves the existence only of a nondescript, first cause, not the personal God of Christian theism. Arguments from design, however, do not, in and of themselves, imply the existence of a first cause; when considered in isolation, rather, they imply merely the existence of a cosmic architect.

Swinburne argues, however, that if this criticism sufficed to defeat all cumulative theistic arguments, it would also suffice to undermine virtually all scientific theories of broad scope. For in arguments for such theories, he asserts:

> each separate piece of evidence [typically] does not make the theory very probable, and indeed taken on its own makes some narrower theory much more probable. . . . Each of the various pieces of evidence that are cited as evidence in favour of the General Theory of Relativity [for example] . . . by itself . . . was evidence in favour of some rival but far less wide-ranging hypothesis than General Relativity. Thus the movement of Mercury's perihelion taken by itself would suggest only that there was a hitherto unknown planet lying between Mercury and the sun or that the sun was of an odd shape, rather than that General Relativity was true. Taken by itself it would not have given much probability to General Relativity; but taken with other pieces of evidence it did its bit in supporting the latter.[47]

Likewise, observes Swinburne, some theistic arguments do indeed, when considered in isolation, imply only the existence of a demiurge. This does not debar the same arguments, however, from supporting the actual existence of God in the context of a larger, multifaceted argument.

G. Is Polytheism More Plausible than Monotheism?

Swinburne addresses, seventh, the objection that arguments for the existence of God do not necessarily indicate that there is only one God; 100 gods, for example, might seem no less, or perhaps even more, competent to construct the cosmos than the one God of monotheism. Those who advance this objection are naturally aware of the difficulty posed by the principle that one ought to postulate no more causes for an event than the data require. The objectors believe, nevertheless, that considerations of probability outweigh considerations of simplicity in this instance.

The hypothesis of polytheism appears more probable than that of monotheism to the persons in question because a multiplicity of gods would correspond more closely to that which human beings experience in the world—large numbers of entities endowed with finite powers, none of which is infinite in power. To the extent that the probability of hypotheses about unobservable entities increases proportionally with

---

[47] Ibid., 19.

these entities' similarity to items of human experience, therefore, polytheism does seem to excel monotheism in probability.

1. The irrelevance of similarity to the world

Swinburne's response to this objection is manifold. The similarity of a motley pantheon of creative beings to the world of human experience, he notes first, does not justify one in setting aside the criterion of simplicity, a criterion that heavily favors monotheism, in one's explanation of the world. For one has no reason to suspect that some entity or set of entities capable of creating, sustaining, and governing the universe will resemble to any great degree the particular beings it creates, sustains, and governs. The characteristics of such an individual or collective creator, rather, will presumably diverge from those of its creatures quite as much as it excels them in creative power and control.

Swinburne reinforces this point with the aid of models of explanation used in the philosophy of science. Background knowledge about what other entities are like, he observes, becomes proportionately less important in determining what kind of entities one can reasonably postulate in a theory, as the scope of what a theory is supposed to explain expands. That is, in formulating a hypothesis about what kind of animal leaves a certain kind of track, it is important to postulate the existence of something similar to other animals that leave similar tracks. If one asks a broader question (for example, why does $e=mc^2$), however, considerations of this sort become utterly irrelevant. In Swinburne's words:

> As we deal with theories of larger and larger scope . . . there becomes less reason to postulate entities and properties similar to those that play a role in theories of neighbouring fields. . . . You cannot [for example] suppose that argon is composed of quarks, while other gases are composed of molecules that are not made of quarks. But you can put forward a theory of the constitution of all protons and neutrons, that they are made of quarks, a quite new kind of entity with strange properties not hitherto observed.[48]

Theism, naturally, is a "Theory of Everything" that one posits in order to explain the existence and character of the entire universe. In this case there are no neighboring fields with entities that God should resemble and therefore no reason to expect God or the gods to resemble items of human experience.[49]

2. The indispensability of the criterion of simplicity

Swinburne observes, second, that the criterion of simplicity is of vital importance in deciding between any competing explanations, and especially competing explanations of everything such as monotheism and polytheism.

> The enormous importance of the criterion of simplicity is not always appreciated. Sometimes people ignore it and say that what makes a theory

---

[48] Ibid., 60–61.
[49] Ibid., 66.

probable is just its explanatory power, or, worse still, just the fact that we can deduce from it statements reporting the phenomena that have been observed. . . . The trouble with this claim is that, for any finite collection of phenomena, there will always be an infinite number of theories of equal scope such that from each (together with statements of initial conditions) can be produced statements reporting the phenomena observed with perfect accuracy. The theories [admittedly] . . . disagree in their subsequent predictions. We may wait for new observations of phenomena to enable us to choose between theories. But, however many theories we eliminate by finding them incompatible with observations, we will always be left with an infinite number of theories between which to choose. If there are no theories of neighbouring fields which some theories may fit better than others [and for explanations of the entire universe there are not], the crucial criterion is that of simplicity.[50]

The rule that, when faced with multiple theories of equal explanatory power one ought to choose the simpler is much more than a matter of methodological etiquette; it is an indispensable factor in evaluating any explanation of any phenomena whatsoever. It is relevant therefore to the controversy between monotheism and polytheism as explanations of the universe; and, as seen, it heavily favors monotheism.

3. The uniformity of natural laws

Third, in opposition to this objection, Swinburne notes that monotheism's explanatory power excels that of polytheism in at least one important respect. A monotheist can easily account for the uniform operation of the same natural laws throughout the universe; if only one God governs the universe, it is only natural that He would administer His domain by one set of rules. For the polytheist, however, the uniform operation of physical laws in the entire cosmos is an enigma. "If there were more than one deity responsible for the order of the universe," Swinburne writes, "we would expect to see characteristic marks of the handiwork of different deities in different parts of the universe, just as we see different kinds of workmanship in the different houses of a city."[51] Monotheism renders probable a striking characteristic of the universe that polytheism leaves unexplained.

In the contemporary philosophy of science, Swinburne asserts, four elements are usually regarded as the sole determinants of a theory's overall probability: its simplicity, scope, conformity with background knowledge, and how probable it makes the data to be explained (i.e, the theory's explanatory power).[52] Since both monotheism and polytheism are explanations of the entire universe, they do not differ in scope. For the same reason, there is no background information distinct from the data to be explained. The question of which is more probable, therefore, must be determined by the criteria of simplicity and explanatory power. Monotheism manifestly excels

---

[50] Ibid., 58.
[51] Ibid., 147.
[52] Ibid., 53–57.

polytheism in simplicity; it also excels polytheism in explanatory power in that it renders the uniform operation of natural laws in the universe probable which polytheism does not. Swinburne concludes that monotheism definitely exceeds polytheism in probability. The objection to theistic arguments that the universe is just as likely to have been created by many gods as it is to have been created by one is thus demonstrably unsound.

H. Conclusion

The preceding summaries of Swinburne's refutations of seven common objections to theistic arguments fail to convey the cogency and force of Swinburne's overall case for theism. Even less do they exhaust the range of arguments appropriate for apologetics to what has been labeled the reasonable skeptic. These summaries do, however, at least hint at some of the main tendencies of Swinburne's thought: his preference for a cumulative, probabilistic argument for the existence of God; his high valuation of the criterion of simplicity; and his penchant for evaluating theistic arguments in terms of scientific models of explanation. The summaries do offer some sense of what kind of arguments are likely to appeal to reasonable skeptics, that is, earnest, analytically minded seekers of truth.

V. CONCLUSION

The foregoing has illustrated how the most distinguished of twentieth- and twenty-first-century apologists have addressed the concerns of four groups of persons: (a) persons tempted to waver in their Christian faith, (b) persons disenchanted with nominal Christianity, (c) persons of literary and romantic sensibilities, and (d) those who might be called reasonable skeptics. The foremost apologist to the first audience (doubting Christians) is Alvin Plantinga, eminent advocate and practitioner of the exclusively defensive apologetic associated with Reformed epistemology. Plantinga persuasively answers the objections that language about God is not meaningful; that absolute assent on the basis of partial evidence cannot be warranted; that robust Christian faith is historically naïve; that such faith is incurably arrogant; and that theistic faith, being explicable by appeal to social or psychological factors, is explanatorily idle. By answering these five objections, Plantinga renders yeoman service to all audiences of Christian apologetics and not merely those tempted to forsake their faith.

C. S. Lewis is the twentieth century's most powerful apologist to the second audience, those who have been exposed to nominal Christianity in their youth and have subsequently become disenchanted with the church. Lewis constructs a persuasive version of the argument from moral awareness for the existence of God and poses the famous trilemma, that Jesus is either liar, lunatic, or Lord. This consideration has led many, through the Holy Spirit, to recognize the veracity of Jesus' claims about Himself. For the third audience, those sentimental, romantic souls who feel a great attraction to the arts, G. K. Chesterton seems the most suitable Christian spokesman. The prose of his book *Orthodoxy*, alternately polemical and rapturous, lays bare his own profoundly emotional journey from a hardened agnosticism to an enthusiastic, mystical Christian faith in terms that can hardly fail to appeal to kindred spirits.

For the fourth audience, the tough-minded, conscientious inquirers called reasonable skeptics, Richard Swinburne seems the most persuasive of twentieth-century apologists. His close engagement with the methods and findings of the contemporary philosophy of science renders it impossible to dismiss his views as relics of bygone ages. The moderation, thoroughness, and cogency of his reasoning render his works ideal for the inquirer who insists on rigor in argumentation. In spite of the miserable anti-intellectualism that has engulfed much of evangelical Christendom, the twentieth century offers a range of apologists and apologetic arguments suited to a wide variety of audiences.

Other authors worthy of mention include Karl Heim (1874–1958), who argues in such works as his *Transformation of the Scientific World View* that quantum mechanics has rendered atheistic materialism obsolete; Reginald Garrigou-Lagrange (1877–1964), author of the masterful (and massive) philosophical defense of theism, *God: His Existence and Nature*; J. Gresham Machen (1881–1937), whose works, *The Virgin Birth of Christ* and *The Origin of Paul's Religion*, retain considerable apologetic value; Eric Mascall (1905–93), the Anglican Thomist whose work, *He Who Is*, is a classic of natural theology; and N. T. Wright (b. 1948), author of perhaps the greatest of all historical defenses of Christ's resurrection, *The Resurrection of the Son of God*. While these authors' works seem best suited to persuading those in the fourth category, that is, reasonable skeptics, their arguments are at least potentially relevant to persons in each of the contemporary audiences.

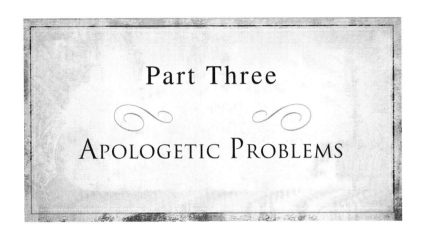

Part Three

APOLOGETIC PROBLEMS

This section deals with some of the problems confronting apologists such as philosophy, the problem of evil, world religions and pluralism, and the Bible's compatibility with modern science. Each of these topics is discussed in detail, as well as how apologists can answer them.

Chapter 16

USE OF PHILOSOPHY IN APOLOGETICS

THE THINKERS STUDIED IN THE PREVIOUS chapters exemplify how one can and should employ philosophy in Christian apologetics. The present chapter discusses in a more systematic way the character and history of philosophy itself and the means by which one can deploy philosophical reasoning in defense of the Christian faith. This chapter offers a provisional definition of philosophy, a thumbnail sketch of the history of philosophy from antiquity to the present, and an account of how Christian apologists can vindicate Christianity's credibility and desirability by philosophical means.

I. WHAT IS PHILOSOPHY?

There is no commonly agreed upon definition of the academic discipline known as philosophy. One might characterize philosophy as the science that appeals to no authority extrinsic to the mind of the philosopher, whose objects include (a) the nature, conditions, and criteria of knowledge; (b) being as such, that is, all beings whatsoever insofar as they are not distinguished by individuating characteristics; (c) universally applicable principles of reasoning and action; and (d) the logical presuppositions of all particular sciences and practices. Philosophy therefore is highly relevant to every activity and area of inquiry. It should come as no surprise, therefore, that philosophy plays a central role in traditional Christian apologetics.

II. EPOCHS IN THE HISTORY OF PHILOSOPHY

To render the foregoing definition more concrete, the present section briefly reviews three central epochs in the history of Western philosophy: the ancient, the medieval, and the modern eras.

A. Ancient Philosophy

1. Platonists

Plato (c. 428–c. 348 BC), a student of Socrates (c. 470–399), was the first Western philosopher to write a substantial literary corpus. He maintained that the truly real cannot be found among changing, sensible things. He said that these constitute mere shadows of the forms (traditionally designated Forms or Ideas), that is, immutable essences such as justice, humanity, truth, and even tableness, to which he ascribed existence apart from things that in some way exemplify them.[1] Plato is also famous for his advocacy of the immortality of the soul,[2] his belief that human knowing consists fundamentally in remembering things known in prior lives,[3] and his disapproval of democratic forms of government.[4] The last position, it is important to note, Plato retracted in large measure in his late dialogue, the *Laws*.[5] Plato's influence was revived in late antiquity by thinkers such as Plotinus (c. AD 205–70) and Proclus (c. AD 410–85). Proclus added substantial religious elements to Plato's philosophy, which many regard as alien to Plato's original thought.

2. Aristotelians

Plato's student, Aristotle (384–322 BC), denied the existence of Platonic Forms[6] and held that essences such as justice or, to choose a more prosaic example, chairness, exist exclusively in individual chairs and persons who are just.[7] Aristotle cogently argued for the existence of a necessary, simple, and immutable supreme being.[8] He denied, moreover, the immortality of the individual human soul.[9] Aristotle consistently praised the ideal of a mixed polity; the ideal, that is, of a state that combines monarchical, aristocratic, and democratic forms of government in such a way that each of these elements checks the excesses of the others.[10] Unlike Plato, Aristotle gave a relatively systematic cast to his ideas and thus offered not mere stimulating hypotheses and arguments but a full-orbed, Aristotelian worldview.

3. Stoics

The Stoics received their name from the Painted Stoa (i.e., Porch) in which the school's founder, Zeno of Citium (c. 335–c. 263 BC), taught. They held, among other things, that all of reality is material,[11] that the divine permeates the universe in a somewhat pantheistic manner,[12] and that the only genuine good is virtue.[13] The last belief led Stoics to inculcate indifference to everything but virtue. Since such indifference required an unemotional disposition and high tolerance for pain, persons even today refer to those who exemplify these personality traits as stoic. Unlike Plato and Aristotle, Zeno left no extensive literary remains. Later generations learn of Stoicism therefore

---

[1] Plato, *Cratylus* 439c–40b; *Republic* 507b–c; *Phaedo* 75b–d; and *Symposium* 210e–211e.

[2] Plato, *Phaedo* 105d–108c; *Phaedrus* 245c–6a; and *Republic* 608d–611a.

[3] Plato, *Meno* 85b–6b; and *Phaedo* 73c–6e.

[4] Plato, *Republic* 558a–c.

[5] Plato, *Laws* 693d–e.

[6] Aristotle, *Metaphysics* 1.9. 990b–992b.

[7] Ibid., 7.13.1038b.

[8] Ibid., 12.7.1072a–1073a.

[9] Aristotle, *On the Soul* 2.4.415b.

[10] Aristotle, *Politics* 4.8.1294a.

[11] Chrysippus, *Stoicorum veterum fragmenta*, ed. H. von Arnim (Leipzig: Tubner, 1903–5), vol. 2, fragment 469.

[12] Ibid., fragments 1042 and 1077.

[13] Seneca, *On Benefits* 7.2.1; see also Cicero's account of Stoic views in his *Academica* 1.10.35–36.

principally by reading works of later philosophers, such as the Roman Stoic Seneca (c. 4 BC–AD 65) and the Stoic teacher Epictetus (c. AD 50–c. 135), whose discourses his pupil Arrian (c. AD 87–after 145) recorded.

4. Epicureans

Epicureans, followers of the philosopher Epicurus (341–270 BC), believed that pleasure is the chief good,[14] that the gods are indifferent to the affairs of human beings,[15] and that the soul does not survive the death of the body.[16] Although the Epicureans themselves did not, as a rule, advocate licentious behavior, the tendency of their philosophy to encourage immoral conduct has led later generations to dub persons bent on self-indulgence as epicurean. The Roman poet Lucretius (c. 96–c. 55 BC), this school's greatest literary advocate, gave its teaching classic expression in his *On the Nature of Things*.

5. Pyrrhonists

The philosopher Pyrrho (c. 360–c. 270 BC) and his followers embraced a thoroughgoing skepticism about everything. The Pyrrhonists believed or rather suspected that any reasons that can be offered for any belief can be counterbalanced by equally persuasive objections to the belief in question.[17] Thus in the Pyrrhonists' view a person who fairly considers both sides of every question will in the end come to believe nothing at all. The Pyrrhonists, moreover, considered this a desirable outcome and sought to obtain it by opposing equally sound arguments for and against particular beliefs to each other.[18] The agnosticism induced by this practice, they believed, leads to "ataraxy," that is, an undisturbed peace of mind.[19]

The ancient world, then, contained persons radically skeptical of all religions and persons who offered a philosophical rationale for immoral behavior. In these respects it was much like the present.

B. Medieval Philosophy

The high moral tone of Stoicism, the otherworldliness of Platonism, and the ambitious system-building of the Aristotelians are notably absent from most twenty-first-century philosophies. The Christian philosophy of the middle ages, however, ennobled and intensified these admirable traits of ancient philosophy and placed them at the service of Jesus Christ.

The medieval philosophical spectrum, broadly speaking, included (a) extreme realists, such as Anselm (1033–1109) and Bonaventure (c. 1217–74), who followed Augustine in advocating a sort of Christianized Platonism; (b) moderate realists, such

---

[14] See the remarks of Epicurus quoted in Diogenes Laertius, *Lives of the Philosophers* 10.128–29.
[15] Ibid., 10.139.
[16] Ibid., 10.125.
[17] Sextus Empiricus, *Outlines of Pyrrhonism* 1.27.202–5.
[18] Ibid., 1.13.31–4.
[19] Ibid., 1.12.25–8.

as Thomas Aquinas (1224–74) and John Duns Scotus (c. 1266–1308), who assimilated Aristotelianism into Christianity; and (c) conceptualists such as William of Ockham (c. 1288–c. 1348) and Jean Buridan (c. 1300–after 1358), who made a clean break with both Platonism and Aristotelianism.

1. Extreme realists

Those who are categorized as extreme realists typically held, with Plato, that human concepts about abstract essences such as justice, goodness, and "chairness" can correspond to reality because these essences actually exist independently of just persons, good things, and chairs. Following Augustine, however, the extreme realists of the middle ages denied that every essence constitutes a being in its own right and identified Plato's Forms, instead, with ideas in the mind of God.[20] These thinkers agreed with Plato in rejecting the idea that human beings naturally derive their knowledge exclusively from the senses. They held, rather, that human beings possess innate ideas, such as those of truth, goodness, and God, and that human beings learn, to a great extent at least, not by turning outward to the world but by turning inward and investigating the ideas that God has implanted in their souls.[21]

2. Moderate realists

Opposed to these thinkers were the moderate realists who held, with Aristotle, that human thoughts concerning abstract essences such as chairness and tableness can correspond to reality but that the realities to which these ideas correspond exist only insofar as they are exemplified in particular beings. Following Aristotle, in other words, these thinkers believed that ideas such as "treeness" corresponded to something real in the world but that this real something consists in treeness as it exists in individual trees, not in an independently existing treeness as such.[22] Moderate realists, moreover, tended to hold that human beings derive all their knowledge from the senses and that the mind, in and of itself, was a blank slate.[23]

3. Conceptualists

Opposed to both of the previously mentioned schools were the conceptualists, who held that human beings do indeed possess universal concepts but that these concepts do not actually correspond to anything in the world.[24] While the conceptualist position borders on nominalism (the view that universals exist neither in extramental reality nor in the mind), it is important in fairness to medieval conceptualists to distinguish between the two.

---

[20] Augustine, *On 83 Diverse Questions*, q. 46; Anselm, *Monologion* 9–11; and Bonaventure, *Journey of the Mind into God* 2.9.

[21] Augustine, *On the Teacher* 11.38; and Bonaventure, *Disputed Questions Concerning Christ's Knowledge*, q. 4.

[22] E.g., Duns Scotus, *Ordinatio* 1, dist. 2, q. 7.

[23] E.g., Thomas Aquinas, *Summa Theologiae* 1, 79, 2 corp.

[24] E.g., William of Ockham, *Summa Totius Logicae* 1.14.

Virtually all Western philosophers of the medieval period considered themselves Christians and attempted to integrate their philosophical views with their concepts of Christianity (which in some cases were inadequate). Christians of today owe to the philosophers of this period an impressive stock of arguments for the existence of God, a clear consciousness of the distinction between philosophy and theology, and cogent answers to philosophical objections to Christian doctrines such as the Trinity and the incarnation.

C. Modern Philosophy

One can reasonably divide philosophers of the sixteenth century and later into five camps, each of which includes enormously diverse viewpoints: rationalists, empiricists, idealists, analytic philosophers, and Continental philosophers. Admittedly these categories partially overlap. Virtually all analytic philosophers, for example, are empiricists, and few if any Continental philosophers are free from all taint of idealism. The categories proposed here, however, do not overlap completely and supply a convenient framework for a brushstroke sketch of the history of modern philosophy.

1. Rationalists

The rationalists, in the specialized sense in which the term is employed here, were philosophers who believed that abstract ideas constitute an adequate starting point for the construction of an accurate portrait of reality. The philosopher Benedict Spinoza (1632–77), perhaps the most extreme exponent of this school, began his *Ethics* with a number of definitions and axioms, which in his view do not require empirical warrant; and he proceeded on this basis alone to deduce numerous and weighty conclusions about God, the world, and the conduct of human life.[25] By the late eighteenth century the Western intelligentsia as a whole had come to regard Spinoza and other rationalist philosophers as ridiculously overconfident in the power of abstract reasoning. The rationalist, quasi-geometrical mode of philosophizing practiced by René Descartes (1596–1650), Spinoza, Nicolas Malebranche (1638–1715), and others largely disappeared from history.

2. Empiricists

The empiricists, unlike the rationalists, insisted that all human knowledge derives from the senses. They tended to regard speculation about anything beyond the ken of human sensibility with intense suspicion.[26] The empiricist mentality, for better or worse, has dominated Anglo-American philosophy since the seventeenth century.

---

[25] B. de Spinoza, *Ethics* (Oxford: Oxford University Press, 2000).

[26] See, e.g., the concluding paragraph of David Hume, *Enquiry Concerning Human Understanding* §12.3.132, in D. Hume, *Enquiries*, 1748; reprint, ed. L. A. Selby-Bigge, rev. P. H. Nidditch, 3rd ed. (Oxford: Oxford University Press, 1975), 165.

3. Idealists

The third major division of modern philosophers, the idealists, either cast doubt on the ability of humans to know anything that exists independently of their own consciousness or they denied the existence of anything but ideas. Idealism is not merely a form of skepticism. In the hands of Johann Gottlieb Fichte (1762–1814) and Georg Wilhelm Friedrich Hegel (1770–1831), idealism of the second sort became a weapon for combating the skepticism engendered by the first form of idealism. If being is knowing, these thinkers claimed, then human beings' inability to know anything other than thought is no liability; thought according to this manner of thinking is all there is.[27] Idealism of the second sort, naturally, is profoundly alien to Anglo-American philosophy and ordinary Anglo-American ways of thinking. It remains influential, however, among philosophers who work in the so-called Continental tradition; the fourth major group of modern philosophers.

4. The Continental-analytic divide

The idea of a distinctively Continental variety of philosophy is inextricably bound up with the antithetical idea of analytic philosophy. This is an empirically oriented, logically sophisticated method of philosophizing characterized by distrust of the imprecise and intuitive methods of philosophizing employed by Hegel and his various successors. The split between the schools is usually dated to the close of the nineteenth century, by which time perceptions of the epoch-making philosophy of Hegel had hardened to a great extent on both sides of the English Channel. Characteristic of Continental philosophy are a deep suspicion of the abstract; an unwillingness to divorce philosophical questions from their political and historical context; a disdain for formal logic; a tendency to equate knowledge and being; and an imaginative, literary sensibility that renders their work relatively entertaining, though frequently unintelligible, to generally educated readers.

Philosophers in the analytic tradition, by contrast, typically employ the methods of formal logic enthusiastically; regard Hegelian idealism as nonsense; and in general seek to delimit the subject matter of their inquiry in such a way as to exclude social, political, and psychological considerations that are not amenable to precise analysis. In general analytic philosophers tend to shy away from sweeping conclusions about matters of existential concern and to establish more modest conclusions by rigorous manners of proof. Continental philosophers, on the other hand, typically brush aside scruples about rigor in argumentation and strive to reach conclusions that are intrinsically interesting and existentially relevant.[28]

---

[27] See, e.g., G. W. F. Hegel, *Phenomenology of Spirit*, trans. A. V. Miller (Oxford: Oxford University Press, 1977), §235, p. 142.

[28] For a fuller account of the Continental-analytic distinction see R. Rorty, *Philosophy as Cultural Politics* (Cambridge: Cambridge University Press, 2007), 120–30.

5. Conclusion

Certain philosophers do not fit neatly within the epochs described above. Michel de Montaigne (1533–92), for example, was neither a rationalist nor an empiricist, as one would expect, but a Pyrrhonist born out of due time. Also thinkers such as John of St. Thomas (1589–1644), Salvatore Roselli (1722–84), Joseph Kleutgen (1811–83), and Jacques Maritain (1882–1973) continued in the traditions of medieval realism well into the twentieth century. Certain philosophers whose philosophy fits the profile of this era are difficult to place within a particular school. J. M. E. McTaggart (1866–1925) and Richard Rorty (1931–2007), for example, qualify as neither unambiguously analytic nor as unmistakably Continental in philosophical orientation. Those who unquestionably belong to the same era and the same category, furthermore, frequently disagree violently among themselves. Hegel and Friedrich W. J. von Schelling (1775–1854), for instance, were both idealistic and proto-Continental in philosophical approach; yet their loathing for each other's ideas and persons is legendary. Understanding even a sliver of this history requires intense thought and research. The labor involved in acquiring such understanding is worthwhile to Christian apologists nonetheless, as will be seen in the next section on philosophy's apologetic value.

III. THE IMPORTANCE OF PHILOSOPHY TO CHRISTIAN APOLOGETICS

Knowledge of philosophy assists apologists in the tasks of comprehending anti-Christian worldviews and of clarifying the philosophical presuppositions of the Christian faith. In addition to these tasks, which are prerequisite to but not constitutive of the actual defense of orthodox Christianity, the following section shows that knowledge of philosophy enables the apologist better to vindicate Christianity's credibility and desirability.

A. Credibility

The famous "five ways" of Thomas Aquinas supply the best examples of how one can deploy philosophical analysis not merely to rebut objections but also to establish the truthfulness of those elements of Christian belief that admit of philosophical proof.[29] The five ways are five arguments for the existence of God that Thomas formulated most succinctly in the third article of the second question of the first part of his *Summa Theologiae*.

1. The argument from motion

In the argument from motion (in the sense of change), Thomas asserted that nothing can be both potential and actual in precisely the same respect. Water, for example, either actually is 80° C, in which case it cannot be merely potentially 80°, or it is merely potentially 80° C, in which case it cannot be 80°. Aquinas reasoned that a be-

---

[29] T. Aquinas, *Summa Theologiae* (reprint, 5 vols., Allen, TX: Christian Classics, 1981).

ing cannot endow itself with what it does not possess; therefore water that is only 40° C cannot attain the temperature of 80° C unless some other being bestows on it the energy equivalent of 40°. No being, in other words, that possesses some status only potentially can bestow on itself that status. An external mover (changer) of sufficient actuality or power must act on that being in such a way as to actualize its potential.

Given this premise, Thomas asserted, a particular change in some finite being might occur as a result of one of two processes. A change might occur as a result of an infinite series of changes by changed changers (or moved movers), each of which receives actuality from a being like itself and passes it on to yet another. Or alternatively a change might occur as a result of some string of changes initiated by an unchanged changer (or unmoved mover) by something so actual (powerful) itself that it can actualize, at least indirectly, the potential of all created things and yet cannot in any way be actualized by it because it already possesses more actuality than the entire creation.

Aquinas regarded the first scenario, in which an infinite series of changed changers bring about particular changes in the world, as inconceivable. For in an infinite series of beings each of which requires to be changed by another being in order to change yet another, no being would be capable of initiating the overall process of change. An infinite series of beings therefore would simply remain inert for want of an agent capable of independently initiating change. Obviously, however, at least minor transformations occur in the world continuously. Thomas concluded therefore that some unchanged changer, which is sufficiently powerful to actualize the potential of all creation, must be responsible for the changes that occur constantly in the cosmos.

2. The argument from efficient causality

In Aquinas's second way, the argument from efficient causality, he observed that nature exhibits a chain of efficient causes. Being "a" brings about the existence of being "b," being "b" brings about the existence of being "c," and so forth. He added that no being can cause its own existence. As in the first way, then, one must reckon with two possibilities: either a chain of caused causes extending infinitely backward in time is responsible for the reality humans experience, or this reality originates ultimately in the creative power of an uncaused cause. As in the first way, Thomas rejects as inconceivable the idea of an infinite regress or infinite chain of causes extending into the past.

> It is not possible in efficient causes to proceed to infinity, because in all ordered efficient causes, the first is the cause of the intermediate, and the intermediate is the cause of the last, whether the intermediate causes are many or only one. When the cause is removed, however, the effect is removed. If, therefore, there were no first efficient cause, there would be neither a last cause nor an intermediate cause. Yet if one proceeds to infinity in efficient causes, there will not be a first efficient cause, nor will there be a last effect, nor will there be intermediate efficient causes, which is obviously false.

229

Therefore, it is necessary to posit some first efficient cause, which all people name God.[30]

3. The argument from contingency and necessity

In the third way, the argument from contingency and necessity, Thomas proposed the following disjunction. Either the universe consists entirely in contingent beings (beings for which it is possible either to exist or not to exist), or the universe contains both contingent beings and at least one being whose existence is necessary. On the first scenario, Aquinas reasoned, a godless universe would extend infinitely backward in time, and in this infinite period of time all possibilities for the universe would be actualized. One possibility for such a universe, he observed, would be that all these beings cease to exist. If therefore the universe consisted entirely in contingent beings, the possibility of all beings ceasing to exist would have been realized in the past, in which case nothing would exist now. Obviously this is not the case. Aquinas concluded therefore that the universe must contain at least one necessarily existent being.

4. The argument from degrees of excellence

In his fourth way, the argument from degrees of excellence, Thomas observed that the various beings of the world possess greater or lesser degrees of truth, goodness, nobility, and so forth. In his view this implies that the universe must contain some independently existing, maximal truth, maximal goodness, and so forth. Aquinas's Aristotelian ontology dictates, furthermore that (a) whatever is greatest among true things is also the greatest among beings, and that (b) whatever is greatest in any classification is the cause of all beings in that classification. Aquinas concluded therefore that a being exists that is the truest being, that this being is also the greatest being, and that this greatest being constitutes the cause of all other beings.

5. The argument from design

In the fifth way, the argument from design, Aquinas observed that subhuman animals, who lack intelligence, nevertheless behave instinctively in such a way as to achieve the desirable ends of warmth, safety, and food. Unintelligent animals, naturally, cannot determine how to achieve these ends by reasoning. Aquinas concluded therefore that some higher, intelligent being must have designed these animals in such a way that they instinctively seek their own good. "Things that lack thought," he wrote, "do not move toward an end unless they are directed by some knowing and intelligent being so to do, as an arrow is directed to its target by an archer. Therefore, some intelligent being exists by whom all natural things are ordered to an end, and this being we call God."

Manifestly one cannot establish the mystery of the Trinity or the incarnation by such means. These subjects are inaccessible to philosophy, a discipline committed to employing only evidence supplied by natural revelation. However, where Christian

---

[30] Ibid., 1, 2, 3 corp. All translations of Aquinas in this volume are those of the authors.

faith and the truths of natural revelation intersect philosophy can be of considerable assistance in establishing the truthfulness of the Christian faith.

B. Desirability

One frequently encounters individuals who are relatively indifferent to the truth or falsehood of the Christian faith but willing to embrace a system of belief that they feel will satisfy their innermost yearnings. For such persons the paramount issue in deciding whether to become a Christian is not the credibility of the Christian faith but rather its desirability. In apologetic efforts to establish the desirability of Christianity philosophy is singularly useful.

To establish the point that Christianity satisfies the natural desires of humans, one must make generalizations about human nature that most analytic philosophers would regard as insufficiently warranted. Nevertheless if the generalizations that make up one's philosophical anthropology are sufficiently plausible, they can, at least arguably, show the desirability of the Christian faith to be probable. To show the desirability of Christianity by philosophical means, one would advance an argument such as the following by Adolphe Tanquerey (1854–1932).

Human beings need some religion. All human beings naturally want to know where they came from and what will happen to them after their death. All human beings, moreover, naturally desire happiness, at least in some sense of the word. Human beings, therefore, need a divine revelation to tell them about their origins and their ultimate destiny; to give them a rule for how they should act in order to attain happiness; and to provide them some guarantee of happiness in another life, where their desires will be completely satisfied and where they need not fear happiness slipping out of their fingers. In order to fulfill their most basic natural longings, therefore, human beings must have a revelation from God.[31]

If there is a God, there is only one because the same natural laws govern the entire universe. If there is only one God, there can be only one true religion, and Christianity is that religion for these reasons: (a) it is monotheistic (this consideration rules out all other major religions except Judaism and Islam); (b) it has the support of the Scriptures of Judaism; (c) it has the support of miracles and fulfilled prophecies, both of which Islam lacks; and (d) it alone among the monotheistic religions explains how God can be perfectly just and perfectly righteous at the same time—by Himself paying the debt human beings owe Him on the cross and forgiving them only on that basis.

Philosophical considerations alone, naturally, do not suffice to show that Christianity is the one true religion. They are sufficient, however, to show that human beings need some religion; and one need add only a few extra-philosophical observations to show that Christianity is the religion that human beings need.

---

[31] My summary of the first part of his argument. See A. Tanquerey, *Synopsis Theologiae Dogmaticae*, ed. J. B. Bord, 26th ed. (Paris: Desclée, 1937), 1:102.

IV. CONCLUSION

The skillful Christian apologist therefore can warrant by philosophical means certain articles of the Christian faith, such as the existence of God, and he can employ philosophical reasoning in such a way as to show human beings that they can fulfill their natural and legitimate desires only by becoming Christians. The Christian apologist needs more than philosophical knowledge and ability if he is to establish the truthfulness of the orthodox Christian religion. Yet if he is to succeed at the two tasks just mentioned, he cannot dispense with the serious study of philosophy.

Chapter 17

SKEPTICISM AND ITS CURE

SKEPTICISM—THE TENDENCY TO DISTRUST THE CLAIMS of others—can be constructive in certain circumstances. Those who followed Sabbatai Sevi (1626–76) and Judah ben Shalom (d. c. 1878), each of whom claimed to be the Messiah, ought to have been skeptical of these persons' assertions. They ought to have demanded evidence for these persons' claims and to have refused, as a matter of principle, to accept either figure as Messiah until he had produced some proof. This sort of skepticism is healthy and virtuous, and Christians study apologetics partially in order to supply evidence for the Christian faith to persons who are rightly skeptical of sweeping claims about the will of God and the plan of salvation.

One ought to distinguish, however, the virtue of skepticism from what passes for skepticism in contemporary Western culture. The latter is an obstinate and frequently bigoted refusal to believe religious claims, regardless of the evidence mustered on their behalf. To this pseudo-skepticism the present chapter offers a cure.

I. VARIETIES OF (PSEUDO-)SKEPTICISM

A. Absolute Skepticism

This kind of skepticism, of which the Pyrrhonism mentioned in the previous chapter is a species, is a refusal to assent to any truth claim. The absolute skeptic, that is, does not acknowledge the fact of his own existence, of the existence of the truth claims whose veracity he denies, or even of his own assertion that he sincerely doubts even the most seemingly self-evident assertions. Naturally no one can maintain such an absolute skepticism consistently in all his thoughts and activities, and the absolute skeptic would be the last person to assert that one could. In fact the absolute skeptic would be the last person to assert, positively and as a fact, anything at all.

Although certain mentally ill persons are tortured by doubts about whether they really exist, one need not suffer from mental illness to be an absolute skeptic. Likewise, an absolute skeptic need not evidence his skepticism by performing obviously imprudent acts such as walking into busy traffic because in his view he does not know that the traffic is really there. Usually persons who profess absolute skepticism practice the lifestyle customary for persons in their position in society on the grounds that this might appear (!) to be the path of least resistance.

Individuals who suspect that absolute skepticism might possibly be rational—an absolute skeptic would never affirm straightforwardly that absolute skepticism is true—typically do so for one or both of two reasons. First, some people embrace absolute skepticism because all arguments that humans know anything at all seem to them highly problematic, as they easily can seem to one who imposes on them unreasonably stringent standards of proof. Second, persons become absolute skeptics because they have been persuaded by authors such as the ancient Pyrrhonist, Sextus Empiricus (c. AD 200), or his Renaissance heir, Michel de Montaigne (1533–92), that by refusing to acknowledge the truthfulness of any claim whatever, they might be able to a certain extent to free themselves from the worries about troublesome realities that torment other human beings.

B. Phenomenalistic Skepticism

When Socrates asserted that he was the wisest man in Athens because he knew that he knew nothing,[1] he might seem to have contradicted himself rather obviously. If, however, by the first "knew," Socrates meant "understand anything whatever," and by the second "knew" he meant "have knowledge of a world external to my consciousness," then Socrates's statement is quite consistent. On this interpretation Socrates anticipated a later school of skeptical philosophers, known as phenomenalists, by stating that he knew that he could not establish that any of his sense perceptions sufficed to enable him to know anything that exists independently of his own thought.[2]

One can envision how a reasonable person could reach this conclusion. One might claim that he does not know, in the proper sense of the term, any truth about which he cannot prove beyond a doubt that he is not mistaken. One might reason, moreover, that, in some possible world one's senses might convey to him precisely the same impression of external reality that he currently possesses, and this impression might be completely false.

Contemporary philosophers, for example, are fond of referring to the hypothesis of a brain in a vat.[3] According to this hypothesis a clever scientist might one day be able to stimulate a brain, floating in a tank of liquids and disconnected from any human body, to produce precisely those mental states that a living, embodied person has in ordinary life. If this is the case, the argument goes, a person experiencing such ordinary mental states cannot know that he is not a brain in a vat. In general skeptical phenomenalists reason that if in some possible, radically different world a human being could have the same experiences he has in the present world, then the human being does not know what kind of world he is experiencing. He does not know that he does not inhabit a world in which his senses constantly deceive him, and therefore

---

[1] See Plato, *Apology* 21d.

[2] The leading figure of this school is David Hume. See his *Treatise of Human Nature* (1739; reprint, ed. L. A. Selby-Bigge [Oxford: Oxford University Press, 1896], §1.2.6, pp. 66–8), for a representative statement of skeptical phenomenalist sentiments.

[3] See, e.g., H. Putnam's famous discussion of this hypothesis in *Reason, Truth, and History* (Cambridge: Cambridge University Press, 1981), 5–15.

regardless of what kind of world he actually inhabits, he does not know this world in the strictest sense at all.

C. Metaphysical Skepticism

The absolute and phenomenalist forms of skepticism considered in the preceding two sections have never been common in any society. This third form of skepticism is by contrast presently the mainstream view in all Western industrialized societies. According to legend the word *metaphysics*, which signifies that of which metaphysical skeptics are skeptical, originated in a decision of Andronicus of Rhodes (fl. c. 60 BC) to place Aristotle's treatise on being as such, physical and otherwise, after Aristotle's *Physics*, that is, *meta* ("after") *physikos*, in his ordering of Aristotle's books.[4] This term has come to refer to the science of being as such, conceived of as including entities beyond the merely physical.

That metaphysics constitutes a legitimate science has come to be widely disputed in the contemporary world. One can know, leading Western intellectuals have long believed, only what is material and observable. Even many Christian believers share secular society's skepticism of metaphysics, holding that one can know nothing of God but can only have faith. Indicative of the modern West's contempt for metaphysics are the application of the honorific title "science" exclusively to the study of the material world and the designation, already in the eighteenth century, of poets who employ far-fetched comparisons as "metaphysical poets."

Metaphysics has fallen into disrepute in the post-Reformation world for three reasons. First, numerous thinkers have followed Immanuel Kant in forging an uneasy compromise between pure phenomenalism and modern, scientific realism. Refusing to decide the question of whether the world as it exists corresponds to human perceptions of it, these thinkers merely acknowledge that human perceptions in some way depend on realities in the external world.[5] This dependence suffices, in these thinkers' view, to allow human beings to discern regularities in nature and so to manipulate it.[6] Mere dependence of perception on sensible reality, however, evidently does not suffice to explain how human beings could learn universal truths about the nature of being that might warrant inferences to the existence of God.[7] The thinkers in question consider themselves justified therefore in placing confidence in the findings of the natural sciences and yet denying that the senses supply human beings with knowledge adequate to warrant conclusions about reality beyond the sensible realm.

Second, the extraordinary success of the natural sciences in achieving consensus about truths within their purview has led countless persons to regard other sciences, such as metaphysics as mere speculation. Third, the enormous contribution made by the natural sciences to the advancement of human well-being over the last several

---

[4] This legend, while charming, is almost certainly apocryphal.

[5] I. Kant, *Prolegomena to Any Future Metaphysics*, trans. P. Carus, rev. J. W. Ellington (reprint, Indianapolis: Hackett, 1977), §13.290–93, pp. 34–37.

[6] Ibid., §19.298–9, pp. 42–43.

[7] Ibid., §55.348, pp. 88–89.

centuries has bred an inordinate admiration for them and a corresponding contempt for sciences such as metaphysics whose conclusions cannot, in the nature of the case, be confirmed by the methods of natural science. Thus skepticism of metaphysical claims (i.e., any claims about realities that transcend the material order) has come to influence vast numbers of people in today's society.

D. Historical Skepticism

Closely related to and perhaps even more pernicious than metaphysical skepticism is historical skepticism. Adherents of historical skepticism, as the term is employed in this chapter, hold to three principles classically articulated by the German theologian Ernst Troeltsch (1885–1923). The first of these, the principle of criticism, consists in the assertion that no historical claim is supported by more than merely probable evidence and that one ought therefore to accord such claims only partial and provisional assent.[8] The second principle of historical skepticism, namely, the principle of analogy, dictates that one ought not to believe testimony to the occurrence of any event that is utterly unlike what one has experienced oneself.[9] According to this principle one ought not to believe the Bible's testimony to Christ's virginal conception and bodily resurrection unless one has directly witnessed similar events.

The third principle of historical skepticism is that of correlation. According to this principle, every event that occurs in the natural world must be explicable by appeal to a strictly natural cause, which in turn arises from strictly natural causes.[10] In other words miracles do not occur. One who adheres to Troeltsch's principle of correlation cannot consistently grant that any event, no matter how extraordinary, results from a supernatural interruption of the ordinary chain of natural events. Obviously one who adheres rigorously to these three principles of historical skepticism cannot be a Christian in the biblical sense of the term.

II. Christian Answers to Unreasonable Forms of Skepticism

Absolute, phenomenalistic, metaphysical, and historical skepticism constitute the tetrad of skeptical ailments to which Christian apologists must offer some cure. Before discussing how apologists might, with the aid of the Holy Spirit, go about curing their patients, one must remember that skepticism can be not only a vice but also a virtue. Besides being an unthinking incredulity that steels human beings against the claims of truth, skepticism can also be a prudent refusal to accept falsehood. In seeking to cure skepticism as a vice, therefore, one must be careful not to depreciate the importance of evidence to sound, rational belief.

---

[8] E. Troeltsch, "Über dogmatische und historische Methode," in *Gesammelte Schriften* 2 (Tübingen: Mohr-Siebeck, 1913), 731.

[9] Ibid., 732.

[10] Ibid., 733.

A. Absolute Skepticism

Absolute skepticism appears untenable for at least four reasons. First, the stance of the absolute skeptic is fundamentally dishonest. His consciousness continually impresses on him truths, such as his own existence and the existence of an external world, to which he involuntarily yields his absolute assent. To the extent that a person's words constitute representations of his inner convictions, therefore, one who states that he knows nothing is simply lying.

Second, absolute skepticism possesses no explanatory power. Alternative belief systems may derive credibility from their ability to explain various occurrences but absolute skepticism explains nothing because it affirms nothing. Third, the absolute skeptic does not adopt the path of least resistance. He commits himself to defying systematically the testimony of his nature that he actually knows many things.

Fourth, by refusing to affirm anything, the absolute skeptic assumes an irresponsible, narcissistic view of the world. An ethically upright realist accepts the view, for example, that innocent persons really are suffering in some part of the globe and that he really is bound in duty to help alleviate their plight. But the absolute skeptic can only suspect that he suspects that some such situation exists and that it might concern him in some way.

In other words the absolute skeptic renders himself incapable of acting on his knowledge of the world in a morally serious way. Absolute skepticism therefore involves its adherents in a fundamentally dishonest worldview that is profoundly contrary to nature and bereft of explanatory power. But it also impairs its adherents' ability to appreciate the reality of their moral obligations. Absolute skepticism therefore constitutes an implausible worldview and an unattractive orientation to life.

B. Phenomenalistic Skepticism

The first, third, and fourth objections to absolute skepticism apply also to thoroughgoing phenomenalism. In the case of phenomenalism, admittedly, the power of these objections is mitigated somewhat by a singularly powerful argument which has already been mentioned, namely, the brain-in-a-vat argument against human knowledge of an external world. The argument is as follows:

1. If one could have the same experience one is presently having in an entirely different world, then his experience would not enable him to know whether he is in the present world or the entirely different one.
2. One does not, in fact, know that one could not have the same experience one is presently having in an entirely different world.
3. One does not therefore know that one's experiences enable him to know whether he is or is not in the present world.

If one allows that a person knows something only if he knows that he knows it, then this argument does invalidate human claims to know truths about the external world. The first objection to absolute skepticism, however, appears to trump the brain-in-a-vat argument. Regardless of whether one can answer the brain-in-a-vat argument, one inevitably believes, on some level at least, that his sense intuitions are reliable and that he possesses some knowledge about the external world. He cannot assert that he is utterly ignorant of external reality, without contradicting himself. And when faced with a choice of committing himself to an evident contradiction and running afoul of an obscure and hypothetical argument, it seems that a rational person would invariably choose to run afoul of the argument. Notwithstanding the brain-in-a-vat objection, which admits of no simple and straightforward refutation, therefore, the involuntary testimony of human nature to the reality of the external world suffices to discredit phenomenalistic skepticism.

C. Metaphysical Skepticism

At least three considerations show that the skepticism of metaphysics, which has become almost universal in the Western world, is unreasonable. First, even secularist practitioners of the natural sciences have come to realize that in order to explain existing, observable realities, one must posit the existence of countless unobservable and yet indispensable events and entities such as the Big Bang, quarks, muons, positrons, and the like. The natural sciences have thus burst the bounds of secular philosophies created to defend them and have shown, through their own intrinsic dynamism and without any religious motivation, that in order to account for the universe as it presently exists, one must be willing to speak of realities that transcend the observable domain.

Second, the argument for the reliability of sense perception employed above, undermines the sort of Kantian half-realism discussed above, that allows for meaningful discoveries in the natural sciences and yet disallows the possibility of metaphysical knowledge. For if one must, on pain of self-contradiction, affirm that he knows the world as it is, he cannot consistently deny that he knows, at least implicitly, what a contingent being is.

If one knows what a contingent being is, he also knows that such a being is not self-subsistent. Such a being does not exist by definition. To explain the existence of such a being, therefore, one must appeal to the agency of some other being; and, unless one wishes to involve oneself in an infinite regress, one must posit the existence of a being that does subsist of itself, whose agency accounts for the existence of all contingent causes. If one admits therefore that he can know what a contingent entity is in itself, he implicitly admits that he can also know that a necessary, self-subsistent entity exists.

Whoever admits that he can know the world as it is thereby admits also that he can attain a singularly important item of metaphysical knowledge, namely, that a self-subsistent being exists, the kind of being Christians call God. If one grants that such a being exists, he also tacitly allows for the possibility of his revealing himself to creatures by supernatural means so that they might obtain a significant store of metaphysical knowledge. Merely admitting that one can know reality in itself, as it actually is, thus suffices to demolish the edifice of metaphysical skepticism.

D. Historical Skepticism

Historical skeptics, as previously noted, adhere to three fundamental principles: criticism, analogy, and correlation. At the outset one may reasonably dismiss the principle of correlation (the view that all events in the natural world are products of merely natural causes) because it seems to presuppose metaphysical skepticism. If metaphysical skepticism is demonstrably false, as argued in the preceding section, then the principle of correlation, which seems to be deduced from it, can hardly be credible.

The principles of criticism and analogy, by contrast, require closer examination. The first of these, the principle of criticism, consists in the prima facie plausible rule that one's judgments in historical matters ought always to be tentative and subject to revision. Since historical evidence is always merely probable and never absolutely certain, the principle states, one ought never to assent unconditionally to a historical claim.

Two arguments, however, discredit this superficially plausible principle. First, the principle of criticism runs contrary to the universal practice of reasonable, intelligent people. Whatever the imperfections of the evidence may be, human beings do not regard the existence of George Washington, Thomas Jefferson, Abraham Lincoln, and others as merely probable; without any reservation everyone grants that these persons existed. At least in cases such as these in which the preponderance of evidence for a claim is overwhelming, it seems unreasonable to insist that one grant only a mere provisional, halfhearted assent.

Second, the circumstances of human life frequently render it rational to yield absolute assent to claims for which the evidence is far from certain. One ought, for example, to believe wholeheartedly that one has married the right person, that one's labor is not in vain, that one's prospects are not hopeless, and so forth. Also at times one must commit himself absolutely to courses of action for the wisdom of which one may possess only shreds of evidence. A fugitive fleeing from his captors, for example, must run in one direction rather than another; a job seeker must accept one position and not another, and so forth.

When existential factors enter into the equation, a precise balancing of degrees of probability and degrees of assent to claims about the past or the present can easily become irrational or impossible. It would be disingenuous to deny, moreover, that such existential factors do come into play when one makes historical decisions with religious implications. When deciding whether Jesus rose from the dead or whether the angel Gabriel dictated the Qur'an to Muhammad, when absolute assent is demanded and partial or equivocal assent is tantamount to denial, when one's eternal blessedness or damnation may hinge on whether he yields an absolute assent to some particular historical claim—no rational person would exercise the restraint in historical judgment that Troeltsch insisted on in his principle of criticism. Troeltsch's principle of criticism therefore does not apply to religiously significant historical judgments.

Troeltsch's principle of analogy—the principle according to which one ought not to credit the testimony of others to events that possess no analogue in one's own experience—appears rather obviously invalid. For one can easily conceive of quite credible testimony that a person who consistently followed the principle of analogy would be obliged to reject. One thinks, for instance, of the proverbial King of Siam who could not be persuaded that water could solidify into ice because he had never experienced anything of the sort. For a more grim example, one might consider the genocides of the twentieth century. The principle of analogy would seem to suggest that since most human beings have never personally witnessed anything like the Holocaust or the genocide of Tutsis in Rwanda, they ought to deny that these genocides ever occurred. However, denial of the historicity of these tragedies would be outrageously perverse. Since the principle of analogy encourages not only irrational but also immoral behavior, it seems abundantly worthy of rejection.

Since no one of these three principles—analogy, criticism, and correlation—seems worthy of credit, historical skepticism is unjustified. Neither historical skepticism nor metaphysical skepticism nor academic skepticism nor absolute skepticism, accordingly, seems worthy of acceptance by a rightfully skeptical, impartial inquirer.

III. CONCLUSION

As noted earlier, skepticism, the tendency to distrust the claims of others, can be a virtue as well as a vice. Although the Christian apologist must protest against the excesses of a destructive, anti-Christian skepticism, he must also sharply distinguish Christian faith from gullible acquiescence in the unproved and unprovable. Through the fulfillment of prophecies, the working of miracles, the survival and expansion of the church against all odds, the benefits of Christianity to civilization, and the religious experience of countless multitudes, God has provided an abundance of evidence for the gospel, which He commands human beings to believe. Christians have nothing to fear therefore from a legitimate skepticism that demands evidence as a prerequisite to responsible belief.

Chapter 18

POSTMODERNISM AND DEFENSE OF CHRISTIANITY

I. INTRODUCTION

THE PRESENT CHAPTER CONSTITUTES AN EXAMINATION of postmodernism: an ideology that is closely interwoven with the controversial claim that the modern era has ended and a new postmodern era has begun. In the following we hope: (1) to delineate the modernism over against which postmodernists define themselves; (2) to describe the characteristic ideas of postmodernism itself; (3) to consider whether postmodernism is or can be a coherent system of thought; and (4) to evaluate postmodernism from a distinctively Christian perspective.

II. MODERNISM

A. Introduction

Before describing postmodernism itself, it seems advisable to clarify what the modernism is against which postmodernists define themselves. In brief the modern era, whose characteristic attitudes constitute modernism, is, as the word is employed by postmodernists: (a) the era of the great secular metanarratives; (b) the era of the subject; and (c) the era of representation.

B. The Era of the Great Secular Metanarratives

Essentially religious worldviews, i.e., worldviews grounded in sacred texts and that endow all of life with religious meaning, are, according to the majority of postmodernists, a premodern phenomenon. Although few would deny that Islam and, to a lesser extent, Christianity, Hinduism, and Buddhism, exert a significant influence in contemporary affairs, postmodernists, on the whole, consider these religions relics of a bygone era, whose adherents have failed for centuries to appreciate or influence the trends of thought driving the development of world civilization.

The modern period, according to the typical postmodernist estimate, is the time in which human beings buried religion and erected atop its grave secular metanarratives that, it was hoped, would bring liberation, unity, and progress to a human race long plagued by divisive and oppressive superstitions. A metanarrative is a claim or set of claims about reality as such that has repercussions for one's thinking about virtually all subjects.

In the Scientific Revolution, for example, one finds the germ that in the late eighteenth and early nineteenth centuries blossoms into the metanarrative of scientism. Scientism is the belief: (a) that the natural sciences alone constitute reliable means of coming to know truth; and (b) and that if human beings would only cultivate and submit to these sciences, the human race could conquer all, or virtually all, of its problems.

Closely related to the metanarrative of scientism is the metanarrative of progress, according to which the human race inevitably advances over time to higher levels of achievement in the material, intellectual, and moral spheres. This metanarrative lent considerable support to the metanarrative of liberty, equality, and fraternity that motivated the French Revolution: the idea that, if human beings brushed aside the old, discredited metanarratives of religion and accepted the new metanarrative of "the rights of man," they could swiftly remedy all injustices, liberate the oppressed masses, and halt the incessant warfare of rival nations and religions.

The collective egotism of races and nations, however, counteracted efforts to achieve world peace and eventually crystallized into the metanarrative of fascism. More importantly in this context, the metanarrative of Marxism exposed, at least to its adherents' satisfaction, the Enlightenment ideology of equal rights and individual liberty as a sham. Marxism, then, constitutes the apex of modernity in the view of most postmodernists: the last of the great metanarratives for which human beings were willing to fight and die, which, according to postmodernists at least, has been happily forgotten by a public now adrift without a metanarrative to guide it.

C. The Age of the Subject

A common theme running through the metanarratives of modernity, postmodernists typically believe, is an emphasis on the at least potential power and aggrandizement of the unified human subject. A unified human subject is simply a person who is responsible for all of his actions and who remains the same person in spite of the passage of time and changes in his body, outlook, and activity.

According to scientism, for instance, the scientific inquirer, conceived of as a unified human subject, can stand over against subhuman nature, know it, and come to dominate it, bending it as he likes to his own purposes. In the metanarrative of progress, likewise, the human subject is envisioned as becoming ever more powerful, ever more capable of determining his own destiny. Again, the Enlightenment ideology of human rights revolves around the dignity of the individual human being, who must be liberated so that he can flourish to his full potential.

Even Marxism, the modern metanarrative to which postmodernist thinkers almost uniformly find themselves most attracted, laments the individual worker's alienation from the products and process of his labor: sc. the immediate removal of the industrial worker's creations from him and the experience of work as a burden imposed by someone else. One cannot so much as conceive of alienation, as postmodernist thinkers rightly observe, if one regards the human being not as a unified subject but as a congeries of events, impulses, chemicals, body parts, and external influences arbitrarily grouped together. Postmodernist thinkers consider it necessary, therefore, to abandon the Marxist idea of alienation: along with, naturally, Marxism's pretension to be true and its claim, as a metanarrative, to explain the chaos of existence.

D. The Age of Representation

Modernity, as postmodernists conceive of it, is not only the age of the secular metanarrative and the subject but also the age of representation. By this, they mean that the human quest to achieve an objective knowledge of the world, a representation in consciousness of things precisely as they are, reached a fever pitch in the modern period. One might object to this portrayal, admittedly, on three grounds. First, the love of truth is not unique to modernity; it flourished among ancient and medieval philosophers long before the modern period. Second, and more importantly, representationalist, "picture" theories of knowledge, according to which ideas represent actual things, gained wide credence long before modernity. Third, and most importantly, such accounts of knowledge as representation have fallen into disrepute since Immanuel Kant's determination in the late eighteenth century that the intellect does not derive its content from things perceived but rather imposes that content, in large measure, on them.[1]

To these objections to their characterization of modernity as the age of representation, postmodernists would reply, first, that, although "picture" theories of knowledge existed before modernity, the frenzied quest for scientific knowledge that marked modernity was unprecedented. As to Kant, second, a postmodernist would presumably assert that Kant did not destroy the modern ideal of knowledge as representation but merely inverted it. Before Kant, that is to say, one possessed knowledge to the extent that one's consciousness reflected reality as it actually is. After Kant, one began to possess knowledge because one's field of perception reflects *a priori* categories imposed by one's own understanding.

Few, if any, postmodernists would deny that Kant significantly altered Western ideas about what constitutes knowledge. Kant retained, however, postmodernists would presumably observe, the conception of knowing as an orderly process governed by laws in which one element in the process reliably reflects another. When one compares this conception of knowing to the ideas of postmodernists, who frequently disavow all distinction between the imaginary and the real, claim that signs can refer only to other signs and never to reality and deny that the knowing, human subject exists; one can see why, to a postmodernist, Kant's theory of knowledge might seem tamely conservative, or "representationalist."

---

[1] Cf. Kant's *Critique of Pure Reason* (trans. N. K. Smith; New York: Palgrave Macmillan, 2003), Bxvi–xx, pp. 22–24.

E. Conclusion

Modernity as postmodernists conceive of it consists in the age of the secular meta-narrative, the age of the subject, and the age of representation. It is important to note, before proceeding to the next section, that postmodernists do not typically repudiate all aspects of modernism or deny that aspects of modernism persist in what they define as the postmodern present. Indeed, postmodernists rarely agree about precisely what modernism is. Since few, if any, postmodernists deny that modernism is characterized by the qualities discussed above, however, the portrayal given here seems adequate to supply a foil for the portrayal of postmodernism in the next section.

III. POSTMODERNISM

A. Introduction

The postmodern era, unlike the modern, is characterized, according to post-modernists, by incredulity toward metanarratives,[2] the death of the subject,[3] and the impossibility of representation.[4] Postmodernists, as one might expect, believe that metanarratives never were credible, that a unified human subject never existed, and that knowledge in the sense of mirror-like representation of worldly realities was never possible. What is distinctive about the postmodern period, they claim, is that these radical conclusions, which would have been unthinkable in other eras, are now the conventional wisdom; and in this estimate the postmodernists may well be correct. In the following, accordingly, attention will be given to why and in what sense postmod-ernists subscribe to the three tenets of postmodernism just mentioned.

B. Incredulity Toward Metanarratives

Postmodernists typically find metanarratives incredible for two principal reasons: (a) a generalized skepticism toward all claims to truth whatsoever and (b) a conviction that metanarratives inevitably become tools of oppression.

1. Skepticism

Postmodernists are typically skeptical of human beings' ability to distinguish be-tween the real and the imaginary and between the real and signs, such as words, that human beings employ to refer to the real.[5] Indeed, if by "reality" one means something

---

[2] J.-F. Lyotard writes, "I define postmodern as incredulity toward metanarratives" (*The Postmodern Condition: A Report on Knowledge*, trans. Geoff Bennington and Brian Massumi, Theory and History of Literature 10 [Minneapolis: University of Minnesota Press, 1984; orig. 1979], xxiv).

[3] "The subject," writes J. Kristeva, "never is. The subject is only the signifying process" (*Revolution in Poetic Language*, trans. M. Waller [New York: Columbia University Press, 1984; orig. 1974], 215).

[4] M. P. Arriaga writes, "Post-modernist philosophy . . . rejects the empirical notion that language can represent reality" (*The Modernist-Postmodernist Quarrel on Philosophy and Justice: A Possible Levina-sian Mediation* [Lanham, Md.: Lexington Books, 2006], 21).

[5] "The thing itself," writes J. Derrida, "is a sign. . . . The so-called 'thing in itself' is always already a *representamen* . . . [which] functions only by giving rise to an *interpretant* that itself becomes a sign and so on to infinity. . . . From the moment that there is meaning there are nothing but signs" (*Of Grammatol-ogy*, trans. G. C. Spivak [Baltimore: Johns Hopkins University Press, 1974; orig. 1967], 49–50).

radically distinct from the imaginary and from signs that point to something other than themselves, then the vast majority of postmodernists deny that "reality" exists.

In part, this skepticism about whether signs refer to something other than more signs reflects traditional philosophical concerns about how one can extricate oneself from the web of language. In the *Meno*, for example, Plato at least implicitly raises the question of whether one can know the actual meaning of any word, since, when he attempts to define a word, he can only do so in terms of other words.[6] Ludwig Wittgenstein's conception of speech as participation in a "language game" in which one does not so much refer to reality as simply play by the rules, constitutes, it seems, a response to much the same concerns.[7]

Partially on traditional philosophical grounds, then, postmodernists usually hold that language and other forms of signification do not refer to a reality outside of the web of signs. Signifiers abound, to borrow a phrase from Jacques Derrida, but there is no "transcendental signified."[8] It seems only natural that persons who hold such views would be skeptical of metanarratives that purport to explain all, or at least a substantial part, of a reality that consists in more than mere signs.

2. *Metanarratives as tools of oppression*

Virtually all postmodernist thinkers, moreover, consider even the most designedly inclusive and liberating metanarratives incapable of doing justice to the perspectives of some marginalized persons. Whenever a society operates according to a metanarrative, in the postmodernists' view, someone, as a matter of necessity, will be excluded and oppressed.

The postmodernist hostility to all metanarratives as inherently oppressive finds its clearest and most extreme expression in work of the historian/philosopher Michel Foucault. In his doctoral thesis, *Madness and Civilization*, for example, Foucault argues that the understanding of madness as mental illness, which became almost universally accepted in the nineteenth century West, does not necessarily constitute as great an advance as commonly believed over prior conceptions of madness as demonic possession or the renunciation of reason. Rather, he argues, the categorization of madness as mental illness merely supplies a soothing, humanitarian rationale for much the same kind of exclusion and coercion of the mad that had occurred since the Renaissance; before the Renaissance, according to Foucault, when leprosy was still common in Europe, lepers rather than the insane fulfilled the role of the other that must be excluded.[9] In Foucault's view, then, the metanarrative of mental illness,

---

[6] In *Meno* 75c, Meno criticizes Socrates' definition of shape as that which always accompanies color on the grounds that Socrates does not define color. Cf. Sextus Empiricus, *Outlines of Pyrrhonism*, 2.207.

[7] Wittgenstein introduces and explores the concept of language games in his *Philosophical Investigations*, trans. G. E. M. Anscombe; 3rd ed. (Oxford: Blackwell, 1958).

[8] Derrida introduces this concept in *Of Grammatology*, 20–23. The "transcendental signified," as Derrida employs the term, refers to something that is real and not merely a sign of some other hypothetical entity. Derrida holds that there is no such thing as a transcendental signified.

[9] Cf. *Madness and Civilization: A History of Insanity in the Age of Reason*, trans. R. Howard (New York: Random House, 1965), 3–7.

although intended to benefit the mad, has merely supplied a pseudo-scientific rationale for institutionalizing them, which Foucault portrays as virtual enslavement.[10]

Foucault's attitude to the metanarrative of mental illness is representative of postmodernist perceptions of metanarratives in general. Since any orderly, consistent account of wide-ranging aspects of reality contains within itself the seeds of brutal oppression, postmodernists consider themselves justified in attacking the most seemingly innocuous metanarratives (e.g., those of prison reform or progress through medical research). In criticizing such metanarratives, moreover, postmodernists believe that they perform, if not a revolutionary act, at least an act of resistance against the oppressors of the poor and marginalized. The postmodernists oppose metanarratives, therefore, for ethical reasons and not merely because they find them incredible.

C. The Death of the Subject

Postmodernists' belief in the absence of a unified psychological-moral subject in the human being is, perhaps, the least original aspect of their ideology. To a great extent, postmodernist antipathy toward the idea of a unified subject derives from the writings of Friedrich Nietzsche, a nineteenth-century German philosopher with whom postmodernist thinkers have significant affinities. In works such as *Human, All Too Human* and *On the Genealogy of Morals*, Nietzsche calls into question the idea that one can reasonably characterize human beings as continuously existing, unified subjects. "Just as the popular mind separates the lightning from its flash and takes the latter for an action, for the operation of a subject called lightning," he writes:

> so popular morality separates strength from expressions of strength, as if there were a neutral substratum behind the strong man, which was free to express strength or not to do so. But there is no such substratum; there is no "being" behind doing, effecting, becoming; "the doer" is merely a fiction added to the deed—the deed is everything.[11]

If the human being does not constitute one, self-identical, unified subject to whom one can justly attribute all actions performed by a given human being at all times, Nietzsche asks, why did it ever occur to human beings to identify themselves as unitary, responsible subjects? To this question, Nietzsche answers, human beings invented the concept of the subject in order, principally, to protect and console the weak,[12] and, secondarily, to render themselves and others competent to make and keep promises.[13] The notion of the subject, Nietzsche concludes, thus constitutes a massive fraud perpetrated for the purpose of securing largely dubious benefits: a fraud in which he, like later postmodernists, refuses to acquiesce.

---

[10] Cf. esp. the final chapter of *Madness and Civilization*, "The Birth of the Asylum," 241–78.

[11] *On the Genealogy of Morals*, trans. W. Kaufmann and R. J. Hollingdale (New York: Random House, 1967), §1.13, p. 45.

[12] Cf. ibid., 45–46.

[13] Cf. ibid., §2.1–2, pp. 57–60.

D. The Impossibility of Representation

Postmodernists question the capacity of the human mind accurately to represent external reality as it is to the human knower for at least four reasons. First and most obviously, if one does relate to the external world through the medium of mental images, then it might seem that one can never know whether these images correspond to reality. For one can never escape dependence on images in such a way as to be able to compare the unmediated reality in itself with one's image of it and so verify that the image accurately represents the reality. The human being seems to be doomed to experiencing only images, sensations, etc., that may indirectly reflect external reality or may not.

Second, if no human subject exists to represent the objects of its perception to itself, then no such representation will occur. The opposition of subject and object that might have rendered such representation conceivable has been dissolved.[14] Third and less radically, Jean-François Lyotard observes that human beings always, and especially in contemporary society, employ multiple language games in their discourse.[15] Yet, notes Lyotard, language games are frequently incommensurable. One cannot, in other words, translate the meanings of one into another, expressing, say, $\pi\iota$ in psychological terms or melancholy in the language of mathematics.[16] It seems, however, that one would have to translate meanings of one language game into another in order to appreciate the interrelations of diverse aspects of one and the same object. Lyotard concludes, accordingly, that reality always contains an overplus that surpasses human beings' representational capacity to a degree that they with their limited capacities cannot determine. Even if it is possible to represent reality, therefore, it is impossible to capture the fullness of reality in representation.

Lyotard argues for the same conclusion, fourth, by noting the felt inadequacy of human language when one attempts to speak of the sublime. When one senses the grandeur of something and yet is unable to express it in words, something has impinged on one's experience that one cannot represent, at least in a certain way. Even if one supposes, therefore, that the signs by which one thinks can convey something of a reality beyond signs, one still must reckon with the evidence of one's own experience that reality contains more, indefinitely more than these signs capture.[17] Whether they

---

[14] The first two objections, naturally, antedate philosophical postmodernism.

[15] *Postmodern Condition*, 9–10, 40–41.

[16] "Languages," writes Lyotard, "are translatable, otherwise they are not languages; but language games are not translatable, because, if they were, they would not be language games. It is as if one wanted to translate the rules and strategies of chess into those of checkers" (Lyotard and J.-L. Thébaud, *Just Gaming* [Theory and History of Literature 20; Minneapolis: University of Minnesota Press, 1985 (orig. 1979)], 53). The work, *Just Gaming*, incidentally, consists in a series of long interviews in which Thébaud poses and Lyotard answers questions.

[17] Lyotard identifies a postmodern aesthetic, in fact, as one that seeks to intensify, rather than to mitigate, the pain human beings experience when they recognize their powerlessness adequately to represent the sublime. "The postmodern," he writes, "would be that which . . . puts forward the unpresentable in presentation itself; that which denies itself the solace of good forms, the consensus of a taste which would make it possible to share collectively the nostalgia for the unattainable; that which searches for new presentations, not in order to enjoy them but in order to impart a stronger sense of the unpresentable" (Appendix: "Answering the Question: What Is Postmodernism?" trans. R. Durand, in *Postmodern Condition*, 81).

consider representation impossible or only inadequate to the reality that it represents, therefore, postmodernists do offer reasonable grounds for questioning or attempting to surpass representational modes of thought.

E. Conclusion

Postmodernists, then, do not hold to their distinctive tenets without some grounds. That all metanarratives, regardless of their content, are false and destructive; that the subject, in the sense of a human being set over against his environment as knower to known and responsible for his actions, does not exist; and that one either cannot, or cannot adequately, represent what is conventionally known as the real—these three theses are intelligible positions for which rational arguments can be advanced and which warrant the attention of the philosophical community, Christian as well as non-Christian.

IV. Criticisms

Although the views of individual postmodernists sometimes diverge wildly, virtually all thinkers who identify themselves as postmodernists unite in rejecting: (a) metanarratives; (b) the idea of a united, human subject; and (c) what they pejoratively describe as representationalist ways of thinking. In addition to uniting the movement, however, this threefold "no" of postmodernism burdens it with both logical and substantive difficulties.

The German philosopher Jürgen Habermas, in his *The Philosophical Discourse of Modernity*, famously indicts postmodernism for a double self-contradiction. First, he argues, postmodernists profess to reject all metanarratives, sc. all universal, totalizing claims; and yet the postmodern denial of the truthfulness of metanarratives is itself a universal, totalizing claim: a metanarrative.[18] Postmodernism, therefore, refutes itself.

Second, observes Habermas, postmodernists who criticize the metanarrative of universal rationality (logic, truth, reality, etc.), as they must in order to sustain their position, cannot do so without employing the basic laws of logic: sc. the tools of that rationality. In the act of criticizing the metanarrative of reason, then, postmodernists make use of it and thus implicitly affirm it.[19] Again, postmodernism refutes itself.

Besides these logical difficulties, moreover, postmodernism substantively contradicts the Christian faith in at least three, relatively straightforward ways. First, in rejecting all metanarratives, it rejects Christianity, which is itself a metanarrative. The incompatibility between Christianity and postmodernism at this point could hardly be more obvious. Second, in rejecting the existence of a unified subject, postmodernists deny that human beings can be justly liable to punishment for their sins. For if human

---

[18] Cf. e.g. Habermas' criticisms of Derrida on 210, G. Bataille on 236, and Foucault on 286 of his *The Philosophical Discourse of Modernity*, trans. F. Lawrence (Cambridge, MA: MIT Press, 1987; orig. 1985).

[19] "The totalizing self-critique of reason," writes Habermas, "gets caught in a performative contradiction since subject-centered reason can be convicted of being authoritarian in nature only by having recourse to its own tools (ibid., 185).

beings are not subjects but merely sites of conflict between varying impulses, they are not free and intelligent beings—the only sort of beings that can incur moral guilt.

Third and finally, Christianity seems to presuppose some form of representationalism. For a consistent Christian cannot admit either: (a) that human beings cannot know beings distinct from them, or (b) that human beings can know beings distinct from them only by overcoming that distinction. Option (a) would explicitly contravene the biblical teaching that all human beings know of God's eternal power and glory (Rom 1:20). Option (b) would allow human beings to know God only if they could somehow partially fuse their being with His divine nature. This does not occur, however, even in the incarnation, in which Christ's divine and human natures, albeit sustained by the same person, remain eternally distinct.

If human beings are to know of things absolutely distinct from themselves, they must be capable of knowing by means of true conceptions: sc. mental contents that correspond to, but do not inhere in, the things known. The notion that human beings know through such conceptions, however, seems to be precisely what the postmodernists mean by representationalism. It appears difficult to avoid the conclusion, therefore, that historic Christianity conflicts with all three of postmodernism's fundamental tenets: viz. the falsehood of all metanarratives, the nonexistence of the unified subject, and the inaccuracy of representationalism.

V.   CONCLUSION

Christians ought, therefore, to repudiate postmodernism. Such a repudiation does not imply, naturally, that Christianity is in any way consistent with modernism, the metanarrative over against which postmodernism defines itself. The secular metanarratives of modernity, rather, uniformly and explicitly reject orthodox Christianity. Enlightenment dreams of liberation and aggrandizement of the human subject, likewise, run directly contrary to Christian ideals of self-denial and self-sacrifice for the glory of God and the good of one's neighbor. Even the distinctively modern variants of representationalism conflict with Christianity.

Cartesian representationalism, for example, according to which one ought to lend credence only to that which is "clear and distinct" to oneself, is evidently inconsistent with Christian acceptance of the Bible on the basis of divinely authenticated testimony. Lockean representationalism, with its insistence of proportioning belief to evidence, likewise precludes authentic Christian faith; and Kantian representationalism, if one can call it representationalism at all, explicitly excludes the possibility that human beings can know anything about God. Both postmodernism and modernism, therefore, are anathema from the perspective of orthodox Christianity.

Chapter 19

THE KNOWLEDGE OF GOD

ALL ORTHODOX CHRISTIANS ACKNOWLEDGE THAT THE heavens declare the glory of God (Ps 19:1) and that His invisible things, His eternal power and deity, are known through the things He has made (Rom 1:20). Precisely how created realities indicate their divine origin to human beings, by contrast, is a point of some contention. Throughout the history of the church, numerous thinkers have proposed theistic arguments not only for the purpose of (a) persuading atheists to become theists, but also and more significantly for the purpose of (b) vindicating the rationality of human beings' spontaneous belief in a higher power. By successfully establishing the fact that data naturally known by almost all people imply that God exists, formulators of theistic arguments seek to show that theism is the natural, healthy condition of humankind and that the atheist is abnormal rather than enlightened.

The present chapter surveys four theistic arguments: the cosmological, ontological, moral, and teleological proofs of the existence of God. This survey, naturally, will convey little of the great variety of arguments within each of these categories, of the arguments' relations to broader systems of philosophy, or of the historical context in which the arguments surveyed have proved effective or otherwise. Some attention will be devoted, however, to objections that could be posed to the various arguments and to how these objections may be answered. Hopefully the arguments discussed will be treated in sufficient detail to give some sense of their cogency, their limitations, and their distinctive appeal.

I.   COSMOLOGICAL ARGUMENTS

Cosmological arguments, that is, arguments from the existence of a cosmos to the existence of a Creator, occur in two types: the conventional and the *kalām*. While each of these, and especially the conventional, occurs in numerous forms, a generic version of each is presented and evaluated in the following section.

A.   The Conventional Version of the Cosmological Argument

Cosmological arguments for the existence of God usually take the following form:

1.   At least one contingent being exists.

2. This contingent being possesses some cause or explanation; the principle of the reason of being dictates that this must be so.

3. The contingent being's cause or explanation is distinct from the contingent being itself; for if the being existed of itself, it would exist necessarily rather than contingently. If the being itself sufficed to explain its own existence, that is, then the presence or absence of other things, conditions, and so forth would not determine whether it existed.

4. The class of things that collectively cause or explain the contingent being's existence either includes a noncontingent (necessarily existing being) or it does not.

5. If no contingent being can account for its own existence, however, then no group of contingent beings can account entirely for the existence of a contingent thing.

6. Therefore the group of things that collectively account for a contingent being's existence must include at least one necessarily existing being.

7. Therefore at least one necessarily existing being exists.

This version of the cosmological argument faces at least four serious objections: (a) the principle of the reason of being is not demonstrably sound; (b) step 5 is a case of the fallacy of composition; (c) the cosmos is demonstrably contingent only with respect to its form; and (d) the argument does not necessarily entail the truthfulness of monotheism. The first three criticisms are answered in the present section; the fourth has already been addressed in the discussion of Richard Swinburne's apologetics in chap. 15, "Contemporary Apologetics."

1. The principle of the reason of being

The principle of the reason of being, also known as the principle of sufficient reason, states that every being has a cause or explanation either in itself or in some other being. A critic of the argument above might object that the argument's soundness hinges on whether this principle is in fact true. The critic may challenge a proponent of this argument either to demonstrate the principle of the reason of being or to admit that his argument is less than demonstrative.

The proponent of such arguments could avoid the unattractive second option, however, if he could show that denying the principle of the reason of being implies absurd consequences. One could accomplish this, by arguing as follows.

1. A being exists, which possesses a cause or explanation neither in itself nor in another being (this is another way of saying that the principle of the reason of being is false).

2. This being has no cause or explanation in another being.

3. If that is the case, however, the being is independent of all other beings and is therefore self-sufficient.

4. If the being is self-sufficient, then it possesses an explanation of its being in itself (self-sufficiency).

5. The being therefore is not such that it possesses a cause or explanation neither in itself nor in another being.

Since proposition 1 implies proposition 5, which is its contrary, proposition 1 is absurd. That is, one cannot deny the principle of the reason of being without falling into absurdity. The dependence of step 2 in the cosmological argument above on the principle of the reason of being therefore in no way undermines the demonstrative character of the argument.

2. The fallacy of composition

The fallacy of composition consists in ascribing to two or more things, when combined, properties that they exemplify only when they are separated. One would commit the fallacy of composition, for example, if one reasoned:

1. Five is odd and two is even.
2. Five and two are seven.
3. Therefore seven is both odd and even.

Also if one were told that a building is composed of small bricks and assumed that the building itself is therefore small, one would be committing the fallacy of composition. Critics of the cosmological argument commonly charge that its proponents commit the fallacy of composition when they assert in step 5, "If no contingent being can account for its own existence, however, then no group of contingent beings can account entirely for the existence of a contingent thing."[1] It is difficult to deny, moreover, that a certain analogy exists between the argument from the smallness of its bricks to the smallness of a building and the argument from one contingent thing's inability to account for its existence to the inability of numerous contingent things to account completely for one contingent thing's existence.

The two cases, however, are not strictly parallel. The reasoning in step 5 resembles an argument from the statement, "Every part of the building is a brick," to the conclusion, "The building is a brick building." The crucial difference between argument "a," from the smallness of the bricks to the smallness of the building, and argument "b," from the "brickness" of the bricks to the brickness of the building is relatively simple. Smallness is an accidental property of bricks; with sufficient clay, equipment, and ingenuity, one could construct a brick as large as Stonehenge. Because smallness is accidental to bricks, it can be overcome by adding more bricks. Brickness, however, that is, whatever makes a brick a brick, is essential to bricks. Regardless of how many bricks one compiles, therefore, one will never build a palace of gold with bricks. By the same token oddness and evenness are accidental to sets of numbers; one need merely add an odd set of numbers to an even set to transform an even set into an odd. Regardless of

---

[1] B. Russell, e.g., levels this charge in his famous debate over the existence of God with F. C. Copleston. See the transcript of the debate in J. Hick's anthology, *The Existence of God* (New York: Macmillan, 1964), 175.

how many numbers one adds to a set of numbers, however, one can never construct a triangle simply by adding numbers.

Contingency cannot constitute an accidental or merely contingent property. For if a being is "contingently contingent" (i.e., if the being might have been necessary, but is not), then one must allow for the possibility that this being could be "contingently necessary." Necessity and contingency, however, are mutually exclusive. Since the existence of a "contingently contingent" being would imply the possibility of a "contingently necessary" being—and the very idea of a "contingently necessary" being is self-contradictory nonsense—it is inconceivable that a "contingently (i.e., accidentally) contingent" being might exist. If a being is contingent at all, therefore, it is essentially contingent; and, as seen, an argument from the character of the parts to the character of the whole is valid when essential properties are concerned. Proponents of the cosmological argument, accordingly, do not commit the fallacy of composition when they reason from the contingency of individual beings to the contingency of these beings as a group.

3. Contingency only as to form?

One might argue in opposition to the cosmological argument that its first premise, "At least one contingent being exists," requires qualification. For the law of conservation of mass-energy dictates that the amount of mass-energy in the universe remains constant; mass-energy, that is, never ceases to exist but rather periodically mutates from mass to energy and vice versa. Mass-energy, therefore, while radically contingent in its form, is indestructible and therefore is necessary as to its existence.

A number of considerations, however, call this conclusion into question. First, the law of conservation of mass-energy does not take into account the possible effects of nonphysical causes (God, angels, etc.) and thus does not establish the indestructibility of mass-energy. Second, indestructibility does not constitute necessary existence. For, in order to exist necessarily, a being must be not merely incapable of ceasing to exist, once it exists; but it must also be incapable of coming into existence because necessarily it always already exists. Third, atheistic versions of Big Bang cosmology require that the law of conservation of mass-energy fail to operate in the initial state of the universe in which the sum total of mass-energy in the cosmos increases exponentially. If the law of the conservation of mass-energy itself does not hold necessarily, it can hardly suffice to establish the necessity of mass-energy's existence.

Fourth, it is not at all evident that a composite entity, that is, something made up of many parts (like mass-energy), can exist necessarily, at least in the sense of "necessary existence" employed in the above version of the cosmological argument. Admittedly one could conceive of a God who eternally and necessarily gives life to an inferior, composite being. In this case it would be possible intelligibly to speak of a being that is composite, dependent on another being, and yet also necessarily existent. Such a being would be necessarily existent, however, only in a derivative sense. It would exist necessarily only because the superior being, whose existence is necessary in a nonderivative sense, i.e., in and of itself, necessarily bestows existence on it.

This kind of necessary but dependent being could not play the role of the necessary being whose existence is affirmed in the conclusion, step 6 of the cosmological argument employed here. To explain: step 4 of the argument poses the question of whether those things that completely account for a contingent being's existence are (a) a set of contingent beings alone or (b) a set of beings that includes at least one necessary being. Step 5 then excludes option "a" on the implicit grounds that a group of contingent beings cannot completely account for its own being and therefore cannot completely account for the being of anything else. Step 5 thus implies that one requires at least one being that can account for its own existence to account for the existence of a contingent entity. The necessary being demanded by step 6 therefore must be such that it accounts for its own being, and the kind of dependent yet necessary being whose existence was hypothesized in the last paragraph cannot meet this qualification. A dependent entity, whether necessary or not, by definition fails to account for its own being.

Every composite being (i.e., every being that consists in parts in any sense) is a dependent being; for the existence of the whole depends logically speaking on the existence of the parts. The entity that accounts for its own being, which is demanded by step 6, therefore must be incomposite, utterly lacking in parts. Anything that is incomposite, however, is incapable of changing. For as Thomas Aquinas observed, anything that changes becomes partly different and remains partly the same, which is inconceivable for a being that has no parts.[2]

It is inconceivable therefore that an entity that is necessary in the sense demanded by step 6 (i.e., an entity that accounts for its own existence) could be contingent in one respect and necessary in another as the objection under consideration suggests. Because step 6 demands the existence of an entity that accounts for its own being, and not merely any conceivable necessary being and because an entity that accounts for its own existence must be incomposite, the necessary being demanded by step 6 must be changeless and thus necessary not only in its existence but in every aspect of its being. The idea that an entity necessary in its being but contingent in its form might constitute this necessary being is thus excluded.

The following seven points summarize the reasoning of this section.

1. The cosmological argument above demands the existence not merely of a necessary being but also of a necessary being that accounts for its own existence.
2. Since a composite being is dependent on its parts for its existence, it cannot account for its own existence.
3. The necessary being demanded by the argument above must therefore be incomposite.
4. Since change consists in becoming partly different while remaining partly the same, an incomposite being cannot change in any way.
5. Since the necessary being demanded by the argument must be incomposite, it must also be unchangeable.

---

[2] Thomas Aquinas, *Summa Theologiae* 1, q. 9, a. 1 corp.

6. The necessary being demanded by the argument is thus necessary in every aspect of its being and not merely in its existence.
7. Mass-energy, or anything else that one might consider necessary in existence but contingent in form, cannot therefore constitute the being demanded by the argument.

4. Less than reasonable objections

While the following three objections do not qualify as serious objections, they carry great weight with many unbelievers.

a. Who created God?

First, when one argues that God must have created the world, a skeptic sometimes retorts, "Who created God?" This objection is less than serious because it arises solely from a misunderstanding of the principle of the reason of being, according to which every being possesses a cause or explanation of its existence either in another being or in itself. The objector who asks, "Who created God?" supposes that the cosmological argument employs not the principle of the reason of being but the much simpler and patently absurd principle that everything has a cause. If the cosmological argument appealed to this principle, it would indeed be ludicrous. To reach the conclusion that God exists, the person who employed this principle in a cosmological argument would be compelled either (a) to except God from the principle, in which case someone could reasonably ask why some more mundane reality might not be excepted as well, or (b) to conclude that God caused Himself, which is manifestly impossible.

To refute this objection, one need merely note that the cosmological argument depends not on the view that everything has a cause but on the principle of the reason of being, according to which again everything has a cause or explanation of its existence either in itself or in another. This principle applies unambiguously to God and impels one to assert only that God is His own explanation; His existence is self-explanatory as a being whose existence is by definition necessary and self-existent. The principle of the reason of being in no way implies that God is His own cause.

Unlike the rather arbitrary hypothesis that everything has a cause, moreover, the principle of the reason of being is demonstrably true. For, as already stated, one cannot deny the principle of the reason of being without contradicting himself. The quip, "Who created God?" therefore constitutes more of a misrepresentation of the cosmological argument than an objection that requires refutation.

b. An infinite chain of causes extending backward

Another less-than-serious objection is the assertion that the chain of causality responsible for the universe's existence need not stop at a self-existent God but could rather extend backward from one caused being to another caused being infinitely. This is a legitimate objection to cosmological arguments whose premises include the impossibility of an infinite regress. The argument set forth above, however, supposes no such thing. Rather, step 5 notes that a group of contingent beings, such as the members of the hypothetical infinite chain, cannot account for their own existence any more than a particular contingent entity can account for its own. Since, according to the principle of the reason of being, an explanation of the contingent entities' existence must be found either in themselves or in some other being, and it is not found in themselves, then the argument concludes that some noncontingent being that explains their existence must itself exist. Whether the group of contingent beings considered is a series of beings each of whom causes the next infinitely in both directions is irrelevant to this argument. Such an infinite chain by itself fails to satisfy the requirements of the principle of the reason of being.

c. Backward causality

A third unserious objection, that the universe itself might have effected its own origin (the Big Bang theory in most scenarios) through backward causality, suffers from precisely the same difficulty as the previous two objections. The person who argues in this way does not realize that many versions of the cosmological argument, such as that proposed here, do not seek to prove that the chain of causes responsible for today's universe requires a first cause capable of acting independently.

The form of the cosmological argument advocated here, rather, leads to the existence of a being who transcends the entire chain and whose action accounts for the existence of everything in the universe at all times. The God to whom the argument advanced here concludes does not in any sense create by tipping over the first in a fantastically long series of dominoes. Whether some of the dominoes might exercise backward causality is therefore irrelevant to the question of whether this argument is sound. Whether contingent entities can exercise backward causality or not, the principle of the reason of being indicates that contingent entities alone cannot account for their own existence. This implies that some noncontingent being must exist who accounts both for the contingent beings' existence and for his own. Arguments for the possibility of backward causation or circular chains of causality, even if successful, would in no way impact the credibility of the cosmological argument proposed here.

5. Conclusion

The version of the cosmological argument advocated here appears immune to the most common criticisms, reasonable and otherwise. Its most notable premise is unquestionably the principle of the reason of being. Since one can demonstrate the principle's soundness without appealing to empirical evidence, it enables one to bypass disputes about whether, given human beings' limited experience of the universe, they actually know that all finite things require a cause. Likewise this principle enables one to construct a cosmological argument whose soundness does not depend on the impossibility of an infinite regress, which is widely questioned by ordinary people. One could reasonably argue therefore that the principle of the reason of being constitutes a key feature of conventional cosmological arguments capable of withstanding the suspicion of contemporary skeptics.

B. The Kalām Version of the Cosmological Argument

The *kalām* cosmological argument constitutes a medieval Islamic form of the cosmological argument, which was rediscovered and popularized in the West by William Lane Craig.[3] This argument consists of four steps:

1. Everything that begins to exist has a cause.
2. The universe began to exist.
3. The universe therefore has a cause.
4. Since this cause created the universe at a certain point, the cause must be personal.

Since everything that begins to exist is contingent, the conventional cosmological argument above verifies the *kalām* cosmological argument's first step. The third step follows necessarily from the first two. Premises 2 and 4, however, may seem highly questionable and thus worthy of serious evaluation.

1. Did the universe begin to exist?

For the claim that the universe began to exist, Craig presents two arguments, one relatively strong and one rather weak. The strong argument is his inference from the present expansion of the universe to its origin in a Big Bang. Craig argues that if the universe has been continuously expanding at the present rate of acceleration (the expansion seems to be speeding up) throughout its life cycle, then the universe, being finite, must have come to be through some kind of explosion from an infinitely small whole or from nothingness. Revealed data about the universe's origins, admittedly, might call into question Craig's uniformitarianism, that is, his assumption that the universe has always behaved as it behaves now. If one excludes revealed data, however, as one must in order to produce an argument that is designed to persuade unbelievers, then uniformitarianism seems like a reasonable assumption. A merely empirical argument, such as Craig's argument from the expansion of the universe, naturally can at best render its conclusion overwhelmingly probable. As seen in previous chapters, however, rational persons, at least in certain circumstances, ought to yield their assent to probable statements. On the whole therefore, Craig's scientific case for the earth's beginning to exist at some point in the past seems persuasive.

Craig's philosophical argument for this point, however, seems weak. Absurd consequences would follow, he maintains, if an actually infinite series, such as a series of moments extending from the present time infinitely into the past, actually existed. Infinity equals infinity, Craig reasons, in accord with standard mathematical understandings of the subject. If an infinite stamp collection existed and if it were composed of equal sets of French and German stamps, the number of French stamps would nevertheless equal the total number of stamps in the collection. This kind of scenario strikes Craig as so profoundly counterintuitive that he discounts the possibility of an actually infinite series.

---

[3] W. L. Craig, *The Kalām Cosmological Argument* (London: Macmillan, 1979).

As Richard Swinburne has observed, however, the moments during which an infinitely old universe has existed would constitute an actual infinite only if they were all presently actual, and this appears counterintuitive as well. If all moments past are presently actual moreover, then the infinite series of periods of time—one-half an hour + one-fourth an hour + one-eighth an hour + one-sixteenth an hour and so forth—that has elapsed over the past sixty minutes is presently actual as well. In this case it is demonstrable that an actually infinite series can occur in reality. Craig's argument for the a priori impossibility of an actually infinite series is thus fallacious and only obscures the strength of his scientific argument that the universe has a beginning.

2. Must the cause of the universe be personal?

The shortcomings of his philosophical case for the finite duration of the universe notwithstanding, Craig's appeal to Big Bang cosmology does render it probable that the universe had a beginning. Since one can establish absolutely that what has a beginning is caused and probably that the universe has a beginning, the *kalām* argument appears sufficient to establish that the universe probably has a cause. Whether the argument also suffices to prove this cause personal, however, is a different question.

Initially some may doubt the claim that because the cause of the universe created it at one point rather than another, this cause is therefore personal. For if God is unchangeable and space-time consists fundamentally in distinct events, which do not occur in the unchangeable God, then there is no time before creation. God did not create the universe at a certain time; rather He created time by creating a universe in which distinct events occur. It might seem anthropomorphic to assert that God created the universe at a certain point.

This claim, however, has a certain logic. Though God certainly did not and could not have created the universe at a specific point in time, He did create it in such a way that a unique, finite amount of time has elapsed from its beginning to the present. An impersonal God, it seems, who creates out of necessity rather than choice, would have created an omnitemporal universe, a possibility Craig's understanding of the actual infinite excludes. Thus it is probable that the cause to whose existence the first three steps of the *kalām* cosmological argument point is personal.

3. Conclusion

On the whole Craig's *kalām* cosmological argument seems successful. However, his speculations about the impossibility of an actual infinite both weaken the overall argument's credibility and distract attention from his strong case for the universe's beginning in a Big Bang. Also, the introduction of empirical evidence for a Big Bang deprives Craig's argument of the austere elegance in argumentation for which philosophers often strive. The inclusion of such data in the *kalām* cosmological argument, however, is critically important, not only because it gives Craig a viable means of confirming that the universe had a beginning but also because such evidence gains a hearing among contemporary people that philosophical reasoning does not. One frequently finds, even among relatively educated people, the view that what purports to be scientific proof is unassailable, whereas philosophy is mere speculation. Craig's formulation of the *kalām* cosmological argument, therefore, although far more vulnerable to critique than the conventional cosmological argument formulated above, may also prove more effective in the practical task of winning atheists to theism.

C. Summary

The present section has examined one of the conventional forms of the cosmological argument for God's existence and William Lane Craig's formulation of the *kalām* cosmological argument. On scrutiny, both forms of the cosmological argument prove adequate to motivate rational belief in the existence of a deity, although the conventional argument excels the *kalām* in rigor, and the *kalām* excels the conventional in appeal to contemporary persons.

II. Ontological Arguments

Ontological arguments for the existence of God come in numerous forms. The three most common are those proposed by Anselm, Descartes, and Leibniz.

A. Anselm's Version of the Ontological Argument

Anselm (1033–1109), archbishop of Canterbury, proposed the paradigmatic form of the ontological argument in his *Proslogium* 2, in which he defines God as "a being than which nothing greater can be conceived."

> Even the fool, who has said in his heart, "There is no God" (Pss 14:1; 53:1), is convinced that something exists in the understanding, at least, than which nothing greater can be conceived. For, when he hears of this, he understands it. And whatever is understood, exists in the understanding. And assuredly that, than which nothing greater can be conceived, cannot exist in the understanding alone. For, suppose it exists in the understanding alone: then it can be conceived to exist in reality; which is greater. Therefore, if that, than which nothing greater can be conceived, exists in the understanding alone, the very being, than which nothing greater can be conceived, is one, than which a greater can be conceived. But this is obviously impossible. Hence, there is no doubt that there exists a being, than which nothing greater can be conceived, and it exists both in the understanding and in reality.[4]

Anselm argued, in other words:

1. The fool understands the meaning of "that, than which nothing greater can be understood" (=TTWNGCBU).
2. Therefore TTWNGCBU exists in the fool's understanding.
3. It can be conceived that TTWNGCBU exists in reality.
4. To exist in reality is greater than to exist in the fool's mind alone.

---

[4] Anselm, "Proslogium," 2, in *St. Anselm: Basic Writings*, ed. and trans. S. N. Deane (Chicago: Open Court, 1962), 54.

5. If TTWNGCBU existed in the fool's mind alone, it would not be TTWNGCBU.
6. It is evident, however, that TTWNGCBU is TTWNGCBU.
7. TTWNGCBU therefore exists not only in the fool's understanding but also in reality.

This form of the ontological argument is fallacious, among other reasons, because it does not distinguish between the idea of TTWNGCBU and TTWNGCBU itself. It attempts, rather, to infer the existence of TTWNGCBU from a property of an utterly different being, namely, the *idea* of TTWNGCBU. A parody of Anselm's argument by his contemporary, Gaunilo of Martmoutiers, illustrates the fallacious character of Anselm's reasoning. After proposing the idea of an "island more excellent than all lands," Gaunilo wrote:

> You can no longer doubt that this island which is more excellent than all lands exists somewhere, since you have no doubt that it is in your under- standing. And since it is more excellent not to be in the understanding alone, but to exist both in the understanding and in reality, for this reason it must exist. For if it does not exist, any land which really exists will be more excellent than it; and so the island already understood by you to be more excellent will not be more excellent.[5]

No reasonable person would believe that such an island exists, at least on the basis of this kind of argumentation. One's idea of an entity, no matter how exalted an idea, can- not prove that the entity exists. Countless persons have followed Gaunilo's example in parodying Anselm's argument. Especially during the twentieth century, one finds ontological arguments for the nonexistence of God, for the nonexistence of the devil, for polytheism, and for many other outlandish conclusions. Suffice it to say that these arguments are no more valid than Anselm's and that the value of this endless stream of parodies is highly dubious.

B. Descartes' Version of the Ontological Argument

While René Descartes advances something similar to Anselm's ontological argu- ment at various places in his writings, he also formulates an argument that Anselm seems not to have anticipated, namely, that the idea of God is so sublime that no other being could have caused it than God. Descartes states his reasoning most succinctly perhaps in his "First Set of Replies" to objections directed to his *Meditations on First Philosophy*. Here Descartes writes, "Since we have within us the idea of God, and contained in the idea is every perfection that can be thought of, the absolutely evident inference is that this idea depends on some cause in which all this perfection is indeed to be found, namely a really existing God."[6] Descartes' argument, which has struck many readers as quite daring, depends on two presuppositions.

---

[5] Gaunilo, "What Someone on Behalf of the Fool Replies to These Arguments," in Deane, *St. Anselm*, 309.

[6] Descartes, *Meditations on First Philosophy*, in *Philosophical Writings of Descartes*, trans. J. Cotting- ham, R. Stoothoff, and D. Murdoch (Cambridge: Cambridge University Press, 1984–85), 2:76.

First, Descartes assumed, as he explained in the third of his *Meditations*, that "in order for a given idea to contain such and such objective [i.e., representational] reality, it must surely derive it from some cause which contains at least as much formal [i.e., actual] reality as there is objective reality in the idea."[7] In other words Descartes extended the commonsensical principle that the effect cannot be greater than the cause to the relation between extramental entities and ideas. In order for him to have an idea as great as the idea of God, he maintained, there must really be a God who corresponds to this idea and who caused it.

One might wonder, however, why Descartes does not suspect that his idea of an infinite, maximally excellent being derives from his simply conceiving of a lesser being and negating all of that being's limitations. Descartes supplied the answer to this question when he clarified the second key assumption of his distinctive version of the ontological argument. In his "Fifth Set of Replies" to objections Descartes asserted, "It is false that the infinite is understood through the negation of a boundary or limit; on the contrary, all limitation implies a negation of the infinite."[8] To the extent that this positive concept of infinity can be extended to all the other perfections in his idea of God, then Descartes can be assured that this idea does not derive from mere negations of finite perfections.

Descartes' second assumption obviates a fairly grave objection to his version of the ontological argument. The argument as a whole, however, fails because Descartes's first assumption is not valid. In presupposing that some extramental reality, which is as great as or greater than anything he can conceive, exists, Descartes confused the ideal and the real orders no less than Anselm. Although Descartes's version of the ontological argument differs drastically from Anselm's, it ultimately miscarries for much the same reason.

C. Leibniz's Version of the Ontological Argument

Gottfried W. Leibniz (1646–1716) disapproved of Descartes's version of the ontological argument for the same reasons as those just set forth. "This argument," he writes, "does not adequately prove that the idea of God, if we do have it, must come from that of which it is an idea."[9] Leibniz was more sympathetic, however, to Anselm's argument and Descartes's revival of it.

> It is not fallacious, but it is an incomplete demonstration which assumes something which should also be proved in order to render the argument mathematically evident. The point is that it is tacitly assumed that this idea of a wholly great or wholly perfect being is possible and does not imply a contradiction.[10]

---

[7] Ibid., 28–29.

[8] Ibid., 252.

[9] G. W. Leibniz, *New Essays on Human Understanding*, trans. P. Remnant and J. Bennett (Cambridge: Cambridge University Press, 1996), §4.10.7, p. 308.

[10] Ibid.

261

Leibniz might seem rather bold in asserting that all one must do to render Anselm's argument valid is to prove that God might possibly exist. Strictly speaking, however, he is correct. For if Anselm's God exists, He exists necessarily. Necessary existence is one of the attributes Anselm ascribes to TTWNGCBU. If this sort of God does not exist, however, it must be impossible for Him to exist. A necessarily existent being, by definition, cannot fall, like contingent beings, anywhere between these two extremes. If therefore one establishes that it is not impossible for God to exist, one establishes not merely that He does exist but that He exists necessarily.

Human beings, however, cannot verify in any direct way that the divine perfections are compatible with each other, that, for example, perfect justice and perfect love can coexist in one and the same entity. Proving that it is not impossible for God to exist, accordingly, is no mean task. Leibniz proposed to accomplish this by the following argument, which appears in his note of 1676, "That the Most Perfect Being Exists."[11]

1. Something that cannot be defined cannot be analyzed.
2. Something can be defined only if it is in some way limited.
3. Perfections express whatever they express without any limitation.
4. Therefore perfections cannot be defined.
5. Therefore perfections cannot be analyzed.
6. A proposition such as "A and B are incompatible" cannot be demonstrated if neither A nor B is analyzable.
7. Therefore no proposition, "Perfection A and Perfection B are incompatible" can be demonstrated; perfections, as already shown, are "unanalyzable."
8. Any proposition that is true is either demonstrable or self-evident.
9. The proposition, "Perfection A and Perfection B are incompatible," is neither demonstrable nor self-evident.
10. The proposition, "Perfection A and Perfection B are incompatible," is therefore false.
11. The proposition, "Perfection A and Perfection B are compatible," is consequently true.
12. If the divine perfections are compatible, then it is not impossible for God to exist.
13. God's existence is either necessary or impossible.
14. God's existence is therefore necessary.
15. God necessarily exists.

The principal weaknesses of this argument are three. First, Leibniz equivocated in his use of the term *define*. In step 1 he correctly asserted that something that cannot even be assigned a nominal definition, something that words cannot even in a halting and inadequate way express, cannot be analyzed. In step 2, however, he stated that something can be defined only if it is in some way limited. This claim also is quite true if

---

[11] G. W. Leibniz, "That the Most Perfect Being Exists," Appendix 10, in *New Essays Concerning Human Understanding*, trans. A. G. Langley (Chicago: Open Court, 1916), 714–15.

by "define" one means "capture the essence of something in such a way as to render it comprehensible."

Numerous entities that defy definition in the sense of step 2 seem susceptible to definition in the sense of step 1. One will never be able to comprehend the divine essence, for example, but one can certainly discern the meaning of the word *God*. The divine perfections, likewise, could be unlimited and so indefinable in the sense of step 2 without being unanalyzable, a quality that attaches only to things indefinable in the sense of step 1.

However, the putative "unanalyzability" of the divine perfections renders the proposition, "Perfection A and Perfection B are incompatible," indemonstrable and therefore false; and the statement, "Perfection A and Perfection B are compatible," correspondingly true. The entire argument, accordingly, depends on a confusion of two radically distinct concepts of definition.

Second, Leibniz's assumption that simply because a statement is indemonstrable it must therefore be false is gratuitous. A statement might be indemonstrable, after all, not because it is false but because it is meaningless. In this case the indemonstrability of a statement would by no means imply the accuracy of its negation. Third, it seems that one could substitute the word *compatible* for *incompatible* in steps 6 and 7 and employ precisely the same argument to prove that the divine perfections are incompatible and that the existence of God is therefore impossible.

Leibniz deserves credit for recognizing that Anselm's proof is incomplete because Anselm did not prove the existence of God possible and for recognizing that God's existence cannot be merely possible but must be either impossible or necessary. Leibniz's version of the ontological argument, however, is as problematic as those of Anselm and Descartes.

D. Conclusion

On the whole, then, ontological arguments for the existence of God seem so problematic as to be of little practical use to the Christian apologist. The method of reasoning about God developed by Anselm in his *Proslogium*, frequently referred to as "perfect-being theology," however, can be helpful in clarifying the nature of the divine attributes. A typical argument in perfect-being theology would proceed along the following lines.

1. God is the being than which no greater can be conceived.
2. If God were X, then God would not be the being than which no greater can be conceived.
3. Therefore God is not X.

Arguments from the concept of a perfect being to its existence may be uniformly unsound. Yet arguments from the concept of a perfect being to that being's character, if He exists, can be illuminating.[12]

---

[12] For a contemporary defense and exploration of perfect-being theology, see K. A. Rogers, *Perfect Being Theology* (Edinburgh: Edinburgh University Press, 2000).

III. MORAL ARGUMENTS

Moral arguments for the existence of God come in two forms: arguments from the existence of the moral law itself and arguments from moral awareness, that is, human knowledge of the moral law. The latter constitutes, strictly speaking, a kind of abductive, teleological argument. This variety of argument is discussed in another section below, and a sterling example of a sound argument of this sort appears in the discussion of C. S. Lewis's apologetics in chap. 15, "Contemporary Apologetics." The present context then does not discuss arguments from moral awareness; instead the section discusses theistic arguments based on the existence of a moral law itself.

Arguments from the very existence of a moral law to God's existence are typically as follows.

1. There is a moral law.
2. The existence of a moral law presupposes the existence of a moral lawgiver.
3. There is therefore a moral lawgiver.

Such arguments admittedly have the advantage of being easily comprehensible. Along with arguments from moral awareness, moreover, they gain a readier hearing than many other theistic arguments because they base their appeal on a concrete and undeniable fact, namely, the individual human being's consciousness of moral obligation.

A. The Euthyphro Dilemma

Arguments from the existence of a moral law to the existence of a moral lawgiver raise what is known as the "Euthyphro dilemma" in an especially pointed way. In Plato's brief dialogue *Euthyphro,* Socrates and his friend Euthyphro discuss among other things, the question of "whether what is pious or holy is beloved by the gods because it is holy, or holy because it is beloved of the gods."[13] Socrates, as one might expect, concluded early in the dialogue that the holy (just, good, etc.) is beloved of the gods because it is holy.

One who argues that there can be no moral law if there is no moral lawgiver, however, seems to take the opposite side. Those who employ the moral argument seem to think that nothing is right or wrong in itself and that something can become right or wrong only by virtue of God's arbitrary decree.

One can reasonably argue that the second position is unbiblical and un-Christian. For if the moral law were the product of an arbitrary decree, if some moral principles were not simply fixed, then in some possible universe it would be virtuous to blaspheme, murder, cheat, lie, steal—in short, to do everything that is forbidden in the present universe. Obviously, then the view that the contents of the moral law depend wholly on God's decision is unacceptable.

The position that morality is somehow independent of God, an authority to which even He must submit, however, is equally unacceptable. Moral arguments for the ex-

---

[13] Plato, *Euthyphro* 10a.

istence of God place the unbeliever face-to-face with a terrible dilemma for theism. It seems that one cannot truthfully say either that justice is just because God declares it just or that God declares it just because it is just.

Naturally one need not become an atheist to escape this dilemma. Rather, one can recognize that since God is incomposite, or simple, as noted earlier, He is not really distinct from the virtues He possesses. Unlike a creature who can be good, just, holy, loving, and so forth, God *is* justice, He *is* goodness, He *is* holiness, He *is* love itself. When God declares an act just, He does not submit to a standard of justice outside Himself. He is justice itself. The doctrine of divine simplicity resolves the Euthyphro dilemma for Christianity.[14] In apologetic contexts, however, it seems that one ought not raise this issue at all.

B. Conclusion

Arguments from the reality of the moral law to the reality of a moral lawgiver, therefore, seem deficient, inasmuch as they apparently presuppose that the moral law is a product of God's arbitrary decree, and they raise uncomfortable questions about the ethical implications of theism that distract attention from the intrinsic credibility of the Christian message.

IV. TELEOLOGICAL ARGUMENTS

Teleological arguments, also known as arguments from design, appeal to evidence in nature that it was designed for a purpose, or *telos*, in order to establish the existence of a purposeful designer, God. The nature of and objections to such arguments have been discussed in the sections on William Paley's and Richard Swinburne's accomplishments as apologists. Therefore a brief discussion of teleological arguments here suffices to fulfill the purposes of this section.

A. Analogical Arguments

Teleological arguments for the existence of God typically take one of three forms: analogical, deductive, or abductive. Arguments of the first type premise that various natural items closely resemble the products of human artifice. Since the latter obviously issue from intelligent human designers, one may reason that the former also issue from one or more superhuman, intelligent designers. While such arguments are not utterly without value, many question the soundness of its foundational assumption, namely, that naturally produced things resemble human artifacts in such a way as to suggest that they originate from a similar source. The usefulness of analogical arguments from design therefore appears limited at best.

---

[14] This resolution of the Euthyphro dilemma is stated in N. Kretzmann, "Abraham, Isaac, and Euthyphro: God and the Basis of Morality," in *Philosophy of Religion: The Big Questions*, ed. E. Stump and M. J. Murray (Oxford: Blackwell, 1999), 417–27.

B. Deductive Arguments

Deductive teleological arguments are inferences from the existence of certain observable entities, which random processes could not conceivably produce, to the existence of a transcendent, intelligent designer.

This argument is immune from the objection we have just noted, which severely reduces the credibility of teleological arguments of an analogical character. One cannot reasonably dismiss every teleological argument, therefore, as a simpleminded application of ill-conceived analogies. Deductive teleological arguments frequently generate difficulties of their own, however. Specifically some deductive teleological arguments purport to prove not only (a) that certain natural entities are probably intelligently designed or (b) that one cannot reasonably suppose that certain natural entities are not intelligently designed, but also (c) that it is strictly inconceivable that certain entities are not intelligently designed.

One might, it seems, have strong and perhaps even compelling reasons for believing in intelligent design without being able to prove an assertion as sweeping as point "c" above. Yet if one presented these reasons as evidence for a proposition like "c," which might seem almost impossible to prove, one might thereby profoundly obscure the evidential force of one's reasons. It seems prudent therefore to err on the side of modesty and avoid claims to the effect that any alternative to the design hypothesis is strictly inconceivable.

C. Abductive Arguments

The easiest way to bolster the credibility of deductive teleological arguments seems to be by converting them into an abductive form. Abductive arguments seek to prove not that certain conclusions follow inexorably from their premises but rather that a given solution constitutes the most reasonable, available explanation for a given set of data. Since this is precisely the kind of argumentation that one employs in experimental science, abductive arguments should prove familiar and, to a certain extent at least, credible to educated unbelievers. Such arguments do admittedly fall short of the absolute standard of proof demanded by many incorrigible opponents of Christianity. If well conceived, however, such arguments can suffice to move reasonable persons to embrace theism as the best explanation of the data available to them.

D. Conclusion

All teleological arguments naturally possess the virtues of being concrete and drawing on data from the natural sciences. Nevertheless, as seen, abductive arguments—arguments according to which theism constitutes the most reasonable explanation of the data presented by the universe—(a) excel deductive arguments in credibility because they make more modest claims and (b) excel analogical arguments in that they do not depend on analogies of dubious value. While all forms of the teleological argument can be useful in persuading individuals of the existence of God, the abductive variety seems to be the least problematic.

V. CONCLUSION

One form of the moral argument for God's existence and one form of the ontological argument, then, constitute embarrassments to the Christian apologist. He possesses potent tools of persuasion nevertheless in the cosmological and teleological arguments, which are sufficient for the purpose of verifying Scripture's claim that God's creation testifies to His existence and nature. One ought not be naively confident in the persuasive power of these arguments in a jaded and hostile culture. One can reasonably hope, however, that these arguments will continue to assure at least some human beings of the essential truths of natural revelation.

Chapter 20

THE PROBLEM OF EVIL

THE TITLE OF THIS CHAPTER, "THE Problem of Evil," may appear somewhat misleading. For what one refers to as "the" problem of evil may assume countless forms and fuel an enormous variety of arguments. An atheist, for example, might argue for the incompatibility of God's existence with any degree of evil in the world. Or he might argue that the kind, the amount, or the unequal distribution of evils in the world, or all of these considered together, preclude the possibility that a benevolent, omniscient, and omnipotent God oversees the workings of the universe. The atheist might also shift attention from the amount, nature, and distribution of evils in the world to the divine act of permitting evil to occur, indicting God not for the consequences of His action or lack thereof but for the putative immorality of a particular failure to act. Again the atheist could shrink from saying that the considerations he raises render God's existence logically impossible, and argue only that, given the evils in today's world and God's alleged failure to counteract them, one might seem irrational or perhaps even immoral if one believed in or worshipped Him. Once more a non-Christian theist might argue that some teachings of Christianity (e.g., the doctrine of eternal punishment or that of God's causing the innocent Christ to suffer on behalf of guilty human beings) portray God as a bloodthirsty tyrant in a way that his own religion or philosophy does not.

In thinking about the problems of evil, therefore, one ought never to assume that a single argument or manner of approaching the subject will suffice to answer every skeptic's accusations about the Christian God's supposed complicity in evil. So this chapter includes a brief inquiry into the nature of evil and then presents seven responses to objections of this nature: (a) the free will defense, (b) the "problem of good" counterobjection, (c) the divine wisdom defense, (d) the counterargument from the inevitable imperfection of created universes, (e) the "vale of soul-making" defense, (f) the appeal to divine justice, and (g) the *felix culpa* defense. One can employ these arguments, some of which are more valid than others, singly or in tandem, to address a wide variety of objections related to the problem of evil.

I. THE NATURE OF EVIL

The Christian who holds that God created all things "very good" (Gen 1:31) cannot consistently regard evil as a kind of being of some sort, which would require its own creator. Whatever evil is, it must constitute some declension from God's creation, a lack of being of some sort. Nor can the Christian consistently identify evil with a mere lack of being. In that case it would be evil for mushrooms not to have eyes, for human beings not to have wings, and for all creatures not to be divine.

From a Christian perspective, then, the nature of evil must consist neither in a substance, nor in a generalized lack of being, but in a lack of a particular sort of being. This particular sort of being cannot be something that a creature does not need or that it ought not to have; lack of the former is harmless, and lack of the latter is positively beneficial. Evil, then, as Augustine concluded long ago, must consist in a privation of being, a lack of being that something ought to have.

It is notoriously difficult to establish the correctness of this conclusion without assuming the existence of a morally upright God. For if God were either evil or imaginary, then one would possess little reason for regarding being as intrinsically good. The Christian definition of evil as the privation of being does constitute something of a defense against antitheistic arguments from evil. However, it seems difficult if not impossible to establish that evil is a privation of being on grounds acceptable to atheists.

II.   THE FREE WILL DEFENSE

The free will defense, by contrast, appears well suited to the task of satisfying certain persons' concerns about the compatibility of Christian theism with the existence of evil. The defense, as the name suggests, consists essentially in two claims. First, God could not endow human beings with libertarian free will, that is, the putative ability of human beings to pursue other courses of action than those they actually pursue, without empowering them to generate enormous amounts of evil. Second, libertarian free will in human beings constitutes a good so precious that it more than counterbalances the evils wrought by human beings. Some apologists attempt to strengthen the argument by conjecturing that there may be no possible world in which human beings could both possess libertarian free will and also refrain from giving rise to horrific evils.[1]

Unquestionably this argument can prove persuasive to an atheist if the atheist believes both that human beings possess libertarian free will and that this kind of freedom constitutes a tremendously important good. The free will defense nevertheless (with or without the additional conjecture mentioned in the previous paragraph) suffers from acute difficulties of which one ought to be aware before employing it in argument. First, the free will defense fails adequately to account for natural evils such as earthquakes and tsunamis, which are not related to moral evil, that is, evil freely committed by human acts. Second, libertarian free will seems incompatible with the doctrine of God's comprehensive foreknowledge of future events and with a correct understanding of the relationship between human and divine action.

---

[1] See, e.g., A. Plantinga, *God, Freedom, and Evil* (New York: Harper and Row, 1974), 45–53.

A. Divine Foreknowledge

Christians of all denominations have historically believed that God knows everything that occurs in the history of creation, past, present, or future, with unerring accuracy. That belief in divine omniscience precludes the possibility of libertarian free will in creatures appears from two considerations: (a) the impossibility of God's deriving His knowledge of creatures' actions from those actions themselves and (b) the incoherence of Molinism, the theory most frequently invoked to resolve the first difficulty.

1. The independence of divine knowledge

If God cannot derive His foreknowledge of creatures' actions from the history of what creatures actually do, it seems that divine foreknowledge cannot depend on what creatures freely decide to do. Instead, what creatures freely decide to do must depend on what God foreknows they will do.[2] In other words God's foreknowledge, conceived of not as receptive but as causal, determines what creatures do.

The timelessness of God, incidentally, does not invalidate this conclusion. For if the key assumption of this section is correct, then the "fore" in divine foreknowledge signifies a real ontological priority of God's knowledge over human actions; the actions depend on the knowledge and not vice versa. If this is the case, then God's atemporal, yet definite and unchanging, knowledge of what creatures freely decide determines what they freely decide and not vice versa. If God cannot derive His knowledge of what creatures do from the creatures themselves, then it follows inexorably that the free will, which rational creatures unquestionably possess, does not consist in libertarian free will. Free creatures cannot do otherwise than they actually do.

The radical nature of this conclusion, when considered in the context of certain traditions, might lead some to question whether it is true that God's knowledge of creaturely acts can in no way depend on those creaturely acts. The doctrine of creation ex nihilo, however, entails precisely this doctrine. For if one cannot bestow on another what he does not have, and creation receives the entirety of its being from God, then creation possesses no actuality, which God does not already possess. The idea that creation could enrich God, cognitively or in any other way, thus appears absurd.

If God, however, draws His knowledge of what occurs in creation from the creation itself, then He supplements His stock of knowledge from resources without Himself; He is cognitively enriched by that on which He bestowed all of the reality, cognitive or otherwise, that it possesses. The thought of this, again, is absurd. One may object that what God creates is the being of things and that actions are something in addition to this that God does not bestow in creation. Nevertheless a being cannot derive its existence from something without also deriving the mode of its existence: in the case of a human being, that is, existence as uttering certain words, performing certain activities, and so forth.

---

[2] In the words of Thomas Aquinas, "the divine mind, unlike ours, does not gather its knowledge from things, but rather by its knowledge is the cause of things" (*Summa Contra Gentiles* 1.65.6). See also Aquinas, *Summa Theologiae* 1, 14, 8 corp.

One may object, again, that although this might apply in the case of creation (e.g., if God created Adam in a standing position, Adam commenced his existence standing), preservation is distinct from creation. Preservation differs from creation, however, only in that preservation presupposes that the creatures preserved already exist.[3] Creatures, do not, when created, become self-subsistent in any sense.[4] God, and not the creatures themselves, thus causes creatures to subsist no less in preservation than in creation. God therefore causes the precise mode of creatures' existence no less in preservation than in creation.

Therefore even in thinking and acting, creatures do not add something to what God, their Creator and Sustainer, gives them. What He gives, He must Himself possess, albeit in a higher, divine manner. Thus it is inconceivable that a creature could enrich God with knowledge or anything else, and it is therefore correspondingly inconceivable that God might derive His knowledge of creatures from the creatures themselves. This implies that human beings do not possess the ability to refrain from doing what they actually do and that the free will defense accordingly rests on a false premise. The difficulties the position advocated here poses for human freedom and God's righteousness will be addressed in the sections on the relation between divine and human action.

2. Molinism

Those who wish to avoid both the conclusion that God depends on creatures for His knowledge of them and the conclusion that human beings lack libertarian free will might invoke a theory known as Molinism, crafted by the sixteenth-century Jesuit Luis Molina (1535–1600). Molina distinguished between what he called natural, free, and middle knowledge. Natural knowledge constitutes the knowledge that God must possess, regardless of whether He decides to create or not to create or of what kind of creation He chooses. By natural knowledge God knows all possibilities whatever. God's free knowledge consists in His knowing events because He Himself intends to cause them, the kind of knowledge ascribed to God in the previous section. Middle knowledge, however, consists in God's knowledge of what a being of a certain nature, who possesses libertarian free will, would freely decide to do in any conceivable situation.[5] According to the Molinist God knows precisely what rational creatures will do, not because He has ordained that they do this or that but because by virtue of His

---

[3] "Conservation is the same as creation, except that creation has a certain newness which conservation lacks and creation lacks a preceding existence which conservation implies" (W. Ames, *The Marrow of Theology*, trans. J. D. Eusden [1623; reprint, Philadelphia: United Church Press, 1968], §1.9.18, p. 109). "The preservation of things by God," in the words of Thomas Aquinas, "is a continuation of that action whereby he gives existence" (*Summa Theologiae* 1, 104, 1 and 4).

[4] Any view, according to which God does not at least indirectly cause every creaturely event, is implicitly polytheistic. For if an event does not at least indirectly derive from God, it either possesses no cause whatever or derives ultimately from an entity or event that, although distinct from God, is without a cause. Aseity, the property of being causeless, however, is conventionally taken to be an exclusively divine attribute. If some entity or event other than God is *a se*, i.e. uncaused, therefore, it seems that the universe must contain more than one deity (cf. F. Turretin, *Institutes of Elenctic Theology*, trans. G. M. Giger, ed. J. Dennison, 3 vols. [Phillipsburg: P & R, 1992–97], 1:503, §6.4.9).

[5] See Molina's *Disputation* 52.9 in his *On Divine Foreknowledge: Part IV of the Concordia*, trans. A. J. Freddoso (Ithaca, NY: Cornell University Press, 2004), 168.

middle knowledge He can project the entirety of human history from His knowledge of Adam and Eve's initial conditions, which He does in fact ordain.

Molinism fails to harmonize the doctrine that human beings possess libertarian free will with God's comprehensive foreknowledge, however, because its own assumptions are implicitly determinist. That is, if it is true that a human being will, without exception, perform a certain action X when confronted with the specific situation Y, then this human being lacks libertarian free will. Once the situation is given, he will unquestionably do what God's middle knowledge dictates that He would do in that particular situation. It will be impossible for the human being to do otherwise, for if he did, he would falsify God's middle knowledge. According to Molinism the human being, although by no means determined to particular courses of action in the manner envisioned above, is, however, no less determined because his nature is such that he will perform one and only one action in any given situation. Molinism, consequently, does not harmonize the notion of libertarian free will with God's complete and nonderived knowledge of human actions.[6]

3. Conclusion

In summary then, comprehensive divine foreknowledge of human decisions and the possession of libertarian free will (i.e., the ability to refrain from doing what one actually does) seem mutually exclusive for two reasons. First, God's knowledge of creaturely acts cannot depend on those acts themselves. God's knowledge that each creature will perform one, and only one, determinate set of actions is in no way subject to the whims of a creature who may decide not to perform the determinate set of actions God's omniscience assigns him. Since God's knowledge of what a creature does is fixed independently of the creature's action, it seems that the creature cannot do otherwise than he actually does. God's nonderived foreknowledge of creaturely actions therefore precludes the possibility of libertarian free will.

Second, Molinism implicitly excludes libertarian free will as well. For if a human being is constituted in such a way that, when faced with some particular situation, he will unfailingly take one and only one course of action, then it is not objectively possible for him to refrain from doing as he actually does. Even if the Molinist understanding of divine foreknowledge were correct, human beings would still lack libertarian free will. It seems overwhelmingly likely that God's comprehensive foreknowledge of human actions excludes the possibility of libertarian free will and thus undermines a key premise of the free will defense.

B. Divine and Human Action

The postulate of libertarian free will also appears incompatible with a proper understanding of the relationship between divine and human action. As already seen, existence never becomes essential to creatures; otherwise they could not be destroyed. God must cause creatures to exist, therefore, just as much in His continuous act of preserving them

---

[6] For a more extensive refutation of Molinism along much the same lines, see W. Hasker, *God, Time, and Knowledge* (Ithaca, NY: Cornell University Press, 1998), 39–52.

as in His instantaneous act of creating them. Creation and preservation, then, are equivalent with the sole exception that preservation brings no new object into being.

To cause a being to exist in the divine manner, that is, to give a being every iota of what it is, as God does in creation and preservation, is to determine the precise mode of that being's existence. When God causes a human being to exist in preservation, therefore, He causes the human being to exist as sleeping, standing, shouting, and the like. He causes the human being to exist, in other words, as an agent who is thinking whatever he is thinking and doing whatever he is doing. God thus constitutes a determinative cause of every human thought and action whatever. In this case libertarian free will on the part of human beings is inconceivable.

The argument just rehearsed for the thesis that God causes every human act in such a way as to determine everything about that act has been regarded as sound by countless theologians, including Thomas Aquinas.[7] Some persons may deny the argument's conclusion, because in their view it implies that God is the author of sin and that human beings possess no free will. In the remainder of this section, therefore, these objections will be addressed.

1. The author of sin?

To see that God's determinative causality does not render Him the author of sin, one must attend to the distinction between God's primary causality of sinful human acts and the secondary causality of the human, sinful agent. Neither God nor the human being, it is important to note, constitutes a partial cause of a sinful human act; each, rather, is the whole cause, albeit in different respects. God is the whole ultimate and originating cause; and the human being is the whole proximate and instrumental cause.[8]

When a human being commits a sinful act, the defect in the act that renders it sinful necessarily lies in the instrumental cause rather than the originating cause. God relates, that is, to a human being who sins as a man who swings an axe relates to the axe whose head flies off in the process of the swing. The outcome of the act may be horrific (Deut 19:5 and 2 Kgs 6:5), but the defect on account of which the act is evil lies completely in the instrumental cause. God, like the human being who swings the axe, is entirely innocent of the harm inflicted by His defective instrument.[9]

One might object that the two cases are not parallel. The human being who swings the axe does not know that its head will fly off, whereas God knows fully that the human act He causes will be sinful. To tell a long tale in a short compass, the classic answer to this objection is that, according to the latter half of Romans 1, sin itself is a punishment of sin.[10] As punishment for the idolatry and thanklessness of the Gentiles, Paul wrote, "God delivered them over in the cravings of their hearts to sexual impurity,

---

[7] In addition to the passages cited above, see Aquinas, *Summa Contra Gentiles* 3.67, 89.

[8] Ibid., 3.70.

[9] Ibid., 3.163.4.

[10] Augustine, *On Nature and Grace* 24, in *Nicene and Post-Nicene Fathers*, Series 1, ed. P. Schaff (Peabody, MA: Hendrickson, 1994), 5:129.

so that their bodies were degraded among themselves" (Rom 1:24) and "delivered them over to degrading passions" (v. 26). Paul also wrote, "Because they did not think it worthwhile to acknowledge God, God delivered them over to a worthless mind to do what is morally wrong" (v. 28).

Since Adam's sin in the fall is imputed to all of his descendants conceived in the ordinary manner (5:12–21), all divine causality of sinful human acts can be justified as punishment of humankind's first sin. God's causality of Adam's initial, sinful act, the so-called *felix culpa* ("happy fault"), which necessitated Christ's redemption of human beings, is typically excused as an evil far outweighed by the goods wrought by the Redeemer. This account naturally possesses its own difficulties as do virtually all defenses of divine justice; these will be addressed in coming sections. It suffices for the present to demonstrate that the divine act of causing a human being's sin does not contain the defect on account of which the human act caused is sinful. God's act is therefore intrinsically stainless; He commits no sin. God is not, therefore, in the narrowest sense of the term at least, the author of sin.

2. No free will?

If God is the determinative cause of every human action, then it might seem that the freedom of the human will is excluded; and it is in fact excluded if one conceives of this freedom in libertarian terms. Divine omnicausality, however, seems compatible with an alternate concept of freedom associated with Augustine and the contemporary philosopher Harry Frankfurt. According to this concept, one possesses sufficient freedom to be morally responsible for one's actions so long as he does what he wants. If someone compels the human being to act in a manner contrary to his wishes, then, the act in question is not free. So long as a human being does what he wants, within the limits of his capacities, however, he is free and thus responsible for what he does.

This understanding of freedom may admittedly seem insubstantial to persons accustomed to conceiving of freedom in libertarian terms. The advocate of libertarian free will ought to consider, however, that persons find it necessary to ascribe freedom to other persons, primarily because a certain measure of freedom constitutes an indispensable prerequisite of moral responsibility. God or the state can justly hold a human being accountable only for those acts that he commits freely. If a concept of freedom implies that all acts that human beings intuitively recognize to be wrong and worthy of punishment are free, this coheres with human beings' moral intuitions. However, if a concept of freedom implies that such acts are not free, it conflicts with the moral intuitions of human beings and is thus implausible.

John M. Fischer demonstrates, by means of a famous example, that the libertarian concept of free will fails the test of correspondence with human beings' moral intuitions.[11] Suppose, he says, that one person wants to murder another, and a mad scientist implants a computer chip in the would-be murderer's brain, which is programmed to

---

[11] See Fischer's "Responsiveness and Moral Responsibility" in his *My Way: Essays on Moral Responsibility* (Oxford: Oxford University Press, 2006), 63–83 at 65–66.

counteract any twinges of conscience the murderer-to-be might have about committing the fateful act. Given the microchip, it is not possible for the aspiring murderer to repent of his criminal intentions. Moreover, suppose the person in question suffers no pangs of conscience and that instead he willingly carries out the act. If a person must be able to refrain from doing what he actually does in order to be responsible for his actions, then the person in question does nothing wrong in committing murder. If he cannot decide to act otherwise, he lacks libertarian free will. Obviously, however, the act is wrong and the murderer is guilty. Moral intuition therefore suggests that the libertarian concept of free will is much too robust, and that in order to count all such blameworthy acts as free, one must have recourse to a milder concept of freedom such as that of Augustine and Frankfurt.

One may protest that human beings conceive of freedom in libertarian terms not only because they require a concept of liberty adequate to undergird moral responsibility but also because they are conscious of possessing libertarian freedom. Human beings, one may reasonably respond, are certainly conscious of their ability to do what they want. They are, moreover, generally aware that they possess adequate mental and physical capacities to perform a variety of actions at any one time.

Awareness of these capacities, however, does not constitute awareness of an objective possibility that they might act otherwise than they do. Human beings know, rather, that they must choose among the spectrum of activities for which they are mentally and/or physically qualified and that they will choose one course of action to the exclusion of others. None of this seems to exclude the possibility that the same humans are caused by a power unknown to themselves to make one determinate set of choices and no others.

One can conceive of instances, moreover, in which human beings are conscious of acting freely although they cannot act otherwise. The example of a man whose hands and feet are tied to a stake and who is comforted in the misery of his bondage by the sweet smell of flowers nearby proves otherwise. The man cannot put his hand to his nose, and he cannot hold his breath long enough to prevent his smelling the flower. In this respect he cannot do otherwise than he actually does. Yet it seems perverse to describe the act of smelling the flowers, an act that gives him pleasure and that he undertakes gladly, as unfree.[12]

Likewise, Augustine notes, everyone desires to be happy or blessed, at least in the broadest senses of those terms. Even a person who attempts to mortify one of his desires does so in order to fulfill another, and a person who inflicts pain on himself or even death does so, again, to fulfill his desires, that is, to achieve what he regards as blessedness or happiness for himself. It seems unnatural, however, to characterize a person's desire for blessedness, a person's desire to fulfill his overall goals, as unfree.[13] One can therefore be conscious of acting freely when one cannot do otherwise than one actually does. The

---

[12] Augustine, *On Nature and Grace* 55, in *Nicene and Post-Nicene Fathers*, 5:140.
[13] Ibid., 54; cp. 57.

notion that he can be free only insofar as it is possible for him to do otherwise than he actually does thus fails both the test of experience and the test of moral intuition.

By contrast, Augustine and Frankfurt's concept of freedom identifies both the actions mentioned above and the actions in which human beings imagine they exercise libertarian free will, as free. This view of freedom, which seems preferable to the libertarian view, moreover, does not mean that actions God causes human beings to perform are unfree. For example God does not force people who desire to remain seated to walk across the room in spite of themselves. Rather, He moves the human will to *desire* to perform the action that He moves the entire person to perform.[14] God's causality of every aspect of every human action, therefore, does not violate the freedom of human beings to do what they want, which Augustine and Frankfurt equate with the freedom of the will. In conclusion therefore it seems that the claim that human beings are free only if they possess libertarian free will is demonstrably false, and that, unless and until the Augustinian/Frankfurtian understanding of freedom is found to be genuinely problematic, God's omnicausality is not inconsistent with the freedom of the human will.

C. Summary

A correct understanding of the relation between divine and human action, then, entails that both God and the human being are whole causes of every human act, albeit in different respects. This conclusion follows inexorably from the truth that God's creation and his preservation of creatures differ only in that the latter presupposes the prior existence of the beings preserved. Although the view that God causes every human act might seem both to render God the author of sin and to abolish the freedom of the human will, moreover, scrutiny of these charges has shown them to be, at best, unproved. For, first, a rightly understood distinction between primary and secondary causality shows that the defect in which consists the sinfulness of any illicit act inheres entirely in the secondary and human cause, rather than in the primary and divine. Second, examination of several limit cases of human freedom reveals the inadequacy of the libertarian conception of free will to describe human freedom in all its fullness. An alternative conception of human freedom, the Augustinian/Frankfurtian, however, accounts for the freedom of the acts depicted in the limit cases without qualifying divinely caused human acts as unfree. If one adopts the Augustinian/Frankfurtian view, then, one can reasonably affirm both divine omnicausality and the freedom of the human will.

1. Conclusion

The free will defense possesses considerable appeal in today's culture because it affirms human autonomy, something persons in the West consider valuable. As a purely negative device employed to persuade a person that the evils in the world do not necessarily disprove the existence of the Christian God, this view can be of some use. The free will defense is highly problematic, however, in that it fails to account for the presence of natural evils such as tornadoes, volcanic eruptions, birth defects,

---

[14] Augustine, *On the Spirit and the Letter* 54, in *Nicene and Post-Nicene Fathers*, 5:107.

and others, which do not derive in any direct way from the evil decisions of free moral agents. Also the reliance of the free will defense on the concept of libertarian free will precludes the possibility that the free will defense might constitute a true explanation of why God allows evil to pervade the world. For God's comprehensive foreknowledge of all human acts and His causation of those acts, as seen, renders libertarian free will unthinkable in creatures. One may legitimately employ the free will defense in a negative, tactical manner to shake the certainty of atheists in the incompatibility of the Christian God's existence with the presence of evil in the world. But one cannot responsibly teach that the free will defense resolves any of the problems posed for Christian theism by the existence of evil.

III. THE PROBLEM OF GOOD

Popular, contemporary apologists frequently counterpose to the problem of evil what they call "the problem of good." They claim that although the existence of the Christian God may seem difficult to harmonize with the existence of evil, it is even more difficult to account for all of the good in the universe without postulating the existence of a God. This argument tends to level the playing field between the Christian and the atheist in arguments over the problem of evil. It constitutes a simplistic and superficial means of bolstering Christian theism's credibility when the Christian theist is overwhelmed by atheistic arguments from evil that he cannot answer. One should note, however, that appeals to "the problem of good" merely pose a difficulty for the atheist; they by no means resolve the difficulties for Christian theism posed by the problems of evil.

IV. DIVINE WISDOM

A more cogent response is the counterargument from divine wisdom. This argument is that God's comprehensive knowledge of human affairs and needs may warrant actions that, when evaluated from a human perspective, appear perverse. This argument finds its classic expression in the Qur'an (Sura 18:65–82).[15]

The text depicts Moses as stumbling upon a wise man and asking if he could travel with the wise man so as to gain knowledge. The wise man, however, rebuffs Moses with the words, "You will not bear with [in some renderings, be patient with] me.... For how can you bear that which is beyond your knowledge?" (18:67–68). Moses insists on traveling with the wise man, however, and the latter instructs Moses not to question him about anything unless he raises the subject.

While he travels with Moses, the wise man performs three deeds, two of which Moses considers criminal and the third of which he considers impractical. The wise man bores a hole in the bottom of a ship, slays a young stranger without any provocation, and repairs a wall in a city whose residents had just refused to offer hospitality to

---

[15] All Qur'anic quotations are taken from *The Koran*, trans. N. J. Dawood, 5th ed. (London: Penguin, 1990).

Moses and himself. For the first two acts, Moses sharply rebukes the wise man, and for the last he observes that the wise man could have demanded wages for his labor. Three times, then, Moses questions the advisability of the wise man's actions.

After these three episodes, then, the wise man tells Moses that he must part from him but that he will first explain his rationale for performing the three acts that Moses criticized.

> Know that the ship belonged to some poor fishermen. I damaged it because at their rear there was a king who was taking every ship by force. As for the youth, his parents are both true believers, and we feared lest he should plague them with wickedness and unbelief. It was our wish that the Lord should grant them another in his place, a son more righteous and more filial. As for the wall, it belonged to two orphan boys in the city whose father was an honest man. Beneath it their treasure is buried. Your Lord decreed, as a mercy from your Lord, that they should dig up their treasure when they grew to manhood. What I did was not done by my will. That is the meaning of what you could not bear to watch with patience [18:79–82].

The moral of the story, naturally, is that God's knowledge enables Him to benefit the good by actions that, when viewed from a merely human perspective, appear cruel and unjust. One ought to respond to such actions, the story suggests, by silently submitting to God's will and trusting that He knows better than any human being what is good for the righteous.

The divine wisdom defense seems more persuasive than the free will defense or appeals to "the problem of good." However, it raises three questions: May God legitimately seek other ends than the benefit of human beings? May God do evil that good may come? Can human beings justly imitate God in employing, say, scientific knowledge to justify acts that normally would be considered immoral?

As to the third point, for example: if physicians could determine from infants' genetic codes which infants, if allowed to survive, would lead tormented lives as a result of mental disorders, would physicians be justified in aborting the infants with the problematic genes?[16] If scientific knowledge enables one to know that life, or the rest of life, will be more of a burden than a privilege, does this authorize one to kill an innocent person? If the sixth commandment means anything, then the answer is an unequivocal no. If human beings are not allowed to perform actions of this nature, however, what justifies God in providentially bringing about the commission of terrible crimes?

This, of course, is the concern raised by the second question. If doing evil that good may come is wrong for human beings, parity of reasoning suggests that it would be wrong for God as well. What might seem like evildoing for a noble purpose in God, however, differs radically from this all-too-familiar behavior in human beings. As seen in the discussion of the free will defense, the defect in sinful acts lies entirely in their human, instrumental cause. God's causality, rather, resembles that of a river

---

[16] This example derives from David Ford of Cambridge University.

that moves a gigantic barge more slowly than it does lighter crafts; the barge moves slowly not because of a defect in the river but because of its own bulkiness.[17]

Human evildoing in order to bring about good, therefore, differs from God's causality in that the human action involved is intrinsically and culpably defective. One might object, however, that, it is wrong to cause another agent to perform an evil deed. This assumption seems highly problematic, however. The evangelist who preaches on a street corner, for example, provokes rather directly the blasphemies hurled at him by raucous passersby, and yet his preaching is a virtuous act. The Christian missionary who works in a brutally oppressive Islamic state is more than a little complicit in others' sinful acts of jailing, torturing, and killing him; acts that would not have occurred had the missionary chosen to work in Britain or the United States. Nevertheless the missionary's self-sacrificial decision to work in an Islamic state constitutes, other things being equal, a virtuous act.

Admittedly the analogy between the acts of the missionary and the street evangelist and the divine act of causing a human being to commit some sin is not perfect. In the cases of the missionary and the street evangelist, however, their actions seem justifiable by appeal to the principle of double effect: the principle, that is, that one may legitimately perform an intrinsically good act, even if that act brings about some evil result, if the good intended clearly outweighs the evil results.

One may object again, however, that causing a human being to sin brings about no good result. This conclusion seems reasonable, however, only if the answer to the first question above is an unqualified no. That is, if the only good that God may legitimately seek is the benefit of human beings, then it seems implausible to suppose that He could justifiably cause anyone to sin. Such an act unquestionably harms the sinner, and the omnipotent God, it seems, could bestow benefits to humanity associated with the sin in some other way. If, however, God may act in order to achieve goods other than the welfare of human beings, such as the manifestation of His glory, then it does not seem obvious that the principle of double effect would never justify him in causing a human being to sin. If one objects that countless human sins in no way discernibly advance the cause of God's glory, moreover, it seems that one ignores the moral of the Qur'anic tale above. God frequently seeks goods that are not discernible to human beings. Human beings ought not therefore presumptuously condemn His acts, whose purposes and implications they cannot fully understand.

V. The Inevitable Imperfection of Created Universes

Atheists may further object, however, that if God is perfect, one cannot acquit Him of wrongdoing simply by pointing out the possibility that in actions with evil effects He brings about even greater goods. If God is perfect, the atheist could reason, everything He makes must be, if not absolutely perfect, at least as good as it could be.

---

[17] G. W. Leibniz, *Theodicy* (London: Routledge & Kegan, 1951; reprint, LaSalle, IL: Open Court, 1985), §1.30, p. 141.

The fact that evil effects in creation may bring about tremendous goods may therefore seem irrelevant to the debate about whether God created the present universe. For one can certainly conceive of an intrinsically better universe than the present. Since, then, the present universe cannot be the best possible universe, it might seem absurd to identify its creator as the Christian God.

This argument might carry considerable weight if the notion of a best possible universe were coherent. That it is not coherent, however, appears from the following argument. If God "created" something absolutely perfect, as perfect as He, it would be indistinguishable from Him. So to create something distinct from Himself, God must create something inferior to Himself. To be inferior to the absolutely infinite, a being must be in some respect finite.

God's rationality dictates that He must choose the universe He created over all other possible universes for some reason. This reason cannot consist, however, simply in the fact that universe X is intrinsically better than universe Y. For an infinite number of possible universes could excel any possible universe in inherent goodness. Since relative goodness cannot constitute the sole criterion by which God chooses universes, it seems unreasonable to state that God could not have created some possible universe simply because it is not as good as another.

VI. THE VALE OF SOUL-MAKING

The "vale of soul-making" defense takes its name from a phrase in a letter by the poet John Keats, in which he declared that the world is not a vale of tears, as Christians typically claim, but a "vale of soul-making"; that is, it is a place in which persons develop noble character by struggling through the myriad obstacles they face in life.[18] The characters human beings form by struggling with evil may be of sufficient value to outweigh the sum total of evils in the world. An omnipotent God, nevertheless, as critics of this argument are wont to observe, could produce the same fantastically valuable characters without imposing any burden of evil at all on the world. The "vale of soul-making" argument thus seems to avail little in the quest to justify God's tolerance of horrendous evils in the world.

VII. DIVINE JUSTICE

A more cogent defense, though one that appeals more to Christians struggling with the problems of evil than to unbelievers, is the appeal to divine justice. According to Rom 5:12–21 God imputed Adam's first sin to all those who descend from him by way of ordinary generation. Since offenses against an infinitely good God are infinitely grievous, they merit infinite punishment. Adam's sin alone therefore might

---

[18] For the origin of John Keats's phrase, "vale of soul-making," see J. Hick, *Evil and the God of Love* (New York: Harper & Row, 1966), 295, n. 1. Hick sketches the "vale of soul-making" theodicy itself in ibid., 289–400.

seem sufficient, within a certain framework of understanding, to warrant the infliction of infinite evils on the entirety of mere human beings.

Admittedly this arrangement might seem unfair to Adam's descendants. Careful examination of the nature and circumstances of Adam's representation of the human race in the garden of Eden, however, shows that a consistently rational human being who was unaware of Adam's failure would prefer being represented by Adam before God to representing himself. Reformed theologians hold that if Adam had succeeded in obeying God's commandments for a specific duration, he would thereby have attained eternal salvation for himself and for all his descendants. Presumably most human beings would prefer the eternal salvation of all human beings through one ancestor's obedience to the salvation of some human beings and the damnation of others after everyone is subjected to a potentially grueling trial.

The first scenario could be conceivable only if human beings also faced the risk of their representative ancestor's failing his trial and so incurring eternal punishment for the whole. Human beings nevertheless have great reason to believe that Adam stood a greater chance of succeeding in his trial than they would stand if God subjected each of them to an individualized test. Human beings born in the natural manner, for example, begin life as infants and must slowly learn how to be responsible adults, a process in which they commit numerous errors. But Adam began life as an adult in full possession of his faculties. If God tested each human being individually, moreover, many would fall. Each human being, while undergoing his test, would thus face the additional burden of enduring temptations emanating from fallen human beings around him. Adam, however, faced no such difficulties.[19]

Thus the divine justice defense successfully accounts for all or virtually all evils visited on the world since Adam's fall. It does not explain, however, why a wise and benevolent God would decree that Adam's initial fall occur. To answer this question one must turn to a different argument, which indicates what benefits might accrue from such a seemingly catastrophic event. The *felix culpa* defense is just such an argument.

VIII. *Felix Culpa*

A *felix culpa* ("happy fault") theodicy is simply an argument that Adam's fall occasioned much greater good than evil, that it was authentically a *felix culpa*. A sound argument of this nature does not merely assert that Adam's fall occasioned Christ's salvific work on behalf of humanity. For Christ could have become incarnate and bestowed unspeakable blessings on the human race even if Adam had not sinned. John Duns Scotus (c. 1266–1308) and his numerous followers, in fact, insisted that Christ would have done just this if Adam had refrained from sinning. If one takes into account goods other than the betterment of human beings, however, then one can construct a

---

[19] For why one should prefer representation by Adam over being subjected to an individual trial of character, see part 4, chap. 3 of Jonathan Edwards, *The Great Christian Doctrine of Original Sin Defended,* ed. Edward Hickman, 2 vols. (London: Billing & Sons, 1834; repr., Edinburgh: Banner of Truth, 1979), 1:222.

credible *felix culpa* defense. In particular the manifestation of God's virtues of mercy and justice both presuppose some significant culpability on the part of creatures and outweigh in importance the evils human guilt engenders. Only because Adam sinned was God able to manifest His self-sacrificial mercy on the cross. Only because Adam sinned is God able to manifest His unbending justice in condemning the lost. If, then, God's primary end in creation is the manifestation of his perfections, it would seem rational for God to decree that the fall occur as a means to this more important end.

In combination with the divine justice defense, therefore, a *felix culpa* response to the problems of evil appears adequate to account for the presence of horrendous evils in the world. Two factors nevertheless make it unlikely that these responses will prove persuasive to actual atheists. First, each of these defenses presupposes that retributive justice constitutes a virtue: a view that virtually no contemporary secularists share. Second, the *felix culpa* argument presupposes that the individual human being's dignity and welfare are of trifling importance in comparison with God's glory, a view average persons are likely to find distasteful. The divine justice and *felix culpa* defenses, then, even when used in tandem (as indeed they ought to be), seem insufficient to squelch the impression that the existence of evil in the world renders Christian theism problematic. These defenses seem adequate, nonetheless, to the tasks of dispelling anxieties about the problems of evil among committed, conservative Christians, and of demonstrating that one can answer hard questions about evil if one approaches them from the vantage point of a Christian worldview.

IX. CONCLUSION

The present chapter is a brief inquiry into the nature of evil and an examination of seven responses to the difficulties evil poses for the thesis that the world's Creator is an omniscient, omnipotent, and perfectly good God. Evil does not constitute a distinct variety of being or substance. Instead, evil consists in an entity's lack of some being that it ought to possess: darkness where there ought to be light, coldness where there ought to be love and the like.

Among the seven answers to the problem of evil, only the free will defense and the "vale of soul-making" theodicy appear profoundly flawed. "The problem of good" argument showed itself to be potentially useful but shallow, and the arguments from divine wisdom and the impossibility of a "best possible world" proved cogent, though exclusively negative. The divine justice defense offers more of a positive rationale for God's allowance of evil but fails to account for Adam's fall, the source of most of the universe's evils. The final argument, the *felix culpa* defense, however, justifies God's provision for Adam's fall on the grounds that the fall supplied otherwise unattainable opportunities for the manifestation of God's justice and mercy. While none of the responses examined here supplies a comprehensive answer to the problems of evil that would satisfy skeptics, the arguments, at least when considered together, constitute a formidable bulwark against antitheistic arguments based on the problem of evil.

Chapter 21

CAN MIRACLES OCCUR AND DO THEY?

OVER THE LAST THREE CENTURIES A consensus has steadily emerged among thinking people in all parts of the Western world that miracles do not occur. According to this consensus one cannot reasonably believe that miracles occur: (a) because contemporary persons do not encounter miracles in their own experience and (b) because, if one admits the possibility that certain events come about through supernatural agency, then one possesses a simple explanation for every heretofore unexplained phenomenon in nature: "God did it." Contemporary persons, accordingly, tend to equate belief in the miraculous with total rejection of scientific inquiry.

When a Christian proposes reintegrating the idea of the miraculous into Western society's collective worldview, secular hearers of today take this to mean abandoning the scientific enterprise. In the secularist's mind, therefore, widespread acceptance of the miraculous among the educated, ruling classes in the West would rule out the possibility of a vaccine for malaria, of hydrogen-fueled cars, of genetically engineered crops that need no pesticides—in short any scientific advance that might in any way benefit humanity. The average thinking person in industrialized societies thus believes that broad support by thinking persons of a miracle-based religion like Christianity would be disastrous for the future of humankind.

This explains, to some extent, the quasi-religious zeal of atheists like Richard Dawkins, who consider the notion of the miraculous not merely deceptive but evil. These considerations also partially explain why the upper echelons of the Western intelligentsia almost universally abhor evangelical Christianity. In response Christians of today must show through their writing and their conduct that authentic Christianity in no way retards the progress of the sciences and that contemporary persons' miracle-free experience of the world does not falsify a properly Christian understanding of miracles.

This chapter, then, discusses (a) the technical, theological definition of "miracle"; (b) the compatibility of Christian belief about miracles with secular persons' everyday experience; (c) how one might go about reconciling a belief in the miraculous with a progressive and affirming attitude toward the natural sciences; and (d) an analysis and refutation of David Hume's influential argument against the knowability of miracles.

I.   THE DEFINITION OF "MIRACLE"

A. The Ideal Definition

The ideal definition of "miracle," at least in theological contexts, may be the following: An event that (a) is manifestly contrary to the ordinary workings of nature, (b) exceeds the capacities of human beings and demons, (c) occurs in a religious context, and (d) attests that the words of one or more persons constitute divine revelation.

This definition is not intended to designate the meaning of any specific biblical term. It identifies, rather, "My Father's works" of which Jesus spoke in John 10:37–38: "If I am not doing My Father's works, don't believe Me. But if I am doing them and you don't believe Me, believe the works. This way you will know and understand that the Father is in Me and I in the Father."

This admittedly restrictive definition excludes as nonmiraculous many phenomena sometimes referred to as miracles. The first criterion, that an authentic miracle must be "manifestly contrary to the ordinary workings of nature," excludes as miracles heartwarming but entirely natural events such as the birth of children. The second criterion, that an authentic miracle exceeds the capacities of all nondivine beings, precludes the possibility that a demon could work an authentic miracle. The third criterion, that authentic miracles occur "in a religious context," bars events with no apparent religious significance from the category of the miraculous; and the fourth criterion identifies as nonmiraculous any event that does not certify a human being's authority to speak on behalf of God.

B. Examples

In concrete terms the medically inexplicable recovery of a person from cancer following prolonged prayer and fasting for him by friends does not qualify as a miracle in the sense of the term employed here. For, first, God may have accomplished the healing through natural means presently unknown to medical science. Second, even if God had employed strictly supernatural means to bring about the healing, He would not have publicly accredited anyone as His messenger. Pious individuals could justly interpret the healing as an answer to prayer, and yet the healing supplies no compelling evidence that any person associated with the healing possesses prophetic authority.

By contrast Jesus' healing the servant of the centurion, who bid Him not to come under his roof but simply to say the word, qualifies as a miracle according to the above definition. For here one finds not only an occurrence for which the natural sciences cannot account but also the extraordinarily improbable conjunction of the occurrence with a claim of responsibility for the occurrence by a person of unimpeachable character, who possessed no natural means of knowing about the occurrence or of bringing it to pass. These data, along with Jesus' explicit proclamation that "My Father's works," which He performed, authenticate His prophethood, render it overwhelmingly likely that the work in question does constitute a miracle.

One may object that a demon could perhaps accomplish a healing of this nature and that Jesus' healing of the centurion therefore does not qualify as miraculous in the sense of the above definition. To answer this objection, however, one need merely attend to the character and claims of the person who heals. Jesus healed for the purposes of glorifying the true God, manifesting His own prophetic commission, and serving unworthy human beings. Satan does not heal for these purposes. Though he masquerades as an angel of light (2 Cor 11:14), his kingdom is not divided against itself (Matt 12:25–26; Luke 11:17–18). Although the healing of the centurion might not exceed the capacities of demons for altering matter in a short time, the healing definitely exceeded the moral capacities of demons. Although the healing may not exceed the moral capacities of human beings, it unquestionably exceeds their capacity for sudden transformation of matter. The above definition of miracle is thus sufficient to cover all of "My Father's works."

II. MIRACLES AND EVERYDAY EXPERIENCE

As already noted, secularists find implausible the notion that miracles occur, partially because contemporary people do not experience miracles, in the sense defined above, in their everyday lives. One can answer this concern by noting that miracles, simply in order to be miracles, must be extremely rare—in the words of the above definition, "manifestly contrary to the ordinary workings of nature." For if people walked on water, turned rivers into blood, or foretold events in the distant future everyday, the performance of such feats by Jesus, Moses, and Isaiah would be utterly unremarkable. A miracle, in the sense defined above, occurs for the purpose of astonishing human beings into recognizing that God endorses the teaching of one of his messengers, and this it cannot accomplish unless it is at least virtually unprecedented in the experience of those who witness it.

This is not to say that God does not intervene frequently in the lives of believers, first regenerating and then progressively sanctifying them. The Christian faith teaches that He does. Such instances of divine intervention, however, are in no way public; indeed, God's working in a person's heart is rarely perceptible even to the person himself. God's rendering Himself present in a supernatural way to the souls of believers does not constitute a miracle, for it neither accredits any human being as a messenger from God nor runs contrary to the ordinary course of nature. Without in any way denying the existence of close communion between the Christian and God and of God's continual intervention in the Christian's life, the Christian can and ought to affirm that miracles, in the technical sense of the term employed here, scarcely ever occur. The secularist's experience of a substantially miracle-free world does not constitute evidence against the occurrence of miracles; this experience confirms, rather, that a miracle would be truly extraordinary if one occurred.

III. MIRACLES AND THE NATURAL SCIENCES

The second source of secularist unease about Christian belief in miracles is the fear that such belief undermines respect and enthusiasm for the natural sciences. But this point can easily be dispelled, much like the previous difficulty. First, the inevitable scarcity of miracles, discussed in the last point, implies that one who grasps the true nature of a miracle will not attribute unexplained phenomena exclusively to miraculous intervention. Second, the notion of miracles presupposes that nature acts according to uniform physical laws; if it did not, then radical variations in nature's course would not astonish.

Third, the definition of miracle above dictates that in order to be a miracle an extraordinary event must occur in a religious context and in some way ratify the words of God's messengers. If a supernova inexplicably exploded, therefore, no one who properly understood the nature of the miraculous would so much as consider whether this event might constitute a miracle. In fact the entire subject of miracles is irrelevant to what one ordinarily regards as the domain of the natural sciences. A reasonable belief in miracles therefore poses no threat whatever to the continued flourishing of the natural sciences.

IV. HUME'S ARGUMENT AGAINST MIRACLES

In his work *An Enquiry Concerning Human Understanding,* the Scottish philosopher David Hume (1711–76) articulated perhaps the most influential argument ever formulated against the rationality of belief in miracles. Since answers to his argument suffice to answer all other major arguments against miracles, the following section is limited to analyzing and refuting this argument.

A. The Essence of Hume's Argument

Hume's argument consists essentially of the following assertion: "A miracle is a violation of the laws of nature; and as a firm and unalterable experience has established these laws, the proof against a miracle, from the very nature of the fact, is as entire as any argument from experience can possibly be imagined."[1] The argument, at least when stated in this form, suffers from at least two flaws. First, Hume begged the question when he invoked "unalterable experience" as evidence against the occurrence of miracles. For experience testifies unalterably against the occurrence of miracles only if no one has ever witnessed a miracle, which is tantamount to saying that a miracle has never occurred. By including "unalterable experience" of the nonoccurrence of miracles among his premises, therefore, Hume presupposes what he pretends to prove. He argues in a circle.

Second, Hume operates with a profoundly unsatisfactory definition of miracle. First, "the laws of nature" are not commands that one can transgress; they are rather generalizations about what actually occurs. If something occurred, which a supposed law of nature dictated could not happen, this event would not violate the law of nature; it would show rather that what one had erroneously taken to be a law of nature

---

[1] D. Hume, *An Enquiry Concerning Human Understanding* (1748; reprint, Oxford: Oxford University Press, 1999), §10.1, 90.

was not a law of nature at all. Second, the "laws of nature," as the phrase suggests, presumably describe what occurs when only natural causes operate. Events wrought by a supernatural agent would thus seem to be not contrary to natural laws but outside of their scope. Hume could presuppose that natural causes are the only causes that operate. He could do so, however, only by assuming that acts of divine intervention such as miracles cannot occur. This, however, would be to place the conclusion of his argument in its premises and, once more, to argue in a circle.

Prima facie, Hume's argument appears weak. When one considers a key presupposition of Hume's argument, however, it becomes relatively easy to see why he and those committed to similar principles find the basic argument mentioned above persuasive. The presupposition in question is Hume's belief that the testimony of other human beings possesses evidential value only insofar as it is analogous with one's own experience.

B. Testimony and Experience

Hume expressed this belief in the following words:

> The reason why we place any credit in witnesses or historians, is not derived from any *connexion*, which we perceive *a priori*, between testimony and reality, but because we are accustomed to find a conformity between them. But when the fact attested is such a one as has seldom fallen under our observation, here is a contest of two opposite experiences; of which the one destroys the other, as far as its force goes, and the superior can only operate on the mind by the force, which remains. The very same principle of experience, which gives us a certain degree of assurance in the testimony of witnesses, gives us also, in this case, another degree of assurance against the fact, which they endeavor to establish; from which contradiction there inevitably arises a counterpoize, and mutual destruction of belief and authority.[2]

Hume stated, in other words, first, that the testimony of another human being derives its force from the listener's experience of correspondence between testimony and reality. Second, he proposes that to the extent that the reality testified to is dissimilar from what one has experienced, experience itself (the authority from which testimony derives whatever credibility it possesses) renders the testimony incredible.

One who evaluates human testimony to the occurrence of miracles in accord with these principles can hardly fail to reject such testimony as false. For miracles, by definition, diverge radically from the course of nature one ordinarily experiences. If, then, (a) testimony borrows its authority exclusively from one's experience and (b) one's experience discredits any account of realities that bear little or no analogy to realities experienced by oneself, then, testimony to miracles can hardly fail to appear preposterous. For one who accepts propositions "a" and "b," Hume's argument seems plausible. One who would adequately refute Hume's argument against miracles must therefore discredit at least one of these propositions.

---

[2] Ibid., §10.1, 89 (italics his).

1. The evidential value of testimony

The first proposition, that testimony derives its authority exclusively from the human experience of conformity between testimony and fact, seems implausible. First, human beings can verify hardly any testimony without consulting, at least implicitly, yet more testimony. For example, if Sue tells Sarah that Sally is around the corner, Sarah can verify the truthfulness of Sue's testimony by rounding the corner and seeing Sally only if Sarah already knows (a) that sense perception in general is a reliable source of information and (b) that the words Sue utters mean what she thinks they mean. If Sarah wants to test the reliability of sense perception in general, however, she must consult the testimony of other human beings about the subject. Likewise, in order to know what Sue's words mean, Sarah must rely on others' testimony as to what the terms mean and, in particular, as to the name of the person she seeks, that is, Sally. Even in such a straightforward case of verifying testimony with sense perception as this, the person verifying the testimony must depend extensively on yet more testimony.

If one cannot verify the correspondence of testimony with reality without consulting other testimony, one must possess some other reason for placing confidence in testimony than experience of this correspondence. Like sense perception and memory, the testimony of others commends itself to human belief simply on the basis of itself.[3] Contrary to Hume, testimony does not derive its trustworthiness from experience, and one cannot reasonably disregard testimony's evidence simply because it concerns realities that one has not experienced.

2. Analogy with personal experience

The second proposition, that one cannot reasonably credit testimony to events that contrast starkly with one's own experience, seems even less plausible than the first. Hume nevertheless finds this proposition credible because it follows directly from his distinctive understanding of causality. According to Hume, one comes to believe, say, that a hammer drives a nail that it strikes into wood only because one has seen on many occasions a nail penetrate wood on the occasion of a hammer striking it. That is, Hume holds that human beings do not perceive a relation of cause and effect between the hammer striking the nail and the nail's penetration. They only see that one event constantly follows another, and it is only this experience of one event following another that justifies them in expecting the nail to penetrate wood when struck and in supposing that a nail driven into wood came to be such by the action of a hammer.

> This idea of a necessary [causal] connexion between events arises from a number of similar instances which occur of the constant conjunction of these events; nor can that idea ever be suggested by any one of these instances, surveyed in all possible lights and positions. But there is nothing in a number of instances, different from every single instance, which is

---

[3] This argument is that of C. A. J. Coady, *Testimony: A Philosophical Study* (Oxford: Clarendon, 1992), 79–100.

supposed to be exactly similar; except only, that after a repetition of similar instances, the mind is carried by habit, upon the appearance of one event, to expect its usual attendant, and to believe that it will exist. This connexion, therefore, which we *feel* in the mind, this customary transition of the imagination from one object to its usual attendant, is the sentiment or impression from which we form the idea of power or necessary connexion [of cause and effect]. Nothing farther is in the case.[4]

In Hume's view, accordingly, there are no causes and no effects in the conventional senses of those terms. Events designated effects merely follow events designated causes, and inferences from cause to effect and effect to cause are valid only because and to the extent that a human being has seen the so-called effect follow the so-called cause in numerous instances.

Hume, therefore, rejects the notion that one must account for extraordinary testimony such as the apostles' witness to Christ's resurrection either by accepting it as true or by assigning it some other, more probable cause than the resurrection's actual occurrence. For Hume considers custom, rather than the supposed law of cause and effect, the criterion by which one ought to determine what one does or does not believe. If one has experienced human beings giving false testimony, as everyone has, and if one has never experienced a miracle, the rule of custom dictates that one ought always to believe that testimony to miracles is false and never that a miracle has occurred.

By denying the reality of causation, then, Hume gives the skeptic a rationale for rejecting accounts of miracles without so much as consulting the concrete evidence for or against their veracity. Since reason, according to Hume, does not dictate that events require causes, the enormous difficulties one encounters when one attempts, say, to account for the history of the earliest church without supposing that Christ rose from the dead are in Hume's view simply irrelevant to the question of whether Christ actually rose.

Two factors, however, suffice to discredit the skepticism about cause and effect, which enables Hume thus to evade the force of historical evidence for miracles' occurrence. First, as seen in chap. 19 ("The Knowledge of God"), one cannot deny the principle of the reason of being without contradicting oneself; and this principle dictates that everything, which does not exist by virtue of its essence, requires a cause. One cannot deny that contingent events require causes, therefore, without implicitly contradicting oneself. Second, Hume's skepticism seems to imply that even one who directly witnessed a miracle could not justifiably believe that a miracle has taken place. For, according to Hume, one can justly infer the action of a cause from its effect only if one has seen the two conjoined many times. God, however, is invisible. According to Hume's principles, then, neither Naaman, nor the man born blind, nor the paralytic whom Jesus commanded to stand up and walk ought to have believed that he had experienced the miracle that occurred. Hume's skeptical stance with regard to causality thus contradicts the self-validating principle of the reason of being and leads to the

---

[4] Hume, *An Enquiry Concerning Human Understanding*, §7.2, 59 (italics his).

preposterous conclusion that one who witnesses a miracle does not actually witness a miracle. To the extent that Hume's argument against the knowability of miracles presupposes his conception of causality, then, the argument is unsustainable.

C. Summary

Hume's argument fails on four counts. First, his denial that human beings perceive causal relations—the premise that underlies Hume's refusal to admit the occurrence of events that diverge radically from one's own experience—is implausible for the reasons just stated. Second, Hume's understanding of testimony as dependent for its authority on experience leads to an infinite regress; one cannot verify any testimony, that is, without consulting other testimony.

Third, Hume's definition of a miracle as a violation of the laws of nature distorts the authentic character of both miracles and the laws of nature. Miracles do not conflict with, but rather presuppose, the regular operation of nature's laws. An occurrence, which the laws of nature show to be naturally impossible, either falsifies one or more putative laws of nature or derives from supernatural causality, in which case it is beyond the scope of these laws. Neither a miracle nor anything else therefore can violate a law of nature.

Fourth, Hume's argument fails because it includes its conclusion in its premises. The argument, that is, presupposes that universal experience testifies against the occurrence of miracles. This proposition is virtually equivalent to "Miracles do not occur." And one can verify an alleged miracle only by inspecting the experience of everyone at all times. Naturally Hume cannot accomplish this task. His argument therefore depends on two false premises and a false definition, and it is an instance of the fallacy of arguing in a circle.[5]

V. Conclusion

As noted at the outset, the Christian apologist in today's industrialized West must argue for belief in the miraculous in the face of an overwhelming consensus to the contrary. Nevertheless the most influential philosophical argument against the knowability of miracles, in which most other such arguments are contained as in a germ, seems thoroughly implausible. The present chapter has shown, moreover, that the absence of miracles from everyday life poses no threat to an intelligent belief in miracles and that such belief in no way imperils the progress of scientific research. The Christian position on this subject, therefore, seems manifestly superior to that of the secularist. This position will not attain a hearing among thinking people, however, unless Christian apologists, in a simultaneously sensitive and persistent manner, give it voice.

---

[5] For a more thorough refutation of Hume's case against belief in miracles see J. Earman, *Hume's Abject Failure: The Argument Against Miracles* (Oxford: Oxford University Press, 2000).

Chapter 22

How Reliable Are the Sources for Christian Truth?

THE HISTORICAL RELIABILITY OF THE OLD and New Testaments is of crucial importance. As heirs of the Enlightenment, biblical scholars following two major streams of thought are colliding in opposition with apparently little hope of a synthesis of any dialectical nature, although the attempt has been ongoing for decades. This chapter examines the foundations of belief in the historical validity of both the Old and New Testaments. Because of the vastness of the topic, however, this study can be only a survey of the major concerns that occupy biblical historians in this field.

Part 1 of this chapter examines the nature of historical investigation, such as presuppositions in historical research, historical methodology, and how much certainty historical research is expected to yield. Part 2 explores the case for the historical reliability of the Old Testament. Is the Old Testament a collection of ancient documents written and collected by a diverse assortment of sources with no divine direction, or is it the very "words of God" (Rom 3:2 NIV). Part 3 explores the case for the historical reliability of the New Testament.

The study of the historical reliability of the Bible is even more critical today than ever before. Some biblical scholars, for example, have accepted in large part a modern approach to the study of the Bible, which does not allow for the role of divine inspiration or even a providential oversight from God. They argue that the evangelical view is not a serious approach to the study of Scripture and is too reliant on a supernatural role that cannot be historically verified. Conservative scholars, however, argue vigorously for a direct role by the living God in ordering and directing the historical development and transmission of the biblical text. These conservative scholars argue that their modernist counterparts have adopted a purely materialistic approach to the study of the historical veracity of the Scriptures that is foreign to its nature as the "words of God." Modern scholars, however, insist that the Scriptures must be subjected to the same historical criticism as any other literary writing, particularly those from antiquity. By accepting the validity (either in whole or in part) of historical criticism, for example, many modern biblical scholars have adopted an alien paradigm that is antithetical to the nature and purpose of the Scriptures. F. David Farnell has argued, "Ingrained in the discipline [of historical criticism] is a prevailing antisupernaturalism that intuitively suspects any document describing the miraculous. Historical Criticism is in reality an ideology whose very nature negates the Scriptures."[1]

The issue, then, has to do ultimately with whether one accepts the supernatural origin of the Bible. If the Old and New Testaments are indeed inspired by the living God, then the issue of their historical reliability is settled. If the Old and New Testaments are not the product of an eternal mind, however, then they are merely collections of interesting human documents telling their own several stories of imagined encounters with an ever-evolving concept of a nationalistic God of Israel.

I. THE NATURE OF HISTORICAL INVESTIGATION

A. Presuppositions in Historical Research

Is history objectively knowable? That is, can one come to know any historical event or epoch purely on the basis of the facts? Throughout the centuries the general argument in defense of the Christian faith has been traditionally based on the historicity of the Old and New Testaments, particularly the New Testament.[2] This was based on the general assumption (held for centuries until after the Enlightenment period) that history is objectively knowable. If there is an absolute mind that overarches all facts in the world, then conformity to that mind would give ultimate meaning and objective interpretation to the facts. In the modern era, however, people are faced with a host of objections to objective history.

Three main epistemological objections are raised by the historical "relativist" that argue against a purely objective knowledge of history. Epistemology deals with the question of how one can know anything either concretely or abstractly. The historical relativist argues that the conditions by which one comes to know history are so subjectively conditioned that he can never possess an objective knowledge of it.

1. History is not observable

This presupposition holds that the substance of history is no longer directly observable. The study of history is not like the study of empirical science because it can never be repeated again. The historian deals not with past events but with records of past events. Since the historian is not bound to actual historical events as they actually occurred, he has a certain freedom of recounting how a particular historical event unfolded. Historical relativists insist that historical facts exist only within the historian's creative genius. Because the historical event is past and can never be repeated, only the creative historian can impose meaning on the fragmentary text.

The modern historical relativist argues for only indirect access to past events for two reasons. First, the historian's own world is composed only of written records of past events, not the events themselves. By reconstructing a picture of the past, the his-

---

[1] F. D. Farnell, "Philosophical and Theological Bent of Historical Criticism," in *The Jesus Crisis,* by R. L. Thomas and F. D. Farnell (Grand Rapids: Kregel, 1998), 85.

[2] N. L. Geisler, "Objectivity of History," in *Baker Encyclopedia of Christian Apologetics* (Grand Rapids: Baker, 1999), 320–29.

torian projects the past into the present. Second, because the past can never be verified (as in empirical science), it becomes the shape of one's own creative imagination. As Geisler explains, "It will be a subjective construction in the minds of present historians but cannot hope to be an objective representation of what really happened."[3]

2. Historical records are fragmented

Another epistemological presupposition about historical research is that the historian can never hope to attain a complete recounting of historical events themselves. Documents of the past are fragmentary at best. The fragmentary nature of the documents presents only an interpretation of the events as mediated by their recorders, but they are not a full account of the events as they actually happened. At best people have only a fragmentary record of what someone else thought happened.

3. Historians are historically conditioned

A third presupposition held by historical relativists is that the historian is a product of a particular time and place and therefore he is conditioned and is subject to unconscious programming. Because one is enmeshed in the historical process, the historian cannot stand above that process and be objective about any period of history. In this sense one must study and understand the mind of the historian before one can understand the historian's history. The best one can hope for is a successive recounting of each generation's historical interpretations viewed from each generation's perspective.

B. Historical Methodology

Opponents raise three objections against the assertion that history is sufficiently objective to establish the truth of Christianity. All three objections are relatively recent in the field of historical research, and none achieve their intended goal.

1. Historical research is selective

The selection of secondary and fragmentary historical records, it is argued, are based on subjective considerations alone, namely, the presuppositions and prejudices of the researcher. It is impossible for the researcher to rise above subjective influences, personal beliefs, knowledge of languages, and social conditions. Therefore it is not the facts of history that speak but the later fragmentary opinions of the researcher about those events. "The original facts or events have perished. So, by the very nature of the project, the historian [it is alleged] can never hope for objectivity."[4]

2. Structuring the facts

Because historical knowledge is full of gaps, it becomes necessary for the researcher to fill in those gaps with his own imagination. The historian's imagination provides the continuity of the historical events described. Further, the historical

---

[3] Ibid., 321.
[4] Ibid.

researcher is never content simply to explain "what" happened but to elaborate "why" something happened. Without the imaginative structure provided by the historian, history becomes merely a chronicle without a sufficient structure to connect the events into a unified whole.

3. The necessity to select and arrange

Historical relativists argue that every historian selects the material for historical study based on the vantage point of that historian's own generation. The topics selected for study are in accord with the researcher's subjective preferences. The project is predetermined from the start. The final written product will be prejudiced by what is selected and what is excluded from fragmentary, secondhand accounts based on personal preference and the subjective arranging of the historical material.

C. The Results of Historical Research

The above examples serve to illustrate the dire situation that faces the reader of history today. The extent and force of such antiobjectivistic arguments seem so formidable that the tendency is to abandon any hope of achieving the ability to learn from history. This becomes even more problematic when considering the historical accounts in the biblical text. How certain can one be about the reliability of any historical document? In answering such a question the modern reader need not resort to a purely subjective understanding of any particular historical account.

True, there is no such thing as a completely objective account of history. But one need not recoil to the opposite extreme of a complete solipsistic understanding of either secular or biblical history. One can indeed know to a high degree of probability that not only did Julius Caesar in fact cross the Rubicon, for example, but also that it is possible to know to a high degree of probability that Moses led the Israelites out of Egypt and that Jesus Christ became incarnate and lived on the earth. These events were written to posterity as actual historical events. To doubt them without possessing solid and historical counterevidence is to prejudge them irrationally.

II. THE HISTORICAL RELIABILITY OF THE OLD TESTAMENT

A. Who Borrowed from Whom?

In the nineteenth century a new debate raged over the question of the origin of the oral and written accounts found in the Old Testament. Theologians from Europe (primarily Germany) began to reexamine their long-held assumptions regarding the origin of the stories found in the Old Testament, such as the accounts of creation, the patriarchs, the exodus, and the conquest of Canaan, to name a few. Swayed by the new Darwinian paradigm of human evolution, a new breed of theologians questioned everything about the origin of the ancient "myths" found in the Old Testament. In the ancient Near East a number of cosmological accounts of the creation of the world were recorded. The creation account described in Genesis 1–2 is not the earliest written in history, and some accounts composed in Mesopotamia preceded the Genesis account by many centuries.[5]

1. Ancient cosmological accounts

Before Moses led the early Israelites out of Egypt to a new future, the ancient world was already rich with cosmologies of creation.[6] The Akkadian Atrahasis Epic, composed around 1635 BC, parallels the Genesis account of creation, population growth, and the flood with an ark. The Akkadian Enuma Elish account of creation also parallels the biblical account. The Egyptian Theology of Memphis, composed during the thirteenth century BC, parallels the Genesis account of creation by postulating that the creation was created by the spoken word of the deity. The question posed by numerous scholars since the nineteenth century was whether the biblical account of creation was borrowed by various literary genres already in existence in the ancient world and edited to form the Hebrew account of creation.

The answer posed by the vast majority of European scholars was an emphatic *yes.* However conservative scholars have rightly pointed out that such an assumption is not supported by evidence but is based on a predisposition to discount any supernatural influence on history by an eternal God and that the Bible cannot be an accurate record of God's dealings with humanity. Recently this assumption that Jewish redactors borrowed from pre-Hebrew cosmologies has been challenged, and there is now no unified consensus.

Even though there are some striking similarities between ancient Mesopotamian cosmologies and that of Genesis, far more important distinctions are fatal to the conclusion that the Hebrews borrowed from their pagan neighbors for their own creation cosmology. In comparing the Genesis account of creation to that of the Enuma Elish (1100 BC), one sees pronounced differences that argue against a theory that the Jewish redactors lifted material from pagan cosmological accounts. For example in the Genesis account God is seen as the ultimate source of divine power which transcends creation, but in the Enuma Elish magic incantations are the ultimate source of power and the gods are subject to nature. In Genesis God created all things by speaking them into existence (Gen 1:3,6,9,11,20); in the Enuma Elish the creation is formed out of formerly existing matter. In Genesis God separated the primeval waters above and below by a firmament (Gen 1:6–8); in the Enuma Elish the corpse of the god Tiamat is divided in two and set up as waters above and below. In Genesis man is created to rule creation as God's regent; in the Enuma Elish man is created to do the service of the gods so that they would not need to work so hard. In Genesis man is created from the "dust" (Gen 2:7); in the Enuma Elish, man is created from the blood of the slain hero, Kingu.

These examples show that it is more rational to conclude that the Genesis account is the "pure" strain of ancient cosmology in contrast to the pagan cosmologies. The

---

5 Conservatives correctly affirm that Genesis was written by Moses during the fifteenth century BC.

6 The following material is based on J. H. Walton, *Chronological and Background Charts of the Old Testament* (Grand Rapids: Zondervan, 1994), 80–82.

later devolved into distorted echoes of what was once held by the early survivors of the flood from Noah's progeny. Also Jesus Christ Himself held to the Mosaic authorship of Genesis and the Pentateuch, and therefore His belief that the Scriptures, including the writings of Moses, are indeed the living oracles of God, should be definitive in informing one's own understanding and appreciation of the eternal nature of Scripture, including the Pentateuch.

2. Ancient flood accounts

Also numerous parallels exist between the flood account in Genesis and flood accounts in Mesopotamian cosmologies. The ancient Sumerian Gilgamesh Epic, written around 2000 BC, describes an amazing account of the flood complete with the surviving family, the ark, and birds. The Akkadian Atrahasis Epic mentioned above also describes a flood with the ark as lifeboat for a remnant of humanity. As in the creation accounts, many modern scholars since the nineteenth century have suggested that Jewish redactors also borrowed from their pagan neighbors in writing their flood account. But again, such a conclusion is not based on any literary evidence. Rather, the flood record is automatically discounted as untrue simply because it is a miraculous event caused by the God of the Bible. This is a bias against the supernatural, not because the miraculous is impossible but because it is a part of the Judeo-Christian tradition of cosmology.

Like the creation accounts, the distinctions between the various flood accounts of pagan nations and that of the Hebrew Scriptures are telling. In the Genesis account God planned the flood; in the Gilgamesh Epic (c. 2000 BC), the flood was planned during a council of the gods Anu, Enlil, Ninurta, Ennugi, Ea, and Ishtar. The reason for the flood outlined in Genesis was the sin of man; in the Gilgamesh Epic the flood was because man's noisiness disturbed the gods' rest. In Genesis God informed the hero of the flood, Noah, that he would destroy all life on earth, but in the Gilgamesh Epic the plan was carried out secretly. In Genesis the ark was a flat-bottomed vessel, rectangular-shaped, 300 x 50 x 30 cubits, with three levels, a door, a window, and a pitch coating, but in the Gilgamesh Epic the "ark" is ziggurat-shaped, 120 x 120 x 120 cubits, consisting of seven levels, nine sections, a door, a window, and a pitch coating. In Genesis the ark landed on the mountains of Ararat; in the Gilgamesh Epic the ark landed on Mount Nisir. In Genesis Noah and his family worshipped God in thanks for their preservation; in the Gilgamesh Epic a sacrifice was offered as an appeasement to the gods to assuage their great anger. In Genesis God blessed Noah and his family with an earthly covenant and a promise never to destroy the earth with water again; in the Gilgamesh Epic mankind was offered the opportunity to share in divinity and immortality with the gods.

The differences are striking. In the Genesis account God possesses a profound majesty and dignity unmatched in any other religious system, something that is utterly lacking in the description of the gods in the pagan Gilgamesh Epic. One need not stretch credulity to believe that what Moses received on Mount Sinai from God was the complete, unabridged version of divine historiography. The pagan nations surrounding the Israelites distorted the beginning of creation and the flood in their cosmologies. But God gave Moses this information in its unadulterated form. What Moses wrote down is an eyewitness record of what God showed him during their one-on-one encounters on Mount Sinai. Those encounters between Moses and God became the written record of what actually transpired since the creation of the cosmos to the giving of the Law. Every major doctrine in the New Testament would be incoherent and even irrelevant unless a flawless record of the past was the basis of God's plan of redemption.

B. The Documentary Hypothesis

Not until the rise of Deistic philosophy in the eighteenth century did the Christian church begin to doubt the claims of the Pentateuch to have been written by Moses of the fifteenth century BC.[7] The documentary hypothesis is the theory that the Pentateuch was a compilation of sections of writings from different documents composed at different times and places over a span of some 500 years—long after Moses. This theory had its genesis with Jean Astruc, a French physician who became fascinated by the literary structure of Genesis wherein God's name in Genesis 1 is Elohim and in chap. 2 it is usually Yahweh. In his *Conjectures Concerning the Original Memoranda Which It Appears Moses Used to Compose the Book of Genesis* (1753), he attempted to make sense of the use of two different names by appealing to the notion that Moses utilized two different sources for the story of creation. Moses supposedly quoted from one author who knew God only by the name of Elohim and from another who knew God only as Yahweh. While Astruc's proposal found little support in his own day, it set in motion a scholarly movement that was already used to dissect ancient texts (such as Homer's epics) into various sources. This was the beginning of the documentary hypothesis: the presumption of the criterion of divine names.

In the latter half of the nineteenth century, the movement took off and spread like wildfire. In England it was W. Robertson Smith (*The Old Testament in the Jewish Church,* 1881) who first popularized the newer documentary theories of Julius Wellhausen (1844–1918) to the public. Samuel R. Driver provided the classic formulation for the English-speaking world (*Introduction to the Literature of the Old Testament,* 1891). In the United States the most notable exponent of the documentary hypothesis was Charles Augustus Briggs of Union Seminary (*The Higher Criticism of the Hexateuch,* 1893). As Gleason Archer rightly notes, "[N]o other systematic account of the origin and development of the Pentateuch has yet been formulated so lucidly and convincingly as to command the general adherence of the scholarly world."[8] As will be seen in more detail, this movement decimated the long-held belief in a unified compilation of ancient oracles inspired by God.

---

[7] Portions of this discussion are based on G. L. Archer, *A Survey of Old Testament Introduction,* rev. ed. (Chicago: Moody, 1985), 83–108, 147–61.

[8] Ibid., 90.

1. Evolution of religion in the ancient world

The scholarly world was awash in the heady methodology of Hegelian philosophy and Darwinian evolutionism, which were at their pinnacle of popularity in philosophical circles of the late nineteenth century. The "documentarians" found a useful scientific methodology in these twin philosophical catalysts of change to explain how the alleged garbled traditions of the patriarchs and Moses could yield studies that could separate legend from fact. The idea of evolution had caught the imagination of the scholarly world, and the nineteenth century was caught up by an anthropocentric worldview. The Darwinian theory was thought to provide the key to the understanding of history as well as nature. Any idea of a special revelation from God to man was discounted, and the religious aspect of man was to be explained on the basis of a natural process of development as an expression of his cultural behavior.[9] According to the documentarians, progress toward monotheism as expressed in the national life of Israel was simply part of a general evolutionary process through which Israel passed, like that of any other nation or culture. As mankind evolved from the slime of his primordial past, so man's religious development also evolved from its most primitive forms to the pinnacle of religious expression found in monotheism.

2. The JEDP theory—assumptions and critique

Space does not permit an exhaustive recounting of the historical development of the documentary hypothesis. However, it is worthwhile to point out briefly how the JEDP theory came to be the documentarians' stock in trade of biblical historicism. Not long after Jean Astruc's *Conjectures Concerning the Original Memoranda* was published, the next phase of development of the divine names criterion came with the publication of Johann Gottfried Eichhorn's five-volume *Einleitung in das Alte Testament* ("Introduction to the Old Testament"). He divided the entire book of Genesis and the first two chapters of Exodus between the Jahwist[10] and the Elohist (E).

The third stage came with the publication of Wilhelm M. L. De Wette's *Dissertation Critico-Exegetica* (1805) and his two-volume *Beiträge zur Einleitung in das Alte Testament* (1806–1807) concerning Deuteronomy. He proposed that none of the Pentateuch came from a period earlier than David's time.[11] Deuteronomy was the book of the Law which was found in the Jerusalem temple during King Josiah's reform (2 Kings 22). Wette proposed that this book was concocted to unify the kingdom and politically unify all parts of the realm and thereby ensure that all revenues would pour into Jerusalem priesthood.[12] In other words, it was a means to serve the campaign of Josiah, and its discovery was planned for the maximum dramatic impact on the people. This is document D (as it came to be called), which was completely separate in origin

---

[9] Ibid., 147–48.

[10] "Jahwist" is a German equivalent to "Yahwist," referring to one who is responsible for writing portions of the Pentateuch, particularly Genesis, in which the divine name Yahweh (Jahweh, Jahveh) is found rather that the generic term Elohim.

[11] Ibid., 84.

[12] Ibid., 84–85.

and purpose from J and E. The list of Pentateuch "sources" now included three: E (the earliest), J, and the late seventh-century D document.

Hermann Hupfeld's groundbreaking work (1853) was *Die Quellen der Genesis* ("The Sources of Genesis"). His contribution to the documentary discussion resulted in what has been referred to as the "Copernican revolution in the history of the documentary theory." His contribution led to the understanding of the final documentary source known as the Priestly source, or P, based on an earlier conjecture among scholars of a division of sources within the E sources. A Dutch scholar, Abraham Kuenen, in his *De Godsdienst van Israel* ("The Religion of Israel," 1869) argued for the essential unity of P. This source allegedly received its final form under the influence of Ezra, who assembled the entire corpus of the Pentateuch in time for the public reading ceremony described in Nehemiah 8. Julius Wellhausen restated the documentary hypothesis with skill and persuasiveness and gave it its classic expression. He supported the JEDP sequence of sources from an evolutionary assumption during the heady days of Charles Darwin's *On the Origin of Species*,[13] which was capturing the allegiance of the scientific and scholarly world. This also presumably was consistent with the theory of man's religious development from animism to sophisticated monotheism.[14] The impact of this theory was felt throughout Germany and Britain and gained increasing acceptance in America.

Following is a brief description of the characteristics of each of the JEDP sources.[15]

J—Written around 850 BC[16] by an anonymous writer in the southern kingdom of Judah. He had a penchant for personal biography and vivid descriptions of personalities. He often referred to God in anthropomorphic terms (as if He possessed a body, parts, and passions like a man). The author had an interest in theology and ethics but little in sacrifice and ritual.

E—Written around 750 BC by an anonymous writer in the northern kingdom of Israel. He wrote more objectively than J and was less concerned about ethics and theology. In Genesis, E exhibited an interest in ritual and worship and represented God as communicating to human beings indirectly through dreams and visions. In Exodus through Numbers, E promoted Moses to the status of a miracle worker, with whom God could communicate in anthropomorphic guise.

Around 650 BC an unknown redactor (or "editor") combined J and E into a single document called J-E.

D—Composed possibly under the direction of the high priest Hilkiah as propaganda for an official program of reunification of the northern and southern kingdoms of Israel and Judah. Its objective was to compel all inhabitants to cease worshipping on the "high places" and to bring all their sacrifices and religious contributions to the

---

[13] The full title of Darwin's work reads, "Or the Preservation of Favoured Races in the Struggle for Life."

[14] Ibid., 89.

[15] Following Archer, *A Survey of Old Testament Introduction,* 91–92.

[16] These dates are those suggested by S. R. Driver in his *Introduction to the Literature of the Old Testament* (New York: Scribner's Sons, 1891), 111–23.

temple in Jerusalem. D was under the strong influence of the prophets, particularly Jeremiah. Devotees of this same Deuteronomic school were later responsible for re-working the historical narratives found in the books of Joshua, Judges, Samuel, and 1–2 Kings.

P—Written during various stages, from Ezekiel, with his holiness code (Leviticus 17–26) around 570 (known as H), to Ezra, "a scribe skilled in the law of Moses" (Ezra 7:6), under whose direction the latest priestly sections were added to the Pentateuch. P is concerned with presenting a systematic history of the origins and institutions of the Israelite theocracy. The document shows a particular interest in origins, genealogies, and the minutiae of sacrifice and ritual.

3. Assumptions of historical criticism

Historical criticism of the Bible seeks to understand the ancient biblical text in light of its historical origins, the time and place of its writing, its sources, the events, dates, persons, places, customs, and so forth, mentioned in the text.[17] Primarily its goal is to determine the primitive—or original—meaning of the text in its historical context.

The *historical-critical method* refers to those specific procedures used by advocates of historical criticism. This method rests on an underlying concept of the nature and power of historical reasoning in understanding the past. This underlying assumption encompasses the following beliefs: (a) reality is universal and uniform, (b) reality is accessible to human reason and investigation, (c) all historical and natural events occurring within reality are interconnected and comparable by analogy, and (d) one's present experience of reality can provide objective criteria by which to determine what happened in the past. Obviously the historical-critical method rests on presuppositions that cannot be validated by historical investigation alone. These presuppositions are philosophical in character. They are antithetical to the possibility of divine revelation being accessible to humanity as genuine knowledge.

The historical-critical method by definition rules out God as an agent in history. This makes it of no use in the church on a practical level for understanding the Bible and for spiritual formation. Despite this, the rise of historical criticism, which began in the seventeenth century and achieved full maturity in the nineteenth and twentieth centuries, has become the major transformation of biblical studies in the modern era. Historical critics have often regarded themselves as the true heirs of the Protestant Reformation with respect to historical criticism's commitment to the validity of the literal (or original) sense of the text, and the necessity of interpreting the Bible without any influence of ecclesiastical tradition. Historical criticism has not achieved its goals because it embraces an equally burdening tradition of biblical skepticism, absent the church's guidance. It also fails to give proper credence to the words of the text as they were written, but rather seeks to substitute critical reconstructions. Moreover, the

---

[17] The following discussion follows R. N. Soulen and R. K. Soulen, "The Historical Critical Method" and "Historical Criticism" in *Handbook of Biblical Criticism*, 3rd ed. (Louisville: WJK, 2001), 78–80.

critic gives little consideration to the place of the Holy Spirit in understanding the text. Reared in the seedbed of presuppositional naturalism, the goal of historical-criticism is to find ways of reading God and the supernatural "out" of the Bible. God and the attendant supernatural events found in the Bible are anachronisms and religious embellishments that must be expunged from the text in order for one to arrive at its original meaning. Far from being a legitimate method for evangelical scholarship, historical criticism and the historical critical methods that follow it are an ideology founded on the principle of pure reason not on divine revelation.

C. Did the Early History of Israel Actually Happen?

If one followed the conclusions of the documentary hypothesis, the answer to this question would be no. According to proponents of that view, the events in Israel's early history are fabrications of a political and cultic nature. Advocates of the documentary hypothesis say people today must strip away the mythological accretions from the text to reach the original meaning. What is left, however, is something rather sterile and cold. How profoundly sad to realize that the greatest stories ever written down and preserved for centuries are nothing more than legends at best. If the Bible is not true, then there never was a figure called Moses who led hundreds of thousands (if not millions) of Israelites out of Egypt through the desert, through a miraculously parted Red Sea, then on to Mount Sinai to meet their God face-to-face. There never was in historical fact a man named Samson who had been endowed with superhuman strength by the Holy Spirit, and who killed thousands of Philistines in one battle with the jawbone of a donkey but who was defeated ironically through the wiles of a Philistine prostitute. Thankfully the Bible is not a mere hodgepodge collection of religious and political musings by unknown writers.

The following section examines one of the events in the Old Testament to consider its historical value. If these are true historical accounts of events portrayed for centuries in the Bible, what evidence might one expect to find that they really happened? That is, what evidence would convince even the most ardent skeptic of the truth of these events?

1. The Exodus and wandering in the desert

As Walter C. Kaiser has accurately observed regarding the importance to the Jews of this one singular event, "[T]he Exodus from Egypt was to Israel what the *Odysee* was to the Greeks or the stories about the Pilgrim fathers and the Revolutionary War is to Americans."[18] The significance of this one event cannot be overestimated for its importance to the identity of all Jews throughout history. Israel's national identity was intimately associated with their actual deliverance from the cruel tyranny of the pharaoh of Egypt. But establishing the historicity of the exodus is perhaps one of the most

---

[18] W. C. Kaiser, *A History Of Israel from the Bronze Age Through the Jewish Wars* (Nashville: B&H, 1998), 95.

vexing problems facing biblical scholars.[19] The reason for this is that there is scant to no archaeological evidence that the event ever occurred. Biblical critics never tire in bringing up the fact that one of the most important historical events ever recorded in the Bible has virtually no physical evidence in support of it. Because it was the most pivotal event on which God's plan turns, if it never occurred, then the theological bonds between the Old and New Testaments unravel. If there is no archaeological evidence in support of such an event, how can anyone be confident that it ever happened?

One solution comes from biblical archaeologist and scholar Randall Price. He explained that at the commencement of the exodus, when the Israelites left Egypt, the most direct route would have been to the north along the present-day Gaza Strip in a direction that would take them to the heart of Canaan.[20] In fact God led them on a much longer southern route in order to avoid military opposition along the northern route. God's reason for this was rather cryptic: "The people will change their minds and return to Egypt if they face war" (Exod 13:17). Not until recently did anyone come up with a plausible answer to the riddle of the southern route. Egyptian military outposts have been discovered along the northern route along "the Way of the Philistines." Excavations by Israelis at Deir el-Balah have confirmed this. Thus "the Way of the Philistines" mentioned in Exodus is also "the Way of Horus," mentioned in reliefs at the Egyptian temple at Karnak. The inexperienced Israelites would have panicked and fled back to Egypt at the first occasion of a military encounter with seasoned Egyptian garrison troops, and the exodus would have failed soon after it got started.

No matter how impressive the archaeological or historiographical evidence supports any of the events in the Old Testament, no one will necessarily accept that evidence if he is predisposed to discount the evidence as either irrelevant or unconvincing. Jesus knew this personally. Despite the many wonderful miracles He performed during His earthly ministry, many Jews refused to accept Him as their Lord and Messiah. One particular story Jesus told (Luke 16:19–31) highlights this problem. After the rich man and Lazarus died, the former was in torment in hades. He begged Abraham to send Lazarus to relieve his discomfort (which was refused) and then to send Lazarus to his five remaining brothers so that they may be warned of the perils of hades. This was also refused by Abraham, who reminded the rich man that his brothers had Moses and the prophets. The rich man countered with the notion that a man raised from the dead and testifying of the reality of hades would convince his brothers of the reality of the place. Abraham responded that if they would not listen to Moses and the prophets, then they would not be persuaded though one were to go to them from the dead. This is a stunning indictment of the invincibility of unbelief.

2. The authoritative teaching of Jesus on the Old Testament canon

Jesus placed His personal imprimatur on the divine authority of all the Old Testament. Many recorded instances show Jesus affirmed the absolute authority of the

---

[19] R. Price, *The Stones Cry Out: What Archaeology Reveals about the Truth of the Bible* (Eugene, OR: Harvest House, 1997), 129.

[20] Ibid., 134–36.

words of the biblical text.[21] For example He affirmed that Scripture is *unbreakable*, or *infallible.* After quoting Ps 82:6 to the Jews He said, "Scripture cannot be broken" (John 10:35). This conveys the idea that the Scriptures possess an authority so absolute in character that *it cannot be destroyed.* Such an idea of biblical inspiration also conveys the thought that everything recorded in the Bible is recorded accurately and truthfully without error of any kind. Therefore anything in the Old Testament is absolutely true (the historical truths as well as the moral truths) for the primary reason that Jesus, who can never be mistaken on any truth claim, expressed absolute confidence in their authenticity. This is evident when Jesus established a direct link between vital spiritual truths and Old Testament events that He represented as historically accurate. For example He employed a strong comparison when He said, "For as Jonah was in the belly of the huge fish three days and three nights, so the Son of Man will be in the heart of the earth three days and three nights" (Matt 12:40). When Jesus said the words "as" and "so," He was not making a casual connection between some mythological event recorded in the Bible and what He expected to experience. Both the occasion and the manner of His comparison make clear that He was affirming the historicity of Jonah in connection with His own impending death and resurrection.

For the same reason historical events such as the creation; the flood; the calling of Abraham; the lives of the patriarchs; the conquest of Canaan; the era of the judges; the reigns of Saul, David, and Solomon; and the entire corpus of historical narratives in the Old Testament are true and historical, readers can place absolute trust in the veracity of the narratives without fear of being embarrassed or shamed.

III. The Historical Reliability of the New Testament

A. Prolegomena on Authority

The appeal for confidence in the Bible's inerrancy and infallibility is not an emotional appeal to the sentimental aspirations of one's fundamentalist roots. The appeal instead is to the heart of the authority of the entire biblical corpus, the Old and New Testaments. Jesus lived on the earth and spoke words of truth that will never be revoked. His disciples said it best when they declared, "Now You're speaking plainly and not using any figurative language. Now we know that You know everything and don't need anyone to question You. By this we believe that You came from God" (John 16:29–30).

The following paragraphs reveal that the testimony of the New Testament to its own divine inspiration begins with the words of Christ, the core and heart of the New Testament.[22] In a real sense Jesus is the key to the inspiration and canonization of the Old and New Testaments. He confirmed the divine inspiration of the Old Testament,

---

[21] For a thorough study of this subject, see N. L. Geisler and W. E. Nix, *A General Introduction to the Bible,* rev. and exp. ed. (Chicago: Moody, 1986), 21–191, for which I am indebted for portions of this discussion.

[22] See ibid., 89–97.

and He promised that the Holy Spirit would direct the apostles into "all the truth" (John 16:13), which resulted in the New Testament.

Jesus never committed His own teachings to writing.[23] He did promise on several occasions during His earthly ministry that His apostles would be directed by the Holy Spirit in recording His teachings. This promise was fulfilled during the life of Christ and well into the apostolic era until the last apostle died. For example, Jesus promised that the Holy Spirit would guide the apostles in what they *would say about Him*. "But when they hand you over, don't worry about how or what you should speak. For you will be given what to say at that hour, because you are not speaking, but the Spirit of your Father is speaking through you" (Matt 10:19–20; cf. Luke 12:11–12).

Later, after the Last Supper, Jesus encouraged His apostles and elaborated further about how they would be Spirit-directed.

> But the Counselor, the Holy Spirit—the Father will send Him in My name—will teach you all things and remind you of everything I have told you. (John 14:26)

> When the Spirit of truth comes, He will guide you into all the truth. For He will not speak on His own, but He will speak whatever He hears. He will also declare to you what is to come. He will glorify Me, because He will take from what is Mine and declare it to you. Everything the Father has is Mine. This is why I told you that He takes from what is Mine and will declare it to you. (John 16:13–15)

Next Jesus promised His apostles *guidance in teaching*. In Matthew's account of the Great Commission, Jesus said the supernatural direction of the Holy Spirit would extend to what the apostles taught about Christ. "Then Jesus came near and said to them, 'All authority has been given to Me in heaven and on earth. Go, therefore, and make disciples of all nations, baptizing them in the name of the Father and of the Son and of the Holy Spirit, teaching them to observe everything I have commanded you. And remember, I am with you always, to the end of the age'" (Matt 28:18–20).

Obviously if the apostles were not supernaturally directed by the Holy Spirit, they would never be able to teach—much less remember—"all things" that He commanded them. Therefore from the promise of the Holy Spirit to remind them of "everything" (John 14:26) and to lead them into "all the truth" (16:13), it follows that the promise applies to the fullness of apostolic teaching as well as preaching.

The book of Acts further confirms this unique ministry of the Holy Spirit, which was the record of what Jesus "began to do and teach" (Acts 1:1). The book of Acts is the record of the acts of the Holy Spirit through the works and *words* of the apostles. The teaching ministry of the Holy Spirit through the apostles is seen in the fact that the first church continued in "the apostles' teaching" (2:42). Apostolic teaching (2:42; 6:4)

---

[23] This was undoubtedly intended to prevent us from "worshipping" the writings themselves. Even possessing the original copies of the apostles' New Testament writings would have encouraged quasi-worship of them rather than a desire to follow their teachings.

and preaching (Acts 2, 4, 10) were the foundation of the early church. In this sense, then, the church was "built on the foundation of the apostles and prophets, with Christ Jesus Himself as the cornerstone" (Eph 2:20). The church is built on the teaching of the apostles, which was the result of the ministry of the Holy Spirit through them, as Jesus Christ repeatedly promised. As Norman L. Geisler and William E. Nix observe, "Thus, the New Testament is the only primary source for study of the Spirit-directed teaching of the apostles, which teaching was promised by Christ in the gospels."[24] Thus one may conclude that the claim for the divine inspiration of the New Testament follows logically from Jesus' promise to His disciples that He would guide them into all truth by the Holy Spirit.[25] Therefore the New Testament is the result of a supernatural activity of God for the preservation of Christ's teachings that lead to salvation. Unfortunately this conclusion is not tolerated among scholars who have swallowed entirely the antisupernaturalistic claims of methodological naturalism. This is why the historical-critical method is hostile to any supposition of the supernatural, for that method too is based on the claims of naturalism.[26]

B. The Gospel Accounts

The Gospels are by nature a crucial part of Scripture, since they are the only reliable sources of the church's detailed knowledge of Jesus and His teachings.[27] If one successfully attacks the historical reliability of the four Gospels, then one has effectively decimated the very foundation of knowledge of Jesus Christ.

The Jesus Seminar, an opponent of biblical inerrancy, has attracted extensive media attention in the last decade of the twentieth century. This seminar, composed of liberal scholars under the leadership of Robert Waller Funk, began its twice-a-year meetings in 1985. They deny the authenticity of 82 percent of what the four Gospels indicate Jesus said during His ministry. Their conclusions about the authenticity of Jesus' sayings appeared in 1993 in *The Five Gospels: The Search for the Authentic Words of Jesus.* The reactions from evangelical scholars has been swift and forceful against the Seminar's pronouncements. Yet many of the evangelical responses come from those who employ the same method in the study of the Gospels as do those in the Jesus Seminar. To a degree these evangelical scholars, Thomas and Farnell argue, must attack the same presuppositional paradigm they themselves employ.[28]

Ever since the historical-critical method made inroads into evangelical scholarship, New Testament studies have been in a crisis. The historical reliability of the

---

[24] Geisler and Nix, *A General Introduction to the Bible,* 91.

[25] Ibid., 97.

[26] Naturalism is the philosophy that assumes that nature is the product of undirected forces. In the beginning were the particles that compose matter, energy, and the impersonal laws of physics. No personal God created the cosmos and governs it as an act of free will. This evolutionary process is responsible for all life, including humankind. This philosophy controls academia not only in science, but in many fields, including law, literature, psychology, and even religion.

[27] Thomas and Farnell, *The Jesus Crisis,* 14. This source provides an excellent study of the current crisis in evangelical New Testament scholarship.

[28] Ibid.

four Gospels has been undermined by well-meaning evangelical scholars who, quite frankly, should know better. Outspoken evangelical critics have been engaged in the same kind of dehistoricizing activity as the Jesus Seminar personnel. Following is a list that, unfortunately, many evangelical scholars would subscribe to as an accurate rendering of their position regarding the Gospel accounts.[29]

1. The author of Matthew, not Jesus, created the Sermon on the Mount.
2. The commissioning of the Twelve in Matthew 10 is a group of instructions compiled and organized by the author of the first Gospel, not spoken by Jesus on a single occasion.
3. The parable accounts of Matthew 13 and Mark 4 are anthologies of parables that Jesus gave on separate occasions.
4. Jesus did not preach the Olivet Discourse in its entirety, as found in three of the Gospel accounts.
5. Jesus gave His teaching on divorce and remarriage without the exception clauses found in Matt 5:32 and 19:9.
6. In Matt 19:16–17, the writer changed the words of Jesus and the rich man either to obtain a different emphasis or to avoid a theological problem involved in the wording of Mark's and Luke's accounts of the same events.
7. The scribes and Pharisees were in reality decent people whom Matthew painted in an entirely negative light because of his personal bias against them.
8. The genealogies of Jesus in Matthew 1 and Luke 3 are figures of speech and not accurate records of Jesus' physical and/or legal lineage.
9. The magi who, according to Matthew 2, visited the child Jesus after His birth were fictional, not real, characters.
10. Jesus uttered only three or four of the eight or nine beatitudes in Matt 5:3–12.

Robert L. Thomas has commented on this situation among the majority of evangelical scholars:

> Granted, their reduction of historical precision in the Gospels is not the wholesale repudiation of historical data as is that of the original Jesus Seminar, but that it is a repudiation is undeniable. An acceptance of imprecision is even more noticeable in light of the fact that the above questions are only the tip of the iceberg. An exhaustive list would reach staggering proportions.[30]

How then should believers regard the historical accuracy of the Gospel accounts? In light of the earlier focus on the Spirit-directed ministry of the apostles, one can conclude that the historical reliability of each of the four Gospels is beyond doubt. They are more than a biographical sketch of Jesus Christ because they also include an understanding of the uniqueness of His life and teachings in light of the fulfillment of Old Testament prophecy. Even though they accurately portray facts about Jesus, they also include interpretation of those facts in light of Israel's religious history. Although the

---

[29] Ibid., 15.
[30] Ibid.

Gospels include the accounts of Jesus' miracles, the Gospels record intelligently and reverently what the writers remembered of them. The disciples were just as amazed at what they saw in Jesus' miracles as were their contemporaries. Contrary to what Rudolf Bultmann (1884–1976) believed and taught, the writers of the four Gospels were just as incredulous of the miraculous as many people are today. Indeed the noteworthiness and impact of Christ's miracles were dependent on the incredulity of His contemporaries. They knew that God was up to something significant in their generation, but it was not until Christ's resurrection that they finally saw the significance of His life and teachings.

C. The Book of Acts

The book of Acts (or the Acts of the Apostles) records the history of the early church from the ascension of Christ to the end of Paul's two-year imprisonment in Rome. This is the second volume of the earliest history of the Christian church, of which the first volume is the Gospel of Luke.[31] Acts is the historical and theological transition between the Gospels and the Epistles, without which there would be an impassable gulf of confusion. Without the book of Acts, there would be no explanatory link between the ministry of Jesus to the doctrine of evangelism in the early church.[32]

The historical value of Acts is inestimable. The modern historical-critical movement has sought endlessly to repudiate the historical reliability of Acts. For example the Tübingen School of the nineteenth century assigned the book to the middle of the second century, believing it to be an apologetic attempt to gloss over differences in the church that preceded it.[33] Others postulated that Acts was written late in the first century on the assumption that the writer used material from the works of Josephus, which were not written before AD 90.

To the contrary, the accuracy of Luke's allusions to places, persons, and events has been corroborated by archaeology and history and testify that he was a contemporary of what he described. Therefore Acts is a document of primary historical importance both for the history of the church and of the ancient world. Practically all of the authentic extant information about the apostolic leaders and the geographical extent of their mission is gleaned from this book. Although Acts does not give an exhaustive account, it does give facts and general principles that assist historical interpretation.[34]

D. The Pauline and General Epistles

Paul and the other writers of the New Testament Epistles all utilized an ancient form of letter writing characteristic of Greco-Roman practice. The Epistles, a collection of letters on theology and practical Christian living, form the second great division of the New Testament. These letters were written by five of the apostles: Paul, James,

---

[31] M. C. Tenney, "The Book of Acts," in *The Wycliffe Bible Dictionary*, ed. C. F. Pfeiffer et al. (Peabody, MA: Hendrickson, 1998), 21.
[32] Ibid., 23.
[33] Ibid.
[34] Ibid.

Peter, John, and Jude. The apostles wrote these letters to new converts or to individuals in a variety of situations. They agreed, however, regarding facts and doctrine. In this they constitute an authentic and invaluable commentary on the meaning of the life and teachings of Jesus Christ.[35]

E. The Revelation

This last book of the New Testament is a prophetic vision of the future. Biblical scholars have interpreted the book differently throughout church history, and Revelation still remains one of the most controversial books of the Bible. The early church fathers unanimously reported that the apostle John wrote this book. And unless the book is approached with a predisposition to doubt the church fathers, no sufficient reason exists to doubt their word.

F. Canon, Manuscript, and Transmission Issues

The integrity of the Old Testament text has been established in the transmission of the Masoretic tradition and was recently confirmed in the discovery of the Dead Sea Scrolls. The accuracy of the Old Testament is largely the result of the painstaking care taken by rabbinical scholars in the transmission process over the centuries.[36]

The integrity of the New Testament text, however, relies on different factors, namely, a vast number of manuscripts. Counting only the Greek manuscripts alone, the New Testament text is preserved in some 5,366 partial and complete manuscript portions that were copied by hand from the second through the fifteenth centuries. By way of contrast, most all other ancient books survive in only a few late manuscript copies.

A few of the New Testament manuscript fragments date early, from the second century. By contrast the manuscripts for most other ancient works date from about a thousand years after their original composition. Some 362 New Testament uncial manuscripts and 245 uncial lectionaries date from the second through the tenth centuries and constitute nearly 11 percent of all New Testament and lectionary manuscripts.

The John Rylands Fragment, a papyrus fragment, is the oldest known copy of any portion of the New Testament. It dates from around AD 117–38. Adolf Deissmann argues that it could be even earlier. The papyrus fragment, written on both sides, contains portions of five verses from John 18:31–33,37–38.

The Chester Beatty Papyri (c. AD 250) is an important collection of New Testament papyri, now in the Chester Beatty Museum in Dublin. It contains three codices and contains most of the New Testament. But the most important discovery of New Testament papyri since the Chester Beatty manuscripts was the Bodmer Papyri, dating about AD 200 or earlier, and now in a museum in Cologny, Switzerland, near Geneva. The text is a mixture of the Alexandrian and Western types and appears to be a private collection of canonical and apocryphal writings.

---

[35] "Outline of the Books of the Bible," in *Nelson's Illustrated Encyclopedia of Bible Facts*, ed. J. I. Packer et al. (Nashville: Thomas Nelson, 1995), 595.
[36] Geisler and Nix, *A General Introduction to the Bible*, 385.

The oldest uncial on parchment or vellum manuscript of the New Testament is the famous Codex Vaticanus (c. 325–50), now in the Vatican of Rome. It is one of the most important witnesses to the text of the New Testament. This manuscript copy of the whole Bible was probably composed by the middle of the fourth century. The Codex Sinaiticus, dating from the fourth century, is one of the most complete manuscripts. Half of the Greek Old Testament has survived, along with the complete Greek New Testament. It is located in the British Museum, London.

This is only a sampling of the amount of manuscript evidence that exists for the text of the New Testament. The only reason one could doubt the historical reliability of the New Testament witness is because of an irrational bias against it from the outset. The amount of manuscript evidence is impressive and almost overwhelming in its implications. This should instill within everyone a confidence that the New Testament is essentially the equivalent of what the apostles wrote down in their original autographs.

Are the New Testament documents historically reliable? Yes, for there is no rational basis on which to doubt their veracity. Are the New Testament documents theological in their emphasis? Yes, otherwise they would not be included in the New Testament. And there is no reason to suppose that being both historical and theological is mutually exclusive. Only in the mind of the rational critic can a theological document be viewed as unhistorical. Unfortunately for modern critics, the historical is synonymous with naturalism, a repudiation of anything supernatural.

The apostolic writers presumed that what they transmitted in writing was the absolute truth. They were writing down the received word of God as delivered to them by the Holy Spirit as promised by the Lord Jesus. All the New Testament documents were written by eyewitnesses of the events they described and are therefore supernatural to their core. Only among modern biblical critics is there a prevailing naturalism or antisupernaturalism that is intuitively suspicious of any document containing stories of miracles.[37]

IV. CONCLUSION

If the sources used to determine Christian truth are not reliable, then Christian truth is not reliable. Fortunately this is not the case. The fact is that people can know history, and even more so the historical events recorded in the Bible. The historical accounts in the Bible have stood up to centuries of criticism. As a result the Bible is the most thoroughly studied and verified example of an ancient historical document. However, unless supernaturalism is accepted, some critics will never accept the biblical account, no matter how reliable the account is.

---

[37] Ibid., 440.

Chapter 23

ANSWERING THE CHALLENGES
OF THE JESUS QUESTS

NEAR THE END OF THE EIGHTEENTH century, the philosophy of the enlightenment had become popular in Western Europe. The Roman Catholic Church had lost the control it had enjoyed in the medieval period. The Reformation had released a tidal wave of change, so that scholars were now allowed to think and teach apart from the authority of the Roman Church. No subject was safe from fresh investigation and rejection in favor of either agnostic or deistic notions, including the nature and work of Jesus.

The average Christian reading the New Testament might not see any distinction between the Jesus presented by the authors of the Gospels and the Epistles and the so called "historical Jesus." To many scholars, though, influenced by the principles of the Enlightenment, a plain reading of Jesus in the Bible is unacceptable. Because of their radical naturalism, the miracles and other supernatural events of the Gospels are discounted as incongruent with modern knowledge. This trend from the historic view of Jesus as God who entered human history has been expressed in three quests of the historical Jesus. Jesus scholar, Darrell Bock, describes these three quests as "an 'antidogmatic' first quest; a second, 'new' quest grounded in historical and tradition criticism as well as in Greco-Roman background; and a third quest rooted in the study of Jesus in his Jewish context."[1]

These quests overlap somewhat. Some hold to older quests while other quests are in progress. For example after Albert Schweitzer declared that the first quests had failed, not all scholars immediately abandoned their positions. Today many scholars adhere to the method and assumptions of the first and second quests, including the later radical positions reflected in the Jesus Seminar, while more constructive work on Jesus and the Gospels continues, including the work of many evangelicals, within the third quest.

Each of these quests has challenged the orthodox understanding of Jesus, so it is important to interact with their work and to evaluate their arguments. While there has been and continues to be fruitful information stemming from the quests, there has also been much speculation and many false arguments about the works and person of Jesus. The Christian apologist needs to be able to challenge the assertions made

---

[1] D. L. Bock, *Studying the Historical Jesus: A Guide to Sources and Methods* (Grand Rapids: Baker, 2002), 141.

by these quests, especially since these assertions have permeated the general public's knowledge of Jesus and Christianity.

I. THE FIRST QUEST

A. A Radical Proposition

The first quest for the historical Jesus may be traced to 1778 when Gotthold Lessing published the work of Hermann Samuel Reimarus (1694–1768) entitled *Fragments*.[2] The book was published posthumously because Reimarus feared recriminations against himself over the content of the work. Reimarus argued that the Jesus who really lived and the way in which the writers of the Gospels presented Him are incongruous. Jesus Himself had no intention of beginning a new religion, and He was very much a follower of first-century Judaism, whereas the Gospel authors portrayed Him according to their own perspectives. Yet according to Reimarus Jesus did see Himself as a political Messiah. The picture of Jesus began to become more and more amazing after His death and burial, when His disciples, in order to foster a Jesus movement, stole His body from the tomb and then proclaimed His resurrection.

B. The Consequences of Reimarus's Efforts

This effort by Reimarus to deny the Jesus of the Gospel accounts, as the risen Lord and God, flourished in the rationalism of the early nineteenth century. Several scholars began to doubt the supernatural elements in the life and teaching of Jesus, including K. F. Bahrdt (1741–92)[3] and K. H. Venturini (1768–1849).[4] Albert Schweitzer, in his monumental work *The Quest of the Historical Jesus*, said of them that they "first attempted to apply, with logical consistency, a non-supernatural interpretation to the miracle stories of the Gospel."[5] Both Bahrdt and Venturini saw Jesus as a member of the Essene sect. Schweitzer called this effort of theirs to make Jesus an Essene "the Earliest Fictitious Lives of Jesus."[6]

Bahrdt saw Nicodemus and Joseph of Arimathea as secret Essenes. With help from the Essenes Jesus was able to fake His miracles. Luke assisted in the various healings and was also involved with providing necessary drugs that enabled Jesus to survive the crucifixion. After Jesus had recovered, He made visits to His disciples.

Venturini's view was similar to that of Bahrdt, believing that in His youth the Essenes trained Jesus. Similar to Barhdt's belief, he said Jesus' miracles were not supernatural. Differing from Bahrdt, Venturini did not believe the crucifixion was a

---

    [2] H. S. Reimarus, *Fragments*, ed. C. H. Talbert, trans. R. S. Fraser (Philadelphia: Fortress, 1970).

    [3] K. F. Bahrdt, *Versuch eines biblischen Systems der Dogmatik*, 2 vols. (Leipzig: Heinsius, 1769–70).

    [4] G. A. B. van Eysinga, *Radical Views About the New Testament*, trans. S. B. Black (London: Rationalist, 1912), 22.

    [5] A. Schweitzer, *The Quest of the Historical Jesus* (New York: Macmillan, 1968), 38. See K. F. Bahrdt, *Ausführung des Plans und Zwecks Jesu*, 4 vols. (Berlin: n.p., 1784–93); and K. H. Venturini, *Naürliche Geschichte des grossen Propheten von Nazareth,* 3 vols. (Bethlehem: n.p., 1800–1802).

    [6] Schweitzer, *The Quest of the Historical Jesus*, 38–47. See also Bahrdt, *Ausführung des Plans,* and Venturini, *Naürliche Geschichte*.

plot, and he believed that Jesus actually expected to die on the cross. However, after Nicodemus and Joseph of Arimathea observed signs of life in Jesus as they were preparing Him for burial, they contacted the Essenes, who took away His body. After Jesus recuperated, He visited His disciples.

C. The First Quest's Titan

Perhaps the most notable scholar of this post-Reimarus period was David Friedrich Strauss (1808–74).[7] In his work *The Life of Jesus Critically Examined*,[8] he denied the historical reliability of the Gospel records, especially regarding supernatural events. Strauss considered the Gospels as mostly mythical tales rather than accounts about the historical Jesus. Rather than seeing the miracles described in the Gospels as actual events, he believed they should be understood as fabrications of the Gospel writers who wished to construct Jesus as the promised Messiah. According to Strauss these myths, such as the virgin birth, are legends that sought to honor Jesus in the same way the Greeks sought to extol their historical figures in myths.

D. The Dawn of Source Criticism

Paralleling this new criticism of the life of Jesus, there arose what is known as "the Synoptic problem," a critique of the first three Gospels. The word *Synoptic* comes from two Greek words meaning "to see together." Because Matthew, Mark, and Luke share much of the same sayings and events in the life of Jesus, they are thought of as congruent. Before the rise of source criticism in the mid-nineteenth century, the majority of scholars held to the priority of Matthew among the Gospels. This view was practically unrivaled from the earliest part of the patristic period until this new perspective was proposed. The first theory of Synoptic criticism was called the two-source hypothesis, advocated in 1863 by H. J. Holtzman (1832–1910). He rejected Matthean priority, substituting Mark as the first Gospel, and argued that Matthew and Luke depended on Mark's Gospel, along with an undiscovered (to this day) hypothetical source of the sayings of Jesus, to construct their Gospels. Later, Holtzman's unnamed source document was given the title Q (from the German *Quelle*, "source") by Johannes Weiss (1863–1914) in 1890, the title that survives today. There exists no written source document representing Q, but most critical scholars believe that either this alleged document or oral tradition of Jesus' sayings was used to write the Synoptic Gospels. Today scholars have postulated other sources, in addition to Q, sometimes called M and L, to reconstruct Matthew and Luke. This is because scholars are seeking to explain the sources of the seemingly unique data in each of the Synoptic Gospels.

E. Conservative Reaction

Not all scholars followed the abandonment of the Jesus portrayed in the Gospels

---

[7] Other scholars who are important in this period were C. Weisse (who is famous for his advocating Marcan priority), B. Bauer, and E. Renan, but space does not permit examination of each person's contribution.

[8] D. F. Strauss, *The Life of Jesus Critically Examined,* 2nd ed., trans. G. Eliot (New York: Macmillan, 1892).

as the historically accurate Jesus. Two who did not were Adolf Schlatter (1852–1938)[9] and Alfred Edersheim (1825–89).[10] Edersheim was a Jewish convert to Christianity and professor at Oxford University, and his *Life and Times of Jesus the Messiah* is still useful to students of the New Testament. Edersheim's argument was similar to Schweitzer's years later, though coming to a considerably different alternative, as to why Jesus was portrayed in such ways. He argued that these various critical scholars' conclusions were greatly influenced by their worldview. The Jesus they discovered at the end of their studies was already determined by the only Jesus they would allow at the beginning of their research. Rather than a true critical study of the Gospels, they were bound to an antisupernaturalist view of reality that overarched and clouded their understanding of Jesus and the Gospels.

F.   The Jesus of the First Quest

Critical scholars of the eighteenth and nineteenth centuries were united in the belief that the Jesus portrayed in the Gospels was in large part fabricated by His followers in the first and second centuries after His death. However, they were divided as to who they thought was the "real" Jesus. Two primary pictures of Jesus emerged. The majority perspective was that Jesus was a moral reformer who taught the brotherhood of man and the fatherhood of God. His teachings emphasized how to live one's life in service to God and one's fellowmen. In the liberalism of the nineteenth century, this teaching was the essence of the Christian religion.

Johannes Weiss expressed the minority view. He taught that Jesus was an eschatological prophet who expected the end of the world in His own time. This emphasis of Jesus caused many during His time, who were not concerned with such an apocalyptic message, to be unreceptive to His teaching. Also sharing this view was the above-mentioned Albert Schweitzer. He argued that the ethical emphasis of many of the first-quest scholars was in reality simply an imposition of the liberalism of those who were writing on Jesus. They brought their own philosophies to the Jesus quest. Schweitzer convincingly argued that there was insufficient information in the Gospel accounts to construct a complete life of Jesus. Instead, he believed the proper view of Jesus was that He was an apocalyptic prophet of a failed attempt to bring in the kingdom of God. Schweitzer's book proved to be the death knell of the first quest.

II.   THE PERIOD OF NO QUEST

A.   End of the First Quest

Three major scholars mark the end of the first quest of the historical Jesus, William Wrede (1859–1906), Albert Schweitzer (1875–1965), and Martin Kähler (1835–

---

[9] A. Schlatter, *The History of the Christ: The Foundation of New Testament Theology*, trans. A. J. Köstenberger (Grand Rapids: Baker Books, 1997).

[10] A. Edersheim, *The Life and Times of Jesus the Messiah* (1883; updated reprint, Peabody, MA: Hendrickson, 1993).

1912). The last of these three wrote the first major critique of the first quest in *The So-Called Historical Jesus and the Historic Biblical Christ.*

> I wish to summarize my cry of warning in a form intentionally audacious: *The historical Jesus of modern authors conceals from us the living Christ.* The Jesus of the "Life-of-Jesus movement" is merely a modern example of human creativity, and not an iota better than the notorious dogmatic Christ of Byzantine Christology. One is as far removed from the real Christ as is the other.[11]

At the center of of Kähler's argument is that the Gospels are not objective reports of Jesus but are records of beliefs by Jesus' early followers.[12] He said the Jesus of history being pursued by the first quest is little like the Christ of faith.

The thought of scholars prior to Wrede was that Mark represented the most accurate information about the historical Jesus and that Matthew and Luke were merely supplemental, and John inconsequential. Wrede questioned even the historical credibility of Mark. In his *The Messianic Secret in the Gospel*[13] Wrede argued that the identification of Jesus as Messiah was a theological interpolation by the church after the resurrection.

In contrast to Wrede, Schweitzer considered Mark's portrayal as basically historical in agreement with earlier scholars in the Jesus quest.[14] Although Schweitzer agreed with earlier scholars against much of Wrede's view on Mark, yet he dismantled the arguments of the first quest because he believed it was impossible to separate the Jesus of the Gospels from the historical Jesus. But he then erected a Jesus of his own who was eschatological in nature.

Schweitzer argued that the rationale behind much of the quest for the historical Jesus was to do away with the orthodox beliefs about Jesus taught in the church for nearly two millennia, which made critical studies of Jesus impossible. Schweitzer pointed out that the scholars of the first quest decried the methodology of orthodoxy while at the same time ignoring their own portraits of Jesus reflecting their idealist, rationalist, socialist, or romanticist philosophies. He said that if the mistake of orthodoxy had been not to ask questions about the Jesus of history, the failure of the historical quest had been to mold Jesus into a modern figure matching the ideology of the biographer.[15]

---

[11] M. Kähler, *The So-Called Historical Jesus and the Historic Biblical Christ*, trans. C. E. Braaten (Philadelphia: Fortress, 1964), 43 (italics his).

[12] Ibid., 92.

[13] W. Wrede, *The Messianic Secret in the Gospel* (Gottinzen: Vandenhoick & Ruprecht, 1911; reprint), trans. J. C. G. Greig (Cambridge: James Clarke, 1971). There have been a plethora of discussions on the messianic secret of Mark. Two helpful explanations have been offered. W. R. Telford suggested that the claim of secrecy actually goes back to Jesus rather than being invented by Mark (*The New Testament: A Short Introduction* [Oxford: Oneworld, 2002], 139). Perhaps this was done to deflect from the notion that Jesus would be the political Messiah often expected by the people. Or possibly His purpose was to provide for Himself and His disciples some measure of privacy. See J. L. Blevins, *The Messianic Secret in Markan Research, 1901–1976* (Washington, DC: University Press of America, 1981).

[14] C. C. Anderson, *Critical Quests of Jesus* (Grand Rapids: Eerdmans, 1969), 73.

[15] Ibid., 72–73.

Schweitzer sought to rescue Jesus from the mélange of the nineteenth and twentieth centuries, which fit the image of a modern ethical teacher or idealist, and to place Him back in the context of the first century AD. He believed, with Wrede, that Mark had a strong messianic element. The question to be decided, however, was the nature of the Messiah in the book. Schweitzer believed that Jesus, along with many in His day, strongly held to an imminent coming of God and came to believe that He was the Messiah to bring this coming. However, before Jesus was able to bring about this coming kingdom of God, He was arrested and put to death.[16]

How does this eschatological Jesus who died in the first century relate to the current day, according to Schweitzer? For him the significance of Jesus is not His history but His spirit. Hugh Anderson concludes the importance of Schweitzer's work in these words: "Whereas the Liberals, in their search for the truly human lineaments of Jesus, lost the Christ-character or the kerygma-character of his history, Schweitzer, himself no less resolved on scientific objectivity, all but submerged the historical Jesus in the dogmatic 'concept of the Christ.'"[17]

B. The Jesus of Strauss

David Strauss represents an optimistic classical liberalism that had considerable appeal in the nineteenth century. Those who held this philosophy were not concerned about the Gospel portrayal of Jesus; they were more interested in Him as the great example of how to live. Thus supernatural elements in the Gospels were unimportant to him, including a belief in the deity of Jesus. Strauss doubted those events he deemed inconsistent or impossible (in keeping with the denial of the supernatural characterized by classical liberalism). However, these nonhistorical accounts were not there by accident but were purposeful fabrications designed to make Jesus fulfill the expectations of the Messiah. Ultimately for Strauss the Gospels are useful only for their example of morality.[18]

The optimism of this period was brought to a screeching halt with the horror of World War I, and the idea of moral evolutionary progress was crushed. Man's sinfulness could not be denied, and although weakened, the inherent goodness of man central to classical liberalism was still not entirely abandoned.

C. The "Big Nasty Ditch"

The first quest of the Jesus of history ended in doubt that the historical Jesus could be discovered. As Charles Anderson concludes: "The liberals saw difficulties in places, but were certain that through literary criticism they could arrive at an accurate picture of the historical Jesus. As a result of the work of Wrede, German scholarship became much more skeptical of the possibility of such an achievement."[19] Scholars

---

[16] Ibid., 74.

[17] H. Anderson, *Jesus and Christian Origins* (New York: Oxford, 1964), 21–22.

[18] C. H. Roth, "Lives of Jesus: Books," Varieties of Unreligious Experience Blog, http://vunex .blogspot.com/2006/05/lives-of-jesus-books.html (accessed January 28, 2008).

[19] C. C. Anderson, *Critical Quests of Jesus* (Grand Rapids: Eerdmans, 1969), 71.

who abandoned the first quest held that it was too optimistic in their efforts to uncover the Jesus beneath the myth. Further they believed there was little possibility through the power of historical investigation to disconnect the faith of the church from the Jesus who lived. Moreover, the abandonment of the quest was all but inevitable because of the embracing of existentialism in religious studies, in which the attempt to discover the historical Jesus was irrelevant and illegitimate. This was because the Christian faith was thought to be built on belief in Christ rather than having certain knowledge of the historical Jesus. Thus it was unimportant who the historical Jesus really was.

This existentialism grew from the ideas argued by Søren Kierkegaard (1813–55),[20] who, in an attempt to protect Christian theology from rabid rationalism of the Enlightenment, separated faith from fact. Kierkegaard is impressive with the warmth of his devotion to the Christian faith, but his attempt to guard the faith actually opened it to the charge of having nothing to say about truth, since it was merely subjective. Some after Kierkegaard, such as Martin Heidegger (1889–1976), Bultmann's teacher, argued similarly. Sixty years before Schweitzer's pronouncements on the first quest, German philosopher Gotthold Lessing, mentioned earlier, had declared that there was a "nasty big ditch" between history and faith.[21] This division is similar to the two-story universe, to use Francis Schaeffer's illustration,[22] in which fact, science, history, the physical, and truth lie in the lower story, while faith, theology, myth, the spirit, and speculation reside in the upper story. Theological truth divided from history and fact becomes little more than questionable speculation about what it addresses. Unlike scientific truth, considered to speak about real, objective matters, theological truth is considered as only personal and speculative, unable to be taken seriously since it was only personal opinion.

With World War I (1914–18), liberalism had lost its footing, allowing for the rise of the brilliant theologian Karl Barth. His commentary *Epistle to the Romans* (*Der Römerbrief*)[23] in 1919 shook the liberal theological world with his emphasis on the sovereignty of God and the sinfulness of man. Though Barth did not bring theology back to an affirmation of earlier classic theology, his neoorthodoxy gained the upper hand on liberal theology. However, Barth and his followers had no interest in the historical Jesus. His existential or *encounter* theology was interested only in a personal encounter with God in a Word of God beyond or above the written words of the text of the Bible.

D. Rudolf Bultmann and the "No Quest" Period

Rising to prominence in the "no quest" attitude and the existential philosophical scene was form critic Rudolf Bultmann. A Lutheran scholar known as a powerful preacher, Bultmann said the desire for facts and history to support the Christian

[20] F. D. E. Schleiermacher (1768–1834) held to existential philosophy before Kierkegaard.

[21] As stated by N. T. Wright, *Who Was Jesus?* (Grand Rapids: Eerdmans, 1992), 6–7.

[22] F. Schaeffer, *Escape from Reason* (Chicago: InterVarsity, 1968).

[23] K. Barth, *Der Römerbrief* (Bern: G. A. Baschlin, 1919; reprint, *The Epistle to the Romans*, trans. E. C. Hoskins [London: Oxford University Press, 1933]).

gospel was an expression of unbelief. His concern was to communicate the good news of Jesus as the Savior of mankind. This message must be presented without the myths surrounding the story of Jesus in the Gospels (hence the coined term "demythologization") that were no longer acceptable to "scientific humans" who had moved past belief in miracles. Since faith negates need for proof, the desire to build Christianity on knowledge of the historical Jesus was actually detrimental to Christian belief. Also Bultmann argued that the first Christians also had little interest in knowing the Jesus of history. He said, "I do indeed think that we can know almost nothing concerning the life and personality of Jesus, since the early Christian sources show no interest in either, are moreover fragmentary and often legendary; and other sources about Jesus do not exist."[24] For Bultmann the early church believed in a Christ of faith, rather than a Jesus of history. Bultmann sought to find this faith by discerning the written sources and oral traditions that developed around Jesus. Rather than finding the historical Jesus, the proclamation (*kerygma*) about the Christ of faith was the focus. Although Barth and Bultmann disagreed on many things, they both believed that a quest for the "historical Jesus" was contrary to faith and perhaps not even possible.

III. THE SECOND QUEST (THE NEW QUEST)

A. New Methodology

After World War I many scholars began to move from literary or source criticism to what is known as form criticism. Literary criticism attempts to determine the sources behind the final form of a literary text, such as the New Testament, giving consideration to the temporal proximity of the event to the recording of the event. Form criticism, on the other hand, concerns itself with different patterns or forms that can be discovered within the text (genre like psalms, parables, hymns), usually developing from oral tradition, and how they fit into the historical context.

Then after World War II biblical critics added another type of analysis of biblical texts, redaction criticism. Those who use redaction criticism are interested in the theological ideas of the authors of given texts and how the author has used these to shape the textual material. In discovering an author's molding of a passage, a critic looks to vocabulary, style, comparison of similar accounts, and repetition of themes.

B. The Beginning of the Second Quest

The second quest of the historical Jesus began with Ernst Käsemann (1906–98), a student of Rudolf Bultmann, with the publication of his essay, "The Problem of the Historical Jesus"[25] in 1954. He believed that a new quest was both historically and theologically necessary, one that should avoid the errors of the past.[26] Käsemann

---

[24] R. Bultmann, *Jesus and the Word*, trans. L. P. Smith and E. H. Lantero (New York: Scribner, 1958), 8.

[25] E. Käsemann, "The Problem of the Historical Jesus," reprinted in *The Historical Jesus: Critical Concepts in Religious Studies*, ed. C. A. Evans (New York: Routledge, 2004).

[26] Evans, "Introduction," in *The Historical Jesus*, 7.

offered two methods to approach the new quest. He developed a theory to find the Jesus who truly lived in human history in Israel, sometimes called the "criterion of dissimilarity." He thought scholars could arrive at the historical Jesus by discounting material that is "is not derived either from primitive Christians teachings or from Judaism. When Gospel material originates from neither of these sources, one can be reasonably sure that the material is historical."[27]

His second criterion to determine an authentic story or saying of Jesus is to find multiple attestations of the words in independent traditions and stories that simultaneously are in agreement with material already determined to be reliable.

C. Differences in the New Quest from the First Quest

This new quest is not only different in methodology from the old quest, but its focus on Jesus and history is different. The first quest sought to find evidence for elements within the Gospels that could substantiate knowledge of the historical Jesus, while the second, accepting the inseparable distance between faith and history, was not interested in substantiating the historical Jesus and was focused instead on the *kerygmatic* Christ, the Christ preached by the church. Anderson explained that this was because "the significance of Jesus for faith was the great overriding factor in the life of the early church. He [Käsemann], feels that this was so much the case that it almost completely replaced his earthly history."[28] Käsemann, according to Anderson, questioned whether the phrase "historical Jesus" is valid to use because of his concern that some might believe that a life of Jesus can be written. Having said this, he did believe that the Christ of faith did have an earthly existence. He said it would be wrong to neglect the important primitive Christian recognition of the identity between the exalted Christian and the earthly Jesus. Second, he had concern that such de-emphasis of the earthly Jesus might give rise to a docetic view of Jesus. Last of all, within the Gospel tradition there is compelling evidence of some things in Jesus' life as being historical.[29]

Even more important than Käsemann's analysis is the work of Günther Bornkamm (1905–90). He also denied the possibility of constructing a biographical or psychological life of Jesus. He accepted form criticism in which the events of the life of Jesus are given thematically rather than connected in a sequential account. Thus the Gospels are not given to provide history but to proclaim Jesus. On the other hand to abandon interest in history altogether is to lose the earthly Jesus. He believed that a balance could be maintained through the use of historical criticism. He also believed that Jesus did not believe Himself to be a Messiah, but Bornkamm did think His ethical teaching was authentic.[30] For Bornkamm Jesus was a "transcendent personality who called people to repent."[31]

---

[27] G. R. Habermas, *The Historical Jesus: Ancient Evidence for the Life of Christ* (Joplin, MO: College Press, 1996), 23.

[28] Anderson, *Critical Quests of Jesus*, 166.

[29] Ibid., 167.

[30] Bock, *Studying the Historical Jesus*, 146.

[31] Ibid.

The second quest, then, distrusted the Jewish context for Jesus and believed that the writers of the canonical Gospels had created a Jesus different from what He really was.

D. The Jesus Seminar

The Jesus Seminar was begun in 1985 by the Westar Institute, a think tank set up by several liberal academics. According to the official Web site of the Westar Institute, "The Jesus Seminar was organized under the auspices of the Westar Institute to renew the quest of the historical Jesus and to report the results of its research to more than a handful of gospel specialists."[32] The Seminar included approximately 70 scholars from North America, though the number of people working on the project varied over time. Few if any could be considered conservative. Most are radical critics of the Bible, and only a handful are well-known scholars in the field of New Testament studies. The Jesus Seminar is not sponsored by either the Society of Biblical Literature (SBL) or the Society for the Study of the New Testament (SNTS), two major scholarly organizations in biblical studies.[33] Several members of the group, however, such as Robert Funk, John Dominic Crossan, and Marcus Borg, have garnered some celebrity from their work.

The desire for media attention makes this "quest" important for apologetics and deserving of more attention here. While all the quests have had some impact, the Jesus Seminar, though widely criticized in scholarly circles, has focused on popularizing their findings, sidestepping normal academic channels. While stating they simply wish to expand the audience of Jesus research, in reality they have actively pursued the attention of popular media and the achievement of celebrity status. To this end their arguments have become widely assumed to be what *all* scholars view as the truth concerning the "real Jesus." As will be seen, this is not the case.

1. Starting Points

The Jesus Seminar, as with some previous quests and despite claims of complete objectivity, operated under certain prejudices and presuppositions. Their starting point is a total rejection of the supernatural, a throwback to the first quest. Robert W. Funk wrote:

> Biblical scholars and theologians have learned to distinguish the Jesus of history from the Christ of faith. . . . The distinction between the two figures is the difference between a historical person who lived in a particular time and place and was subject to the limitations of finite experience, and a figure

---

[32] "The Jesus Seminar: Phase I" (Salem, OR: Polebridge, 1985), http://www.westarinstitute.org/Seminars/seminars.html (accessed May 27, 2010). Though the Jesus Seminar is the most famous of its projects, the Westar Institute projects include The Jesus Seminar on Christian Origins, the Seminar on the Acts, and the Literacy and Liturgy Seminar. These projects are at various stages of progress, but according to records on their Web site, the last yearly "reports" were given in 2008.

[33] B. Witherington III, *The Jesus Quest: The Third Search for the Jew of Nazareth* (Downers Grove, IL: InterVarsity, 1997), 43–45.

who has been assigned a mythical role, in which he descends from heaven
to rescue human kind and, of course, returns there.[34]

Their rejection even includes anything Jesus said that is seen to be supernatural. Any
miracle is considered a myth, added later to reflect later beliefs. Thus there can be no
virgin birth, walking on water, or resurrection. Before they even began their work, the
Jesus Seminar decided that anything in the Gospels that supports Jesus being more
than just a human cannot possibly be true.

Besides rejecting anything miraculous about Jesus, they also reject the Gospel
writers themselves. As Funk said, "Whenever scholars detect detailed knowledge of
post-mortem events in sayings and parables attributed to Jesus, they are inclined to
the view that the formulation of such sayings took place after the fact."[35] The Seminar
rejects verbal inspiration outright but goes even further by asserting that there is no
possibility the Gospel writers could have remembered everything Jesus said, so they
made up large portions of the writings in order to "fit" what they thought Jesus should
have said. These inventions are said to be taken from the "fund of common lore or the
Greek scriptures."[36] The Gospel writers, attempting to make Jesus into the Messiah,
"began to search the sacred writings or scriptures . . . for proof that Jesus was truly the
messiah." This led them to "make the event fit the prophecies lifted (and occasionally
edited) from the Old Testament."[37] On the other hand the Seminar also lampoons the
intelligence of the Gospel writers, calling them "technically illiterate"[38] while giving
no evidence of their assertion. They do not address the apparent contradiction of the
assertion that illiterate Jewish fisherman carefully studied ancient writings and formulated fictional accounts of Jesus' activities to make Him meet the messianic requirements of those writings.

Following their rejection of any supernatural origins of the Gospel writings, the
Seminar was also characterized by approaches that minimize the credibility of the
canonical Gospels while giving unusual credence to Gnostic texts from the second
century, texts they have tried to date far earlier than is generally accepted by scholars.
Again this is based on pure assumption. Apparently those who assembled the canon
were not as qualified as the Seminar personnel to evaluate the texts. They argue, rather,
that the individuals (including some considered heretics by the early church, such as
Valentinus) and the councils that assembled the canon were utterly biased, as are the
many, many scholars who have upheld the canon through the centuries. Only the Jesus
Seminar is objective enough to find the actual words of Jesus, even if those words differ from what has been considered authentic for almost 2,000 years.

The perspective of the Jesus Seminar presupposes that both canonical and noncanonical scriptures have equal value in determining the historical Jesus. Prominent

---

[34] R. W. Funk et al., *The Five Gospels: What Did Jesus Really Say?* (San Francisco: Harper, 1997), 7.

[35] Ibid., 25. In fact the seminar is 100 percent so inclined, which indicates something far less than objectivity; it's a commitment to only one view.

[36] Ibid., 27–33.

[37] Ibid., 23.

[38] Ibid., 27.

among these extracanonical texts is the Gospel of Thomas. This text was used by Gnostic Christianity and formerly assigned to the second century and therefore was not considered by some within the Third Quest as preceding, or at least competing with, Matthew, Mark, Luke, and John.

2. *Methodologies reflecting presupposition*

The above discussed presuppositions directly affect the Seminar's methodology. In fact their adoption of presupposition actually extends to their methods of study. The Seminar's stated goal is to arrive at what Jesus really said, as opposed to what the Gospel writers invented in order to make Jesus into the promised Messiah. But before they ever encounter a single text, they have already decided to throw out most of what is recorded about Jesus in the canonical Gospels. From this starting point they utilized "seven pillars of scholarly wisdom" to evaluate the texts. Each of these "pillars" themselves has significant and erroneous presuppositions.

The first pillar is an assumed dichotomy between the Jesus of history and the Christ of the church. They accept the previous quest's assertion that the Jesus of history cannot be the same as the Christ of faith and further that the Christ of faith is automatically wrong. However, one cannot separate faith from history because faith must have an object. If the "Christ of faith" as He is seen in the Gospels is not the real Jesus, then there is no reason for the existence of Christianity. Genuine faith is not an unreasonable faith (1 Corinthians 15); it is based on evidence that explains the facts. The overwhelming evidence supports Jesus as He is presented in the canonical Gospels.

In the second pillar, alluded to above, the Jesus Seminar says that the Synoptic Gospels, along with the *Gospel of Thomas*, are much closer to the original sayings and deeds of Jesus than the Gospel of John. Again this is a pure assumption. They argue that the Gospel of John is the "spiritual" Jesus.[39] This is understandable, considering that the "Christ of faith" from the creeds looks similar to the Jesus found in John's account. However, the Seminar has already assumed that the church created the "Christ of faith." Further the Seminar refuses even to consider the arguments about dating John's Gospel, simply asserting it is much later than the other writings. Moreover, they are seemingly oblivious to the thought that the "spiritual" element in John's Gospel could simply be a matter of a different emphasis on the same Jesus.[40]

The third and fourth pillars relate to how the Synoptic Gospels came together. The Jesus Seminar assumes with certainty that Matthew and Luke simply copied Mark's Gospel, and that material common to Matthew and Luke but not found in Mark is from the Q document described earlier. In this view Matthew and Luke mostly contain words copied from other sources and are not authentic sayings of Jesus. Certainly it can be surmised that Matthew and Luke used *something* as a source to write their Gospels, but it could have been an oral tradition known to both of them and not a

---

[39] Ibid., 3.
[40] Groothuis, *Searching for the Real Jesus* (Minneapolis: Harvest House, 1996), 97. See also ibid., 41–50.

document. This view also assumes Mark and the mythical Q document are themselves not authentic, and yet there is no justification for holding this view.

These two methodologies show the Seminar's erroneous use of continuity, the discipline of looking for authentic evidence of an event by finding things common among each account. They in fact turn continuity on its head. In a normal legal case one looks for continuity to corroborate a story. Three witnesses with the same story are better than two. The more witnesses, the more likely their story is true. The Jesus Seminar has argued the exact opposite. Stories that are similar among the Gospel writers are said to be *inauthentic* because they have so much in common. The only way for this to be true is if all the writers collectively fabricated Christianity by copying one another (except apparently John, who did not go along with the "conspiracy"). This would have been quite a feat if the Seminar's assertion of the Gospel writers' illiteracy were true.

The fifth column is one point of disagreement with some previous quests. They assume that Jesus never said anything about the end of the world. According to the Jesus Seminar John the Baptist preached this message of impending judgment and cataclysm, whereas Jesus is said to have "rejected that mentality in its crass form, quit the ascetic desert, and returned to urban Galilee." The disciples misunderstood everything Jesus taught them, so when Jesus died, they reverted back to the things John the Baptist taught them. This, coupled with the disciples' desire to transform Jesus into a cultic figure akin to the "hellenistic mystery religions," led them to fill in their own "memories" of Jesus around His actual sayings and parables. For the Seminar this means the "Jesus of the gospels is an imaginative theological construct." The Seminar sees this fifth pillar as "liberation" for Jesus from the traditional majority view. For them modern scholarship is a "search for the forgotten Jesus."[41] Again this argument is almost entire assumption, devoid of actual fact. The Seminar assumes that at an undisclosed time before Jesus began His ministry the apostles learned a great deal from John the Baptist and then went back to their daily lives. Yet, apparently, they had learned nothing from Jesus, whom they had followed for three years. This view also assumes that the disciples were heavily influenced by Greek paganism, rather than being thoroughly Jewish. The Seminar totally disregards the possibility that Jesus spoke about the coming kingdom because He actually knew about it. This view assumes that the "illiterate" Gospel writers were involved in some conspiracy to add to what Jesus actually said in order to construct their own theological system.

The sixth pillar assumes that an oral culture is incapable of preserving the original words of Jesus, unlike our writing culture today. Therefore only those sayings that are memorable, short, provocative, and repeated often are considered authentic. The Jesus Seminar people are simply not able to remember long dialogues, let alone whole stories. This pillar, however, betrays the underlying elitism of the Jesus Seminar. It is as if they are completely ignorant of oral cultures.

This sixth pillar further typifies their dismissal of the supernatural. Jesus Himself said, "But the Counselor, the Holy Spirit—the Father will send Him in My name—will

---

[41] Funk, *The Five Gospels*, 4.

teach you all things and remind you of everything I have told you" (John 14:26).[42] Even if one were to grant, contrary to what this verse says, that the writers of the Gospels were not supernaturally assisted in their recalling Jesus' words and deeds, the Jesus Seminar completely fails to acknowledge human capacity for memorization.[43]

The seventh pillar claims there has been a reversal of the burden of proof. The Jesus Seminar says that previously people assumed that the Gospel narratives are true, and the burden of proof was on proving false the sayings and events that are recorded there false. The Jesus Seminar argues this is no longer the case. They assume that since academia has done such a thorough job of proving the Gospel accounts false, it is now up to scholars to recover the sayings of Jesus that are true (or at least close to true), and they are the real defenders of the Gospel accounts.[44]

Many scholars would deny this point, as will be seen from the discussion of the Third Quest. The existence and need for a third quest proves this point. There is simply too much evidence for the orthodox view of Jesus, and more continues to be discovered as time goes on. So it is not possible to disprove the Gospels, let alone arrogantly assume it has already been done.

Having implemented this highly assumptive methodology, the Jesus Seminar then voted on how to decide which sayings of Jesus were authentic. "Voting was adopted, after extended debate, as the most efficient way of ascertaining whether a scholarly consensus existed on a given point."[45] Concerning this method Ben Witherington III says, "Only in a thoroughly democratic society where the assumption that the majority view is likely to be right and to reflect a true critical opinion on the 'truth' could the idea of voting on the sayings of Jesus have arisen."[46] They implemented a complex system of weighting the results, heavily biased against inclusion. Based on these criteria, the Seminar concluded that 82 percent of the sayings of Jesus in the Gospels are not authentic. In fact only ten verses are considered to be "virtually certain" sayings of Jesus!

The Jesus constructed by the Jesus Seminar is a disjointed sage, dispensing short wisdom sayings. Witherington rightly charges that the Jesus of the Jesus Seminar was no prophet or even a radical reformer, was passive until questioned or criticized, was not controversial, never claimed to have a part in God's final plans for man, never claimed to be Messiah, and did not come to save.[47] The Jesus of the Jesus Seminar is

---

[42] The Jesus Seminar voted this verse black (meaning they considered it inauthentic), as they did for all but one saying in their version of John.

[43] J. Nightengale has memorized word for word several books of the New Testament, including John's Gospel. He makes a living reciting these books at churches or college chapels. See http://www.wordsower .org/index.htm.

[44] Funk, *The Five Gospels*, 5.

[45] Ibid., 35.

[46] Witherington, *The Jesus Quest*, 44

[47] Witherington offers this critique, "So we might ask how anyone as inoffensive as this could have generated so much hostility much less get himself crucified. The Jesus of Jesus Seminar could never have ended up on Golgotha nailed to the cross. Yet the crucifixion of Jesus is one of the basic historical givens of what we know about Jesus. . . . Since Jesus is characterized by the seminar as a man with a laconic wit given to exaggeration, humor, and paradox, he seems a much better candidate for a late-night visit with David Letterman or Jay Leno" (ibid., 56–57).

radically different from the Jesus who is presented in the canonical Gospels and embraced by the church from the first century until now.

The Seminar's book, *The Five Gospels*, includes a discussion of their ideology as well as the canonical Gospels and the *Gospel of Thomas*. The Gospel writings are color-coded based on their voting and weighting. Red letters are "most likely" Jesus' words, pink are "likely," gray are "not likely," and black words are "very unlikely" Jesus' actual words.

3. Evaluating the Jesus Seminar

The Jesus Seminar makes sweeping and radical assumptions based on outdated liberal ideas, leading them to disregard normal textual-critical arguments and evidence and to commit logical fallacies. While claiming to be a fresh look at Jesus scholarship, the Jesus Seminar is actually a return to (largely outdated) liberal thinking. Moreover, the Jesus Seminar does not give any rationale for the adoption of these criteria, much of which are circular in reasoning. The Seminar comes to its work with an elitist view of themselves in regard to scholarship and history, seeing themselves as more objective and having better insight than previous scholars. In the end their use of questionable methods reveals their underlying skepticism and their desire for attention from the media, rather than an objective desire to find the "authentic" sayings of Jesus. Based on how they set up the Jesus Seminar to appeal to the popular media and on their success at garnering attention from that media, it is not a far stretch to see them molding Jesus into what they themselves wish to be, namely, wise sages whom the public can seek out for "countercultural wisdom."[48] They seem to have fallen into the same trap Schweitzer accused the First Quest of, imposing their own philosophies onto Jesus. They claim objectivity which they deny to the original writers of the Gospel. But they are actually engaging in what they accuse the original writers of, reinventing Jesus to suit their own needs.

IV. THE THIRD QUEST

A. Why a Third Quest?

Because of its radically narrow character, Second Quest has provided scant information. The Jesus of the Second Quest became an obscure sage having little or nothing to do with the faith that arose after His lifetime. Many saw this conclusion with skepticism and began what has been called the Third Quest. The beginning of this new quest is generally dated to 1970. Unlike previous quests that mainly centered on single interests, such as literary or form criticism, the Third Quest is an interdisciplinary approach, gaining information from archaeology, history, and texts. These are then judged against the disciplines of anthropology and sociology to seek to understand

---

[48] Ibid., 57.

Jesus and are much broader in possible perspectives of Jesus and reflect a large variety of visions of Jesus.[49]

B. The Third Quest: More Positive Approach but Still Not Correct

The Third Quest has more support across liberal and conservative scholarship and has overall been more constructive in understanding the Jesus who actually lived. A number of scholars, such as E. P. Sanders, Ben Meyer, Geza Vermes, Bruce Chilton, and James Charlesworth, have been seeking to reconnect Jesus to His Jewish heritage, recognizing Him as a Jewish teacher in the first century who embraced Judaism and reflecting Jewish thinking.

N. T. Wright commented on this difference between the Second and Third Quest:

> One of the most obvious features of this "Third Quest" has been the bold attempt to set Jesus firmly into his Jewish context. Another feature has been that, unlike the "New Quest," the writers I shall mention have largely ignored the artificial pseudo-historical "criteria" for different sayings in the gospels. Instead, they have offered complete hypotheses about Jesus' whole life and work, including not only sayings but also deeds. This has made for a more complete, and less artificial, historical flavour to the whole enterprise.[50]

A few examples of the shift to place Jesus back in His cultural context will suffice. Geza Vermes, a Jew, considers Jesus a Galilean rabbi and holy man. Ben Meyer sees Jesus as a preacher to God's chosen people Israel, offering community. E. P. Sanders argues that Jesus' cleaning of the temple offended His Jewish audience and eventually brought His death.[51]

Another shift from the previous quest is the return to traditional source material. Conservative scholars such as N. T. Wright and I. Howard Marshall give much more credibility to the Gospel materials and eyewitness testimony, giving the new quest more credability than the Second Quest.

---

49 The perspectives of Jesus have been categorized under numerous rubrics:
   Jesus, the Myth: Heavenly Christ (E. Doherty, T. Freke, P. Gandy)
   Jesus, the Myth: Man of the Indefinite Past (A. Ellegard, G. A. Wells)
   Jesus, the Hellenistic Hero (G. A. Riley)
   Jesus, the Revolutionary (R. Eisenman)
   Jesus, the Wisdom Sage (J. D. Crossan, R. Funk, B. Mack, S. J. Patterson)
   Jesus, the Man of the Spirit (M. Borg, S. Davies, G. Vermes)
   Jesus, the Prophet of Social Change (R. Horsley, H. Maccoby, G. Theissen)
   John, the Apocalyptic "Prophet" (B. Ehrman, P. Fredriksen, G. Lüdemann, J. P. Meier, E. P. Sanders)
   Jesus, the Savior (L. T. Johnson, R. H. Stein, N. T. Wright)
   See "Historical Jesus Theories," http://earlychristianwritings.com/theories.html#doherty (accessed January 29, 2008).
50 N. T. Wright, *Who Was Jesus?* (Grand Rapids: Eerdmans, 1992),14.
51 E. P. Sanders, *Jesus and Judaism* (Philadelphia: Fortress, 1985), 24–25.

V. AN EVALUATION OF THE QUESTS FOR THE HISTORICAL JESUS

Criticisms of the historical quests for Jesus may be leveled in three ways: (a) presuppositions that underlie the study, (b) the methodology used in dealing with the Gospels, and (c) misunderstanding of the value and authenticity of noncanonical works.

A. Presuppositions of the Quests for Jesus

Excepting the current conservative resurgence, all the quests have been built on false premises that are simply assumed to be true. These include the following five elements.[52]

1. Antisupernaturalism. A foundational assumption of the quests is that any event deemed to be supernatural in nature is rejected without further investigation. Because of their absolute faith in science, their claim is that supernatural occurrences violate natural law and violate the principle of improbability (that the most statistically probable explanation is likely to be the correct one). Therefore anything Jesus said or did that is deemed supernatural is rejected out of hand. This presupposition does not take into account that miracles are miracles for the very reasons they reject them. They are supernatural because they transcend (not violate) natural law. They are miracles because they are not normal everyday occurrences. Further, science has yet to prove that miracles cannot and do not happen so denying them is a matter of faith.

2. Denial of historicity. The quests deny the historical reliability of the Gospels. But the historicity of the Gospels has been substantiated beyond that of almost all other ancient books. To deny the Gospels' historical value would mean denying every other ancient source of knowledge from Roman history to Buddha's teachings.

3. Fact/value dichotomy. Kant's assumption that one can separate fact from value is clearly false. There is no spiritual significance in the virgin birth unless it is a biological fact. It is impossible to separate the fact of Christ's death from its value. Nor can one separate the fact of a human life from its value; a murderer inescapably attacks the individual's value as a human by taking the person's life.

4. A false separation. The quests fail to prove their assertion of the disjunction between the Christ of faith and the Jesus of fact. As mentioned above, they doubt that the Gospels are historical, and therefore they do not set out the historical person of Jesus. They presuppose that "the Jesus of history" was a different person from the "Christ of the church's faith." David L. Bartlett comments on this separation, by way of an instructor, saying:

> My irenic teacher Nils A. Dahl represents a kind of middle ground between the most extreme positions. That faith is *relatively* uninterested in the historical Jesus research does not mean that it is *absolutely* uninterested in it. To draw this conclusion would be a kerygmatic theological Docetism, or

---

[52] Condensed from Geisler, *Baker Encyclopedia of Apologetics;* and Bock, *Studying the Historical Jesus,* 149–50.

even a denial of faith in God as creator, under whose worldly rule even the historian does his service as a scholar. The fact that Jesus can be made an object of historical critical research is given with the incarnation and cannot be denied by faith, if the latter is to remain true to itself.[53]

5. Misunderstanding of "myth." The quests have failed to understand the nature of "myth." That an event is more than empirical does not mean it is less than historical. For example the miracle of Jesus' resurrection is more than simply the resuscitation of His body; however, it is not less than that. To claim the New Testament is myth is to misunderstand completely both the New Testament and mythology. Myths are attempts to explain the nature of things, how they came to be. They generally do not teach requirements for belief and behavior, as the Gospels certainly do.

B. Methodologies of the Quests for Jesus

The First Quest, immersed in the empiricism that had become popular at the time, tried applying strictly empirical rules to studying the Gospels. In the end they gave up the quest, as discussed above. For them there was simply no way to verify the historicity of the Gospels using standard empirical methods. However, since their time vast amounts of archaeological and textual discoveries have made many of their assumptions outdated. Unfortunately this fact has not stopped some modern scholars from using their methodologies.

The Second Quest attempted to peel away all the later information in the Gospels that added to strengthen the church's position. They also wanted to isolate Jesus from His Jewish context, arguing that the Gospel writers were attempting to prove Jesus is the promised Messiah. As a result they accepted as historically accurate only those things in the Gospels that were not directly supporting church doctrine and were not overly Jewish. This practice, in conjunction with their other presuppositions, left the Second Quest with scant actual information. They also gave noncanonical writings more credibility than is deserved. This has resulted in bizarre claims. Martin Hengel, reviewing B. Thiering, says:

> What is new is the distorted, idiosyncratic, polemical approach to Christian Origins based on an eisegesis of the Dead Sea Scrolls, especially the Pesharim, by B. Thiering. She claims to be able to discover—from reading the New Testament in light of her interpretation of the Dead Sea Scrolls—that Jesus was married, divorced, and remarried. Her precision is astounding: Jesus was betrothed to Mary Magdalene at Ain Feshka (= Cana) at 6:00 p.m. on Tuesday, June 6, 30 C.E. Mary Magdalene decided to divorce Jesus in March 44, after "the birth of Jesus' third child." This reconstruction is imaginative eisegesis. Readers of this Festschirft [*sic*] need no demonstrations

---

[53] N. A. Dahl, *The Crucified Messiah and Other Essays* (Minneapolis: Augsburg, 1974; italics his), in D. L. Bartlett, "The Historical Jesus and the Life of Faith," http://www.religion-online.org/showarticle .asp?title=180 (accessed January 29, 2008).

that Thiering has offended the science of historiography, which at best can approximate probabilities.[54]

The Third Quest's method is greatly improved over the previous two. Using modern research techniques involving a broad cross-section of disciplines, modern scholars are seeking to reestablish Jesus in His historical context. Unfortunately some in this new Quest continue to use false presuppositions and an unjustifiable use of extra-biblical sources. To further complicate the issue, scholars have fallen prey to "media scholarship," leading to doubtful conclusions based not so much on the evidence but on what will sell.

C. False Understanding about Extrabiblical Documents

As noted earlier, extrabiblical material continues to be used in the quest for the historical Jesus. Geisler says:

> In the most recent radical quest there is a misdirected effort to date the New Testament late and to place extra-biblical documents of Q and The Gospel of Thomas. But it is well-established that there are New Testament records before 70, while contemporaries and eyewitnesses were still alive. Further, there is no proof that Q ever existed as a written document. There are no manuscripts or citations. The Gospel of Thomas is a mid-second-century work too late to have figured in the writing of the Gospels."[55]

The document Q is an assumed writing. As Geisler alluded, it is a hypothetical document thought to be the source for some of the Gospels' material. The Gospel of Thomas is a text included in the Nag Hammadi Library found in Egypt. It is widely seen as written by Gnostics to give credence to their beliefs. Neither of these works deserves equal consideration with the canonical Gospels. The Gospel of Thomas is far too late to be a contemporary of the Synoptic Gospels. Further, it is known from only one full copy and a fragment (but of the Synoptic Gospels there are more than 5,000 copies and fragments in Greek alone). To utilize it as a reliable source for the historical Jesus violates normal guidelines of ancient historical research. The Q document does not even exist, so it is impossible to study it. Such unreliable and hypothetical evidence would not be acceptable in any other area of scholarship.

VI. CONCLUSIONS

The Quests have all failed to disprove that the Jesus of history differs from the Jesus of the New Testament. Their conclusions are derived from erroneous presuppositions and poor methodology. Unfortunately this has not stopped the newest Quest from forming different versions of the "Jesus of history." However, this does not mean there

---

[54] M. Hengel, quoted in *Geschichte-Tradition-Reflexion: Festschrift für Martin Hengel zum 70 Geburtstag*, ed. H. Cancick and P. Schäfer (Tübingen: Mohr Siebeck, 1996), 27.
[55] Geisler, *Baker Encyclopedia of Christian Apologetics*, 386.

is nothing of value to be gained from the Third Quest. In fact the renewed interest in Jesus gives opportunities for further historical exploration.

A. Opportunities for Research Arising from the Third Quest

N. T. Wright offers important questions he believes must be addressed by modern scholars, many of which have been studied only partially. First, how does Jesus fit into the context of the Judaism of His day? Were Jesus' desires the same as that of His contemporaries, what was their reaction to Him, and what did He say or do that related to their hopes for the immediate future?[56]

Second, what were Jesus' true aims? Though Jesus is sometimes portrayed as only coming to save the world through His death, were there other more mundane things that motivated Him? What did He want people to do in responding to Him?[57]

Third, why did Jesus need to die? On one extreme is the view that He was executed as a political revolutionary against Rome, while on the other is the perspective that He was a "bland Jesus, the mild Jesus, the Jesus who was so thoroughly like any other ordinary Jewish holy man that it is hard to see why anyone would have wanted to oppose him, let alone crucify him."[58] Wright asks whether Jesus believed He was called to a violent death.[59]

Fourth, what caused the origin of the early church? Related directly to this issue is the meaning of Easter, a question that Wright says has received little serious historical research.[60]

Fifth, Wright seeks to form a distinction between the issue of what the Gospels are and whether they are in fact true. He says that the fact of whether they were written by Christians is irrelevant to whether they are true. Further he would like to see more study into what genre they were written, and whether this tells anything about the authors of the Gospels. He concludes:

> These, I suggest, are the questions that ought now to be addressed in serious historical study of Jesus. They are also the starting-point for serious *theological* study of Jesus. It will not do, as we have seen many writers try to do, to separate the historical from the theological. "Jesus" is either the flesh-and-blood individual who walked and talked, and lived and died, in first-century Palestine, or he is merely a creature of our own imagination, able to be manipulated this way and that.[61]

B. How Jesus Is Presented in the Gospels—Some Scholarly Insight

Most critical scholars would say gaining a true understanding is not possible because the Gospels themselves are not historical documents but are statements of the

---

[56] Wright, *Who Was Jesus?* 17.
[57] Ibid.
[58] Ibid.
[59] Ibid.
[60] Ibid.,17–18.
[61] Ibid., 18 (italics his).

church's faith, with only small fragments of true historical fact. Wright answers this by acknowledging that the Gospels are products of theological reflection, but he says that this fact alone does not invalidate them as historical. He admits that they are written from a particular perspective but argues that this is true of all history. All people, not just Christians, write this way, and, like anyone who writes, they do so from a particular worldview. Wright asserts that though the Gospels are not strict biographies according to first-century standards, since their focus is theological, they are "theologically reflective *biographies*."[62]

Second, Jewish thought was fully steeped in history. History to the Jews was an integral part of their identity. They looked to Abraham and the fathers, to the exodus, their connection to David the king; and they anticipated God entering into the historical time-space plane to usher in His kingdom. Wright argues that the Jews would not have considered their redemption by God accomplished since they were ruled by Rome, and disobedience to the Law was rampant, and the world was still sinful.

> Something had to happen in the real world. . . . A "spiritual" redemption that left historical reality unaffected was a contradiction in terms. If the gospels, seen in terms of the pagan culture to which the church went in mission, are inescapably *biographies*, then, seen in terms of the Jewish culture which gave them their theological depth, they are inescapably *theological history*.[63]

The accusation that the Gospels' lack of chronological order indicates that they are nonhistorical is without merit. Wright calls those who make such arguments naïve, since this is what actual history looks like.[64]

C. What May Come of It

So far the Third Quest has been useful for scholars and laity alike. By putting to use modern methods of research, one may be able to gain a better insight into these "theological histories" and the Jesus portrayed in them. This is not to suggest that this research proves the New Testament true, but it certainly argues against the claim that it is *not true*. Much of the work done by the Third Quest completely disproves the claims made by the previous two. Further, despite claims to the contrary, the Third Quest overall is using much more sound research methods and fewer assumptions and prejudices than the previous quests.

After 230 years of intense scrutiny and criticism, the New Testament account of Jesus has not been proven false. On the contrary, many scholars today are convinced that the testimony of the Gospels is as sure as it has ever been. Scholars have given their best arguments against the historicity of the portrayal of Jesus in the Gospels, and on honest consideration of the evidence they have failed to deny its historicity. Moreover, there is widespread interest in Jesus generated by these quests, and believers should take advantage of the opportunity to present Jesus' true message of salvation.

---

[62] Ibid., 95–96 (italics his).
[63] Ibid., 96 (italics his).
[64] Ibid.

Chapter 24

THE MEANING AND IMPORTANCE OF THE PHYSICAL RESURRECTION OF CHRIST

SOME PEOPLE ARE TEMPTED TO REGARD the church fathers as infallible guides of ancient theology, who stood as bulwarks of early Christian orthodoxy against all attempts to deconstruct the teachings of Christ and the apostles. For the most part this is true, but there are exceptions. Origen (184–254), an early church father of the ante-Nicene period, wrote the following on the nature of the resurrection body.

> Now we ask how can anyone imagine that our animal body is to be changed by the grace of the resurrection and become spiritual? . . . *It is clearly absurd that it will be involved in the passions of flesh and blood. . . .* By the command of God the body which was earthly and animal will be replaced by a spiritual body, such as may be able to dwell in heaven; even on those who have been of lower worth, even of contemptible, almost negligible merit, the glory and worth of the body will be bestowed in proportion to the deserts of the life and soul of each. But even for those destined for eternal fire or for punishment there will be an incorruptible body through the change of the resurrection.[1]

This was not the only occasion when Origen wrote bizarre theological speculations, for which he was rightly criticized by some of his contemporaries and for which he and his writings were condemned at the Fifth Ecumenical Council in Constantinople (AD 553) for his teachings on such subjects as the preexistence of the soul, universal salvation for all sentient creatures (including the devil) and for his denial of the physical nature of the resurrection.[2]

Perhaps Origen's most enduring legacy is his influence on subsequent church practice in biblical hermeneutics.[3] For Origen, Scripture is inspired by the Holy Spirit, including every word. This means for him that every word has a *spiritual* meaning that lies behind or transcends the literal meaning of the word. The same Holy Spirit who inspired the biblical text resides in every believer to enable him to discern its

---

[1] Origen, *De Principis,* II.x, quoted in *The Christian Theology Reader,* ed. A. E. McGrath (Malden, MA: Blackwell, 1995), 357 (italics added).
[2] E. Ferguson, "Origen," in *New Dictionary of Theology,* ed. E. Ferguson, D. F. Wright, and J. I. Packer (Downers Grove, IL: InterVarsity, 1988), 481.
[3] Ibid., 482.

spiritual meaning. Origen said that nonliteral, that is *allegorical* interpretations, were justified because Scripture is itself spiritual. Scripture then must have a spiritual meaning worthy of God and be inerrant despite its apparent difficulties. Everett Ferguson notes, "Controls on the non-literal interpretation of the nature of man and God allowed philosophical ideas to influence the interpretation. The allegorical (spiritual) interpretation was elevated to prominence by Origen's followers, who thereby lost the control exercised by the moral purpose."[4]

The major problem with Origen's allegorical method of biblical interpretation is that it too often led straight into a hermeneutical circle that allowed much less for the objective, literal meaning of a text, and led far more to a *subjective* interpretation justified by the inner-light experience of the interpreter imposed on the text. Thus, because of his reliance on an a priori hermeneutic and because of his predisposed reliance on Greek neo-Platonism, Origen believed he was justified in reaching theological conclusions based on his spiritual interpretive methods. In short he was reading certain meanings "into" the text (eisegesis), rather than reading meaning "out" of the biblical text (exegesis).

Origen's faulty view of the resurrection of Christ was based on his overreliance on the allegorical interpretation of Scripture, which itself was dependent on Greek neo-Platonism popular in the Eastern church at the time. Thus his theology of the resurrection was based not on what Scripture clearly taught about its nature but on what he "presumed" it taught. However, the doctrine of the physical resurrection of Jesus Christ simply will not yield to anything but a literal understanding of the term *resurrection*.

This chapter examines the meaning and significance of the physical resurrection of Jesus Christ as taught throughout the history of the church. Did Jesus rise from the tomb physically or spiritually? What has traditionally been the church's teaching on this doctrine? What significance does Jesus' resurrection have in relation to His own claim to being divine? What does the physical resurrection of Christ have to do with the salvation of believers?

I. THE CLASSICAL TEACHING OF THE RESURRECTION OF CHRIST

A. The Fact of Jesus' Resurrection Body

In 1 Corinthians, one of Paul's earliest works, he provides insight into the importance and nature of the resurrection of Jesus, and its integral relationship to the gospel. In 1 Corinthians 15, Paul reminded his readers of the gospel that he first preached to them, by which they were saved (v. 1). Then he wrote:

> For I passed on to you as most important what I also received: that Christ died for our sins according to the Scriptures, that He was buried, that He was raised on the third day according to the Scriptures, and that He appeared to Cephas, then to the Twelve. Then He appeared to over 500

---

[4] Ibid.

brothers at one time, most of whom remain to the present, but some have fallen asleep. Then He appeared to James, then to all the apostles. Last of all, as to one abnormally born, He also appeared to me" (vv. 3–8).

The content of the gospel is the resurrection victory of Christ over death, which is the guarantee of salvation. If Jesus Christ was not raised *bodily* from the tomb of Joseph of Arimathea, then the faith of the Corinthians and the faith of every believer throughout church history since then is in vain (v. 14)—useless to the point of absurdity, and believers are still dead in their sins (v. 17). If Jesus was not raised from the dead, then His life, ministry, miracles, and atoning death on a Roman cross meant *nothing*. For Paul, who had been dramatically confronted by the risen Christ in all His risen glory on the road to Damascus, the fulcrum of his message was the physical reality of Christ's resurrection from the grave. Jesus had actually defeated death itself forever! Paul's overarching ambition thereafter was "to know Him and the power of His resurrection and the fellowship of His sufferings, being conformed to His death, assuming that I will somehow reach the resurrection from among the dead" (Phil 3:10–11). Paul desired to share in that same spiritual transformation from mortality to immortality like his Master before him, Jesus, the firstfruits from the dead. "But now Christ has been raised from the dead, the firstfruits of those who have fallen asleep" (1 Cor 15:20).

The Epistles depend entirely on the foundational assumption that Jesus Christ is reigning as living Savior over the church, to be trusted, worshipped, and adored, and who will one day return physically as King over the whole earth in power and great glory.[5] Indeed the New Testament Epistles would not make any sense whatever without the underlying fact that Jesus Christ defeated death and rose bodily from the dead to reign as God and King forever.

Jesus Christ did not rise from the dead merely to be subject again to aging and eventual death. He rose to a radically different and new kind of existence, a new life in that His resurrection body was made immortal—and perfect—no longer subject to aging, weakness, or death, but able to live on into eternity in an indestructible existence.[6]

Jesus possessed a corporeal body of flesh and bones, physical in every way to that of humans. After His resurrection His body could be seen, touched, and handled as any other human body. This fact was so true that two of His disciples on the road to Emmaus took Him to be a typical wayfarer (Luke 24:15–18,28–29). He took up bread before them and broke it (v. 30). Later He ate a piece of fish in front of His disciples to show that the body that was hung on a Roman cross now stood before them in reality and that He was not a "ghost" (vv. 39–43). Mary through the partial blindness of her tears thought Him to be the gardener (John 20:15). Again demonstrating the corporeal nature of His resurrection body, Jesus graphically pointed out the nail prints in His hands and feet and the fresh spear wound in His side (v. 20). He prepared breakfast for His disciples along the shore of Galilee (21:12–13). He said to them, "Why are you

---

[5] W. Grudem, *Systematic Theology: An Introduction to Biblical Doctrine* (Grand Rapids: Zondervan, 1994), 608.

[6] Ibid., 608–9.

troubled? . . . And why do doubts arise in your hearts? Look at My hands and My feet, that it is I Myself! Touch Me and see, because a ghost does not have flesh and bones as you can see I have" (Luke 24:38–39). The Gospels and the Epistles are adamant that the body Jesus had after His resurrection was a glorified *physical* body.

B. The Nature of Jesus' Resurrection Body

What is meant by the *physical* resurrection of Jesus? Does this mean that the body that was laid in Joseph's tomb was the same body that walked out of it? Yes! However, Jesus is the firstfruits—or prototype—of a new race of human beings. While Jesus has the same body now that He had before His crucifixion, He has taken on to Himself an added quality of *immortality*. Paul wrote about our anticipated resurrection, "For this corruptible [human body] must be clothed with incorruptibility, and this mortal [human body] must be clothed with immortality" (1 Cor 15:53). A new quality of existence is given to believers' earthly bodies. These bodies are of an eternal nature, a nature of immortality that will suit them for their new existence in the heavenly and eternal realms. Because Jesus now enjoys a glorified body for all eternity, believers will each receive his own "spiritual body" (vv. 44–46) after this mortal body gives out in death. "What you sow does not come to life unless it dies" (v. 36).

In other words a new property will be "added on" to the believers' existence ontologically. They will undergo a major metamorphosis. But in this transformation they will not cease to be themselves in any way. They will be "enhanced" but not changed in their essential properties. For example, if I lose weight, I do not say I have lost "x" amount of myself. Rather, I say I have shed unwanted pounds (from myself). Ontologically and essentially, I did not change; only my physical dimensions altered. Or, if I should lose an arm or leg, I have not become less of myself. Therefore, the new property of immortality in one's resurrection body will not alter his essential humanity. Such an addition will enhance him, but it will not alter his essential human nature.

The property of immortality that is added to the believer's body does not make him more human. The body that Jesus now has in heaven is the same body He had while on earth. Now after His glorious resurrection Jesus is more than the suffering Savior; He is the believers' *living Lord.* Jesus' resurrection was prophesied in the Old Testament (Ps 16:10). After His resurrection He appeared to Peter, the Twelve, to more than 500 witnesses, to James, to all the apostles, and then to Paul himself. He is alive and ministering to His church actively.

If Jesus did not rise from the dead, then the gospel is empty and misleading, since Jesus is at the right hand of God the Father interceding for believers (Rom 8:34). Jesus' resurrection, not His crucifixion, secured justification as a sign of God's approval of Christ's sacrifice for sins (Rom 4:25). As the firstfruits, the prototype, of those who have fallen asleep, Christ serves as an example and a guarantee of what believers who hope in Him can expect. Their dead, physical bodies will be raised to immortality (1 Cor 15:42). In their resurrection bodies they will enjoy existence as both material and immaterial beings. And the power behind this tremendous, mysterious event, is Jesus, who said He is "the resurrection and the life" (John 11:25). Believers' resurrected bodies will be altered and prepared for the new life, capable of as-yet-undreamed-of capabilities. As dramatic a change as the small seed that eventually becomes a mighty tree, so will be the transformation of one's lowly body that dies and then in the resurrection becomes the human equivalent of the mighty tree. As a seed dies and is reborn to a new life, so one's mortal body will likewise die and be resurrected into a glorified body of an incorruptible nature, never to die again. One can scarcely imagine what it will be like on that day when suddenly the believers' bodies are changed from their present lowly estate to one of an eternal, vibrant state of being. As Paul wrote:

> Listen! I am telling you a mystery: We will not all fall asleep, but we will all be changed, in a moment, in the blink of an eye, at the last trumpet. For the trumpet will sound, and the dead will be raised incorruptible, and we will be changed. For this corruptible must be clothed with incorruptibility and this mortal must be clothed with immortality. When this corruptible is clothed with incorruptibility, and this mortal is clothed with immortality, then the saying that is written will take place: Death has been swallowed up in victory. Death, where is your victory? Death, where is your sting?" (1 Cor 15:51–55).

C. Regeneration in Light of Jesus' Resurrection

Jesus' resurrection ensures the believers' regeneration. As Peter wrote, "He has given us a new birth into a living hope through the resurrection of Jesus Christ from the dead" (1 Pet 1:3). Here Peter explicitly linked the believers' new birth and regeneration with Christ's resurrection, although for now their bodies remain subject to all the vicissitudes of mortal existence and eventually aging and death.[7] Yet from day to day and moment to moment, they are being preserved for the last day of their redemption.

Paul also linked this regenerative power of the resurrection to the spiritual power at work in believers when he wrote of "the immeasurable greatness of His power to us who believe" (Eph 1:19). As Wayne Grudem observes, "That power is like the working of his mighty strength, which he exerted in Christ when he raised him from the dead and seated him at the right hand in the heavenly realms."[8] The Holy Spirit also raised Jesus out of the tomb and is now at work in believers. Because of this, Paul urged them to follow not after the lusts of the flesh of our "dead" and corrupted bodies, which have been buried with Him through baptism, but to follow after the self-same Spirit who caused Jesus' dead body to come back to a new and abiding life for all eternity. A dead body cannot do anything; therefore each believer should reckon his body dead to sin. "Therefore we were buried with Him by baptism into death, in order that, just as Christ was raised from the dead by the glory of the Father, so we too may walk in a new way of life" (Rom 6:4). "So, you too consider yourselves dead to sin but alive to God in Christ Jesus" (v. 11). This line of reasoning would have no meaning whatever if Christ had not been bodily raised from the dead. Believers are not exhorted to live the ethereal life of a "spirit" but rather to live as those who are alive in Christ and no longer dead in trespasses and sins.

---

[7] Grudem, *Systematic Theology*, 614.
[8] Ibid.

When the New Testament refers to resurrection (*anastasis*), it is signifying the arising to life of dead bodies. This is a reversal of the awful consequences of the sin of disobedience of our first parents in the garden of Eden. Redemption in Christ is a continuation of God's original plan for human beings, to live on eternally in a physical state of bliss, no longer subject to death.

D. Justification in Light of Jesus' Resurrection

Jesus' resurrection also guarantees the believers' justification. In Rom 4:25 Paul wrote of Christ, who "was delivered up for our trespasses and raised for [or 'because of'] our justification" (this is the only text in which Paul links the resurrection of Jesus with justification). When God raised Jesus from the dead, it was God's approval of His sacrificial death for sins and a declaration that Christ's work of redemption was "finished." Therefore Christ no longer needed to remain in the grave.[9] As Grudem has written, "There was no penalty left to pay for sin, no more wrath of God to bear, no more guilt or liability to punishment—all had been completely paid for, and no guilt remained. In the resurrection, God was saying to Christ, 'I approve of what you have done, and you find favor in my sight.'"[10]

E. Jesus' Physical Resurrection and the "Life-Giving Spirit"

The phrase "life-giving Spirit" in 1 Cor 15:45 has often been misunderstood throughout the history of the church and particularly in modern times by cultists. This Greek phrase (*pneuma zoopoioun*) denotes "the spirit that gives life," or "the spirit that makes alive."[11] After being raised from the dead, Jesus entered into a whole new category of existence because He was "glorified" and simultaneously became a "life-giving spirit." This verse does not say that Jesus became "the Spirit" or "a Spirit," since the second person of the Trinity did not become the third person. Instead, Jesus became a life-giving spirit in the sense that His mortal existence and form were altered into what is "spiritual," which is exactly what Paul wrote in the preceding verses: "So it is with the resurrection of the dead: Sown in corruption, raised in incorruption; sown in dishonor, raised in glory; sown in weakness, raised in power; sown a natural body, raised a *spiritual body*" (vv. 42–44, italics added). In His "glorified" body Christ is no longer subject to His mortal body and the limitations inherent in it. He is now "alive in the spiritual realm" (1 Pet 3:18), giving life to all who believe.

F. Jesus' Physical Resurrection Insures Believers' Physical Resurrection

Jesus' resurrection ensures that believers, too, will receive perfect resurrection bodies. Several New Testament passages link the believer's resurrection bodies with Christ's resurrection. "God raised up the Lord and will also raise us up by His power" (1 Cor 6:14). "Knowing that the One who raised the Lord Jesus will raise us also with

---

[9] Ibid.

[10] Ibid.

[11] E. Radmacher, R. B. Allen, H. W. House, eds., *Nelson's Illustrated Bible Commentary* (Nashville: Thomas Nelson, 1999), 1487.

Jesus and present us with you" (2 Cor 4:14). As noted earlier, Jesus is the "firstfruits" of believers (1 Cor 15:20). Just as the firstfruits are a foretaste of what the general harvest will look like, so Christ in His resurrection is a foretaste of what the believers' resurrection bodies will look like.[12]

Why did Jesus retain the nail and spear wounds in His glorified body (John 20:25–27). They are an eternal reminder of the sacrifice that He made for redemption. The scars of crucifixion are a constant testimony of His great love for mankind. David Garlington has highlighted the significance and uniqueness of Christ's resurrection: "The resurrection of Christ concentrates the whole of salvation into a single event. It is the turning point of the ages and the centre of time. Henceforth not only time but life itself can never be the same."[13]

G. Jesus' Resurrection as Validation of His Testimony

Jesus referred to His resurrection as a means of validating His earthly ministry and claim to deity, the messiahship of Israel, and the Savior of the world. First, Jesus connected the prophecy of Jonah with His resurrection when the Jewish teachers demanded a sign to confirm His messianic claims. Matthew records Christ's words: "But He answered them, 'An evil and adulterous generation demands a sign, but no sign will be given to it except the sign of the prophet Jonah. For as Jonah was in the belly of the huge fish three days and three nights, so the Son of Man will be in the heart of the earth three days and three nights'" (Matt 12:39–40).

Second, Jesus uses the imagery of the Jewish temple to speak of His death and resurrection. He predicted that they would destroy Him but that God would raise Him after three days.

> So the Jews replied to Him, "What sign of authority will You show us for doing these things?" Jesus answered, "Destroy this sanctuary, and I will raise it up in three days." Therefore the Jews said, "This sanctuary took 46 years to build, and will You raise it up in three days?" But He was speaking about the sanctuary of His body. So when He was raised from the dead, His disciples remembered that He had said this. And they believed the Scripture and the statement Jesus had made. (John 2:18–22)

When Jesus rose from the dead after three days, just as He said He would, the early church regarded this as vindication from God that Jesus is who He said He is, the Logos of God, God's own Son. The importance of fulfilling this prophecy was not lost on the Jewish leaders who plotted and finally delivered Him up to death. Remembering His prediction of the temple of His body (John 2:18–22), they approached Pontius Pilate with the following remarkable request:

> The next day, which followed the preparation day, the chief priests and the Pharisees gathered before Pilate and said, "Sir, we remember that while this deceiver was still alive He said, 'After three days I will rise again.' Therefore give

---

[12] Grudem, *Systematic Theology*, 615.
[13] D. Garlington, "Resurrection of Christ," in *New Dictionary of Theology*, 583.

orders that the tomb be made secure until the third day. Otherwise His disciples may come, steal Him, and tell the people, 'He has been raised from the dead.' Then the last deception will be worse than the first." (Matt 27:62–64)

Any suggestion made to a Roman soldier (of which Pilate once was early in his career) of an attempted theft of Jesus' body from a sealed tomb guarded by a Roman guard was not only implausible; it was laughable. No Roman guard would have allowed any number of armed men to overpower them while on duty. No Roman soldier would have been caught dead sleeping at his post, or he would certainly be put to death. Roman soldiers of that period were highly disciplined and expertly trained and would not take any assignment lightly, even if it meant guarding an obscure Jewish tomb. Strict autocratic rule demanded the immediate execution of any soldier found to be derelict in his duties. Moreover, the disciples themselves certainly were in no mental condition to plan—much less attempt—so bold a plot as to overpower a Roman guard bristling with all sorts of weapons and then steal away the lifeless body of their dead Master. The charge offered by the Jewish authorities that the disciples stole the body of Jesus while the guards were asleep is incredible, given the nature of their discipline at that time and given the fact that they were supposed to have been asleep during the theft and therefore could not have possibly known who the thieves were![14]

William Lane Craig offers a forceful argument for the historical incident of the resurrection of Jesus and the resultant truth of Christianity.

> In addition to this fundamental dilemma, the Christian apologist also refurbished the old argument from the origin of the church. Suppose, [Horace] Vernet [French apologist, 1789–1863] suggests, that no resurrection or miracles occurred: how then could a dozen men, poor, coarse, and apprehensive, turn the world upside down? If Jesus did not rise from the dead, declares Ditton [eighteenth-century English apologist], then either we must believe that a small, unlearned band of deceivers overcame the powers of the world and preached an incredible doctrine over the face of the whole earth, which in turn received this fiction as the sacred truth of God; or else, if they were not deceivers, but enthusiasts, we must believe that these extremists, carried along by the impetus of extravagant fancy, managed to spread a falsity that not only common folk, but statesmen and philosophers as well, embraced as the sober truth. Because such a scenario is simply unbelievable, the message of the apostles, which gave birth to Christianity, must be true.[15]

The proclamation of the apostles at the inception of the church was that a most astounding miracle had occurred among them: the Man Jesus Christ was also God's eternal Son who had become human flesh and who had vindicated the truth of His identity by defeating death itself and rising from the dead. In the face of an incredulous and religiously skeptical world, they preached this message. By the power of their

---

[14] W. L. Craig, *Reasonable Faith: Christian Truth and Apologetics* (Wheaton, IL: Crossway, 1994), 264.

[15] Ibid., 264–65.

testimony and on the force of the historical evidence, they convinced the great and the lowly. They suffered horrible persecution, torture, and ultimately all of them (except John, the beloved disciple) paid the highest price, martyrdom. Yet not one of them recanted their original assertion that they were eyewitnesses to the most tremendous event humanity had ever witnessed: the entrance into the world, the life and ministry, the death and resurrection, of the second person of the eternal Trinity, Jesus Christ. Our eternal destiny as a species has been forever altered because of that one pivotal event that occurred over 2,000 years ago.

II.   IF THERE WERE NO RESURRECTION OF JESUS

The apostle Paul was adamantly opposed to a faith in the "Way" (as it was known in the first-century church) without the message of Jesus' physical resurrection from the dead. As Paul explained in flawless logic, "But if there is no resurrection of the dead, then Christ has not been raised; and if Christ has not been raised, then our proclamation is without foundation, and so is your faith. . . . For if the dead are not raised, Christ has not been raised. And if Christ has not been raised, *your faith is worthless; you are still in your sins"* (1 Cor 15:13–14,16–17, italics added). The physical resurrection of Jesus Christ from the dead simply cannot be denied. It is central to the entire apostolic theme of salvation in no other name under heaven except for Christ's. And if Christ is not risen, then our faith in Him is worse than ineffective; *it is futile.* There is no logical reason therefore to believe in a Jesus "of the heart" if that Jesus has not risen in time and history. If the ancient tomb of Joseph of Arimathea is in fact *not* empty and contains the bones of Jesus, then this useless façade of religiosity can be tossed aside and there is no hope beyond the grave.

The truth of the Christian message is intimately related to the historical proclamation of Christ's resurrection. A Jesus who has "risen in our hearts" will not save anyone. Such a Jesus would be an impotent savior, unable to save anyone. Also the notion of a "Christ of faith" is a myth and is not the Jesus of the New Testament. The Christian faith is not true because someone happens to believe in Jesus' resurrection. Instead the Christian faith is true—including Jesus' resurrection from the dead— whether someone believes it or not!

Recently much attention has been devoted to the discovery of the so-called family tomb of Jesus of Nazareth.[16] On *The Today Show* on NBC in February 2007, were these words: "Is this the tomb of Jesus? A shocking new claim that an ancient burial place may have housed the bones of Christ and a son." The segment on *The Today Show* was an interview of James Cameron and an infomercial of Simcha Jacobovici's and Charles Pellegrino's new book titled *The Jesus Family Tomb.* In the foreword to this book, James Cameron writes that the research of the authors was done with "systematic rigor," calling it "brilliant scholarly research," with conclusions that were

---

[16] Discussion on the alleged discovery of the ossuary of Jesus can be found in G. Franz, "The So-Called Jesus Family Tomb," April 4, 2007, http://www.answersingenesis.org/articles/2007/04/04/so-called-jesus-tomb. See also René Lopez, *The Jesus Family Tomb Examined* (Springfield, MO: 21st Century, 2008) for a strong refutation against this heretical view.

"virtually irrefutable" and "extremely convincing." The premise of the book and the documentary is that the family tomb of Jesus was discovered outside Jerusalem, which contained ten ossuaries (bone boxes) holding the bones of various family members of Jesus' family, including Jesus and His son, Judah. Included in this tomb are the remains of his brother Joseph, his mother Mary; Jesus' so-called wife Mariamene (actually Mary Magdalene); and another relative by the name of Matthew. The book also claims that soon after the initial excavation of the tomb one ossuary was missing, which turned up later in the antiquities market with the inscription, "James the son of Joseph, the brother of Jesus."

The thrust of the book and the documentary is of course that Jesus was not resurrected from the dead, as the apostles and the early church first claimed and as Christians have continued to proclaim for 2,000 years. The authors also plant seeds of doubt in the minds of the readers that Jesus therefore could not be divine. This is nothing but a frontal assault on the core of Christianity. If it can be demonstrated that the resurrection of Jesus Christ did not in fact happen, then the entire edifice of the Christian faith falls into useless rubble. Gordon Franz understands the implication of this agenda when he writes:

> The stakes are high in this discussion because the bodily resurrection of the Lord Jesus Christ is a foundational truth to Biblical Christianity. If Jesus was not resurrected from the dead, this would rock Christianity to its very foundation. On the other hand, if the Lord Jesus Christ was resurrected from the dead, then His claim to be God manifest in human flesh would be true, and his people should trust the Lord Jesus as their Savior and then follow Him as they seek to live by His principles and teachings.[17]

There is nothing new about this development because critics have been attacking the historical veracity of Jesus' bodily resurrection from the dead since it occurred 2,000 years ago.

In fact if an enemy of the Christian faith wanted to vitiate its truth and render it obsolete and irrelevant, to demolish successfully the claim that Jesus has risen bodily from the dead would be to destroy Christianity. This is the goal of Cameron, Jacobovici, and Pellegrino. The fact is, however, that the weight of the evidence leads overwhelmingly to the conclusion that Jesus Christ indeed rose from the dead.

III. Conclusion

The historic Christian faith has consistently and faithfully taught that to deny the bodily resurrection of Jesus Christ, or to distort the teaching of the bodily resurrection in any way, is to deny the very basis of eternal salvation. Any attempt to deny or distort the doctrine of Christ's bodily resurrection from the dead would be to destroy

---

[17] Franz, "The So-Called Jesus Family Tomb."

it. If any other Christ or gospel message is presented as authoritative truth, which does not in fact conform to the New Testament teaching of Jesus' bodily resurrection from the dead, then whoever delivers such a message must in the end fall under the divine curse delivered by Paul (Gal 1:6–9). This is a serious warning for anyone who would proclaim any other gospel than that proclaimed by the apostles, which most certainly included the doctrine of Jesus' bodily resurrection from the dead.

Chapter 25

CHRISTIANITY IN COMPETITION
WITH OTHER RELIGIONS

WEBSTER DEFINES RELIGION AS "A CAUSE, principle, or system of beliefs held to with ardor and faith."[1] Certainly under this definition anyone who has a personal conviction regarding the way of the universe could be called religious.

At its heart a religion is an attempt to convey truth. Every religious system is based on a foundation of assumptions of what is true. Many of these truth-claims are in conflict, and contradict one another. Despite this, many argue that all religions are simply different paths to the same destination. This chapter shows that this simply cannot be true because of (a) the nature of truth itself and (b) the vastly different worldviews of various religions and their contrasting versions of "the truth."

Some people, consenting that all religions cannot be true, nevertheless argue that there is universal "truth" in each religion. This chapter also shows why this argument is false, again because of the nature of truth and the worldviews of religions.

The chapter will then show why there is only one true religion, namely, Christianity.

I.   IS THERE MORE THAN ONE WAY TO THE TRUE GOD?

A common refrain one often hears today is, "All religions lead to God." In today's postmodern philosophy people argue that "all religions are true to those who accept them as true, and to the extent to which they give meaning to the life of the group or the individual."[2] In other words many people say that so long as the religion gives meaning to life, it is true. A close corollary to this kind of thinking is the philosophy that no one should criticize another's beliefs. Instead, it is argued, people ought to work together to achieve "a just, peaceful, and multi-religious society—a vision to which all human beings can respond, whether or not they believe in the existence of God."[3] This kind of thinking rests in a view of truth that is fundamentally flawed.

---

[1] "Religion," in *Merriam and Webster's Online Dictionary*, http://www.merriam-webster.com/dictionary/religion (accessed October 27, 2008).

[2] G. W. Cooke, ed., *The Social Evolution of Religion* (Boston: Stratford Group, 1920), xix.

[3] R. Boase, ed., *Islam and Global Dialogue: Religious Pluralism and the Pursuit of Peace* (Burlington, VT: Ashgate, 2005), 1.

A. The Nature of Truth

As seen in chap. 5 ("How Do We Know the Truth?") not only can truth be known, but also the principles of logic guide how we define truth. A belief or even a statement that is self-contradicting is false. If one statement contradicts another or fundamentally disagrees with another, they cannot both be true. This is the law of noncontradiction. Those who argue that all religions lead to God must prove that all religions are noncontradicting. If one religion claims to be the sole possessor of the truth, another religion with a contradictory claim to the truth cannot also be true.

B. Can All Religions Be True?

George Willis Cooke wrote, "Fundamentally, all religions are the same, and answer to the same demands of man's nature."[4] He further explained, "Religion, wherever manifest, answers to the same human demands; and it reaches the responding satisfaction by quite similar methods and to the same primary ends."[5] Since religion was for Cooke simply a way to "answer human demands," any religion achieving this goal was seen as true. This idea has become popular especially among liberal religious thinkers and proponents of New Age philosophy. However, this claim fails to acknowledge the nature of truth described above and in other parts of this book. Even the major religions have claims of objective truths that are contradictory, for it cannot be true that there are many gods if it is true that there is only one god. It also cannot be true that the chief aim of man is submission to Allah if it is true that the chief aim of man is to achieve the denial of self-concern. Therefore all religions cannot all be true.

C. Does the Fact That All Religions Possess Truth Mean They Are All Legitimate?

Many are willing to admit that not all religions are all true in their totality. However, they argue that there are universal truths in each of the world's religions. Scholars study the world's religions, attempting to discover how they are related to each other. This has come to be called "comparative religion." Influenced by Darwinian evolutionary philosophy, many of these scholars have come to believe that all the world's religions evolved along with man.[6] Hence whatever claims are universal are seen to be the result of a common ancestry. This belief has become accepted by religious thinkers, who argue that these universal claims are true, while the exclusive claims were added along the way, perhaps because of social differences, geographical separations, cultural differences, and the like. Following this logic, a person may pick and choose what he believes from among the world's religions and therefore arrive at an

---

[4] Cooke, *The Social Evolution of Religion*, xvii.

[5] Ibid., xviii

[6] This view has come under increasing scrutiny and criticism. Modern scholars are beginning to show that rather than linear development from animism to polytheism to monotheism, religious development was much more complicated. As far back as 1912, W. Schmidt, in the *Origin and Growth of Religion* (1912; reprint, New York: Cooper Square, 1971), powerfully and persuasively shows that monotheism may have been the earliest form of religious belief.

underlying truth to believe. For example a Buddhist monk, Thich Hhat Hanh, says, "When you are a truly happy Christian, you are also a Buddhist. And *vice versa.*"[7] Marcus Borg, a retired professor at Oregon State University, says that both Jesus and Buddha "became teachers of a convention-subverting wisdom flowing out of their enlightenment experiences."[8] He argued "that if Jesus and the Buddha were ever to meet, neither would try to convert the other—not because they would regard the task as hopeless, but because they would recognize each other."[9]

Because of their view that all religions contain truth, many also argue that it is not legitimate to criticize religious beliefs, as Borg hinted at above. Again Cooke wrote:

> No demand is made upon the individual that he shall discard all religion, or that he shall turn aside from that into which he was inducted in childhood; but that he shall become undogmatic, appreciative of all that is human, and willing to consider sympathetically whatever ritual or creed has meaning for the life of another community than his own. Whatever gives meaning and purpose and joy to the life of any individual may be regarded with respect, and should be studied, if studied at all, with sympathy and appreciation.[10]

Unfortunately for those holding this view, the vast majority *within* these religions believe they are the *sole* possessors of the truth and do not accept the notion that other religious traditions are equally legitimate. Certainly this is the case among the three great monotheistic religions, Judaism, Christianity, and Islam. Even among Eastern religions, which are supposedly more open to other faiths, the majority believe they possess the highest form of enlightenment. To them, coming to possess the truth necessarily involves coming to accept Hindu or Buddhist teaching. So rather than all religious traditions being legitimate paths to the same goal, or all containing the truth, these religions are all in competition with one another. The following section shows why Christianity differs from and is superior to the world's other major religions.

Part of the failure of these pluralistic philosophers is a failure to recognize the stark differences of worldviews among religions. Since worldviews are the basis on which religious beliefs are built, those views affect all of what these religions claim is true. Despite the claims of Hanh and Borg, there are fundamental differences in the worldviews of Christianity and Buddhism. The fact that all religions share some characteristics does not mean they are all legitimate, and all possess the truth.

---

[7] T. H. Hanh, *Living Buddha, Living Christ* (New York: Penguin, 1995), 197.

[8] M. J. Borg, "Jesus and Buddhism: A Christian View," in *Buddhists Talk About Jesus, Christians Talk About the Buddha*, ed. R. M. Gross and T. C. Muck (New York: Continuum, 2003, originally published as *Buddhist-Christian Studies 19* [Honolulu: University of Hawai'i Press, 1999], 78).

[9] Ibid., 79.

[10] Cooke, *The Social Evolution of Religion*, xviii–xix.

II.   THE THREE MAJOR RELIGIOUS WORLDVIEWS

When distilled to their philosophical bases, there are three major religious world-views: theism, pantheism, and atheism. These are how religions see the divine, and how a religion sees the divine in guiding its entire worldview. Moreover, since these views are diametrically different and contradictory in nature, they cannot all be true. In fact only one can be true. Again the divine cannot both exist and not exist (theism and atheism), nor can the divine be personal and distinct and at the same time impersonal and nondistinct (theism and pantheism).

A. Theism

Theism is the belief that the divine is personal and distinct. There are two major views under theism: polytheism and monotheism.

1.   Polytheism

Polytheism is the belief in many personal and distinct gods. Although Hinduism on some levels is pantheistic, in practice the majority of Hindus are polytheistic. In this worldview some gods control some part of the universe, such as the sky, the earth, and the ocean. And other gods administer certain activities, such as the god of thunder, the god of war, or the god of love. Devotees of polytheism pray to the various gods of their pantheon for certain favors or protection.

2.   Monotheism

Monotheism is theism that believes in one god, rather than many. This god is distinct from the universe and is personal in nature, which means that he can interact in a personal way with the universe. Examples of monotheism are Islam, Judaism, and Christianity.

B. Pantheism

Pantheism differs from theism in that pantheists see god as being "one" with the universe. God is not distinct from the universe, but He *is* the universe. Many New Age teachings embrace pantheism, calling it the "universal consciousness" or "force." Some forms of Hinduism teach that Brahman is pantheistic and that the "gods" of Hinduism are simply manifestations of Brahman.

C. Atheism

Atheism is the belief that there is no divine. Although mostly associated with Western secular philosophy, some forms of Buddhism are also atheistic, such as the Theravada tradition.

III. The Contrasts of the World's Religions with Christianity

This section focuses on four of the world's religions: Hinduism, Buddhism, Islam, and Judaism and to the major tenants of each religion.

A. Hinduism

Some writers have attempted to show that Christianity is related to Hinduism, even going so far as to claim that Jesus visited India and learned from Hindu holy men. This is argued on the basis of the seeming similarity between the teachings contained in the *Bhagavad-Gita* and the New Testament.

1. God's impartiality

The Hindu theme of God's impartiality—the fact that He does not show favoritism—is common with the New Testament. The *Bhagavad-Gita* 9:29 says, "I envy no one, nor am I partial to anyone. I am equal to all. But whoever renders service unto Me in devotion is a friend, is in Me, and I am also a friend to him."[11] This is compared with Rom 2:11, "There is no favoritism with God." However, the text of *Bhagavad-Gita* bears little resemblance in meaning to Rom 2:11. The Hindu text teaches that those who are balanced, are free from contamination, and have several positive traits are dear to the god Krishna. This is not the meaning of Paul's text. The sense of Rom 2:11 is that God is open to provide evidence of Himself to all people by doing good to them, showing no ethnic partiality.

2. The "kingdom of God"

The phrase "kingdom of God" is found approximately 70 times in the New Testament alone and is also a major theme in the Old Testament. The *Bhagavad-Gita* also speaks of the "kingdom of God" and refers to a stumbling block similar to words found in the New Testament: "If one is thus situated even at the hour of death, one can enter into the kingdom of God."[12] But the meaning of the phrase differs from the New Testament meaning. The Hindu word translated "kingdom of God" here is *Baikuntha* and refers to the "abode of God."[13] The "kingdom of God" in Hinduism is achieved after a person has cleansed himself of all impurities in the soul, through right karma.[14] Entering the kingdom requires that the person leave "bodily human form,"[15] which can never be regained.[16] According to modern interpretation, following Hinduism strictly

---

[11] A.C. Bhaktivedanta Swami Prabhupada, *Bhagavad-gītā as It Is* (Alachua, FL: Bhaktivedanta, 1989), 435.

[12] Ibid., 144.

[13] V. Kumar, "God," http://www.godrealized.com/god.html (accessed January 27, 2008).

[14] Ibid.

[15] V. Kumar, "Hinduism Revelations: Vedas," http://www.godrealized.org/hindu/hinduism_revelations.html (accessed January 27, 2008).

[16] V. Kumar, "John 14:3: Interpretation," http://www.rgveda.com/john/john_chapter_14_verse_3.html (accessed January 27, 2008).

is not necessary: "Having gained enlightenment and finally salvation . . . these man gods reached the kingdom of God in their lifetime. All paths . . . all religions and spirituality lead one towards the one and only final goal . . . the abode of God aka Baikuntha in Hinduism."[17] So *Baikuntha* and the Greek phrase *basiliea tou theou* ("kingdom of God") are not synonymous. In the New Testament, "kingdom of God" always refers to God's rule over His world and specifically over believers, and not, as in Hinduism, to an after-body abode of God. The New Testament promises eternal life to those who believe, a life lived *with* God, not a cessation of being, a loss of personhood, and being absorbed into God, as in Hinduism. In God's eternal kingdom believers are promised to receive glorified actual bodies and will live forever as individuals, enjoying being in the presence of God. In Hinduism those who achieve enlightenment cease being individuals altogether, along with any capacity for enjoyment.

3. *Jesus and Krishna*

Some have claimed that Jesus was a reincarnation of Krishna (a supposed manifestation, or avatar, of the god Vishnu).[18] At first glance many similarities may seem evident. Krishna was supposedly born of a virgin; his birth was announced by angels, wise men, and shepherds; his family traveled to pay a tax; his father was warned to flee; he was pursued by a tyrannical king who killed infants as he chased him; he was the son of a carpenter; he was baptized; he did miracles and told parables; he came to save humanity; he was crucified and rose again, among a number of other alleged similarities.[19] On close examination, however, the events that seem so similar are due in large part to the outlandish and unreliable claims of a nineteenth-century author, Kersey Graves. Without giving any documentation, Graves claimed the preceding events listed were historical facts. In reality the *Bhagavad-Gita* does not describe Krishna's childhood at all, and the only Hindu writings that do so were written between 300 and 900 AD.[20] Despite modern scholarship effectively discrediting Graves, his arguments continue to be used by those seeking to show that Christianity is an offshoot of Hinduism. Moreover, the superficial "similarities" between Krishna and Jesus are far outweighed in light of the actual historical record. Unlike Krishna, Jesus came in fulfillment of Old Testament prophecies, revealed Himself as both the great

---

[17] V. Kumar, "John 14:1: Interpretation," http://www.bible-commentary.org/john/john_chapter_14_verse_1.html (accessed January 27, 2008).

[18] K. Graves, *The World's Sixteen Crucified Saviors* (1875; reprint, Kenpton, IL: Adventures Unlimited, 2001) 279.

[19] K. Williams, "Jesus as a Reincarnation of Krishna," http://near-death.com/experiences/origen047.html (accessed January 27, 2008). See also statements of these comparisons, with little reference to primary sources, by C. Bennett, *In Search of Jesus: Insider and Outsider Images* (London: Continuum, 2001), 340–41.

[20] C. E. Olson and S. Miesel, "Christ, the Early Church, Constantine, and the Council of Nicaea," http://www.envoymagazine.com/PlanetEnvoy/Review-DaVinci-part2-Full.htm (accessed October 29, 2008). See also D. Morals and M. Gleghorn, "Did Christianity Borrow from Pagan Religions?" http://www.probe.org/cults-and-world-religions/cults-and-world-religions/did-christianity-borrow-from-pagan-religions.html#text19 (accessed October 29, 2008). Since there is historical evidence that the apostle Thomas went to India sometime after Christ's resurrection, perhaps Christianity influenced Hinduism, not the other way around.

Table 25.1 Major Beliefs of Four of the World's Religions*

Religion	God	Creation	Man	Sin	Salvation	Scripture and Authority
Christianity	Trinitarian Monotheistic	The Trinity created the universe *ex nihilo* (out of nothing).	Created in perfection by God but lost perfection through sin	Originated in the heart of Satan, usually defined as disobedience against God. Atonement is necessary for sin.	Obtained through the atonement of Jesus Christ's suffering on the cross. Some hold faith is all that is necessary, while others say faith and good deeds are.	The Old and New Testaments of the Bible
Hinduism	Polytheistic (though some forms are pantheistic)	The universe is infinite and without beginning or end.	"Self" is an illusion, and people experience many cycles of reincarnation.	Not taught, although poor moral choices build up bad karma, which can lead to suffering.	Liberation from the cycles of reincarnation, entering into the presence of Brahma	The *Vedas* and the *Upanishads* and the *Bhagavad Gita*
Buddhism	Atheistic (though some forms are polytheistic)	Sometimes described as a series of heavens, although not well defined traditionally	"Self" is often described as an illusion, and people experience multiple reincarnations.	Not taught. Evil is an illusion, but the root of evil is ignorance.	Nirvana, a state of oblivion. Achieved through meditation and other religious practices.	The Pali Canon (called the *Tripitaka*) are central, among others.
Islam	Non-Trinitarian Monotheistic	Allah created and sustains the universe.	Created basically good by Allah and should live in submission to him	Failing to submit to Allah. Forgiveness is granted by repenting of sin, but no atonement is necessary.	Obtained through good deeds (submitting to Allah)	The Qur'an
Judaism	Non-Trinitarian Monotheistic	God created the universe *ex nihilo*.	Created in perfection by God but lost perfection through sin	Originated in the heart of Satan, sometimes defined as human failing. Atonement is necessary for sin.	Traditionally obtained through good works and sacrifices. Good works are weighed against evil deeds.	The Tanakh, consisting of the Law, Prophets, and Writings

*Adapted from H. W. House, *Charts of World Religions* (Grand Rapids: Zondervan, 2006).

God of the universe and as man, died for the sins of humanity, and rose physically from the dead. Since these events are based on the Hebrew Scriptures composed long before Eastern ideology came into the Near East and represent a culture largely hostile to foreign religious viewpoints, there is little likelihood that Jesus reflected a Far Eastern view of the world.

Apart from vague similarities, Christianity and Hinduism teach vastly different worldviews. Christianity affirms that there is only one God and that He is transcendent, omnipotent, omniscient, and personal. In contrast, Hinduism holds to either polytheism or pantheism. The two religions' views of man are in stark contrast. Christianity holds to the personhood of man. Each person is an actual individual who will either remain with God forever or spend eternity in punishment. Under Hinduism, individuality is an illusion, and although its view of salvation may seem similar in some ways to Christianity, in reality, being in the presence of Brahman is the cessation of the illusion of individuality and may take several lifetimes through reincarnation.[21]

B. Buddhism

Perhaps no other religion is more often compared to Christianity than Buddhism. Jesus has often been compared to Siddhartha Gautama, the founder of Buddhism. Some argue that there are striking similarities between their lives, to such an extent that it leads some to conclude that Buddhism and Christianity are two branches of the same tree. However, little is known about the life of Gautama, so little in fact that no one is sure if he even existed. Legend says that Buddha was the son of a ruling family, born sometime in the sixth or fifth century BC, in what is now southern Nepal. He married at age 19 and had one son. Sometime around age 30 Siddhartha ventured out of his sheltered palace and saw for the first time an old man, a sick man, a dead man, and an ascetic. He was so moved by these images that he left his life of leisure, abandoned his family, and became a wandering monk. For six years he traveled, looking for inner peace through asceticism, finally arriving in a northeastern Indian town. There he sat down under a giant Bodhi (fig) tree and decided to stay there until he received enlightenment. After 49 days he was "illuminated" and became the Buddha, meaning "Enlightened One." He began to preach his message through the countryside, converting his fellow ascetic monks and then his family and even a king. He allegedly lived to the age of 80.[22]

Buddhist teaching is usually summarized in the Four Noble Truths and the Eightfold Path. The Four Noble Truths are these: (1) life is suffering, (2) the origin of suffering is attachment and desire, (3) suffering can be eliminated, and (4) there is a path to the end of suffering.

The Eightfold Path includes: Right View, Right Intention, Right Speech, Right Action, Right Livelihood, Right Effort, Right Mindfulness, and Right Concentration.

---

[21] J. V., "Hinduism: Paths to Liberation," http://www.hinduwebsite.com/hinduism/h_enlighten.asp (accessed October 26, 2008).

[22] See P. Harvey, *An Introduction to Buddhism: Teachings, History, and Practices* (New York: Cambridge University Press, 1990), 14–27.

Only by realizing the Four Noble Truths and performing the Eightfold Path can one end attachment and enter nirvana.

C. Similar Lives of Buddha and Jesus

Some argue that the extraordinarily similar lives of Buddha and Jesus means that the latter is a reincarnation of Buddha. They both began their preaching around age 30, both fasted, and it could be said that their ministries both began with a sign (Gautama's "illumination" and the descent of the Holy Spirit at Jesus' baptism). Some legends say that Gautama was born of a virgin,[23] was presented at a temple as an infant, that sages came to worship him, and that he made a triumphal entry.[24] Since Buddha may or may not have lived, and many stories about his life were concocted long after he supposedly lived (sometimes hundreds of years later), it is difficult to affirm with any authority that these similarities are fact. Until fairly recently, the question of the historical veracity of Gautama's life was unimportant. The stories were meant to teach about Buddhism, not to prove Buddhism. But this is not the case with the life of Jesus. Unlike the stories of Buddha, Jesus' life is well attested and is essential to Christianity. Buddhism could survive if Siddhartha Gautama never lived, but this is not so with Christianity and Jesus. Further, many of the miraculous events surrounding Jesus were predicted with remarkable detail in the Old Testament, which, even according to the most liberal dating, were composed far earlier than when Gautama supposedly lived.

D. Similar Teachings?

Perhaps more important than the alleged similarities in the lives of Jesus and Buddha are the supposed similarities in their teachings. Some, like Hahn and Borg, argue that Buddhism and Christianity are similar in their religious views. For example, both teach that suffering exists and has a cause. However, the definition of suffering and what causes it could not be more diametrically opposed. Buddhism teaches that suffering results from people being too attached to the illusion called the universe. Suffering is caused by desire. When a person ceases desiring, he ceases suffering. On the contrary Christianity teaches that suffering is caused by sin, either directly (people sin, therefore they suffer) or indirectly (people live in a sinful world and suffer the consequences). A person's suffering will end only when his life on earth ends. Suffering itself will not end until the universe is put back into a sinless state. In fact Peter, one of Jesus' followers, even taught that some kinds of suffering are a blessing because they serve as a witness to the truth and against those who would defame Christians (2 Pet 3:13–17).

---

[23] This claim appears to be a twisting of the story in order to make it fit better with the argument that Jesus was a reincarnation of Gautama. Actually Gautama's mother was not a virgin. As the story goes, she had a dream that an elephant entered her womb. The Brahmans interpreted the dream, telling her that her already conceived child would "become a very great being." Again this is a legendary story told within a legendary tale of Gautama's life (see ibid., 16).

[24] "Jesus as a Reincarnation of Buddha," http://www.near-death.com/experiences/origen045.html (accessed October 29, 2008).

Borg says:

> Furthermore, imagery of "the way" is central to Jesus and the gospels, pointing to a foundational similarity to the teaching of the Buddha. There is the broad way and there is the narrow way; those who humble (empty) themselves will be exalted; the path to a new way of being involves dying to an old way of being. This emphasis points to an internal spiritual-psychological process very similar to Buddhist "emptying" and "letting go." "Dying" and "letting go" are metaphorical synonyms.[25]

Borg's argument involves a radical reinterpretation of Christianity to make it fit with Buddhism. Jesus' teaching about the broad and narrow way were in reference to accepting Him as the Messiah alone. Jesus' teaching about humbling oneself and dying to self challenges believers to rely on Him alone, rather than through human effort, something in direct opposition to Buddhism. Buddhism teaches that one must work to "let go" of desire in order to achieve enlightenment. Borg further says, "I do not see the understanding of Jesus' death as a sacrifice for sin as going back to Jesus himself, but as one of several post-Easter metaphors interpreting the meaning of his death. The other metaphors include seeing Jesus' death as the defeat of the powers, as disclosure of God's love, and as embodiment of the way or path of transformation."[26] Again, he is viewing Christianity *through* Buddhist teachings in an effort to support the notion that Christian and Buddhist teachings are similar. If Jesus' death on the cross was a "way to transformation" like Buddha's life, then it is troubling that Jesus did not teach that people will be transformed by following His example. In reality Jesus' death on the cross was a historical event, predicted centuries beforehand, and was necessary as an atonement for human sin. Peter, a contemporary of Jesus, wrote, "For Christ also suffered for sins once for all, the righteous for the unrighteous, that He might bring you to God, after being put to death in the fleshly realm but made alive in the spiritual realm" (1 Pet 3:18). Also contrary to Borg, Dalai Lama XIV noted that Christianity and Buddhism, while sounding similar, are not compatible. He said, "I believe it is possible to progress along a spiritual path and reconcile Christianity with Buddhism. But once a certain degree of realization has been reached, a choice between the two paths will become necessary."[27] It seems Borg has not only missed the point of Jesus' teachings and death but also has a mistaken view of Buddhism. In no way are these two religions compatible.

E. Islam

Islam, being strongly monotheistic, is closer to Christianity than Hinduism and Buddhism. This is mainly because Muhammad probably had some contact with Christians (as well as Jews) in Arabia. Islam teaches that God is omnipotent and transcendent and has spoken through prophets (Islam accepts the Old Testament prophets and

---

[25] M. Borg, "Jesus and Buddha: A Christian View," in *Buddhist-Christian Studies* 19 (1999): 94.

[26] Ibid.

[27] Dalai Lama, quoted in a 1993 question-and-answer session in a visit to France, http://hhdl.dharmakara.net/hhdlquotes2.html#candb (accessed October 29, 2008).

teaches that Jesus was a prophet). Islam teaches Jesus was born of a virgin and that Jesus is alive in heaven. However, Islam and Christianity have several significant differences. Islam teaches Jesus was not divine because Allah is singular in essence and cannot exist in persons or as a Trinity. Islam also teaches that Jesus did not die on the cross (someone else died in His place), but He was taken to heaven alive. Islam and Christianity both teach that there is a heaven and a hell. However, in Islam, ultimately attaining heaven or being cast into hell are strictly decided by Allah according to his will. There is a nominal teaching that good deeds outweighing bad deeds earns one entrance into Paradise, but the arbiter of whether deeds are good or bad is Allah, and he does not reveal this to man. To the contrary, Christianity teaches that God has revealed everything humans need to know to gain entrance into heaven. Islam teaches that Allah will not forgive those who turns away from Islam, even if they come back.

Both Islam and Christianity teach that God is sovereign. However, in Islam, Allah is rigidly deterministic. The Qur'an Surah 76:30–31 says, "Whatever you will is in accordance with GOD's will. GOD is Omniscient, Wise. He admits whomever He wills into His mercy. As for the transgressors, He has prepared for them a painful retribution." These transgressors have gone astray not because of their sinfulness, as in Christianity, but because Allah determined them to go astray. They could not do otherwise.

Sura 42:44 says, "For any whom Leaves astray, there is no protector thereafter. And thou wilt see the wrong-doers when in right of the Penalty, Say: 'Is there any way (to effect) a return?'" And Surah 42:46–47 states, "And no protectors have they to help them, other than God. And for any whom God leaves to stray, there is no way (to the Soul). Hearken ye to your Lord, before there comes a Day which there will be no putting back. . . . That Day there will be for you no place of refuge nor will there be for you any room for denial (of your sins)!" In other words a person will have no recourse before Allah on his judgment day because Allah determined what he would do in the first place. This is antithetical to Christianity's view that human sin causes people to stray from God. For this reason God provided Jesus Christ as the sacrifice for sin.

F. Judaism

Since Christianity is a direct descendant of Judaism, the two religions are similar, the main difference being that Judaism does not accept Jesus of Nazareth as the long-awaited Messiah and as the divine Son of God. Also Judaism does not accept the New Testament as Scripture or the concept of a Trinitarian God. The idea of the necessity of atonement for sin being made with sacrifices has also been modified in light of the destruction of the temple in Jerusalem. For the most part Jews believe that forgiveness is now accomplished through repentance in prayer, good works, or by the great suffering of the Jewish people through history. In contrast Christianity recognizes that God did not change His requirements for a sacrifice or for salvation. However, He provided the one sacrifice sufficient for the forgiveness of sins by the sacrificial death of Jesus.

IV. THE SUPERIORITY OF CHRISTIANITY TO OTHER RELIGIONS

George Willis Cooke argued:

> We need but look about us to see that Christianity has no monopoly of virtue in its followers, and that it cannot make better men and women than are to be found developed by Buddhism and Mohammedanism. A noble life must be regarded as the true test for any and every religion; and noble lives are to be found throughout the world, in all communities and under all religions. If we accept this test, we must say that all religions are true as to the results they produce.[28]

His claim is true only if "a noble life" is the only test of truth in religion. Cooke's assessment is that of a pragmatist; if it works, it is true.[29] Even if this criteria is accepted, most of the major world religions do not hold up well under scrutiny. Hinduism has led to massive human suffering under its caste system. Buddhism has produced cultures of indifference toward fellow humans. Recent world events show that fundamental Islam is cold and violent toward those it considers outsiders. Even Christianity, if this test were the only measure of truth, sometimes falls short. In actuality, there are many other factors to consider when approaching religion. Chapter 2 ("Worldviews") and chap. 5 ("How Do We Know the Truth?") discuss various ways to discern truth. These principles of truth must be applied to the world's religions. Of all the world's religions, the only one that meets all the criteria of truth is Christianity.

A. The One and Only

There is one event that no other religion can claim, and this one event sets Christianity above all other religions. The apostle John stated it this way: "The Word became flesh and took up residence among us. We observed His glory, the glory as the One and Only Son from the Father, full of grace and truth" (John 1:14). No other religious belief or practice can claim that the Person who was fully man and fully God was crucified, died, and was resurrected as the one sacrifice for all. This event is a historical fact[30] and is the basis on which all of Jesus' claims are shown to be true.

B. Specific Points

Beyond the great truth of the death and resurrection of Jesus, Christianity is superior to other religions in several other specific ways.

1. Hinduism

Ultimately Hinduism offers no hope. If a person is born into a bad situation, it is because of a past life. When a person dies, he will be returned later to a life on earth. But if he is a member of the priestly class, then he may look forward to ceasing to

---

[28] Cooke, *The Social Evolution of Religion*, xix.
[29] See chap. 5 ("How Do We Know the Truth?") for more on pragmatism.
[30] See chap. 24 ("The Meaning and Importance of the Physical Resurrection of Christ").

exist as an individual. The concept of Brahma is impersonal and uncaring. There is no forgiveness from one's bad Karma (actions), nor any clear understanding of what accumulates Karma. Even if a person somehow attains "liberation," he will not find enjoyment or peace because he will simply cease to exist as an identity. All this seems to contradict man's inherent desire for relationships, and a deep desire for personal interaction. Hindu gurus call this desire a consequence of ignorance, something people will lose if they would simply realize their oneness with Brahma. However, rather than trying to fight against one's intense desire for relationship and personality, Christianity acknowledges this desire and explains how to have the ultimate relationship, a relationship with the Creator of the universe, the living and most holy Lord God. Instead of an impersonal force like Brahma, God is revealed in Christianity as an intimate personal Being, God the Father. Also Christianity gives the ultimate hope for eternity. Rather than the Hindu teaching of reliving countless lives until one ceases to exist, Christianity teaches how to gain eternal life in God's presence and to enjoy Him forever.

2. Buddhism

Buddhism, while acknowledging suffering, attempts to prove that suffering (in fact, the entire universe) is only illusory. Buddhism fails to acknowledge that suffering is real. It also tries to deny a basic characteristic of humanity, namely, desire. Peace will be found only with the cessation of desire. This also seems to contradict a fundamental part of human nature. At their core humans desire things. To deny that desire is inherent to humanity is to ignore human nature. Buddhism also assumes that desire and attachment are always negative. Certainly Christianity teaches that Christians are not to be attached to worldly things or to desire material possessions, but it does teach that people are to desire, among other things, righteousness, love, mercy, justice, and holiness.

Also some forms of Buddhism deny the divine (especially among increasingly popular Western adaptations). Even nonatheistic forms of Buddhism deny that a transcendent Creator of the universe exists.[31] Chapter 4 ("Categories of Apologetics") has discussed the fact that there is no possibility of God not existing. He is a necessary Being.

3. Islam

Islam denies human freedom. Allah, as discussed above, directs all human actions. If Allah wills that a person turn aside from him, he will do so, and there is no recourse. Yet at the same time Islam requires obedience to Allah to obtain his favor. Although Muslim scholars argue that one cannot see the truth of Islam unless one be-

---

[31] Historically there has been much debate about deities within Buddhism. While it is often argued that Buddhism in its original form was atheistic, many have argued that the Buddha himself never denied the existence of deities. See A. M. Blackburn and J. Samuels, eds., *Approaching the Dhamma: Buddhist Texts and Practices in South and Southeast Asia* (Seattle, WA: BPS Pariyatti, 2003), 132; and B. A. Wallace, *Contemplative Science and Neuroscience Converge* (New York: Columbia University Press, 2009), 94–108.

lieves in Islam, the principles of logic are universal and do not depend on faith. Either man is responsible for his actions or Allah is. Either man chooses to serve Allah, or Allah forces man to serve him.

Islam claims that the prophets of the Old Testament and Jesus taught the truth but that it was corrupted. This is why the older prophets do not agree with the "prophet" Muhammad. This may have been a convincing argument in the seventh century, but modern textual criticism has shown that the biblical texts are trustworthy. Thus either the Bible is true, or the Qur'an is true. The Bible was written over the course of centuries by multiple authors in widely varying geographic areas, and yet it does not contradict itself. The Qur'an was written by one author, and yet as is clear from the few verses quoted above, it is full of contradictions. Jesus did not contradict or change the teachings of the Old Testament; He fulfilled them. Muhammad, on the other hand, changed and contradicted the teachings of both the Old Testament and Jesus.

Islam limits Allah. While claiming that Allah is omnipotent, it denies that he can have a son or that he can exist equally in essence but distinct in persons. Christianity acknowledges that the Bible teaches a unified yet Trinitarian God.[32] Islam misunderstands what it means when Christians say that Jesus is the Son of God or talk about God the Father and God the Son. However, simply because Muslims misunderstand the terms used by Christians to describe God, that does not mean that Islam is right.

Islam also does not offer hope. Muslims must live in servitude to Allah, but they have no assurance that they have done enough to gain Allah's favor until they stand before Allah's judgment seat. Christianity acknowledges that man's hope lies in God alone and teaches that God is faithful to those who believe in Jesus Christ as Savior. Islam claims that salvation is in Allah alone but then teaches that man must earn his standing before Allah and thereby gain his salvation. For more on Islam, see chap. 30 ("Engaging the Muslim").

4. Judaism

As stated above, Christianity is rooted in Judaism. However, Christianity is superior to Judaism because it completes God's plan for humans. Judaism is the great foundation on which Christianity is built, but Judaism is incomplete without the teachings of Jesus the Messiah. Judaism teaches the truth about God's attributes, man's sinfulness, and the gulf of separation that has been made because of sin. But Judaism fails to provide an ultimate answer as to how humans may overcome this gulf. In ancient times Judaism taught that the sacrifices made at the temple covered man's sin and kept him in a right relationship before God. With the destruction of the temple, though, this position has been modified. Judaism teaches that good works and repentance of sin are all that are necessary to cover sin. However, God did not rescind His demand for a sacrifice for sin. Since the Old Testament looked forward to the ultimate sacrifice of Jesus on the cross, there was no need to provide an alternative to the sacrificial

---

[32] Some have argued that logically a trinitarian God is a necessity. See B. A. Ware, "Christ's Atonement: A Work of the Trinity," in *Jesus in Trinitarian Perspective: An Introductory Christology*, ed. F. Sanders and K. Issler (Nashville: B&H, 2007), 156–88.

system. Hence Jewish arguments that sacrifices are no longer necessary does not agree with biblical teaching. In reality a sacrifice for sin is still needed and is provided only through Jesus Christ. Further, this sacrifice is effective only for the one who believes in Jesus.

V. CONCLUSION

All religions are not equally true, nor do they point to the same destination. A religion with some truth does not legitimatize the entire religion. Religions must adhere to the rules of logic; they cannot be self-contradicting. Despite the claims of some, Christianity is starkly distinct from the world's other religions. God is not the same as Brahman. Jesus was not a reincarnation of Krishna. God is not all, and man's goal is not the extinction of self. Jesus was not a reincarnation of Buddha, nor was He even enlightened in the same way as Buddha. Jesus taught things distinct from Buddhist teachings, many of which contradict Him. Jesus was more than a prophet of Allah, and He offers the only hope for man. Christianity is the fulfillment of Judaism, completing God's plan for mankind. All this evidence shows that Christianity is not only superior to the world's major religions but is the only true religion.

Chapter 26

The Compatibility of Biblical Truth and Modern Science

Countless persons have renounced Christianity over the past 150 years out of a misguided belief that progress in the natural sciences has rendered Christian faith passé. Quantum physics, as commonly understood, the biology of Darwin and his successors, Darwinism's apparent confirmation by paleontology, and the sheer vastness of the universe revealed by astronomy have rendered Christianity incredible and even pernicious in the eyes of many. This chapter seeks to show that progress in the disciplines of physics, biology, paleontology, and astronomy has not merely failed to falsify the truthfulness of the Christian faith but has actually confirmed it.

I. Physics

The Copenhagen interpretation of quantum mechanics, advocated by Niels Bohr (1885–1962) and Werner Heisenberg (1901–76) among others, requires those who adhere to it consistently to deny three principles taught by natural revelation, which are indispensable presuppositions of Christian belief. The first of these principles is realism, the principle that every truth is true regardless of whether a human is aware of its truthfulness. The second is the principle of contradiction, that is, that x cannot be –x at the same time and in the same sense. The third is the principle of causality, that is, that every effect requires a cause.

One can scarcely overestimate the deleterious consequences that result from a person's sincere rejection of these three principles. If a person denies the principle of causality, for example, if he were consistent he would also deny that he could know of God through creation. For if the principle of causality were false, the existence of creatures would not entail the existence of a Creator. Also someone who disputed the principle of contradiction could not consistently consider himself bound by any moral laws. For if two contradictories could both be true, then a person could reasonably believe that a certain act is both forbidden and obligatory. One who sincerely denies that a person can meaningfully speak about unobservable realities, moreover, could hardly accept the existence of a transcendent God and would categorically reject the possibility of special revelation.

If the Copenhagen interpretation of quantum mechanics does include the rejection of the principles of realism, contradiction, and causality, then it is manifestly dangerous. Before establishing that this is the case and discussing alternatives to the Copenhagen interpretation, however, one should note that the Copenhagen interpretation is by no means integral to quantum mechanics itself. The mathematical apparatus of quantum mechanics, the so-called "mathematical formalism" of the theory, is subject to a variety of essentially philosophical interpretations of which the Copenhagen interpretation is only one.

A. How Does the Copenhagen Interpretation Mandate Abandonment of Realism, the Principle of Contradiction, and the Principle of Causality?

That the Copenhagen interpretation does actually include the problematic conclusions discussed above follows from three considerations.

1. Realism

Erwin Schrödinger (1887–1961) famously illustrates the antirealist implications of the Copenhagen interpretation through a thought experiment popularly known as the paradox of "Schrödinger's cat." In this thought experiment one traps a cat in a steel pen and places a device in the pen with which the cat cannot interfere. The device contains a radioactive substance, and there is a 50 percent probability that one of its atoms will decay within an hour. If an atom does in fact decay, the device causes a poisonous gas to be emitted in the pen that kills the cat instantly. If no atom decays, nothing happens.

After an hour the cat's wave or psi-function will indicate that the cat is 50 percent likely to be alive and 50 percent likely to be dead. In Schrödinger's view the uncertainty about the actual state of the cat in the view of one who knows only its wave function reflects the limitations of the human observer and his equipment; the cat is either entirely alive or entirely dead. If one thinks of the cat in the way that the Copenhagen theorist thinks of the atom, however, then so long as one cannot look into the pen and so collapse the cat's wave function, the cat's actual condition is indeterminate, that is, it is neither alive nor dead. Schrödinger asks rhetorically how the Copenhagen theorist defends this manifestly absurd conclusion, and he answers as follows.

> From this very hard dilemma the reigning doctrine [i.e. the Copenhagen interpretation] rescues itself by having recourse to epistemology. We are told that no distinction is to be made between the state of a natural object and what I know about it, or perhaps better, what I can know about it if I go to some trouble. Actually—so they say—there is intrinsically only awareness, observation, measurement. If through them I have procured at a given moment the best knowledge of the state of the physical object that is possibly attainable in accord with natural laws, then I can turn aside as *meaningless* any further questioning about the "actual state."[1]

---

[1] J. D. Trimmer, "The Present Situation in Quantum Mechanics: A Translation of Schrödinger's 'Cat Paradox' Paper," *Proceedings of the American Philosophical Society* 124 (1980): 328b (italics his).

Theologically the Copenhagen view as Schrödinger describes it is obviously unacceptable. The inability of human beings to examine God's knowledge of the future does not imply that God possesses no such knowledge, just as human beings' ignorance of some astronomical entities does not imply that these entities do not exist. Inasmuch as it rejects realism, therefore, the Copenhagen interpretation should be rejected.

2. The principle of contradiction

The Copenhagen interpretation of quantum mechanics entails the denial of the principle of contradiction, or at least a restriction of its applicability, in that it insists that the wave-particle duality of electrons, photons, and so forth is irreducible. In other words the Copenhagen theorists maintain not merely that elementary particles behave in ways characteristic of both waves and particles but that they literally are both: a wave continuously extended in space and a particle confined to a single point in space.

If the Copenhagen theorists are correct, naturally, then the phenomenon of wave-particle duality proves that the principle of contradiction is false. This simply cannot be the case, however, for two reasons. First, if the principle of contradiction were not true, nothing could possibly prove it false. Evidence contrary to a proposition weighs against it only if one cannot reasonably affirm both a proposition and its negation: only, that is, if the principle of contradiction holds true. Second, the statement, "The principle of contradiction is false" is meaningless; it neither affirms nor denies anything. It denies nothing specifically because, if the principle of contradiction is false, then its falsehood does not imply that it is not also true. This statement affirms nothing, likewise, because falsehood consists simply in untruthfulness; and if the principle of contradiction is false, then the property of falsehood does not entail untruthfulness.

The principle of contradiction therefore is an analytic truth, the kind of truth that one cannot coherently deny. Even if one were unable to devise an alternative explanation of the results of the double-slit experiment, whose results Copenhagen theorists invoke wave-particle duality to explain, one would be justified in rejecting the Copenhagen account as incorrect. No amount of evidence can justify rejection of an analytic truth.

Happily, however, careful consideration of the experiment itself shows that one can explain its outcome without invoking wave-particle duality and thus implicitly rejecting the principle of contradiction. In the double-slit experiment one fires electrons through a screen containing two slits located near each other. The electrons that pass through the slits then strike a screen on the other side of the slits. Surprisingly, however, the electrons do not strike the screen in the manner that their particle nature and the two-slit apparatus would lead one to expect. Although they do strike the screen at discrete points in space, they actually spread out and form an interference pattern resembling the waves of water that would form in a box with two slits if one placed it underwater. Physicist Peter Hodgson describes the dilemma in this way:

> The problem of the double slit is that neither the wave nor the particle picture seems at first to be satisfactory: if the electrons are waves, then why are they detected like particles, each at a particular point on the screen, whereas

if they are particles, then they must go through one slit or the other, and then how does the interference pattern arise?[2]

The Copenhagen theorist resolves this dilemma by ascribing to the electrons incompatible properties. Hodgson, however, along with other skeptics of the Copenhagen interpretation, argues that the interference patterns formed on the second screen (the one without the slits) constitute no more than a probabilistic distribution of particles, which is mathematically predictable by one who takes into account all the factors influencing the electrons' course. David Bohm, in particular, has developed formulae that predict the results of the two-slit experiment on the assumption that electrons are particles that do not in any sense constitute waves.[3]

> The wave-particle duality is thus simply a category confusion. On the one hand we have particles moving along definite trajectories with definite momenta, and on the other we recognize that due to their interactions with the slits and with other matter and radiation these trajectories have a certain probability distribution calculable from Schrödinger's equation. The so-called wave nature of these particles is no more an intrinsic property than, for example, actuarial statements are intrinsic properties of a particular individual.[4]

The fact that numerous individual particles appear in a probability amplitude that resembles interference patterns formed by waves does not imply that the particles themselves are waves. Hence the Copenhagen school's assertion of wave-particle duality and its consequent, implicit denial of the principle of contradiction lack experimental support.

B. The Principle of Causality

According to the Copenhagen interpretation, radioactive decay constitutes an uncaused event and therefore a counterexample to the principle of causality. Copenhagen theorists reach this conclusion, however, only because they suppose (a) that only the observable is real, and (b) that physical events, which do not follow automatically from a certain state of affairs in accord with a known scientific law, are uncaused. The second assumption naturally follows immediately from the first. If only what human beings observe is real, that is, then an unobserved cause is no cause at all, and events that lack presently discernible causes are causeless. Ultimately therefore the Copenhagen interpretation rejects the principle of causation because it rejects realism (the view that the world's existence is not contingent on human beings' perception of it).

The antirealism of the Copenhagen school seems at best counterintuitive. Its consistent application would require one to believe that bacteria did not exist before human beings developed microscopes sufficiently powerful to observe them and that the

---

[2] P. Hodgson, *Theology and Modern Physics* (London: Ashgate, 2005), 141.
[3] D. Bohm and B. J. Hiley, *The Undivided World: An Ontological Interpretation of Quantum Mechanics* (London: Routledge, 1993), 28–42.
[4] Hodgson, *Theology and Modern Physics*, 153.

planet Uranus sprang into existence only when Sir William Herschel (1738–1822) first observed it in 1781. If the Copenhagen interpretation's antirealism is unfounded, however, then its view of radioactive decay is equally unfounded. In any event physicists know why radioactive decay occurs; they simply lack a means of determining which individual nuclei of radioactive substances will decay at what time. If, as many physicists believe, quantum mechanics does not supply an exhaustive description of the quantum world, however, the present inability of physicists to predict these events with precision need not imply that the events lack causes; and to declare causeless all events that are simply unpredictable is to confuse causality with predictability. Like its rejection of realism and the principle of contradiction, therefore, the Copenhagen school's opposition to the principle of causality seems unwarranted.

C. Conclusion

Rejection of the Copenhagen interpretation does not constitute rejection of the mathematical formalism of quantum mechanics. This formalism has proven itself in countless experiments and in numerous practical applications. Devices such as transistors, personal computers, cell phones, MRI machines, and electron microscopes, for example, would not function if the mathematical apparatus of quantum physics were invalid. One can reject quantum mechanics itself only at the cost of evincing scandalous ignorance.

However, one ought to adopt or develop a philosophically and theologically viable alternative to the Copenhagen interpretation of quantum mechanics, among the most plausible of which are David Bohm's hidden variables theory and probability electrodynamics. These and other concepts currently circulating in the scientific literature both preserve the mathematical formalism of quantum mechanics in its entirety and jettison Copenhagenism's objectionable philosophical tenets. One need not choose, therefore, between Christianity and quantum mechanics; in order to integrate the findings of quantum mechanics into a Christian worldview, one must merely adopt or develop a credible alternative to the Copenhagen interpretation.

II. BIOLOGY

The clearest challenge to Christianity that has emerged from the abuse and/or misunderstanding of scientific data in the past two centuries is obviously Darwinian evolutionism. This secular view has captured the allegiance of virtually all highly educated persons on earth. Before addressing what is the most significant item of biological evidence for Darwinism and the three most significant items of biological evidence against it, it is necessary first to clarify the meaning of the terms *Darwinism* and *evolution*.

The term *Darwinism*, at least in nontechnical contexts, signifies not merely the theory articulated by Charles Darwin in *The Origin of Species* and *The Descent of Man* but also the general idea that all living organisms originated from inner-worldly causes operating at random and without supervision. Although the term *Darwinism* thus understood signifies an aggregation of mutually exclusive theories (such as conventional neo-Darwinism, saltationism, orthogenesis, and even Lamarckism), it is useful in discourse in that it supplies a common name for all atheistic accounts of the origin of species.

The term *evolution*, by contrast, is so vague as to be virtually useless. For it encompasses both microevolution, the kind of evolution that, say, bacteria undergo when they develop resistance to a particular antibiotic, and macroevolution, the kind of evolution Darwinists believe brought human beings from fish. No informed person denies that microevolution occurs. Yet, because persons frame the debate over Darwinism as a debate over *evolution*, macroevolutionists can and do claim that well-documented instances of microevolution, such as the development of fruit flies who feed on apples, constitute indisputable evidence for the reality of *evolution*. Thus they persuade countless students every year that the occurrence of macroevolution is an incontestable fact. By drawing the simple distinction between microevolution and macroevolution, one can expose such arguments from microevolution to macroevolution as logical fallacies with ease. Thus the following section speaks of microevolution and macroevolution and shuns the ambiguous term *evolution* altogether.

A. The Miller-Urey Experiment

The most powerful item of evidence for the feasibility of macroevolution is almost certainly the outcome of the Miller-Urey experiment.[5] While a doctoral student, Stanley Miller, working under the supervision of Nobel laureate Harold Urey, attempted to confirm experimentally the Oparin-Haldane hypothesis, which states that life emerged by spontaneous generation through the gradual, accidental formation of the requisite combinations of chemicals. Miller constructed an apparatus in which he attempted to simulate the earth's atmosphere at the time of life's origin. The apparatus was a roughly rectangular glass tube with two spherical enlargements (or flasks), one on the lower left corner and another just beneath the upper right, and at the bottom middle a U-shaped trap similar to the drain traps one sees in plumbing fixtures.

Miller carefully drained all oxygen from his apparatus. Although oxygen is essential to human life, it tends to break down organic compounds and prevent their formation altogether. He placed water in the lower left flask and two electrodes in the flask on the upper right. Then, having placed water vapor, ammonia, methane, and hydrogen in the rectangular tube, he boiled the water in the lower left flask, which caused the gases in the tube to move away from the water, up, right, then down, and so forth. When the gases passed through the flask on the upper right, Miller fired electricity, designed to simulate lightning, through the flask. Then, after the gases passed through the upper right flask, they descended through a cooling device that caused them partially to condense into a liquid solution, which then collected in the U-shaped trap in the lower middle of the apparatus. After the apparatus operated continually for a week,

---

[5] The description and criticism of the Miller-Urey experiment developed in this section relies heavily on P. Davis and D. H. Kenyon, *Of Pandas and People: The Central Question of Biological Origins*, 2nd ed. (Dallas: Haughton, 1993), 43–54.

Miller found that the solution gathered in the trap contained several though not nearly all of the amino acids necessary to sustain biological life. Since the initial publication of Miller's results in 1953, propagandists for macroevolutionism and authors of high school and college biology textbooks have trumpeted the Miller-Urey experiment as scientific confirmation of the Oparin-Haldane hypothesis. A number of difficulties, of which introductory biology students are rarely if ever informed, however, show that the Miller-Urey experiment does not significantly bolster the hypothesis's credibility.

First, the earth's early atmosphere probably contained significant amounts of oxygen, which, as already noted, prevents the synthesis of organic compounds. For (a) organic compounds could not have endured the dissociative effects of ultraviolet radiation if the early earth had not been shielded by a substantial ozone layer, and (b) extensively oxidized rocks appear even in the oldest strata of the geologic column. Yet Miller purposefully excluded all oxygen from the apparatus in which he conducted his experiment.

Second, the trap in Miller's apparatus shields spontaneously synthesized organic compounds from the radiation that formed them. Under natural conditions, however, such organic compounds would be exposed to this radiation continually and therefore destroyed by the radiation that supplied the energy for their synthesis.

Third, Miller's apparatus artificially shielded the organic compounds produced from harmful cross-reactions that, under natural conditions, would greatly hinder the synthesis of molecules useful for life.

Fourth, Miller's experiment yielded a mixture of amino acids in which left-handed and right-handed amino acids occurred in equal quantities. Yet proteins consist exclusively of left-handed amino acids, and genetic material (RNA and DNA) consists exclusively in right-handed amino acids. How all living things came to develop these peculiar preferences is a significant unresolved difficulty for the view that both proteins and genetic material developed by chance.

Fifth, Miller's experiment supplies no explanation for how amino acids could form proteins without enzymes, themselves a kind of protein programmed by DNA, to ensure that the amino acids combine in the correct sequence. If the approximately 100 amino acid units in a small protein lack the correct sequence, the protein cannot perform its function, and the construction of a single protein or DNA molecule requires the work of approximately 60 precisely sequenced proteins acting as enzymes. A cell, the most primitive unit of biological life, moreover, contains itself at least 500 enzymes, each with a precise sequence and a precise function essential to the sustenance of the cell.

Given the dissimilarity between Miller's apparatus and the environment in which life initially emerged and the precise organization exhibited by even the simplest life, Miller's experiment hardly confirms in any significant way Oparin and Haldane's speculations about the origins of life on earth. This item of evidence for macroevolution crumbles when subjected to scrutiny.

B. Irreducible Complexity

Probably the second most compelling item of evidence in favor of intelligent design over against random macroevolutionism is the phenomenon of irreducible complexity. The notion of irreducibly complex organisms or systems has found its most articulate contemporary advocate in biochemist Michael Behe. He defines irreducible complexity as follows:

> By irreducibly complex I mean a single system composed of several well-matched, interacting parts that contribute to the basic function, wherein the removal of any one of the parts causes the system to . . . cease functioning. An irreducibly complex system cannot be produced directly . . . by slight, successive modifications of a precursor system, because any precursor to an irreducibly complex system that is missing a part is by definition non-functional.[6]

An organism that is irreducibly complex, explains Behe, cannot evolve by natural selection, which favors adaptive traits and disfavors others; for, unless every part of the organism is already present and functioning, none of its parts conveys an adaptive advantage. Although Behe offers a multitude of examples of irreducible complexity in his books, *Darwin's Black Box* (the 2006 edition of which includes an afterword with replies to critics of the original 1996 ed.) and *The Edge of Evolution* (2007), it is important to note that rebuttals of Behe's examples available on the Internet and in Darwinist publications are legion. Anyone who thinks he can discern a function for an irreducibly complex organism in some half-developed state has a ready case, albeit frequently not a valid one, against the designation of the fully developed organism in question as irreducibly complex. While Behe's examples are striking, then, they have less persuasive power than the second, and strongest, item of evidence for intelligent design, discussed in the following section.

C. Specified Complexity

The most powerful item of evidence against unsupervised macroevolutionism and for intelligent design is the existence in nature of what William Dembski describes as specified complexity—a virtually unmistakable hallmark of intelligent design.[7] To qualify as an instance of specified complexity, a configuration of parts in an organism or more generally a pattern found in nature must satisfy three conditions. First, it must be contingent in the sense that one cannot reasonably consider it the product of an automatic process. The pattern must be markedly different in other words from, say, the monotonous pattern formed by the emission of radio waves at each rotation of a pulsar.

Second, a pattern must exhibit complexity or improbability. To exclude all reasonable possibility of random origins in probability-theoretical terms, Dembski argues

---

[6] M. Behe, *Darwin's Black Box: The Biochemical Challenge to Evolution,* 2nd ed. (New York: Simon & Schuster, 2006), 39.

[7] This account of Dembski's theory of specified complexity relies heavily on W. Dembski, *Intelligent Design: The Bridge between Science & Theology* (Downers Grove, IL: InterVarsity, 1999), 127–44.

in his mathematically sophisticated work, *The Design Inference*,[8] the probability of a pattern's arising by chance must be less than or equal to 10^{-150}. Even this unimaginably low probability, however, does not suffice unmistakably to identify a pattern as an instance of specified complexity. As Dembski explains, contingency and a profound degree of improbability can characterize completely random events. For example if one tosses a coin 25,000 times, the probability that one will find precisely the sequence of heads and tails that he actually obtains is infinitesimal; nevertheless no one would infer from this that someone had preprogrammed the coin to fall in precisely that pattern.

If the coin came up heads 25,000 times in a row, however, everyone would assume that the coin either has a head on each side or is weighted: in other words, that someone had intelligently designed the coin to yield only heads. For the pattern of 25,000 heads in a row exhibits not only contingency and complexity but a third characteristic essential to valid inferences to design, namely, specification. For an entity to exhibit specification, the pattern on which it is formed must satisfy the additional condition of detachability. The pattern must be such that one could realistically envision its being constructed by a rational agent even if one were ignorant of any item that exemplifies the pattern.

Naturally many items that are intelligently designed might fail to satisfy all of Dembski's conditions for specified complexity. For example someone ignorant of cryptology might mistake a message in a carefully crafted code for a random jumble of letters. Nevertheless when a pattern does satisfy all three of Dembski's criteria for specified complexity, it is virtually certain that the pattern is the product of intelligent design. While Behe's identification of irreducibly complex organisms significantly buttresses the credibility of the claim that nature reflects intelligent design, Dembski supplies a means of rendering this conclusion inescapable. If some naturally occurring pattern exemplifies specified complexity, it seems that one cannot reasonably deny that it springs, at least partially, from intelligent design.

D. Conclusion

The reflections on biology in this segment seem to warrant four principal conclusions. First, it is critically important to distinguish between microevolution, whose reality is observable, testable, and reproducible, and macroevolution, which no one even claims to have observed or tested directly. The former manifestly occurs; those afflicted by drug-resistant bacteria, among others, know this from personal experience. Macroevolution, however, is implausible, even if one considers only the evidence supplied by nature.

Second, the Miller-Urey experiment hardly suffices to render the Oparin-Haldane hypothesis credible. For the experiment (a) presupposes profoundly inaccurate assumptions about the composition of the early earth's atmosphere, (b) artificially shields the amino acids formed from the sustained radiation to which they would have been exposed even in the early atmosphere as Miller envisioned it, and (c) artificially

---

8 W. Dembski, *The Design Inference* (Cambridge: Cambridge University Press, 1999).

protects the amino acids formed from harmful cross-reactions. In addition the experiment (d) yields only a jumble of left- and right-handed amino acids, and (e) it fails to explain how amino acids produced spontaneously could combine to form the proteins essential for the most primitive forms of life. Objectively speaking, therefore, the Miller-Urey experiment supplies little information about how life emerged or could have emerged on earth.

Third, Behe's notion of irreducible complexity exposes as fallacious the view that all complex systems in nature gained their many interlocking parts one by one for reasons largely or entirely unrelated to the function those parts presently perform by working together. For, as Behe argues persuasively, the parts of many of these systems are devoid of independent, functional utility. Apart from the entire system, that is, they supply the organism to which they belong no adaptive advantage, which would account for their development through natural selection.

Fourth, Dembski's theory of specified complexity supplies a mathematically rigorous method of verifying that naturally occurring patterns are the product of intelligent design. If a certain pattern in nature is contingent, highly improbable (10^{-150}), and such that a rational agent might conceivably construct it, one cannot reasonably deny that the pattern in question owes its origin to intelligent design. To the extent that certain patterns in nature fulfill Dembski's criteria, the conclusion that at least certain aspects of nature derive from intelligent design seems certain, even if one considers the evidence of nature alone.

III. PALEONTOLOGY

Paleontology poses serious difficulties for the Christian faith only insofar as paleontologists claim to have unearthed evidence for the occurrence of macroevolution. Yet the massive paleontological discoveries of the last century and a half overwhelmingly favored the Christian view that God created the basic kinds of animals intact, fully equipping them with their basic structures and capacities. These discoveries have shown that the vast majority of phyla (large groups of living things) originated in a small period of time, geologically speaking, during the transition from the Pre-Cambrian to the Cambrian periods. "In a geological moment near the beginning of the Cambrian," writes Stephen Jay Gould, "nearly all modern phyla made their first appearance. . . . The 500 million subsequent years have produced no new phyla, only twists and turns upon established designs."[9]

Transitional forms, that is, now-extinct species that purportedly combined the characteristics of two taxa and constituted stages in the macroevolutionary development of one from the other, moreover, do not seem to exist. Even the most ardent Darwinists, in fact, only claim to have identified a handful. As Gould candidly observes:

---

[9] S. J. Gould, *Wonderful Life: The Burgess Shale and the Nature of History* (New York: Norton, 1990), 64; see also 23–24.

> The extreme rarity of transitional forms in the fossil record persists as the trade secret of paleontology. The evolutionary trees that adorn our textbooks have data only at the tips and nodes of their branches [the places occupied by actual, radically distinct taxa]; the rest is inference, however reasonable, not the evidence of fossils.[10]

Paleontologists' failure, in spite of the most strenuous efforts, to discover the myriads of transitional forms in the fossil record calls Darwinism radically into question. Even if paleontologists had found numerous, apparently transitional forms in the fossil record, moreover, they would have scarcely succeeded thereby in warranting Darwinism. For a species can be morphologically intermediate between two other species without being the descendant of one and the ancestor of the other.[11] It may be, as the intelligent design theorist might propose, that the species in question is designed to perform some function that requires its peculiar combination of traits.[12] No amount of seeming transitional species in the fossil record therefore could constitute proof of unsupervised macroevolution. "Fossils may tell us many things," Colin Patterson pithily observes, "but one thing they can never disclose is whether they were ancestors of anything else."[13]

IV. ASTRONOMY

Astronomy presents the least difficulties for an informed and consistent Christian faith. It does, however, pose one difficulty, which, while easy to dismiss on the theoretical plane, possesses great existential force and has motivated countless conversions to atheism or deism. The difficulty, which constitutes a misunderstanding of contemporary astronomy's implications rather than a finding of the science itself, goes by the names of "the Copernican principle," "the principle of mediocrity," and "the principle of indifference."[14] According to this principle the sheer vastness of the physical universe shows the Christian belief that human beings are the princes of subangelic creation, for whom inferior creatures are made, to be fatuous. Only by an act of monstrous hubris, the Copernican principle dictates, can human beings claim to be anything other than a meaningless detail, a tiny inkblot, as it were, on the universe.

Two observations suffice to refute the so-called Copernican principle. First, it in no way constitutes a logical conclusion of the discoveries of Copernicus, Galileo, Kepler, and others. Second, this principle leads one to expect that certain assertions will hold true, which are demonstrably false.

---

[10] S. J. Gould, *The Panda's Thumb: More Reflections in Natural History* (New York: Norton, 1992), 181.

[11] Ibid., 36.

[12] Ibid.

[13] C. Patterson, *Evolution* (Ithaca, NY: Cornell University Press, 1999), 109.

[14] G. Gonzalez and J. W. Richards, *The Privileged Planet: How Our Place in the Cosmos Is Designed for Discovery* (Washington, DC: Regnery, 2004), 248.

A. Historical Inaccuracy

As to the first point, in the context of the early Copernicans' times, moving the earth from the center to the periphery of the cosmos constituted not a demotion but rather a vindication of the earth's honor. For, as Guillermo Gonzalez and Jay W. Richards explain, in Aristotelian-Ptolemaic cosmology:

> The "center" of the universe was considered no place of honor, any more than we think of the center of the Earth as being such. And Earth was certainly not thought to be "sitting at the center of Heaven itself." . . . Quite the opposite. The sublunar domain was the mutable, corruptible, base, and heavy portion of the cosmos. Things were thought to fall to Earth because of their heaviness, and Earth itself was considered the "center" of the cosmos because of its heaviness.[15]

In essence, therefore, the early Copernicans promoted the earth from the status of cosmic sump to one more befitting the significance that Scripture assigns to humanity. The Copernican principle consequently is a later philosophical conviction foisted on Copernicus and his early modern disciples; it is not an obvious implication of their findings.

B. Scientific Disconfirmation

As to the second point, Gonzalez and Richards formulate six propositions, which the Copernican principle suggests ought to be true. The first of these is that "Earth, while it has a number of life-permitting properties, isn't exceptionally suited for life in our Solar System. Other planets in the Solar System probably harbor life as well."[16] Yet as virtually all contemporary astronomers recognize, the other planets in the Earth's solar system are incapable of supporting advanced life; the only debate is as to whether the most primitive organisms might inhabit Mars or its moons.

Gonzalez and Richards's second proposition is that "our sun is a fairly ordinary and typical star."[17] Nevertheless, as Gonzalez and Richards observe, the sun's mass and properties are by no means average among stars in the Milky Way and elsewhere. If the mass of the sun were significantly higher or lower than it presently is, it would almost certainly render planets surrounding it uninhabitable, at least by advanced forms of life. The sun is by no means an ordinary star; it is peculiarly suited for hosting a life-sustaining planet like Earth.

The third proposition, which one would expect to find true if the Copernican principle were sound, is, "Our Solar System is typical; we should expect other Solar Systems to mirror our own."[18] Nevertheless the relatively few solar systems of which scientists are presently aware seem radically dissimilar to that of the earth. The solar system, for example, has small terrestrial planets relatively close to the sun and gas

---

[15] Ibid., 226. See the quotations of Kepler and Galileo on 238 and 240 respectively.
[16] Ibid., 251.
[17] Ibid., 253.
[18] Ibid., 254.

giants farther out, all with roughly circular orbits. Other solar systems, however, typically contain planets with wildly eccentric orbits. Perhaps the best-known planet in another solar system is 51 Pegasus B. It is a gas giant that is much closer to its sun than Mercury is to its own. Presently available data at least verge on falsifying the third proposition.

The fourth proposition, which the Copernican principle at least suggests ought to be true, is this: "Even if our Solar System is not typical, there are lots of planetary configurations that are consistent with the presence of biological organisms. Variables like the number and types of planets and moons are mainly contingencies that have little to do with the existence of life in a planetary system."[19] As Gonzalez and Richards explain and document with a degree of detail impossible to reproduce in this format, however:

> The existence of a large, well-placed moon, of circular planetary orbits, of a properly placed asteroid belt with felicitous properties, of the early bombardment of these asteroids on Earth, of the outlying gas giants to sweep the Solar System of sterilizing comets later on—all these and more are profoundly important for the existence of complex life on our planet.[20]

Given the data presently available to scientists, therefore, the fourth proposition suggested by the Copernican principle appears to be false.

The fifth proposition, which, if the Copernican principle were correct, would likely prove correct also, is: "Our Solar System's location in the Milky Way is relatively unimportant."[21] As Gonzalez and Richards argue at length, however, Earth's solar system occupies what one might call a Galactic Habitable Zone, which contains properties friendly to the development of biological life and which covers only a small fraction of the Milky Way's total area. The location of Earth's solar system is therefore by no means a matter of indifference for the development of life on Earth.

The sixth proposition that Gonzalez and Richards identify as probable if the Copernican principle is true, is this: "Our galaxy is not particularly exceptional or important. Life could just as easily exist in old, small, elliptical, and irregular galaxies."[22] Again, argue Gonzalez and Richards, this is simply false. As they explain:

> All galaxies in the early history of the universe, and low-mass galaxies forming now, are metal-poor, making them unlikely habitats for life. Similar problems attached to globular clusters and irregular galaxies. We now have reason to suppose [furthermore] that large spiral galaxies like the Milky Way that formed at about the same time are substantially more habitable than galaxies of different ages and types. The metal content of a galaxy is highly dependent not just on its age but also on its mass. Without enough metals, there aren't enough materials for building terrestrial planets.

---

[19] Ibid., 256.
[20] Ibid.
[21] Ibid., 257.
[22] Ibid., 258.

And without terrestrial planets, there are no environments suitable for life. Our very massive, spiral galaxy, then, is an especially suitable home for a habitable planet and Solar System.[23]

The sixth proposition rendered probable by the Copernican principle thus seems rather obviously untrue. Gonzalez and Richards seem to succeed in thoroughly discrediting the Copernican principle.

V.   CONCLUSION

Contemporary opponents of Christianity hold that the religion of the Bible conflicts with the natural sciences in the areas of physics, biology, paleontology, and astronomy. As to quantum physics, however, one can interpret its mathematical formalism in such a way as to render it compatible with orthodox Christianity. It is not quantum mechanics as such but rather the Copenhagen interpretation of quantum mechanics that poses difficulties for the Christian faith.

Similarly, Christianity does not conflict with the hard science of biology but rather with its Darwinist misinterpretation. Given the irrelevance of Stanley Miller's famous experiment to the debate over the origins of life and the phenomena of irreducible and specified complexity, it seems reasonable on purely scientific grounds to repudiate Darwinism and to embrace intelligent design. The sudden emergence of virtually all animal phyla at the outset of the Cambrian period and the marked absence of transitional forms in the fossil record, moreover, suggest that intelligent design supplies a more reasonable explanatory paradigm than Darwinism for paleontology as well.

As for astronomy, the so-called Copernican principle (the view that human beings are in no way integral to the larger purposes of the cosmos) flies in the face of an abundance of evidence. For as noted, the earth, the sun, earth's solar system, and the Milky Way itself are uniquely suitable for the sustenance of human life on the earth. The Copernican principle therefore appears to possess little in the way of warrant.

Assertions of incompatibility between Christianity and the contemporary sciences, therefore, reflect confusion on the part of those who make them: not any authentic disharmony between the sciences and Christian faith. The Intelligent Design movement, it is to be hoped, will eventually gain intellectual respectability and at least partially efface the false impression of conflict between Christianity and the natural sciences.

---

[23] Ibid.

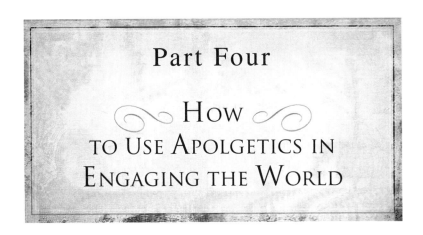

Part Four

How
TO USE APOLGETICS IN
ENGAGING THE WORLD

This section focuses on several worldviews the Christian apologist is likely to encounter. The beliefs of these worldviews are described, and the superiority of Christianity to each worldview is demonstrated.

Chapter 27

ENGAGING THE CULTIST

EVANGELICALS HAVE TRADITIONALLY USED THE WORD *cult* to describe those groups whose teachings diverge from orthodox Christian teaching.[1] This chapter uses the term "new religious movements" unless the term *cult* is preferable in the context.[2] The range of groups that may be included under this designation is legion. They include any group that surrounds itself around an individual(s) with a particular interpretation of the Bible or some other religious authoritative text or a combination of both. Their teachings always differ from orthodox Christian teaching that involve the "essentials" of the faith—teachings on the Trinity, the deity and resurrection of Jesus, and the doctrine of salvation. This chapter explores the major features of the worldviews of devotees of the new religious movements. The chapter also examines the importance and theological bases for orthodox beliefs, why Christians differ so radically from the new religious movements, and what doctrines Christians should be emphasizing. The chapter concludes with a discussion of the most effective ways of approaching cultists in seeking to evangelize them.

I.   WORLDVIEW OF NEW RELIGIOUS MOVEMENTS

Several important elements make up the worldview of typical new religious devotees.[3] At the center of their worldview is a sphere of experiences that set the group off from the rest of the world. These experiences tend to establish the truth or veracity of the group's particular teachings about the nature of reality and of the one true God. These experiences include alleged religious dreams and visions, precognition, extrasensory perception, among others. A well-known example is the alleged vision of Joseph Smith in 1820, in which he claimed to have had a vision of God the Father and God the Son in bodily form appearing to him in the woods of New York State. He said

---

[1] To avoid confusion the word *orthodox* with a small "o" refers to correct theological teaching of the church throughout its history. This is in contradistinction to the alternative use of the word *Orthodox*, with a capitol "O," which refers to the Eastern Orthodox Church.

[2] The term *cult* in the media today tends to refer to a group that is bizarre, or even dangerous, rather than doctrinally aberrant. Consequently social scientists prefer the term *new religious movements*. I. Hexham, "New Religions," in *New Dictionary of Theology*, ed. S. B. Ferguson and D. F. Wright (Downers Grove, IL: InterVarsity, 1988), 460.

[3] Ibid., 460–61.

the Father and the Son advised him (in answer to his fervent prayers) not to join any of the Christian sects of the area because of their universal apostasy from the true faith. This alleged vision of Joseph Smith, when he was only 14 years of age, established the unique position of the "restored faith" of Jesus Christ and Joseph Smith's author-ity to speak on behalf of the "deities" on the earth. In declaring all other Christian denominations and sects to be "an abomination," this fledgling group of "Mormons" set themselves off from the rest of orthodox Christianity by denying every major tenet of the Christian faith.

Another important element in the worldview of a devotee to a new religious movement is the reliance on the leadership of an individual or group of individuals who claim unique ability to interpret properly either biblical and/or other authorita-tive religious texts. A famous example of this phenomenon is the Jehovah's Witnesses and their slavish reliance on the unique and allegedly divine ability of the Watchtower Bible and Tract Society in Brooklyn, New York, to provide the only authoritative and true interpretation of the Bible. A major problem arises in this approach when the interpretation of God's Word is in the hands of a few people who form a spiritual hierarchy of elite interpreters. The *Watchtower* states, "The Bible is an organizational book and belongs to the Christian congregation, not to individuals, regardless of how sincerely they may believe that they can interpret the Bible. . . . The Bible cannot be properly understood without Jehovah's visible organization in mind."[4]

Another typical feature of the worldview of new religious movements is an ani-mosity expressed against the "established churches" of mainline Christianity. Many devotees of new religious groups tend to explain that one of the primary factors that led them to an alternative religious group is a distinct dislike of the organizational structure and worship practices (or lack thereof) of mainline churches. In their new environment new religious devotees testify to having found what they had been miss-ing; a sense of belonging, a zeal for the truth, and an intense devotion to the (usually) simplistic teachings of the group's founder or current teacher. It is no coincidence, for example, that about 80 percent of all converts to the Mormon faith have come out of mainline churches. It would be a mistake, however, to assume that either all or some of the new religious devotees have been somehow "brainwashed" into accepting their new religious beliefs. Such an idea was common about 30 years ago when devotees to the Moonies or Hari Krishna were once thought to have been spirited away and sub-jected to brainwashing techniques.

Another characteristic of a new religious worldview is the "fortress mentality" syndrome. Some of the extreme religious groups take on a more sinister look when they wrap themselves in fortified ideologies that isolate them from the outside world. This mentality is often expressed in extreme forms of isolationism that may lead to violence, as it did in Jonestown in the 1970s and in Waco, Texas, in the 1990s. More

---

[4] *Watchtower,* May 1, 1957, 274.

often, however, the devotees of alternative religious groups exhibit beliefs and behaviors that are irrational by accepting bizarre beliefs that are impervious to sound logic.[5]

All other groups on the outside are considered "the enemy" and "tools of Satan." Those who leave such groups are branded as traitors, and their lives are sometimes put in jeopardy by more extreme members of such groups. Sometimes members of these groups who contemplate leaving are warned that they will be attacked and destroyed by Satan if they leave. The placing of such psychological barriers creates an environment of isolation and antagonism.[6]

II.   Heterodox Beliefs

Heterodox[7] groups and individuals usually reject biblical teaching for differing reasons.[8] For example the orthodox teaching on the Trinity may be rejected by some because of their commitment to the belief in the existence of many gods, or because they reject the deity of Jesus or the Holy Spirit, or because they reject the plurality of the persons of the Godhead, or because they reject the personal nature of God because of their commitment to pantheism.

A common feature of those who reject orthodox teaching is the strength of their sincerity. Most members of new religious groups are sincere in their beliefs. Most are honest, diligent, and personable. They are committed to the promulgation of their faith with a zeal that often puts orthodox Christians to shame. However, the unorthodox beliefs of these people are divergent and even dangerous. Their eternal destiny before God is at stake, and that is a serious matter. It *does* matter what one believes. If a person holds to aberrant and heterodox beliefs about the nature of God and the issue of salvation, then he faces eternal destruction by placing his trust in anything other than the gospel preached by the apostles and delivered to us once and for all as revealed in the New Testament.

How can a person recognize heterodox beliefs?[9] Usually false teaching is expressed in (a) a rejection of the true humanity and or true deity of the Lord Jesus, and (b) the replacement of God's free gift of salvation by faith alone in Christ along with requirements of works or merit. These two Christian orthodox doctrines are primarily the main focus of attack by the new religious groups. Their attempts to justify their anti-Christian teachings usually involve citing portions of Scripture out of context.

Heretical teachings regarding the person of Christ attempt to diminish either His humanity or His deity or to hold one nature above another. In the first few centuries of the history of the church, some Jews known as Ebionites accepted Christ as the human Messiah of Israel but rejected His claims that He is God incarnate. Others in that period (Gnostics) considered Him fully divine but denied that He had a genuine human

---

[5] See N. L. Geisler and R. Rhodes, *When Cultists Ask* (Grand Rapids: Baker, 1997), 11–13.

[6] Ibid.

[7] *Heterodox* or *heterodoxy* means "other doctrine" or "another teaching."

[8] The following discussion is adapted from H. W. House and G. Carle, *Doctrine Twisting: How Core Biblical Truths Are Distorted* (Downers Grove, IL: InterVarsity, 2003), 9–14.

[9] Ibid., 223–25.

nature. Nestorians tried to accept Christ's deity and humanity by separating His person from His nature. Still others (Eutychians) attempted to blend the two natures into a third nature that blurred and confused the human and divine natures. The Arians taught that Jesus was a human being who had been "adopted" into the Godhead and thereby possessed some divine properties but was not the unique, eternal Son of God. Each of these ancient heresies was an attempt to eliminate the built-in tension in the Scriptures' expression of Jesus Christ as fully God and fully man.

Most new religious groups emphasize or deemphasize some aspect of Jesus' nature. The apostle John left no doubt that the major area of contention wherein false religions fail is in reference to the person of Christ: "Who is the liar, if not the one who denies that Jesus is the Messiah? He is the antichrist: the one who denies the Father and the Son. No one who denies the Son can have the Father; he who confesses the Son has the Father as well." (1 John 2:22–23).

John made abundantly clear that Christians are expected to recognize spiritual error.

> Dear friends, do not believe every spirit, but test the spirits to determine if they are from God, because many false prophets have gone out into the world. This is how you know the Spirit of God: Every spirit who confesses that Jesus Christ has come in the flesh is from God. But every spirit who does not confess Jesus is not from God. This is the spirit of the antichrist; you have heard that he is coming, and he is already in the world now. (4:1–3)

Besides distorting Jesus' nature, false religious groups also teach that a person must somehow earn salvation from God. Some work or ritual is the requisite for being made a part of God's kingdom and being declared righteous before a righteous judge. False teachings like these place adherents of new religions under the absolute control of the group or group leader who administers the labor required to spread God's message. Such a mind-set is absolutely foreign to the message of the gospel of God's gracious forgiveness in Christ. True, grateful obedience to God's Word is expected of those who are now God's children, but that does not determine a person's standing before God with regard to his salvation.

Paul also explained how to distinguish truth from error. In his epistle to the Galatians (perhaps the first letter he wrote), he stated denial of salvation by grace alone is an indication of serious error. He was concerned about a group of Jews from Jerusalem who were teaching the Galatian believers that in order to be truly saved, they had to perform various works of obedience to the law of Moses in addition to believing in Christ. In no uncertain terms—and in perhaps the strongest language in the Bible—Paul declared that even if an angel from heaven preached to them a message different from that message that he preached to them, that person deserves eternal damnation (Gal 1:6–10).

Today numerous new religious groups deny the true humanity of Jesus, repudiate His incarnation, or make Him less than God, coequal with the Father. These groups also seek to add to one's salvation by teaching that eternal salvation requires something other than belief in Jesus Christ. Without exception, spiritual counterfeits always involve errors on these pivotal doctrines of the historic Christian faith.

III. Why Do We Differ?

A. On What Hills Do We Die?

Before delving into the means of engaging those from various new religious groups, it is appropriate at this juncture to outline those beliefs of the Christian faith that are *nonnegotiable.* These are doctrines that must be defended always, consistently, and without equivocation. Among genuine orthodox believers there have always been differences of opinion regarding certain aspects of Christian doctrine of a more secondary nature. Yes there is—and has been—unity around the core doctrines of Christianity that distinguish Christian denominations from new heterodox groups and sects.

Orthodox Christians are united in their commitment to the following core doctrines:[10]

1. There is one God who is eternally existent as three persons, Father, Son and Holy Spirit.
2. The Bible, in whole and in part, is the written Word of God and thus is fully authoritative, inerrant, and sufficient for the Christian's beliefs and practices.
3. Jesus Christ is the Son of God, born of the virgin Mary, being both fully God and fully man with neither confusion of His two natures nor division of His person.
4. Jesus died as a substitutionary sacrifice for humanity, His death alone being necessary and sufficient for redemption.
5. Jesus Christ was raised from the dead in the same physical body in which He died; glorified, it is now subject to neither decay or death.
6. Jesus will return physically in the clouds of glory to receive His people and judge the wicked.
7. Justification is by grace alone through faith alone.

These doctrines serve as the basis for evaluating all heterodox belief systems. Other *secondary* doctrines, although important, are minor issues that do not have an impact on one's eternal destiny.[11] These should be avoided when dealing with devotees of new religious groups. When dealing with a Jehovah's Witness, for example, avoid any arguments over the issue of blood transfusions. These are examples of red-herring arguments that detract from the central issues of who Jesus Christ is and what one must do to be saved.

Individuals from new religious groups deny certain biblical teachings for various reasons. The orthodox doctrine of the Trinity, for example, may be rejected by some because they are committed to a belief in the existence of many gods, or because they deny the deity of Jesus Christ, or because they reject the personal nature of God and gravitate toward a pantheistic view of reality and God.

---

10 Ibid., 9–10.
11 Examples of secondary or minor Christian doctrines include the mode of baptism, the form of church organization, views on Christ's second coming, the identity of the antichrist, and the like.

B. Why Should They Be Evangelized?

The question as to why one should consider evangelizing members of cults was succinctly answered by Walter Martin many years ago: *because they are souls for whom Christ died.* Evangelizing members of new religious groups may go against the beliefs of some Christians who say that they should "shun" such individuals for their distortion of true Christian doctrine. Although the New Testament teaches believers to admonish and finally shun members of the Christian community who go off into serious doctrinal error, this does not refer to those who are outside the Christian community, who are just as much in spiritual darkness as any secularist.

Christians ought to love their neighbors as themselves. But how is this to be done? Would it be a loving act to ignore the spiritual condition of cultists? Loving one's neighbor includes helping others reevaluate false teachings on crucial theological issues that will affect their eternal destiny. If someone is heading down a pathway to destruction, led by teachings contrary to the Christian faith, then the loving thing to do is to help to point out the error of those teachings. People cannot be argued into the kingdom of God, but believers are to "set the orthodox Christian record straight."[12] Christians should not attack adherents of false groups. But believers should respond to beliefs that are contrary to sound, biblical teaching.

C. Getting Prepared

The great Christian mathematician, Blaise Pascal, wrote, "Those who do not love truth excuse themselves on the grounds that it is disputed and that very many people deny it."[13] The fact that a doctrine is disputed—even for a long time—does not mean that truth cannot be found. Certain doctrines will continue to be debated. In relation to the core Christian message, however, where the evidence is clear as to what is true, a stand needs to be taken and held without equivocation.

The essential doctrines of orthodox Christianity enumerated above are virtually all denied or distorted by the new religious movements. Most doctrines are categorically rejected, contradicted, and compromised. Another factor that explains why some people are subject to false teachings is a lack of accurate information. Ignorance may result when one relies heavily on the written materials of a new religious organization rather than on an independent reading of God's Word. Ignorance can also result from being poorly schooled in biblical truth. Such ignorance usually often opens the door to confusion. This is why evangelists today should know the Bible, systematic theology (the systematic study of God and His revealed truth), apologetics (the branch of theology that deals with the rational defense of the faith), hermeneutics (the art of biblical interpretation), logic (the art of systematic thought), and rhetoric (the art of persuasive and logical speech).

Another reason for theological confusion is improper biblical interpretation. Even though believers are promised that the Holy Spirit will guide them into all truth, they

---

[12] Ibid., 12.

[13] B. Pascal, *Pensées,* XII.176 (261), trans. A. J. Krailsheimer (New York: Penguin, 1966), 84.

are also admonished to be "rightly dividing the word of truth" (2 Tim 2:15 NKJV). Three principles of biblical interpretation are indispensable for interpreting the Bible properly. First, Scripture must interpret Scripture; that is, unclear Bible passages must be interpreted in light of clear passages. Second, the meaning of each passage must be determined in the light of its context. Third, Scripture should be understood in its plain sense, giving due consideration to grammatical structure, figures of speech, literary genre, and cultural-historical background.[14] If people have never heard of or learned of these basic principles of interpretation, they are more susceptible and vulnerable to unorthodox teachings.

A more dangerous form of ignorance is the *willful* variety. Some people in new religious organizations may have been led to believe that to question their group's teachings is wrong, and now they simply refuse to consider biblical truth. Even worse, some devotees of alternative religious groups face serious threats or other forms of peer pressure that inhibit them from even considering leaving their group. Some, however, recognize biblical truth for what it is, and they *still* respond with a willful denial and disobedience to God.

IV. Approaching the Cultist

Approaching a member of a new religious movement can be as different as the movement to which one belongs. One would not approach a Mormon, for example, in the same way one would approach a Buddhist. Understanding the faith tradition of each member is important in finding an avenue of approach, or some "common ground." When Paul spoke to the philosophers of Athens, he commented on the positive value of their religious expression. Then he quoted from one of their poets about the all-pervading presence and power of the unknown God, for whom the Athenians in ignorance had erected a monument. Thus Paul began his evangelistic presentation by appealing to natural revelation in creation and to certain true statements by an Athenian poet. Paul could hardly have appealed to the Hebrew Scriptures, of which the Athenians had little or no knowledge. So he began with creation itself and wove his presentation within a logical and philosophical framework familiar to his Greek audience.[15]

By employing his knowledge of Greek philosophy, he gained the attention of his audience. By appealing to recognizable features in their culture, Paul was able to introduce the unknown gospel of Jesus Christ with familiar—and hence less intimidating—features of their own surroundings. Witnesses of the gospel today must seek to find common ground by which to gain a hearing for the gospel.

---

[14] House and Carle, *Doctrine Twisting,* 13. See also R. B. Zuck, *Basic Biblical Interpretation* (Wheaton, IL: Victor, 1991; reprint, Colorado Springs: Cook, 1996).

[15] See H. Wayne House, "A Biblical Argument for Balanced Apologetics: How the Apostle Paul Practiced Apologetics in the Acts," in *Reasons for Faith: Making a Case for the Christian Faith,* ed. Norman L. Geisler and Chad V. Meister (Wheaton IL: Crossway, 2007), 64–74.

A. Disarming the Situation

The Scriptures exhort believers to contend earnestly for the faith delivered to the saints (Jude 3) and to be always ready to give a rational defense for their hope (1 Pet 3:15). Peter added that such a defense must be given "with gentleness and respect" (v. 16). Perhaps the first, and most important, principle in presenting the gospel to a religious devotee is to do so in a true spirit of meekness. This is, however, far easier to prescribe than it is to actually follow. Of course maintaining one's "cool" in the presence of spiritual darkness is difficult. Therefore one should pray before such encounters, asking the Holy Spirit to assist him in keeping him calm and serene. First, one must ask the Holy Spirit to give a genuine sense of compassion for the individual in the false movement. When a believer has a genuine love for an individual, he will find that he is in a better position emotionally and spiritually to listen and thereby to put the cult member at ease. Listening and being patient are important. One's first inclination is to jump into the discussion vigorously, but this temptation should be avoided. When engaging a cultist, it is also important not to let him lead the discussion.

B. Putting on Your Armor

In any army wise platoon leaders know the various levels of experience of their fighting men and utilize them accordingly. The same is true of the Christian "army." If a person is a recent Christian, he ought not go to the front rank of a battle line and face the frontal assaults of an experienced enemy. In ancient armies the inexperienced troops were kept at the back of a military unit—close enough to observe and learn the tactics of the more experienced men firsthand, yet far enough in the back to be out of harm's way. Similarly younger Christians can learn about evangelism—even evangelization of cultic members—by observing closely the techniques of experienced, battle-hardened "veterans."

C. Knowing It Better Than They Do

In Walter Martin's long and fruitful career, he mastered the belief systems and historical developments of the majority of all of the more well-known cults, such as the Church of Jesus Christ of Latter-day Saints, the Jehovah's Witnesses, Christian Science, and many more, including more obscure cults. In debate settings Martin would cause great consternation among members of cultic groups by demonstrating a profound mastery of their own theological and historical systems better than their knowledge. Members of these false groups wondered how anyone could know that much about their religion and *not* be a member of it. This question plagued many cultic members unfortunate enough to be the subject of Martin's "attacks." This is the secret of Martin's great success in evangelism: One should know his opponent's religion better than the adherent does. This principle has long been employed by the most prominent Christian apologists and theologians of church history. One example is the early church theologian Irenaeus of Lyons, who lived and ministered in the mid-second century. As bishop of Lyons, Irenaeus devoted himself to mastering the belief systems of numerous Gnostic sects that were plaguing the Christian communities with their heretical teachings, while at the same time masking themselves as true Christians. Inspired by his great love for Christ and by his iron-willed commitment to protect the pure faith of Christianity from heresy, Irenaeus set about systematically to analyze and refute the Gnostics by first becoming an expert of their own convoluted belief systems. Once he mastered their beliefs, he refuted them soundly, elevating the gospel message of Jesus Christ at the same time among his generation. His writings have continued to inspire thousands of Christians to become faithful defenders of God's truth in their own situations.

D. Staying on Track: Keep to the Essentials

Again it is important to avoid debating over secondary doctrines when speaking with a member of a new religious movement. The primary doctrinal issues of eternal importance for any individual are the person and work of Jesus Christ and the issue of salvation. Whether you are speaking with a Mormon, a member of New Age, or with a follower of Baha'i, these two pivotal Christian doctrines—the deity of Christ and the way of salvation—should be the *primary focus of presentation*. The conversation should revolve around who Jesus is and how one becomes righteous before a holy God. All other doctrinal issues are secondary at this point of evangelism.

If a believer finds himself bogged down in some minor doctrinal point of a particular cult, he should steer the conversation back to Jesus Christ and His power to save lost sinners. The book of Acts shows that every recorded speech of an evangelist or apostle before an audience was *always* focused on Jesus Christ and His mission to sinners.

V. Conclusion

The worldviews of new religious movements share a number of features common to most of them, such as defining moments in the movement's beginnings, peculiar social distinctions, and peculiar teachings of the founder. This chapter also examined some of the peculiar heterodox beliefs of some cultic groups, and why the solid core of Christian theological doctrines is rejected by them. Christians are to be as gentle as doves in their debates and evangelistic efforts, while at the same time cultivating a keen and disciplined mind, thoroughly trained in the Scriptures and in the study of Christian theology.

Evangelism for a Christian is not an option. They are to be evangelists in every facet of life, whether as a professional evangelist or not. Although being an evangelist to members of the new religious movements is a rather specialized ministry, one that requires dedication and commitment for such a task, it is not insurmountable. Prayer, preparation, and practice are required. Witnessing to members of new religious groups can be one of the most frustrating of all evangelistic efforts. However, because of the stakes involved and because of the inherent difficulties it presents, the spiritual blessings that come with partnering with the Holy Spirit for such a task and being instrumental in leading precious souls to faith in Christ are nothing less than monumental.

Chapter 28

ENGAGING THE SECULARIST

SECULAR HUMANISM HAS HAD A TREMENDOUS impact on Western culture. The humanist philosophy has been embraced by the overwhelming majority of college professors, who in turn pass on secular humanist beliefs to their students. These professors have been largely successful at removing most opposing viewpoints, and they have been particularly militant against Christianity. Secular humanist groups such as the American Civil Liberties Union (ACLU) and the Americans United for the Separation of Church and State have been on a crusade to remove traditional religion from the public life. Secular humanists have sued to remove the Bible from public schools, blocked creationism being included as a valid theory in school curriculua, removed the Ten Commandments from public buildings, banned prayer from public events, stopped Christians from gathering in public buildings, and a host of other anti-Christian initiatives.

Early in the history of secular humanism those who founded the movement considered it a religion. More recently, as the secular humanists have engaged in an aggressive campaign to win over converts, the humanists have vehemently denied that they are a religious movement. They do not want to be associated with a belief system; they say they are simply adhering to science and logic.

Because of secular humanism's strong impact on today's culture and the movement's militantly anti-Christian attitude, Christians need to be prepared to defend against their claims and to show why Christianity is superior to secular humanism.

I. IS SECULAR HUMANISM A RELIGION?

A. What Is Religion?

1. Secular humanism's attempt to redefine the terms

While secular humanism was begun as an alternative *among* religions, many humanists today argue that humanism is actually an alternative *to* religion. Today, secular humanists expend considerable efforts redefining religion in order to prove that their's is *not* a religion. However, their redefinition restricts the word *religion* to narrow parameters. They define religion as "belief in deities" and "anything supernatural."[1] Skipp Porteous, said, "Humanism is not a religious belief system. This is particularly true when applied to secular humanism, owing to the fact that 'secular' is defined as not religious."[2] Religion, it is argued, is "faith in a being or a power that transcends reason and human desires."[3] By this narrow definition, many other belief systems are not "religions." Some strands of Buddhism could not rightly be called religions since they are atheistic and deny the supernatural.[4] Confucianism would not be a religion. Even some forms of Judaism are not religious, according to the humanist strict definition.[5]

2. A better definition

Chapter 25 ("Christianity in Competition with Other Religions") includes this definition of religion given in *Webster's Dictionary*: "a cause, principle, or system of beliefs held to with ardor and faith."[6] In 1933 the *Humanist Manifesto* was written to elucidate humanist beliefs. In it "religion" is defined as

> those actions, purposes, and experiences which are humanly significant. Nothing human is alien to the religious. It includes labor, art, science, philosophy, love, friendship, recreation—all that is in its degree expressive of intelligently satisfying human living. The distinction between the sacred and the secular can no longer be maintained.[7]

As stated in chap. 25, religion provides a basis for a person's view of the world. This is commonly called a worldview. David Noebel defines "worldview" as "the way we view our world and our place in it."[8] More specifically he argues that worldviews are formed from ten "disciplines": theology, philosophy, ethics, biology, psychology, sociology, law, politics, economics, and history.[9]

3. Why all the trouble?

This move to distance themselves from religion is due, in large part, to secular humanists attempting to assert themselves as the guardians against mixing "religion" and

---

[1] J. D. Fowler, *Humanism: Beliefs and Practices* (Portland, OR: Sussex Academic, 1999), 33.

[2] S. Porteous, "Humanism Is Not a Religion," *Free Inquiry Magazine* (September, 1996), http://find articles.com/p/articles/mi_hb6407/is_/ai_n25620201 (accessed November 3, 2008).

[3] L. Hyman, "What Humanism Means to Me," *Free Mind Magazine* (May/June 1997), http://shsny .org/pique/2003–01.html (Accessed November 10, 2008).

[4] See S. Batchelor, *Buddhism Without Beliefs: A Contemporary Guide to Awakening* (New York: Riverhead, 1997).

[5] See the International Institute for Secular Humanistic Judaism. They are thoroughly secular but also participate and celebrate the various Jewish holidays and ceremonies, http://www.iishj.org/about_iishj .htm#shj

[6] "Religion," in *Merriam and Webster's Online Dictionary*, http://www.merriam-webster.com/dictionary/religion (accessed October 27, 2008).

[7] American Humanist Association, *Humanist Manifesto I*, http://www.americanhumanist.org/about/ manifesto1.html (accessed November 15, 2008).

[8] D. Noebel, *Understanding the Times: The Collision of Today's Competing Worldviews* (Manitou Springs, CO: Summit Press, 1991), 15.

[9] Ibid., 16.

government. The "Secular Humanist Declaration" of 1980[10] asserted that "tax money should not be used to support religious institutions."[11] It also said, "People should not be taxed to support religions in which they do not believe."[12] The *Humanist Manifesto II* of 1973 proclaims:

> The separation of church and state and the separation of ideology and state are imperatives. The state should encourage maximum freedom for different moral, political, religious, and social values in society. It should not favor any particular religious bodies through the use of public monies, nor espouse a single ideology and function thereby as an instrument of propaganda or oppression, particularly against dissenters.[13]

Paul Kurtz wrote, "Religion should not invade the schools, given the multiplicity of denominations in our society; instead it should be a private matter, best left to the parents."[14] If secular humanism is a religion, its proponents would have to include themselves in these assertions. According to the statements above, even if secular humanism is an "ideology," it must excuse itself from governmental involvement. Unfortunately secular humanism has engaged in the very thing it purports to avoid, often being used as an "instrument of propaganda or oppression" in public institutions. In fact one of secular humanism's basic goals is to infiltrate governmental institutions, especially schools. Again Kurtz wrote:

> We secular humanists need to nourish wholesome moral values and principles, which we can then help to grow within our children. More than that, we need to develop institutions, schools, textbooks, and curricula to provide the learning materials and the teachers to instill an appreciation for the good life and some recognition of our moral obligations and responsibilities. Indeed, moral education and cognitive growth should have first place in our agenda for the future.[15]

If this quotation had come from a Christian source, secular humanists would be outraged. Stephan Schafersman, arguing that religious morals should have no place in public schools, wrote, "The religious right advocates such moral instruction in order to sneak their religion back into the schools. It is quite clear, however, that such religious moral instruction is illegal."[16] If secular humanism is a religion, then advocating the teaching of secular humanist morality in schools is also "illegal."

---

[10] P. Kurtz. et al., "A Secular Humanist Declaration," http://www.secularhumanism.org/index.php?page=declaration&section=main (accessed November 15, 2008).

[11] Ibid.

[12] Ibid.

[13] P. Kurtz and E. H. Wilson, *Humanist Manifesto II*, http://www.americanhumanist.org/about/manifesto2.html (accessed November 3, 2008).

[14] P. Kurtz, "Wanted: Moral Education for Secular Children," http://www.secularhumanism.org/index.php?section=library&page=kurtz_27_1 (accessed November 4, 2008).

[15] Ibid.

[16] S. D. Schafersman, "Teaching Morals and Values in the Public Schools: A Humanist Perspective," March 1991, http://www.freeinquiry.com/teaching-morals.html (accessed November 10, 2008).

Another important reason secular humanists do not want to be labeled as religious is their distinct dislike of what they perceive religion to be. John F. Haught charged that "religion is an impoverishment of our life in this world."[17] Religion has become a popular secular humanist scapegoat, upon which they heap all kinds of blame. E. J. Buckner, a secular humanist, claimed, "Religion, including Christianity, directly fosters immorality, and that is among the best reasons for actively opposing it."[18] Lawrence Hyman wrote that religion "has only confused my understanding of what is right and wrong in ethical matters, as well as true about the world."[19] Richard Dawkins, a secular humanist and devout atheistic evolutionist (who believes aliens seeded life on Earth),[20] said, "I think a case can be made that *faith* is one of the world's great evils, comparable to the smallpox virus but harder to eradicate."[21]

B. Is Secularism a Religion?

If religion is defined as a system of beliefs that inform someone's worldview, is secular humanism a religion? Secular humanism has definite beliefs in the "disciplines" listed above and consequently has a definite worldview. Lawrence Hyman, wrote, "Humanism is a philosophy that allows me to understand the world, including human relationships, as clearly as possible, and to make moral decisions that enable me to live in as much harmony as possible with other human beings."[22] He then called it a "worldview." Under the definitions of religion above, and using secular humanism's worldview as a guide, secular humanism *is* a religion. Secular humanists hold to certain beliefs and principles and hold them with fervor.

1. Atheism

Secular humanism is atheistic. While the *Humanist Manifesto I* of 1933 was silent regarding the existence of God, in 1973 the *Humanist Manifesto II* had fully cast God aside: "We find insufficient evidence for belief in the existence of a supernatural; it is either meaningless or irrelevant to the question of survival and fulfillment of the human race. As nontheists, we begin with humans not God, nature not deity."[23]

Secular humanism holds that "the conviction that 'this world,' the immediate environment available to ordinary experience and scientific investigation, is all there

---

[17] J. F. Haught, *What Is Religion?* (Mahwah, NJ: Paulist, 1990) 200.

[18] E. Buckner, "Us Christians have the Good News to spread, whereas you secular humanists only have bad news, even if you're right. So why do you insist on being heard?" http://www.secularhumanism.org/index.php?section=columns&page=news (accessed November 8, 2008). Buckner is on the Council for Secular Humanism.

[19] L. Hyman, "What Humanism Means to Me," in *Free Mind Magazine*, May/June 1997, http://shsny.org/pique/2003–01.html (accessed November 10, 2008).

[20] For an interesting insight into the questionable logic of atheistic theories on the origins of life, including Dawkins', "alien seeding" theory of the origin of life on earth, see B. Stein's film, *Expelled: No Intelligence Allowed* (2008).

[21] R. Dawkins, "Is Science a Religion?" *Humanist Magazine*, January/February 1997 (italics his), http://www.thehumanist.org/humanist/articles/dawkins.html (accessed November 8, 2008).

[22] L. Hyman, "What Humanism Means to Me."

[23] Kurtz and Wilson, *Humanist Manifesto II*.

is to reality. Secularism therefore rejects any idea of God or 'ultimate reality.'"[24] So secular humanism's theology is atheism. It holds with conviction the belief that God does not exist. In fact some humanists go further and deny anything that cannot be observed or tested: "Secularism denies that we need to go beyond the natural and social world to find the sources of confidence that can allow us to accept our existence with confidence."[25]

2. Evolution

Secular humanism believes the doctrine of evolution:

> Modern science discredits such historic concepts as the "ghost in the machine" and the "separable soul." Rather, science affirms that the human species is an emergence from natural evolutionary forces. As far as we know, the total personality is a function of the biological organism transacting in a social and cultural context.[26]

While debate rages over whether evolution has actually been scientifically proven, there can be no argument that at some point, evolutionists must *believe* certain things to be true. Secular humanism *believes* evolution is the answer to the question of how life began on earth. It also *believes* evolution explains how certain traits arose among mankind.

Moreover, secular humanists believe religion arose from evolutionary forces. "Much of it stems from genetically endowed aggressive instincts rooted in our hunter-gatherer ancestors."[27] Arguing that the tendency toward being religious is simply a "temptation," Kurtz wrote, "The hypothesis that I wish to offer is that the belief in the efficacy of prayer and the submission to divine power persists because it has had some survival value in the infancy of the race; powerful psycho-sociobiological factors are thus at work, predisposing humans to submit to the temptation."[28] For Kurtz, the rise of religious belief comes not from a true idea of the workings of the universe but from some ancient genetically driven psychological reaction. He argues that for some unexplained reason, humans with the capacity to believe in the supernatural survived to pass along their genetic predisposition to their offspring.[29]

3. Inherent goodness of man

Secular humanism assumes man is inherently good. Therefore humans inherently conceive moral values without the help of a transcendent deity:

---

[24] Haught, *What Is Religion?* 199.

[25] Ibid.

[26] Kurtz and Wilson, *Humanist Manifesto II*.

[27] F. March, "How to Counter Religion's Toxic Effects," http://www.thehumanist.org/humanist/Fred-March.html (accessed November 8, 2008).

[28] P. Kurtz, "Why Do People Believe or Disbelieve?" *Free Inquiry Magazine*, Summer 1999, http://www.secularhumanism.org/index.php?section=library&page=kurtz_19_3_1.

[29] For further discussion of the evolutionary theory of religion see chap. 4 ("Categories of Apologetics"). For a detailed critique of the theory of evolution, see chap. 26 ("The Compatibility of Biblical Truth and Modern Science").

We affirm that moral values derive their source from human experience. Ethics is autonomous and situational needing no theological or ideological sanction. Ethics stems from human need and interest. To deny this distorts the whole basis of life. Human life has meaning because we create and develop our futures. Happiness and the creative realization of human needs and desires, individually and in shared enjoyment, are continuous themes of humanism. We strive for the good life, here and now. The goal is to pursue life's enrichment despite debasing forces of vulgarization, commercialization, and dehumanization.[30]

Secular humanists *believe* that man, freed from the "constraints" of traditional religion, will strive for "the good life." They believe this results from evolutionary forces, that seeking morality is beneficial to the species of man. They do not generally explain how self-depreciating traits like selflessness, sacrificing oneself for another, or sharing things necessary for survival are traits that aid in the evolutionary model of biology.

C. By Their Own Admonition

The *Humanist Manifesto I* of 1933 assumes that secular humanism is a religion. In the introduction the *Manifesto* says that traditional religion contributed greatly to "this age" but is no longer sufficient. A new religion is needed, "shaped for the needs of this age." The authors of the *Manifesto* argued, "To establish such a religion is a major necessity of the present. It is a responsibility which rests upon this generation."[31] What followed in the *Manifesto* was, in essence, a doctrinal statement. The theme of humanism replacing traditional religion but not religion itself is laced through the document. The *Manifesto* says, "In the place of the old attitudes involved in worship and prayer the humanist finds his religious emotions expressed in a heightened sense of personal life and in a cooperative effort to promote social well-being."[32] In the *Manifesto* the goal of humanism is to infiltrate traditional religion, changing it to fit humanistic philosophy. "Religious institutions, their ritualistic forms, ecclesiastical methods, and communal activities must be reconstituted as rapidly as experience allows."[33] Nowhere in this first declaration is there a denunciation of religion. In fact the *Manifesto I* does just the opposite. It was an active attempt to establish a new religion, that of humanism.

II. Answering the Charges of Secular Humanists

Secular humanists affirm that people who believe in God are ignorant. They claim that theists simply "have not been exposed to the factual critiques of their faith."[34]

---

[30] Kurtz and Wilson, *Humanist Manifesto II*,

[31] R. B. Bragg et al., *Humanist Manifesto I,* American Humanist Association, http//w.w.w.americanhumanist.org/about/manifesto I. html (accessed November 6, 2008).

[32] Ibid.

[33] Ibid.

[34] P. Kurtz, "Why Do People Believe or Disbelieve?"

They argue, "There are alternative naturalistic explanations of the alleged phenomena . . . and if criticisms of the claims were made available to them, they would abandon their irrational beliefs."[35] Certainly this argument is narrow at best. This book effectively falsifies this claim, and it is but one among thousands of other works that deal with criticisms such as these.

While secular humanists theoretically argue against *any* religious belief, most of their criticisms focus on Christian beliefs.

A. The Bible

If secular humanism portrays the truth, and Christianity is false, then the writings Christians rely on for their beliefs must be false. C. Dennis McKinsey argued that there is a plethora of dangers in believing the Bible, all based in severe misunderstanding of the Bible itself. He claims that believing in the Bible causes everything from misogyny to anti-intellectualism, and even war.[36] Thus motivated, he offers a litany of the standard criticisms of the Bible: errors in dates, numbers, and "science," contradictions, borrowing from other religions, and outright deception. McKinsey's lack of literary scholarship is blatant and exemplifies the lengths to which secular humanism goes to argue against the Bible. Actually the Bible is the most reliable ancient document in the world. If what McKinsey and every other secular humanist says is true, then the written history of the ancient world must be relegated to myth. In truth, not only are ancient non-Christian sources used and considered reliable, but the Bible is far more so. For a full discussion of the reliability of the Bible, see chap. 22 ("How Reliable Are the Sources for Christian Truth?").

B. God

As already noted almost all secular humanists are atheists. They argue that science proves God does not exist. This "evidence" consists of the following logical argument. Theists invent God to explain "various phenomena." If these phenomena may be explained by something else, it "proves" God does not exist. Secular humanists claim that "science has shown, however, that these phenomena can be explained without invoking these entities."[37] Thus secular humanists think they have disproven God's existence. Their logical errors are exemplified by the argument, "By demonstrating that these entities are not needed to explain anything, science has proven that they do not exist."[38] This of course assumes that the only criteria for proving the existence of a being is that their existence is needed in order to explain something. The logical construction of their argument goes:

---

[35] Ibid.

[36] C. D. V. McKinsey, *The Encyclopedia of Biblical Errancy* (Amherst, NY: Prometheus, 1995), 482–85.

[37] T. Schick Jr., "Can Science Prove that God Does Not Exist?" in *Free Inquiry Magazine*, Winter 2001, http://www.secularhumanism.org/library/fi/schick_21_1.html (accessed November 8, 2008).

[38] Ibid.

People postulate the existence of things to explain certain phenomena (understood premise).

Things only exist if they explain certain phenomena (understood premise).

Theists postulate the existence of God to explain certain phenomena.

Certain phenomena can be explained by science.

Therefore God does not exist.

Beyond the formal logical fallacies,[39] this argument also suffers from unproven premises. While it is certainly true that myths are born from people attempting to explain certain phenomena, it is not true that *all supernatural things* are. Even more troubling is the assertion that things exist only if they explain phenomena. This makes the being's existence dependent on what it does. Almost anything might be doubted if this were the actual criteria for existence. Finally, the premise that "science" has proved the actual explanation for phenomena is false. One example is the origin of the universe. Secular humanists argue that God does not exist because science explains how the universe came to be, by the famous Big Bang theory. However, science cannot answer what *caused* the Big Bang, nor who or what provided the materials for the event (beyond its own beliefs and postulations). Therefore the phenomena of the origin of the universe, at least from a "scientific" standpoint, remain unexplained. Though this one phenomenon provides a sufficient argument against this premise, there are many, many more. The classical arguments for the existence of God—see chap. 3 ("Approaches to Apologetics") and chap. 17 ("Skepticism and Its Cure")—are not founded on arguable premises (much less formal logical fallacies) and therefore stand up against the logically fallacious secular humanist arguments against them.

C. Man

Secular humanists constantly espouse that man has been suppressed by traditional religion. They contend that the Bible's portrayal of man as a sinful being in need of salvation is wrong and that this is what has caused man's suffering. They argue that man is essentially good and will strive for good of his own accord when not "hindered" by traditional religious morality. Secularists charge that one's perception of morality is conditioned by traditional religion, and if people would free themselves from this bondage, they would realize that many of the things they think of as immoral are actually acceptable. However, history alone shows this is not the case. Almost without exception, removing the moral authority of biblical teaching in a society is detrimental. In those societies where atheism and evolution are promulgated, society suffers. When it is taught that people are simply the result of "an emergence from natural evolutionary forces,"[40] and that morality is nothing more than "generic human needs,"[41] people tend to do whatever they feel meets their needs. Secular governments have little qualm

---

[39] This argument commits a formal syllogistic fallacy of reaching a negative conclusion from positive premises.

[40] Kurtz and Wilson, *Humanist Manifesto II*.

[41] P. Kurtz, "The Ethics of Humanism without Religion" *Free Inquiry*, 1 (Winter 2003), http://www.secularhumanism.org/library/fi/kurtz_23_1_1.htm (accessed November 4, 2008).

over implementing policies that are harmful to people. People themselves increasingly have rank disregard for those around them, acting in their own perceived best interests. The drive for individual gratification at the expense of others has led to a society of ever-increasing pain and suffering. The Bible acknowledges this failing in humanity, ascribing it to mankind's sinful nature. Rather than trying to deny human sinfulness and brushing aside its effects, the Bible shows the only way for man to escape from his sinful state, and the Bible teaches morality that is antithetical to men's "natural" state. Rather than "oppressing" humanity, the Bible actually presents the only way for people to become free.

III. CHALLENGING SECULAR HUMANIST BELIEFS

The Christian apologist need not always be on the defensive. Secular humanist distinctives cannot bear scrutiny and need to be challenged. Though casting itself as the philosophy of "free thinkers" and intellectuals, secular humanism's beliefs are often logically unsound and factually false, often relying on emotion rather than reason (something secular humanists are loath to admit).

A. Atheism

Though secular humanists argue that "scientific advancement" has proven God does not exist, in fact, it is more correct to say secular humanism has *decided* God does not exist. Chap. 19 ("The Knowledge of God") has discussed the logical arguments for the existence of a supreme deity, and that the God of the Bible is the only deity that can logically exist. Secular humanists argue that God's existence is scientifically impossible, and therefore God does not exist. However, they fail to provide what basis they use for making these claims. Have they been able to set up an experiment that definitively proves God does not exist? If they have, they have not shared it. In reality, though, they argue that their denial of God rests in science, it actually rests in philosophy and logic. Their philosophical and logical arguments are easily shown to be false.

B. Evolution

Paul Kurtz wrote:

> The common moral decencies are transcultural in their range and have their roots in generic human needs. They no doubt grow out of the long evolutionary struggle for survival and may even have some sociobiological basis, though they may be lacking in some individuals or societies since their emergence depends upon certain preconditions of moral and social development.[42]

Kurtz lists several of these "elementary virtues" that arise from the human "struggle for survival":

---

[42] Kurtz, "The Ethics of Humanism Without Religion." Kurtz fails to define what these "precursors" are, but one could argue that religion is one of them.

truth telling,
trustworthiness or loyalty,
benevolence, or lack of malevolence, and
fairness.

He does not attempt to explain how these tendencies arose or how these specific virtues came about as a result of the human struggle for survival. Also he does not explain how theoretically there can be evolutionary advantages to lying, serving one's own interests, engaging in violence and cheating others. He fails to account for the tendency of humans to lose these "elementary virtues" when confronted with a struggle to survive.

Moreover, on many occasions "moral decencies" have evaporated after governmental authorities either suppressed or outlawed religious belief. If morality were indeed rooted in "genetic human needs," then removing artificial constraints such as religion would result in even greater morality. Yet this is simply not the case. While secular humanists argue that religion has caused the most conflict and suffering in the world, in truth militantly atheistic governmental regimes are responsible for far more human suffering. These antireligious governments were supposedly the "more evolved" forms of government. According to dialectical materialists (the philosophical forerunners of Frederick Engels and Karl Marx), evolution produces ever more complexity and quality. Societies that are seen as more complex are thought to be more evolved. Thus Marx argued that his theory of society was more evolved than anything that had come before it and should be "better" than "less-evolved" societies.

Applying this principle, however, produces a different result. Primitive societies that are theoretically "less evolved" often have a much greater sense of morality. Using the criteria Kurtz listed, atheistic societies (thought to be more evolved) are far more likely to engage in deception, often must use force to engender the loyalty of their people, often display rank malevolence to the common population, and are often patently unfair. Even in America, where traditional religion has not been outlawed but rather pushed out of public life, morality has declined steeply.

C. Man's Inherent Goodness

Secular humanism insists that ethics and morality are "autonomous and situational, needing no theological or ideological sanction. Ethics stems from human need and interest."[43] If this is the case, then humans should be allowed to decide what their interests should be. For example, it is often said that government cannot legislate morality and that individuals should be allowed to decide their own moral codes. In fact Kurtz argued that humans should be given autonomy. He said, "This means a person's ability to take control of his or her own life, to accept responsibility for one's own feelings, one's marriage or career, how he or she lives and learns, the values and goods one cherishes. Such a person is self-directed and self-governed. A person's autonomy is an

---

[43] Kurtz and Wilson, *Humanist Manifesto II*.

affirmation of one's freedom."[44] Yet Kurtz and Wilson, in the *Humanist Manifesto II,* under the section entitled "Democratic Society," assert the following.

> The principle of moral equality must be furthered through elimination of all discrimination based upon race, religion, sex, age, or national origin. This means equality of opportunity and recognition of talent and merit. Individuals should be encouraged to contribute to their own betterment. If unable, then society should provide means to satisfy their basic economic, health, and cultural needs, including, wherever resources make possible, a minimum guaranteed annual income.[45]

If human beings are basically good and do not need religion, why must "moral equality" be artificially enforced? If "autonomous" humans will naturally strive for the betterment of society, why do secular humanists argue that "society" should provide some a "guaranteed annual income"?

Further, what if a society decides it is in its needs and interest to engage in discrimination? Are they free to implement their morality? Certainly Nazi Germany argued that it was in their best interest to intern and ultimately murder huge numbers of their own society. Later, Chinese communists engaged in vast amounts of situational ethics, imprisoning and even putting to death those who were carrying out the previous commands of the party. These "reactionaries" were simply following the orders of their leaders, but unfortunately the ideology of their leaders changed. Those who were formally enjoying the benefits of obeying the Communist party suddenly found themselves discriminated against when the party decided to change for the "need" and "interest" of China. Those opposed to the civil rights movement in America argued that discrimination was necessary for the nation's societal needs. In 1939 Charles Magnum argued that the Jim Crow laws were "considered necessary to the continued tranquillity of the southern states."[46]

One may think it noble to assert the moral goodness of humanity, but in practice moral relativism resulting from a lack of external religious morality has led to enormous human suffering. When released from moral constraints of religious belief, humans will normally descend into all kinds of activities that are detrimental to themselves and others.[47] Many people, following a pragmatic philosophy, will do whatever they see as beneficial to themselves, and when they have been indoctrinated that they are the sole source of deciding what is beneficial, the result is often tragic.

D.   The Moving Target of Secular Humanistic Morality

On one hand often using words like "should" and "must" when referring to morality, Paul Kurtz seems to give credence to the accusation that secular humanist

---

[44] Kurtz, "The Ethics of Humanism without Religion."

[45] Kurtz and Wilson, *Humanist Manifesto II.*

[46] C. Mangum, *The Legal Status of the Negro* (Chapel Hill: University of North Carolina Press, 1940), 181.

[47] See T. Dalrymple, *Life at the Bottom: The Worldview That Makes the Underclass* (Lanham, MD: Iran R. Dee, 2001), for a vivid portrayal of what impact programs formulated from secular humanist philosophy have on society.

philosophy has no foundational morality. He argues that secular humanist moral values are simply "guidelines" subject to change. He wrote, "Morally developed human beings accept these [moral] principles and attempt to live by them because they understand that some personal moral sacrifices may be necessary to avoid conflict in living and working together."[48] The conclusion that may be drawn from this statement is that moral values may be discarded in the attempt to "avoid conflict" and "working together." Just such a situation was illustrated in the regimes of Nazi Germany and Communist China.

Secular humanism sometimes does acknowledge that Western society has seen a disturbing slide in moral values. Unfortunately the explanation often falls far short. Secular humanists Verne and Bonnie Bullough, in an article written about "moral decay," list several reasons for the increasing scarcity of moral values in society. They claim that "changes in society have undermined many traditional ways of doing things," leading to "the alienation which many feel, and has led to turn to drugs, alcohol, or other form of escape from reality."[49] They add, "We wish we as Humanists could claim responsibility for all of the things attributed to us by our opponents, but realistically it is the changes in society which are far more responsible than the organizational activities of the various Humanist groups."[50] In essence they are blaming the cart for being pulled by the horse. They are arguing that changes in society are to blame for undermining traditional values, rather than the other way around. They apparently do not consider that secular humanism's unrelenting undermining of the foundations of traditional morals may be contributing to these changes in society. In failing to accept blame, they instead say Christians are the problem because they have failed to teach their children "about the Bible they claim to revere." They argue, "They cannot blame that on secular schools."[51] In the end the Bulloughs, unable to accept the blame for the moral degradation that has resulted from the influence of secular humanisms, claim that there has actually been no decline in morality at all. Rather, they argue that "there has been a change in what is defined as moral by large parts of our society."[52] If anything, one could argue the moral degradation is even worse because the definition of what is moral is actually much less restrictive. Activities previously seen as immoral were restricted because of societal pressure against doing those acts.

For example whereas in previous generations pregnancy out of wedlock was viewed as a moral failure, today it is a widely accepted practice. As a result the number of single-parent households has skyrocketed. Secular humanists often argue that traditional models "regarding marriage and family life are liable to involve religious discrimination."[53] They see nothing wrong with "alternative" models of family rela-

---

[48] Kurtz, "The Ethics of Humanism without Religion".

[49] V. L. and B. Bullough, "Is There Moral Decay?" in *Humanism Today* 9 (1995): 4.

[50] Ibid

[51] Ibid., 6. This ignores the fact that the Bible used to be used in schools, until secular humanists were largely successful in removing biblical morality from public school curriculums.

[52] Ibid., 10.

[53] W. Kaminer, "Marriage, Religion, and the Law," in *Free Inquiry Magazine* 21 (2001), http://www.secularhumanism.org/library/fi/kaminer_21_4.html (accessed November 15, 2008).

tionships, and they argue that traditional family values actually leads to child abuse.[54] Yet in reality the societal acceptance of single parenthood has demonstrably led to far greater suffering for children. A recent study found that children living in single-parent households are twice as likely to be physically abused as children in two-parent households.[55]

Secular humanism, while claiming that morality is simply the result of human need, and is subject to change, nevertheless attempts to shift blame, denying declining morality and ignoring the detrimental effects of their arguments, when their philosophies produce negative results.

IV. CONCLUSION

Secular humanism is a religion despite the attempts of humanists to deny it. Humanism is a worldview based on certain beliefs, such as atheism, evolution, and man's inherent efforts to strive for good. Also secular humanism's arguments against Christian beliefs do not stand up. They are logically false and ignore evidence. Also secular humanism's beliefs cannot bear scrutiny. Atheism is not logically tenable; evolution does not explain morality; man is not inherently good, as evidenced by his actions; situational ethics often leads to catastrophic and tragic results.

By contrast, Christianity (as rightly practiced, being guided by the teachings of Jesus and the apostles) is a religion of hope and love that is compassionate toward others, stands up for the oppressed and afflicted, protects others, and seeks to bring the good news of the gospel to the lost and hurting world. Rather than looking inward and deriving worth from simply being human, as secular humanism does, Christianity looks outward and derives worth from glorifying the Creator and Lord of the universe.

---

[54] See R. Boston, "10 Reasons Why the Religious Right Is Not Pro-Family," in *Free Inquiry Magazine* 19 (1999), http://www.secularhumanism.org/library/fi/boston_19_1.html (accessed November 15, 2008). Boston argues that "many Religious Right groups, notably Dobson's Focus on the Family, actually advocate violence toward children. Dobson is a vocal proponent of corporal punishment." Unfortunately he makes this serious accusation without providing any evidence.

[55] According to a University of Pennsylvania Medical School study, quoted in "One-Parent Households Double Risk of Childhood Sex Abuse," *Science Daily*, March 14, 2007, http://www.sciencedaily.com/releases/2007/03/070313114303.htm (accessed November 6, 2008). See also R. B. Zuck, *Precious in His Sight: Children and Children in the Bible* (Grand Rapids: Baker, 1995), 28, 31–32, 36–37.

Chapter 29

ENGAGING THE POSTMODERNIST

THIS CHAPTER EXPLAINS HOW ONE MIGHT reason with a postmodernist and attempt, with the assistance of the Holy Spirit, to persuade him to abandon postmodernism and to embrace Christianity. The chapter reviews and develops in some measure the conclusions of chap. 18 ("Postmodernism and Defense of Christianity") and explores how the Christian might approach the task of evangelizing academic postmodernists, superficial postmodernists, and persons who display postmodernist attitudes without explicitly identifying themselves as postmodernists.

I.   WHAT IS THE POSTMODERN?

Although theorists of postmodernity differ radically in their conceptions of the postmodern era, they generally concur in characterizing it as one in which people no longer believe in (a) any metanarrative whatever; (b) the existence of unified human subjects; and (c) the possibility of accurately representing reality.

Persons who identify themselves as postmodernists recognize that vast numbers of individuals, especially in the developing world, do not share their generalized disbelief. Postmodernists, nonetheless, do accurately diagnose the general thrust of thinking among many academics in the humanities departments of secular universities; and they do not deny that modern and premodern modes of thought coexist with the attitudes they see as typical of postmodernity. One cannot reasonably accuse postmodernists therefore of taking the attitudes of others in their circles to be representative of humanity as a whole.

A.   Common Criticisms of Postmodernism

One can, however, level a number of legitimate criticisms at postmodernists, five of which were discussed in chap. 18. First, as Jürgen Habermas observes, postmodernism is itself a metanarrative and, therefore, undermines itself by repudiating all metanarratives; postmodernism is self-referentially incoherent.[1] Jean-François Lyotard, for

---

[1] J. Habermas, *The Philosophical Discourse of Modernity,* trans. F. Lawrence (Cambridge, MA: MIT, 1985), 125, 210, 286.

example, asked rhetorically, "Are 'we' [postmodernists] not telling the great narrative of the end of great narratives?"[2]

Second, as Habermas also demonstrates, postmodernists involve themselves in a performative contradiction when they attempt to deconstruct conventional logic and canons of interpretation; for they inevitably employ that logic and those canons in the process of their deconstruction.[3] In response, certain postmodernists grant that without the aid of the rules whose validity they contest, they could not mount a meaningful critique. They typically claim to uncover pervasive inadequacies in conventional logic and interpretation that would be problematic even if postmodernism were self-refuting. Suffice it to say that few academics outside of postmodernist circles find these putative inadequacies in conventional rationality at all problematic.

Third, postmodernism's avowed opposition to all metanarratives seems to disqualify it as a serious option for committed Christians; for Christianity is itself a metanarrative.

Fourth, the postmodernist's denial of the existence of unified human subjects renders postmodernism inadmissible for Christians inasmuch as human beings cannot justly suffer punishment or receive deliverance from deserved punishment in view of Christ's suffering, if they are not responsible for their sins.

Fifth, the postmodernist denial that human beings can represent and thereby know reality as it is renders it incompatible with any simultaneously credible and orthodox Christian theology. Admittedly certain Christian theologians regard postmodernity as a boon to Christianity because it smashes what they take to be the idols of universally available, nonnarrative truth and foundationalism: the view that one can legitimately consider justified only those beliefs that have some more or less demonstrable link with reality.[4] In an atmosphere of skepticism about the possibility of universal truths and rational methods of defending and criticizing the claims of faith, such persons contend, a more or less fideistic and irrationalistic theology can gain a sympathetic hearing.

Such "postmodern" theologians, their praiseworthy intentions notwithstanding, seem gravely to underestimate the centrality both of universally available truth and of a moderate foundationalism to orthodox Christianity. As seen in chap. 6 ("The Tension Between Faith and Reason"), Paul argues in Romans 1 that human beings are responsible for their sin of idolatry because they have a knowledge of God. He wrote:

---

[2] J.-F. Lyotard, *The Differend: Phrases in Dispute* (Manchester, UK: Manchester University Press, 1988), 135.

[3] Habermas, *The Philosophical Discourse of Modernity,* 185.

[4] The most distinguished Christian theologian, who is: (a) even nearly sympathetic to the notion of an objectively true gospel that the church ought to propagate; and (b) nevertheless, openly sympathetic to postmodernism, is surely John Milbank, intellectual fountainhead of the movement known as Radical Orthodoxy. His magnum opus is *Theology and Social Theory: Beyond Secular Reason* (London: Blackwell, 1993). Evangelical thinkers sympathetic to postmodernism include John Franke and the late Stanley Grenz (cf. their pioneering joint work, *Beyond Foundationalism: Shaping Theology in a Postmodern Context* [Louisville: Westminster John Knox, 2001]) and James K. A. Smith (cf. his *Who's Afraid of Postmodernism? Taking Derrida, Foucault, and Lyotard to Church* [Grand Rapids: Baker Academic, 2006]).

> The wrath of God is revealed from heaven against all ungodliness and unrighteousness of men, who suppress the truth in unrighteousness, because what may be known of God is manifest in them, for God has shown it to them. For since the creation of the world His invisible attributes are clearly seen, being understood by the things that are made, even His eternal power and Godhead, *so that they are without excuse*. (Rom 1:18–20 NKJV, italics added)

If human responsibility for the sin of idolatry is contingent on knowledge of the one, true God, parity of reasoning suggests, human guilt for offenses committed against all the Ten Commandments must be contingent on knowledge of the moral law as well. Romans 2:15, moreover, implies that human beings naturally possess such knowledge. Paul wrote that when Gentiles obey the dictates of their conscience in some measure, they "show that the work of the law is written on their hearts." The gospel message, furthermore, presupposes in its hearers an implicit awareness of God's existence, His justice, and His truthfulness. Admittedly converts to Christianity almost never possess a well-developed natural theology of their own before they embrace the salvation offered to them in the gospel. Nevertheless to deny the existence of a natural revelation would be to portray the act of faith as a leap into the dark, unsupported by sound reasoning. This would defeat the purpose of apologetics.

B. Conclusions

The postmodernists' denial that one can know of Christianity's truthfulness, then, perverts reasonable Christian faith into the rationally unjustifiable—what one ordinarily refers to as superstition. Along with postmodernism's self-refuting qualities, its opposition to Christianity as a metanarrative, and its denial of individual responsibility for previously committed sins, this consideration warrants a skeptical attitude on the part of Christians to postmodernism.

II. Witnessing to Persons Sympathetic to Postmodernism

The present section provides some guidance for defending one's faith and commending Christianity to three categories of persons associated in some way with postmodernism: academic postmodernists, superficial postmodernists, and persons who display postmodernist attitudes without explicitly describing themselves as postmodernists.

A. Academic Postmodernists

1. Who are the academic postmodernists?

Academic postmodernists are professional academics who understand postmodernism, are well versed in postmodernist literature, and have integrated postmodernism into a carefully thought-out worldview. They bring postmodernist perspectives to bear on the most diverse disciplines and thereby spread postmodernist ideas far beyond the rather narrow circle of persons who would naturally be inclined to read works by Jacques Derrida or Jean-François Lyotard. Disciplines in which postmodernist scholars work include art history,[5] education,[6] film studies,[7] geography,[8] history,[9] lesbigay studies,[10] linguistics,[11] literary criticism,[12] literary theory,[13] musicology,[14] nursing,[15] philosophy,[16] political science,[17] psychiatry,[18] psychology,[19] and sociology.[20] It is unlikely that a student in any discipline, and especially a humanities major, will pass through any secular university without encountering one or more professors with postmodernist sentiments.

2. How to recognize a postmodernist academic

In certain cases it is not difficult to distinguish a postmodernist academic from an ordinary professor. First, postmodernists tend to include relatively frequent references to luminaries of postmodernism such as Jacques Derrida and Michel Foucault. One does not ordinarily expect, for example, the ideas of Derrida to figure prominently in a work on nursing administration. Yet Michael Traynor, a postmodernist professor of nursing at Middlesex University, London, mentions Derrida on 21 of the 192 pages of his *Managerialism and Nursing: Beyond Oppression and Profession*.[21] If a professor peppers his lectures on, say, the history of the American West with references to figures such as Jean Baudrillard and Georges Bataille, one may be reasonably certain that he harbors postmodernist sympathies.

---

[5] I. Sandler, *Art of the Postmodern Era: From the Late 1960's to the Early 1990's* (Boulder, CO: Westview, 1998).

[6] A. de Alba, *Curriculum in the Postmodern Condition* (New York: Peter Lang, 2000).

[7] J. P. Natoli's, *Postmodern Journeys: Film and Culture 1996–1998* (New York: SUNY, 2001).

[8] M. J. Dear, *The Postmodern Urban Condition* (London: Blackwell, 2000).

[9] H. White, *The Content of the Form: Narrative Discourse and Historical Representation* (Baltimore and London: Johns Hopkins University Press, 1987).

[10] L. L. Doan, *The Lesbian Postmodern* (New York and London: Columbia University Press, 1994).

[11] R. Melrose, *The Margins of Meaning: Arguments for a Postmodern Approach to Meaning and Text* (Atlanta: Rodopi, 1996).

[12] C. Caramello, *Silverless Mirrors: Book, Self, and Postmodern American Fiction* (Tallahassee, FL: University Presses of Florida, 1983).

[13] L. Hutcheson, *A Poetics of Postmodernism: History, Theory, Fiction* (New York: Routledge, 1988).

[14] L. Kramer, *Classical Music and Postmodern Knowledge* (Los Angeles: University of California Press, 1996).

[15] M. J. Watson, *Postmodern Nursing and Beyond* (New York: Elsevier, 1999).

[16] M. Luntley, *Reason, Truth, and Self: The Postmodern Reconditioned* (New York: Routledge, 1995).

[17] P. van Ham, *European Integration and the Postmodern Condition: Governance, Democracy, Identity* (New York: Routledge, 2001).

[18] G. G. Globus, *The Postmodern Brain* (Philadelphia: John Benjamins, 1995).

[19] H. Anderson, *Conversation, Language, and Possibilities: A Postmodern Approach to Therapy* (New York: Basic, 1997).

[20] J. Choi, *Postmodern American Sociology: A Response to the Aesthetic Challenge* (Lanham, MD: University Press of America, 2004).

[21] M. Traynor, *Managerialism and Nursing: Beyond Oppression and Profession* (London: Routledge, 1999).

Second, postmodernist academics are notorious for employing postmodernist jargon. If a professor incessantly speaks of alterity, *différance*, logocentrism, "the Other," metanarratives, imbrication, decentering, "the social construction of reality," bricolage, and "the transcendental signifier," he is almost certainly an adherent of postmodernism or some closely related school of thought.

Third, a professor who rails against claims to absolute truth or even against assertions that absolute truth is attainable is, if not a self-styled postmodernist, at least inordinately attached to central tenets of postmodernism: viz. general skepticism and the universal rejection of metanarratives.

3. Why concern oneself with witnessing to postmodernist academics?

Most Christians, admittedly, do not live near secular university campuses and thus have little or no contact with academic postmodernists. Postmodernist academics, moreover, have frequently invested a great deal of their prestige in the superiority of postmodernism. They are aware of common arguments against postmodernism and usually are proficient in rebutting them. If they embrace Christianity, they will almost certainly face ostracism by colleagues, and if they have not yet received tenure, they may face an abrupt end to their academic careers. One might, therefore, think it a waste of time for a pastor or lay Christian to consider arguments that might prove useful in witnessing to academic postmodernists.

A number of considerations, however, suggest that this enterprise may be worthwhile after all. Academics, especially those who spend most of their time writing rather than teaching, can wield an extraordinary amount of influence on society as a whole. Through books and articles they can influence the thinking of professors and students alike. Even moderating such a person's skepticism of and disdain for Christianity can prove enormously beneficial in the long term.

The prejudices against and ignorance about conservative Christianity that characterize most postmodernist academics, moreover, are often so extreme that one can easily correct them. One of us, for example, once heard one of the world's leading experts on the philosophy of G. W. F. Hegel announce to a class that it is uncertain whether Jesus actually existed. It requires only a slight knowledge of historical Jesus studies to disabuse someone of such a misperception. Likewise, numerous postmodernist academics have either not interacted with evangelicals at all or interacted only with persons who reinforced the centuries-old stereotype of evangelicals as narrow-minded ignoramuses. An evangelical Christian who speaks fluently, does not commit grammatical errors, and is aware and appreciative of the difficulties that lead intellectuals to dismiss Christianity as implausible can disabuse a postmodernist academic of some prejudices in the space of a few conversations. Witnessing to the academic postmodernist himself therefore is unquestionably a worthwhile enterprise.

Considering arguments that might be useful when witnessing to a postmodernist academic, moreover, can prove useful for a more obviously pressing task: viz. inoculating college-bound youth against the insidious influence of postmodernist ideas. If students have some sense of what postmodernism is and why it is incorrect, they will be less likely to succumb to attempts to persuade them to adopt a postmodernist worldview. If the pastors of today want to avoid losing the best and brightest of their church's young people to postmodernism or kindred anti-Christian worldviews, they have ample motive to consider, in some detail, how one might attempt to refute the errors of a postmodernist professor.

4. Strategies of argument

Habermas proposes two devastating arguments against postmodernism. First, postmodernism refutes itself by rejecting all metanarratives, since postmodernism itself is a metanarrative. Postmodernism, therefore, is self-contradictory. Second, postmodernists cannot so much as criticize conventional logic, with its principles of noncontradiction, excluded middle, etc., without employing that very logic. In a sense therefore postmodernism is hypocritical; the postmodernist skewers others for placing trust in certain principles and then grounds his own deeply held beliefs in precisely the same principles. The following supplements these points with three additional arguments against postmodernism, two ethical and the last epistemological.

a. Ethical concerns

Postmodernism at least appears to be ethically problematic for two reasons.

i. Relativism. First, if every metanarrative is false, totalitarian, and deserving of relentless critique, then it would seem that no metanarrative about right and wrong can be worthy of obedience. To this charge the postmodernist would presumably respond that in rejecting metanarratives he does not mean to forbid persons from acting on moral concerns. He would affirm that in opposing metanarratives he is taking the moral high ground, defending the marginalized against ideologies imposed by the ruling classes that exclude them.

Be that as it may, the Christian could reply, cultivating suspicion toward metanarratives is likely to deaden one's moral sensibilities. Skepticism about the absoluteness of moral norms invites persons to justify apathy. Would a relativist, one might ask, be as likely as a believer in absolute morality to rescue a child from a burning house, to volunteer to help disaster victims, or to reduce his own standard of living so that others could enjoy the barest necessities? The answer is obvious: of course not.

The postmodernist might retort that by adopting a relativist stance in questions of moral obligation, he does not mean to assert that moral obligation is an illusion but only that it is relative to one's time and culture. He does not want to paralyze moral action but to encourage deliberation before action and to inculcate understanding for offenders against accepted moral codes.

Deliberation, the Christian could reply, is vitally necessary in countless instances and frequently neglected to the detriment of the common good. However, most human beings rarely face complex moral dilemmas. The duties they notoriously neglect are simple and straightforward. It seems clear, therefore, that human beings' moral sensibilities, perhaps especially in the industrialized West, are abysmally dull. Before assenting to some proposed theory of moral obligation, one ought to ask, "Will this theory sharpen the moral sensibilities of the privileged peoples of the world, or will it render them even more immune to all sense of their duty?" A theory of morals (which postmodernism is, at least by default) that leads to the latter outcome is unworthy of acceptance.

ii. Negation of a unified, human subject. Second postmodernism appears ethically problematic because of its rejection of the unity of the human subject. According to the postmodernist, unified human subjects simply do not exist. In other words, no one is a single entity, that endures through time, to which one can reasonably ascribe intentions and acts. That which can neither act nor intend, however, cannot be subject to moral responsibility. Postmodernism seems, therefore, to absolve its adherents of ethical obligations entirely.

A postmodernist might reply that one ought, at least in certain instances, to treat human beings as if they were unified subjects because this is a useful fiction. If, however, one reduces the human and his duty to the status of a useful fiction, one incurs difficulties similar to those explored in the previous objection. One can responsibly adopt the notion of personal unity as a useful fiction, moreover, only after one has answered the question: useful to whom?

The proposal that one act as if all human beings were unified subjects might not appear useful at all to someone facing the prospect of punishment for a previously committed crime. The idea might seem similarly unsavory to someone contemplating performing an act that is morally unacceptable to his community. Admittedly, a postmodernist could observe, moral imperatives override the interests of wrongdoers and might appear therefore to mandate the adoption of the fiction. Yet if the unity of the human subject is a mere fiction, then moral imperatives can hardly be binding; if there are no unified human subjects, no one exists to whom these imperatives might apply. The earnest postmodernist naturally does not mean to cast morality to the wind. When he denies the unity of the human person, however, he seems to be depriving morality of all rational foundation.

b. An epistemological argument

Although the term *epistemological* may suggest that this final argument against postmodernism is complex, it is actually quite simple. Human beings can know of at least some reality external to themselves with a reasonable degree of accuracy and with certainty. This is another way of saying that humans can know some, though perhaps only a few absolute truths. This is an article of sanity. According to postmodernists, however, and especially the disciples of Jacques Derrida, human beings find themselves trapped in a world of signs and cannot by any means gain knowledge of a "transcendental signified": i.e., extralinguistic or, better still, suprasemiotic reality.

The postmodernist position on this subject, admittedly, is not altogether indefensible. Human beings gain knowledge of external reality, at least initially, exclusively through the senses, and no one can escape his senses and verify through some nonsensory mode of perception that reality actually conforms to the senses' impression of it.

Persons tend to perceive data through ideological lenses, moreover, that distort them in such a way as to confirm previously existing worldviews.

After millennia of trial and error, however, human beings have learned reliably to distinguish genuine perceptions from hallucinations and optical illusions. Likewise humans are able to detect ideological bias in the interpretation of data and to differentiate credible from incredible testimony. Beginning from the testimony of his senses as to his immediate surroundings, therefore, the human person can gain a wide swath of knowledge about human events and the natural world. Naturally, one must exercise caution to avoid assenting to plausible falsehoods and dissenting from impalatable but well-documented truths. It is irrational, however, to believe that one lives in an atmosphere not of reality but of hyperreality, that realism is a sham, or that mathematical and scientific commonplaces merit suspicion.

To abandon such a radically skeptical attitude towards human knowledge, however, is to abandon the first and third of the three planks of postmodernism identified in chap. 8 ("Speaking About God and Ultimate Reality"): incredulity toward metanarratives, disbelief in the existence of unified human subjects, and the denial that human beings can accurately represent reality. As to the third, if human beings can attain certain knowledge of the extramental world, then the human mind can represent at least aspects of this world with some reasonable degree of accuracy. As to the first, moreover, one who admits that he can know objective truth thereby commits himself at least implicitly to the metanarrative of realism. In fact to acknowledge that one can know something of the world with certainty involves an implicit rejection of postmodernism's second plank as well; the existence of certain human knowledge presupposes the existence of human subjects who know. Rationality, in sum, mandates assent to realism, and such assent is incompatible with central tenets of postmodernism.

B. Superficial Postmodernists

Superficial postmodernists are undergraduates who declare themselves postmodernists after (a) taking a class from a charismatic, postmodernist professor or listening to a lecture by him or her or (b) reading a book or article, usually one assigned by a professor, whose author argues persuasively for postmodernism. The postmodernism of such persons is, at least initially, superficial because they possess scant familiarity with or understanding of postmodernist writings and ideas. They are impulsively taking up an intellectual fad. The arguments above, addressed to the academic postmodernist, perhaps in tandem with the less complex responses outlined below, should suffice to refute any defenses of his or her new worldview the superficial postmodernist might propose.

C. Persons Who Display Postmodernist Attitudes Without Identifying Themselves as Postmodernists

The following pages include remarks and replies useful in conversing with persons who are not intellectuals but who hold vaguely postmodernist sentiments.

1. *"Christian beliefs about hell are cruel"*

To the accusation, "It is cruel for you to think that people who do not believe as you do will go to hell," one could respond in words such as the following:

> Is it cruel to believe that people with no food will starve? Of course not. It's unpleasant to think about millions starving in the third world, and it bothers my conscience that I don't do more to help them. But it would be wrong for me to soothe my conscience by pretending that everyone has plenty of food. Likewise, it's painful to think about people going to hell; and it's even worse to think that in many cases the suffering of those people is partially my fault. But it would be criminal of me simply to pretend that there's no problem. As a Christian, I know that there's a problem and that it's my responsibility to do something about it.

2. *"Christians are arrogant"*

To the accusation, "It is arrogant of you to believe that your religion is true, and that everyone else's is false," one could reply as follows:

> I have three responses. First, I believe the claims of the Bible are entirely true, but I do not think every one of my religious beliefs is true. The odds are overwhelming that at least some of them are false. Second, I do not believe that everyone else's religion is 100 percent false. Judaism, Islam, and even Hinduism and Buddhism teach many truths that Christianity also teaches, and when they speak on those subjects, I say "Amen." But, third, to get to the heart of the matter, everyone who holds any religious belief or for that matter any belief at all contradicts everyone who believes otherwise than he does. That is not being arrogant; that is being human.

3. *"Religion causes violence"*

To the accusation, "Religion causes violence," one could respond,

> So does law enforcement, but that doesn't mean we can do without it. To the probable reply, "But we need law enforcement," one could reply, "If Christianity is true, we need Christianity even more. The issue between us is not whether Christianity causes violence; the issue is whether Christianity is true."

4. *"Religion causes war"*

To the accusation, "Religion causes war," one might respond:

> All kinds of strongly held beliefs, whether good or evil, cause war. Belief in democracy and the right to self-determination led to the American Revolution and countless other wars; that is a good belief, and yet it led to war. Communism caused the Russian and Chinese revolutions, the Korean War, the Vietnam War, the Cultural Revolution, and the killing fields of Cambodia; that was an evil belief, and it led to war. Both good and evil beliefs can

lead to war. Therefore one cannot reasonably reject religion as such simply because it leads to war.

5. *"Christianity has a bad record of violence"*

To the accusation, "Christianity has a lot of blood on its hands; consider the Crusades, the Inquisition, the Wars of Religion in the seventeenth century, etc.," one could respond:

> Every country that professes to believe in a religion invariably invokes that religion's support when it goes to war. True it's shameful that countries that call themselves Christian, inaccurately in my view, have shed so much of each others' blood. But I don't think for a minute that those nations were led to go to war out of loyalty to Jesus, who taught believers to love their enemies and to do to others what they would want done to them.

6. *"Christianity is a ruse of the powerful"*

To the accusation, "Religion is just something the ruling classes invented to keep the poor under control," one might respond:

> If that's true, why does the Bible say such negative things about rich people? James 5:1–6, for example, says, "Come now, you rich people! Weep and wail over the miseries that are coming on you. Your wealth is ruined and your clothes are moth-eaten. Your silver and gold are corroded, and their corrosion will be a witness against you and will eat your flesh like fire. You stored up treasure in the last days! Look! The pay that you withheld from the workers who reaped your fields cries out, and the outcry of the harvesters has reached the ears of the Lord of Hosts. You have lived luxuriously on the land and have indulged yourselves. You have fattened your hearts for the day of slaughter. You have condemned —you have murdered—the righteous man, he does not resist you."

That doesn't sound like a rich man's religion to me.

7. *"It is pretentious to claim to know that your religion is true"*

To the accusation, "It's insane to say that you know all these details about what God does and does not want; you just can't know about those things," one could respond:

> First, I agree that the Christian's claim that he knows Christianity to be true is a bold claim. It's not half as bold, however, as your claim to know that God could not inform His people of all these things. Second, I don't pretend to be able to prove every article of my creed on the basis of independent evidence; if I know that Jesus is God, everything else follows from that. For that claim I have abundant evidence. God confirmed Jesus' teachings by raising Him from the dead. The birth and early expansion of Christianity would have been impossible if Christianity were not true. Biblical

prophecies uttered hundreds and sometimes thousands of years before the event have proven accurate in the minutest details, and no biblical prophecy has ever been proven false. My own experience, the experience of all other Christians, and the collective wisdom of the Christian tradition, which includes people who know more about these things than you or I ever will, all support this point. I'll grant Christianity's truthfulness is not so obvious that someone determined not to be a Christian cannot find an excuse. But I think that the evidence on the whole is quite substantial and that the Christian position is very reasonable.

This reply alone will lead few, if any, skeptics to take the claims of Christianity seriously. However, it may lead to further conversation about individual items of evidence for the Christian religion, which, given time and the work of the Holy Spirit, may yield eventual persuasion.

III. CONCLUSION

It is unquestionable that the postmodernist ideology cultivated in academia and the relativistic, anti-Christian mentality it fosters in society present formidable challenges to today's Christian apologist. As seen, however, the postmodernist position is untenable for at least five reasons. First, although it vehemently condemns any and all metanarratives, it is itself a metanarrative. Second, it relies on the putatively modern Western logic that it condemns to critique that logic. Third, it undermines all systems of morality by its relativism. Fourth, it exculpates every human being from responsibility for his acts by denying the existence of unified, human subjects. Fifth and finally, postmodernism denies the possibility that humans can know objective reality, which denial, incidentally, is itself a singularly sweeping and implausible claim about objective reality. Postmodernist worldviews, then, are sufficiently vulnerable to critique that the Christian may proceed confidently in engaging and evangelizing persons influenced by postmodernism.

Chapter 30

ENGAGING THE MUSLIM

ISLAM, THE SECOND LARGEST RELIGION IN the world, has emerged as a formidable theological and social alternative to Christianity. Recent statistics have numbered Muslim adherents at over one billion and Christians at two billion, making half the world's six billion people either Muslim or Christian. With statistics like these, Muslims and Christians will inevitably come into contact with each other, placing a higher premium on affective ways to communicate the gospel across theological and cultural boundaries. Both Islam and Christianity are missionary religions offering a comprehensive worldview that demands wholehearted and intellectual commitment of its followers. Despite the similarities between the two Abrahamic religions, there are theological, philosophical, and social differences. The challenge for Christian evangelism and apologetics is to discern crucial Islamic ideas that conflict with orthodox Christianity and to enter into positive conversation without being unnecessarily offensive. In three significant areas Muslims and Christians disagree: theology, philosophy, and society. Successful encounters with Muslims depend somewhat on the degree to which the apologist understands these ideas and can respond to the tenets of Islam.

I.   THEOLOGICAL ENGAGEMENT

A. God

The oneness and unity of Allah, known as *Tawhid*, is considered the theological hub in the wheel of Islam. The Qur'an (Sura 112) reflects this essential doctrine when it reads "He is God, The One and Only; God, the Eternal, Absolute; He begetteth not, Nor is He begotten," thus to associate partners with Allah is to commit a "most heinous sin" known as *shirk* (cp. Sura 4:48). It is here that Islam confronts the Christian notion of the Trinity, which espouses that God is three distinct persons in one essence or nature. The Muslim misunderstanding revolves around two issues: the *identity* of the persons within the Trinity and the apparent logical *contradiction* implied by "three in one." First, one can gently correct the mistaken Muslim view that the Trinity consists of the Father, Jesus, and Mary (Sura 5:119) by asserting the orthodox position as the Father, the Son, and the Holy Spirit. This misunderstanding may be partly due to pseudo-Christian exposure in Arabia such as the Collyridians, which according to

Epiphanius (*d.* 403), were a fourth-century sect of women who worshipped Mary.[1] A second cause of this misunderstanding may be associated with certain Islamic scholars, such as Abdullah Yusuf Ali, who have mistakenly claimed that the worship of Mary was widespread in pre-seventh century AD Christian churches both in the East and the West.[2] Third, the apparent contradiction implied in Trinitarian theology can be clarified by offering the Muslim real objective examples of other three-in-one relationships such as a triangle shape or mathematical equations.

Objective examples are both a positive and nonpartisan method of engagement that many would accept as common ground (cf. Acts 17:22–23,28). For example a *single* triangle is a geometric object with *three* distinct sides and intersecting points. The essence or nature of the geometric figure is one (i.e. a triangle), while simultaneously possessing three distinct sides or intersecting points to the triangle. Each intersecting point is unique to itself, wholly distinct from the other points. The Trinity is much the same, three distinct *persons* (i.e., *who* one is) share one divine *essence* or *nature* (i.e., *what* one is). Moreover, the equation $1 \times 1 \times 1 = 1$ or 1^3 can convey the idea of multiple and distinct numbers equivalent to one and offer a plausible alternative to the Muslim notion of $1+1+1=3$. In addition Muslim ideas of the relationship between the Qur'an and Allah may serve as a theological argument in favor of multiplicity within unity. For example Muslims view the Qur'an as eternal (85:21–22), "the essence of God's Will and Law,"[3] which is not identical to Allah.

The Qur'an is seen as a material and ideological expression and manifestation of Allah yet distinct from him. In a sense Allah has incarnated himself in the Qur'an much the same way God was incarnated in Christ, which calls for some degree of multiplicity within unity. This idea is not foreign to earlier Abrahamic religions (Judaism and Christianity). Of particular importance is the Hebrew vocabulary of the revered Shema of Deut 6:4, which reads, "Listen, Israel: The LORD our God, the LORD is *One*." The Hebrew word for "one" is *echad,* which is closely related to *yahad,* meaning "to be united." The *Echad* stresses unity while recognizing diversity within that oneness.[4] For example Gen 2:24 uses *echad* when referring to the *two*, Adam and Eve, becoming "one [*echad*] flesh," which allows for multiplicity within unity. If the author of Deuteronomy wanted to convey the idea of absolute oneness without multiplicity, then *yacheed* would have been a better choice. Therefore one must allow for the possibility of multiplicity within unity in the Godhead. Unlike Islam's *absolute* monotheism, Christianity possesses a *compound* monotheism.

---

[1] Epiphanius, *Haeracas*, 79, in P. Schaff, *History of the Christian Church* (1914; reprint, Peabody, MA: Hendrickson, n.d.), vol. 3, chap. 7, §82.

[2] Abdullah Yusuf Ali, *The Holy Qur'an: Text, Translation and Commentary* (Tahrik Tarsile Qur'an Inc), 280, n. 829.

[3] Ibid, 616, n. 1864.

[4] R. L. Harris, G. L. Archer, and B. K. Waltke, *Theological Wordbook of the Old Testament* (Chicago: Moody, 1980), 30.

B. The Son of God

As a result of Sura 112, "He [Allah] neither begets nor is begotten," Therefore Muslims emphatically deny that Jesus Christ is the Son of God or is the Messiah of God. As early as AD 691 Muslims inscribed these words of Sura 112 inside the Dome of the Rock in Jerusalem. To the Muslims, the notion of Christ's sonship is repugnant since it ascribes partners to Allah by attributing deity to Christ and it allows the possibility of God procreating a son.[5] Though communication regarding this subject can be highly volatile, it can be overcome by clarifying what is meant by the phrase "Son of God." Traditionally it refers to a functional title identifying His relationship to the other members of the Trinity. In no way does it refer to a procreated son by natural means. The "Son of God" is not referring to *biological* sonship; rather it illustrates His capacity of *office*, meaning that Christ is *eternally* the *relational* and *functional* Son of God. This avoids the Muslim contention that God would need a wife and that a son can only be generated through natural means (Sura 6:101).

Perhaps the most constructive engagement at this point would be to draw on examples that are familiar and acceptable to the Islamic world. Like the English language, which allows for flexibility in the usage of words, the Arabic word *ibn* allows for the metaphorical usage of the word "son," while *walad* conveys the idea of literal sonship. Therefore Christ may be seen as the *Ibn* of God and not the *Walad* of God. Further the Qur'an allows for the possibility of Allah having a son. "Had God wished to take to Himself a son, He could have Chosen whom He pleased Out of those whom He doth create: but glory be to Him! (He is above such things.) He is God, the One, the Irresistible" (39:4). It appears the Qur'an seems to allow for the *possibility* of Allah having a son but rejects the *actuality* of the event. If it is *possible* for God to have a son, as the Qur'an asserts, then one must remove the notion from the realm of impossibility.

In denying Christ's deity and Sonship, Muslims also reject the idea that Jesus Christ is the Messiah. Though Muslims often attribute to Jesus terms of respect as one of their prophets such as "eminence" or "peace be upon him," these terms are not used of Christ in the Qur'an. Eleven times Jesus is referred to in the Qur'an as *Al-masihu Isa* ("the messiah Jesus"; 3:45; 4:157, 171–72; 9:31) along with the definite article ("the") thereby stressing His unique personal title and mission. Although the word for "Messiah" is never used without the article and of no other person except Christ Himself, little explanation is offered by Muslim scholars.[6]

C. The Scriptures

Since Muslims accept the Torah (*Tawrat*), Psalms (*Zabur*), and the four Gospels (*Injil*), constructive engagement based on common scriptural ground can involve discussions of the Christian Scriptures. In addition, figures such as Abraham, Moses, David, and Jesus are revered by Muslims as prophets, among thousands of others. Despite these similarities with Christianity, the biblical books are considered corrupted and

---

[5] Ali, *The Qur'an*, 1237, n. 4246.
[6] G. Parrinder, *Jesus in the Qur'an* (Oxford: One World 1995), 30.

viewed with suspicion, or must be reinterpreted to be consistent with Islamic theology. At this point several areas can be discussed, including manuscripts, archaeology, and Qur'anic testimony to the Bible. Each area offers information that can illuminate the truth and build confidence in the reliability of the Old and New Testaments.

First, one can acknowledge the precision with which medieval Muslim scribes copied the Qur'an through the centuries. The Topkapi Qur'an in Istanbul, Turkey, and the Samarqand Qur'an in Tashkent, Uzbekistan, date to the second century after Muhammad's death with little thematic differences. The Arabic manuscript fragments housed at the British Museum and other institutions around the world are fairly consistent with one another. However, this falls well short of the claim that the Qur'an has been preserved in its original pure and holy Arabic form free from corruption, inventions, and accretions since the time of Muhammad (Sura 15:9; 43:3–4).[7] Scholars have cited several significant differences between the Uthmanic and Ibn Masud texts as well as the Hafs (used in most of the Islamic world) and Warsh (used in West and Northwest Africa as well as Yemen) transmissions of the Qur'an.[8] Islamic scholar Ali Dashti describes the grammatical irregularities (e.g., Sura 4:160; 20:66; 74:1) in the Qur'an when he writes,

> The Qur'an contains sentences that are incomplete and not fully intelligible without the aid of commentaries; foreign words, unfamiliar Arabic words, and words used with other than the normal meaning; adjectives and verbs inflected without observance of the concord of gender and number; illogical and ungrammatically applied pronouns that sometimes have no referent.[9]

Moreover, problems of historical accuracy have arisen. For example, Sura 20:87, 94 identifies a "Samaritan" (*Samariyyu*) as the one responsible for instigating calf worship in Exodus 32, though Samaritans were not a people group until hundreds of years later. In addition, Sura 21:68–69 says Nimrod threw Abraham into the fire in an act of bitter hostility, but Nimrod came in the third generation after Noah while Abraham was in the tenth generation after Noah (Gen 10:22–25; 11:13–25). Sura 7:124 and 12:41 describe Pharaoh threatening to *crucify* those who followed Moses nearly a thousand years before crucifixion was practiced by the Persians, Romans, and Carthegenians from the sixth century BC through the fourth century AD.[10]

By contrast the New Testament's transmission and reconstruction is supported by over 5,700 Greek manuscripts and over 24,000 manuscripts in all languages, with Homer's *Illiad* a distant second place with truly about 643 manuscripts. The quantity and quality of manuscripts led Princeton scholar Bruce Metzger to estimate that the

---

[7] Ali, *The Qur'an*, 638, n. 1944.

[8] See A. Brockett, "The Value of the Hafs and Warsh Transmissions for the Textual History of the Qur'an," in *Approaches to the History of the Interpretation of the Qur'an,* ed. A. Rippin (Oxford: Clarendon Press, 1988).

[9] Ali Dashti, *Twenty-three Years: A Study of the Prophetic Career of Mohammad* (London: Allen & Unwin, 1985), 48–49.

[10] See M. Hengel, *Crucifixion in the Ancient World and the Folly of the Message of the Cross* (Philadelphia: Fortress, 1977).

New Testament is copied at a 99 percent plus accuracy rate. The manuscript quantity and quality comparison between the Bible and the Qur'an becomes more dramatic when one notes that the Bible is an earlier *ancient* book while the Qur'an is a much later *medieval* work. This however, does not persuade the Muslim objector who claims the biblical manuscripts have been changed, altered, or corrupted. But this argument appears to be without foundation since the Qur'anic testimony to the Bible affirms the unchanging nature of Scripture and confirms previously revealed Scripture and its integrity (Sura 5:44–47; 6:92, 115–117; 10:64; 18:27; 35:31). Moreover, the manuscripts available in Muhammad's day (seventh century) are the same manuscripts available to scholars today. In fact Sura 4:136 describes the one who has denied "His Scriptures" (i.e., that were revealed before Muhammad) as having gone "far astray." That is, all who deny the previous Scriptures *in the seventh century* have strayed from Allah's revelation. To prove corruption, there would need to be obvious deviation in content when comparing seventh-century manuscripts to later manuscripts. However, the manuscripts available today date from *before* and *after* the time of Muhammad without deviation except for minor spelling differences and nonessential variants that do not affect meaning or essential doctrines.

Also archaeology has contributed to the reliability debate. Vast amounts of information from Syria, Palestine, Mari, Nuzi, and Ebla substantially confirm the biblical account of the patriarchal narratives.[11] The names of more than 60 individuals mentioned in the Old Testament have been confirmed by either archaeology or non-Christian historical records, including some of the more supposedly "mythical" figures such as Goliath and Balaam the prophet.[12] Confirmation of the New Testament is also impressive, with over 30 names confirmed by archaeological or non-Christian historical records, including Jesus, Pontius Pilate, Herod, John the Baptist, Sergius Paulus, Erastus, Tiberius Caesar, and Caesar Augustus, among others. Historian Colin J. Hemer has documented over 80 details in the book of Acts that have been confirmed through archaeology or non-Christian historical records.[13] This optimism is shared by others such as Roman historian A. N. Sherwin-White, who declared that confirmation of the historicity of the New Testament is "overwhelming," and that any attempt to reject its basic historicity is "absurd."[14]

Approximately 25,000 archaeological finds have directly or indirectly revealed the Bible's reliability. On the other hand Islamic archaeology has not been as fruitful, particularly in the areas of mosque architectural orientation and inscriptions. The mosque's architectural feature known as the *Qibla* is said by Muslim scholars to

---

[11] E. Yamauchi, *The Stones and the Scriptures* (Philadelphia: Lippincott, 1972), 36.

[12] J. M. Holden, *Archaeology and the Bible: A Pictorial Guide to the Amazing Discoveries of the Bible* (Sandy, UT: Aardvark, 2007). The Goliath inscription discovered in 2005 at Tel es-Safi (Gath) by A. Meir and the eighth-century BC Balaam inscription unearthed in 1967 at Deir Alla, Jordan, provide good evidence for these figures.

[13] C. J. Hemer, *The Book of Acts in the Setting of Hellenistic History* (Winona Lake, IN: Eisenbrauns, 1990).

[14] A. N. Sherwin-White, *Roman Law and Roman Society in the New Testament* (Grand Rapids: Baker, 1963), 189.

indicate the direction of prayer toward Mecca. According to the Qur'an (Sura 2:144, 149–150) the direction of the *Qibla* was finalized by c. AD 624. However, research conducted in the Middle East on seventh- and eighth-century mosques in Egypt, Iraq, and North Africa has yielded random directions for the *Qibla*, some of which point more toward Jerusalem than to Mecca.[15] Some Jordanian mosques face north, and some North African mosques face south. The eyewitness testimony of Christian traveler Jacob of Odessa (AD 705) appears to be consistent with these details. He wrote extensively about mosque orientation in Egypt and confirmed that Egyptian Muslims faced eastward toward *their own* Ka'ba in Palestine, not southeast to the Ka'ba located in Mecca.[16] Muslim scholars may attempt to solve this problem by arguing that early Muslims were geographically unsophisticated and had difficulty with direction and navigation. But this seems unlikely since Muslim livelihood came from caravan trading, which involved an intimate knowledge of trade routes, direction, and impeccable stellar navigation. Interestingly the Dome of the Rock possesses no *Qibla*, leading some to believe that Jerusalem, not Mecca, was the *center* of the Muslim world. Others may claim that the Dome is not really a mosque at all and should not be expected to contain a *Qibla*.

In addition to archaeological problems, textual concerns of the Qur'an emerge. Many seventh-century inscriptions, such as the Qur'anic passages written on the tiled walls of the Dome of the Rock (built AD 691) and on Muslim coinage, do not exactly reflect the modern Qur'anic canon. Rather, they contain significant verbal deviations and omissions, implying that the Qur'an was still undergoing transformations in the first century after Muhammad's death. Of equal importance is what scholars have *not* discovered in the Dome of the Rock. There are no inscriptions commemorating Muhammad's miraculous overnight journey from Mecca to Jerusalem and his brief ascension to heaven (Sura 17:1). For this highly significant event to be omitted from the Dome's inscriptions seems to be at odds with historical precedence and introduces doubt as to the historicity of the event.

II. Philosophical Engagement

Historically, many Muslims have been competent philosophers investigating an assortment of questions regarding knowledge, logic, morality, mathematics, and mysticism. Medieval thinkers such as al-Kindi, al-Ghazali, Ibn Sina (Avicenna), Averroes, and al-Farabi contributed to the Muslim understanding of God and formulated arguments for His existence. Here too are many theistic similarities and points of agreement on which one could build substantial discussions. Muslims and Christians agree there is one God who created the world, that God has revealed His will through written

---

[15] For research conducted by Creswell and Fehervari, see http://debate.org.uk/topics/history/bib-qur/ qurarch.htm (accessed May 27, 2010). See also research conducted at the School of Oriental and African Studies (SOAS) at the University of London by Dr. Hawting. As late as 1995, Hawting noted that no seventh-century mosques have been found with the *Qibla* in the direction of Mecca.

[16] Letters of Jacob of Odessa are located in the British Museum in London.

revelation, that obedience to God and the Scriptures is a virtue, that beliefs should work themselves out in everyday life, and that there will be rewards and punishments in the end. Ultimately, however, the philosophical *differences* must be addressed since it is here that the Muslim forms his foundational vision of what God is like and consequently how to work out this vision into life. A. W. Tozer correctly summarizes the importance of having a right concept of God: "What comes into our minds when we think about God is the most important thing about us."[17] The consequences are great since mankind can rise no higher than his concept of God. That is because there is a natural inclination within mankind to become like one's object of worship. The psalmist declared, "The idols of the nations are of silver and gold, made by human hands. They have mouths but cannot speak, eyes, but cannot see. They have ears but cannot hear; indeed, there is no breath in their mouths. Those who make them are just like them, as are all who trust in them" (Ps 135:15–18).

The implications are theological, but they also affect personal sanctification and wholehearted worship (John 4:24). If the foundational truths of God are incorrect, then worship will be in jeopardy of collapsing.

The concept of God offered by Muslims and Christians is radically different not only on theological grounds but also on philosophical grounds. As a fundamental philosophical presupposition "voluntarism" in Islam characterizes their view of God. This view establishes the *will* of God as paramount in legitimizing the morality of a given event or decision. That is, something is good if God wills it. Because of Islamic emphasis on this doctrine, the driving goal in Islam is *obedience* to the *will* of Allah. Abdullah Yusef Ali emphasizes the priority of God's will as the essence of Islam. "Islam is: bowing to the will of God. All who have faith should bow to the will of God and be Muslims."[18]

The will of Allah is crucial since it serves as the deciding factor in the morality and goodness of any action or event. Several problems have been identified with this position. First, voluntarism possesses no accountability structure to provide checks and balances on what God wills to do. In other words, according to Islam the will of God can move in any direction without the risk of immoral or contradictory action. Second, this view of God allows Him to change and become arbitrary. This means God's will is not constrained, for it is free from any internal or external moral and logical constraints. Third, it brings into question the Islamic view of both God's and mankind's personal moral responsibility. If God *necessarily* and *directly* wills all things (Sura 9:51), how then is one morally responsible for doing something he had no choice to avoid? The word *responsibility* implies the "ability to respond" one way or another. Clearly, then, where there is no ability to respond there is no responsibility.

Fourth, the problem of evil becomes an acute issue when attempting to discover the efficient (source), instrumental (tool or vehicle), and final (purpose) causes of pain and suffering. Unlike Islamic voluntarism, Christianity embraces "essentialism," the

---

[17] A. W. Tozer, *The Knowledge of the Holy* (New York: HarperSanFrancisco, 1961), 1.
[18] Ali, *The Qur'an*, 136, m. 392.

belief that something is good, therefore God wills it. That is to say, God is *essentially* (by nature) good, and that goodness is the accountability structure that constrains His will. Thus, God can will only what is in *accord with His good nature*. For example God cannot lie (Heb 6:18), change His mind or nature (Mal 3:6; Jas 1:17), deny Himself or tempt one to do evil (Jas 1:13), among other things. These actions are inconsistent with what and who God is by nature. Essentialism ensures that God wills only what is good without the possibility of contradiction or change. Since God is by nature loving and good (1 John 4:8,16), He must essentially love and be good. Traditionally several objections to this doctrine have emerged. First, some declare that essentialism creates a dualism consisting of the *standard* which God's will must obey and the person of God Himself. Though this may sound formidable, the objection assumes the standard exists *outside* of God as a separate and distinct entity. Though this may be true of Plato's view of essentialism, which places his *Demiurgos* ("god") and *Agathos* ("the good") in two separate realms, this is not true of Christianity. For Christians, God's nature (which includes His mind and will) *is* the standard that exists in and as Himself, never appealing to an *external* standard of morality beyond Himself. This philosophical question bares heavily on ethics, and it also strikes at the core of how Muslims and Christians work out their respective faiths. Unlike the Islamic focus on *obedience,* which flows from one's belief in *voluntarism,* Christianity emphasizes *relationship,* which emerges from one's belief in *essentialism.* Genuine Christian works and obedience *follow from* a relationship with God, whereas in Islam obedience and works *precede* an attempt to be approved by God. The former offers a legal (forensic) standing of righteousness and approval gained by personal relationship with God through faith in Christ (Eph 2:8–9).

III. Social Engagement

Social dimensions of engagement often prove to be fruitful since this aspect of evangelism transcends theological debate and addresses the most basic of human needs such as love, equity, and dignity. Relationships with Muslims can be built in several ways.

First, using the Bible, especially the books of the Law, Psalms, and the Gospels, is always beneficial (Ps 119:130). A Christian should state his beliefs openly while supporting them with Scripture; this places the responsibility on the Word of God. Muslims admire the high value placed on God's revelation and will quickly recognize Christian dedication and faith. This is particularly important since Islam makes no distinction between one's social life and his spiritual life, which is made in the West. The more Muslims are exposed to the way Scripture gives direction, governs life and is integrated into everyday life, the less they will suspect Christians as being "hypocrites" or holding ulterior motives.

Second, making oneself available will indicate that the Christian is a genuine friend. Sometimes saying "hello" is not enough. Instead one should become a good listener, share time with them, escort them to the store, or even help them work through their problems. These actions will build bridges of communication and develop stronger trust and bonds of friendship. Since many Muslims fear that their social, economic, and religious support systems will crumble if they leave Islam, a believer's actions of social support may lessen this fear.

Third, one should focus on positive apologetics, which emphasizes what Christ offers the Muslim (forgiveness, grace, love, relationships, assurance), rather than negative apologetics that tear down Muhammad or the Qur'an. Christianity has more than enough evidence to support its claims. For example the Qur'an declares that Jesus was born of a virgin (Sura 19:16–21), was known as the Messiah (4:172; 9:31), worked miracles (19:29–31), was sinless (3:46; 19:17–19), was called God's "Word" (4:171–73), and was considered a prophet (3:37–40).

Fourth, Muslims should be confronted with common sense regarding their beliefs about Jesus. For example if Jesus was a prophet, and prophets tell the truth, what then should one do in response to Jesus' claim to be "the way, the truth, and the life. No one comes to the Father except through Me" (John 14:6)? Some Muslims have not considered the logical implications of their beliefs since stress is placed upon *memorizing* the Qur'an rather than understanding what is *meant* in the text. A case in point is the repeated usage of the Arabic phrase *al-masihu Isa* ("the *Messiah* Jesus") to describe the prophet Jesus, whereas Muhammad is considered the greater prophet despite his not having this important and unique title.

Fifth, one should become familiar with the *Hadith* (i.e., "traditions"), which contain the words and deeds of Muhammad. This helps one understand Islamic views and practices. Al Bukhari, the most reliable collector of Muslim traditions contained in the Hadith, collected 300,000 such traditions, but only 100,000 might be true. Bukhari narrowed the quantity to 7,275, many of which were repetitions, which makes the total number of recorded traditions closer to 3,000. This means there were errors in more than 295,000 Hadith traditions, which is not considered a reliable basis on which to model one's actions.[19]

Perhaps the best way to reach those in alien religions is to follow the general example of the apostle Paul as he engaged the Athenians on Mars Hill (Acts 17:16–34). At least seven characteristics of his method and message can be helpful to communicating with Muslims.

First, the Greek passive verb in Acts 17:16 indicates that Paul *allowed his heart to be* "troubled," which led to compassion for those who were given over to false religions. This means that evangelism springs from one's love and concern for the spiritual welfare of others. Hearts that remain callus or undisturbed by the more than 200,000 people who die and enter eternity each day around the world will seldom be interested in sharing the good news of the gospel with unbelievers. Christ, the great example, was moved with compassion (from the Latin *cum passio,* meaning to "suffer with") several

---

[19] N. L. Geisler, and A. Saleeb, *Answering Islam: The Crescent in Light of the Cross* (Grand Rapids: Baker, 1993), 170.

times in His ministry to those who were leaderless and hungry (Matt 9:36; 14:14; 15:32; 20:34; Mark 1:41; 6:34; 8:2).

Second, compassion moved Paul to action as he then began sharing the gospel with those available to him in the marketplace (Acts 17:17). If the Lord gives a Christian the *opportunity* to share the gospel along with the *ability* to communicate it, then he has a *responsibility* to convey God's good news to Muslims (Opportunity + Ability = Responsibility). In Paul's approach every day, he "reasoned" (*dielegeto*) with Jesus, meaning He discoursed, argued, disputed, and contended for Christ on a regular basis. The sustained and deliberate communicator will reap his or her rewards since Muslims will soon realize Christians are committed and knowledgeable about what they believe (Rom 1:16).

Third, Paul preached to them Jesus and the resurrection (Acts 17:18). Christians can get sidetracked in their witness to Muslims by addressing issues that are not necessary for salvation. The best thing one can do is focus on the major issues such as the person and work of Christ and His resurrection from the dead (Rom 10:9–10). Of the approximately 20 sermons in the book of Acts, all address Jesus and the resurrection since this was the key salvific message to the lost. Jesus exemplified this unswerving communication when He addressed the Samaritan woman by avoiding her gender ("you being a man and me a woman" [John 4:9]), ethnicity ("you being a Jew and me a Samaritan" [v. 9]), and religiosity ("our fathers worshiped on this mountain, yet you Jews say that the place to worship is in Jerusalem" [v. 20]).

Fourth, Paul placed confidence in the *unique* gospel message of Christ as it is distinguished from all other ways and means of entering heaven; Acts 17:19–21 reveal that the Athenians viewed the gospel as "new" and "strange," ensuring Paul an audience that desired to be "hearing something new." Often Christians attempt to fit into the moral and theological environment around them, which can dilute the main differences between Islam and Christianity. The uniqueness of the gospel makes it attractive, and this fact led Paul to proclaim it boldly, for he knew "it is God's power for salvation to everyone who believes" (Rom 1:16).

Fifth, Paul found common ground with those he was evangelizing when he said, "I see that you are extremely religious in every respect" (Acts 17:22). The same could be said of Paul since his life was consumed with the prospect of sharing the spiritual benefits of the death and resurrection of Christ. Good communicators work from common beliefs and interests to the more diverse and distinct doctrines. This disarms the persons who think a Christian is hostile and antagonistic to his faith; it enables him to see the believer as a balanced proclaimer of truth. Christian evangelists do well to discover something about the unbeliever that is admirable and worthy of praise. For example Muslims do well in integrating their beliefs into their everyday lives. Also, they are passionate about what they believe and correctly challenge polytheism and moral lasciviousness. Moreover, Muslims have formulated excellent arguments for the existence of God (e.g., Kalam cosmological argument), and they have challenging arguments in favor of divine revelation. Paul understood his audience and did everything possible to convince his listeners that he was a man of the Spirit and truth.

Sixth, Paul used ideas and objects present within the Athenian culture to communicate biblical truth. Since people often relate better to things that are familiar to them, Paul discussed the objects of their worship, particularly the alter dedicated to "an unknown God" (v. 23). Nearly 500 years earlier Socrates was executed for leading the youth of Athens away from the state gods. Paul was not about to make the same mistake. He did not deny the Athenians' gods. Instead he positively informed them of the true God. This approach is particularly important with Muslims since any negative statements about Allah, Muhammad, and the Qur'an would most certainly be met with vehement opposition. Instead, conversations surrounding explicit Qur'anic themes regarding Christ's title of *Al-masihu* ("the Messiah"), God's will, obedience to God and his Word in the *Tawrat*, *Zabur*, and *Injil*, would be helpful. Moreover, Paul quoted the pagan poets Epimenides and Aratus, writers familiar to the Greeks, to communicate and confirm biblical truth (v. 28). Undeterred by its source, Paul sought truth wherever it is found since it will always be consistent with God's Word (Phil 4:8).

Some might object to Paul's having quoted pagan poets. However, he was justified in doing so for several reasons. First, to reject something because of its source is to commit what is called the "genetic fallacy." The implications would be staggering since one would have to reject the alternating current motor (Tesla), the Benzene molecule (Kekula), syllogistic logic (Aristotle), and formal collective classroom education (Socrates and Plato), all of which are of pagan origin. Second, the question is not whether ideas are pagan but whether they are true. Third, if God Himself used a fallen animal (Balaam's donkey) to communicate with Balaam (Num 22:22–33), how much more would Paul be justified in using the truths of fallen humanity to communicate or confirm God's message to the world. By familiarizing oneself with the truths of various Muslim theologians, philosophers, and poets, Christians reveal a cultural-theological relevance and avoid the Muslim charge of Christian bias. Fourth, one can expect difficulty as well as triumphs when sharing his or her faith. Some of Paul's hearers began to ridicule him. But others said, "'We'd like to hear from you again about this.' . . . However, some men joined him and believed" (Acts 17:32,34). Unrealistic expectations can set up one for discouragement. So Christians should make it their goal clearly and tactfully to articulate the gospel, while at the same time leaving the conviction of the heart and salvation to God Himself. Christian evangelism is *deontological* (i.e., "duty centered") rather than *teleological* (i.e., "results centered"). In other words evangelism is the *Christian's* duty (Matt 28:19–20), and salvation is *God's* work (John 1:12–13; 3:5–6; Eph 2:8–9). This can relieve Christians of the burden of personally trying to convert a Muslim.

IV. CONCLUSION

Though sharing the gospel with Muslims can be rewarding, it can also try one's resolve and patience. Keeping in mind that the battle belongs to the Lord, believers can most certainly appropriate the skill, love, confidence, and patience in the most difficult situations when engaging Islam.

Chapter 31

ENGAGING NEW AGE MYSTICISM

THE TERM *NEW AGE* DESCRIBES AN almost infinitely wide variety of spiritualism, generally characterized by a belief in the "oneness" of the universe and the desire to become at one with the universe. While the modern movement may be traced to the 1970s, its roots go back to the early nineteenth century with the Theosophist thinkers such as Madame Blavatsky and William Quan Judge. These in turn were followed by others, most famously Shirley MacLaine. Today New Age philosophy has become a strong force in Western culture, from popular psychology to environmentalism, and has even invaded Christian theology. New Age thought seeks to couple itself with all things and thereby to usher in a new period of human history and development. New Age beliefs are seen as compatible with any other belief system so long as that system does not claim to be the sole basis of truth. Here is where it clashes with orthodox Christianity, for Christians claim to possess absolute truth and the only means to true salvation. As New Age becomes more and more accepted in Western culture, Christians must be well informed of its philosophies so they may be prepared to answer the challenges of that movement.

I. THE HISTORY AND BACKGROUND OF THE NEW AGE MOVEMENT

A. Theosophy

The modern New Age movement has a diversified background, with elements from many religious and philosophical beliefs. This is a direct result of the teachings of Madam Blavatsky and the leaders of the Theosophist movement mentioned above.

Helena Petrova Hahn Blavatsky was born in 1831 in Russia. When she was seventeen, she married forty-year-old Nikifor Blavatsky but abandoned him shortly after the wedding. For ten years she traveled, claiming later to have spent two years in Tibet studying spiritism and psychic phenomena with "the masters." After an affair with a Russian opera singer ended with his death in 1871 when he was en route to Cairo, she continued on to Egypt. There she partnered with Emma Cutting (who later became known as Coulomb) to establish Société Spirite. They supposedly dealt in the occult and spiritistic phenomena, but clientele accused the two women of fraud. Blavatsky and Cutting were forced to close their doors. So in 1873 Blavatsky moved to New York

City and once again began advertising her occult practices. She was alleged to have the powers of clairvoyance, clairaudience, levitation, out-of-the-body experiences, channeling spirits, and telepathy. A year after she arrived in New York, she met Henry Steel Olcott and William Quan Judge. Together they formed the Theosophical Society in Wheaton, Illinois. The Society advocated esoteric or hemetic wisdom of God, which they said is the truth that lies at the foundations of all religion. They also espoused the coupling of science and belief and that the evolutionary progress of mankind was tied to the laws of Karma. Eventually the Society settled on three goals: to become a nucleus of the universal brotherhood of humanity; to encourage comparative study of religion, philosophy and science; and to investigate unexplained laws of nature and latent powers possessed by humanity.[1]

Blavatsky began to write, publishing her first book, *Isis Unveiled,* in 1877, and what is considered her greatest work, *The Secret Doctrine,* in 1888. During this time she and Olcott moved to India to study Hindu and Buddhist thought and to establish the Theosophical Society there. In 1879 she began *The Theosophist* magazine, which is still in circulation today.[2]

B. Eastern Religion Comes West

Amid the growing popularity of theosophy and Eastern mysticism in America, Chicago hosted the 1893 World's Fair. In connection with the fair was the first Parliament of World Religions. In describing the climate of the Parliament, Russell Chandler comments, "Spiritual masters, swamis, and gurus washed into American shores en masse for the first time, making Eastern mysticism accessible—and acceptable—to thousands of Americans."[3] Among these "masters, swamis, and gurus" was Swami Vivekananda. Chandler says he was the most popular speaker at the Parliament. He parlayed his popularity into establishing the Vedanta Society, which became a prodigious publisher of Eastern religious material, so much so that the group has had far more influence on the New Age movement than its membership numbers might suggest.[4] In the following decades Hindu teachers continued to come to America, finding a receptive audience. Swami Yogananda was one of these. After graduating from college, Yogananda was invited to speak at the International Congress of Religious Liberals in 1920. He gave an address titled, "The Science of Religion." He was well received at the gathering, and then he toured the nation in 1924. Thousands from Los Angeles to Washington, DC, packed theaters and halls to hear his lectures. He was even invited to President Calvin Coolidge's White House.[5] In 1935 he organized the Self-Realization Fellowship, a group dedicated to, among other things, "encourage 'plain living and high thinking'; and to spread a spirit of brotherhood among all peoples by teaching

---

[1] D. H Caldwell, *The Esoteric World of Madame Blavartsky: Insights into the Life of a Modern Sphinx* (Wheaton, IL: Theosophical, 1991), 69.

[2] According to their Web site: http://www.ts-adyar.org/magazines.html (accessed July 28, 2008).

[3] R. Chandler, *Understanding the New Age* (Nashville: Thomas Nelson, 1991), 48.

[4] Ibid., 27.

[5] Ibid., 67. In India, Yogananda was honored as a hero for "stemming the tide" of Christian missionaries working in Inda. He did this by spreading the message of Hinduism in America.

the eternal basis of their unity: kinship with God."[6] The Fellowship now has temples in several American cities, as well as overseas.

Over the intervening decades Eastern religious figures continued to travel to America to spread their message and teachings. By the 1970s Eastern religion was a countercultural phenomenon. Reacting to perceived excesses of the previous generation, many young people were drawn by the seeming simplicity and community taught by these gurus and spiritual masters. Among these were Swami Muktananda, teaching siddha Yoga; Maharishi Mahesh Yogi, the popular one-time spiritual advisor to the Beatles and founder of Transcendental Meditation; and Maharaj Ji, the founder of the Divine Light Mission.[7] These spiritual gurus brought with them the Hindu and Buddhist ideas of karma and reincarnation important to New Age. Also in recent years Zen and Taoism have become popular, thanks in part to the Eastern mystical roots of the New Age movement.

C. Conglomeration

Theosophical and Eastern religion are the two most influential foundations of the New Age movement. But many other factors have influenced the movement. As stated earlier, almost any religious, philosophical, or even scientific belief can be and is incorporated into New Age. Chandler has identified Gnostic teaching, Hellenistic paganism, American philosopher poets such as Ralph Waldo Emerson and Henry David Thoreau, the spirituality of Franz Messmer, Annie Besant's teachings, the writings and teachings of Ram Dass, Native American shamanism, and even the bizarre thoughts of Carlos Castaneda and his fictional "Don Juan" as contributing to the New Age Movement.[8] Others have seen the influence on New Age by "New Thought" and Christian Science with its spiritual healing, power of constructive thinking, and emphasis on the metaphysical. In fact John P. Newport argues that the "Positive Thinking" movement within certain strains of Christianity, together with "New Thought" and Christian Science led directly to the preparation of a huge audience for the budding New Age movement by the 1970s.[9]

> The initial support given the movement by the many older Spiritualist, Theosophical, and New Thought groups explains the seeming rapid emergence and expansion of the movement. The older occult-metaphysical community also provided a host of additional ideas and practices that gave the new movement increasing substance.[10]

---

[6] S. D. Mata, "Aims and Ideals of Self-Realization Fellowship Set Forth by Pramahansa Yogananda, Founder," http://www.yogananda-srf.org/aboutsrf/aims_ideals.html (accessed July 28, 2008). Mata is the current president of the Self-Realization Fellowship.

[7] Chandler, *Understanding the New Age*, 49.

[8] Ibid., 43–50.

[9] J. P. Newport, *The New Age Movement and the Biblical Worldview: Conflict and Dialogue* (Grand Rapids: Eerdmans, 1998), 29–32.

[10] Ibid., 32.

D. Ferguson and MacLaine

The term New Age came into popular use in the 1970s and '80s through publications by New Age gurus and popular figures in the movement.

Marilyn Ferguson's book *The Aquarian Conspiracy* (1980) has become the unofficial scripture of the movement. It contains a compendium of New Age philosophy and social agenda.[11] The book was almost an instant sensation. In eight years *The Aquarian Conspiracy* had sold over half a million copies and earned Ferguson speaking engagements with all kinds of groups and individuals, such as "the U.S. Army War College, health educators, nuclear physicists, Canadian farm wives, members of Congress, data processing managers, hotel executives, state administrators, medical librarians, college presidents, and international gatherings of youth and business leaders."[12]

Perhaps no single figure associated with New Age has done more to popularize the movement than Shirley MacLaine. Chandler said, "If Ferguson wrote the New Age Bible, Shirley MacLaine has become its high priestess."[13] Because of MacLaine's celebrity, when she began to espouse New Age teaching, her writings became remarkably popular, despite criticism from media and experts alike. She is the author of several books, has appeared in television specials, led conferences, and popularized other New Age figures such as J. Z. Knight.

E. Eckhart Tolle

Before his book was mentioned on Oprah Winfrey's talk show, Eckhart Tolle was a relatively unknown author of *The Power of Now*. Few details are known about him, other than the fact that he was born in Germany in 1948, spent some time at Cambridge University, and now lives in Vancouver, Canada. Tolle claims to have had a "profound inner transformation" at age 29. He says he spent the next 15 years wandering around the streets and parks of London. At some point he began teaching as a "spiritual coach" in England. Later he moved to Vancouver where he met Constance Kellough. Kellough published Tolle's *The Power of Now* under her new publishing company, Namaste. Two years later Tolle's book was produced by New World Library, a New Age publisher in California.[14] Allegedly *The Power of Now* did not even sell all the initial 3,000 copies. Even after Oprah mentioned it in 2002, only 161,000 copies sold. Then in January 2002, Oprah promoted *The Power of Now* as her "book of the month."[15] As of 2008, three million copies of the book had sold, and it "has been translated into 32 languages."[16]

Although he claims he is not a New Age teacher, Tolle has cleverly disguised his New Age teaching as a way to care for others and the world by changing one's focus.

---

[11] Chandler, *Understanding the New Age,* 51.

[12] Ibid., 57.

[13] Ibid., 51.

[14] J. McKinley, "Eckhart Tolle: America's Guru of the Moment," *International Herald Tribune,* March 25, 2008.

[15] "Always Say Yes to the Oprah: What Will Happen When the Power of Now and the World of Winfrey Collide?" *Ottawa Citizen,* March 2, 2008.

[16] According to http://www.eckharttolle.com/eckharttolle-books (accessed on September 5, 2008).

He includes sayings of Jesus among other "religious figures" to give his book a veneer of authoritative religious teaching. His next book, *The New Earth*, was on how to overcome self and achieve the salvation of the world through new consciousness. Even critics within New Age have pointed out that what he teaches is nothing new, but Tolle has simply had the good fortune of being involved with Oprah and her millions of loyal audience members. Tolle has covertly introduced New Age teaching to millions who would not have otherwise sought out New Age philosophy. Since he does not mention New Age, these millions are often unaware that Tolle's teachings fall within that movement, and so they simply follow Oprah's suggestion that his "message will bring you to greater possibilities in your life."[17]

II. NEW AGE BELIEFS

As stated, *New Age* is an umbrella term for many religious and spiritual practices and beliefs. To present all these varying philosophies would constitute an entire book. However, there are some distinctives common to the New Age movement as a whole.

A. Monism

The one overall foundation of New Age is monism, the view that "all is one." The idea of the "oneness" of all things drives the New Age movement to the extent that every other New Age distinctive may be traced directly to monism. The word *universe* in fact carries somewhat this same idea, being derived from the Latin *universum,* meaning "all together." According to New Age, "The cosmos is seen as a pure, undifferentiated, universal, energy-interconnected process."[18] New Age teaching holds that "the notion of separateness, of discrete existence, is illusory."[19] There is an "encompassing reality" that is expressed as an energy or force that binds the universe together. All matter, including the earth and humans, is simply a manifestation of this universal energy. Monism is seen in environmentalism (one's actions can affect the entire globe, and since everything including the environment is one, people are hurting things by hurting the environment), economics (everything is connected in a global village), and politics (national policies should take into consideration the whole world and help foster unity).

B. Pantheism

Closely following the idea that "all is one" is the New Age belief in pantheism. For most people in the New Age movement, God is the unifying principle or force, binding all things together. God is said to be "all that exists."[20] Since God is all, it fol-

---

[17] "Always Say Yes to the Oprah: What Will Happen When the Power of Now and the World of Winfrey Collide?"

[18] Newport, *The New Age Movement and the Biblical Worldview,* 4.

[19] Ibid.

[20] D. K. Clark and N. L. Geisler, *Apologetics in the New Age: A Christian Critique of Pantheism* (Grand Rapids: Baker, 1990), 118.

lows that even seeming opposites are also one. Thus "good and evil coalesce in God."[21] However, this is not how New Agers describe the oneness that is God. They see God "beyond" good and evil. They see God transcending personal and impersonal, being and becoming, being finite and infinite. Following from God being the unifying force of the universe that is beyond distinctions, New Age teaches that God is impersonal. Being "one with God" does not mean being in God's personal presence; it means being one with the unifying principle or force that is God. Since this is the case, all humans are already one with God, but not all humans realize this. This is often expressed as humans having the "spark" of divinity. The goal of New Agers is to come to the realization of their own divinity and therefore of their oneness with God.

C. Reincarnation and Karma

New Age teaches that humans undergo reincarnation. This follows from the idea that all things are evolving toward a new era of spiritual oneness, including humans, and is a development of Eastern ideas of spiritual progression through multiple rebirths. However, for most humans, one lifetime is not long enough to achieve this evolution. Newport says that for the New Ager, "You must progress through many lifetimes to reach oneness with the One—to be reunited with the Ultimate Reality."[22] The way a person progresses toward this reuniting is by accumulating good Karma. Karma is defined as "the fruit of your actions." A person's Karma affects his future lives. Building up too much bad Karma leads to bad consequences and suffering in future lives, whereas building up good Karma in this life can lead to better experiences in the next. Newport argues that belief in Karma serves New Age philosophy several ways: It explains the inequalities and negativities of life; it allows infinite time for spiritual growth and "provides a never-ending source for speculation on past lives, soul mates, and life after death."[23] A quick perusal of the "spiritual" section of many bookstores reveals how lucrative the New Age focus on reincarnation and Karma is.

D. Consciousness

As alluded to above, the goal of New Age philosophy is the realization of oneness. This involves what New Age teachers see as a change in consciousness. According to the New Age movement, most people live under the illusion that they are finite and limited and that they are somehow separated from God. Most people live in ignorance of their unity with all things. New Agers argue, according to Newport, "You need to be enlightened. You have forgotten your true identity. You are the victim of a false sense of a separate identity which blinds you to your essential unity with God. This is the cause of all your problems."[24] By following New Age teaching, a person can transform himself from ignorance to enlightenment. If a person achieves this enlightenment, he can be released from the bad Karma he has built up previously.

---

[21] Ibid.
[22] Newport, *The New Age Movement and the Biblical Worldview,* 4.
[23] Ibid.
[24] Ibid., 7.

421

He can then transcend what the rest of the world calls good and evil. New Age teachers have come up with several techniques for achieving this enlightened state. These are "psycho-spiritual" practices designed to awaken the "divine spark" within the person. Examples of these techniques include Yoga, chanting, music, psychotropic drugs, mystical experiences, meditation, guided imagery with a guru, hypnosis, and martial arts. Several systematized programs have been developed to help individuals achieve enlightenment. These include Erhard Seminar Training, Silva Mind Control, and bioenergy treatments. Tolle's *A New Earth* promises to "shift your conscious" to "something infinitely greater than anything we currently think we are."[25] Just as an almost infinite number of beliefs are under the umbrella of New Age, so there are many programs, methods, techniques, practices, rituals, and other activities practiced by New Age practitioners. Strangely, though, most of these programs come with a price. Newport argues, "New Age is a business, and nowhere is that more evident than in the array of consumer goods New Age groups produce and sell."[26]

III. Answering New Age Adherents

Because of the wide diversity of beliefs in the New Age movement, including the use of Christian terminology and biblical passages (Tolle quotes the Bible throughout his book *A New Earth*), answering particular New Age teaching may seem challenging. However, by answering the *general* beliefs shared by all in the New Age movement, individual beliefs are not difficult to interact with.

A. Monism

1. No value to human life

New Age claims to be assisting individuals in coming to the realization that they are really not individuals because all is one. People then do not have intrinsic value beyond being part of the cosmic oneness. Any care New Age expresses for people is at best superficial. As Newport observes, "Although New Agers assert the value of the individual on the psychological level, their belief system denies this value on the ultimate spiritual level."[27] Clark and Geisler ask, "Why serve a person who does not exist separately from ourselves?"[28] This has in fact led to an entire society historically characterized by apathy toward human suffering, that of India. Hinduism believes in monism, which has led to the belief that there is no intrinsic good in helping others. Monism leads to self-centered living. If the goal of all humans is to realize that they are simply a manifestation of the one force of the universe, then to be concerned with the troubles of others only distracts from this goal. Since monism sees all things as

---

[25] "A NEW EARTH Awakening to Your Life's Purpose," http://eckharttolle.com/a_new_earth (accessed on August 5, 2008).

[26] Newport, *The New Age Movement and the Biblical Worldview,* 16.

[27] Ibid., 605.

[28] Clark and Geisler, *Apologetics in the New Age,* 129.

belonging to one reality and denies intrinsic value to human life, individuals have no more value than a tree, a rock, or a cow. Some radical environmentalists who subscribe to New Age philosophy have no compulsion against destroying property or even causing harm to other people because of their view that nature has equal value with humans or even greater value. However, most New Agers pragmatically do not treat other people the same way they treat a rock or a tree or a cow.

2.   Is everything one, or are there distinctions?

The goal of New Agers is to avoid doing evil in order not to affect their future Karma. In this way New Age must see evil existing separately from good. However, this contradicts the teaching that good and evil are simply illusions. If monism is true, there is no need to avoid evil but simply to transcend it (whatever that may mean). If a New Ager actually attains enlightenment, he would not concern himself with avoiding evil and perusing good because these differentials do not exist. In fact, few who follow New Age actually put this into practice.

Monism teaches that pleasure and suffering are simply illusions. Yet New Age teaches that suffering is real, in that it is a consequence of bad actions committed during a past life, and may be avoided by accumulating "good Karma" during past lives.

The first verse of the Bible points to a dichotomy that shows that pantheistic monism is false: "In the beginning God created the heavens and the earth" (Gen 1:1 NKJV). Under monism God cannot exist apart from the universe because they are one. If God created the universe, then He is separate from that creation.

3.   Everything is true, or is it?

Since New Age advocates believe in monism, they argue that the basic beliefs of all religions are true. Tolle said, "There is only one absolute Truth. All others emanate from it. When you find that Truth, your actions will emanate from it."[29] However, as stated above, New Age rejects any teaching that claims to be the sole possessor of truth. Tolle also wrote, "Many 'religious' people . . . equate truth with thought, and as they are completely identified with their thought (their mind) they claim to be in the sole possession of truth in an unconscious attempt to protect their identity."[30] Which is it? Does Tolle possess the Truth, or is he unconsciously attempting to protect his own "identity"? He completely contradicts his "Truth" claim in these words: "All religions are equally false or equally true, depending on how you use them. If you believe only your religion is the Truth, you are using it in the service of your own ego."[31] Yet Tolle claims his teachings are the Truth, over and against all other truth claims. Is he perhaps simply servicing his own ego?

New Age also teaches that truth is found not by intellectual pursuit but through feelings. If it "feels" right, it is. Again Tolle claims, "Only through awareness—not

---

[29] Tolle, *A New Earth,* 71.
[30] Ibid., 17.
[31] Tolle, *A New Earth,* 70–71.

through thinking—can you differentiate between fact and opinion."[32] If he is correct, people ought not think about his statement but rather how they feel about it. In this way any statement could be considered "truth" so long as the person feels it is truth. However, this practice could lead to disastrous consequences. Suppose someone else might feel that some people are of less value than others (see Tolle's statements about the poor below). Suppose another feels that it is mere opinion that arsenic is deadly. Or someone else may legitimately claim that Mao Tse-tung's Great Leap Forward was good for the Chinese people because Mao's teachings "feel" right.[33] This is absurd. There are things that are objectively and absolutely true and things that are objectively and absolutely false. Someone may feel that $2 + 2 = 5$, but that would still be objectively false. This presents a serious problem for monism. A distinct dichotomy exists between truth and untruth, and this dichotomy is actual, not merely perceived. Therefore all things cannot be "one." Something cannot be both true and false at the same time.

B. Pantheism

1. Is suffering real or an illusion?

Closely tied to monism is the New Age claim that God is impersonal and is the unifying energy or force of the cosmos. And yet New Age adherents claim that realizing oneness with this energy is in effect salvation. Some in the New Age say a person's "suffering" simply results from a lack of awareness of being one with "God." Others relate it to "bad Karma" in a past life. But, as noted above, to remain consistent, New Age must see suffering itself as an illusion. If suffering actually exists, which New Age sometimes does claim, and a person can find ways to cease suffering, then (at least metaphysically) there is a separation within the supposedly unified "God."

2. Pantheism leads to selfishness

Another issue with pantheism is that it places an undue emphasis on self. New Agers are supposed to "find the God within" in order to become enlightened, leading to a self-centered focus. For as much as the New Age talks about love and helping others, in the end New Age teaching is concerned primarily with individual experiences with "God." Their answer to personal crisis is to look inward, to find the energy of the universe residing in themselves for strength. Practitioners are taught they must rely on their inner spirit rather than looking to others for help. This focus on self has led to many people abandoning the movement after experiencing an intense crisis and finding no solace or comfort.

---

[32] Ibid., 69.

[33] Instead the Great Leap Forward led to suffering on an almost unimaginable scale. Estimates suggest that as many as 40 million people starved to death as a direct result of Mao's policies. See M. White, "Source List and Detailed Death Tolls for the Twentieth Century Hemoclysm," http://users.erols.com/mwhite28/warstat1.htm (accessed September 16, 2008).

3. A desire for the personal while claiming to be impersonal

New Age constantly claims that the cosmic "god" is impersonal. God is all things, including trees, rocks, cows, humans, stars, and so forth. Yet New Age teaches that people may seek guidance from this impersonal God and that it can speak to them. Commenting on how to make good decisions, one New Ager says: "Making decisions with the heart involves listening to the voice within. Visualizing each of the choices and its implications, noticing the feelings associated with each. Possibly even observing your dreams, after asking your subconscious for guidance."[34] Why should a person ask himself for guidance? Who is speaking when a person listens to this "inner voice"? Tolle says that God (whom he calls "Life" here) spoke to him:

> When I lived in England and did spiritual teaching on a small scale, sometimes I would say, "Okay, I could do so much more. There's much more I could do." I said, to Life, "I'm ready." But Life just waited and waited and the answer didn't come for several years until that morning when he said, "Move."[35]

Whom does Tolle think was "speaking" to him since God is supposedly impersonal? How does something without any personality make decisions like this and speak to us? New Age claims, "There is no separation between you and God,"[36] yet Tolle's slip of the tongue, ascribing the personal pronoun "he" to this supposed impersonal "Life," betrays the fact that New Age movements cannot reconcile their teaching of pantheism with their desire for something beyond them. New Agers reject the troublesome responsibility of a personal God but long for the intimate relationship of a personal God. Richard Abanes identified this inconsistency within New Age's theology.

> They [New Agers] neither like, nor want, certain aspects of a *personal* God (e.g., commands to be obeyed, an external deity to whom they are accountable, obedience to Scripture), but they long for other aspects of a *personal* God (e.g., an intimate relationship with the Creator, guidance/direction from an external source). So in a blatant display of inconsistency, such individuals attribute personal characteristics to their *impersonal* life force, or Universal Energy.[37]

As Abanes says, they want to have their cake and eat it too.[38] But logically either God is a personal being, distinct from His creation (as the Bible teaches), or God is an impersonal force existing with no distinction from the universe. Both cannot be true. Christianity teaches a personal God, distinct from His creation.

---

[34] "How to Make Good Decisions," http://www.new-age-spirituality.com/selfhelp/decision.html (accessed September 16, 2008).

[35] Tolle, "A New Earth Online Class," March 4, 2008, http://video.oprah.com/podcast/ane/week1/webcast_cc_3_4_2008.wmv (accessed May 27, 2010).

[36] Ibid.

[37] R. Abanes, *A New Earth: An Old Deception* (Grand Rapids: Bethany House, 2008), 67 (italics his).

[38] Ibid.

4. Reincarnation and Karma

New Age proponents teach that people need several (or many) lifetimes to reach oneness with God. New Agers believe people are evolving toward this oneness over time. The way to grow closer toward this goal is by building Karma through a proper lifestyle in successive lives. For New Age, "the key to understanding comes with the realization that our stay in this world is ultimately of utter insignificance. Our bodies eventually cease to function and we pass back (home) to Spirit. All that we take with us is lessons learned."[39] However, while some New Agers claim unusual feelings or vague "memories," they do not claim to have memories of previous lives. Yet they believe they experience suffering because of the actions they do not remember. This would seem to make learning and "progressing" over the span of many lifetimes difficult, to say the least. All a New Ager knows if he suffers is that it because of some failing *during a past life*. They do not know what they did or how to avoid doing it in this life. In an effort to explain away this inconsistency, some in the New Age movement believe enlightened spirits can be channeled to help adherents along this path to enlightenment. However, this would seem to contradict their belief in monism and pantheism. If the goal of New Age is to become one with the universe, to become enlightened by achieving new consciousness, then how would a being who has done so retain any kind of personhood apart from the cosmic force with which it is now supposed to be united? New Age either personifies Karma or makes arbitrary decisions based on universal human morality to decide what is good and bad Karma. Christianity rejects reincarnation and Karma, and it teaches that there is only one life on earth and an eternity to come. Whether one has faith in Jesus Christ determines where a person will spend eternity. There are only two outcomes: "The one who believes in the Son has eternal life, but the one who refuses to believe in the Son will not see life; instead the wrath of God remains on him" (John 3:36).

5. New Age's problem of evil and suffering

New Age fails to answer the problem of human suffering. Because of its pantheistic ideas, New Age "reduces the status of the human individual to the level of grass or bacteria."[40] Basically, New Age cares little for the individual. If one human oppresses another, if one human does unspeakable evil to another, or if someone is suffering, that is of little interest to New Age adherents. One New Ager, giving advice on how to overcome suffering because of pain, taught the following.

> When pain happens, NOTICE it. It's a signal. A piece of information. Hear it. Do what is appropriately do-able, if anything. If you are sitting on a tack, get off the tack! And don't sit down again until you have removed it. Having done the do-able, RELEASE the pain. You heard and responded to the message. You do not have to run it again and again like an old tape. You

---

[39] "Do What Thou Wilt," http://www.new-age-spirituality.com/selfhelp/dowhat.html (accessed September 16, 2008).

[40] V. Mangalwadi, *When the New Age Gets Old: Looking for Greater Spirituality* (Downers Grove, IL: InterVarsity, 1992), 170.

heard it. You responded. Now, let go of it. And finally, SHIFT your attention somewhere else. Put it on what you need to do next and do that with full awareness. That's it. Notice, Release, Shift. It works. And it works immediately. Oh, not forever. Some pains return and you'll have to Notice, Release and Shift your attention again. And like any habit or skill, you'll get better at it the more you practice it; and, if you don't practice it, you won't get better at it. But you don't have to wait until all the habits of suffering have been overcome, until you've finally reached enlightenment and Nirvana.[41]

This pithy advice to "Notice, Release, Shift" rings hollow in the face of the loss of a loved one, debilitating and painful illness, catastrophic natural disasters, the memories of vicious warfare, and any number of other events that cause tremendous suffering.

6. License to indulge

New Age is popular because it gives people license to engage in total self-indulgence. Charles Colson and Nancy Pearcey observed, "It assuages the ego by pronouncing the individual divine, and it gives a gratifying sense of 'spirituality' without making demands in terms of doctrinal commitment or ethical living."[42] New Age makes no attempt to reach out to the less fortunate, the sick, the oppressed, the hurt, or the needy because their afflictions are of no concern to the amoral philosophy of New Age. Under New Age philosophy, man is already perfect; he simply has not yet realized it. Rather than focusing on improving the person through obedience to God, New Age teaches that the *perception of one's self* is all that needs to change. Tolle goes so far as to reinterpret the Gospel as "the good news of the possibility of a radical transformation of human consciousness."[43]

7. Religion of the wealthy

The inward focus of New Age also tends to lead to elitism for many involved in the movement.[44] When asked about the poor during a radio interview, Tole admitted that his work is not applicable or useful for those "who are just trying to survive." According to Tolle, "they don't have time to be unhappy."[45] Apparently for him, New Age is only for relatively affluent members of Western culture who have nothing better to do than try to "find inner peace." Because of the mass commercialism that seems to go hand in hand with New Age, could it be that the reason Tolle disregards the poor is that they are not the ones who will be buying his books? Is a belief system valid if it is at most irrelevant and at least unavailable to the vast majority of the human population?

---

[41] M. Young, "Pain Is Inevitable. Suffering Is Optional," http://home.hawaii.rr.com/uuchurch/sermons/111295.htm (accessed September 16, 2008).

[42] C. Colson and N. Pearcey, *How Now Shall We Live?* (Wheaton, IL: Tyndale, 1999), 264.

[43] E. Tolle, *A New Earth* (New York: Penguin, 2005), 13.

[44] Although Tolle claims that he is not part of the New Age movement, his teaching lines up perfectly with the tenets we discussed in this chapter. He even says he is "beyond New Age," which is quintessential New Age language.

[45] E. Tolle, radio interview with K. Tippett, on "Speaking of Faith," National Public Radio, August 12, 2008.

8. Suffering and Karma

Because of New Age's focus on Karma, suffering is the result of one's actions in his past life and is inevitable. There is no motivation to seek to end this suffering because it is simply the way things are. At best, suffering is the result of bad Karma. At worst, some New Age proponents say suffering is necessary for spiritual growth, provoking a "spiritual crisis" that aids in one's "evolution" toward new consciousness.[46]

9. Naïve reaction to events of terrible suffering

The tsunami of December 2004 ravaged much of the coast around the Indian Ocean. It was a horrible and tragic event, costing the lives of more than 200,000 people and leading to the suffering of many more. Yet New Age's answer to the suffering and destruction is not one of compassion. One New Ager described the event as "our planetary watershed adventure."[47] She quipped:

> As we embrace the wildness within, love our primal essence in the same way we thrill to the power of nature to transform and renew, we become spiritual warriors, transmuting the wound within us into wonder. With a subtle shift in perception, we move from scarred and scared to sacred, from density to destiny, from being exclusive to becoming inclusive."[48]

The horrendous destruction of human lives is to her simply nature's power to "transform and renew." The selfish attitude of her comment underscores New Age's refusal to acknowledge real human suffering.

10. Christianity's compassion versus New Age's indifference

In contrast to Roase's view, Christianity is at heart focused on individuals and their relationship to God. Human suffering is of great concern to Christianity because it believes in a God of love and mercy. Christianity is equally applicable to the rich and the poor, the affluent and the starving, the healthy and the sick. Christian morality is the driving force behind relieving human suffering. Jesus taught, "I give you a new command: Love one another. Just as I have loved you, you must also love one another. By this all people will know that you are My disciples, if you have love for one another" (John 13:34–35).

Suffering, according to Christianity, is a result of sin in the world. Although God uses suffering sometimes for the benefit of humans, evil and suffering were not original to His creation. Suffering, while real and actual now, will eventually be ended by God when He renews His people and His creation. Until then, Christianity offers hope, based not on the possibility to do better in another life but on the possibility of living forever with God.

---

[46] "A Christian Reflection on the 'New Age'" (The Vatican: Pontifical Council for Inter-religious Dialogue, 2003), http://www.vatican.va/roman_curia/pontifical_councils/interelg/documents/rc_pc_interelg_doc_20030203_new-age_en.html#FOREWORD (accessed September 5, 2008).

[47] A. Roase, "Watershed," New Age Journal (January 2005), http://www.newagejournal.com/watershed.shtml (accessed September 5, 2008).

[48] Ibid.

IV. CONCLUSION

Although New Age philosophy has become popular, in the end it is a shallow, convoluted, and ultimately disappointing belief system. Its monism and pantheism is impersonal and causes indifference toward others. Its belief in Karma and reincarnation leaves people without hope and frustrated. It ignores the cause of human suffering and cannot answer the question of evil. Since most New Agers trust experience over reason, these false teachings alone may be enough to convince many of them that New Age does not present the truth. Nor can New Age stand logical scrutiny. By contrast, Christianity stands up to both experiential and rational scrutiny.

Name Index

433

Subject Index

SCRIPTURE INDEX